Lecture Notes in Computer Science 3231

Commenced Publication in 1973
Founding and Former Series Editors:
Gerhard Goos, Juris Hartmanis, and Jan van Leeuwen

T0180861

Hans-Arno Jacobsen (Ed.)

Middleware 2004

ACM/IFIP/USENIX International Middleware Conference
Toronto, Canada, October 18-22, 2004
Proceedings

 Springer

Volume Editor

Hans-Arno Jacobsen
University of Toronto
Department of Electrical and Computer Engineering and
Department of Computer Science
10 King's College Road, Toronto, ON, M5S 3G4, Canada
E-mail: jacobsen@eecg.toronto.edu

Library of Congress Control Number: 2004113129

CR Subject Classification (1998): C.2.4, D.4, C.2, D.1.3, D.3.2, D.2, H.4

ISSN 0302-9743
ISBN 3-540-23428-4 Springer Berlin Heidelberg New York

Springer is a part of Springer Science+Business Media

springeronline.com

© 2004 IFIP International Federation for Information Processing, Hofstrasse 3, A-2361 Laxenburg, Austria
Printed in Germany

Typesetting: Camera-ready by author, data conversion by Olgun Computergrafik
Printed on acid-free paper   SPIN: 11333388   06/3142   5 4 3 2 1 0

Preface

Middleware systems comprise programming models, abstractions, protocols, and services to facilitate the design, the development, the integration, and the deployment of distributed applications in heterogeneous computing environments. Conceptually, the term "middleware" refers to a layer of software above the networking substrate and the operating system and below the (distributed) application. In practice these boundaries are not clear cut, with middleware functionality moving into and out of these layers. Remote communication, publish/subscribe, messaging, and (distributed) transaction constitute examples of common middleware abstractions and services.

Middleware research encompasses, builds on and extends a wide spectrum of concepts, techniques and ideas from a broad range of fields, including programming languages, distributed systems, operating systems, networking, and data management.

Following the success of the past conferences in this series in the Lake District, UK (1998), in Palisades, NY (2000), in Heidelberg, Germany (2001), and in Rio de Janeiro, Brazil (2003), the 5th International Middleware Conference in Toronto, Canada aimed to be the premier conference for middleware research and technology in 2004. The broad scope of the conference included the design, the implementation, the deployment, and the evaluation of distributed systems platforms and architectures for emerging computing environments. The conference gave an overview of research on middleware for peer-to-peer computing, middleware for mobility, middleware for replication and transactions, on publish/subscribe systems, on routing protocols and overlay networks, on application servers, resource management, and software engineering, and on Web services.

This year, the technical program of Middleware drew from 194 submitted papers, among which 13 were explicitly submitted as work-in-progress papers. At the program committee meeting on Saturday and Sunday, June 5th and 6th in Toronto, 25 research papers and 1 invited paper were selected for presentation at the conference. Two, as research papers designated submissions, were recommended for inclusion in the conference's work-in-progress paper program. The work-in-progress paper committee selected 6 papers among the 13 submitted and the 2 recommended papers for inclusion in the program. The paper selection was based on the papers' technical merit, originality, projected impact on the field, and pertinence to the scope of the conference. Each research paper was reviewed by at least three reviewers. A PC-authored paper (i.e., one or more authors on the paper was a Middleware committee member) was reviewed by at least four reviewers.

Finally, I would like to express my deepest gratitude to the authors of submitted papers, to all program committee members for their active participation in the paper review and selection process, to all external reviewers for their help in evaluating submissions, to Mark Hau and Microsoft Research for providing us with the Conference Management System and support, and finally to the members of the organizing committee and the steering committee for their efforts towards making Middleware 2004 a successful conference.

October 2004   Hans-Arno Jacobsen

Organization

Middleware 2004 was organized under the auspices of IFIP TC6 WG6.1 (International Federation for Information Processing, Technical Committee 6 [Communication Systems], Working Group 6.1 [Architecture and Protocols for Computer Networks]).

Steering Committee

Joe Sventek (chair)	(University of Glasgow, UK)
Gordon Blair	(Lancaster University, UK)
Markus Endler	(PUC-Rio, Brazil)
Rachid Guerraoui	(EPFL, Switzerland)
Peter Honeyman	(CITI, University of Michigan, USA)
Guy LeDuc	(University of Liege, Belgium)
Jan de Meer	(IHP-Microelectronics, Germany)
Doug Schmidt	(Vanderbilt University, USA)

Sponsoring Institutions

 ACM (Association for Computing Machinery)
www.acm.org

 IFIP (International Federation for Information Processing)
www.ifip.or.at

 Advanced Computing Systems Association
www.usenix.org

Corporate Sponsors

Diamond Level

Cybermation, Inc.
www.cybermation.com

IONA, Inc.
www.iona.com

Silver Level

BBN Technologies
www.bbn.com

IBM Research
http://www.research.ibm.com

Siemens Corporate Technology
http://www.ct.siemens.com

Supporting Institution

Zero Gravity Design House
Middleware Logo Design
http://www.sungmarketing.com/

Organizing Committee

General Chair	Steve Vinoski (IONA Technologies, Inc.)
Program Chair	Hans-Arno Jacobsen (University of Toronto, Canada)
Work-in-Progress Chair	Jean Bacon (University of Cambridge, UK)
Posters Chair	Eyal de Lara (University of Toronto, Canada)
Advanced Workshops Chair	Fabio Kon (University of Sao Paulo, Brazil)
Tutorials Chair	Stefan Tai (IBM T.J. Watson, USA)
Local Arrangements Chair	Baochun Li (University of Toronto, Canada)
Publicity Chair	Cristiana Amza (University of Toronto, Canada)
Travel Grants Chair	Daby M. Sow (IBM T.J. Watson, USA)

Program Committee

Gul Agha	(Univ. of Illinois, Urbana-Champaign, USA)
Gustavo Alonso	(ETH Zürich, Switzerland)
Cristiana Amza	(University of Toronto, Canada)
Jean Bacon	(Cambridge University, UK)
Mark Baker	(Canada)
Guruduth Banavar	(IBM T.J. Watson, USA)
Alejandro Buchmann	(Darmstadt Univ. of Technology, Germany)
Andrew Campbell	(Columbia University, USA)
Roy Campbell	(Univ. of Illinois, Urbana-Champaign, USA)
Harold Carr	(Sun, Inc., USA)
Geoff Coulson	(Lancaster University, UK)
Prem Devanbu	(University of California at Davis, USA)
Jan DeMeer	(IHP-Microelectronics, Germany)
Naranker Dulay	(Imperial College, London, UK)
Markus Endler	(PUC-Rio, Brazil)
Mike Feeley	(University of British Columbia, Canada)
Chris Gill	(Washington University, St. Louis, USA)
Aniruddha Gokhale	(Vanderbilt University, USA)
Peter Honeyman	(University of Michigan, USA)
Bettina Kemme	(McGill University, Canada)
Fabio Kon	(University of Sao Paulo, Brazil)
Doug Lea	(SUNY Oswego, USA)
Joe Loyall	(BBN Technologies, USA)
Edmundo Madeira	(University of Campinas, Brazil)
Keith Moore	(HP Laboratories, USA)
Hausi Muller	(University of Victoria, Canada)
Klara Nahrstedt	(Univ. of Illinois, Urbana-Champaign, USA)
Dennis Noll	(Boeing, USA)
Kerry Raymond	(DSTC, Australia)
Luis Rodrigues	(University of Lisbon, Portugal)
Isabelle Rouvellou	(IBM T.J. Watson, USA)
Michael Stal	(Siemens, Germany)
Rick Schantz	(BBN Technologies, USA)
Douglas Schmidt	(Vanderbilt University, USA)
Jean-Bernard Stefani	(INRIA, Grenoble, France)
Joe Sventek	(University of Glasgow, UK)
Janos Sztipanovits	(Vanderbilt University, USA)
Stefan Tai	(IBM T.J. Watson, USA)
Peter Triantifilou	(RA Computer Technology Institute and University of Patras, Greece)
Nalini Venkatasubramanian	(University of California, Irvine, USA)
Werner Vogels	(Cornell University, USA)
Martina Zitterbart	(University of Karlsruhe, Germany)

External Referees

Ioannis Aekaterinidis
Jalal Al-Muhtadi
Filipe Araujo
Damin Arregui
Michael Atighetchi
Vidhya Balasubramanian
Stefan Behnel
Stefan Berger
Chatschik Bisdikian
Gordon Blair
Erik-Oliver Blass
Marion Blount
Tom Brown
Ioana Burcea
Kan Cai
Richard Cardone
Fernando Castor Filho
Paul Castro
Emmanuel Cecchet
Shiva Cehtan
Renato Cerqueira
Dan Chalmers
Ellick Chan
Kai Chen
Liping Chen
Shiva Chetan
Mariano Cilia
Yvonne Coady
Norman Cohen
Michael Conrad
Fábio M. Costa
Curt Cramer
John Davis
Lou Degenaro
Jauvane C. de Oliveira
Mayur Deshpande
Judah Diament
Daniel Dietterle
Gary Duzan
Ludger Fiege
Arlindo Flávio da Conceição
Ivo J. Garcia dos Santos
Ashvin Goel
Paul Grace

Xiaohui Gu
Sebastian Gutierrez-Nolasco
Dabiel Hagimont
MyungJoo Ham
Qi Han
George Heineman
Asher Hoskins
Shuang Hou
Danny Hughes
Bernhard Hurler
Stoney Jackson
Jingwen Jin
Lasaro Jonas Camargos
Ackbar Joolia
Patric Kabus
Apu Kapadia
Dimka Karastoyanova
Rania Khalaf
Richard King
Alexander V. Konstantinou
Samuel Kounev
Sudha Krishnamurthy
YoungMin Kwon
Kevin Lee
Geoffrey Lefebvre
Baochun Li
Guoli Li
Jin Liang
David Lie
Honghui Lu
Fabio Luciano Verdi
Heiko Ludwig
Kaloian Manassiev
Prakash Manghwani
Vance Maverick
Oliver Maye
Kirill Mechitov
Thomas A. Mikalsen
Thomas Mikalsen
Hugo Miranda
Archan Misra
Amr Abdel Momen
Gero Muehl
Jonathan Munson

Table of Contents

Publish/Subscribe

Web Services: Composition, Integration and Interoperability

Middleware for Mobility

Application Servers, Enterprise Computing, and Software Engineering

Middleware and Web Services for the Collaborative Information Portal of NASA's Mars Exploration Rovers Mission

Elias Sinderson[1], Vish Magapu[2], and Ronald Mak[3]

[1] Computer Sciences Corporation
NASA Ames Research Center, M/S 269-3
Moffett Field, California 94035
esinderson@mail.arc.nasa.gov
[2] Science Applications International Corporation
NASA Ames Research Center, M/S 269-3
Moffett Field, California 94035
vmagapu@mail.arc.nasa.gov
[3] Research Institute for Advanced Computer Science
NASA Ames Research Center, M/S 269-3
Moffett Field, California 94035
rmak@mail.arc.nasa.gov

Abstract. We describe the design and deployment of the middleware for the Collaborative Information Portal (CIP), a mission critical J2EE application developed for NASA's 2003 Mars Exploration Rover mission. CIP enabled mission personnel to access data and images sent back from Mars, staff and event schedules, broadcast messages and clocks displaying various Earth and Mars time zones. We developed the CIP middleware in less than two years time using cutting-edge technologies, including EJBs, servlets, JDBC, JNDI and JMS. The middleware was designed and implemented as a collection of independent, hot-deployable web services, providing secure access to back end file systems and databases. This service-oriented approach to developing an integrated system is an example of cutting edge middleware design. Throughout the middleware we enabled crosscutting capabilities such as runtime service configuration, security, logging and remote monitoring. This paper presents our approach to mitigating the challenges we faced, concluding with a short review of the lessons we learned from this project and noting some of the things we would do differently and why.

1 Introduction

The 2003 Mars Exploration Rover (MER) mission was the latest in a series of science missions to the planet Mars. The primary goal was to search for irrefutable evidence of liquid water existing on the surface in the Martian past. The mission was composed of two redundant (dual launch, dual lander) mobile science platforms, or rovers, outfitted with a variety of instruments. NASA

H.-A. Jacobsen (Ed.): Middleware 2004, LNCS 3231, pp. 1–17, 2004.

Fig. 1. Artists rendition of a MER mobile science platform (rover)

launched two spacecraft carrying these rovers in June 2003, and in January 2004 they landed safely on Mars. After landing the rovers at two separate locations, they proceeded to take numerous images of their surroundings and collect data from the Martian rocks and soil. Intermittently throughout each Martian day, or sol, the rovers transmitted their data back to Earth where it was collaboratively analyzed and activities were planned for the next sol. This analysis and planning cycle had to be completed in time for the next set of command sequences to be uplinked as the sun is rising on Mars.

The MER Collaborative Information Portal (CIP) was conceived of to provide mission personnel a sense of situational awareness, allowing the MER scientists, engineers and managers to accomplish their daily tasks by facilitating access to various mission data products, schedules, broadcast announcements, and the like. This paper focuses on the middleware and web services that were developed for CIP. The rest of this section presents a brief overview of the day-to-day mission operations, and describes previous work at Ames that both led to and influenced the CIP project. Sec. 2 outlines the overall approach to systems development that was employed. Sec. 3 provides an initial, high-level overview of the client application functionality and back end data stores before proceeding on to the details of the CIP middleware. Sec. 4 looks at the crosscutting functionality that was implemented across all of the CIP middleware services. We conclude the paper by identifying several of the lessons learned on the project.

1.1 MER Operations

The MER operations (Ops) environment is stressful, to say the least. The turn-around time from downlink to uplink is approximately 14 hours, barely enough time for the teams of scientists and engineers to analyze the recent data, plan the next sols activities, and then generate and verify the command sequences before uplink radiation. To make matters worse, a sol is approximately forty minutes longer than a day is on Earth, so each day's activities, meetings, etc. occur a little later than they did the previous day. What this means, practically, is that the time of telemetry downlink, and all associated activities occurring afterwards, moved forward by approximately an eight-hour shift every other week, making it extremely difficult for mission personnel to maintain a sense of situational awareness about the mission. Operations proceeded in this fashion 24x7 for the duration of each rover's life. The cumulative stress on Ops personnel makes it exceedingly difficult for them to remember when activities are to occur or where data products are located.

The total amount of data associated with the MER mission is quite large. The 1996 Mars Pathfinder mission, for reference, produced 2.3 gigabits of data in over 17,000 data products in the nineteen days the rover was active. With two rovers in operation during MER, several GB of data was being produced every day, including Experimental Data Records (EDRs) from the rovers themselves, Reduced Data Records (RDRs) as a result of EDR analysis, and the planning documents and command sequences produced within Ops. This volume of data not only needs to be archived, but also catalogued and tagged with metadata for ease of indexing, location and retrieval. Furthermore, the interdependencies of the various teams make the challenges of cooperative and collaborative work more difficult than they would be otherwise. For example, if modifications are made to a given resource then others who depend on that information must be notified as quickly as possible. Subsequent modifications to data products ripple outwards through other resources and people as the awareness of the changes spreads.

1.2 Background

In the mid 1990s, the DARWIN project focused on the problem of providing real-time access to aeronautical data captured during wind tunnel testing over the internet [6]. DARWIN provided secure access to wind tunnel data, allowing researchers at remote facilities to collaboratively analyze experimental results using a standard web browser [11]. This system was implemented using Common Gateway Interface (CGI) scripting and Java applet technologies to access underlying data repositories [12]. One of the aspects of this work that the CIP project inherited was the D3 metadatabase schema [10].

The initial prototypes of the CIP tools were developed as applets and delivered within a commercial portal package, however we quickly identified several drawbacks to this approach. The reloading of applets on hyperlink traversal and web page refresh was problematic from a user experience perspective as well as making it difficult to maintain state in the tools. Further, testing of this environment, with multiple browsers, browser versions and Java plugin versions was extremely resource intensive. Lastly, applets did not offer the sort of rich and flexible client UI that was desired for CIP. For the above reasons, it was decided that the CIP client should be developed as a full-fledged Java application.

2   CIP Development

As mentioned previously, CIP provides an enhanced sense of situational awareness to mission personnel. Of primary importance was to allow secure local and remote access to mission data products and scheduling information. The system was specified to be available 24x7, with better than a 99% availability over the course of the mission, while handling a load of 150 or more concurrent users. Furthermore, addressing the needs of a diverse user community including scientists, engineers, and managers posed a challenge in and of itself.

The basic principles we followed during the CIP development were to (a) apply applicable industry standards, (b) utilize existing COTS software and (c) use available commercial development tools. Essentially, we wanted to avoid reinventing the wheel, as we were working against hard deadlines (i.e. launch dates) that quite simply could not be pushed back.

CIP needed to be platform-independent, so we naturally chose to use Java throughout the system, with J2EE [9] being used for the middleware and SOAP-based web services [2] providing the client interface to the middleware EJBs [3]. A major benefit in the tools we selected was that the IDE we used was tightly integrated with the application server, making it possible to deploy and test our code from within the IDE. Further, both the client and server web service interfaces were automatically generated simply by invoking build utilities provided with the application server. This saved us much effort in the long run in not having to code these by hand whenever we had to change an interface.

The decision to pursue a Service Oriented Architecture (SOA) built on SOAP-based web services was, at the time, felt to contain some risk, especially given the relative immaturity of the associated technologies and the nature of the system under development. However, the benefits offered in terms of firewall negotiation, stateless connections and security made our early adoption of these technologies a reasonable gambit. This approach has since been validated in several ways, not the least of which by other MER applications utilizing the CIP web services for authentication, authorization and data access in ways that we had not originally anticipated.

3   CIP Architecture

In this section we provide an expose of the CIP architecture. The first two subsections outline the client application functionality and the back end data stores before presenting the CIP middleware and web services in detail. We conclude

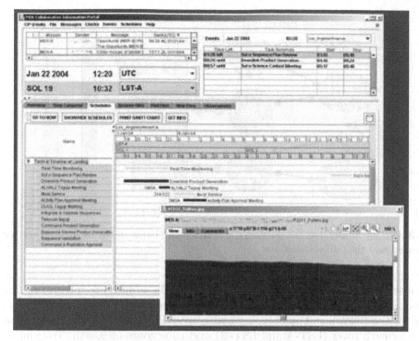

Fig. 2. Screenshot of the CIP client application

this section by examining how crosscutting functionality such as security and logging was implemented across all of the web services.

3.1   Client Application

CIP employs a three-tier client-server model in which the client is a desktop application and the server is a J2EE compliant middleware platform consisting of a number of web services. The server maintains user preferences and profile data [1] in order to provide a consistent interface and behavior from one session to the next. The suite of tools within CIP facilitated increased communication, improved situational awareness and provided a greater exposure to mission information than would otherwise have been possible.

The CIP client application is divided into different information panels as shown in Fig. 2, with broadcast messages and clocks displayed in the upper left, the event horizon in the upper right, and lower tabbed pane for doing time conversions, displaying event and personnel schedules, browsing data files, searching for files, monitoring the arrival of new files, and displaying observations. In this screen shot, part of the tactical timeline schedule is visible with the time scale showing both Earth and Mars times. The auxiliary window is displaying an image of the martian horizon that has been selected in the data file browser.

In essence, mission management, operations and science team members used CIP to retrieve the various data products, staffing and event schedules and main-

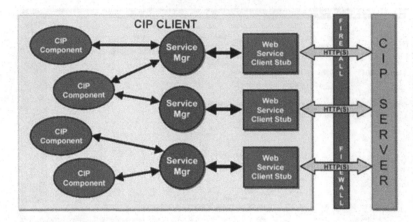

Fig. 3. CIP client architecture showing the relationship between the tools, their service managers and the CIP middleware

tain a sense of what was going on in the mission. In addition to integrating the various mission data repositories into a common interface, CIP provided custom tools for the following: Time keeping and conversion between Mars Local Solar Time for each rover (LST-A and LST-B) and time zones on Earth. Tracking of strategic and tactical events with an event horizon and schedule viewer that is linked to information about science teams and data products. Access to mission broadcast announcements and lastly, the ability to manage subscriptions to different types of notifications about new resources.

The CIP Client was implemented as a layered architecture, with each tool panel relying on one or more of the middleware web services. Each service had a *service manager* which ran in its own thread and served to manage the connection to the service. Each web service connection utilized a service adapter which translated between data formats and mediated the exception handling for the service manager. A number of different design patterns [4] were used throughout the CIP client architecture, including singletons, factories, proxies, decorators and iterators, among others.

CIP Client Tools. The CIP clocks maintain the correct time to within minute accuracy (due to network latency) and convert between different time zones on Earth as well as two Mars time zones LST-A and LST-B. An Event Horizon panel is also provided to display upcoming, ongoing and recent events, including communication windows, shifts and handovers, activity planning and approval meetings, communications windows, press conferences, etc.

The schedule viewer is an interactive tactical event timeline. The time zones supported by the scheduler are the same as those supported by the CIP Clocks. Tactical events are displayed in the schedule viewer, which can also display staffing information for mission personnel, press conferences, etc. The schedule is hyperlinked such that when a user clicks on an event, information about the associated teams, processes, and data products is displayed in a pop-up window.

The Browse Files and Find Files tabs provide tools for searching and browsing mission data products and resources by name, type, date, etc. In addition, the New Files tab allows users to subscribe to notification about active data products that they are interested in. The mission resources of interest include generated summary reports, rover health information, and strategic and activity plan summaries among other things. The data products reside on mission specific file systems, while annotations and other resource metadata are maintained in a metadata database. These repositories are described in more detail in the next subsection.

The broadcast announcements panel allows CIP users to communicate about mission announcements, news, events, and plans. Past messages are archived to a database and accessible through a message browser utility located in a pull down menu. Using the message browser, users can delete messages from their view or make important announcements 'sticky' so that they don't scroll off the screen as new messages appear.

3.2   Data Repositories

A critical aspect of the CIP application is being notified when new resources become available or when existing resources are modified. This allows the metadata cache to be kept up to date, in turn ensuring that mission personnel are using the most recent versions of resources to make important decisions. Maintaining a sufficient level of situational, group, and workspace awareness in a distributed system required a reliable event notification infrastructure.

For simplicity and responsiveness under extreme user loads, MER utilized several flat NFS file systems to store mission data products, hence the amount of control over the repository was limited when compared to other, more robust content management systems. To provide CIP with information about active resources, the Solaris NFS logging daemon, nfslogd, was used to trap file operations. Information is written to a log file that is monitored by a data acquisition daemon running on the CIP server.

When a given resource is active, a notification is sent to the CIP middleware in the form of a JMS message. The notifications contain enough information to update the CIP metadata repository appropriately. Subsequently, a notification was sent to any concerned clients about the update. The CIP metadata is maintained in an Oracle database on a dedicated server. This database also maintains schemas for scheduling information and archival storage of broadcast messages.

3.3   Middleware

CIP is a three-tier enterprise system based on the Java language. The client tier consists of a desktop application developed with Java Swing components, while the J2EE middleware tier consists of Enterprise Java Beans (EJB) and servlets. Web services acted as the interface between the client applications and

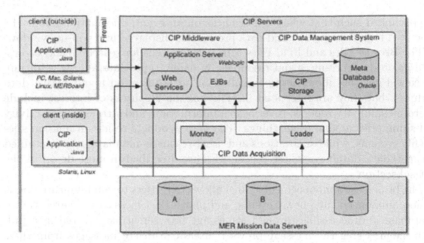

Fig. 4. CIP middleware architecture

the EJBs. The data repository tier included the mission file system, the Oracle databases, and data monitor and data loader utilities. The middleware EJBs used JDBC calls to access the databases. The Java Message Service (JMS) provides asynchronous messaging among the three tiers.

The CIP middleware architecture and its' relationship with the client application and back end data repositories is shown in Fig. 4. In the final deployed configuration, the CIP middleware, data acquisition and data management system ran on separate machines, with the MER mission data servers were NFS mounted as shown.

The CIP middleware consisted of a number of independent services, forming an example of a service oriented architecture. Each service had a public interface implemented by a stateless session EJB, acting as a session facade [7], that was the service provider. Each service provider had a SOAP processor to handle incoming web services requests and their responses. CIP used the HTTPS protocol to ensure secure communications between the client applications and the middleware. A general representation of the CIP web service architecture is presented in Fig. 5.

The following web services were exposed to the client application: User management, Time, Database query, File streaming, and JMS messaging. These services were chosen based on logical groupings of functionality present in the system requirements. The primary goals of the middleware included scalability, reliability, extensibility, and security. For the most part, these goals were fulfilled by our use of J2EE and web services over HTTPS. Our other goal for the middleware was that it remained invisible to the end client, giving each user the illusion of having direct and exclusive access to the data. It was evident that we had achieved this latter goal when users asked, "What server?", not realizing that they were connected to one in the first place.

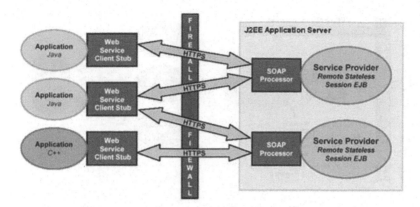

Fig. 5. CIP Web Services

User Management Service. The CIP User Management Service provides authentication and authorization services for CIP clients and is designed to be an independent vertical service that can be used for either purpose across several MER subsystems apart from CIP. The requirements for other MER subsystems to use the CIP User Management Service was inclusion of the user management service client stubs by way of a jar file.

Time Service. It was important for everyone working on the MER mission to be able to answer the question "What time is it?". The mission ran on Mars time, and since a Sol is about 40 minutes different than an Earth day, regularly scheduled events drifted later from day to day relative to Earth time. Moreover, two Martian time zones, one per rover were used extensively throughout the mission.

The CIP application displayed clocks that showed Mars and Earth times in various time zones chosen by the user. The CIP middleware supplied accurate times, which went over the Internet to the CIP applications. Due to network latencies, the times displayed by the CIP applications could be a few seconds off; we only guaranteed accuracy to the minute. The middleware obtained accurate Earth time via a Network Time Protocol server and computed the Mars times from the Earth time.

Query Service. The middleware query service accessed schedules and metadata stored in the Oracle databases of the data repository tier. CIP client applications displayed staff and event schedules, which they requested from the middleware. The applications also allowed users to browse data and images sent by the rovers. This information was categorized according to metadata fields, such as which rover, which sol, or which instrument. Users could also do searches based on metadata field values. The metadata was generated and loaded into the database by the data loader utility in the data repository tier.

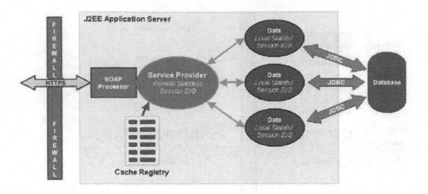

Fig. 6. The CIP query service

As shown in Fig. 6, the query service used stateful session EJBs to perform the queries via JDBC calls. Each session EJB stored the query results. By keeping track of these stateful session EJBs in a registry – a hash table keyed by the query strings – the middleware was able to cache query results in memory. As of this writing, the middleware cache has achieved a cumulative hit rate of 65% over the longest recorded server uptime.

Streamer Service. A user of the CIP client application often requested downloads of data and images. The middleware responded to such a request by accessing the desired file from the mission file servers in the data repository tier.

The middleware transmitted each file in small blocks, with the web services interface converting each block of binary data into ASCII – two characters per original byte – using base 64 notation. The block was then encrypted and sent over HTTPS to the requesting client application. The web services client stub decrypted the block and converted it back to binary. The application received all the blocks sequentially, and so it was simple for it to reassemble the data or image.

Despite all the data conversions and the encryption and decryption, files downloaded at the rate of around 100 MB per hour. Most of the data or image files were smaller than a few megabytes, although some data products were quite large – panoramic mosaics, for example, that were composed of many smaller images being stitched together.

Message Service. The CIP Message Service provided JMS messaging capabilities between the CIP client and the middleware. The clearest example of this functionality is the broadcast announcements tool, which allowed managers to send messages out to the mission. Many of the CIP components, however, were able to take advantage of this framework so that the information they displayed was the freshest possible.

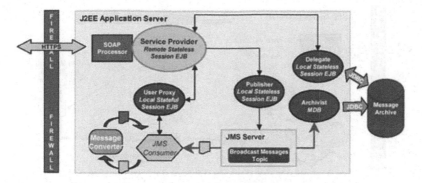

Fig. 7. CIP Message Service

The Schedule Viewer subscribed to messages about modifications to the mission schedules. When a new schedule is uploaded to the server, or an existing schedule is modified, a message is published to 'schedules' topic. When the client receives the message, the display is updated to reflect that new scheduling information is available. Similarly, the New Files tab allows users to subscribe to active resources by their type and when they were last modified. When resources are modified or added to one of the mission repositories, an active resource notification message is published to a 'resources' topic and if a client has subscribed to notifications of that type, it is notified.

On the data acquisition side of things, the database loader subscribes to a 'monitor' topic, which carries messages about NFS operations on mission data products. This information is used to keep the metadata about the mission resources accurate and up to date. Thus, when the loader receives a notification that new data products are available it populates the metadata database with information about them.

The decoupling of event producers and event consumers within the overall system is perhaps one of the greatest benefits of using messaging oriented architectures. This approach redeemed itself when it became necessary to migrate the data acquisition components to another machine in order to lighten the load on the primary machine that clients connected to. Without the decoupling of system components provided by JMS, this would have required a fair amount of effort.

One of the difficult challenges in designing the CIP Message Service was in allowing multiple clients to connect using the same user ID. This situation would arise, for example, whenever a user left an instance of the CIP client application running in their office or at home and then subsequently attempted to log in at a terminal in one of the science areas. This posed a problem because the application used durable subscriptions for several of the system services. As the JMS specification states, durable subscriptions require a unique client ID to be used consistently from one session to the next and only a single client can use this client ID at any given time [5]. The solution was to use a client proxy on

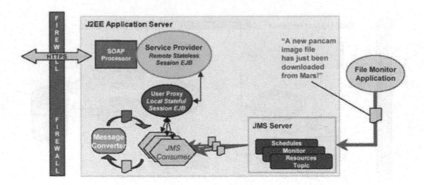

Fig. 8. CIP file notification process

the server to connect to the JMS server in the J2EE container of the application server. In this way, when a user logged in more than once, we could detect that this was the case and manage the JMS subscriptions appropriately.

4 Crosscutting Functionality

In this section we take a look at the crosscutting functionality that was implemented across all of the CIP middleware services. At the time CIP was being developed, the current approaches to SOA did not address overarching issues such as logging, system monitoring, runtime configuration and security. Whereas more recent activities focus on specifying additional application tiers for these activities, [8], our solutions to these issues were considerably less formal, although sufficient for their intended purpose. The monitoring and logging methods described below all rely upon the use of shared data structures, referenced by the application server classpath setting.

4.1 Security and Authorization

According to Sun Micro Systems J2EE specification there are two ways to control access to application resources using the J2EE architecture, declarative authorization and programmatic authorization. In the declarative authorization the application permission model is defined in a deployment descriptor. In the programmatic authorization the container makes access control decisions before dispatching method calls to a component. The CIP User Management Service uses programmatic authorization. In this architecture, the J2EE container serves as an authorization boundary between the components it hosts and their callers

The CIP authentication process is as follows. The CIP client sends a login request by sending username and password on HTTPS (or HTTP if the client is inside the Ops firewall). The User Management Service authenticates the credentials by interacting with the J2EE container. If the authentication is successful, the service generates an access token and returns the token to the client. If the request fails the service returns a null token.

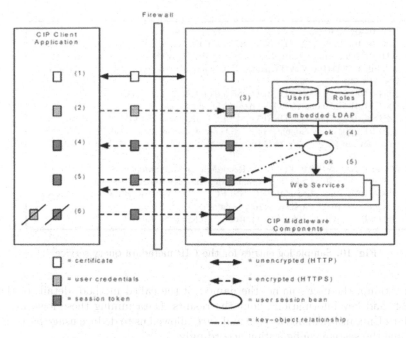

Fig. 9. CIP Authentication and authorization scheme in which (1) SSL certificate is exchanged, (2) user credentials are submitted over a secure channel, (3) user credentials are verified against the embedded LDAP store, (4) a user session EJB is created along with a corresponding session token, which is passed back to the client, (5) subsequent requests for middleware web services include the user session token, which is used by the middleware to look up the user session EJB and authorize the request against the associated roles and privileges, and (6) the expiration of the session token and removal of the user session EJB upon client logout. The actions in (6) may also occur if a CIP client is idle for too long and their session expires

The CIP user authorization procedure is accomplished through the definition and enforcement of user roles. The authorization process for a CIP client is as follows. When a CIP client requests a CIP middleware service, it supplies the login token obtained in a prior authentication request. The token is validated and then user is checked against the roles for granting permission to access the service requested. If the check is successful, the service request will be allowed to proceed, otherwise an authorization error will be returned to the client. The complete life cycle of CIP authentication and authorization described above is depicted in Fig. 9.

4.2   Logging and System Monitoring

Extensive run time logging and real time monitoring enhanced the middleware's reliability. The middleware web services logged every user request and it's subsequent processing within the system. As shown in Fig. 10, the log entry contains

14   Elias Sinderson, Vish Magapu, and Ronald Mak

```
2004-04-01 12:09:32,225 INFO : rmak: Metadata.query()
2004-04-01 12:09:32,230 DEBUG: SELECT file_view.* FROM MER_B.file_view
WHERE ((file_view.modified >= 1080806949117) AND (file_view.category =
'dataFile') AND (file_view.filename LIKE '/%/merb/ops/ops/surface%/%/rcam/%'
ESCAPE '\'))
2004-04-01 12:09:33,126 DEBUG: Records fetched: 0, skipped: 0
2004-04-01 13:50:06,816 INFO : rmak: Metadata.query()
2004-04-01 13:50:06,820 DEBUG: SELECT file_view.* FROM MER_B.file_view
WHERE ((file_view.seqnum = 66) AND (file_view.category = 'dataProduct') AND
(file_view.owner = 'opgs') AND (file_view.type LIKE '%/jpeg/MER-B' ESCAPE
'\'))
2004-04-01 13:50:10,073 DEBUG: Records fetched: 1, skipped: 0
2004-04-01 13:50:11,546 INFO : rmak: Metadata.getObjectsByParent()
2004-04-01 13:50:11,550 DEBUG: SELECT * FROM MER_B.file_view WHERE
(parent_pk = 16127) AND (category = 'dataFile')
2004-04-01 13:50:12,108 DEBUG: Records fetched: 5, skipped: 0
```

Fig. 10. Sample log entries for the CIP metadata query service

a time stamp, the user's name, the named of the called method, details of the request, and key information about the results. Data mining these logs, using standard Unix utilities such as *grep* and *sort*, allowed us to deduce usage patterns and tune the system configuration accordingly.

A separate utility monitored the status of the middleware and graphically reported statistics such as memory usage and response times. Knowing the health of server at all times enables system administrators to correct any problems before they became serious. This monitoring was made possible by writing status information for each of the web services to a static data structure that was made available via inclusion on the application servers' main classpath. Fig. 11 shows a screenshot of the graphical monitoring utility. In addition to the statistics tab shown, the Users tab displayed the users currently logged in, the file tab showed which files had recently been accessed by users, and the cache tab showed the metadata that was currently cached from users interaction with the system. In addition to the GUI monitoring utility, a cron job was set up to report the same information to an administrative email address as well.

4.3   Runtime Configuration

An important measurement of software reliability is how long a system stays up and running. An application can unexpectedly crash, or system administrators can bring it down for maintenance. A common maintenance operation is to reconfigure an application to meet some change in operational usage or deployed configuration.

A key feature that has allowed the CIP server to stay up and running for extended periods (over 70 days at a time) was dynamic reconfiguration. CIP's middleware design allowed individual services to be hot redeployable. In other words, it was possible to reconfigure and restart a given service while the rest

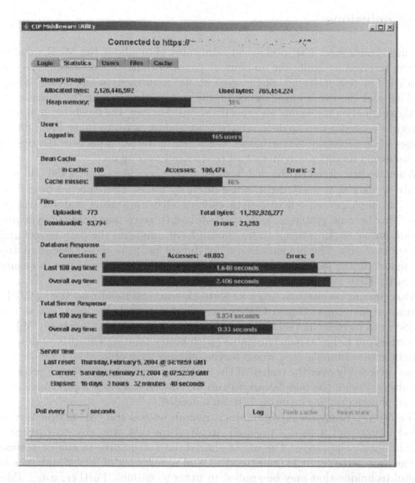

Fig. 11. The CIP Middleware monitoring utility, displaying the primary statistics tab, showing the current memory profile, number of users logged in, cache data, file upload / download statistics, database and server response times, and server uptime. The other tabs displayed the currently logged in users, recently downloaded files and cached metadata

of the middleware web services (and CIP as a whole) continued to run without interruption. To reconfigure a service, a system administrator first edited the service's configuration file and then redeployed the service, causing it to read in the new configuration. Redeploying a service typically took only a few seconds, and often users did not notice any service interruptions even though they had active clients up and running. When the CIP client was unable to connect to a service, the request was queued until the service was reachable.

5   Conclusions

All things considered, CIP performed admirably throughout the MER mission and has received a significant amount of praise for the broad functionality it provided. The responsiveness of the system, its' robustness in the face of heavy user load and the overall availability of the system throughout the mission all met the original requirements and specifications. Further, the flexibility and ease of runtime configuration made it relatively straightforward to make last minute changes when necessary. Nevertheless, there are, of course, aspects of the design that we would do differently if we had to do it all over again.

When we first designed the middleware, a very complex data model [10] was already in place that precluded the use of entity EJBs. Therefore, as described above, we implemented our own data caching algorithm using stateful session EJBs. This became problematic in that we had to solve many thread synchronization problems. In retrospect, we should have simplified the data model and used entity EJBs. The obvious lesson for future projects is to (re)design the data model at the same time as the middleware is being developed to ensure that entity EJBs can be used.

After proving its worth during a series of Operational Readiness Tests at JPL, the mission managers deemed CIP to be mission critical. By then, it was too late for us to increase its reliability by clustering the middleware servers. While CIP turned out to be extremely reliable (with better than 99.9% uptime) despite the middleware running on a single server, admins were obliged to monitor the system extensively over the course of the mission. The lesson for future projects is to always design the middleware to run on clustered servers if possible, since one can always disable clustering if it isn't needed.

Despite the recognized shortcomings, overall we feel the CIP middleware is a good example of a service oriented architecture that was able to overcome several difficult challenges. The use of shared data structures to enable session management across multiple web services and monitoring of server statistics is a useful technique that may be applied in other situations. Further, using JMS to integrate the data acquisition components proved to be a wise design choice, providing the necessary flexibility to migrate these components to another system for performance reasons. Lastly, we were able to effectively unify multiple web services into a single client application, giving many of the users the distinct impression that the CIP client was a unified application with direct and immediate access to the mission data repositories. CIP continues to be one of the primary tools used by MER mission personnel, both remotely and within mission control.

References

1. Joshua Bloch and Mark Pozefsky. Jsr 10: Preferences api specification. Technical report, Sun Microsystems, Inc. and International Business Machines Corporation (IBM), May 2002. http://www.jcp.org/en/jsr/detail?id=10.

2. Don Box, David Ehnebuske, Gopal Kakivaya, Andrew Layman, Noah Mendelsohn, Herik Nielsen, Satish Thatte, and Dave Winer. Simple object access protocol (soap) 1.1. Technical report, World Wide Web Consortium, http://www.w3.org/TR/2000/NOTE-SOAP-20000508/, May 2000.
3. Linda DeMichiel. Jsr 19: Enterprise javabeans 2.0. Technical report, Sun Microsystems, Inc., June 1999.
http://www.jcp.org/en/jsr/detail?id=19.
4. Erich Gamma, Richard Helm, Ralph Johnson, and John Vlissides. *Design Patterns: Elements of Reusable Object-Oriented Software*. Addison-Wesley, 1995.
5. Mark Hapner, Rich Burridge, Rahul Sharma, Joseph Fialli, and Kate Stout. *Java Message Service*. Sun Microsystems,
http://java.sun.com/products/jms/docs.html, April 2002.
6. D. J. Koga, D. J. Korsmeyer, and J. A. Schreiner. Darwin information system of nasa – an introduction. In *19th AIAA Advanced Measurement and Ground Testing Technology Conference*, New Orleans, LA, June 1996. AIAA.
7. Floyd Marinescu. *EJB Design Patterns*. Wiley Computer Publishing, 2002.
8. Mike P. Papazoglou. Service-oriented computing: Concepts, characteristics and directions. In *Proceedings of the Fourth International Conference on Web Information Systems Engineering*. IEEE Computer Society, 2003.
9. Bill Shannon. *Java2 Platform Enterprise Edition Specification, v1.3*. Sun Microsystems, Inc., July 2001.
10. Joan Walton, Robert E. Filman, Chris Knight, David J. Korsmeyer, and Diana D. Lee. D3: A collaborative infrastructure for aerospace design. In *Workshop on Advanced Collaborative Environments*, San Francisco, CA, August 2001.
11. Joan Walton, Robert E. Filman, and David J. Korsmeyer. The evolution of the darwin system. In *Symposium on Applied Computing*, pages 971–977, Como, Italy, March 2000. ACM.
12. Joan Walton, D. Korsmeyer, R. Batra, and Y. Levy. The darwin workspace environment for remote access to aeronautics data. In *35th Aerospace Sciences Meeting*, Reno, NV, January 1997.

A Content Model for Evaluating
Peer-to-Peer Searching Techniques

Brian F. Cooper

Center for Experimental Research in Computer Systems
College of Computing
Georgia Institute of Technology
cooperb@cc.gatech.edu

Abstract. Simulation studies are frequently used to evaluate new peer-to-peer searching techniques as well as existing techniques on new applications. Unless these studies are accurate in their modeling of queries and documents, they may not reflect how search techniques will perform in real networks, leading to incorrect conclusions about which techniques are best. We describe how to model content so that simulations produce accurate results. We present a content model for peer-to-peer networks, which consists of a tripartite graph with edges connecting queries to the documents they match, and documents to the peers they are stored at. Our model also includes a set of statistics describing how often queries match the same documents, and how often similar documents are stored at the same peer. We can construct our tripartite content model by running queries over live data stored at real Internet nodes, and simulation results show that searching techniques do indeed perform differently in simulations using this "real" content model versus a randomly generated model. We then present an algorithm for using real content gathered from a small set of peers (say, 1,000) to generate a synthetic content model for large simulated networks (say, 10,000 nodes or more). Finally, we use a synthetic model generated from World Wide Web documents and queries to compare the performance of several search algorithms that have been reported in the literature.

Keywords: peer-to-peer search, simulation, modeling, performance evaluation

1 Introduction

A flurry of recent research activity has centered on peer-to-peer search networks and their applications to a variety of tasks. A consensus has emerged that initial protocols (such as Gnutella's flooding protocol) are not scalable enough, and this has spurred a great deal of interest in developing new search protocols and strategies. However, it is difficult to accurately evaluate the performance of these new techniques, since it is hard for research groups to deploy and test a real peer-to-peer network of any significant size (i.e., more than a few hundred nodes). As a result, many investigators use simulations of large peer-to-peer networks to evaluate either new techniques or existing techniques for new applications [1, 3, 5, 6, 12, 18, 16, 17, 24, 26].

Our focus is primarily on so-called "unstructured" peer-to-peer networks like those in Gnutella or Kazaa. Although "structured" networks (such as CHORD [23] and CAN

H.-A. Jacobsen (Ed.): Middleware 2004, LNCS 3231, pp. 18–37, 2004.

[20]) have important strengths, research interest in unstructured networks remains high because of their ability to do content-based searches; see for example [6]. In unstructured networks, peers process searches over locally stored content. An overlay network is used to forward search messages between peers according to some routing protocol.

Simulations of unstructured peer-to-peer networks must model both the topology of the network and the content within the network. The topology model describes how peers are connected, while the content model describes two things: the documents that different queries match, and at which peers documents are located. In this context, a "document" is any atomic piece of content, such as a text document, music file, video file, and so on. The topology model is important, since the topology of a network determines how queries will be forwarded, and several recent techniques rely explicitly on certain topology characteristics for performance [1, 6]. However, the content model is equally important, since a simulator must be able to determine when a query reaches a peer with documents matching that query.

There are two general approaches for creating a content model for use in P2P simulations. One approach is to collect real documents and process real queries over these documents [3, 12, 24, 26]. When the simulation runs, the matching between real queries and documents is used to determine when a corresponding simulation query matches a simulation document. In the simulation, documents are assigned to nodes either randomly, or to follow the real location of the collected documents. This approach accurately captures the characteristics of real content, but it is difficult to collect very large sets of real documents. Typical studies examine tens of thousands of documents [12] or perhaps hundreds of thousands of documents [24, 26]. However, existing deployed networks may have many more documents; Kazaa for example has reported as many as hundreds of millions of documents. Techniques that work well at a relatively small scale may not work well at a much larger scale.

The second approach is to generate the content model randomly. In this approach, the matching between simulation queries and simulation documents follows some random distribution, such as uniform [1, 6] or Zipfian [5, 18, 16, 17]. The choice of which peers documents are assigned to is again random, although several existing techniques involve replicating content proactively [7]. While a random approach can be used to generate content models for simulations of very large networks, the model may not accurately reflect the distribution of queries and documents in real applications. In simulation studies described in Section 4, we found that several techniques appeared to perform significantly better using a random content model than when using a content model that matched real documents and queries. For example, a simple random walk search over a power law network topology required twice as many messages when using a real content map than when using a random map.

Our goal is to develop a content model that 1. matches query and document distributions from real applications, and 2. can be scaled up for use in simulations of very large networks. Our approach is to measure useful statistics using small but real collections, and then generate large synthetic content models that match the measured statistics. First, we model content as a tripartite graph: vertices in the graph represent queries, documents and peers, and edges represent the documents that queries match and the peers that documents are stored at. Then, we measure two kinds of statistics about the graph: *degree* statistics, such as the number of documents that a given query matches, and *similarity* statistics, such as the number of common documents matched by two different queries. Using these statistics, we can generate a tripartite content graph of the desired size. This content graph can be used as the input to a simulation of peer-to-peer searching techniques. Our model is general enough to capture content distributions found in existing networks, such as filesharing networks, where it has been observed that a few "popular" documents are replicated widely [6]. At the same time, our model can represent content in other applications that may have different characteristics.

We have developed a simulator for peer-to-peer systems to evaluate the performance of various searching techniques. This simulator uses our content model to determine when a searching technique has found matching results. We present a case study of generating a large synthetic content model and using it with our simulator to evaluate several techniques that have been proposed in the literature. However, our content model is a general model, and can be used with any simulator to evaluate peer-to-peer systems.

In this paper, we discuss our content model and how it can be used in simulations of large peer-to-peer networks. In particular, we make the following contributions:

- We define the Map-Degree-Similarity content model (or *MDS content model*). This model includes the tripartite graph representation of queries, documents and peers (the "map"), and formal definitions for the degree and similarity statistics. (Section 2)
- We present an algorithm, SynthMap, for synthesizing large MDS content maps from degree and similarity statistics. SynthMap treats degree statistics as constraints, and uses hill climbing to form a map that best approximates the similarity statistics. (Section 3)
- We present simulation results that demonstrate the need for an accurate content model by showing the discrepancy in performance of several existing algorithms on "real" and "random" maps. We also validate our model by showing that the performance of these algorithms on a synthetic MDS content map closely matches their performance on the "real" map. (Section 4)
- We present a case study of generating a large synthetic MDS content map from a smaller real map, and using it in simulations to compare the performance of several search techniques reported in the literature. (Section 4)

We have implemented a set of tools for gathering statistics from real content and generating synthetic content models, and these tools are available to researchers who wish to use them. In Section 5 we examine related work, and in Section 6 we discuss our conclusions.

2   Map-Degree-Similarity Content Model

Our content model consists of two components. The *map* represents queries matching documents, and documents located at peers. The *statistics* describe the properties of the map.

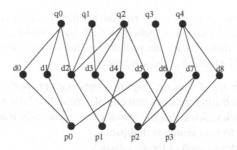

Fig. 1. Example content map.

2.1 Map

The *map* M is defined as a 5-tuple $< Q, D, P, qd, dp >$:

- Q is a set of queries
- D is a set of documents
- P is a set of peers
- qd is a set of pairs over the domain $Q \times D$, where a pair $(q_i \in Q, d_j \in D)$ represents the fact that query q_i matches document d_j
- dp is a set of pairs over the domain $D \times P$, where a pair $(d_j \in D, p_k \in P)$ represents the fact that a copy of document d_j is stored at peer p_k.

The Q, D and P sets are disjoint; that is, $Q \cap D = \emptyset$, $Q \cap P = \emptyset$ and $D \cap P = \emptyset$.

In other words, a map is a tripartite graph with vertices for queries, documents and peers. Edges from queries to documents represent the documents that each query matches, and edges from documents to peers represent the peers that each document is stored at.

The set Q contains distinct queries. For example, if the system uses keyword queries, each query $q_i \in Q$ would have a different combination of keywords. In a run of a simulation, each q_i may be submitted multiple times, possibly at different peers. Similarly, the documents in D represent distinct documents. If the same document d_j is replicated at multiple peers, this is represented by several dp edges incident on d_j.

A simple example map is shown in Figure 1. This content map represents five queries, nine documents and four peers. Query q_0 matches documents d_0, d_1 and d_2. If query q_0 reaches peer p_0, the query will find matching documents d_0 and d_1; if the query reaches peer p_1 it will find matching document d_2. Some documents in this example are located at only one peer (i.e., d_0) while some documents have copies at multiple peers (i.e., d_5).

2.2 Statistics

We define four statistics as part of the MDS model:

- *query-degree* represents the number of documents matched by each query.
- *document-degree* represents the number of peers at which each document is located.

- *query-similarity* represents the similarity between pairs of queries, defined by the number of common documents matched by each query in the pair.
- *query-peer-similarity* represents the probability that multiple documents matching a given query will be located at the same peer.

We believe that our choice of statistics captures important properties of content maps. There may be other interesting statistics that can also be defined. However, in Section 4, we present results which validate that the statistics we have chosen are useful for accurately simulating peer-to-peer search techniques.

We now formally define each of these statistics.

Query-degree counts the number of documents matched by a given query. Formally,

$$query\text{-}degree(q_i) = |\{(q, d) \in qd | q = q_i\}|$$

where $|A|$ denotes the number of elements in set A. In Figure 1, $query\text{-}degree(q_2) = 4$.

Document-degree counts the number of peers at which a given document is stored. Analogously to *query-degree*,

$$document\text{-}degree(d_j) = |\{(d, p) \in dp | d = d_j\}|$$

In Figure 1, $document\text{-}degree(d_7) = 2$.

By measuring the distribution of these statistics in addition to their average, we can capture the variance present in real networks. For example, some queries will match large numbers of documents, while others may only match one or two. Since the distribution of these statistics for a real set of queries, documents and peers may not match a smooth distribution, such as the normal or Zipfian distributions, exactly, we represent these statistics as histograms.

The next two statistics attempt to capture notions of similarity. *Query-similarity* represents the similarity between pairs of queries. Two queries are defined to be highly similar if they match many of the same documents. Query-similarity measures the property often observed in real collections that related queries will match some (though not necessarily all) of the same documents. Consider two keyword queries, "apple" and "banana." Both queries are likely to match documents about fruit, but "apple" may also match documents about "Apple Computer" while "banana" may not. Query similarity measures the amount of overlapping documents matched by pairs of queries. The amount of query similarity can affect the performance of search protocols that route queries based on past results, such as "intelligent search" [12] or routing indices [8].

In order to formally define query-similarity, we must first define a related statistic, *query-overlap*. The query-overlap for a pair of queries q_a and q_b is the number of shared documents between q_a and q_b. Formally,

$$query\text{-}overlap(q_a, q_b) = |\{d \in D | (q_a, d) \in qd \land (q_b, d) \in qd\}|$$

We could simply use query-overlap as the definition of query-similarity, but this definition is unsatisfactory since query-overlap is unnormalized. For example, if q_a and q_b both match the same single document, and q_c and q_d both match the same ten documents, $query\text{-}overlap(q_a, q_b) = 1$ and $query\text{-}overlap(q_c, q_d) = 10$. However, intuitively, q_a is as similar to q_b as q_c is to q_d, since for each pair, each query matches all of the documents of the other query. We therefore normalize query-overlap to define query-similarity. To do so, we divide query-overlap by the query-degree of the queries. Since the queries might have different query-degrees, we get

$$query\text{-}similarity(q_a, q_b) = query\text{-}overlap(q_a, q_b)/query\text{-}degree(q_a)$$

$$query\text{-}similarity(q_b, q_a) = query\text{-}overlap(q_a, q_b)/query\text{-}degree(q_b)$$

In other words, the query-similarity statistic is not symmetric. Intuitively this makes sense; if the query-similarity statistic were symmetric then it would not capture the difference between pairs of queries with overlapping sets of matching documents and pairs of queries where one query's matching documents are a subset of the other query's matching documents. In the map in Figure 1, $query\text{-}similarity(q_1, q_2) = 2/2 = 1$, while $query\text{-}similarity(q_2, q_1) = 2/4 = 0.5$.

The fourth statistic, $query\text{-}peer\text{-}similarity$, captures the notion that queries are likely to find multiple matching documents at the same peer. Since users tend to collect multiple documents on each topic they are interested in, if a query matches one document at a peer it will probably match several others as well. Query-peer-similarity measures the probability of such co-occurrence of matching documents for a given query. The query-peer-similarity impacts the performance of protocols that attempt to find results by routing searches to a promising subset of peers, such as in [13, 15], since the query-peer-similarity determines the probability that multiple matching documents are indeed found in that promising subset.

The query-peer-similarity for a given query q_i is defined as the probability that if q_i matches two documents, those two documents are located at the same peer. Formally,

$$query\text{-}peer\text{-}similarity(q_i) =$$

$$\frac{\left| \begin{array}{c} \{(d_a, d_b); d_a, d_b \in D | \; d_a \neq d_b \wedge (q_i, d_a) \in qd \wedge (q_i, d_b) \in qd \wedge \\ \exists p((d_a, p) \in dp \wedge (d_b, p) \in dp)\} \end{array} \right|}{query\text{-}degree(q_i) \times (query\text{-}degree(q_i) - 1)}$$

The numerator of this expression calculates the number of ordered pairs of documents (d_a, d_b) such that d_a and d_b both match q_i and are stored at the same peer. The denominator calculates the total number of ordered pairs of documents (d_c, d_d) such that d_c and d_d both match q_i. Thus, the statistic calculates the probability that an ordered pair of documents (d_a, d_b) that q_i matches is stored at the same peer. The definition is the same if we consider unordered pairs of documents; then, both the numerator and the denominator in the expression above overcount by a factor of two, and the factors of two cancel. In Figure 1, $query\text{-}peer\text{-}similarity(q_0) = 2/6 = 0.3333$.

As with the degree statistics, we can measure the distribution of values of query-similarity and query-peer-similarity for a given map. These distributions capture the diversity of query, document and peer similarities. For example, in one map there may be groups of related queries that all match roughly the same set of documents alongside individual queries that are the only ones to match certain documents. Similarly, for some queries, the matching documents may be clustered at a few sites, while for others matching documents may be scattered all over the network.

3 Synthesizing Content Maps from Statistics

We want to generate large synthetic content maps that we can reasonably expect will accurately model real applications. In this section, we describe how to generate a synthetic map from a set of degree and similarity statistics. Probably these statistics will be computed by analyzing a map representing real content. However, it is possible that researchers may want to generate maps that have arbitrary properties not found in an existing map. For example, a researcher may postulate that an as yet undeveloped application would use content distributed in a certain way. The researcher could generate statistics matching his assumptions and then construct a synthetic content map matching those statistics. As such, our techniques do not require the original, real content map in order to generate the synthetic map. Instead, only the degree and similarity statistics are required.

The quality of the generated map depends on the quality of the statistics. If the statistics are generated from inaccurate samples of real data, then the resulting synthetic content map will be flawed. Therefore, researchers using our model must be careful to gather an accurate sample of data before generating statistics. Similarly, a synthetic content map for a new application will produce accurate results only if the underlying statistics accurately model the new application.

First, we describe how we scale the values of the statistics to the size of the synthetic map by treating the statistic histograms as vectors and multiplying by a constant. Next, we present an iterative algorithm based on hill climbing, called SynthMap, for generating the synthetic map from the statistic vectors.

3.1 Scaling MDS Statistics

Recall that the MDS content model uses four statistics: *query-degree*, *document-degree*, *query-similarity* and *query-peer-similarity*. Since the distribution of these statistics may not be smooth, we manipulate the distribution of each statistic using histograms.

The query-degree statistic histogram has one bin for each degree $0, 1...MQD_M$, where MQD_M is the maximum query-degree in map M. The count in bin i is the number of queries in M that have query-degree i. For convenience, we represent this histogram as a vector; the value in position i of the vector is the count for bin i, and the vector has $MQD_M + 1$ elements. Similarly, the histogram for the document-degree statistic has one bin for each degree $0, 1...MDD_M$, where MDD_M is the maximum document degree in M. The vector for document-degree has $MDD_M + 1$ elements, where element i is the number of documents with degree i. In our discussion, we call the query-degree histogram vector *qd-histo*, and the document-degree histogram vector *dd-histo*.

The similarity statistics query-similarity and query-peer-similarity have values in the interval $[0, 1]$. Therefore, we must choose a *bin-interval* BI that represents the width of the histogram bins for these statistics. For example, we use $BI = 0.1$, so we have bins $(0, 0.1], (0.1, 0.2] ... (0.9, 1]$, and the counts in each bin represent the number of items within the intervals of the bin. Note that we assume that all bins are of equal width and are contiguous. In general, histograms can be constructed with varying intervals and non-contiguous intervals, but we do not necessarily need this generality for our purposes. However, we do find it useful to have a special "zero" bin that represents the interval $[0,0]$. For the query-similarity statistic, the bin counts represent the number of ordered pairs of queries that have a query-similarity within the bin interval. For the query-peer-similarity statistic, the bin counts represent the number of queries whose query-peer-similarity falls within the bin interval. In our discussion, we call the query-similarity histogram vector *qs-histo*, and the query-peer-similarity histogram vector *qps-histo*.

The histogram counts depend on the size of the map from which the histograms were derived. For example, the sum of the elements of qd-histo equals the number of queries in the map. Before we can generate a synthetic map, we need to scale the histogram counts to the size of the map we are generating. We choose a scaling factor S, and the histograms will represent a map with S times as many queries, documents and peers as the map for the original histograms. We make a simplifying assumption that empty bins in the small histogram remain empty in the scaled histogram. In general, this may not be true; increasing the number of samples in a distribution may add samples to previously empty histogram buckets, especially in the tail of the distribution. However, since we do not attempt to derive a smooth distribution for our histograms, it is impossible to predict the probability that bins which were empty in the small histogram would have samples in the large histogram. Therefore, we make our simplifying assumption.

For the qd-histo, dd-histo and qps-histo, the sum of the counts is equal to the number of queries, documents, and queries (respectively) in the map. We can therefore generate scaled histograms by multiplying the histogram vectors by S. Thus, to generate histograms for a synthetic map M' from histograms representing map M:

$$qd\text{-}histo_{M'} = S \times qd\text{-}histo_M; \quad dd\text{-}histo_{M'} = S \times dd\text{-}histo_M; \quad qps\text{-}histo_{M'} = S \times qps\text{-}histo_M$$

In contrast, the qs-histo represents all ordered pairs of queries (excluding queries paired with themselves; e.g. (q_i, q_i)). Thus, the sum of counts in the qs-histo is equal to $|Q| \times (|Q|-1)$, and the scaled histogram must have counts summing to $S \times |Q| \times (S \times |Q|-1)$. Therefore, to scale the qs-histo:

$$qs\text{-}histo_{M'} = \frac{S \times |Q| \times (S \times |Q| - 1)}{|Q| \times (|Q| - 1)} \times qs\text{-}histo_M = \frac{S \times (S \times |Q| - 1)}{|Q| - 1} \times qs\text{-}histo_M$$

3.2   Generating Synthetic Maps

We want to generate a synthetic map $M' = <Q', D', P', qd', dp'>$ with MDS statistics matching a set of histograms. These histograms may be scaled versions of histograms from a real map M, although $S = 1$ is also possible. For example, in Section 4, we validate our model by comparing a real map and a synthetic map "scaled" with $S = 1$.

Our *SynthMap* algorithm takes as input qd-histo, dd-histo, qs-histo and qps-histo histogram vectors, and produces a synthetic map M' with MDS statistics whose distributions closely approximates these histograms. It is straightforward to generate maps that exactly match the qd-histo and dd-histo distributions by randomly generating edges. For example, to create a random query-document mapping matching a given qd-histo:

1. For each query $q_a \in Q'$, choose a non-empty qd-histo bin i
   (a) Create i edges from q_a to randomly chosen documents $d \in D'$.
   (b) Decrement the count in qd-histo bin i

A random document-peer matching that matches dd-histo can be constructed in a similar way. However, it is more difficult to generate maps that match the qs-histo and qps-histo distributions, since those statistics represent multiple interacting objects.

Our approach is to generate a map matching dd-histo and qd-histo exactly, and that is as close as possible to qs-histo and qps-histo. As such, we treat the problem of generating a map as an optimization problem where dd-histo and qd-histo act as constraints, and we want to maximize the similarity to qs-histo and qps-histo. The general idea of the algorithm is that we generate an initial map according to dd-histo and qd-histo, and then use hill climbing to successively improve the map until it closely matches qs-histo and qps-histo.

The SynthMap algorithm, shown in Figure 2, creates sets of queries, documents and peers. The sizes of these sets are specified by the user in the $Q\text{-}size_{M'}$, $D\text{-}size_{M'}$, $P\text{-}size_{M'}$ parameters; these parameters should describe the same size map as that modeled by the histogram parameters. SynthMap then generates a query-document matching qd', using the SynthMap-QD algorithm, and a document-peer matching dp', using the SynthMap-DP algorithm.

In SynthMap-QD, we iterate, producing a series of matchings that are better and better matches to qs-histo. In each iteration, we try to replace each query-document edge with an edge that reduces the "badness" of the matching. To see if a matching qd'_x with a changed edge is better than the current qd', we calculate a histogram $qs\text{-}histo^x$ for the query-similarity of qd'_x. We define the "badness" of a matching qd'_x as the Euclidean distance between the $qs\text{-}histo^x$ vector and the goal $qs\text{-}histo^{M'}$ vector. Formally:

$$badness(qs\text{-}histo^x, qs\text{-}histo^{M'}) = \sqrt{\sum_{i=0}^{n-1}(qs\text{-}histo_i^{M'} - qs\text{-}histo_i^x)^2}$$

where n is the number of buckets in a histogram, and $qs\text{-}histo_i^{M'}$ and $qs\text{-}histo_i^x$ represent histogram buckets. Eventually, we will find a matching that minimizes badness, and this matching is used as the qd' for our synthetic map M'. (Since we are trying to minimize badness, our algorithm is more properly described as "gradient-descent" rather than "hill-climbing.") Ideally, we find a matching with $badness = 0$ and the synthetic map matches $qs\text{-}histo^{M'}$ exactly. However, if we cannot match $qs\text{-}histo^{M'}$ exactly, we iterate SynthMap-QD until the badness is satisfactorily small; e.g., less than some $target\text{-}badness$. Note that the algorithm is not guaranteed to converge to a matching with a badness less than the $target\text{-}matching$. In particular, the algorithm might reach a local minimum in the search space whose badness is undesirably high. In practice, if the algorithm stops making progress we can terminate it early. Then we must decide whether to accept the matching it has produced, or to restart with the hope that it will find a better search space minimum. In our experiments, the algorithm produced matchings with satisfactorily small badness.

SynthMap(qd-$histo_{M'}$, dd-$histo_{M'}$, qs-$histo_{M'}$, qps-$histo_{M'}$, Q-$size_{M'}$, D-$size_{M'}$, P-$size_{M'}$)
  returns M' {
    Create Q', D' and P' sets with Q-$size_{M'}$, D-$size_{M'}$, P-$size_{M'}$ elements respectively
    qd' = SynthMap-QD(Q', D', qd-$histo_{M'}$, qs-$histo_{M'}$)
    ds' = SynthMap-DP(Q', D', P', qd', dd-$histo_{M'}$, qps-$histo_{M'}$)
    return $M' = <Q', D', P', qd', ds'>$
}

SynthMap-QD(Q', D', qd-$histo_{M'}$, qs-$histo_{M'}$)
  returns qd' {
    qd'=createInitialMatching(Q', D', qd-$histo_{M'}$)

    Calculate query-similarity histogram qs-$histo_{qd'}$ for qd'

    // Iterate
    while ($badness(qs$-$histo_{qd'}$,qs-$histo_{M'}$) > $ target-badness) {
      For each edge $(q_a, d_j) \in qd'$ {
        Choose a random document $d_k \in D'$, such that $(q_a, d_k) \notin qd'$

        // qd'_x represents removing the edge (q_a, d_j) from qd' and replacing it with (q_a, d_k)
        $qd'_x = (qd' - (q_a, d_j)) \cup (q_a, d_k)$
        Calculate query-similarity histogram qs-$histo^x$ for qd'_x

        Choose a random number $pick$ on the interval $[0, 1)$

        // If changing the edge decreases the badness, make the change
        // If changing the edge leaves the badness the same, make the change with some
        // probability $pick$-$probability$
        If $[badness(qs$-$histo^x$,qs-$histo_{M'}) < badness(qs$-$histo_{qd'}$,qs-$histo_{M'})]$ OR
        $[badness(qs$-$histo^x$,qs-$histo_{M'}) = badness(qs$-$histo_{qd'}$,qs-$histo_{M'})$ AND
        $pick < pick$-$probability]$ {
          $qd' = qd' - (q_a, d_j)$
          $qd' = qd' \cup (q_a, d_k)$
          Set query similiarity histogram qs-$histo_{qd'} = qs$-$histo^x$
        }
      }
    }

  return qd'
}

Note: SynthMap-DP is similar to SynthMap-QD and is omitted.

Fig. 2. SynthMap and SynthMap-QD algorithms for generating synthetic content maps.

The initial matching is created by calling some function createInitialMatching().
This function could create a matching randomly from the qd-histo (as described above).
Alternatively, any easy to create matching can be produced. For example, createInitial-
Matching() could just assign queries to documents by iterating through documents in

round robin order. In fact, in our experience, SynthMap-QD converged more quickly in some cases by using this round robin approach rather than the random approach. Our approach in our implementation is to start by using the random initial matching, and try other easy to construct initial matchings if the rate of convergence is not satisfactory.

The SynthMap-QD algorithm always replaces an edge if the replacement reduces the badness of the map. However, sometimes it replaces an edge with another that leaves the badness unchanged. The *pick-probability* constant determines the probability that the algorithm takes such a "horizontal" move in the search space. The reason we include this possibility in the algorithm is that in our experience the algorithm frequently reaches a "plateau" in the search space. Horizontal moves allow the algorithm to move off of the plateau and resume gradient descent. Adding the horizontal moves to the algorithm results in consistently better qd' matchings.

The most expensive step in this algorithm is the repeated calculation of the query-similarity histogram qs-histo, shown in boldface in Figure 2. Constructing a qs-histo requires computing the overlap for $O(|Q'|^2)$ pairs of queries, and for large $|Q'|$, repeated calculation of this step takes a prohibitively long time. To address this problem, in our implementation we avoid the full histogram computation. Instead, we determine which pairs of queries are affected by the change, and then incrementally update the old $qs\text{-}histo_{qd'}$ histogram by updating the affected bins to produce the new $qs\text{-}histo_{qd'_x}$ histogram. To support this optimization, we maintain two lookup tables for qd': one that maps from a query to its matching documents, and one that maps from a document to its matching queries. We also memoize as many query overlap counts as will fit in memory, preferring query overlaps involving queries with the highest query-degree, as these queries have a high probability of being affected by changing edges. When an edge is changed, the affected memoized overlaps are updated. The combination of incremental histogram updates and overlap memoization significantly sped up our algorithm.

Next, SynthMap-DP takes the qd' query-document matching produced by SynthMap-QD, and produces a dp' document-peer matching to closely approximate $qps\text{-}histo^{M'}$. SynthMap-DP is very similar to SynthMap-QD, and is omitted from Figure 2. SynthMap-DP iterates, generating successive dp'_x matchings, until the badness of the matching is satisfactorily small. Again, we use the Euclidean distance to measure the "badness" of the dp'_x matching, which is defined analogously to the badness for the qd'_x matching. When SynthMap-DP terminates, we have generated synthetic qd' and dp' matchings, and the process of generating M' has completed.

In our experience, an initial dp' matching that works well is to assign edges so that all of the documents are clustered on a small number of sites. This is because the maps we tried to synthesize had high query-peer-similarity, and assigning documents to a small number of sites creates a matching with higher query-peer-similarity than a random matching. As a result, the algorithm converges more quickly (and to a matching with lower badness) than when using a random initial matching.

The most expensive step in the SynthMap-DP algorithm is again the histogram calculations. In this case, the histogram calculation required comparing all pairs of documents matched by a given query to see which were co-located on the same peer. If the average number of documents matched by a query is $|qd'|/|Q'|$, then the number of comparisons needed to calculate the histogram one time is $O(|Q'| \times (|qd'|/|Q'|)^2) =$

Table 1. Content sets used in our experiments.

	Gnutella set	Web set
Queries	321	1,000
Documents	30,247	31,066
Peers	2,000	999
Content	Music files	HTML pages

$O(|qd'|^2/|Q'|)$. Again, incremental histogram updates and memoization sped up the algorithm. For each query $q_i \in Q'$, we memoize the number of co-located documents, and the total number of matching documents. When a document-peer edge is changed, the affected memoized counts are updated.

4 Experiments

In this section, we report the results of two types of experiments. First, in Section 4.3 we describe experiments we conducted to validate our MDS content model. These validation experiments measure the performance of several peer-to-peer search techniques on real content maps generated from Gnutella and Web search traces, content maps generated randomly using a uniform or Zipfian distribution, and synthetic content maps generated using our SynthMap algorithm. These validation experiments show:

- The performance of several search techniques differs widely between the real and random maps, with some techniques sending two or three times as many messages when using the real map than when using the random map. One technique's performance differed by almost a factor of 10.
- The performance of these search techniques on the synthetic content map closely matches their performance on the real map.

Thus, our validation experiments demonstrate both the need for an accurate content model and the effectiveness of the model we propose.

Second, Section 4.4 describes a case study of simulations using a synthetic content map for a 10,000 node network generated from a smaller map representing a trace of queries over 1,000 web sites. The results of this study show that in such large networks there is a tradeoff between search cost and search response time, and demonstrates the value of the MDS content model in simulating peer-to-peer search techniques.

4.1 Content Sets and Simulation Setup

We used two different content sets for our experiments representing two different applications of peer-to-peer search. The characteristics of these content sets are summarized in Table 1. The first, called *Gnutella*, was generated from a trace gathered from the Gnutella network by Yang and Garcia-Molina in September 2001 [26][1]. This trace was gathered by running a Gnutella peer and logging queries and query responses. We used

---

[1] We would like to thank Beverly Yang and Hector Garcia-Molina for the Gnutella trace.

a subset of the full trace representing 2,000 randomly chosen peers. The Gnutella set represents content from the traditional peer-to-peer application, multimedia filesharing.

The second content set, called *Web*, was generated from web pages we downloaded from 1,000 web sites in March 2004. We downloaded between 1 and 2,303 pages per site by crawling the first two levels of the site. Then, we generated a set of keyword queries from the downloaded pages using term frequencies commonly observed in information retrieval systems (from [4]). We used standard information retrieval techniques to determine which queries matched which documents; namely, TF/IDF weights and the cosine distance [2]. The Web set represents an application of peer-to-peer techniques to World Wide Web information discovery and retrieval, where web sites connected in a peer-to-peer network perform searches over their own content.

For our simulations, we generated peer-to-peer search network topologies that match a power law distribution. Peer-to-peer systems are frequently simulated with power law topologies [1, 16], as a power law topology is a good (but not perfect) model of the Gnutella topology [22]. To generate the power law network, we used the PLOD algorithm [19] with an average degree of 5 and a maximum degree of 10.

We used an event-based peer-to-peer simulator that we have developed to conduct the experiments. This simulator takes as inputs a network topology, MDS content map, and list of (query,site) pairs, and generates for each pair a search message at the listed site. A message handler implementing a given search protocol (such as flooding or random walks) is registered with the simulator, and determines how search messages are routed. One time tick in our simulator represents the time for a peer to process a query and then forward it one hop in the overlay network according to the routing protocol. The simulator counts the total number of search messages generated, as well as the total search processing time (measured in ticks). Note that our MDS content model is not restricted to use with our simulator but is general enough for use with any peer-to-peer simulator.

4.2 Searching Techniques

We used four different search techniques for our experiments.

Flooding is the original Gnutella search protocol. When a peer receives a search message, it both processes the message and forwards it to all of its neighbors in the overlay network. Each message is given a time-to-live value *ttl*, and search messages get flooded to every node within *ttl* hops of the source.

Iterative deepening [26] is like flooding, but search messages are sent from the source with a progressively higher *ttl* until "enough" content is found (where "enough" is defined by the user.)

Random walks avoids sending messages to all nodes [1]. When a peer receives a search message, it processes the message and then forwards it to one randomly chosen neighbor. Messages continue random walking until either a predefined number of results are found (again, predefined by the user), or a *ttl* is reached. Random walk *ttl* values are high and exist mainly to prevent searches from walking forever [16].

Biased random walks adapts random walks to leverage the power law nature of search networks [1]. Peers forward search messages to the neighbor that has the most overlay links. Messages are annotated with a list of where they have been, and are only

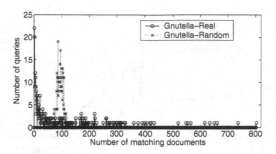

Fig. 3. Query-degree for the Gnutella maps.

forwarded to a given node once if possible. Moreover, every peer tracks the content of its neighbors. As a result, the peers with many neighbors track a large amount of content, and by seeking out those peers searches are likely to quickly discover matching content.

4.3 Validating the Content Model

We ran a set of experiments to validate our content model. We wanted to determine 1. if the statistic distributions differed between real and randomly generated maps, 2. if the performance of search techniques differed between real and randomly generated maps, and 3. if the performance of search techniqes on synthetic maps matched their performance on real maps. We compared several content maps:

- *Gnutella-Real*: a content map representing the real content and query traces collected from the Gnutella network.

- *Gnutella-Random*: a content map generated randomly, with the same number of queries, documents and peers as the Gnutella-Real map. Also, the average number of documents matched by queries, and the average number of copies of documents, were the same as in the Gnutella-Real map.

- *Gnutella-Zipfian*: a content map generated randomly, where the "popularity" of documents (e.g., the number of queries that match them) matched a Zipfian distribution. The number of queries, documents and peers were the same as in the Gnutella-Real map, and the average number of documents matched by queries, and the average number of copies of documents, were also the same as in the Gnutella-Real map.

- *Gnutella-Synth*: a synthetic content map generated from MDS statistics collected over the *Gnutella-Real* map.

Similarly, we compared *Real*, *Random*, *Zipfian* and *Synth* versions of the Web map.

Statistic Distributions. First, we asked whether the MDS statistics differed for real and random maps. The query-degree distributions for the maps are shown in Figure 3. As the figure shows, queries in the Gnutella-Random map have an average query degree clustered around the mean degree, while the distribution of the query degrees in the Gnutella-Real map is much more skewed. The random assignment of edges naturally leads to a Gaussian degree distribution. Because our SynthMap algorithm gen-

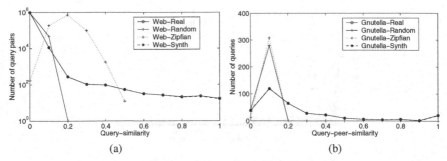

Fig. 4. Similarity statistics: (a) query-similarity for the Web maps, (b) query-peer-similarity of the Gnutella maps.

erates maps with the exact query-degree distribution of the real maps, the distribution of the Gnutella-Synth map matches that of the Gnutella-Real map and is omitted from Figure 3. The query-degree distribution of the Gnutella-Zipfian map is also omitted because it closely matches that of the Gnutella-Random map: the queries matched by a document follow the Zipfian distribution but the documents matched by a query is uniformly distributed. The difference between the query-degree distributions in the Web maps are similar to that in Figure 3.

For both the Gnutella and Web traces, each found document was stored only at one site. Although it has been noted elsewhere [6] that content is often replicated at multiple sites, we did not observe such replication in our traces. Therefore, the document-degree distribution was identical in the real, random, Zipfian and synthetic maps for both the Gnutella and Web data.

The distribution of query-similarity values for the Web-Real, Web-Random and Web-Zipfian maps is shown in Figure 4(a). This figure also shows, for comparison, the query-similarity distribution in our generated Web-Synth map, which almost completely overlaps that of the Web-Real distribution. Note that the vertical axis in the figure has a logarithmic scale. As the figure shows, most pairs of queries in the random map have little or no query-similarity. In other words, if a query matches a document, it is unlikely that any other queries will also match the document. In the Zipfian map, there is more query-similarity due to the large popularity of some documents, with most pairs of queries having a similarity around 0.2. In contrast, in the real map, the query-similarity distribution is more spread out, with several pairs of queries having similarity as high as 1. The figure also shows that our SynthMap algorithm is able to produce a synthetic map with a query-similarity closely matching that of the real map. The results are similar for the Gnutella maps, except that the query-similarity of the Gnutella-Real and Gnutella-Synth maps is somewhat closer to that of the Gnutella-Random map.

The query-peer-similarity distributions are also different between the real, random and Zipfian maps. The distributions for the Gnutella maps are shown in Figure 4(b); the distributions for the Web maps are similar. As the figure shows, the real map has more query-peer-similarity than either the random map or the Zipfian map, since real sites tend to store similar documents, while the random and Zipfian maps scatter similar documents all over the network. The figure also shows that the query-peer-similarity of

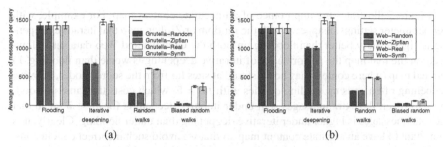

Fig. 5. Cost of search techniques on various maps: (a) Gnutella set, (b) Web set.

the synthetic map closely matches that of the real map (in fact, overlapping it in the figure), again showing the effectiveness of our algorithm at generating synthetic maps that match real statistics.

Query Performance. Next, we examined whether the performance of search techniques on the random, Zipfian and synth maps matched their performance on the real map. In these experiments, we generated 50 search network topologies. For each topology, we injected 10,000 randomly chosen queries at randomly generated source peers, and we measured the average number of messages required per query for each search technique as well as the average time for each query to complete. The goal for each search technique was to find 10 results. For flooding and iterative deepening, we set the *ttl* to 5, and for random and biased random walks we set the *ttl* to 1,000. We also conducted simulations where we varied these parameters; while the absolute results differed, we reached the same conclusions as those reported below.

First, the number of messages sent per query is shown in Figure 5(a) for the Gnutella maps, and Figure 5(b) for the Web maps. In both figures, the error bars represent 95 percent confidence intervals. As the figures show, the performance of search techniques on the random and Zipfian maps (dark gray bars) differs from the performance on the real map (white bars), sometimes radically. For example, the difference in performance between the random and real Gnutella maps is a factor of two for iterative deepening, a factor of three for random walks and a factor of 9.6 for biased random walks. The exception is flooding, which always sends the same number of messages from a given source node regardless of the query or results. The search techniques also require more messages on the real Web map than on the random or Zipfian Web maps, by a factor of 1.5 or more. The reason that the techniques appear to perform better on the random map is that content is scattered uniformly throughout the network, making it easier to locate. In the real map, content matching a query is concentrated at a few sites, which can pose problems for random walks and biased random walks in particular. If the query misses those few sites along its walk then it may walk for a long time without finding content. Although we might think that the Zipfian maps would do a better job of capturing the skewed distribution of real content, our results show that Zipfian maps do not produce performance results comparable to the real maps. The reason is clear from Figure 4; the Zipfian maps do not accurately model the distribution of queries, documents and peers in the real content sets.

Figure 5 illustrates the importance of an accurate content map. For example, with our parameter settings, it appears with the random or Zipfian map that iterative deepening is significantly better than flooding on both the Gnutella and Web data sets. However, on the real map the performance of iterative deepening is worse than flooding. In the real map (where content may be clustered at sites far from the source node), iterative deepening often ends up sending queries with $ttl = 5$, which costs the same as flooding. However, the extra messages sent under iterative deepening for $ttl < 5$ mean that the total messages is higher under iterative deepening than under flooding. Clearly, it is important to have an accurate content map so that we avoid such incorrect conclusions.

In contrast, Figure 5 shows that the search techniques perform comparably using the real map (white bars) and synthetic map (light gray bars). Because the synthetic content map accurately models the distribution of content in the network, it provides a better framework for evaluating the performance of the different techniques.

Next, we calculated the time required to process each query. Recall that a time tick represents the time for one node to process a query and forward it one hop in the overlay network, and we measured the time for a query in terms of the number of simulation time ticks before all results reached the source. The results (not shown) are similar to the results for the number of messages: the search techniques require less time on the random map or Zipfian than they do on the real map, by a factor as high as 10, while the search techniques require the same amount of time in the real and synth maps.

All of these results demonstrate the usefulness of the MDS content model for accurately simulating the performance of peer-to-peer search techniques.

4.4   Case Study: Evaluating the Performance of Search Strategies

We now describe a case study of using a synthetic content map to examine existing techniques for a new application: peer-to-peer web search, where web sites themselves process and route web searches. This application was suggested by Li et al. [14] who proposed using structured DHT networks to perform search. Our study considers unstructured search techniques. There are a number of motivations for such an application. First, the web is quite large and growing, and a peer-to-peer architecture has the potential to be far more scalable than a centralized search engine. Second, long crawling times cause search engines to be out of date, while a peer-to-peer search system can locate the most up to date content. Third, decentralization puts search back in the hands of web site owners, who resent the power of large search engines like Google.

We used the HTML pages from the Web set, as described in Section 4.1. We generated a synthetic 10,000 peer content map using the MDS statistics from the real Web content map. Certainly, this is a relatively small map when compared to the actual size of the Web. However, it represents a useful first step in studying this application, as we can rule out techniques that do not even scale to 10,000 sites. In ongoing work we are constructing even larger maps for simulation.

In this experiment, our goal was to find 10 web pages matching a query, roughly equivalent to the first page of query results. The search mechanism can continue running if the user wants more results. Because of the size of the network, we set the ttl for flooding and iterative deepening to 6, and the ttl for random walks and biased random

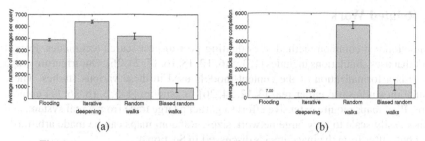

Fig. 6. Web search case study: (a) messages sent, (b) query processing time.

walks to 20,000. We also set the first iteration of iterative deepening to $ttl = 3$. By using an initial ttl larger than one, we can reduce the total number of messages [26].

The total number of messages for each technique is shown in Figure 6(a), with 95 percent confidence intervals. As the figure shows, the best performance was achieved by biased random walks, which required 915 messages per search on average. Surprisingly, flooding is the second best technique, requiring 4,895 messages per search, a factor of 5.3 worse than biased random walks. We might expect random walks to perform better than flooding, but it does not, requiring 5,188 messages per query. Analysis of the data reveals that random walks perform well for queries that match many documents but perform poorly for queries that match few documents. This variance is reflected in the large confidence interval. As before, iterative deepening performed worse than flooding, despite the optimization of starting with $ttl = 3$.

However, flooding is far superior to biased random walks when we consider the time to process queries, which is shown in Figure 6(b). (In this figure, the bars for flooding and iterative deepening are so small we print the number of time ticks above where the bars would be.) The flooding technique required only 7 time ticks to complete (one tick to submit the query and six ticks to forward it six hops) but the biased random walks required 915 time ticks. This is because flooding allows many peers to process the searches in parallel, while biased random walks requires queries to be processed sequentially, one peer after another. As a result, for an improvement of a factor of 5.3 in message cost, biased random walks causes two orders of magnitude degradation in response time over flooding. Very long response times may be unacceptable to users accustomed to quick response times from Google. It has been suggested to use parallel random walks to improve response time [16]. However, if we simulate multiple parallel walks, the response time does not approach that of flooding unless we create so many walks that the message cost becomes prohibitive. We might proactively replicate content to improve the cost and response time of walks [7]; but unless a large number of web site owners are willing to store mirrors of each other's content proactive replication will not be effective. Overall, we may not believe that flooding is scalable enough, but we can conclude from simulations using the MDS model that random and biased random walks are even less scalable for this application due to the long response time.

5 Related Work

Simulation is a common method of evaluating peer-to-peer search techniques. Recent work that uses simulations includes [1, 3, 5, 6, 12, 18, 16, 17, 24, 26]. Our tripartite graph model is a formalization of the content models used in these various studies. These simulation studies use either real [3, 12, 24, 26] or random [1, 5, 6, 18, 16, 17] content maps. Real maps require extensive effort to gather a large trace from a real system, and cannot easily scale to very large network sizes. Random maps can be made arbitrarily large but suffer from the inaccuracies discussed in Section 4.

There are several interesting traces of real peer-to-peer systems available, including [11, 21, 22, 26]. These traces can be used to inform accurate simulations. Similarly, topology models have been well studied [9, 25], as have models for download traffic [11] and peer behavior [10]. Content models for peer-to-peer networks, to our knowledge, have received less treatment. Chawathe et al [6] discuss the properties of Gnutella content but do not derive a general model as we do.

6 Conclusions

Accurate simulations of peer-to-peer techniques require both a topology model and a content model. We have presented the MDS model, a general model of content in peer-to-peer systems which allows researchers to simulate large networks whose content shares the characteristics of content in real networks. The MDS model represents queries, documents and peers as a tripartite graph, with edges representing documents matching queries and documents stored at peers. A set of degree and similarity statistics describes the properties of the tripartite graph. Our approach is that researchers can generate a large synthetic tripartite graph that has statistics matching a smaller graph generated from real data. To this end, we present an algorithm, SynthMap, that takes a set of statistics and produces a synthetic map matching those statistics.

In a set of simulation experiments we demonstrate two conclusions. First, simply generating a random content map results in inaccurate simulation results. Second, generating a synthetic map using our techniques produces results that closely match the results obtained using a real map. This validation study shows that the MDS model is an effective one for peer-to-peer simulations. We also present a case study of peer-to-peer web search that uses a 10,000 peer synthetic content model produced using SynthMap. As this study shows, the MDS content model is a useful tool for evaluating the performance of peer-to-peer search techniques.

References

1. L. Adamic, R. Lukose, A. Puniyani, and B. Huberman. Search in power-law networks. *Phys. Rev. E*, 64:46135–46143, 2001.
2. R. Baeza-Yates and B. Ribeiro-Neto. *Modern Information Retrieval*. ACM Press, New York, N.Y., 1999.
3. B. Bhattacharjee. Efficient peer-to-peer searches using result-caching. In *Proc. IPTPS*, 2003.

4. B. Cahoon, K. S. McKinley, and Z. Lu. Evaluating the performance of distributed architectures for information retrieval using a variety of workloads. *ACM Transactions on Information Systems*, 18(1):1–43, January 2000.
5. A. Carzaniga and A. L. Wolf. Forwarding in a content-based network. In *Proc. SIGCOMM*, 2003.
6. Y. Chawathe, S. Ratnasamy, L. Breslau, N. Lanham, and S. Shenker. Making Gnutella-like P2P systems scalable. In *Proc. ACM SIGCOMM*, 2003.
7. E. Cohen and S. Shenker. Replication strategies in unstructured peer-to-peer networks. In *Proc. SIGCOMM*, August 2002.
8. A. Crespo and H. Garcia-Molina. Routing indices for peer-to-peer systems. In *Proc. Int'l Conf. on Distributed Computing Systems (ICDCS)*, July 2002.
9. M. Faloutsos, P. Faloutsos, and C. Faloutsos. On power-law relationships of the internet topology. In *Proc. SIGCOMM*, 1999.
10. Z. Ge, D.R. Figueiredo, S. Jaiswal, J. Kurose, and D. Towsley. Modeling peer-peer file sharing systems. In *Proc. INFOCOM*, 2003.
11. K.P. Gummadi, R.J. Dunn, S. Saroiu, S.D. Gribble, H.M. Levy, and J. Zahorjan. Measurement, modeling and analysis of a peer-to-peer file-sharing workload. In *Proc. SOSP*, 2003.
12. V. Kalogeraki, D. Gunopulos, and D. Zeinalipour-Yazti. A local search mechanism for peer-to-peer networks. In *Proc. CIKM*, 2002.
13. M. Khambatti, K. Ryu, and P. Dasgupta. Structuring peer-to-peer networks using interest-based communities. In *Proc. International Workshop on Databases, Information Systems and Peer-to-Peer Computing*, 2003.
14. J. Li, B.T. Loo, J.M. Hellerstein, M.F. Kaashoek, D.R. Karger, and R. Morris. On the feasibility of peer-to-peer web indexing and search. In *Proc. IPTPS*, 2003.
15. A. Loser, F. Naumann, W. Siberski, W. Nejdl, and U. Thaden. Semantic overlay clusters within peer-to-peer networks. In *Proc. International Workshop on Databases, Information Systems and Peer-to-Peer Computing*, 2003.
16. Q. Lv, P. Cao, E. Cohen, K. Li, and S. Shenker. Search and replication in unstructured peer-to-peer networks. In *Proc. of ACM Int'l Conf. on Supercomputing (ICS'02)*, June 2002.
17. Q. Lv, S. Ratnasamy, and S. Shenker. Can heterogeneity make Gnutella scalable? In *Proc. of the 1st Int'l Workshop on Peer to Peer Systems (IPTPS)*, March 2002.
18. W. Nejdl, M. Wolpers, W. Siberski, C. Schmitz, M. Schlosser, I. Brunkhorst, and A. Loser. Super-peer-based routing and clustering strategies for RDF-based peer-to-peer networks. In *Proc. WWW*, 2003.
19. C. Palmer and J. Steffan. Generating network topologies that obey power laws. In *Proc. of GLOBECOM 2000*, Nov. 2000.
20. S. Ratnasamy, P. Francis, M. Handley, R. Karp, and S. Shenker. A scalable content-addressable network. In *Proc. SIGCOMM*, Aug. 2001.
21. M. Ripeanu and I. Foster. Mapping the Gnutella network: Macroscopic properties of large-scale peer-to-peer systems. In *Proc. of the 1st Int'l Workshop on Peer to Peer Systems (IPTPS)*, March 2002.
22. S. Saroiu, K. Gummadi, and S. Gribble. A measurement study of peer-to-peer file sharing systems. In *Proc. Multimedia Conferencing and Networking*, Jan. 2002.
23. I. Stoica, R. Morris, D. Karger, M. F. Kaashoek, and H. Balakrishnan. Chord: A scalable peer-to-peer lookup service for internet applications. In *Proc. SIGCOMM*, Aug. 2001.
24. C. Tang, Z. Xu, and S. Dwarkadas. Peer-to-peer information retrieval using self-organizing semantic overlay networks. In *Proc. SIGCOMM*, 2003.
25. H. Tangmunarunkit, R. Govindan, S. Jamin, S. Shenker, and W. Willinger. Network topology generators: Degree-based vs. structural. In *Proc. SIGCOMM*, Aug. 2002.
26. B. Yang and H. Garcia-Molina. Efficient search in peer-to-peer networks. In *Proc. Int'l Conf. on Distributed Computing Systems (ICDCS)*, July 2002.

Foreseer: A Novel, Locality-Aware Peer-to-Peer System Architecture for Keyword Searches*

Hailong Cai and Jun Wang

Computer Science and Engineering, University of Nebraska-Lincoln
{hcai,wang}@cse.unl.edu

Abstract. Peer-to-peer (P2P) systems are becoming increasingly popular and complex, serving millions of users today. However, the design of current unstructured P2P systems does not take full advantage of rich locality properties present in P2P system workloads, thus possibly resulting in inefficient searches or poor system scalability. In this paper, we propose a novel locality-aware P2P system architecture called Foreseer, which explicitly exploits *geographical* locality and *temporal* locality by constructing a *neighbor* overlay and a *friend* overlay respectively. Each peer in Foreseer maintains a small number of neighbors and friends along with their content filters used as distributed indices. By combining the advantages of distributed indices and utilization of two-dimensional localities, the Foreseer search scheme satisfies more than 99% of keyword search queries and realizes very high search performance, with a low maintenance cost. In addition, query messages rarely touch free-riders, and therefore avoid most meaningless messages inherent in unstructured P2P systems. Our simulation results show that, compared with current unstructured P2P systems, Foreseer boosts search efficiency while adding only modest maintenance costs.

Keywords: geographical locality, temporal locality, Foreseer, Bloom filter

1 Introduction

Unstructured peer-to-peer (P2P) system becomes one of the most popular Internet applications at present, mainly resulting from its good support for file lookup and sharing. Its system architecture is categorized as either centralized or distributed. Centralized system architectures like Napster [1] require a central index server, which limits the system scalability and incurs a single point of failure [2]. Without centralized administration, recent systems like Gnutella [3] construct a totally decentralized overlay (at the application level) on top of the Internet infrastructure. Search schemes in these systems can be *blind* or *informed*. Blind search schemes are based on message flooding and thus suffer poor system scalability. To address this problem, some researchers have proposed random walks [4, 5] as well as several improved versions of this scheme, such as Directed BFS [6], GIA [7] and Interest-based shortcuts (IBS) [8]. However, these schemes are still blind to some extent because they lack any indexing information. As a result, they cannot prevent a peer from repeatedly trying multiple walks due to previous walk failures or meaningless walks toward free-riding peers. This is because the

---

* This research is supported in part by a University of Nebraska Lincoln Layman Fund.

H.-A. Jacobsen (Ed.): Middleware 2004, LNCS 3231, pp. 38–58, 2004.
© IFIP International Federation for Information Processing 2004

sender does not know what contents, if at all (a free-rider shares nothing), are shared on the receiver before the query is actually transmitted. A straightforward solution to resolve the blindness without using a centralized index server is to maintain distributed indices among peers, which are used in the informed search technique that trades off distributed indices storage management for search performance. Intelligent BFS [9], APS [10], Local Indices (LI) [6] and Routing Indices [11] are examples of this class. In order to intelligently direct searches and obtain an acceptable hit rate, however, the indices to be maintained would be extraordinarily large, and hence the overhead involved in indices' update may become prohibitively expensive, thus partially offsetting the benefits of the indices themselves.

Previous studies [12, 13] have shown that current P2P systems have both *geographical* locality and *temporal* locality. For node A, its geographically nearby node B exhibits geographical locality if it is likely to offer service to node A in the near future. This is because the objects on node A's neighbors are more likely to be reached by queries from A than those objects located on distant nodes from A. Similarly, node C, which has successfully served requests from node A in the past, exhibits temporal locality if it is likely to be able to offer further service to node A in the near future. The main reason why current search schemes cannot simultaneously realize high search efficiency and good scalability is that they do not or not fully exploit such an inherent two-dimensional locality in P2P systems. For example, an interest-based shortcut approach [8] attempts to exploit the temporal locality, but only to improve the blind flooding. LI [6] introduces a simple way to implement indices in unstructured P2P systems but does not consider any kind of localities. These search schemes introduce inefficient blind traffic in P2P network or require very expensive maintenance to manage distributed indices, especially in support of keyword searches, and therefore seriously compromise the search performance and system scalability. A good design of a P2P system that supports keyword searches must organize distributed indices more efficiently and exploit two-dimensional locality awareness intentionally.

In this paper, we attempt to design a novel unstructured P2P system architecture for keyword searches called *Foreseer*. Our design fully exploits two-dimensional localities. *First*, unlike Gnutella-like systems that simply organize live peers into an overlay with small-world property[1], Foreseer constructs two orthogonal overlays on top of the Internet infrastructure: a neighbor overlay based on geographical locality, and a friend overlay based on temporal locality which also has small-world properties. The neighbor overlay is built with network proximity while the friend overlay is maintained according to the online query activities. Each peer maintains a small number of links to its neighbors and friends that serve its future queries more efficiently. *Second*, we use Bloom filters [15] to compactly represent the contents shared on each peer and distribute the content filters, so that each peer saves copies of the content filters of its neighbors and friends as well as their IP addresses. *Third*, due to the native locality properties, one peer's neighbors and friends provide a much better chance of serving its query requests than other "strange" peers do. Therefore, Foreseer employs a locality-aware search scheme to answer queries more efficiently. The search is performed in two

---

[1] A network exhibiting the small-world property is one with high level of clustering and a small characteristic path length. For more details, please refer to [14].

phases on each involved node on the route path: 1) *local matching* to resolve the query (*i.e.,* find the node that seems to have the requested objects) on behalf of its neighbors and friends using their content filters, and 2) *selective dispatching* to forward the query to the destination peer if it has been resolved, or otherwise to the node's friends or neighbors. Foreseer is not only able to answer queries within few hops, but also reduces a lot of redundant flooding messages and skips most free-riders. In addition, using a Bloom filter index minimizes the maintenance overhead, making it even more suitable for a highly dynamic environment. Trace-driven simulation results show that Foreseer can boost the search performance by up to 70% and significantly reduce the search cost by up to 90%, compared with state-of-the-art P2P systems.

2   Related Work

We review several representative search schemes in Gnutella-like decentralized P2P system architectures in this section.

2.1   Blind Searches

Gnutella does not scale well because of its message flooding scheme. One way to improve its scalability is to reduce the number of redundant messages by forwarding queries only to a subset of neighbors. The neighbors are either randomly picked or selectively chosen based on their capability of answering a query. Lv *et al.* [5] suggest a *random walk* scheme, in which a query is forwarded to a randomly chosen neighbor at each step until there are sufficient responses. Adamic *et al.* [4] recommend that the search algorithm bias its walks toward high-degree nodes. *GIA*, designed by Chawathe *et al.* [7], exploits the heterogeneity of the network and employs a search protocol that biases walks toward high-capacity nodes. Although these approaches are effective in reducing the number of flooding messages, the system performance is compromised. The search may require multiple walks due to previous walk failures or meaningless walks toward free-riders. By estimating neighbors' potential capabilities according to their past performance, a *Directed BFS* approach [6] selects neighbors that have either produced or forwarded many quality results in the past. This approach intuitively reuses the paths that were effective in previous searches. However, if any peer on a path departs, the path is lost. Sripanidkulchai *et al.* [8] exploit temporal locality to employ interest-based *shortcuts*. These shortcuts are generated and updated after each successful query, and are used to serve future requests. The authors claim that the destination peer who hosts requested objects can be found in just one hop for many queries. Unfortunately, this approach may delay other queries that cannot be satisfied by the shortcuts. This is due to the fact that the peer has to contact all the peers marked as shortcuts before it sends the query to its neighbors.

2.2   Informed Searches

Considering the benefits of indices for object location, another way to improve Gnutella-like systems' performance is to build distributed indices. *Intelligent BFS* [9] maintains query-neighbor tuples on each peer. These tuples map classes of queries to neighbors who have answered most of the queries that are related. This technique tries to reuse paths that were used for previous queries of the same class. Unfortunately, this technique cannot be easily adapted to object deletion and node departures. In addition, its search accuracy highly depends on the assumption that nodes specialize in certain documents. In *APS* [10], each node keeps a local index of the relative probability for each object it requests per neighbor. This approach saves bandwidth but may suffer long delays if the walks fail. *Local Indices*, proposed by Yang *et al.* [6], suggests each node's index files are stored at all nodes within a certain radius r, and queries are answered on behalf of all of them. If r is small, however, the indices cannot satisfy many queries; whereas if r is big, the indices' update will be very expensive. In *Routing Indices* [11], each node stores an approximate number of documents from every category that can be retrieved through each outgoing link. This technique can be efficient for searches, but requires too much flooding effort for the indices to be created and updated. Therefore it may not work well in a highly dynamic environment.

3   Foreseer Design and Implementation

Foreseer comprises three components at different layers, as shown in Figure 1. The neighbor and friend overlays are built on top of the Internet infrastructure by exploiting geographical and temporal localities, respectively. The indices implemented by Bloom filters are distributed according to the relationships between peers within the two over-lays. By directing searches along the overlay links and resolving queries by the dis-tributed indices, the searching module provides high performance for keyword searches with a low maintenance cost.

The rationale behind Foreseer comes from our daily life. Everyone has neighbors who live nearby and friends who live further away. Neighbors and friends constitute one's social relationships. One gets to know his neighbors upon settlement, and makes new friends when interacting or doing business with someone else. Suppose each per-son has a business card and knows about others only through their business cards. When someone has a new business request, he looks at his the business cards of his friends and neighbors first. If these cards imply that a friend and/or neighbor can help, he im-mediately contacts that person. If none of them can help, he passes the request to his friends and/or neighbors who, in turn, seek help from their friends and neighbors.

We present the detailed design of Foreseer in this section. First, we explain the creation of peers' content filters represented by Bloom filters. Then we show how to explicitly exploit both geographical and temporal locality and construct the neighbor and friend overlays. In Section 3.3, we present the Foreseer search algorithms. The system maintenance cost is detailed in Section 3.4.

3.1   Bloom Filters as Content Filter

In Foreseer, the business card refers to a peer's content filter derived by computing the Bloom filter [15] on all its shared contents. A Bloom filter is a hash-based data structure for representing a set to support membership queries. The membership test

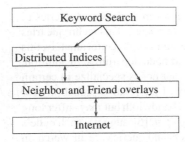

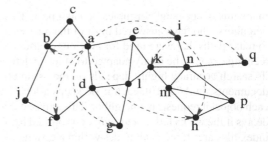

Fig. 1. System architecture of Foreseer built on top of the Internet infrastructure.

Fig. 2. Illustration of the neighbor overlay and friend overlay. For clarity, this figure only shows the friend links from node a and i.

returns false positives with a predictable probability, but it never returns false negatives. With an optimal choice of hash functions, we can obtain the minimum probability of false positive as $(\frac{1}{2})^k$, or $(0.6185)^{\frac{m}{n}}$, where k is the number of hash functions used, m is the number of bits in the filter and n is the number of elements in the set.

In this paper, we use Counting Bloom filters proposed by Fan *at al.* [16] to summarize the contents shared with each peer. Assume D_p is the set of documents shared on node p, and $K_p = \{kw_i \in d_j | d_j \in D_p\}$ is the set of keywords that appear in any documents in D_p. The kw_i is a keyword that appears in document d_j. The content filter of node p, denoted by $\mathcal{F}_{content\_p}$, is initialized by hashing all the keywords in K_p and setting the corresponding bits to 1. Free-riders have a null content filter, which can be easily recognized by other peers. If the number of hash functions in use is fixed, the cardinality of the maximum keywords set K_{max} determines the space requirement for the filter with the least false positive rate as $m = \frac{nk}{\ln 2} = \frac{|K_{max}|k}{\ln 2}$. We believe that the size of the maximum keyword set will not be arbitrarily large for several reasons. *First*, the number of shared files on most peers is limited. Saroiu *et al.* [17]'s measurement studies on Gnutella indicate that about 75% of the clients share no more than 100 files, and only 7% of the peers share more than 1000 files. The results in [12] show that 68% of 37,000 peers share no files at all (free-riders), and most of the remaining clients share relatively few (between 10 and 100) files. *Second*, the documents on the same peer tend to share common topics. The overlap of semantics among documents on one peer reduces the number of unique keywords to be mapped to the content filter. *Third*, according to [12, 13], most files shared in current P2P systems are multimedia streams, where only a few unique keywords can be derived from one document. Even with $|K_{max}| = 10,000$ and $k = 8$, the length of the filter with least false positive rate is $m = \frac{10,000 \times 8}{\ln 2} = 114,416$ bits $= 14.4KB$. When transmitted over the network, this filter can be packed into several IP packets. However, as the network size increases, some peers may share so many files that the cardinality of their keyword sets become greater than current K_{max}. This problem can be solved in two ways. If only a few peers begin to share a large number of files, a workload migration mechanism can be used to move some of these shared files to their neighbors and/or friends. If a lot of peers want to share a large number of files, we can deliberately increase the length of the Bloom filters according to the size of the maximum keyword set K_{max}. For those peers who share few files and keywords, we use a compressed representation of the filter as a collection of 2-tuples (i, x), which means that the ith bit is set for x times. Only the first number in each tuple (location of a 1 in the filter) is transmitted over the network.

To facilitate keyword queries, each peer keeps an inverted file created from its keyword set by information retrieval techniques. In addition, a counter is locally maintained for each bit in its content filter to record the current number of objects mapped to this bit by any of the k hash functions. Notice that this counter does not need to be transmitted over the network since it is only used in local file insertion and deletion.

3.2   Two-Dimensional, Locality-Aware Overlay Construction

Two orthogonal overlays are constructed in this system: 1) the neighbor overlay, which captures geographical locality, and 2) the friend overlay, which captures temporal locality. In addition to maintaining its own local content filter, each node p saves copies of the content filters of the peers in both its neighbors list $N(p)$ and friends list $F(p)$. If a peer becomes a neighbor and a friend at the same time, it is allowed to act as both a neighbor and a friend. To limit the number of filters one peer maintains, we restrict the size of N and F as follows: for node p, $n_{min} \leq |N(p)| \leq n_{max}$, $f_{min} \leq |F(p)| \leq f_{max}$, where n_{min}, f_{min} and n_{max}, f_{max} are the lower bound and upper bound for the number of neighbors and friends respectively. Figure 2 illustrates the two overlays in a simple network where $N(a) = \{b, c, d, e\}$ and $F(a) = \{b, f, g, h, i\}$. Node a maintains a copy of the content filter for each node among $N(a) \cup F(a)$. Together with its own local filter, node a maintains nine content filters in total, which greatly strengthens its ability to serve future queries.

Finding and Maintaining Neighbors. The bidirectional neighbor overlay is constructed with network proximity, so that only peers that are physically proximate can become each other's neighbors. Network latency is used as a simple metric to measure the physical distance between peers because it reflects the performance directly seen by end hosts and can be easily measured in an end-to-end, non-intrusive manner. As in Gnutella, a new node joins the system by contacting well-known bootstrapping nodes, and builds up its neighbors according to the replies. To ensure network proximity, a new peer, upon receiving replies from peers who can accept more neighbors, will always choose peers with lower latencies as neighbors. The content filters are transmitted along with the replies so that the new peer can initialize its neighbors list quickly. If the number of its neighbors is smaller than the lower bound, the node issues a PING_NEIGHBORS message to its current neighbors. The current neighbors, in turn, propagate this message to their neighbors. Upon receiving this message, peers with less than the maximum number of neighbors reply positively along with their content filters. This process repeats until the new arrival peer has a minimum number of neighbors. When a peer makes a planned departure, it notifies its neighbors so that they can remove it from their neighbors list and discard its content filter. In case of a node failure, the node does not have a chance to notify other peers. However, its neighbors will realize this when trying to contact it later, and make updates accordingly.

Geographical locality implies that an object near the querying peer is more likely to be reached than distant objects, thus minimizing network latency and bandwidth consumption. The construction of the neighbor overlay ensures that each peer keeps a list of its nearby peers, and resolves the query locally if the requested object can be found on any of its nearby peers.

Making and Refreshing Friends. The friend overlay is constructed as a directed graph independent of the physical network topology. Unlike bidirectional friendships in real life, the friend relationship in this paper is designed to be unidirectional. The unidirection of the friend relationship does not affect the small-world property of the subgraph induced by the friend links, as we will prove in our experiments. Each peer knows a number of friends. Each peer may also be a friend of other peers, who are called *back friends*. In addition to the neighbors and friends lists, each peer also maintains a list (including IP address) of its back friends denoted as F^{-1}, but without any content information. Tracking a reverse direction of the friends relationship, the list is used to notify those back friends peers of its content filter update when necessary. In Figure 2, $\{a, i\} \subseteq F^{-1}(h)$, and any filter update on node h would cause node a and i to take corresponding action: updating filter copies of node h accordingly.

It is obvious that a peer who has ever answered a request from node p should be a candidate of p's friends, according to temporal locality principles. However, when a brand new peer issues its first query, it has no friends to consult. To mitigate this problem, we recommend an active "friends making" stage for the new node as soon as it builds up its neighbors list. To find potential friends, new node p sends out a PING_FRIENDS message to its neighbors, who in turn forward this message to their friends. Upon receiving this request, peer q checks to see if it can be accepted ($|F^{-1}(q)| < f_{max}^{-1}$, where f_{max}^{-1} is the maximum number of a peer's back friends) or not. Those peers who can accept this "friends making" request will reply to p along with their content filters. Based on these replies, p can fill out its initial friends list by selecting those peers who have more 1's in their content filters, because the documents shared on these peers contain more keywords. Since free-riders have nothing to share, no friend link will point to them (*i.e.,* they have an empty F^{-1} list). Therefore, they will never see PING_FRIENDS messages except as a neighbor at the first step. Updating the friend overlay due to node departure/failure can be done in a similar manner as the neighbor overlay.

Node p's friends are ordered and replaced in an LRU manner as new information is learned. After each download, p has a chance to refine its friends list. If the serving peer is already one of p's friends, this peer comes to the top of the list because it is the most recently used. If the serving peer is not on p's friends list, and $|F(p)| < f_{max}$, this peer becomes a new friend of p with the highest priority. However, if $|F(p)| = f_{max}$, p has to remove a least recently used friend and insert the new friend as the most recently used. When an old friend is replaced, p sends a message to that node so that it is removed from that node's back friends list. For partial searches that result in multiple responses, we can use a counter to record the number of results each friend returns for previous X queries, and find a victim that returns the fewest number of results when a newly recognized friend asks for a replacement. Accordingly, the counters are updated when a query is answered.

To attain a better performance, we can speed up the node join procedure by employing a caching scheme. Before a node departs the system, the addresses of its neighbors and friends are saved on its local disk. When the node rejoins the system, it tries to contact its old neighbors and friends directly and asks for their current content filters. Recent research results [13, 18] show that the node departure-and-rejoin pattern is a common feature of current P2P systems. Not only is the join process simplified in this way, but the workload of bootstrapping nodes is also reduced.

3.3   Two-Dimensional, Locality-Aware Search Algorithm in Foreseer

Algorithm Design. The keywords extracted from documents work as metadata to be mapped to the content filters in our design, although the extraction method is beyond the scope of this paper. Existing systems use either *local* or *global* [19] indexing to retrieve or place a document's metadata. As described above, Foreseer uses local indexing so that multi-term queries are as easy to be processed as single-term queries. Foreseer avoids the inefficiency of local indexing by orienting the queries intelligently instead of flooding every node in the system.

The main process of object location is simple. When initiating a new query request or receiving an unresolved query message that contains one or more terms $kw_1, kw_2, ...kw_r$, node p runs a search algorithm that consists of two phases: *local matching* and *selective dispatching*. In the local matching phase, node p computes the query filter $\mathcal{F}_{query}$ by mapping all the query terms, and compares it with the content filter $\mathcal{F}_{content\_q}$ for each node $q \in N(p) \cup F(p)$ by the logical "AND" operation. If $\mathcal{F}_{query} \wedge \mathcal{F}_{content\_q} = \mathcal{F}_{query}$, then there is a match, indicating that node q seems to have the document containing all the keywords with a high probability. Otherwise, none of p's neighbors or friends has the requested document. This matching is conducted on node p locally and requires no network bandwidth. The query message is then selectively forwarded based on the results of the first phase. If there is a match, *i.e.*, the query has been resolved and is likely to be answered by one of p's neighbors or friends q, the message is flagged as *resolved* and forwarded to q, which looks up its local inverted file for the document that matches the query. If a false positive occurs, however, the query is flagged as *unresolved* and returned to node p. In either situation, whether the local matching fails or a match turns out to be a false positive, the query message is forwarded according to the system searching policy $P_1 = \{F^{h_1} N^{h_2}\}$. Let h be the current hop count of the query message. In P_1 policy, given $h < h_1$, the query is forwarded to its friends. If $h_1 \leq h < h_1 + h_2$, the query will be forwarded to its neighbors. The query stops traveling when $h = h_1 + h_2$. Because of the locality properties in P2P system workloads, a large number of queries are resolved locally (when $h = 0$) at the nodes who issue the requests. For other queries that need to travel more hops, Foreseer runs an intelligent, light flooding procedure: the query messages are forwarded along the friend links for up to h_1 hops and then along the neighbor links for up to h_2 hops until they are successfully resolved and answered by some nodes in the system, or otherwise fail with an exception.

We search along the friend links before the neighbor links based on several intuitive reasons. *First*, suppose $q \in F(p)$ and $r \in F(q)$, files shared on node r, which tend to interest node q, may also interest node p because p is likely to download more files from

q in the near future according to temporal locality principles. On the other hand, geographical locality only ensures that objects *near* node p are more likely to be reached than *distant* objects, but does not mean that node p's neighbors have a better chance of answering the query. This implies that peers reached through friend links have a better chance of answering the query than peers reached through neighbor links. *Second*, the construction of the friend overlay implies that the friend links point to peers who share many objects and never refer to free-riders. These peers have a better chance of answering the query than other peers sharing few or no files. *Third*, the small-world property of the friend overlay ensures that by following friend links, the query quickly scatters over a large network diameter and reaches distant peers in few hops. Because of its construction, however, the friend overlay may consist of disconnected subgraphs. To ensure a high success rate for searches, Foreseer propagates the query along neighbor links after h_1 hops in the friend overlay. At this stage, free-riders may serve as an intermediate router for the query messages.

We also develop and examine other possible search policies that can be employed in our two-dimensional overlays. By directing the query along neighbor links first and then friend links, we have a policy $P_2 = \{N^{h_1} F^{h_2}\}$. However, this policy suffers a low success rate since the neighbor overlay is built with network proximity. Therefore, going through neighbor links first cannot reach distant peers who may have the requested document. We could also forward the query messages to neighbors and friends simultaneously, as denoted by policy $P_3 = \{F^{h_1}//N^{h_2}\}$. However, propagating through neighbor links at the beginning does not incur much benefit since only peers within a local area will be touched. For the same reason, a more complicated policy like $P_4 = \{N^{h_1} F^{h_2} N^{h_3}\}$ does not attain a better result. Other policies like $P_5 = \{F^{h_1} N^{h_2} F^{h_3}\}$ do not work better than P_1 since propagating the query along the friend links again after it has traveled along the neighbor links does not capture the temporal locality. Our experiments also prove that P_1 attains the best outcome among all the policies mentioned above. Therefore, we adopt P_1 as our default search policy in all experiments without explicit specification.

In short, the key ideas (major procedures) in our search scheme are three-fold: 1) The peer who issues the query tries to resolve the query instantly by local matching. If successful, only one more message will be involved in this search. 2) If 1) fails, the query will be selectively forwarded along the friend links and then the neighbor links, and will never touch free-riders until traveling along the neighbor links. 3) As soon as the local matching is successful at some nodes, the query is resolved and only one more message is needed for success confirmation in case of no occurrence of false positives.

Algorithm Efficiency. For any peer p issuing a query, if the requested object can be found on any peer $p_0 \in N(p) \cup F(p)$, this query can be resolved locally and reach the destination peer within only a single hop with a high probability. Such kind of queries are resolved with $O(1)$ complexity. In other cases, the query needs to be spread out as is examined here. We use $F^i(p)$ to denote the set of peers with i hops distance along friend links from node p, and let $F^0(p) = \{p\}$. Formally,

$$F^i(p) = \{q|r_0 = p, r_i = q, r_{k+1} \in F(r_k), 0 \leq k \leq i-1\}$$

Table 1. The search efficiency in the friend overlay.

Hop	Nodes touched	Nodes foreseen	Messages produced
0	1	$f+n$	0
1	f	$(f+n)f$	f
...	...	...	...
i	f^i	$(f+n)f^i$	f^i
...	...	...	...
h_1	f^{h_1}	$(f+n)f^{h_1}$	f^{h_1}

Table 2. The search efficiency in the neighbor overlay.

Hop	Nodes touched	Nodes foreseen	Messages produced
0	1	$(f+n)f^{h_1}$	0
1	n	$(f+n)nf^{h_1}$	n
...	...	...	...
j	n^j	$(f+n)n^j f^{h_1}$	n^j
...	...	...	...
h_2	n^{h_2}	$(f+n)n^{h_2}f^{h_1}$	n^{h_2}

If the requested object resides on any peer

$$p_i \in N(f^i(p)) \cup F(f^i(p)), \forall f^i(p) \in F^i(p), 0 \le i \le h_1$$

it can be resolved in i hops and reach the destination peer in $i+1$ hops with a high probability. At each hop, the query touches some new nodes along the friend overlay, and checks the content filters of their neighbors and friends. Table 1 shows the number of peers touched, the number of peers foreseen, and the number of messages produced at each hop, in which f and n denote the average number of one peer's friends and neighbors respectively. We do not consider revisited peers for simplicity.

If the query fails in the friend overlay, it spreads by following the neighbor links. Similarly, we use $N^j(f^{h_1}(p))$ to denote the set of peers with j hops distance along the neighbor links from node $f^{h_1}(p)$, where $f^{h_1}(p) \in F^{h_1}(p)$. Formally,

$$N^j(f^{h_1}(p)) = \{q|r_0 = f^{h_1}(p) \in F^{h_1}(p), r_j = q, r_{k+1} \in N(r_k), 0 \le k \le j-1\}$$

If the requested object resides on any peer

$$p'_j \in N(n^j(f^{h_1}(p))) \cup F(n^j(f^{h_1}(p))), \forall n^j(f^{h_1}(p)) \in N^j(f^{h_1}(p)), 1 \le j \le h_2$$

it can be resolved in h_1+j hops and reach the destination peer in h_1+j+1 hops with a high probability. Table 2 shows the the number of peers touched, the number of peers foreseen, and the number of messages produced at each hop along the neighbor links.

As long as the shortest distance between the query source peer and the pre-destination peer that has a successful local matching is not longer than h_1 hops in the friend overlay plus h_2 hops in the neighbor overlay, this query is satisfied by our algorithm. Similar to other flooding approaches, a randomly generated identifier is assigned to each query message and saved on passing peers for a short while so that the same message is not handled by the same peer again. Our experiments suggest that 5 hops in the friend overlay ($h_1 = 5$) and 1 hop ($h_2 = 1$) in the neighbor overlay suffice for more than 99.9% of queries. As shown in Figure 2, where $N(a) = \{b, c, d, e\}$ and $F(a) = \{b, f, g, h, i\}$, a query from node a for objects shared on these nodes can be resolved locally and reach the destination peer in one hop. Since $j \in N(b), l \in N(g), m \in N(h), p \in N(h), n \in N(i)$, and $k \in F(i), q \in F(i)$, a query for objects shared on any of these peers can be resolved in one hop by one of a's friends, and reach the destination in two hops. Compared to other blind search algorithms, Foreseer conducts searches more aggressively with the help of distributed content filters by checking $(f + n)$ times more nodes at each hop. Compared to current distributed indexed approaches, Foreseer directs searches more intelligently by well exploiting temporal and geographical locality properties, namely following the friend links and then neighbor links accordingly.

Skipping Free-Riders. Previous studies have shown that a large portion of participating nodes are free-riders. Although any node can issue queries to the system, only non-free-riders can contribute objects and are helpful in answering queries. The friend overlay ensures that free-riders cannot be friends of any peer, and thus a query will never touch them when traveling along the friend links for h_1 hops. If the query is not yet resolved, Foreseer continues the search in the neighbor overlay and may touch some free-riders. By giving search priority to the friend overlay, Foreseer reduces a lot of meaningless messages that are unavoidable in many blind search schemes.

Effects of False Positives. When a false positive occurs, the peer that resolves the query receives a negative reply from the "matching but false" peer, and the query is further forwarded. However, this only incurs some extra workload with a very low probability, and does not affect the correctness of the search algorithm. To reduce the side effects of false positives, when a peer finds that more than one neighbor or friend may have the requested document, it forwards the query to two or more of them. The probability of obtaining multiple false positives at the same time is very slim. For partial keyword searches that require multiple responses, the query can be forwarded to all of its neighbors and friends that seem to have the requested documents.

3.4   System Maintenance

Object Publishing and Removal. When a peer is going to share new files, this information should be quickly made visible to its neighbors and back friends peers. To do this, the peer extracts keywords from new documents, and selects new keywords from all extracted keywords, if any, to map to its content filter. Any change in the filter is recorded and sent in an update message to all peers in its lists N and F^{-1}. Only a small amount of location information (less than k bits per new keyword contained in the file) that reflects the changed bits is transmitted over the network, and thus the involved network traffic is minimized. At the same time, the inverted file and counters associated with corresponding bits are also updated locally on the peer. Upon receiving an update message, peers make necessary changes on their filter copies of the sender node. The process of removing a document is similar to this object publishing procedure. Compared to current indexed search schemes or DHTs, only a small amount of location information specifying the changed bits in the content filter is transmitted when publishing or removing a document, thus making Foreseer perform an efficient maintenance job in a highly dynamic environment.

An additional benefit from this instant publishing is that popularly requested files are advertised widely and quickly. As a result, they will have more and more copies available in the network as more peers conduct such downloading and publishing processes. Therefore, queries for this kind of files can be served more efficiently and the query hot spot may not occur at all.

Node Join and Departure. When a new node joins the system, it needs to set up its neighbor and friend relations as described in Section 3.2. When a node departs, it notifies all its neighbors and back friends. A total of $(|N| + |F^{-1}|)$ small messages are involved per update if necessary. The nodes that receive this notification message simply remove this node from their neighbors or friends lists, along with the corresponding content filter copies. In the meantime, the departing node caches its neighbors and friends on its local disk. When it rejoins the system, it first tries to contact its old neighbors and friends to build up its initial relations quickly. When a node fails unexpectedly, it has no chance to notify other nodes of its absence. But when live nodes try to contact it, they would find this node has already departed. Since each node maintains multiple neighbors and friends, random node failures do not affect the overall system performance. A more aggressive approach would be adoption of PING-PONG messages to proactively check the live status of each peer's neighbors and friends.

4 Experimental Methodology

We develop a trace-driven simulator to evaluate the performance of Foreseer compared with other baseline P2P systems. We describe the experimental methodology in this section and present the simulation results and our analysis in the next section.

4.1 Set Up Experiments

To evaluate Foreseer's performance compared with other popular search schemes, we carefully choose several representative systems, such as Gnutella, Interest-based Shortcuts (IBS) [8], and Local Indices (LI) [6] as baselines. For the LI scheme, where each node maintains an index over the data of neighbors within r hops, we choose two practical configurations, LI-1 with $r = 1$ and LI-2 with $r = 2$ without loss of generality. LI-1 maintains fewer indices than LI-2, but its indices are not able to satisfy enough queries. LI-2 maintains more indices but has a high maintenance cost. We configure each baseline system according to its default configuration to guarantee a fair comparison. For systems without indices such as Gnutella and IBS, we set $TTL = 7$. For LI-1, LI-2 and Foreseer, which maintain indices on each node, we set $TTL = 6$. As suggested by Yang et al. [6], a policy $P = \{0, 3, 6\}$ is adopted in both LI-1 and LI-2 to gain good performance. This policy suggests that the query is processed by nodes at depth 0, 3 and 6, while nodes at other depths simply forward the query to the next depth. In IBS, each node maintains at most 10 shortcuts as specified by the authors [8]. In Foreseer, unless explicitly specified, we have $2 \leq |N(p)| \leq 10$, $4 \leq |F(p)| \leq 8$, and $|F^{-1}(p)| \leq 20$ for any node p. The default search policy in Foreseer is $P_1 = \{F^5 N^1\}$.

In order to best simulate the system performance, we choose the Transit-Stub model [20] to emulate a physical network topology for all testing systems. This model constructs a hierarchical Internet network with 51,984 physical nodes randomly distributed in an Euclidean coordinate space. We set up 9 transit domains, with each containing, on the average, 16 transit nodes. Each transit node has 9 stub domains attached. Each stub domain has an average of 40 stub nodes. Nine transit domains at the top level are fully connected, forming a complete graph. Every two transit or stub nodes in a single transit or stub domain are connected with a probability of 0.6 or 0.4 respectively. There is no connection between stub nodes in different stub domains. The network latency is set according to the following rules: 100 ms for inter transit domain links; 20 ms for links between two transit nodes in a transit domain; 5 ms for links from a transit node to a stub node; 2 ms for links between two stub nodes in a stub domain. We randomly choose peers from these 51,984 nodes to construct the testing P2P systems in our experiments. Notice that only some of the physical nodes participate in the P2P system while all nodes contribute to the network latency for messages passing by.

For baseline systems that require a Gnutella-like network overlay, we apply the crawled Gnutella network topology data downloaded from the Limewire website [21], and then set up the logical network connections. Foreseer needs to build its own neighbor and friend overlays that are different from the baseline systems. To construct the neighbor overlays with network proximity in Foreseer, we find nearby nodes and create neighbor links for a new peer according to the network latency between this peer and other present peers that may accept more neighbors. This process repeats until each peer has a sufficient number of neighbors. The initialization and online evolution of the friend overlay are described in Section 3.2. In each run of the trace replaying, we randomly select 5% node departures and 5% node failures on the fly to emulate dynamic activities in P2P systems.

Trace Preparation. Because there is no real-world publicly accessible trace that contains the keyword query and download history information required in our experiments, we carefully rebuild a trace that contains original query terms associated with each event by preprocessing a content distribution information trace of an eDonkey [22] system obtained from [12]. The eDonkey trace contains the names of 923,000 files shared among 37,000 peers, and was probed during the first week of November 2003. To restore the keyword query trace, we do two preliminary jobs (calculating keyword weights and restoring a download trace) and then transform the download trace into the keyword query trace with keyword weight information. To do the first job, we conduct a simple lexical analysis and extract keywords from each document by converting its file name into a stream of words. We then calculate the total number of occurrence per keyword, which indicates the weight of the keyword among the entire document set. For the second job, we process the same eDonkey trace to restore a download trace, where each event consists of a peer that issues a query, a peer that answers the query, and the document that is transferred. During the restore process of the download trace, we assume that only one copy of each document is shared in the system before any query and download, and the content distribution of the eDonkey trace reflects the system status after the completion of all queries and downloads. This assumption is only used to derive a reasonable downloading trace, and does not disallow a file to have multiple copies in the system during the trace replay. When the two jobs are finally completed, we transform the download trace into a keyword query trace used in our experiments. During the transform process, we add query terms that have relatively high weights out of the requested file in each event, since these terms are more effective to improve search precision than those with light weights. The number of query terms is controlled within a limit so that most of the queries involve 1 to 4 keywords. The maximum number of terms for each query is limited by 10, as suggested by Reynolds *et al.* [23]. When the keyword query trace is restored, we feed it into each testing system, replay the queries, and collect the results.

Metrics in Use. We measure the search efficiency using the following metrics:

- *Success rate*: the percentage of successfully resolved (*i.e.*, can be satisfied) queries among all submitted queries.
- *Response time*: the average response time to find the first matching document. Since the processing time at a node is negligible compared to the network delay, we ignore the queuing latency and Bloom filter computation times.
- *Relative distance*: the distance actually traveled by consecutive nodes encountered along the route normalized to the shortest distance between the source and the destination node, as defined in [24]. This metric tells the search cost, in terms of distance traveled in the proximity space, and indicates how well the system exploits the geographical locality, while the average hops only count the number of P2P nodes along the route.
- *Messages produced*: the average number of messages produced while searching for an object that matches a query.
- *Nodes touched*: the average number of nodes touched by the query messages during the search.
- *Free-riders touched*: the average number of free-riders touched by the query messages during the search.

The first three metrics demonstrate how well a system conducts searches for a given query (search performance), while the last three metrics indicate the bandwidth consumption involved in a query (search cost) that can be used to indirectly justify the system scalability. The success rate is the most important factor in choosing searching policies. Besides these metrics, we also compare the indices' maintenance overhead involved in both LI schemes and Foreseer because their work in updating indices for object addition and deletion impacts the entire system performance and its scalability.

5 Experimental Results

5.1 Search Policy

We conduct experiments to find an optimal search policy of Foreseer by running 20,000 queries on a 10,000-peer network and comparing the performance of each policy as shown in Table 3. On the average, most policies in class P_1 and P_3 show better performance than other policies, because temporal locality is fully exploited by traveling along the friend links in the early stages. The table also indicates that $P_1:\{F^4N^2\}$,

Table 3. Performance of different search policies of Foreseer.

Policy	Success rate	Average hops	Average response time	Relative distance	# of query messages	# of node touched	# of free-riders touched
$P_1 : \{F^3 N^3\}$	93.64%	3.01	426	3.91	194	164	56
$P_1 : \{F^4 N^2\}$	99.7%	2.95	453	4.22	234	175	18
$P_1 : \{F^5 N^1\}$	99.9%	2.97	459	4.29	262	177	2
$P_1 : \{F^6 N^0\}$	99.34%	2.95	457	4.24	250	169	0
$P_2 : \{N^4 F^4\}$	28.3%	5.64	482	4.36	181	163	5
$P_3 : \{F^4//N^2\}$	94.87%	2.77	402	3.70	191	150	7
$P_3 : \{F^4//N^3\}$	98.25%	2.75	382	3.42	210	170	28
$P_3 : \{F^4//N^4\}$	99.29%	2.74	374	3.36	228	187	42
$P_4 : \{N^2 F^2 N^2\}$	96.46%	4.14	442	4.01	228	181	18
$P_5 : \{F^2 N^2 F^2\}$	98.1 %	3.35	403	3.65	208	174	47

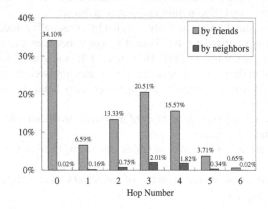

Fig. 3. Distribution of queries served by friend links and neighbor links at each hop, with policy $P1 : \{F^5 N^1\}$.

$P_1:\{F^5 N^1\}$, $P_1:\{F^6 N^0\}$ and $P_3:\{F^4//N^4\}$ achieve a success rate higher than 99%. Among these policies, $P_3:\{F^4//N^4\}$ achieves the best search performance in terms of average hops per query, average response time per query and relative distance per query, but still touches a lot of free-riders in a search. Due to its high success rate and good performance (although not best), we use $P_1:\{F^5 N^1\}$ as our default policy when running our experiments.

In order to demonstrate the different functions of neighbor and friend links at each hop, we collected the number of queries resolved by friend links and by neighbor links respectively at hop $h = 0, 1, ..., 6$. Notice that $h = 0$ indicates a successful local matching at the peer who issues the query. If the query is resolved at node p, and the destination peer is both a neighbor and a friend of p, this is considered as a contribution of both links. The results are shown in Figure 3, which illustrates that more than 34% queries are resolved locally (h=0) due to temporal locality in the workloads. When $h > 0$, the number of nodes touched at each hop dominates in answering the queries. As the hop number increases and the search touches more peers in the friend overlay, both the friend and neighbor links serve an increasing number of queries until the hop number reaches 3. When the hop number exceeds 3, however, the number of served queries by either type of links decreases since most of the queries are already satisfied. This figure also shows that for each hop number, the friend links serve many more queries than the neighbor links. One reason for this is that the friend links established by temporal locality are more likely to serve future requests, while the neighbor links constructed with geographical locality only help reduce the search cost. Another reason is that each peer maintains up to 8 friends while the average number of neighbors is only around 2.43, which implies that there are many more friend links existing in the system than neighbor links. Although it seems that the neighbor links do not contribute much to the search performance, they play a critical role in Foreseer. They increase the success rate by connecting isolated nodes without many friend relationships, and reduce the search cost in relative distance by network proximity, as shown in Table 3.

5.2   Search Efficiency

In this section, we compare the search efficiency of Foreseer against the baseline systems in terms of search performance and search cost. By running the query traces, we found that, with the configurations mentioned above, all the baseline systems have an average success rate around 98%, while our Foreseer achieves an even higher success rate of 99.9%. Because of the uncontrolled data placement and finite TTL for query messages, no current search algorithms in unstructured P2P systems can guarantee a 100% success rate. However, only a small percentage (less than 0.06%) queries may fail in Foreseer, which is quite satisfactory for most users.

Search Performance. The average response time and relative distance of each algorithm to find the first matching document are shown in Figure 4 and Figure 5, respectively. By exploiting temporal locality, both IBS and Foreseer can answer a lot of queries (around 34% in our experiments) within just one hop. Compared to IBS, however, Foreseer reduces the average response time and relative distance by up to 70%. It is clear that IBS obtains such one-hop successes with the cost of a longer response time and a farther relative distance. In IBS, a peer first contacts all of its shortcuts to see if they can answer the query. If no shortcut peer has the requested object, the search is already delayed before the peer floods the query to its neighbors. In contrast, Foreseer does not need the flooding algorithm as a backup. Compared to other baseline systems like Gnutella and Local Indices, Foreseer reduces the average response time by up to 40% and the average relative distance by up to 45%. The benefit stems from Foreseer's ability to exploit both temporal and geographical locality at the same time to propagate queries. Following the friend links enables Foreseer to reach the destination peer within few hops. Furthermore, if the local matching indicates a neighbor seems to have the object, the peer forwards the query to that neighbor, which is physically nearby according to network proximity. However, the neighbor in other systems only indicates a logical connection and may point to a distant node.

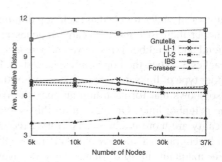

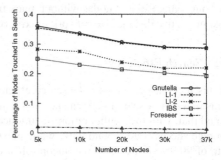

Fig. 4. Comparison of search performance in average response time.

Fig. 5. Comparison of search performance in relative distance.

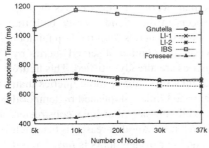

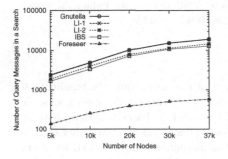

Fig. 6. Comparison of search cost in the number of messages produced in a search.

Fig. 7. Comparison of search cost in the percentage of nodes touched in a search.

Search Cost. Gnutella has poor system scalability because its blind flooding results in a large number of redundant messages and touches too many unrelated peers during the object searches. Other baseline systems also require a lot of messages if the query is not satisfied by the shortcuts (in IBS) or the local indices (in LI schemes). We collected the total number of query messages and touched nodes in all the queries, and computed the average number of messages produced and the average percentage of touched nodes in a search, as shown in Figure 6 and Figure 7 respectively. Compared with IBS, which shows the best results among the baseline systems, Foreseer can reduce both the number of messages and the percentage of touched nodes by more than 90%. In our experiments, Foreseer only touches less than 2% live nodes for each query on average. From the two figures, we can see that both IBS and LI-2 show capabilities of reducing the number of redundant messages and touched nodes. IBS achieves this improvement by exploiting temporal locality, while LI-2 by maintaining abundant index information. By combining their advantages, Foreseer improves the search performance and simultaneously slashes the search cost.

One of the valuable features of our friend overlay is that no free-riders are pointed by any friend links since they share nothing and cannot serve any query. Therefore, the search will never touch free-riders while propagating along friend links. If the query

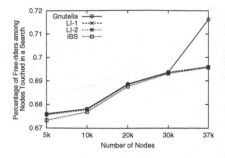

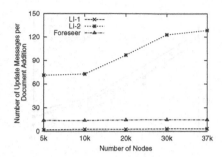

Fig. 8. Comparison of search cost in the percentage of free-riders among the touched nodes in a search.

Fig. 9. Comparison of indices maintenance cost in the number of update messages produced for this purpose.

is not satisfied in the friend overlay, then it will touch free-riders along the neighbor links. In other systems, however, even a peer knows that some of its neighbors are free-riders (by looking at the indices as in LI schemes), it still sends the query to them when fanning out the query. We conducted experiments and calculated the percentage of free-riders among nodes touched in a search. Figure 8 depicts the results we obtained when running queries on the baseline systems. The result of Foreseer, not shown in the figure, is less than 1% in the experiments.

5.3 Maintenance Costs

When a query is answered, the peer who issued that query has a new document to be published to other peers (we assume this is a requirement). We compared the number of messages used to update indices in LI schemes and Foreseer, as shown in Figure 9. It is clear that LI-1 only needs to send several update messages after a query on the average, because only a small number of peers need to be reached for indices update. But for LI-2, since each peer stores the indices of files shared on all the nodes within radius $r = 2$, an index update will result in a large number of update messages. With an average of 13 update messages after each query, Foreseer pays a modest cost for its good search performance as seen in the previous sections. Furthermore, by using Bloom filters, the update messages are quite small and do not consume much network bandwidth. For an object addition, a peer only needs to transmit the locations of changed bits in its content filter. Suppose $T = 100$ unique keywords can be extracted from this document and $k = 8$, $m = 8KB$ for the Bloom filter. Each changed bit requires $B = 2Bytes$ to specify its location in the filter. The information to be sent is limited by $L \leq T \times k \times B = 1.6KB$ *bits*, which can be easily packed in few IP packets.

5.4 Scheme Optimization

We studied Foreseer's sensitivity to the number of neighbors and friends by running 20,000 queries on a 10,000-peer network with various configuration parameters. Since peers keep making new friends after their queries until they have the maximum number of friends, the upper bound of friends (Max $|F|$) indicates the number of friends each

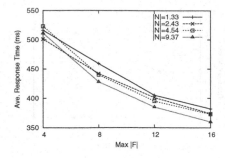

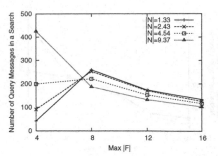

Fig. 10. Sensitivity of search performance to peer's number of neighbors and friends, in terms of response time.

Fig. 11. Sensitivity of search cost to peer's number of neighbors and friends, in the number of query messages produced.

node maintains in the system. On the other hand, a peer may have a lower bound number of neighbors and will not look for new neighbors until some of its current neighbors depart. We collected the number of neighbors for each node and computed the average value as $|N| = 1.33$ for $n_{min} = 1$ and $n_{max} = 5$, $|N| = 2.43$ for $n_{min} = 2$ and $n_{max} = 10$, $|N| = 4.54$ for $n_{min} = 4$ and $n_{max} = 20$, $|N| = 9.37$ for $n_{min} = 8$ and $n_{max} = 40$. Due to space limitation, we only present the results in terms of response time for these configurations as the evaluation of search performance, as shown in Figure 10. The results for other metrics follow the same trend. Similarly, the number of query messages produced in a search is plotted in Figure 11 to show the search cost with various configurations. We noticed that when $Max|F| = 4$, a large portion of queries failed because the query could only reach a small number of nodes due to the upper bound for the number of friends. When $Max|F| > 4$, as shown in the two figures, the search performance keeps increasing, and the number of query messages produced keeps decreasing as more neighbors and more friends are allowed on each peer. This is straightforward since a peer can have the content filters of more peers and outgoing links if allowed to maintain more neighbors and friends. However, a larger number of neighbors and friends results in more indices update workloads, as shown in Figure 12.

Figure 13 shows the number of free-riders touched in each query when varying the number of neighbors and friends in our experiments. It is notable that when $Max|F| = 8$, a query, on the average, touches less than 23 free-riders, indicating that some of the queries are not resolved until they propagate along the neighbor links. However, when $Max|F| \geq 12$, the query will never touch the free-riding peers, which implies that all the queries have been resolved within the friend overlay. This also indicates that the number of friends is not necessarily too large, considering the maintenance cost of updating a peer's content filters.

6   Conclusions and Future Work

In this paper, we propose a new P2P system architecture called Foreseer, which constructs two orthogonal overlays based on geographical and temporal localities and main-

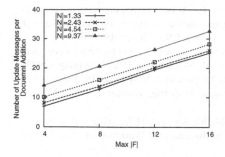

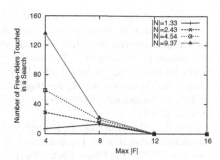

Fig. 12. Sensitivity of indices maintenance cost to peer's number of neighbors and friends, in the number of update messages.

Fig. 13. The number of free-riders touched in a query with varying number of neighbors and friends.

tains distributed indices for objects shared on peers' neighbors and friends. By selectively directing searches along the friend links and neighbor links, Foreseer achieves a high search efficiency with a modest maintenance overhead. We conduct a comprehensive set of trace-driven simulations and perform an in-depth analysis of the results. Our experiments show that Foreseer can boost the search performance by up to 70%, with regard to response time and relative distance, and slash the search cost by up to 90% in terms of the number of query messages produced and nodes touched, compared with state-of-the-art P2P systems. In future work, we will study the system performance of Foreseer when different searching policies are employed and/or standard information retrieval traces are fed. In addition, we would like to measure its benefits for partial keyword search applications with multiple responses required.

References

1. Napster: (http://www.napster.com)
2. Milojicic, D.S., Kalogeraki, V., Lukose, R., Nagaraja, K., Pruyne, J., Richard, B., Rollins, S., Xu, Z.: Peer-to-peer computing. Technical Report HPL-2002-57, Hewlett Packard Laboratories (2002)
3. Gnutella: (http://www.gnutella.wego.com)
4. Adamic, L.A., Lukose, R.M., Puniyani, A.R., Huberman, B.A.: Search in power-law networks. Technical report, Physical Review E, vol.64(4), 046135 (2001)
5. Lv, C., Cao, P., Cohen, E., Li, K., Shenker, S.: Search and replication in unstructured peer-to-peer networks. In: Proceedings of 16th ACM International Conference on Supercomputing(ICS'02),New York, NY. (2002)
6. Yang, B., Garcia-Molina, H.: Efficient search in peer-to-peer networks. In: Proceedings of the 22nd International Conference on Distributed Computing Systems (ICDCS), Vienna, Austria,. (2002)
7. Chawathe, Y., Ratnasamy, S., Breslau, L., Lanham, N., Shenker, S.: Making gnutella-like p2p systems scalable. In: ACM SIGCOMM'03, Karlsruhe, Germany. (2003) 407–418
8. Sripanidkulchai, K., Maggs, B., Zhang, H.: Efficient content location using interest-based locality in peer-topeer systems. In: IEEE INFOCOM'03, San Francisco, USA. (2003)

9. Kalogeraki, V., Gunopulos, D., Zeinalipour-Yazti, D.: A local search mechanism for peer-to-peer networks. In: Proceedings of the 11th international conference on Information and knowledge management, (CIKM'02), McLean, Virginia, USA. (2002) 300–307
10. Tsoumakos, D., Roussopoulos, N.: Adaptive probabilistic search (aps) for peer-to-peer networks. In: Proceedings of the 3rd IEEE International Conference on P2P Computing. (2003)
11. Crespo, A., Garcia-Molina, H.: Routing indices for peer-to-peer systems. In: Proceedings of the 22nd International Conference on Distributed Computing Systems (ICDCS), Vienna, Austria,. (2002)
12. Fessant, F.L., Handurukande, S., Kermarrec, A.M., Massoulie, L.: Clustering in peer-to-peer file sharing workloads. In: Proceedings of the 3rd International Workshop on Peer-to-Peer Systems (IPTPS), San Diego, USA. (2004)
13. Gummadi, K.P., Dunn, R.J., Saroiu, S., Gribble, S.D., Levy, H.M., Zahorjan, J.: Measurement, modeling, and analysis of a peer-to-peer file-sharing workload. In: the 19th ACM Symposium on Operating Systems Principles (SOSP-19), Bolton Landing, NY. (2003) 314–329
14. Watts, D.: Small worlds : the dynamics of networks between order and randomness. Princeton University Press, Princeton (1999)
15. Bloom, B.H.: Space/time trade-offs in hash coding with allowable errors. In: Communications of the ACM, 13(7). (1970) 422–426
16. Fan, L., Cao, P., Almeida, J., Broder, A.Z.: Summary cache: a scalable wide-area web cache sharing protocol. IEEE/ACM Transactions on Networking 8 (2000) 281–293
17. Saroiu, S., Gummadi, P.K., Gribble, S.D.: A measurement study of peer-to-peer file sharing systems. In: Proceedings of Multimedia Computing and Networking (MMCN), San Jones, CA. (2002)
18. Sen, S., Wang, J.: Analyzing peer-to-peer traffic across large networks. In: Proceedings of the second ACM SIGCOMM Workshop on Internet measurment, Marseille, France. (2002) 137–150
19. Tomasic, A., Garcia-Molina, H.: Query processing and inverted indices in shared-nothing document information retrieval systems. VLDB J. 2 (1993) 243–275
20. Zegura, E.W., Calvert, K.L., Bhattacharjee, S.: How to model an internetwork. In: Proceedings of the IEEE Conference on Computer Communication, San Francisco, CA. (1996) 594–602
21. Limewire: (http://www.limewire.org)
22. Edonkey: (http://www.edonkey2000.net/)
23. Reynolds, P., Vahdat, A.: Efficient peer-to-peer keyword searching. In: Proceedings of International Middleware Conference. (2003) 21–40
24. Rowstron, A., Druschel, P.: Pastry: Scalable, decentralized object location, and routing for large-scale peer-to-peer systems. In: the 18th IFIP/ACM International Conference on Distributed Systems Platforms (Middleware), Heidelberg, Germany. (2001) 329–350

Guiding Queries to Information Sources
with InfoBeacons

Brian F. Cooper

Center for Experimental Research in Computer Systems
College of Computing
Georgia Institute of Technology
cooperb@cc.gatech.edu

Abstract. The Internet provides a wealth of useful information in a vast number of dynamic information sources, but it is difficult to determine which sources are useful for a given query. Most existing techniques either require explicit source cooperation (for example, by exporting data summaries), or build a relatively static source characterization (for example, by assigning a topic to the source). We present a system, called *InfoBeacons*, that takes a different approach: data and sources are left "as is," and a peer-to-peer network of *beacons* uses past query results to "guide" queries to sources, who do the actual query processing. This approach has several advantages, including requiring minimal changes to sources, tolerance of dynamism and heterogeneity, and the ability to scale to large numbers of sources. We present the architecture of the system, and discuss the advantages of our design. We then focus on how a beacon can choose good sources for a query despite the loose coupling of beacons to sources. Beacons cache responses to previous queries and adapt the cache to changes at the source. The cache is then used to select good sources for future queries. We discuss results from a detailed experimental study using our beacon prototype which demonstrates that our "loosely coupled" approach is effective; a beacon only has to contact sixty percent or less of the sources contacted by existing, tightly coupled approaches, while providing results of equivalent or better relevance to queries.

Keywords: source discovery, integration, peer-to-peer search

1 Introduction

There is an explosion of useful data available from dynamic web sources, such as "deep-web" data sources [7], web services, web logs and personal web servers [3]. One reason that this information is so useful is that it is being constantly maintained and updated by a huge number of humans and software programs. The Internet and web standards make it possible and easy to contact a source and retrieve information. But the proliferation of sources creates a challenge: how to find the right source of information at a given point in time? Search engines are a useful tool for searching the "surface web" but most deep web data is not reachable via crawling, and much of it changes more quickly than search engines can keep up with.

A system which allows users to find the right information sources must deal simultaneously with four challenges.

H.-A. Jacobsen (Ed.): Middleware 2004, LNCS 3231, pp. 59–78, 2004.
© IFIP International Federation for Information Processing 2004

- *Scale* - there are millions of potential sources and a huge amount of aggregate data
- *Dynamism* - new sources are appearing and old sources are disappearing frequently, and the information in many sources is being updated constantly
- *Heterogeneity* - information structure and semantics vary widely between sites
- *Limited source cooperation* - while sources are willing to provide basic search and retrieval via HTML forms or a web services interface, they are frequently unwilling to export all of their data, change their query model, run foreign software, or otherwise modify their functionality

Existing source discovery systems deal with some of these challenges, but the most utility comes from addressing all of them.

We are developing a peer-to-peer middleware system called *InfoBeacons* to guide users to information sources while dealing with these four challenges. The functionality of InfoBeacons is based on that of a search engine over static web pages: a user submits a query to a *beacon*, and the beacon returns results. The user can then use these results, and may go directly to the information sources and perform more complex queries or browsing. If the beacon is unable to provide enough results, it routes the queries to neighbor beacons in the peer-to-peer overlay. Our InfoBeacons prototype operates on keyword queries, a "lowest common denominator" approach that works across a variety of sources, including text [1], XML [26] and relational data [21] and is intuitive to users.

The InfoBeacons system is designed around two basic principles. First, the system is composed of a set of *beacons*, lightweight middleware components that are loosely-coupled to several information sources. The loose coupling means that the beacons use the source's existing search and retrieval interface, without attempting complex semantic integration or requiring extra functionality on the part of the sources. This principle allows InfoBeacons to make the best of the limited cooperation from heterogeneous sources. Second, the system pushes most of the query processing to the sources themselves, while the beacons act mainly to choose sources and retrieve results. This principle ensures that the system scales to many sources, by utilizing the aggregate resources of the sources themselves and minimizing the load on each beacon. Also, processing queries at the sources ensures that the most current information is available to users.

One distinguishing feature of our system compared to other peer-to-peer systems is that the beacon cannot expect information sources to cooperate by exporting content summaries or notifying the beacon of changes. How can we choose good sources for queries in this situation? It is too expensive to broadcast the user query to all of the sources. Our approach is that beacons remember the results of previous user queries, and use these results to guide future queries. Unlike previous caching schemes (such as [27]), the InfoBeacons cache is not used to answer queries but instead to direct queries to the sources themselves. We introduce a function, called *ProbResults*, that ranks sources for a given query based on past results stored in the beacon's cache. We have also developed a heuristic, called *experience weighting*, that dynamically adapts the beacon cache based on the changing results returned by sources. Experiments with our InfoBeacons prototype on data gathered from the World Wide Web shows that a beacon using *ProbResults* and experience weighting can find high-quality information, without having to query a large number of sources and despite having limited information. For example, a beacon using *ProbResults* contacts less than one quarter of the sources compared to a beacon using a random ordering, and only sixty percent of the sources compared to a beacon using a more tightly-coupled approach, even if sources are frequently changing their information. This results in less load on sources, as well as more than a factor of two decrease in query response time.

This paper presents the InfoBeacons architecture and explores our design choices. We then focus on one challenge faced by our architecture: how can a beacon choose good sources for a query despite limited cooperation from those sources? Since the beacon is the basic unit of functionality in our system, we must address this challenge before we can explore other aspects of the system. In ongoing work, we are addressing other issues, such as techniques for using multiple beacons to answer a query, and preliminary results are discussed in [13].

1.1 Related Work

Several peer-to-peer systems have been developed to provide information discovery, including multimedia filesharing systems (such as Kazaa and Gnutella), "unstructured" networks [11, 25] and distributed hash tables [31]. Each of these systems assumes the active participation of information sources to export content summaries to aid in source selection and query routing. However, many sources are unwilling to export their data, even those that provide free searching over their information. These sources may not want to expend the bandwidth necessary, may wish to protect their intellectual property by only serving individual results and not the whole collection, or may simply be unwilling to modify their existing server infrastructure. Our approach deals with sites that offer such limited cooperation. Also, our approach goes beyond previous P2P routing strategies that leverage result information (such as [25]) since we use whole document contents to achieve higher accuracy.

Similarly, several peer-to-peer systems have been developed to provide source integration [20, 22, 29]. Such systems can provide high retrieval accuracy but require either complex schema mappings between sites [4] or assume that all data is structured similarly [22]. In a large scale system such as the Web, it is too expensive to construct all the required mappings, and data is structured in a wide variety of ways.

The "source discovery" problem has been examined by a variety of investigators, including those in the fields of information retrieval [8], databases [17] and distributed systems [33]. Again, the dominant approach is to ask the source to export all of its data to a central broker, as in GlOSS [18] or CORI [16], or at least to export a summary of its data, as in YouSearch [3] or Galanis et al [17]. Such tight coupling works only if sources are willing to export data, and many are not. An alternate approach is to use query probes to build source content summaries or classify uncooperative sources [9, 19]. However, in a highly dynamic network, with lots of sources appearing and disappearing, and sources constantly updating their information, it may be difficult and expensive to keep these classifications accurate. In Section 5 we present experimental results comparing this approach to our techniques. Some systems assume a consistent classification scheme or topic hierarchy to which sources can be assigned (such as in [23, 32]), but it is not clear that sources can always be assigned a single, unambiguous topic or that a single hierarchy is equally useful to all users. Some systems combine these two approaches, such as BrightPlanet [7]. The Harvest system was an early pioneer in database selection, with "brokers" similar to our beacons [6]. Harvest combined source data export with search engine-style crawling of static content through modules called "gatherers." Other systems focus on the mechanics of extracting structured data once a source has been found; an example is DeLa [34]. Such an extraction and transformation component could be added to the InfoBeacons system, which currently returns data to users in its raw form.

Caching of data to improve performance has been well studied in many contexts, including the web [2], database systems [15] information retrieval [27] and peer-to-peer search [5]. The most common use of caching in these systems is to cache data from a known source to hide latency. Search engines, such as Google or BrightPlanet, can be thought of as web caches that have the same goal as ours: directing users to sources that the users did not previously know about.

There are other types of systems that search across multiple sources, including data integration systems [10] and search engines [30]. Again, we are designing the InfoBeacons system to be more loosely coupled, so that tight data integration or centralized search engine summaries are not required. While the query semantics in InfoBeacons is consequently weaker than in a federated database, the system is more able to scale to very large numbers of sources since it avoids expensive schema and data integration. Moreover, search engines have difficulty dealing with frequently changing sources and data stored in "deep-web" databases, and our InfoBeacons architecture aims to address these challenges.

1.2 Contributions and Overview

In this paper, we examine InfoBeacons and show that a beacon can make good decisions about which sources to contact, without being tightly coupled to sources or building an *a priori* source classification. In particular, we make the following contributions:

- We describe the InfoBeacons architecture and our implemented prototype, and describe its benefits for finding web information sources (Section 2).
- We present *ProbResults*, a function for ranking sources based on previous results cached by the beacon (Section 3).
- We present *experience weighting*, a heuristic for online adaptation of the beacon cache to deal with changes at sources (Section 4).
- We report the results of a detailed experimental study that examines the performance of our beacon prototype on real web data. These experiments demonstrate that a beacons system, despite being loosely coupled to sources and having partial information, can find high quality information sources at low cost (Section 5).

Finally, in Section 6, we discuss conclusions and future work.

2   InfoBeacons Architecture

The InfoBeacons architecture is comprised of three basic elements: autonomous information sources, users and a peer-to-peer network of *beacons*. This architecture is shown in Figure 1.

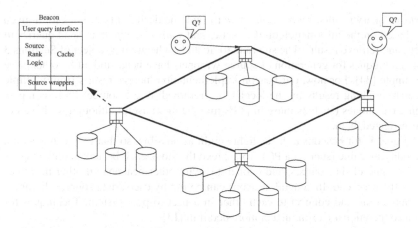

Fig. 1. InfoBeacons architecture.

Information sources provide an interface for searching and retrieving information. Examples of sources include databases searchable via HTML forms or web services that provide a SOAP interface. Each source has its own interface and query language, although we assume that they provide at least basic keyword search. Each source also has its own locally-defined semantics for keyword searching. For example, some sources may return documents matching all of the keywords, while others may return documents that are most similar to the query (even if some query words are missing). We envision that the InfoBeacons network should scale to at least thousands of sources and eventually to millions. We assume that sources process searches and return results free of charge, as many web sources do. The *documents* returned by sources may be of a variety of types, including HTML files, XML files, PDF files, relational tuples, and so on. Our current prototype deals with documents encoded in ASCII, although filters can be added to deal with other document types (such as PDF).

Users pose keyword queries in order to locate information sources. Users in our system are very similar to users of a traditional web search engine. For example, if they do not like the returned results, they will refine and resubmit their query. On the other hand, when a user gets a result that he likes, he may simply retrieve the matching document, or may go directly to the result source to browse and/or search more directly.

Users are directed to sources by *beacons*. Beacons have several responsibilities:

- Maintaining connection information for multiple sources
- Providing a uniform search interface to the user for all of the beacon's sources
- Submitting the user's queries to appropriate sources and returning results to the user
- Caching query results to aid in selecting appropriate sources for future queries
- Submitting the user's query to other beacons if the local beacon's sources provide inadequate results

As shown in Figure 1, each beacon contains several components in order to fulfill these responsibilities: a *user query interface* that allows the user to submit keyword queries, a *cache* of query results, *source rank logic* to rank the desirability of sites for a given query based on the information on the cache, and *source wrappers* to send queries to sources and retrieve results. The site rank logic and cache are the subject of Sections 3 and 4. Techniques for generation of source wrappers have been studied by others; see for example [34]. For now, our beacon implementation merges results from multiple sources by ranking results by the local score returned by the source. More complex merging techniques (such as those in [14]) may be more useful although we have not yet investigated them.

Our goal is for beacons to be as lightweight as possible, so that they can run on a commodity machine (such as a PC). To achieve this goal, each beacon is only responsible for some of the sources, and cooperates with other beacons on other machines to share the user load. In general, beacons can be run by users, data sources, libraries, ISPs, and so on, and connect to each other in a peer-to-peer system. Techniques for beacon cooperation are examined in more detail in [13].

Note that beacons are loosely-coupled to sources. That is, a beacon needs only to know how to submit keyword queries to sources and retrieve results. The beacon does not need other information, such as the database schema or query processing paradigm, in order to guide users to sources. This allows beacons to manage multiple, heterogeneous sources without extensive data integration, and allows a beacon to add and remove sources from its list with minimal effort. There must be a mechanism for beacons to discover new sources. For example, the beacon can probe UDDI registries or search engines to find web sources. Alternatively, a specialized service can be developed to discover sources and assign them to beacons.

Consider an example system with multiple beacons $B_1, B_2...B_n$, each of which is responsible for several sources. A user might submit a query "houses for sale" to beacon B_3. Beacon B_3 may be responsible for sources $S_1, S_2...S_m$, and must choose an order in which to contact these sources. The beacon may decide to first submit the query "houses for sale" to S_5. Source S_5 may not return any results, and so the beacon next sends the query to S_{19}. Source S_{19} may return 15 results, which the beacon returns to the user. If the user wants more results, then the beacon will go to the next source on its list, perhaps S_{11}, and submit the query again. This process continues until the user has gotten enough results. The number of desired results may be specified when the query is first sent to the beacon, or may be determined interactively, with the user requesting "more results" until he is satisfied. If the beacon B_3 cannot find enough results, it would forward the query to other beacons, say, B_1 and B_9, to find more results. Our techniques must balance efficiency with the need to retrieve "good" results. As with a search engine, a beacon may not return the "best" results in the system, but as long as the results are good the user will be satisfied. In our experimental results (Section 5) we see that the quality of the beacon's results is in fact quite high.

The beacon must decide for each query which sources are most appropriate. To do this, the beacon sorts its sources in decreasing order of "desirability" on a per query basis, and then contacts the most desirable sources in order until enough results are found. The beacon, which both submits queries to the source and retrieves results for the user, can cache these results to aid source selection. If an information source returns only a URL (and possibly an abstract) for each document, the beacon can use that

URL to retrieve and cache the actual document. The issue of a good ranking function is examined in Section 3, where we propose several alternative ways to use the result cache to rank sources. If the beacon's sources do not provide enough information, the beacon must forward the query to other beacons until enough information is found. There are several possible ways to choose remote beacons for a query, and we are examining this issue in more detail in ongoing work [13].

2.1 Architecture Rationale

The InfoBeacons architecture provides a number of key advantages that allows it to scale to large numbers of information sources despite the limited cooperation from sources and a highly dynamic information environment.

First, InfoBeacons minimizes the requirements on sources. Sources continue to process queries (as they were already doing) but do not have to run extra foreign software to participate in the peer-to-peer system. Sources are not required to export their data to the peer-to-peer system for indexing, which is something many sources are unwilling to do for bandwidth or intellectual property reasons. Moreover, by intelligently selecting sources, InfoBeacons avoids the load on sources associated with sending them lots of irrelevant queries.

Second, new sources can be integrated into the system and searched by users with a minimum of effort. By avoiding complex semantic integration and focusing on keyword search, InfoBeacons reduces the problem of integrating a new source to the task of connecting to the source, submitting keyword queries and retrieving results. As with a search engine that intelligently selects sources, our middleware can provide high quality results without understanding the data semantics.

Third, the system can scale to large numbers of sources simply by adding new beacons. Each beacon is only responsible for some of the sources in the system, and thus the processing and storage requirements for a beacon is limited. Also, most of the processing is done by the information sources, as they process and answer keyword searches, further reducing the load on the beacons themselves. Therefore, it is feasible to deploy lots of lightweight beacons on commodity hardware scattered throughout the web.

Finally, beacons hide the complexity of connecting to and searching multiple information sources for most users. Only users that want to dig deeper into a particular source need to contact that source directly and search it themselves.

3   Choosing Data Sources

Beacons must intelligently choose which information sources will be sent user queries. The simplest approach, which is to send the query to all sources, is too expensive, both for the sources and for the beacons. Another simple approach is to contact the sources in random order until the user has received enough results. The random approach may reduce the cost, but beacons may potentially contact many sources that do not return results. Our approach is for the beacon to rank the sources for each query based on the likelihood that the source will return results for the query, and then contact the sources in that order. Previous results are used to estimate the usefulness of a given source for the current query.

Although the beacon cache could retain whole documents, doing so may require a large amount of memory, and our goal is to minimize the resource requirements of the beacon. For this reason, the cache consists only of a set of statistics about the result data. Specifically, for each source s, the beacon cache consists of a set of pairs $((W_1, CW_1^s), (W_2, CW_2^s), ...)$, where W_i is a word and CW_i^s is the count of W_i for source s. The exact meaning of CW_i^s is tied to the definition of *ProbResults* and is described below. To update the cache with a new document, the beacon must parse the document and extract its terms. Because the beacon cache stores only aggregated counts, and not whole documents, the cache is very compact. Experimental results in Section 5 show that high selection accuracy can be achieved with a cache that is only a few tens of megabytes. We may want to place an upper limit on the size of the cache, and then it is necessary to eject some of the (W_i, CW_i^s) pairs to save space if the cache becomes too large. We examine this possibility in Section 5.5.

In this section, we examine *ProbResults*, a technique that we have developed for using the beacon cache to rank sources. Our goal is to minimize the number of information sources contacted, while still providing useful results to users despite the incompleteness of the cached data. We also compare qualitatively to existing techniques for source selection. In Section 5 we present experimental results over real web data to compare techniques quantitatively.

3.1   ProbResults

The *ProbResults* ranking is based on the probability that an information source will return documents containing the query words if it is sent a query Q. We call this probability the *ProbResults score* for the site for a given query. The beacon will rank the information sources in order of decreasing *ProbResults* score. Sites with the same *ProbResults* score should be chosen in random order so that all sites that appear equally good have a chance of being chosen.

More formally, a query Q is a set of n_Q keywords $(QW_1, QW_2, ...QW_{n_Q})$. Different queries may have different numbers of keywords. Consider a source s that we have previously sent k_s queries too. Each query may contain different words, and may differ from Q. For each of these queries, s has returned zero or more results. The number of results that contain word W_i (whether or not it was part of the query) is stored in the cache as CW_i^s. The expected number of results from s containing query word QW_i is $PW_i^s = CW_i^s/k_s$.

The *ProbResults* score is the product of the PW_i^s values of the query words:

$$ProbResultsScore_Q^s = \prod_{i=1}^{n_Q} PW_i^s = \prod_{i=1}^{n_Q} CW_i^s/k_s$$

Taking the product gives higher weight to sources that will return results relevant to all of the query words than to sources that are particularly relevant to one or two query words but not to the others. As a result, taking the product resulted in better experimental performance than the other ways we tried to combine the PW_i^s values into one score, including sum, max and min.

A beacon using *ProbResults* depends on cached result data to choose sources, and this may bias the beacon toward sources that have returned many results in the past at the expense of new sources or sources with less content. It may be possible to mitigate this bias by giving "extra credit" to new sources, by probabilistically choosing a low score source over a high score source, or by proactively probing new sources. We are examining these possibilities in ongoing work.

Minimum Probability. The beacon cache contains incomplete information about a source; in particular, it may not contain all of a source's documents. As a result, PW_i^s may be zero for a word that actually does appear in documents at a source. Because *ProbResultsScore*$_Q^s$ is the product of PW_i^s values for a source, the effect is that a source may be given a *ProbResults* score of zero and placed at the bottom of the ranking if there is no cache information for one or more query words for that source.

To see why this is a problem, consider a query for words "exothermic reactions." A beacon may have cached documents from source s_1 containing the word "exothermic," but no documents containing "reactions." The same beacon may have a second source s_2, but no cached documents containing either "exothermic" or "reactions" for s_2. In this case, s_1 should clearly be queried before s_2, since s_1 is more likely to have documents containing the query words. However, the *ProbResults* score for both sources will be zero, as neither contains cached information for "reactions."

We address this problem by using a special constant PW^{min}, $0 < PW^{min} \leq 1$, instead of zero, for the PW_i^s probability when we have no cached information for word QW_i for source s. Formally:

$$PW_i^s = \begin{cases} CW_i^s/k_s \text{ if } CW_i > 0 \\ PW^{min} \text{ otherwise} \end{cases}$$

Our experience in building the InfoBeacons prototype has taught us that choosing a good value for PW^{min} can have a big impact on system performance. In Section 5.2 we investigate appropriate values for PW^{min} using experiments. Alternatively, a good value of PW^{min} can be learned adaptively by each beacon.

Note that other systems have also dealt with incomplete content summaries; see for example [23], which uses a hierarchy of summaries to infer missing information. Our PW^{min} technique is simpler than the techniques used in many of these systems, but still produces good performance in practice.

Existing Techniques. The *ProbResults* ranking function is similar to the *Ind* ranking function used in bGlOSS [18]. *Ind* ranks sources based on the content at sources, while *ProbResults* ranks sources based on the behavior of those sources in response to queries. In other words, if a source returns document D_1 100 times and document D_2 once, *Ind* treats both documents as equally descriptive of a source, while *ProbResults* would place more weight on the words in D_1. This distinction allows *ProbResults* to better predict what a source's response to a query will be. *Ind* was developed to work with conjunctive boolean query sources; that is, sources that only return documents containing all of the query words. Our *ProbResults* function attempts only to characterize the results returned for queries, not the source's query model, and thus works well across a variety of sources, including boolean and vector space model sources (e.g. sources that return documents based on "similarity" to the query rather than exact match of all query words).

Another version of GlOSS, vGlOSS, was designed to work directly with vector space model sources. The vGlOSS system uses the *Max* metric to rank sources. *Max* attempts to predict the scores a source will give different documents for a given query, and then uses these scores to predict the number of documents that will have a score greater than some user-defined threshold l. As a result, vGlOSS must understand the source's query model, and in particular, the source must send a list of documents, words and word frequencies to vGlOSS. The full definition of *Max* given in [18].

In *CORI* [16], each database is ranked as a function of two statistics: df_i^s, the number of documents at source s containing QW_i, and sf_i, the *source frequency* (number of sources that have documents containing QW_i). A source gets a high score for a query if the query contains words that appear frequently in the source and infrequently in other sources. The formula for *CORI* is given in [16].

Ind, *Max* and *CORI* require the source to export all of its data to a central index before any queries are processed. If a source refuses to export its data, Callan and Connell [9] have suggested building a source characterization by sending a set of randomly selected words, or *query probes*, to collect a subset of the source's documents (again, before any queries are processed). Then, *Ind*, *Max* or *CORI* can be used to select sources based on these collected documents.

In contrast, in our approach the beacon cache is continually updated as new results arrive. Therefore, the information the beacon has about each source continually improves as time progresses. Moreover, the beacon cache is updated with data that matches the queries users are actually asking for, so that the cached data is focused on information that users are interested in. In pre-caching, all documents are cached, and in query probing, the set of cached documents depends on randomly chosen query probes. By utilizing the results of past queries to load the cache, beacons can form accurate source characterizations even without explicit source cooperation.

In Section 5 we present experimental results comparing our *ProbResults* ranking and caching techniques against *Ind*, *Max* and *CORI* with both pre-caching and query probing.

4   Cache Forgetting and Experience Weighting

When a beacon cache contains a word for a given source, the beacon has some reason to believe that future queries containing the word will return results from that source. However, experience may prove otherwise for two reasons. First, the data at sources may be changing frequently, and thus the cached information may have become out of date. Second, just because a source returns a document containing a given word does not necessarily mean that the word is a useful query term for that source. For example, a source of weather information may have the word "weather" in all of its documents. However, many searching techniques (such as TF/IDF weighting in information retrieval [1]) give a query term very low weight if it is too common, and a query for "weather" will not produce any results from that source.

A common solution is to use a *forgetting factor* μ to decrease the importance of old samples relative to new samples; this technique is used in areas such as control systems and reinforcement learning [24]. In our context, we would periodically multiply each CW_i^s value in the cache by μ. (Recall that the beacon cache maintains for each source s a set of (word,count) pairs $((W_1, CW_1^s), (W_2, CW_2^s), ...)$.) The effect is that truly stale information (such as that representing documents removed from the system) would slowly be "forgotten," while up to date information (such as that representing new documents or old documents that are still in the system) would be refreshed by the results of new queries. One potential disadvantage of a forgetting factor is that even old information can be useful in characterizing a source, especially if there is little new information. Another potential disadvantage is that the forgetting factor deals primarily with the issue of stale cache data and does not directly address the second issue listed above, that it is difficult to predict the weight a source will assign to a term.

We have developed another technique that allows the cache to dynamically adapt to align with the results that sources are actually producing. We call this heuristic *experience weighting*. The basic idea is that we weight the word counts in the cache based on the beacon's experience with each word as a query term. Then, when a beacon receives a query with a given word, the beacon is more likely to send the query to a source that has produced results before for queries with that term than sources that have been queried with that term and produced no results.

Experience weighting operates as follows. We specify an *experience factor* $EF \geq 1$. After each query, the beacon updates the cache count CW_i^s of each query word QW_i for each contacted source s:

- If the source returned results, CW_i^s is multiplied by EF
- If the source returned zero results, CW_i^s is divided by EF

Note that $EF = 1$ is equivalent to no experience weighting.

After applying the experience weighting heuristic to the cache, the *ProbResults* score no longer has a strict probability interpretation. However, the general intuition behind each function still applies: sources are given a higher score if they are more likely to provide good result for a query.

The magnitude of the impact on the cache from forgetting and experience weighting depends on the value of the forgetting factor μ and the experience factor EF. Appropriate values can be found using experiments, and in Section 5.2 we examine results that identify good values these parameters, as well as examine the effectiveness of forgetting versus experience weighting. Alternatively, EF or μ can be set adaptively, based on the experience of the beacon.

5   Experimental Results

We have run a set of experiments to evaluate our architecture and techniques. We examine two types of metrics: cost and quality. Our *cost* metric is the number of sources that are contacted for each query. Contacting fewer sources is better because the load on sources and beacons is reduced, and response time and throughput are improved.

To measure the quality of results returned by our system, we use the cosine distance with *TF/IDF* weighting, a common measure of relevance in information retrieval sys-

70   Brian F. Cooper

Table 1. Data and workload values.

Number of documents	169,902
Total data size	4.04 GB
Information sources	100
Documents per information source	111...5,517
Queries	100,000
N_Q: Terms per query	1...6
DT: Document turnover	0%, 50%
T: User result threshold	10

tems [1]. In this metric, both documents and queries are represented as term vectors, and the relevance of a query to a document is calculated as the cosine distance between the two vectors (e.g., the inner product). Term vectors are weighted based on the *inverse document frequency* (IDF); terms that appear less frequently are more descriptive and are given higher weights. We calculated IDF over all documents in the system. Thus, the TF/IDF score for a document returned for a query represents how relevant that document is compared to all documents at all sources. The "quality" of a query's results is the total TF/IDF score of documents found by the beacon for the query.

In the following sections, we examine the performance of using a beacon to choose information sources. In summary, our results show:

- The *ProbResults* ranking has lowest cost, especially in scenarios where there are frequent updates of source data (contacting 40 to 45 percent fewer sources than *CORI, Ind* or *Max*).

- The *ProbResults* ranking also find the highest quality documents, with an average total TF/IDF score of 3.1 versus 3.0 or less for *CORI, Ind* or *Max.*

- Our prototype took 4.3 seconds per query on average to select sources for queries, query those sources over the Internet, and retrieve, cache and return results to the user. In comparison, a beacon choosing sources randomly required 11.8 seconds per query.

- The cache of the beacon is quite compact, requiring only a few tens of megabytes in our experiments. If we limit the cache size, the performance degrades gracefully.

- Our conclusions hold even as we change the number of sources.

5.1 Experimental Setup

The characteristics of our data and workload are shown in Table 1. We discuss these values in this section.

Our InfoBeacons prototype is written in C++, and currently runs on Unix and Linux platforms. A beacon accepts user queries and returns results via XML over HTTP.

To ensure our experiments were repeatable, we created our own information sources on machines in our lab, and populated them with HTML documents downloaded from 100 .com, .net, .gov, .edu and .org websites. (In the extended version of this paper [12], we discuss results for searching across larger numbers of sites and sites with different numbers of documents.) Each information source managed documents downloaded from one website, and processed keyword searches using TF/IDF weighting and the inner product of the document and query vectors. We set each source to return only "relevant" documents, that is, those that had a score of at least 0.1 (on a scale from 0 to 1). The beacon contacted each source using XML over HTTP. Some sources had many documents and some had few, just as we would expect to find on the actual web.

We used synthetically generated keyword queries so that we could evaluate our system with a very large query set. For each query, we randomly selected N_Q words from a randomly selected document. Within our query set the N_Q value varied between one and six. The probability that a given word was chosen was a normally distributed function of the total number of occurrences of the term in all documents in the system. The mean μ of the normal distribution was equal to the average number of occurrences of any term in all documents, and the standard deviation was $\sigma = \mu/2$. As a result, the most frequent terms are terms that are neither too common nor too rare in the document corpus. This distribution of query terms matches the observed distribution of several real query sets as reported in [8].

We assume that each user has a threshold T: the number of desired document results. This is similar to a search engine, where users usually only look at the first page or two of results. Although we used $T = 10$ in the results presented here, other experiments (omitted here) show that our results and techniques generalize to other values of T. For example, the number of sources contacted under each ranking function increases with T, but for all values of T, *ProbResults* was the best ranking function in terms of cost, and the advantage of *ProbResults* over other functions increased as T increased. We also experimented with an alternate model, where a user wanted T sources instead of T results; this model is examined in [12].

We examined two scenarios: a *static* scenario and a *dynamic* scenario. In the static scenario, the documents at sources do not change. In the dynamic scenario, some documents are added and removed during querying. The document turnover was 50 percent; that is, 50 percent of the total documents were added and 50 percent of the total documents were removed while queries were being processed. The dynamic scenario models sources that are changing frequently, adding and removing information.

5.2 Tuning *ProbResults* with PW^{min} and Experience Weighting

PW^{min}. First, we examine the effect of using the minimum probability PW^{min} on the beacon's performance. Recall that the PW^{min} value determines the score assigned to a word for a source if that source has no information cached about the word. Figure 2 shows the effect of PW^{min} on the performance of a beacon using *ProbResults* in the static scenario with $EF = 1$. As the figure shows, choosing the right PW^{min} value can have a large effect on performance. The best value, $PW^{min} = 0.0001$, results in only 10.0 sites contacted on average. This represents a 64 percent decrease over $PW^{min} = 0$ (27.8 sites contacted) and an 86 percent decrease over $PW^{min} = 1$ (70.0 sites contacted). In other words, carefully selecting a PW^{min} that is non-zero and less than one is key to achieving good performace. Similar results (not shown) were obtained for the dynamic scenario, and for $EF \neq 1$. These results also show that a carefully chosen PW^{min} is important, and that $PW^{min} = 0.0001$ works best.

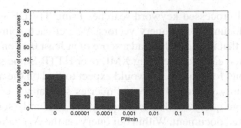

Fig. 2. Effect of PW^{min} on *ProbResults*.

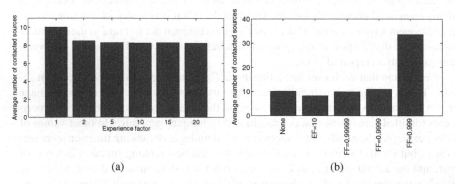

(a)　　　　　　　　　　　　　　　　(b)

Fig. 3. Cache adaptation with *ProbResults*: (a) Experience factor EF, (b) Forgetting factor FF.

Experience Weighting Versus Forgetting Factor. The experience factor is also key to performance. Recall that $EF = 1$ is equivalent to no experience weighting, while $EF \neq 1$ means weighting the cache to reflect the results that sources are returning. Figure 3(a) shows the effect of the experience factor on the performance of *ProbResults* in the static scenario with $PW^{min} = 0.0001$. As the figure shows, using experience weighting can have a significant effect: the best value, $EF = 10$, results in 8.3 sources contacted on average, 17 percent less than no experience weighting ($EF = 1$, 10.0 sources contacted). Note that increasing the experience factor beyond 10 does not provide any further improvement. Again, results are similar for the dynamic scenario.

We also compared the effectiveness of using experience weighting versus a forgetting factor. Figure 3(b) shows the results, with various forgetting factors (FF=X), $EF = 10$, and no cache adaptation at all (neither experience weighting nor forgetting; marked "None"). Again, $PW^{min} = 0.0001$. As the figure shows, the experience factor is more effective than the forgetting factor, with $EF = 10$ resulting in 8.3 sources contacted on average, 17 percent less than the best forgetting factor ($FF = 0.99999$, 9.9 sources contacted on average). In fact, for other forgetting factors, forgetting actually produces worse results than no cache adaptation at all. This is because forgetting can cause the cache to lose what little information it has about some sources, and thus the beacon begins to make bad decisions. Experience weighting retains all cache information, but weights the most useful information most heavily.

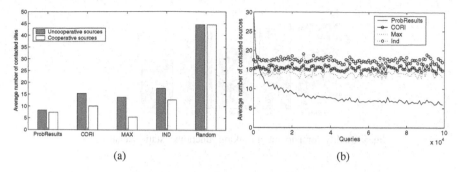

Fig. 4. Comparison of ranking functions - static scenario: (a) overall average, (b) running average.

For the rest of our discussion, we will use $PW^{min} = 0.0001$ and $EF = 10$ for *ProbResults*.

5.3 Comparison – Static Scenario

Performance. We can now examine the performance of various ranking functions used by the beacon. In this section, we first look at the number of sources contacted, and second at the quality of results. We compare four ranking functions:

- *ProbResults*: our ranking function based on the probability that a source returns results
- *CORI*: the ranking function from the CORI system
- *Max*: the ranking function from the vGlOSS system
- *Ind*: the ranking function from the bGlOSS system
- *Random*: sources are selected in random order (similar to a random walk [28])

We found that the *Ind* ranking performed significantly better if we used a minimum probability $PW^{min} = 0.0001$ in the same way as in *ProbResults*. Like *ProbResults*, if a cache count for a query word is zero or missing, the source score will be zero. Using a PW^{min} value avoids ranking promising sources low simply because the cache is incomplete, resulting in a factor of two improvement in performance for *Ind*. Therefore, the result we report represent *Ind* modified to use a minimum probability.

The results for the static scenario, averaged over all 100,000 queries, are shown in Figure 4(a). Consider first the uncooperative source scenario (gray bars), which is our focus in this paper. In our experiment, *CORI*, *Max* and *Ind* use query probing to deal with uncooperative sources. As the figure shows, *ProbResults* performs better than the other functions. A beacon using *ProbResults* contacts 8.3 sources on average, compared to 15.3 for *CORI*, 13.8 for *Max* and 17.4 for *Ind*. Random is significantly worse. By accurately characterizing a source's behavior instead of just its content, *ProbResults* is best able to predict which sources will return results for a given query.

In fact, the performance of *ProbResults* continually improves as its cache becomes more accurate. Figure 4(b) shows a running average of the performance of each function

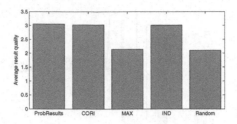

Fig. 5. Quality comparison of ranking functions - static scenario.

in the uncooperative sources scenario, with averages calculated every 1,000 queries. As the figure shows, initially *ProbResults* performs poorly, but after about 6,000 queries, *ProbResults* begins to perform better than all the other functions. After 100,000 queries, a beacon using *ProbResults* only has to contact 6.0 sources on average, less than half of the sources contacted using *CORI*, *Max* or *Ind*. Clearly, the combination of *ProbResults*, result caching and experience weighting is significantly better than previous methods.

Recall that *CORI*, *Max* and *Ind* were originally designed to operate on a full mirror of each source's content, which requires that the sources export all of their data. Although uncooperative sources are unlikely to export data, it is interesting to compare *ProbResults* to the performance of *CORI*, *Max* and *Ind* when using a full mirror. This "cooperative sources" scenario is also shown in Figure 4(a) (white bars). *ProbResults* with or without source cooperation outperforms *CORI* and *Ind*, even when those functions have source cooperation. This is because that characterizing the behavior of sources can be as important as, or more important than, characterizing their content, and *ProbResults* accurately characterizes source behavior. With cooperative sources, *Max* performs best overall, contacting only 5.4 sources on average compared to 7.3 for *ProbResults*. Thus, *ProbResults* is most appropriate for the uncooperative scenario.

Quality. Next, we examine the quality of the results found by the beacon. Recall that we use TF/IDF weighting and cosine distance as our quality metric; this metric is a common measure of relevance in information retrieval. Figure 5 shows the results for the static scenario. As the figure shows, a beacon returns the highest quality documents with *ProbResults* (3.1), *CORI* (3.0) and *Ind* (3.0). *Max* and Random provide lower quality results (2.1 each). While *ProbResults* does not provide significantly more quality than *CORI* or *Ind*, it does provide high quality results when compared to these traditional functions. This result shows that the improved performance of *ProbResults* reported in the previous section does not cause a corresponding decrease in the quality of results.

5.4   Comparison – Dynamic Scenario

In the dynamic scenario, documents are added and removed from sources as the experiment progresses so we can measure the performance of the various techniques for dynamic sources. Due to space limitations, the full results are presented in the extended version of this paper [12]. In summary, the *ProbResults* performance continued to offer the best performance, contacting 45 percent fewer sources than *CORI*, *Max* or *Ind* while still providing the highest quality information.

Table 2. Machine characteristics.

	Internet	*LAN*
Beacon	Dell 4 x 2.0 GHz Xeon, 6 GB RAM	Dell 8 x 550 MHz Xeon, 4 GB RAM
Sources	HP RX2600 2 x 900 Mhz Itanium II 6 GB RAM	HP RX2600 2 x 900 Mhz Itanium II 6 GB RAM
Ping	69.9 ms	< 1 ms

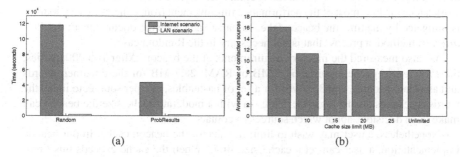

(a)   (b)

Fig. 6. Time and memory: (a) time to process 10,000 queries, (b) limiting cache size.

5.5 Time and Memory

Next, we ran a set of experiments to measure the time and memory requirements for our beacon prototype. To do this, we constructed two scenarios. In the *Internet* scenario, the beacon ran on a machine at Stanford University, while the data sources ran on a machine at Georgia Tech[1]. Thus, the beacon had to communicate with the sources using the Internet, incurring high latency for every roundtrip. In the *LAN* scenario, the data sources ran on the same machine at Georgia Tech, but now the beacon ran on another nearby Georgia Tech machine. In this scenario, the beacon contacted sources via gigabit Ethernet. In both scenarios, a client program, running on the same machine as the beacon, connected to the beacon via HTTP to submit queries and retrieve results. The characteristics of the machines involved are listed in Table 2. The average ping time between the beacon machine and the source machine was 69.9 ms in the Internet scenario, and less than 1 ms in the LAN case. We expect the Internet scenario to be most representative of a system of beacons querying real web sources.

In our experiment, we warmed the beacon's cache using the first 90,000 queries of our query set. (This was done using sources local to the beacon machine to save time in conducting the experiment.) Then, we measured the time required to process the next 10,000 queries of our query set.

The results are shown in Figure 6(a) for *ProbResults* ($MP = 0.0001$, $EF = 10$). The figure also shows the time for the beacon to process the same 10,000 queries using the Random ranking function. As the figure shows, in the Internet scenario, the beacon

---

[1] We would like to thank the Database Group at Stanford University for the use of their machine.

performs 2.7 times as fast using the *ProbResults* function (4.3 seconds per query) than when using the Random ranking (11.8 seconds per query). This difference shows how intelligently selecting sources can improve the response time of beacon queries, in addition to other benefits such as not overloading sources. The response time improvement of *ProbResults* versus Random is not quite as dramatic as the decrease in the number of sources contacted shown in Figure 4(a). While the number of sources contacted is less under *ProbResults*, the amount of data transferred once good sources are found is roughly constant under both methods, and this data transfer incurs large latency.

In the LAN scenario, the two methods perform almost equally: 0.144 seconds per query under *ProbResults* versus 0.158 seconds per query under Random. Because network latency is low, most of the performance improvement from contacting less sources is mitigated by the time the beacon takes to parse and cache the documents in the *ProbResults* method, a process that is not necessary in the Random case.

We also measured the memory requirements of the beacon. After 100,000 queries, the *ProbResults* cache required 64.6 MB of RAM: 28.7 MB for the document words and associated counts, and 35.9 MB for a set of hashtables, one per source, to index the words. These results demonstrate that even with a moderate cache size the beacon can make good decisions about which sources to contact.

Nonetheless, a user may wish to limit the size of the beacon cache. In our beacon implementation, a user can set a cache size limit. When the cache exceeds this limit, the beacon will eject words and associated counts (e.g., (W_i, CW_i^s) pairs) from the cache until the size is under the limit. The beacon ejects words in order of increasing $|CW_i^s - PW^{min}|$ (where $|A|$ is the absolute value of A) so that the counts are closest to PW^{min}, which have the least useful information, are ejected first.

The results are shown in Figure 6(b), where the horizontal axis shows the cache size limit (in terms of the size of the cached document words and associated counts). As the figure shows, the beacon's performance degrades gracefully as the cache becomes smaller. Even for a very small cache of 5 MB, the beacon using *ProbResults* contacts only about twice the sources of a beacon with unlimited cache, and has performance roughly equivalent to a beacon using *Ind*, *Max* or *CORI* (e.g., Figure 4). We can see from these results that the beacon is quite effective at choosing information sources, even with limited cache size.

5.6 Beacon Scalability

In most of our experiments, the beacon was responsible for 100 sources. We also examined results for different numbers of sources to see how the beacon scaled to larger source sets. Due to space limitations, these results are discussed in the extended version of this paper [12]. In summary, the performance of our techniques was not negatively impacted as we increased the number of sources.

6 Conclusions and Future Work

We have presented *InfoBeacons*, a system designed to process information from large numbers of diverse web information sources. The design philosophy behind our system is to loosely couple beacons to web sources, so that no modifications are needed to the sources and so our beacon can adapt quickly to changes. This approach results in a number of benefits: many more sources can participate in the system, the system can scale well despite heterogeneity and dynamism, and the most up to date information can be located and retrieved. However, because beacons have limited information about sources, beacons must make the best of the information they have in order to select sources for queries. We presented *ProbResults*, a ranking function that uses cached information from previous queries to choose sources. We also described experience weighting, a heuristic that allows a beacon cache to adapt effectively to changes at sources. Experimental results show that a beacon using *ProbResults* and experience weighting can find high quality results while contacting forty to forty-five percent fewer sources than existing techniques. Our focus in this paper has been on the architecture and the source selection aspects of InfoBeacons. Another important aspect is the distributed cooperation of multiple beacons. The good performance of the *ProbResults* function suggests that it may be useful as the basis of a routing function that can choose beacons in a manner analogous to how beacons choose sources. We are examining this possibility in ongoing work [13]. Overall, our results show that the InfoBeacons framework is a promising middleware architecture for distributed information source discovery.

References

1. R. Baeza-Yates and B. Ribeiro-Neto. *Modern Information Retrieval*. ACM Press, New York, N.Y., 1999.
2. G. Barish and K. Obraczka. World wide web caching: Trends and techniques. *IEEE Communications Magazine*, May 2000.
3. M. Bawa, R. J. Bayardo Jr., S. Rajagopalan, and E. Shekita. Make it fresh, make it quick — searching a network of personal webservers. In *Proc. WWW*, 2003.
4. P.A. Bernstein, F. Giunchiglia, A. Kementsietsidis, J. Mylopoulos, L. Serafini, and I. Zaihrayeu. Data management for peer-to-peer computing: A vision. In *Proc. WebDB*, 2002.
5. B. Bhattacharjee. Efficient peer-to-peer searches using result-caching. In *Proc. IPTPS*, 2003.
6. C. M. Bowman, P. B. Danzig, D. R. Hardy, U. Manber, and M. F. Schwartz. The Harvest information discovery and access system. In *Proc. 2nd WWW Conference*, 1994.
7. BrightPlanet. Deep content. http://www.brightplanet.com/deepcontent/index.asp, 2003.
8. B. Cahoon, K. S. McKinley, and Z. Lu. Evaluating the performance of distributed architectures for information retrieval using a variety of workloads. *ACM Transactions on Information Systems*, 18(1):1–43, January 2000.
9. J.P. Callan and M.E. Connell. Query-based sampling of text databases. *ACM TOIS*, 19(2):97–130, 2001.
10. S. Chawathe, H. Garcia-Molina, J. Hammer, K. Ireland, Y. Papakonstantinou, J. Ullman, and J. Widom. The TSIMMIS project: Integration of heterogeneous information sources. In *In Proc. of IPSJ Conference*, October 1994.
11. Y. Chawathe, S. Ratnasamy, L. Breslau, N. Lanham, and S. Shenker. Making Gnutella-like P2P systems scalable. In *Proc. ACM SIGCOMM*, 2003.
12. B.F. Cooper. Guiding users to information sources with InfoBeacons (extended version). Technical Report, at http://www.cc.gatech.edu/~cooperb/pubs/infobeaconsext.pdf, 2004.
13. B.F. Cooper. Using information retrieval techniques to route queries in an InfoBeacons network. Technical Report, at http://www.cc.gatech.edu/~cooperb/pubs/beaconrouting.pdf, 2004.

14. R. Fagin, R. Kumar, and D. Sivakumar. Efficient similarity search and classification via rank aggregation. In *Proc. SIGMOD*, 2003.
15. M.J. Franklin and M.J. Carey. Client-server caching revisited. In *Proc. Int'l Workshop on Distributed Object Management*, 1992.
16. J.C. French, A.L. Powell, J. Callan, C.L. Viles, T. Emmitt, K.J. Prey, and Y. Mou. Comparing the performance of database selection algorithms. In *Proc. SIGIR*, 1999.
17. L. Galanis, Y. Wang, S.R. Jeffrey, and D.J. DeWitt. Locating data sources in large distributed systems. In *Proc. VLDB*, 2003.
18. L. Gravano, H. Garcia-Molina, and A. Tomasic. GlOSS: Text-source discovery over the internet. *ACM TODS*, 24(2):229–264, June 1999.
19. L. Gravano, P.G. Ipeirotis, and M. Sahami. QProber: A system for automatic classification of hidden-web databases. *ACM TOIS*, 21(1):1–41, January 2003.
20. A.Y. Halevy, Z.G. Ives, P. Mork, and I. Tatarinov. Piazza: Data management infrastructure for semantic web applications. In *Proc. WWW*, 2003.
21. V. Hristidis, L. Gravano, and Y. Papakonstantinou. Efficient IR-style keyword search over relational databases. In *Proc. VLDB*, 2003.
22. R. Huebsch, J.M. Hellerstein, N. Lanham, B.T. Loo, S. Shenker, and I. Stoica. Querying the Internet with PIER. In *Proc. VLDB*, 2003.
23. P. Ipeirotis and L. Gravano. Distributed search over the hidden web: Hierarchical database sampling and selection. In *Proc. VLDB*, 2002.
24. L. P. Kaelbling, M. L. Littman, and A. W. Moore. Reinforcement learning: A survey. *Journal of Artificial Intelligence Research*, 4:237–285, May 1996.
25. V. Kalogeraki, D. Gunopulos, and D. Zeinalipour-Yazti. A local search mechanism for peer-to-peer networks. In *Proc. CIKM*, 2002.
26. C. Botev L. Guo, F. Shao and J. Shanmugasundaram. XRANK: Ranked keyword search over XML documents. In *Proc. SIGMOD*, 2003.
27. Z. Lu and K. S. McKinley. Partial collection replication versus caching for information retrieval systems. In *Proc. SIGIR*, 2000.
28. Q. Lv, P. Cao, E. Cohen, K. Li, and S. Shenker. Search and replication in unstructured peer-to-peer networks. In *Proc. of ACM Int'l Conf. on Supercomputing (ICS'02)*, June 2002.
29. W. Nejdl, M. Wolpers, W. Siberski, C. Schmitz, M. Schlosser, I. Brunkhorst, and A. Loser. Super-peer-based routing and clustering strategies for RDF-based peer-to-peer networks. In *Proc. WWW*, 2003.
30. L. Page and S. Brin. The anatomy of a large-scale hypertext web search engine. In *Proc. WWW*, 1998.
31. P. Reynolds and A. Vahdat. Efficient peer-to-peer keyword searching. In *Proc. ACM/IFIP/USENIX International Middleware Conference*, 2003.
32. A. Sugiura and O. Etzioni. Query routing for web search engines: Architecture and experiments. In *Proc. WWW*, 2000.
33. C. Tang, Z. Xu, and S. Dwarkadas. Peer-to-peer information retrieval using self-organizing semantic overlay networks. In *Proc. SIGCOMM*, 2003.
34. J. Wang and F. Lochovsky. Data extraction and label assignment for web databases. In *Proc. WWW*, 2003.

The Peer Sampling Service:
Experimental Evaluation
of Unstructured Gossip-Based Implementations*

Márk Jelasity[1,2], Rachid Guerraoui[3],
Anne-Marie Kermarrec[4], and Maarten van Steen[5]

[1] University of Bologna, Italy
jelasity@cs.unibo.it
[2] RGAI, MTA SZTE, Szeged, Hungary
[3] EPFL, Lausanne, Switzerland
Rachid.Guerraoui@epfl.ch
[4] INRIA, Rennes, France
Anne-Marie.Kermarrec@irisa.fr
[5] Vrije Universiteit, Amsterdam, The Netherlands
steen@cs.vu.nl

Abstract. In recent years, the gossip-based communication model in large-scale distributed systems has become a general paradigm with important applications which include information dissemination, aggregation, overlay topology management and synchronization. At the heart of all of these protocols lies a fundamental distributed abstraction: the *peer sampling* service. In short, the aim of this service is to provide every node with peers to exchange information with. Analytical studies reveal a high reliability and efficiency of gossip-based protocols, under the (often implicit) assumption that the peers to send gossip messages to are selected uniformly at random from the set of all nodes. In practice – instead of requiring all nodes to know all the peer nodes so that a random sample could be drawn – a scalable and efficient way to implement the peer sampling service is by constructing and maintaining *dynamic unstructured* overlays through gossiping membership information itself. This paper presents a generic framework to implement reliable and efficient peer sampling services. The framework generalizes existing approaches and makes it easy to introduce new ones. We use this framework to explore and compare several implementations of our abstraction. Through extensive experimental analysis, we show that all of them lead to different peer sampling services none of which is uniformly random. This clearly renders traditional theoretical approaches invalid, when the underlying peer sampling service is based on a gossip-based scheme. Our observations also help explain important differences between design choices of peer sampling algorithms, and how these impact the reliability of the corresponding service.

* This work was partially supported by the Future & Emerging Technologies unit of the European Commission through Project BISON (IST-2001-38923) and by the Swiss National Fond project 2100-064994.01/1.

H.-A. Jacobsen (Ed.): Middleware 2004, LNCS 3231, pp. 79–98, 2004.

1   Introduction

Motivation. Gossip-based communication protocols have been applied success-fully in large scale systems. Apart from the well-known traditional application for information dissemination [6, 9], gossiping has been applied for aggregation [16, 14, 13], load balancing [15], network management [29], and synchronization [20]. The common property of these protocols is that, periodically, every node of the distributed system exchanges information with some of its peers. The underlying service that provides each node with a list of peers is a fundamental distributed component of gossip-based protocols. This service, which we call here the *peer sampling* service is usually assumed to be implemented in such a way that any given node can exchange information with peers that are selected following a uniform random sample of *all nodes* in the system. This assumption has led to rigorously establish many desirable features of gossip-based broadcast protocols like scalability, reliability, and efficiency (see, e.g., [24] in the case of information dissemination, or [16, 14] for aggregation).

To achieve this uniform random selection, many implementors opt for the solution where every node *knows* all other nodes of the system [4, 11, 17]. Prac-tically speaking, every node maintains a membership table, also called its *view*, the size of which grows with the size of the system. The cost of maintaining such tables has a non-negligible overhead in a dynamic system where processes join and leave at run time. In short, whereas the application and its underlying gossip-based protocol are supposed to be scalable, it is wrong to assume that this is also the case for the underlying peer sampling service.

Recently, much research has been devoted to designing scalable implemen-tations of this service. The basic idea is to use a gossip-based dissemination of membership information naturally integrated into the service [8]. The continu-ous gossiping of this information enables the building of unstructured overlay networks that capture the dynamic nature of distributed peer-to-peer systems and help provide very good connectivity in the presence of failures or peer dis-connections.

Interestingly, there are many variants of the basic gossip-based membership dissemination idea, and these variants mainly differ in the way new views are built after merging and truncating views of communicating peers (see, e.g., [12]). So far, however, there has never been any evaluation of and comparison between these variants, and this makes it hard for a programmer to choose the implemen-tation of the peer sampling service that best suits the application needs. More importantly, it is not clear whether any of these variants actually lead to *uniform sampling*, which, as we pointed out, lies at the heart of all analytical studies of gossip-based protocols. In search for an answer to these questions, this paper introduces a generic protocol scheme in which known and novel gossip-based implementations of the peer sampling service can be instantiated, and presents an extensive empirical comparison of these protocols.

Contribution. First, we identify a new abstract service, the peer sampling service, which is a fundamental building block underlying gossip-based protocols. This peer sampling service is thus indispensable for gossip-based implementations of a wide range of higher level functions, which include information dissemination, aggregation, network management and synchronization.

Second, as a result of identifying this service and performing its logical separation in a class of existing applications, we present a generic protocol scheme, which generalizes the gossip-based peer sampling service protocols we are aware of. Our scheme makes it possible to implement new protocols as well.

Third, we describe an experimental methodology to evaluate the protocols in question. A key aspect of the methodology is that we focus on the *overlay network* that is induced by the peers that the service returns to nodes. In particular, we examine if these overlays exhibit *stable properties*, that is, whether the corresponding protocol instances lead to the *convergence* of important properties of the overlay. We also measure the extent to which these communication topologies deviate from the desirable uniform random model mentioned earlier. We do so by looking at several static and dynamic properties: degree distribution, average path length and clustering coefficient. We also consider the reliability of the service by examining its self-healing capacity and robustness to failure.

The behavior of the protocol instances we evaluate shows a rather wide variation. A common characteristic, however, is that no instance leads to a uniform sampling, rendering traditional theoretical approaches invalid when these protocols are applied as a sampling service. This result is surprising, as uniform randomness has long been generally assumed based only on (wrong) intuition. As a result of our work, all previous theoretical results about these protocols assuming randomness will have to be revised to properly describe the observed behavior.

Roadmap. In Section 2 we define the peer sampling service. Section 3 describes our generic protocol and the various dimensions according to which it can be instantiated. Section 4 presents our experimentation methodology. Sections 5, 6 and 7 discuss our results in different simulation scenarios. In Section 8 we interpret the result of the experiments. Related work is discussed in Section 9. Finally, Section 10 concludes the paper.

2   Peer Sampling Service

The peer sampling service is interpreted over a set of nodes that form the domain of the gossip-based protocols that make use of the service. The same sampling service can be utilized by multiple gossip protocols simultaneously, provided they have a common target group. The task of the service is to provide a participating node of a gossiping application with a subset of peers from the group to send gossip messages to.

The API of the peer sampling service is extremely simple consisting of only two methods: init and getPeer. While it would be technically straightforward to provide a framework for a multiple-application interface and architecture, for a better focus and simplicity of notations we assume that there is only one application. The specification of these methods is as follows.

init() Initializes the service on a given node if this has not been done before. The actual initialization procedure is implementation dependent.

getPeer() Returns a peer address if the group contains more than one node. The returned address is a sample drawn from the group. The specification of this sample (randomness, correlation in time and with other peers) is implementation dependent (one research goal of the present paper is exactly to give information about the behavior of this method in the case of a class of gossip-based implementations).

Many times an application needs more than one peer. To maintain focus we define getPeer to return only one peer. Applications requiring more peers can call this method repeatedly. We note however that allowing getPeer to return more peers at the same time might allow for optimizations of the implementation of the service.

Note that we do not define a stop method. The reason is to ease the burden on applications by propagating the responsibility of automatically removing non-active nodes to the service layer.

The design of the service should take into account requirements with respect to the quality of peer sampling, as well as the costs involved for providing a certain quality.

Based on the growing body of theoretical work cited above, the service should ideally always return a peer as the result of independent uniform random sampling. However, we note that although this quality criterion is useful to allow rigorous analysis, it is by no means the case that all gossiping applications actually require uniform randomness. For example, some applications require only good mixing of random walks, which can also be established without demanding that peers are sampled uniformly. On the other hand, applications such as those that do aggregation do at least require that samples are not drawn from a fixed, static subset of all possible nodes.

These two examples illustrate that the costs of sampling may be reduced if near-uniformity is good enough for the application that makes use of the sampling service. In short, for an implementation of the service there is a trade-off between the required quality of sampling and the performance cost for attaining that quality. Uniform randomness can be conveniently treated as a baseline to compare protocols to, and in particular the quality of the sampling service.

3   Evaluation Framework

To study the impact on various parameters of gossip-based approaches to peer sampling, we define an evaluation framework. A wide range of protocols fits into this framework and in particular the peer sampling components of the protocols Lpbcast [8] and Newscast [12] are specific instances of protocols within this framework.

System Model. We consider a set of nodes connected in a network. A node has an address that is needed for sending a message to that node. Each node maintains addresses by means of a *partial view*, which is a set of c *node descriptors*. The

```
do forever                                 do forever
  wait(T time units)                         (p, view_p) ← waitMessage()
  p ← selectPeer()                           view_p ← increaseHopCount(view_p)
  if push then                               if pull then
    // 0 is the initial hop count              // 0 is the initial hop count
    myDescriptor ← (myAddress, 0)             myDescriptor ← (myAddress, 0)
    buffer ← merge(view,{myDescriptor})       buffer ← merge(view,{myDescriptor})
    send buffer to p                          send buffer to p
  else                                       buffer ← merge(view_p,view)
    // empty view to trigger response        view ← selectView(buffer)
    send {} to p
  if pull then
    receive view_p from p
    view_p ← increaseHopCount(view_p)
    buffer ← merge(view_p,view)
    view ← selectView(buffer)
          (a) active thread                        (b) passive thread
```

Fig. 1. The skeleton of a gossip-based implementation of a peer sampling service.

value of c is the same for all nodes. Besides an address, a node descriptor also contains a *hop count*, as we explain below.

We assume that each node executes the same protocol, of which the skeleton is shown in Figure 1. The protocol consists of two threads: an active thread initiating communication with other nodes, and a passive thread waiting for incoming messages. The skeleton code is parameterized with two Booleans (push and pull), and two function placeholders (selectPeer() and selectView()).

A view is organized as a list with at most one descriptor per node and ordered according to increasing hop count. We can thus meaningfully refer to the *first* or *last* k elements of a particular view (note however that all hop counts do not necessarily differ so the first and last k elements are not always uniquely defined by the ordering). A call to increaseHopCount($view$) increments the hop count of every element in *view*. A call to merge($view_1$,$view_2$) returns the union of $view_1$ and $view_2$, ordered again by hop count. When there is a descriptor for the same node in each view, only the one with the lowest hop count is inserted into the merged view; the other is discarded.

This design space enables us to evaluate in a simple and rigorous way the impact of the various parameters involved in gossip-based protocols along three dimensions: *(i)* Peer selection; *(ii)* View propagation; *(iii)* View selection. Many variations exist along each of these dimensions; we limit our study to the three most relevant strategies per dimension. We shall now define these dimensions.

Peer Selection. Periodically, each node selects a peer to exchange membership information with. This selection is implemented by the function selectPeer() that returns the address of a *live* node as found in the caller's current view. In this study, we consider the following *peer selection* policies:

rand	Uniform randomly select an available node from the view
head	Select the first node from the view (the one with the *lowest* hop count)
tail	Select the last node from the view (the one with the *highest* hop count)

View Propagation. Once a peer has been chosen, the peers may exchange information in various ways. We consider the following three *view propagation* policies:

push	The node sends its view to the selected peer
pull	The node requests the view from the selected peer
pushpull	The node and selected peer exchange their respective views

View Selection. Once membership information has been exchanged between peers and merged as explained above, peers may need to truncate their views in order to adhere to the c items limit imposed as a protocol parameter. The function selectView(*view*) selects a subset of at most c elements from *view*. Again, we consider only three out of the many possible *view selection* policies:

rand	Uniform randomly select c elements without replacement from *view*
head	Select the first c elements from *view*
tail	Select the last c elements from *view*

These three types of policies give rise to a total of 27 combinations, each of which we express by means of a 3-tuple (ps, vs, vp) with ps indicating one of the three possible peer selection policies, vs the view selection policies, and vp the chosen view propagation policy. As an example, Lpbcast corresponds to the 3-tuple (rand,rand,push), whereas Newscast is described by (rand,head,pushpull). In the following, a DON'T CARE value (i.e., a wild card) is denoted by the symbol "*".

Implementation of the Peer Sampling API. The implementation of method init() is done by initializing the view of the node by an arbitrary peer node. This obviously involves a bootstrapping problem, which can be solved by out-of-band methods, for example through well-known nodes or a central service publishing contact nodes, or with any other convenient method. We will experimentally evaluate different bootstrapping methods in Section 5. As the simplest possible implementation, method getPeer() can return a random sample of the current view. Obviously, more sophisticated implementations are also possible that e.g. maximize the diversity of the set of peers returned by consecutive calls to getPeer. From our point of view in this paper the only important feature is that getPeer utilizes the local partial view to return a peer.

4   Experimental Methodology

As already mentioned in Section 2 the baseline of our evaluation will be the ideal independent uniform random implementation of the sampling service. It is far from trivial to compare a given sampling service to this ideal case in a meaningful way. Statistical tests for randomness and independence tend to hide the most important *structural* properties of the system as a whole. Instead of a statistical approach, in our methodology, we switch to a graph theoretical framework, which provides richer possibilities of interpretation from the point of view of reliability, robustness and application requirements, as Section 4.2 also illustrates.

To translate the problem into a graph theoretical language, we consider the *communication topology* or *overlay topology* defined by the set of nodes and their views (recall that getPeer() returns samples from the view). In this framework the directed edges of the communication graph are defined as follows. If node a stores the descriptor of node b in its view then there is a directed edge (a, b) from a to b.

In the language of graphs, the question is how similar this overlay topology is to a random graph in which the descriptors in each view represent a uniform independent random sample of the whole node set?

4.1   Targeted Questions

There are two general questions we seek to answer. The first and most fundamental question is whether, for a particular protocol implementation, the communication graph has some stable properties, which it maintains during the execution of the protocol. In other words, we are interested in the *convergence behavior* of the protocols. We can expect several sorts of dynamics which include chaotic behavior, oscillations or convergence. In case of convergence the resulting state may or may not depend on the initial configuration of the system. In the case of overlay networks we prefer to have convergence toward a state that is independent of the initial configuration. Sometimes this property is called *self-organization*. In our case it is essential that in a wide range of scenarios the system should automatically produce consistent and predictable behavior.

Related is the question is that *if* there is convergence then what kind of communication graph does the protocol converge to? In particular, as mentioned earlier, we are interested in what sense do these graphs deviate from certain random graph models.

4.2   Selected Graph Properties

In order to find answers to the above problems we need to select a set of observable properties that characterize the communication graph. In the following, we will focus on the *undirected* version of the communication graph which we get by simply dropping the orientation of the edges. The reason for this choice is that even if the "knows-about" relation that defines the directed communication graph is one-way, the actual information flow from the point of view of the applications of the overlay is potentially two-way, since after initiating a connection the passive party will learn about the active party as well. Now let us turn to the properties we will examine.

Degree Distribution. The degree of a node is defined as the number of its neighbors in the undirected communication graph. We will consider several aspects of the degree distribution including average degree, the dynamics of the degree of a node, and the exact degree distribution. The motivation for looking at degree distribution is threefold and includes its direct relationship with reliability to different patterns of node failures [2], its crucial effect on the exact way epidemics are spread (and therefore on the way epidemic-based broadcasting is performed) [23] and finally its key role in determining if there are communication hot spots in the overlay.

Average Path Length. The shortest path length between node a and b is the minimal number of edges that are necessary to traverse in the graph in order to reach b from a. The average path length is the average of shortest path lengths over all pairs of nodes in the graph. The motivation of looking at this property is that, in any information dissemination scenario, the shortest path length defines a lower bound on the time and costs of reaching a peer. For scalability, small average path length is essential.

Clustering Coefficient. The clustering coefficient of a node a is defined as the number of edges between the neighbors of a divided by the number of all possible edges between those neighbors. Intuitively, this coefficient indicates the extent to which the neighbors of a are also neighbors of each other. The clustering coefficient of the graph is the average of the clustering coefficients of the nodes, and always lies between 0 and 1. For a complete graph, it is 1, for a tree it is 0. The motivation for analyzing this property is that a high clustering coefficient has potentially damaging effect on both information dissemination (by increasing the number of redundant messages) and also on the self-healing capacity by weakening the connection of a cluster to the rest of the graph thereby increasing the probability of partitioning. Furthermore, it provides an interesting possibility to draw parallels with research on complex networks where clustering is an important research topic (e.g., in social networks) [30].

4.3 Parameter Settings

The main goal of this paper is to explore the different design choices in the protocol space described in Section 3. That is, the parameters which we want to explore are peer selection, view selection, and symmetry model. Accordingly, we chose to fix the network size to $N = 10^4$ and the maximal view size to $c = 30$.

During our preliminary experiments some parameter settings turned out not to result in meaningful overlay management protocols. In particular, (head,∗,∗) results in severe clustering, (∗,tail,∗) cannot handle dynamism (joining nodes)

Table 1. Protocols where partitioning was observed in the growing overlay scenario.
Data corresponds to cycle 300.

protocol	partitioned runs	average number of clusters	average largest cluster
(rand,head,push)	100%	58.36	4112.09
(rand,rand,push)	33%	2.27	9572.18
(tail,head,push)	100%	38.19	7150.52
(tail,rand,push)	1%	2.00	9941.00

at all and (∗,∗,pull) converges to a star topology, which is highly undesirable.
These variants are therefore excluded from further discussion.

5   Convergence

We now present experimental results that illustrate the convergence properties
of the protocols in three different bootstrapping scenarios. The first is the case
of a growing overlay discussed in Section 5.1. The second is the initialization of
the overlay with a structured large diameter topology (Section 5.2) and finally
the initialization with a random topology (Section 5.3).

   As we focus on the dynamical properties of the protocols, we did not wish
to average out interesting patterns so in all cases the result of a single run is
shown in the plots. Nevertheless, we ran all the scenarios 100 times to gain data
on the stability of the protocols with respect to the connectivity of the overlay.
Connectivity is a crucial feature, a minimal requirement for all applications. The
results of these runs show that in all scenarios, every protocol under examination
creates a connected overlay network in 100% of the runs. The only exceptions
(shown in Table 1) were detected during the growing overlay scenario.

5.1   Growing Overlay

In this scenario the overlay network initially contains only one node. At the
beginning of each cycle, 100 new nodes are added to the network until the
maximal size is reached in cycle 100. The view of these nodes is initialized with
only a single node descriptor, which belongs to the oldest, initial node.

   This scenario is the most pessimistic one for bootstrapping the overlays. It
would be straightforward to improve it by using more contact nodes, which
can come from a fixed list or which can be obtained using inexpensive local
random walks on the existing overlay. However, in our discussion we intentionally
avoid such optimizations to allow a better focus on the core protocols and their
differences.

   Figure 2 shows the dynamics of the properties of the communication topology. Protocols (rand,head,push) and (tail,head,push) are not plotted due to their
instability in this scenario with respect to connectivity of the overlay (see Table 1). A non partitioned run of both (rand,rand,push) and (tail,rand,push) is
included however.

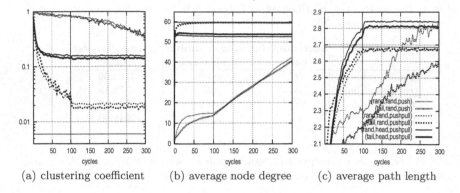

(a) clustering coefficient   (b) average node degree   (c) average path length

Fig. 2. Dynamics of graph properties in the growing scenario. Horizontal line indicates the property in a uniform random topology, vertical line indicates end of growth.

The partitioning of the push version of the protocols is due to the fact that it is only the first, central node that can distribute new links to all new members. For the same reason convergence is extremely slow when push is applied, while the pushpull versions do show fast convergence. Protocols (∗,rand,pushpull) are seemingly closer to the random topology, however, we will see that this is misleading and is a result of a highly non-balanced degree distribution (see Section 6).

5.2 Ring Lattice Initial Topology

In this scenario, the initial topology of the overlay was a ring lattice, a structured topology. The motivation behind this experiment is to examine if the overlay properties converge to the same random structure with a low average path length even if the initial topology is highly structured and has a large average path length.

We build the ring lattice as follows. The nodes are first connected into a ring in which each node has a descriptor in its view that belongs to its two neighbors in the ring. Subsequently, for each node, we add additional descriptors of the nearest nodes in the ring until the view is filled.

Figure 3 shows the output of this scenario as well. As in the case of the growing scenario, 300 cycles were run but here only 100 are shown to focus on the more interesting initial dynamics of the protocols. We can observe that all versions result in quick convergence which is particularly well illustrated by path length in Figure 3(a) (note the logarithmic scale), but also by the other observed properties.

5.3 Random Initial Topology

In this scenario the initial topology was defined by a random graph, in which the views of the nodes were initialized by a uniform random sample of the peer

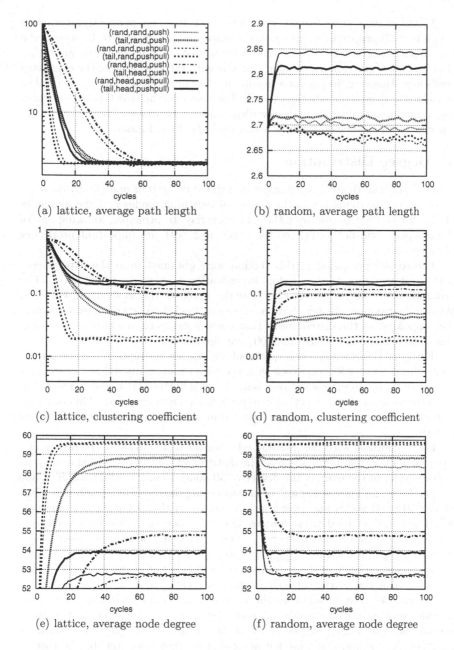

Fig. 3. Dynamics of graph properties. Horizontal line shows uniform random topology.

nodes. Figure 3 includes the output of this scenario as well. As in the other scenarios, 300 cycles were run but only 100 are shown.

The most interesting feature we can notice is that independently of starting conditions, all properties converge to the same value. This cannot be seen in the case of path length, but it is also true. We can also see that the values are rather close to that of the random topology, maybe with the exception of the clustering coefficient. However, to put these results in the appropriate context, we need to consider the degree distribution as well. For instance, the star topology – which has a maximally unbalanced degree distribution – also has a low diameter and low clustering coefficient, while it is obviously far from random.

6   Degree Distribution

When describing degree distribution in a dynamic system one has to focus on two aspects: the dynamics of the degree of individual nodes and the dynamics of the degree distribution over the whole overlay. In principle, knowing one of these aspects will not determine the other, and both are important properties of an overlay.

The results presented in this section were obtained from the experiments performed according to the random initialization scenario described above. The evolution of the degree distribution over the whole overlay is shown in Figure 4. We can observe how the distribution reaches its final shape starting from the random topology, as the distributions that correspond to exponentially increasing time intervals (cycle 0, 3, 30 and 300) are also shown.

This time the behavior of the protocols can clearly be divided into two groups according to view selection. Note that previous experiments did not reveal this difference. Random view selection results in an unbalanced distribution and slow convergence while head selection is more balanced and very fast. This is a very important difference and it will be reflected in most of the following experiments as well.

Let us continue with the question whether the distribution of the degree of a fixed node over time is the same as the distribution of the converged overlay at a fixed cycle. In the overlay the degree of 50 nodes were traced during $K = 300$ cycles. Table 2 shows statistical data concerning degree distribution over time at the 50 fixed nodes and over the full overlay in the last cycle (i.e. in cycle K). The notations used are as follows. Let $d(i,j)$ denote the degree of node i in cycle j. Let $\overline{d_i}$ be the mean degree of node i over K consecutive cycles. Now, let $\overline{d} = \sum_{i=1}^{50} \overline{d_i}/50$ and $\sigma = \sum_{i=1}^{50} (\overline{d_i} - \overline{d})^2/49$, where $\overline{d}$ is the average and σ is the empirical variance of the time-averages of the degree of the traced 50 nodes. Finally, $\overline{D_K}$ is the average of node degrees in cycle K over all nodes.

We can see that in all cases the degree of all nodes oscillates around the overall average, in other words, all nodes tend to have the same degree, there are no emerging higher degree nodes on the long run. On the other hand, we again observe a major distinction according to view selection. In the case of random selection the oscillation has a much higher amplitude, the network is less stable.

The last question we consider is whether the sequence of node degrees during the cycles of the protocol can be considered a random sequence drawn from the

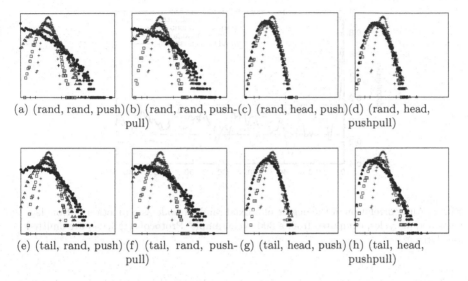

(a) (rand, rand, push) (b) (rand, rand, push- (c) (rand, head, push) (d) (rand, head,
                        pull)   pushpull)

(e) (tail, rand, push) (f) (tail, rand, push- (g) (tail, head, push) (h) (tail, head,
                       pull)   pushpull)

Fig. 4. Degree distributions on the log-log scale, when starting from a random topology.
The ranges are [30,300] for the degree axis (horizontal), and [1:1000] for the frequency
axis (vertical). Note that degree is guaranteed to be at least 30. The symbol + denotes
the random graph (cycle 0). Empty box, empty triangle and filled circle belong to cycle
3, 30 and 300, respectively.

Table 2. Statistics describing the dynamics of the degree of individual nodes.

protocol	$\overline{D_{300}}$	$\overline{d}$	$\sqrt{\sigma}$
(rand,head,push)	52.623	52.703	1.394
(tail,head,push)	54.785	55.519	2.690
(rand,head,pushpull)	52.717	52.933	1.756
(tail,head,pushpull)	53.916	53.888	2.176
(rand,rand,push)	58.404	60.804	19.062
(tail,rand,push)	58.844	58.746	17.287
(rand,rand,pushpull)	59.569	61.306	13.886
(tail,rand,pushpull)	59.666	58.616	9.756

overall degree distribution. If not, then how quickly does it change, and is it perhaps periodical? To this end we present autocorrelation data of the degree time-
series of fixed nodes in Figure 5. The band indicates a 99% confidence interval
assuming the data is random. The autocorrelation of the series $d(i,1), \ldots d(i,K)$
for a given time lag k is defined as

$$r_k = \frac{\sum_{j=1}^{K-k}(d(i,j) - \overline{d_i})(d(i,j+k) - \overline{d_i})}{\sum_{j=1}^{K}(d(i,j) - \overline{d_i})^2},$$

which expresses the correlation of pairs of degree values separated by k cycles.

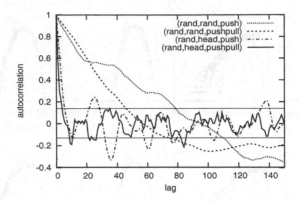

Fig. 5. Autocorrelation of the degree of a fixed random node as a function of time lag, measured in cycles, computed from a 300 cycle sample. Protocols (tail,*,*) are omitted for clarity.

For the correct interpretation of the figure observe that (rand,head,pushpull) can be considered practically random according to the 99% confidence band, while the time series produced by (rand,head,push) shows some weak high frequency periodic behavior. The protocols (*,rand,*) appear to show low frequency periodic behavior with strong short-term correlation, although to confirm that further experiments are necessary. This means that apart from having a higher oscillation amplitude, random view selection also results in a much slower oscillation.

7   Self-healing Capacity

As in the case of the degree distribution, the response of the protocols to a massive failure has a static and a dynamic aspect. In the static setting we are interested in the self-healing capacity of the converged overlays to a (potentially massive) node failure, as a function of the number of failing nodes. Removing a large number of nodes will inevitably cause some serious structural changes in the overlay even if it otherwise remains "usable," that is, at least connected. In the dynamic case we would like to learn if and how the protocols can repair the overlay after a severe damage.

The effect of a massive node failure on connectivity is shown in Figure 6. In this setting the overlay in cycle 300 of the random initialization scenario was used as converged topology. From this topology, random nodes were removed and the connectivity of the remaining nodes was analyzed. In all of the $100 \times 8 = 800$ experiments performed we did not observe partitioning until removing 69% of the nodes. The figure depicts the number of the nodes outside the largest connected cluster. We observe consistent partitioning behavior over all protocol instances: even when partitioning occurs, most of the nodes form

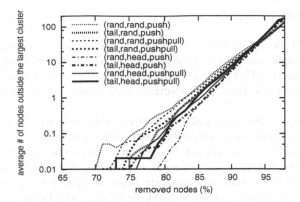

Fig. 6. The number of nodes that do not belong to the largest connected cluster. The average of 100 experiments is shown.

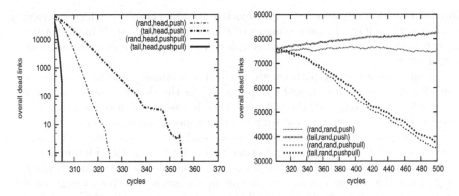

Fig. 7. The evolution of the number of dead links in the overlay following the failure of 50% of the nodes in cycle 300. The (∗,head,pushpull) protocols fully overlap. Note the different scales of the two plots.

a single large connected cluster. Note that this phenomenon is well known for traditional random graphs [21].

In the dynamic scenario we made 50% of the nodes fail in cycle 300 of the random initialization scenario and we then continued running the protocols on the damaged overlay. The damage is expressed by the fact that, on average, half of the view of each node consists of descriptors that belong to nodes that are no longer in the network. We will call these descriptors dead links. Figure 7 shows how fast the protocols repair the overlay, that is, remove dead links. Based on the static node failure experiment it was expected that the remaining 50% of the overlay is not partitioned and indeed, we did not observe partitioning with any of the protocols.

8   Discussion

In our analysis of the output of the experiments presented above we first concentrate of the two main questions we posed: convergence and randomness. Then we move on to discuss the effects of the design choices in the three dimensions of the protocol space: peer selection, view selection, and symmetry of communication.

Convergence. Figures 2(a), 3(c) and 3(d) illustrate especially well that the protocols converge to the same clustering coefficient from extremely different starting conditions. Although it is somewhat less evident due to the different scales of the plots in Figure 3, average path length and average degree converge just as well. Note that the (∗,∗,push) protocols are unstable and converge very slowly in the growing overlay scenario. We will return to this issue below.

Also note that in the case of the lattice initialization scenario the initial diameter is very large but even in that case we observe rapid convergence to the desirable low diameter topology (Figure 3(a)).

Randomness. Let us compare the overlays with random graphs in which the view is filled with uniform random samples of the other nodes. The behavior of the protocols we examined shows a rather colorful picture with respect to different graph properties.

In the case of average path length, clustering coefficient and average degree it is clear that protocols (∗,rand,pushpull) give us the closest approximation of the random topology, with the tail peer selection being slightly more random (see Figure 3). However, when looking at other aspects, we see a rather different picture. Degree distribution protocols (rand,head,∗) are the closest to random distribution while protocols (∗,rand,∗) are rather far from it (see Figure 4).

In all cases, we can observe that the clustering coefficient is significantly larger than that of the random graph and at the same time the average path length is almost as small. This adds all our overlay topologies to the long list of complex networks observable in nature, biology, sociology, and computer science that have a so-called "small-world" topology [1].

View Selection. The view selection algorithms are significantly different. Head view selection results in a more random degree distribution than the others, and it results in much less autocorrelation of the degree of a fixed node over time (Figures 4 and 5 and Table 2). These properties make the overlays using head view selection much less vulnerable to directed attacks targeting large-degree nodes because there are no nodes with very large degree and the degree of a node changes very quickly anyway. This also means that there are no communication hot-spots in those overlays, which could result in scalability problems.

Also, head view selection repairs the overlay exponentially fast whereas random view selection can at best achieve linear speed, which can hardly be considered scalable (Figure 7). The only scenario when head view selection is not desirable is temporary network partitioning. In that case, with head view selection all partitions will forget about each other very quickly and so quick self-repair becomes a disadvantage. In practical applications the slow and quick self-healing mechanisms should be combined.

Symmetry of Communication. The symmetry of communication is also an important design choice. In particular, push has severe problems dealing with "bottleneck" topologies, like the star-like topology implicitly defined by the growing overlay scenario. In that case, some protocols using the push communication model were not even stable enough with respect to connectivity to participate in the experiments (Table 1), and even those that were included showed very slow convergence. The reason is that nodes that join the network in the growing scenario can get information only if the contact node pushes it to them which is very unlikely to happen because the contact node communicates only once in each cycle, just like the other nodes.

It appears that this parameter plays a more prominent role in characterizing the overall behavior of the various protocols. In general, the performance of push-pull is clearly superior compared to push-only approaches.

Peer Selection. In the case of peer selection we cannot observe drastic differences. In general, applying the tail selection algorithm results in slightly more randomness and slightly slower convergence at the same time. The only scenario in which opting for tail selection results in clear performance degradation is self-healing (Figure 7). In that case, (tail,head,push) converges significantly slower than (rand,head,push), although both converge still very quickly. Also, (tail,rand,push) slowly *increases* the amount of dead links which is especially undesirable.

9   Related Work

Complex Networks. The assumption of uniform randomness has only fairly recently become subject to discussion when considering large complex networks such as the hyperlinked structure of the WWW, or the complex topology of the Internet. Like social and biological networks, the structures of the WWW and the Internet both follow the quite unbalanced power-law degree distribution, which deviates strongly from that of traditional random graphs. These new insights pose several interesting theoretical and practical problems [3]. Several dynamic complex networks have also been studied and models have been suggested for explaining phenomena related to what we have described in the present paper [7]. This related work suggests an interesting line of future theoretical research seeking to explain our experimental results in a rigorous manner.

Unstructured Overlays. There are a number of protocols that are not covered by our generic scheme but that are potentially useful for implementing peer sampling. An example is the Scamp protocol [10]. While this protocol is reactive and so less dynamic, an explicit attempt is made towards the construction of a (static) random graph topology. Randomness has been evaluated in the context of information dissemination, and it appears that reliability properties come close to what one would see in random graphs. Some other protocols have also been proposed to achieve randomness [18,22], although not having the specific requirements of the peer sampling service in mind.

Structured Overlays. A structured overlay [26,25,27] is by definition not dynamic so to utilize it for implementing the peer sampling service random walks or other additional techniques have to be applied. It is unclear whether a competitive implementation can be given considering also the cost of maintaining the respective overlay structure. Structured overlays have also been considered as a basic middleware service to applications [5]. Another issue in common with our own work is that graph theoretic approaches have been developed for further analysis [19]. Astrolabe [28] needs also be mentioned as a hierarchical (and therefore structured) overlay which although applies (non-uniform) gossip to increase robustness and to achieve self-healing properties, does not even attempt to implement or apply a uniform peer sampling service. It was designed to support hierarchical information dissemination.

10   Concluding Remarks

In this paper we have identified peer sampling as an abstract middleware service. We have shown that dynamic gossip-based unstructured overlays are a natural candidate for implementing this service due to their reliability and scalability. Whereas there has been a lot of work in analyzing the behavior of structured overlay networks, this is the first attempt to analyze the behavior of a class of unstructured overlays, which so far have been simply assumed uniform random.

The main conclusion of our experiments is that the gossip-based constructions of overlays through partial views leads to many different topologies, none of which actually resembles traditional random graphs. Instead all these constructions belong to the family of small-world graphs characterized by small diameter and large clustering. Besides, many of the implementations result in highly unbalanced degree distribution. This observation indicates that gossip-based peer sampling implementations have strong links to the field of complex networks and self-organizing systems, and more generally to statistical physics, a fact which has been largely overlooked so far. This links give hope for the possibility of the adaptation of the well established theoretical results of dynamic complex networks [7].

When considering the stable properties of various protocols, that is, which emerge from convergent behavior, it also becomes clear that different parameter settings lead to very different properties, which can be exploited according to the needs of the targeted application. For example, a strong self-healing topology may not be appropriate in the presence of temporary network partitions. In many cases, combining different settings will be necessary. Such a combination can, for instance, be achieved by introducing a second view for gossiping membership information and running more protocols concurrently.

References

1. R. Albert and A.-L. Barabási. Statistical mechanics of complex networks. *Reviews of Modern Physics*, 74(1):47–97, January 2002.
2. R. Albert, H. Jeong, and A.-L. Barabási. Error and attack tolerance of complex networks. *Nature*, 406:378–382, 2000.
3. A.-L. Barabási. *Linked: the new science of networks*. Perseus, Cambridge, Mass., 2002.
4. K. P. Birman, M. Hayden, O. Ozkasap, Z. Xiao, M. Budiu, and Y. Minsky. Bimodal multicast. *ACM Transactions on Computer Systems*, 17(2):41–88, May 1999.
5. F. Dabek, B. Zhao, P. Druschel, J. Kubiatowicz, and I. Stoica. Towards a common API for structured peer-to-peer overlays. In *Proc. of the 2nd International Workshop on Peer-to-Peer Systems (IPTPS'03)*, Berkeley, CA, USA, February 2003.
6. A. Demers, D. Greene, C. Hauser, W. Irish, J. Larson, S. Shenker, H. Sturgis, D. Swinehart, and D. Terry. Epidemic algorithms for replicated database management. In *Proc. of the 6th Annual ACM Symposium on Principles of Distributed Computing (PODC'87)*, pages 1–12, Vancouver, August 1987. ACM.
7. S. N. Dorogovtsev and J. F. F. Mendes. Evolution of networks. *Advances in Physics*, 51:1079–1187, 2002.
8. P. T. Eugster, R. Guerraoui, S. B. Handurukande, A.-M. Kermarrec, and P. Kouznetsov. Lightweight probabilistic broadcast. *ACM Transactions on Computer Systems*, 21(4):341–374, 2003.
9. P. T. Eugster, R. Guerraoui, A.-M. Kermarrec, and L. Massoulié. Epidemic information dissemination in distributed systems. *IEEE Computer*, 37(5):60–67, May 2004.
10. A. J. Ganesh, A.-M. Kermarrec, and L. Massoulié. Peer-to-peer membership management for gossip-based protocols. *IEEE Transactions on Computers*, 52(2), February 2003.
11. I. Gupta, K. P. Birman, and R. van Renesse. Fighting fire with fire: using randomized gossip to combat stochastic scalability limits. *Quality and Reliability Engineering International*, 18(3):165–184, 2002.
12. M. Jelasity, W. Kowalczyk, and M. van Steen. Newscast computing. Technical Report IR-CS-006, Vrije Universiteit Amsterdam, Department of Computer Science, Amsterdam, The Netherlands, November 2003.
13. M. Jelasity, W. Kowalczyk, and M. van Steen. An approach to massively distributed aggregate computing on peer-to-peer networks. In *Proc. of the 12th Euromicro Conference on Parallel, Distributed and Network-Based Processing (PDP'04)*, pages 200–207, A Coruna, Spain, 2004. IEEE Computer Society.
14. M. Jelasity and A. Montresor. Epidemic-style proactive aggregation in large overlay networks. In *Proc. of the 24th International Conference on Distributed Computing Systems (ICDCS 2004)*, pages 102–109, Tokyo, Japan, 2004. IEEE Computer Society.
15. M. Jelasity, A. Montresor, and O. Babaoglu. A modular paradigm for building self-organizing peer-to-peer applications. In G. Di Marzo Serugendo, A. Karageorgos, O. F. Rana, and F. Zambonelli, editors, *Engineering Self-Organising Systems*, number 2977 in LNCS, pages 265–282. Springer, 2004.
16. D. Kempe, A. Dobra, and J. Gehrke. Gossip-based computation of aggregate information. In *Proc. of the 44th Annual IEEE Symposium on Foundations of Computer Science (FOCS'03)*, pages 482–491. IEEE Computer Society, 2003.

17. A.-M. Kermarrec, L. Massoulié, and A. J. Ganesh. Probablistic reliable dissemination in large-scale systems. *IEEE Transactions on Parallel and Distributed Systems*, 14(3), March 2003.
18. C. Law and K.-Y. Siu. Distributed construction of random expander graphs. In *Proc. of the 22nd Annual Joint Conference of the IEEE Computer and Communications Societies (INFOCOM'2003)*, San Francisco, California, USA, April 2003.
19. D. Loguinov, A. Kumar, V. Rai, and S. Ganesh. Graph-theoretic analysis of structured peer-to-peer systems: Routing distances and fault resilience. In *Proc. of ACM SIGCOMM*, pages 395–406, 2003.
20. A. Montresor, M. Jelasity, and O. Babaoglu. Robust aggregation protocols for large-scale overlay networks. In *Proc. of the 2004 International Conference on Dependable Systems and Networks (DSN)*, pages 19–28, Florence, Italy, 2004. IEEE Computer Society.
21. M. E. J. Newman. Random graphs as models of networks. In S. Bornholdt and H. G. Schuster, editors, *Handbook of Graphs and Networks: From the Genome to the Internet*, chapter 2. John Wiley, New York, NY, 2002.
22. G. Pandurangan, P. Raghavan, and E. Upfal. Building low-diameter peer-to-peer networks. *IEEE Journal on Selected Areas in Communications (JSAC)*, 21(6):995–1002, August 2003.
23. R. Pastor-Satorras and A. Vespignani. Epidemic dynamics and endemic states in complex networks. *Physical Review E*, 63:066117, 2001.
24. B. Pittel. On spreading a rumor. *SIAM Journal on Applied Mathematics*, 47(1):213–223, February 1987.
25. S. Ratnasamy, P. Francis, M. Handley, R. Karp, and S. Schenker. A scalable content-addressable network. In *Proc. of ACM SIGCOMM*, pages 161–172, 2001.
26. A. Rowstron and P. Druschel. Pastry: Scalable, distributed object location and routing for large-scale peer-to-peer systems. In R. Guerraoui, editor, *Middleware 2001*, volume 2218 of *LNCS*, pages 329–350. Springer, 2001.
27. I. Stoica, R. Morris, D. Karger, M. F. Kaashoek, and H. Balakrishnan. Chord: A scalable peer-to-peer lookup service for internet applications. In *Proc. of ACM SIGCOMM*, pages 149–160, 2001.
28. R. Van Renesse, K. P. Birman, and W. Vogels. Astrolabe: A robust and scalable technology for distributed system monitoring, management, and data mining. *ACM Transactions on Computer Systems*, 21(2), May 2003.
29. S. Voulgaris and M. van Steen. An epidemic protocol for managing routing tables in very large peer-to-peer networks. In *Proc. of the 14th IFIP/IEEE International Workshop on Distributed Systems: Operations and Management, (DSOM 2003)*, number 2867 in LNCS. Springer, 2003.
30. D. J. Watts and S. H. Strogatz. Collective dynamics of 'small-world' networks. *Nature*, 393:440–442, 1998.

Directed Flood-Routing Framework
for Wireless Sensor Networks

Miklós Maróti

Institute for Software Integrated Systems (ISIS), Vanderbilt University,
Box 1829, Station B, Nashville, TN 37235, USA
miklos.maroti@vanderbilt.edu

Abstract. The directed flood-routing framework (DFRF) for wireless sensor
networks is introduced in this paper that allows the modeling and rapid development of application specific routing protocols based on directed flooding.
Flood-routing protocols are probabilistic methods that make only the best effort
to route data packets. The presented family of protocols can route regular sized
data packets via broadcast messages according to customizable, state machine
based routing policies that govern the way intermediate nodes rebroadcast messages. The framework supports automatic data packet aggregation, and allows
in-network data packet filtering and alteration.

1 Introduction

Routing protocols for wireless sensor networks are proliferating. Unlike wired networks, where the TCP/IP is dominant, wireless sensor networks have no prevailing
routing protocol. Even well designed and tested routing protocols can exhibit subpar
performance under a different application load, in a certain deployment scenario, or
on a new hardware platform. We argue that this is unlikely to change in the near future, and current research shall focus on developing and classifying broad families of
routing protocols that are easily adaptable to a wide variety of real word applications.

The connectivity and topology of the wireless network, as well as the characteristics of the medium access control (MAC) of the operating system, fundamentally
influence the design of any routing protocol. Separating the essential part, called the
policy, of a routing protocol from the implementation techniques common to a family
of protocols, and expressing it in a compact representation reap substantial benefits.
First, protocols become easier to understand. Second, automatic optimization techniques can be utilized to find the best policy that adapts the protocol to the target
network topology and to the particular implementation of the MAC. Third, the engine
that coordinates and executes these routing policies becomes a general middleware
service that bridges the gap between the application requirements and the characteristics of the underlying networking services.

We have identified a rich family of routing protocols based on directed flooding
that can be parameterized by policies, as described above. Flood-routing protocols are
probabilistic methods that make only the best effort to route data packets. On the
other hand, they are particularly resistant to node and link failures because data packets can reach their destination through different routes.

In an acoustic shooter localization application [5] we have successfully used several flood-routing protocols to reconfigure the nodes of the network and to gather

H.-A. Jacobsen (Ed.): Middleware 2004, LNCS 3231, pp. 99–114, 2004.
© IFIP International Federation for Information Processing 2004

sensor readings, the time of muzzle blast and shock wave events. Designing a routing protocol that can handle this load is especially challenging, since a large subset of nodes detects these acoustic events approximately at the same time and has to report back to the base station under real time constraints. The routing protocols that achieved the requirements of the acoustic shooter localization application were developed using the proposed directed flood-routing framework (DFRF).

The framework consists of an engine and several flooding policies. The engine stores and manages data packets enroute to their destination, while routing policies define state machines that describe which packets need to be rebroadcasted by intermediate nodes and when. The framework supports automatic data packet aggregation, and allows in-network data packet filtering and alteration.

In the next section we introduce the targeted hardware platform, and then survey the available routing protocols on this hardware. Next, we formally define the directed flood-routing framework. Finally, we present a set of selected flooding policies that can be used to build robust wireless sensor network applications. Among these a novel spanning tree based convergecast routing policy is introduced that routes messages in a "*lane*" consisting of the nodes at most one hop away from the shortest path from the sender to the root. The resulting routing policy is (1) robust to node and link failures, (2) energy efficient as the maximum number of routing messages increases only linearly with the distance of the sender, and (3) has no data or message overhead compared to simple spanning tree based routing.

2   The Target Platform

The directed flood-routing framework was evaluated on the Berkeley Mica motes [1], the most widely used platform for researching ad-hoc wireless sensor networks with limited resources. This platform exemplifies the class of resource constrained platforms having a broadcast medium which the proposed framework was designed for. We highlight the main characteristics of this platform now. The second generation Mica2 version features a 7.3 MHz microcontroller, 4 KB of RAM, 128 KB of flash memory, and a 433 MHz wireless radio transceiver. The motes are powered by two AA batteries, which last for a few days under continuous operation. A wide variety of pluggable sensor boards containing light, temperature, magnetic and other sensors are available. The Mica motes run a small, embedded, open source operating system, called TinyOS, specifically designed for resource limited sensor networks [2]. TinyOS applications are statically linked graphs of event-driven operating system and application components written in the nesC language, a variant of C [4].

The characteristics of the radio transceiver and the radio stack of the target platform are of special importance to the performance of any multi-hop communication protocol. The radio chip (CC1000) of the Mica2 mote utilizes a single radio channel, has 38.4 Kbps transfer rate and maximum 500-foot communication range in open space. Close to or on the ground the range drops dramatically to tens of feet. TinyOS employs up to 36-byte long radio messages. Seven bytes are reserved by the OS to store the length, the cyclic redundancy check (CRC) and other parameters of the message, leaving only 29 bytes for application data at most. The MAC is based on the carrier sense multiple access (CSMA) technique with random backoff [3]. The Mica2 mote can transmit or receive up to 30 messages per second provided no radio collisions occur. Due to manufacturing differences and fading effects, there are more "polite" motes that will not transmit at all if nearby motes are constantly occupying the radio channel. Others are more prone to start transmitting messages in the middle of other transmissions causing radio collisions.

3 Existing Approaches

Conventional routing protocols are insufficient for ad-hoc wireless sensor networks because of their routing related communication overhead. Examples of a few proposed protocols are: dynamic source routing (DSR) [6], ad-hoc on demand distance vector routing (AODV) [7], temporally ordered routing algorithm (TORA) [8], and the zone routing protocol (ZRP) [9]. On the other hand, routing protocols for sensor networks can exploit the physical properties of the environment where the network is deployed. For example, the location of nodes and their sensor readings in these networks are typically more important than their node IDs.

Existing research mostly focused on location-aware routing protocols allowing routers to be nearly stateless: each node needs to know only the position of its neighbors to make the right forwarding decisions. The greedy perimeter stateless routing protocol (GPSR) use perimeter forwarding to get around voids [10]. Location-aided routing (LAR) improves the efficiency of on-demand route-discovery algorithms by restricting routing-packet flooding to "request zones" [11]. This particular protocol could be developed in the proposed DFRF. The Stateless protocol for real-time communication (SPEED) [12] provides soft real-time communication based on feed-back control.

There are several other routing protocols in the literature relevant to the DFRF. The gradient broadcast (GRAB) protocol builds and maintains a gradient field on a particular subgraph of the network describing the direction sensory data is forwarded to a sink [13]. The gossip routing protocol performs a reliable network broadcasts, probabilistically [14]. These two protocols fit precisely the proposed DFRF. Flooding policies achieving similar functionalities will be presented in Sections 5.1 and 5.2. The rumor routing protocol is a combination of two flooding algorithms: query and event flooding. This protocol utilizes available power resources well [15]. A similar algorithm can possibly developed in DFRF. Constraint based routing (CBR) is another directed flood-routing protocol [16]. TinyDiffusion [17] is another flooding based routing protocol with a publish-subscribe interface that utilizes route reinforcement. Broadcasting protocols are compared in [18] and [19]. The AODV, GPSR, SPEED, CBR and TinyDiffusion protocols are already implemented in TinyOS, and many others are in development [20].

A wide range of other middleware services related to routing were proposed for wireless sensor networks. A new group management middleware and distributed programming paradigm was introduced EnviroTrack [21]. Database management middleware services for wireless sensor networks, such as TinyDB [22] and COUGAR [23], are also actively researched and can offer greater abstraction than traditional routing middleware services. Most existing services for sensor networks however are not readily reconfigurable to meet application requirements and to fully exploit the capabilities of the underlying hardware and networking services, which distinguishes the proposed directed flood-routing framework from other middleware services.

4 The DFRF Algorithm

The directed flood-routing framework is built around a flood-routing engine middle-ware service that manages the routing messages on all nodes in the network. Application components using the flood-routing engine can send and receive regular sized data packets according to a flooding policy. Flooding policies specify the "direction" of flooding and how intermediate nodes rebroadcast messages. The DFRF engine keeps the recently received data packets in a table together with their *priority* (which is managed by the policy), periodically selects the packets with the highest priority, packs them into a single radio message and broadcasts it to the neighboring nodes. In the rest of this section we will describe this algorithm.

4.1 System Architecture

The modules that implement the DFRF algorithm on each node and their interactions are depicted in Fig. 1. Each node has a single routing engine module that can serve several application modules. Application modules register data packet types and corresponding flooding policies with the engine. The same policy can be registered for several data packet types. The modules interact with each other through method invocations, which are depicted as arrows originating from the caller. These methods will be covered in detail in the following sections.

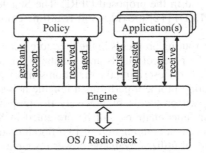

Fig. 1. The architecture of the directed flood-routing framework.

4.2 The Data Packet

Most applications of wireless sensor networks must send and receive different types of data packets, but each of these data types has a well defined internal structure. Typically, data packets of the same type have the same size, as well. For the ease of implementation, and to maximize the available radio message space, we made this a requirement. The lack of variable length data packets allows the DFRF algorithm to aggregate many very small (e.g. 2-byte) data packets into a single radio message. The DFRF engine does not need to know the internal structure of each data packet, only its length.

In directed flooding the same data packet originating from a single node can reach its destination through different routes. This necessitates that the final node, as well as intermediate nodes, be able to uniquely identify the same data packet in order to discard multiple messages. Most routing protocols append a globally unique identifier to each data packet for this purpose, which adds extra data overhead, typically 2-3 bytes. However, this is not necessary for some applications where the data packet is either already globally unique, or the source of the data packet is unimportant. For example, if nodes send time-stamped sensor readings to a base station, then the node ID (or the 3D coordinates of the sensor) together with the time stamp can serve as a unique identifier of the data packet. Or in a multi-hop network reprogramming application, which uploads a new executable image to each node in the network, the missing capsule ID can be used as the unique identifier of the missing capsule message sent to the base station, since it is unimportant which node did not receive a particular capsule of the image.

Because of these considerations, the DFRF engine does not generate globally unique identifiers but requires the user of the algorithm to employ data packets that can be uniquely identified by their first few bytes. This requirement does not put a lot of burden on the user, as generating unique IDs where necessary is trivial. The number of bytes used to uniquely identify data packets is called the *unique length* of the data packet. We say that two data packets are *analogous* if their unique parts (the first unique length of bytes) are identical. Note that analogous data packets are not necessarily identical, as for example, intermediate nodes can modify data packets enroute to the destination.

Each node in the network must know about all packet types used in a particular wireless sensor application. The packet types are identified by a type ID, and they define the length and the unique length of the packet. The type ID is transmitted with each radio message (which can contain several data packets of the same type), and used by the engine to slice the radio message to the appropriate type of data packets, identify the data packets by their unique part, and notify the corresponding application component.

4.3 The Node Rank

When the DFRF engine (re)broadcasts a radio message, it does not include the node ID of the sender in the message, instead a policy dependent value, called the *rank* of the node, is inserted. The rank describes the progress of a data packet in a policy dependent way, and is used to determine what to do with incoming data packets. For the DFRF engine, the rank is simply a (possibly empty) array of bytes, which is passed to the flooding policy when a data packet arrived. The broad possibilities of what the rank can describe are best illustrated through examples.

For the converge-cast policy that routes along a gradient vector to a base station, the node rank is the hop-count distance from the root. In this policy, when the rank of the sender is smaller than that of the receiver, the receiver simply drops the data packet because it comes from a node closer to the root than itself. For the network-wide broadcast policy, the rank is an empty array. It does not matter where the data packet was received from, it will be rebroadcasted if this is the first time this node has received it. For the spanning tree policy that routes message along a spanning tree to a base station, the node rank can be the node ID of the parent node. Here the parent does not care which of its children sent the data packet. There is a robust variation of this policy where the rank is the node ID of the grandparent, which will be covered later. For a geographic routing protocol the rank of the node can be the coordinates of the node. A data packet is sent further if the receiving node is closer to the final destination (which is contained in the data packet) than the sender.

It is important to note that the rank does not depend on the data packet, thus the single rank value is used for multiple aggregated data packets of the same type. On the other hand, it is allowed for the rank of a node to change over time. For example, the gradient vector can change if the root of the converge-cast is mobile. It is even possible to provide flow control through ingenious use of ranks. For example, the rank of a node can include a flag indicating that temporally the node cannot store further data packets for retransmission. Neighboring nodes can detect this and delay transmitting new data packets.

The flooding policy has to implement two methods (or commands in the nesC language) that are used by the DFRF engine. First, the *getRank* method has to return the current rank of the node in this flooding policy. This method is invoked for each transmitted radio message. Second, for each received radio message the policy is consulted via the *accept* method whether the message should be processed at all based on the rank of the sender.

4.4 The Priority

Apart from defining the rank of nodes, the flooding policy has the primary role to govern the life-cycle of data packets at each node. Typically, analogous data packets are received multiple times at each node because radio messages are always broadcasted. An intermediate node first receives the data packet from a node further from the destination, next it rebroadcasts it, and then it will normally hear the packet from a node closer to the destination. This shows that each data packet (or more precisely, the family of analogous data packets) has a life cycle at each node. This life-cycle is governed by the flooding policy.

The life-cycle of a particular data packet is described by a finite state machine. There are states in which the data packet is eligible for retransmission, and there are states in which the data packet must be remembered but should not be retransmitted. For example, if an intermediate node A retransmits a data packet D and then hears the same packet from a node closer to the target than A, then it should remember D for some time, but not retransmit it again to prevent receiving and consequently retransmitting an analogous data packet from some node further from the target than A.

The DFRF engine periodically selects, packs and sends data packets from its internal table to the neighbors. Since nodes have very limited memory, an existing data packet from the table might have to be evicted when a new data packet arrives. The flooding policy directs these two selection processes in the following way. The life-cycle states are numbered, typically from 0 to 255, and these numbers are regarded as the *priority* of data packets. The DFRF engine selects data packets for sending or evicting based on their priority.

We have said that in a subset of states data packets are not retransmitted. It can be very important to keep and remember a data packet on a node even if we do not want to retransmit it immediately. The priorities of these data packets must be high, to avoid eviction, and marked as non-transmittable. To have a dense set of non-transmittable states, we selected the odd number priorities for this purpose.

The DFRF engine holds a table of data packets together with their priority or state in which they are currently in. It selects the data packet with the highest even priority (the smallest number) for sending, and with the lowest priority (the largest number) for evicting. There are two special priorities, the smallest and largest values. The value 0 is the initial state of the state machine, while the value 255 is considered the terminal state. If the DFRF engine has a data packet in the terminal state then the packet is considered invalid and the corresponding slot empty.

4.5 The Policy Actions

The flooding policy defines the transitions of the finite state machine that describes the life-cycle of data packets. There are three events: *sent, received* and *aged*. The first is fired when a data packet has been (successfully) broadcasted, the second when a new or an analogous data packet has been received, and the third is fired at regular time intervals. The flooding policy implements three corresponding methods: *sent, received* and *aged* that compute the new state of a data packet based on the old state (and on the rank of the sender for the *received* event).

When the method *sent* is invoked, the corresponding data packet has been already successfully broadcasted. Note that the data packet had to pass the selection criteria for it to be sent, that is, it had to have one of the highest even priorities. However, by the time this method is called, it might not have the same (or even an even numbered) priority since other actions could have modified it between the two events. As radio links are naturally unreliable due to collisions and fading, flooding policies typically retransmit the same data packet a few times by stepping through even numbered priorities in increasing order, e.g. from 0 to 2, then to 4, etc. This way, the same data packet gets gradually lower priorities and could become evicted if the engine is short on memory.

The *received* method is called for each incoming data packet. If this is the first time this data packet is received at this node, then priority 0, otherwise the priority of the existing analogous data packet is passed as an argument to this method. The rank of the sender is also available on which the flooding policy can base its action. Normally, the rank of the sender and that of the current node is compared, and if the flooding policy determines that the packet was heard from a node "closer" to the target than the current node, then it either drops or remembers the packet, but it will never become eligible for retransmission. The packet can be dropped by entering state 255 that makes the corresponding slot free. It can be remembered by walking through a high valued chain of odd priorities, e.g. 201, 203, etc., incremented in the *aged* method.

The *aged* method is invoked periodically for all valid (with priority other than 255) data packets. Typically, policy implementations should decrease the priority of the packet by increasing this number and eventually drop the packet by entering priority 255.

4.6 Message Layout

Each radio message contains one or more data packets of the same type. The layout of the message is as follows. The first field is the type ID (1 byte) followed by the rank of the sender node. The rank is stored in zero or more bytes depending on the flooding policy that corresponds to the type ID. After these two fields come the data packets. On the selected platform the number of data packets is not included in the message, because it can be calculated from the length of the radio message and the type ID. The priority of the data packet is not transmitted, as it is maintained locally and separately by each of the nodes that participate in the routing. This compact representation keeps the number of extra bytes at the absolute minimum, which allows several data packets to be aggregated into a single radio message. The message layout on the TinyOS platform is depicted in Fig. 2.

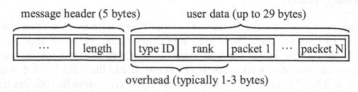

Fig. 2. The message layout on TinyOS. The overhead imposed by the DFRF is typically 1-3 bytes depending on the choice of flooding policy.

4.7 The Data Packet Table

The DFRF engine maintains a table for each type of data packets. This table includes the data packets and their priorities. This table holds at most one data packet from any family of analogous packets at any given time. Currently, this table is held in a fixed size array, but a hash table based implementation (based on the unique first bytes of data packets) is also possible. If a data packet has priority 255, it is considered invalid and the corresponding slot free. The engine has three basic activities: broadcasting and receiving radio messages, and aging data packets in the table.

When a message has been sent, the engine invokes the *sent* method to calculate the new state for each data packet contained in the message. Then it selects the next batch of data packets. It looks for the highest (lowest number) even priority data packets and packs them into a radio message buffer until it is full. Then it obtains the current rank of the node from the flooding policy and passes the radio message buffer to the radio stack for transmission. The engine stops sending messages if there are no more even numbered data packets in any of the tables.

When a new radio message is received, the engine first identifies the data type of the packets contained in the message, then invokes the *accept* method of the corresponding flooding policy to determine if further processing is necessary. If so, it unpacks each data packet contained in the message. For each packet, it locates an analogous data packet in the table. If there is no match, then the user of the flooding algorithm is notified of the newly arrived data packet via the *receive* method. The engine then finds a place for this packet by evicting an existing packet with the lowest priority from the table. Note that this selection includes available free slots as their priority is 255, the lowest. This evicted packet is overwritten by the newly arrived data packet with priority 0. Once the packet (or an analogous packet) is in the table, the *received* method of the flooding policy is invoked to calculate the new state of the packet, and the next packet in the message is considered.

Finally, the DFRF engine periodically ages all valid data packets in the table by invoking the *aged* method of the flooding policy.

4.8 Initialization

Since the type description and the corresponding policy of data packets are not passed around in radio messages, all nodes in the network (or that part of the network that routes a particular type of data packet) must initialize the DFRF engine with the same configuration for each data type. This configuration consists of the type ID, the length and the unique length of the data packet, and the selected flooding policy. Given that the target platform does not support dynamic memory allocation, the configuration includes the address and length of a user provided memory buffer where the engine will store the data packets. The engine keeps track of all registered data types and it can route data packets of different types concurrently. Typically, the types of data packets do not change during the lifetime of the application. Nevertheless, it is possible to register and unregister configurations dynamically.

4.9 Sending and Receiving Data Packets

The user of the directed flood-routing protocol interacts with the DFRF engine. When the user wants to send a data packet it simply passes it to the *send* method of the DFRF engine. Similarly to the case of data packets received via the radio, the engine first checks if an analogous data packet is already in the data table. If yes, then it simply returns (with an error code) because this packet is already being transmitted. If it is not in the table, then it evicts an already existing packet with the lowest priority from the table, as described before, and inserts the new data packet with priority 0. The actual transmission and life-cycle management is taken care of by the engine.

The *receive* event is fired by the DRFR engine to notify the user of the arrival of a new data packet. This event is fired exactly once for each family of analogous data packets, at the time when the packet was inserted into the table. Unlike in other routing algorithms, the *receive* event is fired at each intermediate node towards the target. This allows the user to modify or even drop the data packet enroute to the destination, a critical feature used in smart data aggregation protocols. We will present examples exploiting both of these features in the following sections. Note that this notification scheme does not complicate the use of the routing protocol, as the user can easily consult the particular routing policy at each node to check if it is the true destination of the packet.

The application component implementing the *receive* method gets a pointer to the data packet as a parameter and returns a boolean value. The received pointer can be used to read the data and possibly update its content (other than the first unique length bytes that must not be changed). If the *receive* method returns false, the engine drops the newly arrived data packet by not inserting it into its table. Otherwise, the data packet enters its life-cycle on this node, as described in Section 4.7.

5 Flooding Policies

Flooding policies have two central functions. First, they define the meaning and compute the value of the node rank. Second, they implement the state machine that governs the life-cycle of individual packets on every node. Flooding policies can be classified by either of these two traits. We can speak of, for example, broadcast policies where the node rank is vacuous (an empty array), or energy-aware policies where the actions of the state machine depend on the available power of the node and its neighbors. We grouped our selection of routing policies according to their definition of rank.

5.1 Broadcast Policy

The broadcast policy is used to route data packets from an arbitrary source node to all nodes in the network. A data packet is rebroadcasted one or more times at every node until all nodes received it with a high probability. There are several variations where the target area is limited in an application specific manner.

The node rank in the broadcast policy is void. There are several ways intermediate nodes can retransmit data packets. First, we present the simplest version where each intermediate node retransmits the data packet exactly once, as soon as possible. The nodes remember each data packet as long as possible to avoid receiving the old packet and classifying it as new. The corresponding state machine is depicted in Fig. 3.

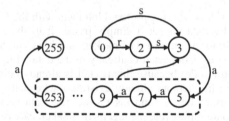

Fig. 3. The state machine of the broadcast policy.

Each circle represents a state. The states are numbered by their unique priority, from 0 to 255, but possibly not all of them are used. State 0 and state 255 are always the initial and terminal states, respectively. The arrows represent state transitions. The label of the arrow describes the corresponding type of event: 's' for *sent*, 'r' for *received*, and 'a' for *aged*. State transitions that do not change the state are not shown. For example, the *aged* event does not change the state of the machine in states 0 and 2. Arrows originating from a composite state, a dashed rounded rectangle, represent transitions from each of the contained states. Recall that a data packet is eligible for transmission only in even numbered states.

A data packet always starts its life-cycle in state 0, either because the packet originates from this node (the user called the *send* method of the engine), or when it is received for the first time by this node. If it is the latter, then its state is immediately changed to state 2 by the flooding policy, because we want packets originating from this node to have higher priority (i.e. 0) than those that we received from another node. Once the packet is in either state 0 or 2, we wait until it gets selected and transmitted by the engine. After transmission, we enter state 3. The sequence of states, starting from 3 up to 255, is used to remember the same packet for 126 aging actions (63 seconds in the current implementation) before dropping it. If during this period the node receives the same packet again, we start counting again from state 3. Note that in general this procedure does not prevent a data packet getting into an infinite cycle in a large dynamic network. However, the user can terminate this broadcast when handling the *receive* event.

As an application of the broadcast policy, we outline how to measure the hop-count distance from a root node to all other nodes in the network. The data packet shall contain a field for the "current" hop-count, and possibly others for the node ID of the root, etc. The unique part of the packet should not include the hop-count field. When the root initiates the network-wide broadcast, it fills in 0 for the hop-count in the packet. Upon receiving a data packet of this type, the application code should increment the current hop-count value in the *receive* event. The DFRF engine will not change this value, even if it later receives an analogous message with a different hop-count value, and will retransmit it with the incremented value. To get a more valuable estimate of the hop-count distance, the application should measure the hop-count distance from the root several times and the nodes should use the average of the measured values.

The range of the broadcast can also be limited in a similar way. For example, the root enters the required maximum number of hops into the hop-count field of the original message. Upon receiving the message, the hop-count fields needs to be decremented. If it reaches zero, then the *receive* method should return false, which will terminate the retransmission of the packet.

We found this basic policy to work very well on the Mica2 platform for planar networks with average degree of five or higher. This can be attributed to the sensible connectivity of the network and to the excellent radio collision avoidance of the radio stack. However, the same policy does not perform well on linear networks or on platforms with erratic radio collision avoidance. Nevertheless, this can be overcome by retransmitting each data packet two or more times on each node, with random delay in between. One particular implementation of this modified broadcast policy is shown in Fig. 4.

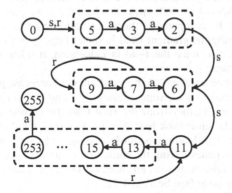

Fig. 4. The state machine of the reliable broadcast policy.

Arrows pointing to a composite state stand for transitions that enter one of the contained states based on a random choice. There are several subtle design choices that make this broadcast policy more robust than the one pictured in Fig. 3. First, note that the composite states (2,3,5) and (6,7,9) facilitate the random delay via the aging event. Not only does it wait for a random number of aging events, but also the aging events are executed asynchronously in the network. Second, the priority value is decreased inside these composite states, because if the engine is short of memory, we want to keep those packets that we can retransmit sooner. What is more, the 'r' self-loop at the composite state (6,7,9) implements a random backoff functionality. Observe that the 's' arrow to state 11 does not come from state 6, the only even numbered state in (6,7,9) allowing retransmission, but from the whole composite state. The reason is that the engine can select the packet in state 6 for transmission, pass the radio message buffer to the OS, receive an analogous message that restarts the backoff delay, and only then does the OS complete the transmission of the previously packed message. As a final point, the source node of the broadcast transmits the packet three times in contrast to relaying nodes, which transmit every packet only twice.

5.2 Gradient Convergecast

Convergecast policies are used to route data packets from all nodes of the network to a selected node, called the root. Intermediate nodes rebroadcast a data packet zero, one or more times until it is received from a node "closer" to the root than the current node. In the gradient convergecast policy, being closer means that the hop-count distance from the root is smaller. Thus, the rank of each node is the hop-count distance from the root, and the hop-count distances of the sender and receiver are compared. The same data packet can reach the root through several different paths, always descending in the gradient field. This guarantees robustness and fast message delivery at the expense of higher communication overhead. The data packet typically arrives at the root first through unreliable "long" links, then through more reliable "short" links.

The hop-count distance can be calculated, for example, by an application of the broadcast policy, as described in Section 5.1 above. The gradient convergecast policy implements this functionality and allows the user to set and query the current root in the network. Data packets of several types can share the same gradient field, or different gradient fields can be computed if there are multiple roots in the network. The overall cost of calculating the gradient field is rather large; possibly several network-wide broadcasts. However, once the field is calculated, it takes very little memory space, 1 or 2 bytes, to store it.

Fig. 5 depicts the state machine of the gradient convergecast policy. The receive action has been split into two separate actions: 'r⁻' and 'r⁺' for messages received from nodes closer to and further from the root than the current node, respectively. Note that nodes with the same rank have been explicitly excluded from this list, because we want to direct the flooding as mush as possible by preventing the same data packet to spread among nodes having the same hop-count distance. The policy avoids this case by returning false in the *accept* method for radio messages with the same rank as of the receiving node (see Section 4.7).

Each node retransmits a data packet up to three times, with two and one aging actions in between. The delay between the first and second transmissions is relatively long but it leaves the nodes receiving the first transmission enough time and radio channel bandwidth to retransmit the packet. The transition labeled by 'r⁻' on the left hand side in Fig. 5 implements implicit acknowledgment in the following way. If node A sends a packet that is received by node B that is closer to the root than A, and then B rebroadcast this packet, which is received, among others, by A, then the state of the packet on A becomes 7 and A will not retransmit the packet again. The policy remembers each data packet for a certain time period since the last time it was received from a node further from the root. This is enough, because even if the node receives an analogous packet from a node closer to the root later, it will immediately enter state 7 again.

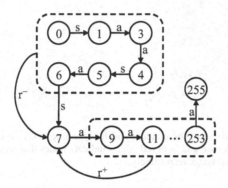

Fig. 5. The state machine of the gradient convergecast policy.

Clearly, this policy does not guarantee message delivery, but best effort only. This is not a serious limitation for most wireless sensor network applications because they have to prepare for message loss as the result of failing nodes and unreliable links. However, a variation of this policy can guarantee message delivery in connected networks provided the hop-count distance gradient field remains accurate. This variation retransmits the packet on each node other than the root until it is received from a node closer to the root.

The gradient convergecast policy yields a very fast and robust routing protocol to deliver messages to a root node, but at the expense of significant message overhead. Depending on the topology of the network, the number of transmissions during the routing of a single data packet can grow as the square of the distance between the sender and the root.

5.3 Fat Spanning Tree Convergecast

The major shortcoming of the gradient convergecast is its message overhead. The optimal solution, with respect to the number of messages, would be to route the data packet along a spanning tree towards the root. However, this algorithm is inherently fragile: the radio links are not reliable causing message loss in any fixed path. Moreover, a single node failure close to the root can cut off a large portion of the network from the root. The speed and robustness of the gradient convergecast and the low message overhead of the spanning tree routing protocol can be combined in the following way. Instead of utilizing a single path starting from the source node towards the root, define a small neighborhood of this path and flood the data packet in this "*lane*". The lane can be defined as all nodes one hop away in the spanning tree from the nodes of the path. The resulting routing policy is called the fat spanning tree con-

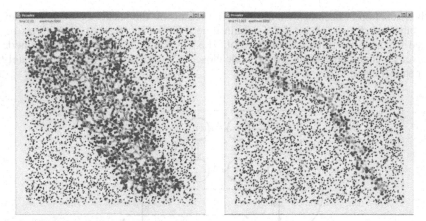

Fig. 6. The message overhead of the gradient and fat spanning tree converge cast policies in a 5000-node network. Dark blue and light red colors indicate nodes that received or received and retransmitted the routed message, respectively.

vergecast. The message overhead of the gradient and fat spanning tree policies is illustrated in Fig. 6, where a single data packet is routed from a node in the bottom right corner to the root in the top left corner. Red nodes retransmitted the packet, while the blue ones received it but did not retransmit it.

This particular definition of the lane allows a strikingly simple implementation of directed flood-routing in the lane with minimal storage requirement. Each node has to know the node IDs of its parent, grandparent, great-grandparent and great-great-grandparent. The node rank is simply the node ID of the grandparent. The relationship between the sender and the receiver of a radio message can be computed by the receiver from the rank of the sender, which is stored in the message, as follows:

(1) If the rank of the sender is the node ID of the receiver or its parent, then the sender is further from the root than the receiver. The corresponding event will be denoted by 'r⁺'.

(2) If the rank of the sender is the node ID of the grandparent of the receiver, then the sender is at the same distance from the root as the receiver. These types of message are also denoted by 'r⁺'.

(3) If the rank of the sender is the node ID of the great-grandparent or its parent of the receiver, then the sender is closer to the root than the receiver. The corresponding event will be denoted by 'r⁻'.

(4) If the rank of the sender is none of the above, then the receiver is either not in the lane of the source, or more than two steps away from the sender. In both cases we ignore the message by returning false in the *accept* method of the policy.

The spanning tree can be constructed and the node IDs of the four ancestors found by a simple network-wide broadcast, or by other methods. Finding the spanning tree that best supports directed flood-routing is possibly a challenging problem and is not addressed here.

Once the spanning tree is formed and the 'r⁺' and 'r⁻' receive events defined, we can reuse the state machine of the gradient convergecast policy (see Fig. 5) for the spanning tree convergecast policy. The performance of the spanning tree convergecast for arbitrary networks will be similar to that of the gradient convergecast for essentially linear networks. In particular, the number of messages required to route a data packet from the source to the root is proportional to the hop-count distance of the source from the root.

6 Conclusion

We have introduced the directed flood-routing framework for wireless sensor networks. We demonstrated that the state machine based language describing routing policies is rich enough to capture a wide variety of existing flood-routing protocols. The supporting engine and flooding policies were implemented for TinyOS and extensively tested on the Mica and Mica2 platforms. The gradient convergecast policy was used in an acoustic shooter localization application to route acoustic events back to a base station. A network of 60 motes covering a 100 by 40 meter urban area with diameter of 10 hops was used to evaluate the performance of both the routing and shooter localization algorithms. Typically, 25-30 motes were triggered by a shot, half of them managed to report their events in the first second, and the other half in the next second.

There are several research opportunities in directed flood-routing in general and flooding policies in particular. For example, it seems possible to design convergecast flooding policies that implement flow control by delaying retransmission of data packets if nodes closer to the root are overloaded. Another challenging research area is the study of topology changes with respect to convergecast policies. For example, is it possible to dynamically update the gradient field or the spanning tree if the root node is mobile?

The state machines of flooding policies can clearly be optimized for different hardware platforms and network configurations, as well as for speed, reliability and power consumption. Since these state machines have a limited number of actions and are relatively small, it seems possible that they can be mechanically optimized utilizing a simulator to compute the fitness of policies.

Acknowledgment

The DARPA/IXO NEST program (F33615-01-C-1903) has supported, in part, the activities described in this paper.

References

1. J. Hill and D. Culler, "Mica: A Wireless Platform for Deeply Embedded Networks," IEEE Micro., vol 22(6), Nov/Dec 2002, pp 12–24.
2. J. Hill, R. Szewczyk, A. Woo, S. Hollar and D. C. K. Pister, "System architecture directions for networked sensors," ASPLOS, November 2000.
3. A. Woo and D. Culler, "A Transmission Control Scheme for Media Access in Sensor Networks," Mobicom 2001, July 2001, Rome.

4. D. Gay, P. Levis, R. von Behren, M. Welsh, E. Brewer and D. Culler, "The nesC Language: A Holistic Approach to Networked Embedded Systems," Proceedings of Programming Language Design and Implementation (PLDI) 2003, June 2003.
5. Gy. Simon, M. Maroti, A. Ledeczi, Gy. Balogh, B. Kusy, A. Nadas, G. Pap, J. Sallai and K. Frampton, "Sensor network-based countersniper system," accepted to SenSys 2004.
6. D. B. Johnson and D.A. Maltz, "Dynamic Source Routing in Ad Hoc Wireless Networks." In Mobile Computing, Chapter 5, pages 153–181, Kluwer Academic Publishers, 1996.
7. C. E. Perkins and E. M. Royer, "Ad-hoc On Demand Distance Vector Routing." In WMCSA'99, February 1999.
8. V. D. Park and M.S. Corson, "A highly adaptive distributed routing algorithm for mobile wireless networks." In Proceedings of IEEE INFOCOM, April 1997.
9. M. R. Pearlman and Z.J. Haas, "Determining the Optimal Configuration for the Zone Routing Protocol," IEEE JSAC, special issue on Ad-Hoc Networks, Vol. 17, No. 8, August 1999.
10. B. Karp and H. T. Kung. "GPSR: Greedy Perimeter Stateless Routing for Wireless Networks." In IEEE MobiCom, August 2000.
11. Y. B. Ko and N. H. Vaidya. "Location-Aided Routing (LAR) in Mobile Ad Hoc Networks." In IEEE MobiCom 1998, October 1998.
12. T. He, J. A. Stankovic, C. Lu and T. F. Abdelzaher, "SPEED: A Stateless Protocol for Real-Time Communication in Sensor Networks", In International Conference on Distributed Computing Systems (ICDCS 2003), Providence, RI, May 2003.
13. F. Ye, G. Zhong, S. Lu and L. Zhang, "GRAdient Broadcast: A Robust Data Delivery Protocol for Large Scale Sensor Networks," accepted by ACM WINET (Wireless Networks).
14. M. Lin, K. Marzullo and S. Masini, "Gossip versus deterministic flooding: Low message overhead and high reliability for broadcasting on small networks." UCSD Technical Report TR CS99-0637.
15. D. Braginsky and D. Estrin, "Rumor Routing Algorithm for Sensor Networks," ACM WSNA, 2002.
16. Yi Shang, M. P. J. Fromherz, Y. Zhang and L. S. Crawford: "Constraint-based Routing for Ad-hoc Networks." IEEE Int. Conf. on Information Technology: Research and Education (ITRE 2003), Newark, NJ, USA, Aug. 2003, pp. 306–310.
17. Osterweil, E. and Estrin, D, "Tiny Diffusion in the Extensible Sensing System at the James Reserve," May 2003; see www.cens.ucla.edu/~eoster/tinydiff/.
18. Jie Wu and Fei Dai: "Broadcasting in Ad Hoc Networks Based on Self-Pruning." IEEE Conf. on Computer and Communications Societies (INFOCOM), 2003.
19. B. Williams and T. Camp: "Comparison of broadcasting techniques for mobile ad hoc networks." Proceedings of the 3rd ACM international symposium on Mobile ad hoc networking & computing (MOBIHOC) June 2002, pp. 194–205.
20. P. Levis, S. Madden, D. Gay, J. Polastre, R. Szewczyk, A. Woo, E. Brewer and D. Culler, "The Emergence of Networking Abstractions and Techniques in TinyOS," NSDI, 2004.
21. T. Abdelzaher, B. Blum, Q. Cao, Y. Chen, D. Evans, J. George, S. George, L. Gu, T. He, S. Krishnamurthy, L. Luo, S. Son, J. Stankovic, R. Stoleru and A. Wood, "EnviroTrack: Towards an Environmental Computing Paradigm for Distributed Sensor Networks," International Conference on Distributed Computing Systems, Tokyo, Japan, March 2004.
22. S. Madden, J. Hellerstein, and W. Hong, "TinyDB: In-Network Query Processing in TimyOS," Intel Research, IRB-TR-02-014, October 2002.
23. P. Bonnet, J. Gehrke, and P. Seshardi. Towards sensor database systems. In 2nd International Conference on Mobile Data Management, pp. 3–14, Hong Kong, January 2001.

On Exploring Performance Optimizations in Web Service Composition

Jingwen Jin and Klara Nahrstedt

Department of Computer Science
University of Illinois at Urbana-Champaign, USA
{jjin1,klara}@cs.uiuc.edu

Abstract. The importance of service composition has been widely recognized in the Internet research community due to its high flexibility in allowing development of customized applications from primitive services in a plug-and-play manner. Although much research in defining architectures, choreography languages and etc, has been conducted, little attention has been paid to composite services' runtime performance-related aspects (e.g., network bandwidths, path delay, machine resources), which are of great importance to wide-area applications, especially those that are resource-consuming. Service composition in the wide area actually creates a new type of routing problem which we call *QoS service routing*. We study this problem in large networks and provide distributed and scalable routing solutions with various optimization goals. Most importantly, we propose ways to reduce redundancies in data delivery and service execution through explorations of different types of multicast (service multicast and data multicast) in one-to-many application scenarios.

Keywords: service composition, QoS, multicast, application-level routing, overlay networks

1 Introduction

The Internet has long been recognized as an environment with heterogeneity everywhere and in every aspect, and this heterogeneity problem has been further exacerbated with the increasing popularity of small devices using wireless connections in recent years. With a diverse spectrum of devices (ranging from powerful desktops, to less powerful and energy-sensitive laptops, hand-held computers, PDAs, and mobile phones etc) communicating over networks of different bandwidths by using different protocols, there is a strong need to perform protocol and content translations between communicating parties to bridge the gaps. Value-added, transformational services have been created for such purposes [1, 2]. However, given the range of diversity involved in the Internet, developing monolithic transformational services to bridge all conceivable end-to-end heterogeneities would be some task that requires tremendous amount of effort, if not totally impossible.

Fortunately, the *component service* model, which allows complex services to be dynamically and rapidly aggregated from primitive ones, has been proposed

H.-A. Jacobsen (Ed.): Middleware 2004, LNCS 3231, pp. 115–134, 2004.

and started to be adopted in the Internet (e.g., the Web and peer-to-peer networks) for service flexibility and reusability [3–5]. This new, flexible service model has triggered many interesting and useful Internet applications. Imagine a mobile phone user that wants to retrieve the content of a Web document written in Latin and hear it through speech in English, the original data can flow through a sequence of services (such as an html2txt converter, a Latin2English translator, and a text-to-speech converter) to get itself transformed before being delivered to the destination (Figure 1(a)). We call an end-to-end network path comprising a sequence of primitive service instances in a one-to-one scenario a *service path.*

At the service deployment time, for the sake of robustness, each service needs to be replicated in multiple network locations (i.e., have multiple instances). Service composition should happen at the runtime, and it is desirable to select service instances based on current network and machine conditions, so that the service path not only meets service functional requirements, but also satisfies certain performance requirements (e.g., ensuring that there is sufficient network bandwidth between the output and input of every pair of consecutive components). Since service composition includes a broad range of issues (e.g., architecture, language standard), we create and use the terminology *service routing* for focus on functional correctness and performance aspects involved during the run time of service composition. We will assume Web services are deployed at *proxies* (be them regular caching proxies or dedicated application-specific proxies).

Interesting composite services can be also useful in one-to-many application scenarios. Imagine the Web news video distribution application that involves a

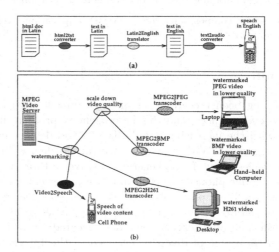

Fig. 1. Two Web scenarios that make use of composite services: (a) A mobile phone user retrieves a Web document written in Latin and hears it through speech in English; (b) news video from CNN or Yahoo server is customized within a service network according to end users' network and machine capacities. When there are multiple end users interested in receiving the same source data, service multicast can be employed for resource optimization purposes.

single sender and multiple receivers, each of which requiring the original video content to be customized according to its own resource conditions (Figure 1(b)). Although it is feasible to have end-to-end service paths individually built, such a unicast delivery model may incur waste of bandwidths (due to redundancies in data delivery) and machine resources (due to redundancies in service execution). We propose to build a single service tree, rather than multiple independent service paths, through which the data should be delivered to save both network bandwidths and machine resources. We term such a group delivery model *service multicast*, to distinguish it from the traditional (data) multicast. To differentiate the two delivery modes, hereafter we will use the terminologies *service unicast (routing)* and *service multicast (routing)* for service routing in one-to-one and one-to-many scenarios, respectively.

For composite services to be widely acceptable and useful, automating the service routing process at the middleware layer has become critical to enable seamless provisioning of integrated services at the application layer despite the fact that an integrate service might be actually distributed over multiple hosts in wide-area networks. Service unicast routing has been reasonably addressed in the literature [6–9]. Some of the existing work, e.g., [8, 9], adopt a global planning approach which, concerning its limited scalability, is not suitable for the current Web. Scalable routing falls into two approaches: hierarchical [6] and distributed [7], each with its own advantages and disadvantages. The routing approach to be adopted in this paper follows the latter category, because distributed routing based on on-line probing involves with more updated (thus more accurate) routing state. In the unicast context, a distributed solution based on local heuristics has been described in [7]. However, the local optimality alone often will incur long service paths. We remedy this shortcoming by using the geometric information of the network hosts as guidance to compute more delay-efficient paths.

Our major focus would be on the less investigated, more challenging *QoS service multicast routing* problem, whose usefulness has been illustrated in Figure 1(b), and whose importance is undubious due to resource constraints. While source-based (pure) service multicast has been proposed and studied in [10, 11] for small service networks, in this paper, we consider the problem in the current Web scale. In such a large scale, centralized planning is certainly not a viable solution, for it becomes infeasible for a single network node to maintain full state information of the whole network. For better scalability, we devise a fully distributed approach for service multicast. Moreover, we propose to further optimize resource usages by integrating data multicast into service multicast. We call such a combined multicast delivery mode *hybrid multicast*.

The remainder of this paper will be structured as follows. We first describe some background and related work in Section 2, followed by the foundation of our solution design in Section 3. We present our distributed solutions for service unicast, pure service multicast, and hybrid multicast in Sections 4, 5, and 6, respectively. The solutions are implemented in the well-known network simulator *ns-2* and in Section 7 we provide some performance results. Section 8 gives some concluding remarks of this paper as well as directions for our future research.

2   Background and Related Work

To realize service composition in the Internet, many important issues need to be addressed. (1) **service description:** When a developed service component is to be deployed, it needs to be described by an unambiguous name and/or an interface describing the component's inputs and outputs. WSDL (Web Service Description Language) is an XML-based language for describing Web services. (2) **service discovery:** Service components need to be published and later on discovered before being composed. UDDI (Universal Description, Discovery and Integration) creates a standard interoperable platform that enables companies and applications to publish and find Web services. Scalable ways of performing service discovery have been also investigated in peer-to-peer networks [12, 13]. (3) **service request compilation:** At the application design or run time, given service specifications of two communicating ends, it needs to be further verified which service components are to be composed and in which order, i.e., to obtain a compositional service model or a *service request*[1]. Research in this area can be found in [14, 5].

Since a service discovery system's task is only to locate instances of single services, and a QoS compiler's task is only to obtain a system-independent service graph, there needs to be a process, which we call *service routing*, that resides above these tasks and that can choose appropriate service instances (returned by a discovery system) for the basic components in a service request (returned by a QoS compiler), so that users at the application layer will see the application as an integrated service, rather than separate components (Figure 2).

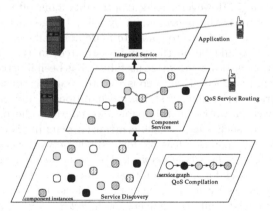

Fig. 2. The *service routing* substrate is resided between the application layer and the service discovery/QoS compilation layer to make component services transparent to the application layer.

[1] The literature has used different terminologies, e.g., logical service path [3] and plan [5].

A sample service request is shown in Figure 3. The functional part of a service request will be denoted as $r = (p_s, s_1 \rightarrow s_2 \rightarrow s_3 \rightarrow \ldots, p_d)$, which is to find a service path between the source p_s and the destination p_d containing s_1, s_2, and s_3, in sequence. A service path will be denoted as $sp = (p_s \rightarrow s_1/p_\alpha \rightarrow s_2/p_\beta \rightarrow s_3/p_\gamma \rightarrow \ldots \rightarrow p_d)$, where s_i/p_θ means service s_i is provided by proxy p_j (mapping of a service onto a proxy). Note that different from the traditional data routing, where paths should be loop-free, in service routing, data loops are allowed, in the sense that a single network node is allowed to be visited multiple times in case it is capable of serving multiple (either consecutive or inconsecutive) services in the request. Therefore, when we refer to "a service node", it means mapping of a service onto a proxy (s_i/p_θ). We define *service neighbor* of a service s_i as s_i's proceeding service in service graphs. For instance, if $SG_1 = s_1 \rightarrow s_2 \rightarrow s_3$ and $SG_2 = s_1 \rightarrow s_4$, then s_1's service neighbor can be either s_2 or s_4, depending on which service graph is in use. We also define *next service hop* of a node n to be an instance of n's preceding service in the request. Thus, if $sp = (p_s \rightarrow s_1/p_\alpha \rightarrow s_2/p_\beta \rightarrow s_3/p_\gamma \rightarrow \ldots \rightarrow p_d)$, then p_s's next service hop is s_1/p_α, and s_1/p_α's next service hop is s_2/p_β and so forth.

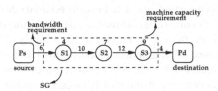

Fig. 3. A service request with linear service graph (SG): from the *source* to the *destination*, locate a QoS-satisfied path that encompasses $s_1 \rightarrow s_2 \rightarrow s_3$ in sequence.

Service unicast has been investigated extensively in different domains (e.g, Web, peer-to-peer networks, or company networks) and in different levels of the network (e.g., physical network level or overlay network level). Depending on the size of the network, computations of service routing can be performed in different ways, e.g., centralized or distributed. In [8,9], a single network node is required to maintain the global routing state (QoS and service availability information) of the network, so that computation of service paths can be performed locally. However, such an approach does not scale because the associated state maintenance overhead increases quickly with the network size. A remedial step for increasing scalability is to introduce hierarchies into the network, so that topology abstraction and state information become possible to significantly reduce the state maintenance overhead. A hierarchical solution was developed in [6]. Alternatively, scalable service routing can take a distributed approach by having the network nodes maintaining state information of a limited neighborhood. [7] describes a distributed, hop-by-hop approach whose routing decision is based on local heuristics.

Service multicast was proposed in our previous work [10], and two algorithms for building service trees have been devised and their performances compared. However, since both the construction and the maintenance of service trees take a source-based approach, the solution is suitable only for small-scale networks. A source-based approach is simple, and allows service trees to be computed quickly, and usually path/tree optimizations are better achieved. However, due to the rapidly increasing routing state maintenance overhead with the network size, scalability is constrained.

Overlay network routing can be performed either on top of structured topologies [15, 10] or on top of unstructured topologies [16, 9]. The former approach views the overlay network topology as a partial mesh, so that routing protocols (such as OSPF and MOSPF) designed for the IP layer can be directly employed at the overlay layer. In the latter approach, hosts are considered fully connected, and for each application, a special topology (e.g., a multicast tree) is built and maintained.

3   Foundation of Our Solution Design

A service discovery system's task is to return service instances' locations (typically the IP addresses of the hosts in which instances are resided). However, with only the IP address information, it is hard to estimate how far away service instances are located from each other, thus making distributed routing decisions also hard if communication delay is a concern. We address this weakness by associating each Internet host with geometric coordinates and using it to estimate Internet distances (communication delays) between hosts. The relative geometric coordinates of a machine can be automatically assigned by the method described in [17] and, as will be clear later, the added geometric location information will serve us as guidance in finding more delay-efficient service paths/trees.

To maximize path performances at the overlay layer, in this paper we do not set network topology constraints (i.e., the initial network is a fully connected, unstructured topology), and a service path/tree is built for each application scenario. However, while service paths/trees are built on top of an unstructured overlay topology, another structured mesh topology is maintained for general control messages. Note that the tree and the mesh are employed for different purposes: the former is used for content distribution and the latter is used for control messages. This design choice is similar to that of YOID [16]. For communication efficiency, we connect the overlay network nodes into a Delaunay triangulation [18], because Delaunay triangulation is a spanner graph that possesses some nice properties: a path found within a Delaunay triangulation has length bound by a constant times the straight-line distance between the endpoints of the path. By using such a geometric topology, control messages can be routed by using an on-line routing method, such as the greedy approach or compass routing approach [19].

In a large, unstructured service overlay network where service neighbors are not defined until the runtime, we do on-line probing of the service instances' resource conditions (e.g., bandwidth and machine capacity) to identify the best next service hop according to the request, instead of maintaining routing state. By distributed, we mean not only the construction of service paths/branches, but also the maintenance of multicast group tree information, will be performed distributively. In [10], the functional service tree is centrally maintained at the root. Thus every join request had to go to the root to learn its functionally graftable service nodes. Such a centralized approach introduces both a single point of failure and a bottleneck. In this research, the functional service tree will be maintained by all on-tree nodes, so that each of them can individually look for graftable service nodes for other join requests (more details later).

4   Service Unicast

In QoS data routing, starting from one end, the shortest network path towards the other end is usually probed for QoS. If, at certain point, insufficiency of resources is detected, the probe will detour to other neighboring links/nodes [20]. While in data routing, there is always the shortest network path (maintained by, e.g., the distance vector or link state protocol) that serves as guidance for distributed QoS path finding so that the computed QoS-satisfied path is not unnecessarily long, in service routing, due to the complex dependency relations among services, no similar shortest *service* paths can be maintained as to allow a node to quickly lookup for the *best* next service hop[2].

Lacking maintenance support, next service hop needs to be discovered at the runtime. Specifically, starting from the source, we gradually add to the path instances of required services as we route toward the destination. The source may first discover the locations of all requested services' instances by invoking a service discovery system. A service path can be thus resolved in a hop-by-hop manner as follows. Each hop sends QoS probe messages to all instances of its service neighbor, and then among the instances that satisfy resource requirements, the current hop will select the best one according to its selection criteria.

However, existing solutions in unicast QoS service routing that follow the distributed approach are not satisfactory. For example, in [7], selection of next service hop is solely based on local heuristics, where the next service hop is the one whose aggregate value of available bandwidth, machine resources and machine's up time is optimum. The local heuristics alone, however, would only help balance the network and machine loads and potentially optimize the path's overall concave or multiplicative metrics (e.g., the path's bottleneck bandwidth or robustness), but would not pose any constraint on the overall service path length, which is an additive metric that requires global optimizations. As a consequence, service paths computed hop-by-hop by adopting local heuristics tend to be long, and inevitably consume more network resources. We will name this approach *local resource-amplest (LRA)* approach.

The weakness of the *LRA* approach can be remedied by using the hosts' geometric location information as guidance when performing the hop-by-hop routing computation. At this point, let us temporarily ignore the load balancing issue, and concentrate on path delays. We first describe how a QoS-satisfied delay-efficient service path can be computed. In Section 3, we mentioned Internet

---

[2] By *best*, we mean the QoS-satisfied service instance that leads to a shortest service path.

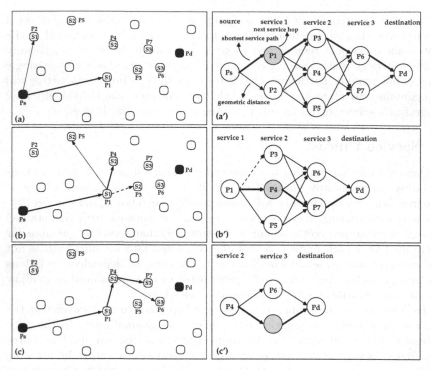

Fig. 4. Finding a QoS-satisfied and potentially shortest service path hop-by-hop from p_s to p_d that satisfies the service graph $s_1 \rightarrow s_2 \rightarrow s_3$.

hosts can obtain their geometric information as described in [17]. Such information can then be easily incorporated into a service discovery system, so that the discovery system is able to tell also the locations of the service instances. With this location information, we resolve the service path in a hop-by-hop manner as follows. Each hop sends QoS probe messages to all of its service neighbors, and then among the instances that satisfy all resource requirements, the current hop will select the one that potentially leads to the most delay-efficient service path as the next service hop, by doing some extra computation as shown in Figure 4.

Figure 4 depicts a case where we want to find a path, between the source p_s and the destination p_d, in which services s_1, s_2, and s_3 are to be included in sequence. In Figure 4(a), starting from the source, p_s probes resource conditions of both instances of next service in the request, s_1/p_1 and s_1/p_2. Resource conditions in this case may be available bandwidths from p_s to p_1 and from p_s to p_2, and p_1 and p_2's available machine capacity. Assuming both instances have sufficient resources, p_s chooses the one that potentially leads to a shorter service path. This can be computed as shown in Figure 4(a'): by deriving the correspondent service DAG (Directed Acyclic Graph) based on the service request and service instances' availability (returned by a discovery system), and applying a shortest paths algorithm [21] on top of it, a shortest service path (shown in bold lines) can be calculated, and after which next service hop (shown in shadow) that optimizes the overall path length is chosen. In Figure 4(b), once at p_1, p_1 probes the resource conditions of three instances of next service in the request - s_2/p_3, s_2/p_4, and s_2/p_5. Figure 4(b') shows how p_1 chooses the most delay-efficient and QoS-satisfied next service hop. Note that in this case, the probed bandwidth between p_1 and p_3 does not meet the requirement, thus the correspondent link is deleted (shown in dashed line) from the service DAG. Such a hop-by-hop process continues until all of the services in the request are resolved. We name such an approach GLG, which stands for *geometric location guided*.

Since LRA and GLG are intended for individual optimization goals (load balancing and delay respectively), it can be predicted each one will perform poorly in terms of the non-optimized metric. For example, LRA would have poor performance in terms of delay, and likewise, GLG would perform poorly in terms of load balancing. If we are to consider both metrics at the same time, then combining LRA and GLG would be necessary. Two derivatives exist: LRA-GLG and GLG-LRA. In the first one, each hop first identifies the next service hops that potentially lead to shortest service paths, and then among them, it makes its selection based on their resource conditions. As an example, if at a network node p, p detects that both $sp_1 = (p \rightarrow s_1/p_\alpha \rightarrow \dots \rightarrow p_d)$ and $sp_2 = (p \rightarrow s_1/p_\beta \rightarrow \dots \rightarrow p_d)$ are two potential shortest service paths, then p may decide which one to go, either p_α or p_β, based on p_α and p_β's resource conditions. The second derivative, LRA-GLG, is different from GLG-LRA just in the order of application of two routing features.

5   Pure Service Multicast

When a multimedia stream is delivered to a group of users that require different transformational rules on the stream, then instead of having the stream transformed and delivered through multiple independent service paths, a more efficient way is to construct a service multicast tree for the transformation and delivery purposes. To support the dynamic membership feature of many multimedia applications, we take an incremental approach for service multicast tree building, which means that one service path/branch is constructed at a time to cover the newly joining member.

A key issue in multicast tree building is the *graftable on-tree node* concept. For example, in the PIM protocol, a newly joining member m's request is forwarded towards the source. If the request hits some on-tree node n before reaching the source, then n is said to be the *graftable on-tree node* for m, and a branch starting from n and ending at m is usually constructed to cover m.

Unlike the conventional data multicast, where every on-tree node functionally qualifies as a graftable node for all other group members, in service multicast, due to the functionality issues, not all on-tree nodes functionally qualify as graftable nodes for other joining members. Rather, an on-tree node n only qualifies as a graftable node for a member m (whose service request is r) if n's up-tree service path (the service path from the root to n) is a prefix of r. Let $sp = (p_s \rightarrow$

$s_1/p_\alpha \rightarrow s_2/p_\beta \rightarrow s_3/p_\gamma \rightarrow s_4/p_\delta \ldots \rightarrow p_{d1})$ denote a service path, and let $r = (p_s, s_1 \rightarrow s_2 \rightarrow s_3 \rightarrow s_5 \rightarrow \ldots, p_{d2})$ denote a service request, then several nodes in sp qualify as functionally graftable service node for r: p_s, s_1/p_α, s_2/p_β, and s_3/p_γ. To maximize service sharing, we use the *longest match* (prefix) [10] criterion when selecting a graftable service node. We call the graftable service node selected by the longest prefix criterion the *best functionally graftable service node*. In this case, s_3/p_γ is the best functionally graftable service node, because the longest prefix of sp and r is *prefix* $= s_1 \rightarrow s_2 \rightarrow s_3$ and *prefix*'s last service s_3 is mapped onto p_γ.

Construction of our service multicast tree will take the following procedures (an example will be shown later in the section). Each member joining the multicast group would send its request r towards the source through the organized overlay network topology (Delaunay triangulation) by using compass routing. For each overlay node n_i that is hit by the request, it is verified if n_i is an on-tree node. If it is not, then n_i simply forwards the original request to the next hop (computed by compass routing) towards the source, and if it is, it tries to match r with the locally maintained functional service tree T_f (maintenance of T_f will be discussed further later) to identify the best functionally graftable service node n, and forwards the request accordingly. Between n and m, a service branch can be constructed hop-by-hop by using a unicast service routing solution described in Section 4. Note that with a prefix of r satisfied by the found graftable node, we only need to find a service branch for the suffix of r between n and m.

We now briefly describe the tree maintenance issue. In data multicast, routers express their join/leave interests through IGMP (Internet Group Management Protocol), and since a router has one single function (to forward data as is), it basically needs to be only aware of its children in the multicast tree. However, the similar does not hold in service multicast due to service functionality constraints. Rather, to enable an on-tree node to identify graftable service nodes for others, it needs to keep the functional tree information of the multicast group. This implies that whenever the functional aspect of the service tree has been modified, tree state needs to be updated in all current on-tree proxy nodes by broadcasting adequate control messages. Although because of the possible loop issue in service routing, a single proxy may appear in multiple positions of a functional service tree, only one copy of the tree needs to be maintained *per proxy*.

Figure 5 depicts an example of how a pure service multicast tree is built and maintained. In Figure 5(a), assume p_{d1} is the first member who joins the group. After p_{d1} has joined the group, the on-tree proxy nodes p_s, p_1, p_4, p_7, and p_{d1} will maintain a functional service tree T_f depicted at the right side of Figure 5(a). When p_{d2} joins, a service request $r_2 = (p_s, s_1 \rightarrow s_2 \rightarrow s_4, p_{d2})$ is sent from p_{d2} towards the source by using compass routing, and the request hit an on-tree node p_1 before it reaches p_s. Since every on-tree node maintains T_f, p_1 found that p_4 is the best functionally graftable node for the current request, thus the request is forwarded to p_4. In Figure 5(b), a service branch is established hop-by-hop from the graftable node p_4 to p_{d2}. Since the graftable node p_4 already satisfied

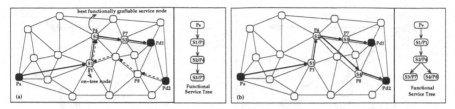

Fig. 5. (a) A service request message is sent from the newly joining member p_{d2} towards the source by using compass routing, and the request hit an on-tree node p_1 before it reaches p_s. Since every on-tree node maintains T_f, p_1 found that p_4 is the best graftable node for the current request, thus the request is forwarded to p_4; (b) a service branch is established hop-by-hop from the graftable node p_4 to p_{d2}.

a prefix of r_2, only the correspondent suffix needs to be satisfied by the service branch from p_4 to p_{d2}. After p_{d2} joins, the functional service tree T_f maintained by all on-tree nodes becomes that on the right-side figure of Figure 5(b). Note that T_f only needs to be updated if the functional aspects of the tree have been modified. If, a third join request has the form $r_3 = (p_s, s_1 \rightarrow s_2 \rightarrow s_3, p_{d3})$, then p_{d3} can get attached to p_7, and the functional service tree remains unchanged.

It is easy to see that service multicast definitely helps to save machine resources because each service in the functional service tree gets executed only once. It should also reduce network bandwidth usages compared to service unicast, as in most of the cases, we can expect the length of a service branch (satisfying only the suffix of the request) to be shorter than an individually built service path that needs to satisfy the whole request.

6 Hybrid Multicast

In pure service multicast, each service branch gets directly attached to its best functionally graftable node. However, in such an approach, bandwidth usage may not have been optimized. An example is illustrated in Figure 6(a): the proxy offering the MPEG2H261 transcoding service needs to send four separate copies of transformed data to its downstream nodes. Likewise, the node of quality filter will send two separate copies of filtered data to the downstream nodes. This may cause data delivery in those sub-groups to be sub-optimal. First, it may be expensive to do so, because bandwidths need to be separately allocated. Second, after a node's (e.g., the one offering MPEG2H261) outbound network bandwidth usage reaches its limitation, then no new service branches can be created starting from this point.

We address these weaknesses by further employing data multicast in the local sub-groups. Although IP-layer multicast would be an option, in this research, we will only exploit data multicast at the application layer because the real deployment of multicast at the IP layer has been hindered by its need of change in the infrastructural layers. Two feasible application-layer data multicast trees (for subgroups 1 and 2) can be built as shown in Figure 6(b). In addition to boosting the overall cost efficiency of the service tree, exploring data multicast would also

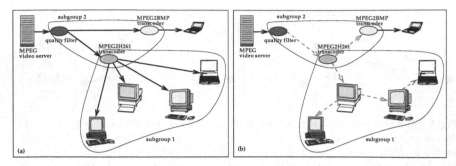

Fig. 6. (a) Pure service multicasting; (b) hybrid multicasting (service multicasting + data multicasting).

increase the success rate in finding QoS service branches when resources are scarce.

To realize such a hybrid multicast scenario, the distributed approach requires each on-tree proxy and/or service node to keep two trees: one for the global functional service tree, and the other for local data distribution tree, which we denote as T_f and T_d respectively. Since two types of tree exist in the hybrid multicast case, we will call nodes on the functional tree T_f *on-functional-tree nodes* to explicitly mean they are nodes providing specific functionalities, rather than nodes that only perform relay of data. The same as in pure service multicast, each on-functional-tree *proxy* will keep an updated T_f, which is the functional service tree of the whole multicast group. In addition to T_f, each on-tree *service node* n also keeps a T_d, whose root is itself, and whose lower-level members are its children in T_f (T_d should also maintain the location information of its nodes, for some purpose that will be clear soon). While T_f is global and its maintenance is still to enable on-functional-tree nodes to individually search for functionally graftable nodes for other joining requests, T_d is local and is maintained for exploiting benefits of data multicast in subgroups.

When a new service branch b gets attached to a graftable node n, initially, n's T_d will have b's first node (say n') attached to itself. However, as n is aware of the geometric locations of its T_d's nodes, it will be able to identify which nodes are closer to n' than itself. If there is any such node, then n will initiate a *parent switching protocol*, so that at the end, n' gets attached to a closer parent with sufficient network bandwidth. Note that the parent switching protocol is only for switching parent in the local data distribution tree, it does not affect the global functional service tree.

The *parent switching protocol* works as follows. First, n sends n' a list of nodes which are closer in an increasing order of distance. Upon receiving the list, n' starts to probe the listed nodes for the bandwidth conditions one by one in an increasing order of distance. Once it finds a node whose outbound bandwidth to n' is sufficient for supporting the data stream, n' sends a request of *parent switching* to n, so that n will update n''s parent in its T_d. Different from T_f, which is maintained by every *on-functional-tree proxy*, a different T_d needs to be maintained by every *on-functional-tree service node*. This means that if a

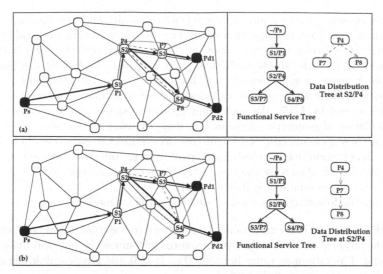

Fig. 7. Exploring data multicast in a service multicast scenario: (a) a new service branch's first node, p_8, is initially directly attached to the graftable service node p_4 (p_4 as p_8' parent in the local data distribution tree); (b) p_8 gets parent-switched to p_7 in the data distribution tree.

single proxy offers different services in the multicast group, then it needs to keep multiple data trees (one per each service it offers).

Figure 7 depicts what the global functional service tree and the local data distribution tree would look like in the scenarios. In Figure 7(a), right after P_{d1} and P_{d2} have successfully joined the multicast group, the functional service tree kept by all on-tree service nodes and the data distribution tree at s_2/p_4 are shown on the right side of Figure 7(a). Subsequently, inside the subgroup (circled), the *parent switching protocol* will take place. Suppose p_7 is closer to p_8 than p_4, and suppose from p_7 to p_8 there is sufficient bandwidth to support the data stream, then p_8 will ask p_4 to switch parent, after which p_4's data distribution tree becomes the one shown on the right side of Figure 7(b).

It is clear that with the employment of local data multicast, end-to-end service paths may become longer than in pure service multicast. However, such a performance degradation is justified by savings on network bandwidths.

7   Performance Study

We implemented service routing (service unicast, pure service multicast, and hybrid multicast) in the well-known network simulator *ns-2*. This section is devoted to performance studies of the proposed approaches.

7.1   Evaluation Methodology

Our physical Internet topologies are generated by the *transit-stub* model [22], by using the GT-ITM Topology Generator software. A number of physical nodes are randomly chosen as proxy nodes, whose service capability and machine capacity are randomly assigned by some functions. The end-to-end available bandwidth from an overlay proxy node a to another overlay proxy node b is the bottleneck bandwidth of the shortest physical path from a to b. Among the physical network nodes, a small set of them are chosen to be the landmark nodes – L, based on which the proxies can derive their coordinates in the geometric space defined by L[17]. We use planar geometric spaces in our simulations, and calculation of geometric coordinates is done by using the software available at http://www-2.cs.cmu.edu/~eugeneng/research/gnp/. Construction of the Delaunay triangulation overlay mesh for control message purposes is aided by the Qhull software developed by the Geometry Center at University of Minnesota (http://www.geom.umn.edu/software/qhull).

We use the following performance metrics in the evaluations:

– *Link Utilization:* is the ratio of used bandwidth to the total initial bandwidth of the physical network links that measures how much the physical links are loaded. The ratio may range between 0 to 1: at 0, the physical link has zero load; at 1, the link is fully loaded.
– *Proxy Utilization:* is the ratio of amount of machine resources in use to the machine's total initial amount of resources. In simulations, we represent a machine's computing capacity as a single numerical value, although in reality, it should be a resource vector of multiple parameters (e.g., memory, cpu).
– *Service Path Length:* is the sum of individual virtual link lengths that make up the service path, where the virtual link lengths are end-to-end delays.
– *Delay × Bandwidth Product:* The purpose of this metric is to measure the volume that the data occupies in the network. For example, if the streaming data requires 2MB of bandwidth on a physical link whose single trip delay is 10ms, then the volume of data is said to be 20MB*ms.
– *Path Finding Success Rate:* is the rate of finding service paths successfully. Service path finding failures may occur when resources are scarce, or when there is no instance of the required service(s). However, in our following tests, there will be always at least one instance of each service in the system, thus failures can only be caused by resource scarcity.

7.2   Performances of Different Service Unicast Approaches

In this section, we measure performances of the different service unicast approaches (*GLG, LRA, GLG-LRA,* and *LRA-GLG*) described in Section 4 in terms of all listed performance metrics.

The simulation settings for these tests are as follows. The physical networks contain 300 nodes, and among them, 10 are landmarks and 250 are proxies. We randomly generated 1000 service path requests between randomly selected pairs of proxies. We compare the performances under two different resource settings: one with sufficient resources to admit all service requests, and the other with insufficient resources, where late join requests may be rejected because of resource scarcity. For each scenario, we run two test cases.

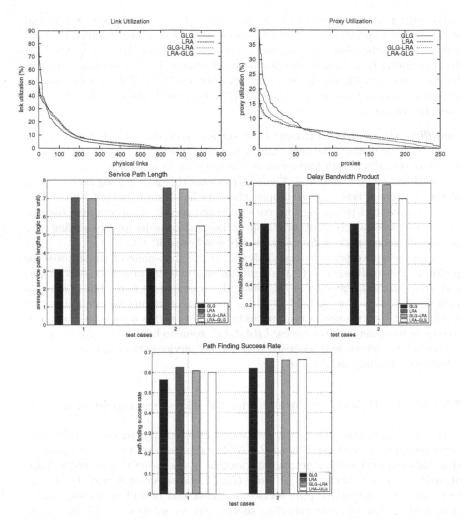

Fig. 8. Comparisons of: (a) *physical link utilization*; (b) *proxy utilization*; (c) *service path length*; (d) *delay bandwidth product*; and (e) *path finding success rate* among the different service unicast approaches.

Sufficient-resource settings: In this case, since all service requests get successfully admitted, the performance metrics of interest are *link utilization*, *proxy utilization*, *service path length*, and *delay bandwidth product*. Figure 8 (a) and (b) show the physical network link and proxy utilization of the different approaches. As has been predicted, since *GLG* genuinely seeks shortest QoS-satisfied service paths, load balancing in both respects is poor. This is indicated by the fact that the *GLG* curves are steepest. *LRA* does in fact help to keep a more balanced network and machine load, as the next service hop is the one that maximizes an aggregate function of available bandwidth and machine capacity. On the other hand, LRA performs poorly in terms of *service path length* (Figure 8 (c)) and *delay bandwidth product* (Figure 8 (d)), because service paths computed by LRA are long, and therefore demand more network resources. However, this time GLG performs best, because service paths computed by this approach tend to be short, and as such, require less network resources. GLG-LRA's performances are quite close to those of LRA, and LRA-GLG has the best performances in these two respects.

Insufficient-resource settings: After certain resources get exhausted, a join request may be denied. The performance metric of interest in such an insufficient-resources scenario is *path finding success rate* which, in some way, indicates how well load balancing is achieved. Figure 8(e) shows the path finding success rates of the different service unicast approaches. As has been expected, since GLG does not take load balancing into consideration, certain resources may become exhausted more quickly than other approaches that consider load balancing, and as a consequence, *path finding success rate* was lowest in GLG.

From the above performance analyses, we see that none of the approaches performs best in all aspects: GLG's performances in terms of *service path lengths* and *delay-bandwidth product* are significantly superior to others', but is worst in *path finding success rates*; LRA is one of the best in finding service paths successfully, but incurs longer service paths than others and as a consequence, tends to require more network resources. LRA-GLG seems to have best balanced these contradictory factors, as it incurs relatively short service paths while maintaining a high path finding success rate.

7.3   Service Unicast *vs* Pure Service Multicast *vs* Hybrid Multicast

In this section, we study the performance benefits of employing pure service multicast and hybrid multicast. Since LRA-GLG is the best service unicast approach that balances load and optimizes path lengths at the same time, constructions of multicast tree branches adopt LRA-GLG when selecting service hops. The two multicast approaches, pure service multicast and hybrid multicast, will be compared against the corresponding service unicast solution, which is unicast LRA-GLG.

Sufficient-resource settings: Simulations are run for multicast group size of 100, where service requests are drawn from a pool of size 20. As we can see from Figure 9 (a), hybrid multicast yields better bandwidth (link) utilization than pure service multicast. However, there is not too much difference in proxy utilization between pure service multicast and hybrid multicast (Figure 9 (b)). This is expected, because local data multicast does not further diminish the number of service executions. Compared to service unicast, both types of multicast incur longer end-to-end service paths (Figure 9 (c)), but less total tree lengths (Figure 9 (d)) due to service path sharing. Not surprisingly, the two multicast cases yield tremendous delay bandwidth product savings compared to unicast (Figure 9 (e)). While it is intuitive that advantages of hybrid multicast over service

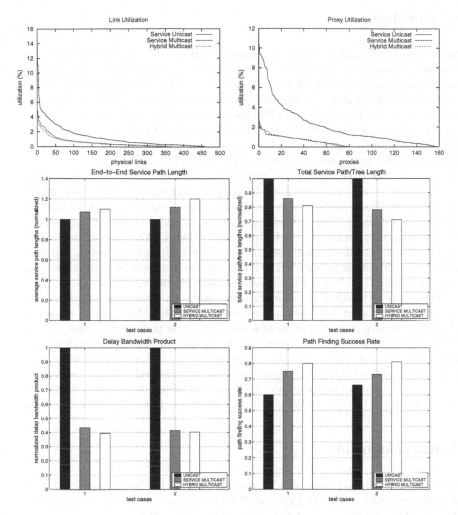

Fig. 9. Comparisons of: (a) *physical link utilization*; (b) *proxy utilization*; (c) *end-to-end service path length*; (d) *total service path/tree length*; (e) *delay bandwidth product*; and (f) *path finding success rate* among the different delivery modes: *service unicast, pure service multicast*, and *hybrid multicast*.

multicast (and multicast over unicast) increase with the multicast group size, it would be interesting to quantify the gains in the future work.

Insufficient-resource settings: Since the major purpose of designing hybrid multicast was to make even better network bandwidth usage than pure service multicast, in this test, we only make bandwidth scarce. As Figure 9 (f) shows, service path finding success rate increases dramatically from unicast to the two cases of service multicast, and hybrid multicast over-performs pure service multicast.

8   Conclusions

In this paper, we have explored performance optimizations in Web service composition in several respects. First, we made an improvement over an existing hop-by-hop service unicast solution – LRA – that makes routing decisions based on local heuristics only, by introducing and using the geometric location information of the Internet hosts. The geometric location guidance (GLG) can significantly reduce service path lengths compared to LRA. We studied different combinations of GLG and LRA in terms of several performance aspects. The simulation performances showed that LRA-GLG best balances the trade-offs. Second, the paper proposed a fully distributed approach for incrementally building service multicast trees, by identifying and solving several key differences (e.g., graftable node, tree maintenance) between service multicast and the conventional data multicast. Advantages of pure service multicast over service unicast were also verified through simulations. Third, We proposed to further explore benefits of data multicast inside service multicast scenarios, and provided a hybrid multicast solution. We showed how this can be realized, and by how much hybrid multicast can outperform pure service multicast.

Due to space limitations, failure recovery issues have been left out. Recovery operations are called for when a physical node or link fails. Since loops are allowed in service routing, failure of a single physical node may trigger failures of several points in the service path/tree. As an example, assume a single service path $sp = (p_s \rightarrow s_1/p_\alpha \rightarrow s_2/p_\beta \rightarrow s_3/p_\alpha \rightarrow \ldots \rightarrow p_d)$, if p_α fails, then two service nodes (s_1/p_α and s_3/p_α) need to be repaired. Failure recovery is even more complex in multicast scenarios; special failure detection and recovery mechanisms will be needed. We plan to address these issues in our future work.

Acknowledgments

This material is based upon work supported by NSF (under Awards No. CCR-9988199 and EIA 99-72884 EQ) and NASA (under Award No. NAG2-1406). Any opinions, findings, and conclusions or recommendations expressed in this publication are those of the authors and do not necessarily reflect the views of the awarding agencies. The authors would like to thank the anonymous reviewers for their helpful comments.

References

1. Rakesh Mohan, John R. Smith and Chung-Sheng Li. Adapting Multimedia Internet Content for Universal Access. *IEEE Transactions on Multimedia*, Mar 1999.
2. Surendar Chandra, Carla Schlatter Ellis, and Amin Vahdat. Application-Level Differentiated Multimedia Web Services Using Quality Aware Transcoding. *IEEE Journal on Selected Areas in Communications*, 18(12), Dec 2000.

3. S. D. Gribble, M. Welsh, R. von Behren, E. A. Brewer, D. Culler, N. Borisov, S. Czerwinski, R. Gummadi, J. Hill, A. Joseph, R.H. Katz, Z.M. Mao, S. Ross, and B. Zhao. The Ninja Architecture for Robust Internet-Scale Systems and Services. *Special Issue of Computer Networks on Pervasive Computing*, 2001.
4. A. Ivan, J. Harman, M. Allen, and V. Karamcheti. Partitionable Services: A Framework for Seamlessly Adapting Distributed Applications to Heterogeneous Environments. In *Proc. of IEEE International Conference on High Performance Distributed Computing (HPDC)*, Edinburgh, Scotland, Jul 2002.
5. Shankar R. Ponnekanti and Armando Fox. SWORD: A Developer Toolkit for Web Service Composition. In *the Eleventh World Wide Web Conference (Web Engineering Track)*, Honolulu, Hawaii, May 2002.
6. Jingwen Jin and Klara Nahrstedt. Large-Scale Service Overlay Networking with Distance-Based Clustering. In *ACM/IFIP/USENIX International Middleware Conference (Middleware2003)*, Rio de Janeiro, Brazil, Jun 2003.
7. Xiaohui Gu, Klara Nahrstedt. A Scalable QoS-Aware Service Aggregation Model for Peer-to-Peer Computing Grids. In *Proc. of High Performance Distributed Computing*, Edinburgh, Scotland, Jul 2002.
8. Sumi Choi, Jonathan Turner, and Tilman Wolf. Configuring Sessions in Programmable Networks. In *Proc. of IEEE INFOCOM*, Anchorage, Alaska, Apr 2001.
9. Liangzhao Zeng, Boualem Benatallah, Marlon Dumas, Jayant Kalagnanam, Quan Z. Sheng. Quality Driven Web Services Composition. In *The Twelfth International World Wide Web Conference*, Budapest, Hungary, May 2003.
10. Jingwen Jin and Klara Nahrstedt. On Construction of Service Multicast Trees. In *Proc. of IEEE International Conference on Communications (ICC2003)*, Anchorage, Alaska, May 2003.
11. Zhichen Xu, Chunqiang Tang, Sujata Banerjee, Sung-Ju Lee. RITA: Receiver Initiated Just-in-Time Tree Adaptation for Rich Media Distribution. In *13th International Workshop on Network and Operating Systems Support for Digital Audio and Video (NOSSDAV03)*, Monterey, CA, Jun 2003.
12. Ion Stoica, Robert Morris, David Karger, M. Frans Kaashoek, Hari Balakrishnan. Chord: A Scalable Peer-to-Peer Lookup Service for Internet Applications. In *ACM SIGCOMM*, San Diego, California, Aug 2001.
13. Sylvia Ratnasamy, Pau Francis, Mark Handley, Richard Karp, Scott Shenker. A Scalable Content-Addressable Network. In *Proc. of ACM SIGCOMM*, San Diego, CA, Aug 2001.
14. Duangdao Wichadakul. *Q-Compiler: Meta-Data QoS-Aware Programming and Compilation Framework*. PhD thesis, Computer Science Department, University of Illinois at Urbana Champaign, Jan. 2003.
15. Y. Chu, S. G. Rao and H. Zhang. A Case For End System Multicast. In *Proc. of ACM SIGMETRICS*, pages 1–12, Santa Clara, CA, Jun 2000.
16. Paul Francis. Yoid: Extending the Internet Multicast Architecture, Apr 2000.
17. T. S. Eugene Ng, Hui Zhang. Predicting Internet Network Distance with Coordinates-Based Approaches. In *Proc. of IEEE INFOCOM*, New York, NY, Jun 2002.
18. J. Liebeherr, and M. Nahas. Application-Layer Multicast with Delaunay Triangulations. In *Proc. of Sixth Global Internet Symposium (IEEE Globecom 2001)*, San Antonio, Texas, Nov 2001.
19. Evangelos Kranakis, Harvinder Singh, Jorge Urrutia. Compass Routing on Geometric Networks. In *Proc. of the 11th Canadian Conference on Computational Geometry*, Vancouver, CA.

20. Shigang Chen, Klara Nahrstedt, Yuval Shavitt. A QoS-Aware Multicast Routing Protocol. *IEEE Journal on Special Areas in Communication*, 18(12):2580–2592, Dec 2000.
21. Jingwen Jin, Klara Nahrstedt. QoS Service Routing for Supporting Multimedia Applications. Technical Report UIUCDCS-R-2002-2303/UILU-ENG-2002-1746, Department of Computer Science, University of Illinois at Urbana-Champaign, USA, Nov 2002.
22. E. Zegura, K. Calvert, S. Bhattacharjee. How to Model an Internetwork. In *Proc. of IEEE INCOFOM*, Apr 1996.

iOverlay:
A Lightweight Middleware Infrastructure for Overlay Application Implementations

Baochun Li, Jiang Guo, and Mea Wang

Department of Electrical and Computer Engineering
University of Toronto
{bli,jguo,mea}@eecg.toronto.edu

Abstract. The very nature of implementing and evaluating fully distributed algorithms or protocols in application-layer overlay networks involves certain programming tasks that are at best mundane and tedious – and at worst challenging – even at the application level. In this paper, we present *iOverlay*, a lightweight and high-performance middleware infrastructure that addresses these problems in a novel way by providing clean, well-documented layers of middleware components. The internals of iOverlay are carefully designed and implemented to maximize its performance, without sacrificing the simplicity of application implementations using iOverlay. We illustrate the effectiveness of iOverlay by rapidly implementing a set of overlay applications, and report our findings and experiences by deploying them on PlanetLab, the wide-area overlay network testbed that iOverlay conveniently supports.

1 Introduction

Existing research in the area of application-layer overlay protocols has produced a sizable collection of real-world implementations of protocols and distributed applications in overlay networks. Examples include implementations of structured search protocols such as Pastry [1] and Chord [2], as well as overlay data dissemination such as Narada [3], NICE [4], SplitStream [5] and Bullet [6]. However, an interesting observation is that most of the existing work has resorted to simulations to evaluate the effectiveness of the proposed protocols.

The recent availability of global-scale implementation testbeds for application-layer overlay protocols, such as PlanetLab [7] and Netbed [8], makes it feasible to design, implement and deploy overlay protocols in a wide-area network, so that they may be evaluated in realistic environments rather than simulations. However, there still exist roadblocks that make it impractical to deliver a high-quality, high-performance and fully distributed real-world implementation of overlay applications entirely from scratch: such an implementation involves many software components that must work together, including certain programming tasks that are at best mundane and tedious – and at worst challenging – to code.

H.-A. Jacobsen (Ed.): Middleware 2004, LNCS 3231, pp. 135–154, 2004.

We observe that, among all the components of a distributed application or protocol implementation, only a few specific areas are interesting for research purposes, and are subject to changes and innovations. On the other hand, any realistic implementation of overlay applications must include a significant number of largely uninteresting elements, such as (1) bootstrapping wide-area nodes from a centralized authority; (2) implementing a multi-threaded message forwarding engine; (3) monitoring facilities to control, debug, and record the performance of distributed algorithms. The necessity of writing such supporting infrastructure slows down the pace of prototyping new applications and protocols.

In this paper, we present *iOverlay*, a lightweight and high-performance middleware infrastructure that is specifically designed from scratch to support rapid development of distributed applications and protocols over realistic testbeds. The design objectives of *iOverlay* are as follows. First, it seeks to provide a high-quality and high-performance implementation of a carefully selected number of features that are common or useful to most of the overlay application implementations. Second, it seeks to be as *generic* as possible, and minimizes the set of assumptions with respect to the objectives and nature of new applications. Third, it seeks to significantly simplify the implementation of distributed applications, to the extent that only the logics and semantics specific to the application itself need to be implemented by the application developer. In addition, it should not be necessary for the application developer to have any prior knowledge about the internal details of iOverlay, before starting a successful implementation. Finally, it seeks to design a well-documented, straightforward and clean interface between the application and iOverlay.

The remainder of this paper is organized as follows. In Sec. 2, we present the design and implementation of the iOverlay architecture. In Sec. 3, we present our own experiences with rapidly prototyping a set of overlay applications as case studies. Finally, we discuss iOverlay in light of related work (Sec. 4), and conclude the paper in Sec. 5.

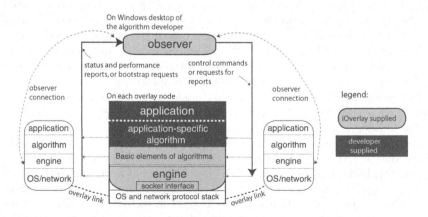

Fig. 1. The iOverlay architecture.

2   iOverlay: Design and Performance

iOverlay considers three layers in a distributed application: (1) the *message switching engine*, which performs indispensable tasks of switching application-layer messages. (2) the *algorithm*, which implements the application-specific distributed protocol beyond mundane tasks in the engine; and (3) the *application*, which produces and interprets the data portion of application-layer messages at both the sending and the receiving ends. This may include global storage systems that respond to queries, or publish-subscribe applications that produce events and interests. The ultimate objective is for the application developer to build new *algorithms* based on the engine, and to select an application to be deployed on top of the algorithm.

Architecturally, the iOverlay middleware infrastructure provides support to the application developer in all of these aspects. First, it implements a fully functional, virtualizable and high performance message switching engine, upon which the application-specific algorithm is built. Second, it implements common elements of selected categories of algorithms that are completely optional for the application developer to use. Third, it implements typical applications, which the algorithm developer may choose to deploy. Finally, it provides a centralized Windows-based graphical utility, referred to as the *observer*, for the purpose of monitoring, debugging, visualizing and logging various aspects of the distributed application. The iOverlay architecture, as discussed, is illustrated in Fig. 1.

2.1   Highlights

The iOverlay middleware design features the following highlights.

Simplified Interface. iOverlay is designed to have the simplest interface possible between the application-specific algorithm and the engine on each overlay node, in order to minimize the cost of entry to use iOverlay. The application developer only needs to be aware of *one* function of the engine: the *send* function, used for sending data or protocol messages to downstream or peer nodes. In addition to this function, the entire interface is designed to be completely *message driven*, in the sense that the algorithm only needs to *passively* process messages when they arrive or are produced by the engine. Since messages are distinguished by their *types*, a *message handler* that handles possible types is all that is required for the algorithm implementation. Further, the entire implementation of the application-specific algorithm is guaranteed to be executed in a single thread, and therefore does not need to use thread-safe data structures (those guarded with semaphores and locks).

Virtualized nodes. iOverlay features complete *virtualization* of overlay nodes in a distributed application. Each physical node in the wide-area network may easily accommodate from one to up to dozens of iOverlay nodes, depending on available physical resources such as CPU. Each iOverlay node has its own bandwidth specifications, such as the total bandwidth available to and from the node, separate upload and download available bandwidth, or per-link bandwidth limits. This adds to the flexibility of iOverlay deployment: if necessary, iOverlay may be entirely deployed in a local area network with a cluster of servers; or, for small-scale tests, on just a single server.

Maximized Performance and Flexibility. Finally, iOverlay is designed to maximize its performance. The engine is implemented from scratch with the C++ programming language and the native POSIX thread library in UNIX. It is portable across many UNIX variants. The observer is implemented in Windows using the C# programming language, guaranteeing rapid development of additional interface elements.

2.2   Internal Design

In iOverlay, we assume that all communication is in the form of *application-layer messages*, containing application data of a maximum length in bytes. Each message maintains a fixed 24-byte header, which includes the type and sender of the message, the application identifier that it belongs to, the sequence number and the size of the payload. To keep it simple, the content of a message is mostly immutable, and is initialized at the time of construction. In addition, the notion of a *node* in iOverlay is uniquely identified by its IP address and port number. The port number may be explicitly specified at start-up time; otherwise, the engine chooses one of the available ports.

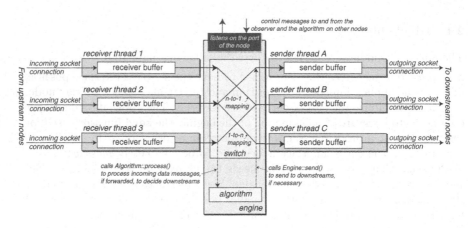

Fig. 2. The internal design of the engine.

The Message Switching Engine: A Close Examination

The engine of iOverlay is an application-layer message switch. We seek to design the engine such that it supports multiple competing traffic sessions, so that the application developer may easily test the performance of distributed algorithms under heavy cross traffic. It also has the capability to concurrently process both application data and protocol-specific messages.

We deploy a multi-threaded architecture to concurrently handle multiple incoming and outgoing connections, application-specific messages, as well as messages to and from the observer. Specifically, we use a thread-per-receiver and a thread-per-sender design, along with a separate *engine* thread for processing and switching messages using the application-specific algorithm. All receiver and sender threads use blocking receive and send operations, and the sender thread is suspended when the buffer is empty, to be signaled by the engine thread. We use a thread-safe circular queue to implement the shared buffers between the threads. Such a design is illustrated in Fig. 2.

We adopt such a design to avoid the complex wait/signal scenario where the receiver or sender buffer is shared by more than one reader or writer threads. Unlike the receiver and sender threads that "sleep" when the the buffer is full (receiver) or empty (sender), the engine thread constantly monitors the publicized port of the node (by using the non-blocking `select()` function) for incoming control messages from the observer, or from the algorithms of other nodes. If they exist, they are either processed within the engine, or sent to the algorithm to be processed, by calling the `Algorithm::process()` function. Next, it switches data messages from the receiver buffers to the sender buffers in a weighted round-robin fashion, with dynamically tunable weights (implemented in the `Engine::switch()` function). The skeleton of the engine thread is shown in Table 1.

Table 1. Design of the engine thread.

```
start the TCP server on the publicized port;
bootstrap from observer;
while not terminated
    if there are incoming messages on the port detected
    using non-blocking select()
        if the message is engine-related
            call Engine::process();
        else
            call Algorithm::process();
    call Engine::switch();
stop the TCP server.
```

Obviously, when the switch attempts to forward messages to downstreams, the choice of downstream nodes is at the sole discretion of the algorithm. Therefore, the engine consults with the algorithm by calling `Algorithm::process()`. There are two possibilities. First, the algorithm may locally process and consume the message. Second, the algorithm continues to forward the message to one or more downstream nodes, by calling the `Engine::send()` function. Only in the latter case does the engine forward the message to the sender buffers.

The tight coupling of the algorithm's and the engine's message processing components is intentional by design. First, they must reside in the same thread, since we prefer to avoid the cases where the developer needs to use thread-safe data structures when algorithms are developed with iOverlay. It is impossible to design a typical two-thread solution – where the engine processes control messages in one thread, and switches data messages in another – and still achieve such a favorable property of accommodating thread-unaware algorithms. Second, the seemingly complex "paradox" – at times the engine calls the algorithm, and at other times the algorithm calls the engine – is in fact straightforward, since the algorithm is always *reactive* and never *proactive*.

There are further complexities involved in the design of a switch. As a first example, there may be cases where messages are successfully forwarded to only a subset of the intended senders, but fail to be forwarded to the remaining ones, since their buffers are full. In this case, we label each message with its *set of remaining senders*, so that they may be tried in the next round. As a second example, in some scenarios a set of states needs to be shared and exchanged between active threads. For example, a receiver thread needs to notify the engine when a failed upstream node has been detected, such that the engine thread can clear up its data structures related to this node. To avoid complex thread synchronization between active threads, we extensively take advantage of the mechanism of passing application-layer messages across thread boundaries via the publicized port. Without a doubt, these complexities are completely transparent to the algorithm developer.

Finally, we may not only wish to forward verbatim messages in an application-layer switch, but also wish to merge or code multiple incoming messages into one outgoing message. In order to implement the most generic n-to-m mapping (such as coding messages from n multiple incoming connections to m downstreams), we allow `Algorithm::process()` to return a *hold* type, instructing the engine that the message is buffered in the algorithm, but its processing should be put on hold to wait for other messages from other incoming connections. It is up to the algorithm to implement the logic of merging or coding multiple messages after requesting a hold on them, and eventually producing a new message to be sent to downstreams. Using the *hold* mechanism, we have successfully implemented algorithms that perform overlay multicast with merging or network coding [9].

Salient Features

Handling of Failures. In iOverlay, we assume that the nodes themselves, the virtual link between nodes, as well as the application data sources may all fail prematurely. Transparent to the algorithm developer, iOverlay supports the automatic detection of failed nodes and links, and the automatic tear-down of relevant links after such failures. For example, if an upstream link in a multicast tree has failed, it causes a "Domino Effect" that fails all downstream links from this point. The engine is able to appropriately tear down these links without affecting any of the other active links, and to notify the algorithm of such failures. All terminations are graceful, and all affected links are smoothly dropped without side effects.

We have implemented a collection of exception handling mechanisms to detect and process such failures. Depending on the state of the sockets at the time of premature failures, we rely on a combination of mechanisms to detect that a node or a link may have failed: (1) exceptions thrown and timeouts at the socket level; (2) abnormal signals caught by the engine, such as the *Broken Pipe* signal; and (3) long consecutive periods of traffic inactivity, detected by throughput measurements. To avoid overhead, we do not use any forms of active probes or "heartbeat updates" for this purpose. Still, we are able to implement very responsive detections of link and node failures in most cases. In addition, the observer may choose to terminate a node at will, in which case all the data structures and threads in both the engine and the algorithm will be cleared up, and the program terminates gracefully.

Measurement of QoS Metrics. At the socket level, we have implemented mechanisms to measure the TCP throughput of a connection, as well as the round-trip latency and the number of bytes (or messages) lost due to failures. The results of these measurements are periodically reported to the algorithm and the observer. Upon requests from the algorithm, the available bandwidth and latency to any overlay nodes can be measured.

Emulation of Bandwidth Availability. In some cases, the algorithm developer prefers to test a preliminary algorithm under controlled environments, in which node characteristics are more predictable. iOverlay explicitly supports the emulation of bandwidth availability in three categories: (1) per-node total bandwidth: the total incoming and outgoing bandwidth available; (2) per-link bandwidth: the bandwidth available on a certain point-to-point virtual link; and (3) per-node incoming and outgoing bandwidth: iOverlay is able to emulate asymmetric nodes (such as nodes on DSL or cable modem connections) featuring disparate outgoing and incoming bandwidth availability. The emulated values may be specified at node start-up time, or within the observer at runtime. In the latter case, artificially emulated bottlenecks may be produced or relieved on the fly, in order to evaluate the adaptivity of the algorithm. To implement such emulations, we have wrapped the socket `send` and `recv` functions to include multiple timers in order to precisely control the bandwidth used per interval (the length of which may be specified by the algorithm).

Performance Considerations

The performance objective of the engine design is to "push" messages through the engine as quickly as possible, with the lowest possible overhead at the switch. Towards this objective, we have considered three directions of performance optimizations, and successfully implemented them in the current engine.

Persistent Connections. In order to avoid the unacceptable overhead of thread-level context switching at the operating system when a large number of threads are used, we implement both incoming and outgoing socket connections as *persistent connections*, in the sense that all the messages between two nodes are carried with the same connection, regardless of the applications they belong to. With persistent connections, we have avoided the creation of more threads when new distributed applications are deployed; instead, existing connections are reused.

Zero Copying of Messages. In order to avoid deep copying of entire messages when they pass through the engine, we have implemented a collection of mechanisms to ensure that only the references of messages are passed from the incoming socket all the way to the outgoing socket, and *no messages will be copied* in the engine at all. The algorithm may choose to copy messages, if necessary, supported by the copy constructor of the `Msg` class. In order to appropriately destruct messages whose references are shared by multiple threads, an elaborate thread-safe reference counting mechanism is in place in the core of the engine.

Footprint. The engine is meticulously designed and tested so that the memory footprint is minimized and stable (without leaks). For example, with a message size of 5 KB and a buffer capacity of 10 messages, the footprint of the engine is only 4 MB per active connection[1]. The optimized binary executable of the engine (with a simple testing algorithm) is only 100 KB. Such a footprint guarantees the scalability of iOverlay, especially when a large number of virtualized nodes are deployed on the same physical server.

The Observer

As a centralized monitoring facility, we have implemented the observer as a graphical tool in Windows. The observer implements the first level of bootstrap support, by responding to any bootstrap requests (messages of type *boot*) with a random subset of existing nodes that are alive. The number of initial nodes in such a subset is configurable. Once a node is bootstrapped, the observer periodically sends it a *request* message to request for status updates, which include lengths of all engine buffers, measurements of QoS metrics, and the list of upstream and downstream nodes. With these status updates, the observer may visually illustrate the current network topology of each of the applications with geographical locations of all nodes, on either the world or the North American map.

Further, the observer serves as a control panel and may take the following actions to control the status of the network: (1) controlling the emulated per-link and per-node bandwidth availabilities; (2) deploying an application; (3) asking a node to join or leave a particular application; and (4) terminating an application data source or a node. For the sake of flexibility, the observer is also able to send new types of algorithm-specific control messages to the nodes, with two optional integer parameters embedded in the header.

Basic Elements of Algorithms

Despite the tight coupling between the algorithm and the engine, the algorithm is placed in its own namespace with an object-oriented design. The basic and com-

---

[1] This is the case in Linux, which may be inferior with respect to footprint since `clone()` is usually used to support user-level POSIX threads.

monly used elements of an algorithm is defined and implemented in a generic base class referred to as *iAlgorithm*. We present two examples. First, it implements a default message handler, that handles known messages from the observer and the engine with a default behavior. For example, upon receiving the bootstrap message from the observer, it records the set of initial nodes in a local data structure referred to as KnownHosts. Second, *iAlgorithm* implements a disseminate function, which disseminates a message to a list of overlay nodes, with a specific probability *p*. This resembles the *gossiping* behavior in distributed systems. The default implementations of a library of functions in the *iAlgorithm* class serve as a set of basic utilities, and since application-specific algorithms are classes that inherit from *iAlgorithm*, the developer may choose to override any default behavior with application-specific implementations.

2.3   Interface Between iOverlay and Algorithms

Given the iOverlay design we have presented, how do we rapidly develop an application using iOverlay? Many design choices are made to reduce the complexity of developing new application-specific algorithms. First, the algorithm namespace extensively uses object orientation such that new algorithms may be built based on existing algorithm implementations. As we have discussed, a few basic elements of algorithms have already been provided by iOverlay. Second, the algorithm only needs to call *one* function of the engine: the *send* function. This greatly improves the learning curve of the interface. Finally, the algorithm is designed as a message handler, in the form of a *switch* statement on different types of messages. While processing each incoming message, internal states of the algorithm may be modified. The message handler should reside in the process() function. The skeleton of an algorithm is shown in Table 2.

In such a skeleton, it is not necessary for an algorithm to handle all the known message types from the engine or the observer. If a message type is not handled in the algorithm, the default process() function provided by the base *iAlgorithm* class takes this responsibility. In fact, the only message type that the algorithm must handle is the type data, indicating a data message. iAlgorithm provides default handlers for all other types of messages. It is also not necessary for an algorithm to handle abnormal return values when invoking the send() function. In fact, send() has a return type of void, and all abnormal results of sending a message are handled by the engine transparently. For example, if the destination node of the message fails, the algorithm is notified appropriately, again via messages produced by the engine.

Another important design decision is related to the destruction of messages. In order to completely eliminate memory leaks, we need to carefully assign the responsibilities of message destruction. Particularly, consider a message passed to the algorithm (by pointers) as a parameter in the *process* function. Should the engine or the algorithm be responsible for destructing the message after it has been processed? Further, when a message is constructed in the algorithm and passed to the *send* function of the engine, should the engine or the algorithm be responsible for destructing the message after it is sent? To simplify the tasks of

Table 2. Skeleton of the algorithm using iOverlay.

```
process(Msg * m)
   switch (m -> type())
   case sDeploy: (from observer)
      deploy an application source;
   case request: (from observer)
      send algorithm status updates to observer;
   case sTerminate: (from observer)
      terminate an application source;
   case BrokenSource: (from upstream)
      clear up internal states corresponding to the application
      source at upstream, since it has failed;
   case data: (from the engine)
      process, consume or forward the message using
      send(Msg * m, Node dest);
   case UpThroughput: (from the engine)
      record or process the throughput from an upstream;
   ... (process other engine or algorithm-specific types)
   default: (use the default behavior from iAlgorithm)
      iAlgorithm::process(m);
```

algorithm developers, we stipulate that *all message destructions are the respon-sibility of the engine*. The algorithm developer should never destruct messages, even if they have been constructed in the algorithm.

However, there exist a subtle problem with this solution even it works well at most times. When the algorithm receives a pointer to an engine-created message as a parameter of the *process* function, what if the algorithm passes the pointer back to the engine by using the *send* function? We distinguish treatments of this scenario depending on the type of the message. If the message is of type `data`, we have developed the engine carefully such that the algorithm can directly invoke *send* with the same message, guaranteeing zero copying of data messages. However, if the message is of any other type, we require the algorithm developer to clone the message before invoking *send* on the new copy. Performance-wise this is not a problem, since most protocol messages are very small in size.

2.4   Performance

With C++ on Linux, C# on Windows, and around 25, 000 lines of code in total, we have completed a stable implementation of the entire iOverlay middleware infrastructure that we have presented. We now evaluate the results of such an implementation, focusing on the raw message switching performance of iOver-lay nodes, especially when they are virtualized nodes on the same server. For this purpose, we execute iOverlay nodes on a single dual-CPU server with two Pentium III 1GHz processors, 1.5GB of memory, and Linux 2.4.25. The iOverlay engine is compiled with `gcc 3.3.3` with the most aggressive optimizations.

Since iOverlay nodes are multi-threaded user-level programs, the bottleneck of such switching performance under heavy load is the overhead of context switching among a large number of threads. We create such a load using a chain topology, and we test iOverlay with different number of nodes in the network. Before we deploy an application on the chain topology, we observe that the CPU load is 0.00, which shows that iOverlay does not consume CPU resources without traffic. After we deploy an application that sends back-to-back traffic from one end of the chain to the other as fast as possible, we measure the end-to-end throughput, as well as the total bandwidth in the chain, calculated by the end-to-end throughput multiplied by the number of links. The total bandwidth represents the actual number of messages per second that have been switched or in transit in the network. Fig. 3 shows the iOverlay engine performance in this test, with a chain from two nodes to 32 nodes.

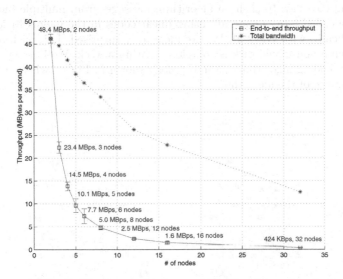

Fig. 3. The raw performance of the iOverlay engine.

We have two noteworthy observations from this experiment. First, if we compare the two-node total bandwidth of 48.4 MBps and the three-node bandwidth of 46.8 MBps, the overhead of one user-level message switch is only 3.3%. Second, as the number of nodes increases, the overhead of context switching becomes more significant, due to the Linux implementation of POSIX threads using `clone()`. Still, even with a 32-node configuration, the sustained throughput is still 424 KBps, which is higher than the typical throughput of wide-area connections. This implies that we may potentially deploy dozens of nodes on a single physical node in a local-area or wide-area testbed, making it feasible to test the scalability of new applications in terms of the number of participants. Such performance is simply not achievable if, for example, Java is used rather than C++, or zero message copying is not enforced.

3   Case Studies

We believe that iOverlay is useful to support the rapid implementation of a wide range of applications and distributed algorithms in application overlay networks. In this paper, we undertake three case studies to highlight our own experiences of rapidly prototyping new algorithms and ideas using iOverlay as the middleware infrastructure.

3.1   Network Coding

The advantages of application-layer overlay networks arise from the fundamental property that overlay nodes, as opposed to lower-layer network elements such as routers and switches, are end systems and have capabilities far beyond basic operations of storing and forwarding. In the first case study, we implement a novel message processing algorithm that performs *network coding* on overlay nodes, using iOverlay. In such an algorithm, messages from multiple incoming streams are coded into one stream using linear codes in the Galois Field (and more specifically, with $GF(2^8)$). We are pleasantly surprised that, with one developer, such a non-trivial task is completed within a week. We have evaluated the network coding algorithm in the topology shown in Fig. 4, where we show the performance of the algorithm.

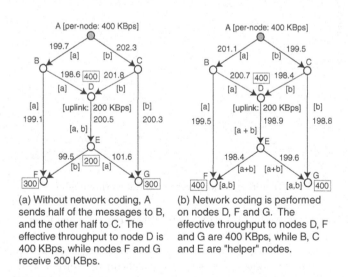

(a) Without network coding, A sends half of the messages to B, and the other half to C. The effective throughput to node D is 400 KBps, while nodes F and G receive 300 KBps.

(b) Network coding is performed on nodes D, F and G. The effective throughput to nodes D, F and G are 400 KBps, while B, C and E are "helper" nodes.

Fig. 4. Performance of network coding: an iOverlay case study.

Fig. 4(a) shows the results without using network coding. Node A is the data source with per-node bandwidth of 400 KBps, and node D has an uplink bandwidth of 200 KBps. Node A splits its data into two streams sent to B and C, respectively. In this case, B and C are not able to receive both streams, and are referred to as *helper* nodes. Based on iOverlay throughput measurements, the nodes D, E, F and G have received $400, 200, 300, 300$ KBps, respectively. In comparison, Fig. 4(b) shows the case where the coding algorithm $a + b$ in $\mathrm{GF}(2^8)$ is applied at node D on the two incoming streams. In this case, the nodes F and G are able to receive both streams a and b by decoding $a + b$ with a, achieving a throughput of 400 KBps. The trade-off, however, is that node E becomes a helper node, in addition to B and C. Our experiences with this case study have demonstrated both the advantages and the trade-offs of applying network coding on overlay nodes. We believe that such an experiment-based evaluation of network coding algorithms is not possible within such a short time frame, if iOverlay is not available as a substrate. For more details of our implementation on network coding, the interested reader is referred to our companion paper [10].

3.2   Construction of Data Dissemination Trees

In this case study, we are interested in the development and evaluation of new algorithms that construct data dissemination multicast trees in overlay networks, particularly in the scenario that the "last-mile" available bandwidth on overlay nodes is the bottleneck. With iOverlay, we have implemented a *node stress* aware algorithm to construct such multicast trees, where *node stress* is defined as the degree of a node in a data dissemination topology divided by the available "last-mile" bandwidth of the node.

The outline of this algorithm is as follows. Periodically, each node in the existing multicast session exchanges node stress information with its parent and child nodes. As a node A joins the multicast session, it first locates a node *that is currently in the tree* by using one of the utility functions supported in iOverlay, which disseminates a *sQuery* message. As the message is relayed to the first such node B in the tree, B compares its own node stress with its parent and child nodes. If B itself has the minimum node stress, it responds with an *sQueryAck* message, so that A becomes a new child of B in the tree. Otherwise, it recursively forwards the message to the node with the minimum node stress (parent or children), until the message reaches the minimum-stress node who sends the acknowledgment.

In order to evaluate such an algorithm in a comparative study, we have also implemented the *all-unicast* and *randomized* tree construction algorithms as control. In the all-unicast algorithm, node B – or any node who is aware of the source of the session (e.g., from the *sAnnounce* message in iOverlay) – simply forwards the *sQuery* to the data source of the session. In the randomized algorithm, node B directly sends the *sQueryAck* acknowledgment to A, and A will join the tree on receiving the first such acknowledgment.

We first experiment with a five-node data dissemination session, shown in Fig. 5, in which the data source is deployed on node S, and nodes A – D joins the session in the order of D, A, C, and B. The figure has been annotated with the per-node available bandwidth, as well as the throughput that we have obtained in our experiments. The node degree and stress are summarized in Table 3. It is very clear that, with respect to end-to-end throughput, our new

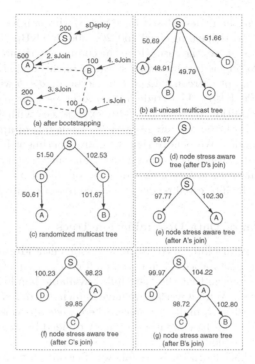

Fig. 5. Tree construction algorithms: throughput (in KBytes per second).

algorithm has the upper hand. We have also observed that the topology of the node stress aware tree is not *optimal*, there may be better trees with respect to throughput. For example, in Fig. 5(g), if D is a child of A rather than S, throughput may be further improved, leaving possibilities for further research. Such experiment-based insights would not be possible without the substrate that iOverlay provides.

In the next experiment, we choose to evaluate the performance and stress tolerance of the node stress aware algorithm in large-scale overlay networks, by deploying it to a total of 81 wide-area nodes in PlanetLab. The per-node available bandwidth has been specified to a uniform distribution of 50 to 200 KBps for all the nodes, with the source node set at 100 KBps. By taking advantage of the deployment scripts in iOverlay, we are able to deploy, run, terminate and collect data from all 81 nodes, with one command for each operation. Fig. 6 shows the North American portion of the wide-area topology after 30 nodes have joined the data dissemination session.

The results we have obtained from these PlanetLab experiments are illustrated in Fig. 7. With respect to node stress, we may observe that the node stress aware algorithm has managed to approach the ideal case (*i.e.*, the vertical line at node stress 20) much better than the other cases. With respect to end-to-end throughput, we may observe that the throughput is much higher with the node stress aware algorithm.

Table 3. Tree construction algorithms: node degree and stress.

Node	node degree			node stress (1/100 KBps)		
	unicast	random	ns-aware	unicast	random	ns-aware
S	4	2	2	2.0	1.0	1.0
A	1	1	3	0.2	0.2	0.6
B	1	1	1	1.0	0.98	0.97
C	1	2	1	0.5	1.0	0.51
D	1	2	1	1.0	1.98	1.0

Fig. 6. The real-time wide-area topology produced by the node stress aware algorithm after 30 nodes have joined (only nodes that reside in North America have been shown, some nodes may reside in the same geographical location).

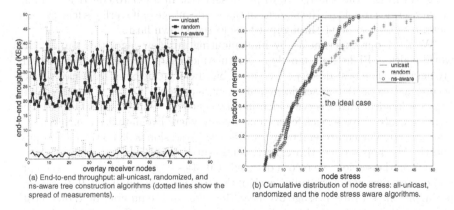

(a) End-to-end throughput: all-unicast, randomized, and ns-aware tree construction algorithms (dotted lines show the spread of measurements).

(b) Cumulative distribution of node stress: all-unicast, randomized and the node stress aware algorithms.

Fig. 7. Performance of the node stress aware algorithm using 81 wide-area nodes in PlanetLab. (a) end-to-end throughput; and (b) the cumulative distribution of node stress.

3.3   Service Federation in Service Overlay Networks

In some applications, data messages may need to be transformed (such as media or web data transcoding) by a series of third-party nodes (or *services*) before they reach their destinations. The process of provisioning a complex service by constructing a topology of a selected group of primitive services is known as *service federation* (or *composition*), within what is referred to as *service overlay networks* consisting of instances of primitive services. In order to start a service federation process, a specific *service requirement* needs to be specified, which includes the required primitive services in order to compose the federated service. As a case study, we have designed and implemented a new distributed algorithm, referred to as *sFlow*, to federate complex services that require service requirements in the generic form of directed acyclic graphs, with the aid of iOverlay and over a period of three weeks.

We outline the gist of the algorithm as follows. When a new service is established by the *sAssign* message from the observer, it locally maintains a *service graph* that represents the producer-consumer relationships among different types of services, and disseminates its existence to all its known hosts via the *sAware* message. The message is further relayed until an existing service node is reached, which forwards the message to the direct upstream and downstream nodes of the new service in its service graph. When a service federation session is started using the observer, the requirement for the complex service is specified in a *sFederate* message to the designated source service node. As this message is forwarded, each node applies a local algorithm to select the most bandwidth efficient downstream service node according to the requirement, until the sink service node is reached. The federation process is concluded with the deployment of actual data streams through the selected third-party services. In order to construct a high-quality service topology, the algorithm takes advantage of iOverlay's feature that measures point-to-point throughput to selected known hosts.

We start our experiments by implementing our new algorithm on 16 real-world nodes in PlanetLab, mostly in North America, to construct a service overlay network. The best-quality – *i.e.,* most bandwidth efficient – federated service according to a particular service requirement is presented in Fig. 8. Each node in Fig. 8 is labeled with a service identifier assigned to them by the observer. The edges indicate a live service federation session where live data streams are being transmitted. The end-to-end delay of this service session is 934.547 milliseconds, and the last hop average throughput is measured as 69374 bytes per second.

During the session, we record detailed statistics on bandwidth measurements and control message overhead on each of the 16 nodes, shown in Fig. 9. In this experiment, the sAware message overhead depends on the number of known hosts of each node, and the overhead of sFederate messages is sufficiently small, compared to that of sAware messages. The per-link and total per-node bandwidth are illustrated in Fig. 9(b) in descending order. Evidently, the overhead incurred by the algorithm is sufficiently small, and seven nodes are left untouched during the entire session of the protocol, since they do not host services or are not involved in the service federation process.

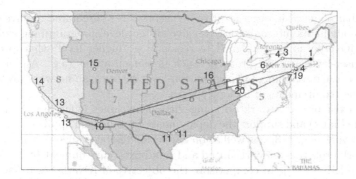

Fig. 8. The constructed complex service in a service overlay network.

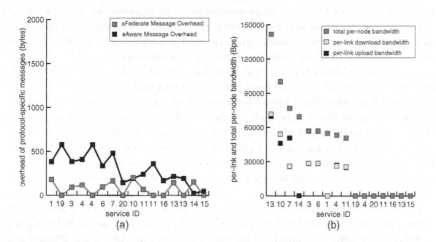

Fig. 9. Service federation: (a) control message overhead; (b) per-link and per-node bandwidth measurements on each of the overlay nodes. The overlay nodes are sorted by their per-node bandwidth availability.

4   Related Work

iOverlay was originally motivated by our own experiences of implementing distributed application implementations on overlays, when we have failed to locate a suitable middleware framework for such developments. The idea behind iOverlay originates from the *Flux OSKit* project [11] in operating system design, where a modular set of OS components are designed to be reusable, and to facilitate rapid development of experimental OS kernels. iOverlay provides a reusable set of components in the domain of overlay rather than OS implementations, and seeks to achieve similar design objectives that support rapid prototyping of new overlay-based distributed applications. Particularly, iOverlay is designed to minimize the bar of entry: in order for it to be useful, it is *not* required to have either knowledge about its internals, or extensive system-level programming skills. In addition, iOverlay is also designed to reside at a "higher level" than previous work on user-level network protocol stack implementations (e.g., Alpine [12]), and aims at the development of application-layer rather than network protocols, without the requirements of root privileges.

There exist previous work on using virtual machines (such as VMWare or User-Mode Linux) and support the deployment of full-fledged applications over a virtual network (e.g., [13]), as well as on emulation testbeds and environments to test network protocols in a virtualized and sandboxed environment (e.g., Netbed [8] and ModelNet [14]). In comparison, the objective of iOverlay is to facilitate the development of distributed applications and algorithms at the application layer, and iOverlay assumes the availability of a wide-area network testbed such as PlanetLab. Although iOverlay supports virtualizing multiple overlay nodes on a single physical node, all implementations are achieved at the user level beyond the abstraction of sockets. iOverlay is designed to be tightly coupled with applications and distributed algorithms, rather than a supporting infrastructure based on either virtual machines or emulation environments.

In particular, ModelNet [14] has introduced a set of ModelNet core nodes that serve as virtualized *kernel-level packet switches* with emulated bandwidth, latency and loss rates. Such kernel-level modifications may not be achievable in wide-area testbeds due to the lack of root privileges. The iOverlay engine, in contrast, implements *application-layer message switches*, that may be bundled with any new algorithms and deployed in the user space of any UNIX hosts. Thanks to the virtualization of iOverlay nodes, it is not required to have access to a large-scale network in order to experiment with large-scale application topologies.

To the best of our knowledge, there exist two previous papers that present similar objectives to iOverlay. First, the *PLUTO* project [15], an underlay topology service (or routing underlay) for overlay networks, based on PlanetLab. PLUTO is a layer between the overlay algorithms and the network, that exposes topological information to the algorithms. More specifically, it may expose information on connectivity, disjoint end-to-end paths between overlay nodes, as well as the distance between nodes in terms of a particular metric such as latency or router hops. We believe that iOverlay and PLUTO are completely *complementary* with each other, and that it is straightforward for the algorithm to simultaneously take advantage of both architectures. From the viewpoint of PLUTO, iOverlay is simply an overlay application. When it comes to measurement of metrics, iOverlay focuses on measuring the performance of active or potential overlay links, while PLUTO focuses on obtaining insights on the underlay physical topology. From this perspective, iOverlay operates at a higher level than PLUTO does, and PLUTO may be easily integrated into the overall iOverlay middleware architecture.

Second, the *Macedon* project [16] offers a common overlay network API by which any Macedon-created overlay implementation may be used. It features a new language to describe the behavior of an overlay algorithm, from which actual code can be generated using a code generator. As a result, Macedon allows algorithm designers to focus their attention on the algorithm itself, and less on tedious implementation details. Despite the similarities between the design objectives of Macedon and iOverlay, the design principles are drastically different. Macedon attempts to minimize the lines of code to be developed by the algorithm developer, by providing a new language to specify the characteristics of the algorithm. In contrast, iOverlay seeks to maximize the freedom and flexibility when designing new algorithms, by minimizing the API between the middleware and the application. While Macedon is able to support Distributed Hash Table based searching and overlay multicast algorithms, iOverlay is sufficiently generic to accommodate virtually any applications to be deployed on overlay networks, while still encapsulating tedious and common functional components such as message switching, throughput emulation, fault detection and recovery, as well as a centralized debugging facility. Our recent experiences of successfully and rapidly deploying a Windows-based MPEG-4 real-time streaming multicast application on iOverlay have verified our claims.

5   Concluding Remarks

We have been pleasantly surprised at how phenomenally rapidly one can develop fully distributed overlay applications using iOverlay. The evolution of features we have presented have been entirely demand-driven: rather than being designed *a priori*, with inevitably flawed vision of what new applications may need, iOverlay has been constantly refined and augmented, driven by the needs of new application implementations. From this experience, we conclude that research and implementation of overlay applications and algorithms are significantly aided by having reusable, extensible and customizable components that iOverlay provides. As a matter of fact, the burden on the application developer is completely shifted to the core portion of the application-specific algorithm, rather than subtle and mundane details that iOverlay has encapsulated. We are convinced that the full potential of iOverlay has yet to be realized. For example, the library of prefabricated algorithms may be significantly extended, in the form of new classes derived from the base *iAlgorithm* class. These new extensions may become foundations of similar categories of algorithms, which may further simplify the process of new application implementations. In addition, the PLUTO routing underlay may be integrated into the iOverlay framework as additional reusable components in the form of libraries, in order to support algorithms that need topological knowledge of the underlying IP topology.

References

1. Rowstron, A., Druschel, P.: Pastry: Scalable, distributed object location and routing for large-scale peer-to-peer systems. In: Proc. of IFIP/ACM International Conference on Distributed Systems Platforms (Middleware 2001). (2001)

2. Stoica, I., Morris, R., Karger, D., Kaashoek, F., Balakrishnan, H.: Chord: A Scalable Peer-to-Peer Lookup Service for Internet Applications. In: Proc. of ACM SIGCOMM. (2001)
3. Chu, Y., Rao, S.G., Seshan, S., Zhang, H.: A Case for End System Multicast. IEEE Journal on Selected Areas in Communications (2002) 1456–1471
4. Banerjee, S., Bhattacharjee, B., Kommareddy, C.: Scalable Application Layer Multicast. In: Proc. of ACM SIGCOMM. (2002)
5. Castro, M., Druschel, P., Kermarrec, A.M., Nandi, A., Rowstron, A., Singh, A.: SplitStream: High-Bandwidth Multicast in Cooperative Environments. In: Proc. of the 19th ACM Symposium on Operating Systems Principles (SOSP 2003). (2003)
6. Kostic, D., Rodriguez, A., Albrecht, J., Vahdat, A.: Bullet: High Bandwidth Data Dissemination Using an Overlay Mesh. In: Proc. of the 19th ACM Symposium on Operating Systems Principles (SOSP 2003). (2003)
7. Peterson, L., Anderson, T., Culler, D., Roscoe, T.: A Blueprint for Introducing Disruptive Technology into the Internet. In: Proc. of the First Workshop on Hot Topics in Networks (HotNets-I). (2002)
8. White, B., Lepreau, J., Stoller, L., Ricci, R., Guruprasad, S., Newbold, M., Hibler, M., Barb, C., Joglekar, A.: An Integrated Experimental Environment for Distributed Systems and Networks. In: Proc. of the Fifth Symposium on Operating Systems Design and Implementation (OSDI 2002), to appear. (2002)
9. Ahlswede, R., Cai, N., Li, S.Y.R., Yeung, R.W.: Network Information Flow. IEEE Trans. on Information Theory IT-46 (2000) 1204–1216
10. Wang, M., Li, Z., Li, B.: A Case for Coded Overlay Flows. Technical report, Department of Electrical and Computer Engineering, University of Toronto, submitted for review to IEEE INFOCOM 2005 (2004) http://iqua.ece.toronto.edu/papers/case-coding.pdf.
11. Ford, B., Back, G., Benson, G., Lepreau, J., Lin, A., Shivers, O.: The Flux OSKit: A Substrate for Kernel and Language Research. In: Proc. of the 16th ACM Symposium on Operating Systems Principles (SOSP 1997). (1997)
12. Ely, D., Savage, S., Wetherall, D.: Alpine: A User-Level Infrastructure for Network Protocol Development. In: Proc. of the the 2001 USENIX Symposium on Internet Technologies and Systems (USITS 2001). (2001)
13. Jiang, X., Xu, D.: vBET: a VM-Based Emulation Testbed. In: Proc. of ACM Workshop on Models, Methods and Tools for Reproducible Network Research (MoMeTools 2003). (2003)
14. Vahdat, A., Yocum, K., Walsh, K., Mahadevan, P., Kostic, D., Chase, J., Becker, D.: Scalability and Accuracy in a Large-Scale Network Emulator. In: Proc. of 5th Symposium on Operating Systems Design and Implementation (OSDI 2002). (2002)
15. Nakao, A., Peterson, L., Bavier, A.: A Routing Underlay for Overlay Networks. In: Proc. of SIGCOMM 2003. (2003)
16. Rodriguez, A., Killian, C., Bhat, S., Kostic, D., Vahdat, A.: MACEDON: Methodology for Automatically Creating, Evaluating, and Designing Overlay Networks. In: Proc. of the USENIX/ACM Symposium on Networked Systems Design and Implementation (NSDI 2004). (2004)

Ganymed: Scalable Replication
for Transactional Web Applications

Christian Plattner and Gustavo Alonso

Department of Computer Science
Swiss Federal Institute of Technology (ETHZ)
ETH Zentrum, CH-8092 Zürich, Switzerland
{plattner,alonso}@inf.ethz.ch

Abstract. Data grids, large scale web applications generating dynamic content and database service providing pose significant scalability challenges to database engines. Replication is the most common solution but it involves difficult trade-offs. The most difficult one is the choice between scalability and consistency. Commercial systems give up consistency. Research solutions typically either offer a compromise (limited scalability in exchange for consistency) or impose limitations on the data schema and the workload. In this paper we introduce Ganymed, a database replication middleware intended to provide scalability without sacrificing consistency and avoiding the limitations of existing approaches. The main idea is to use a novel transaction scheduling algorithm that separates update and read-only transactions. Transactions can be submitted to Ganymed through a special JDBC driver. Ganymed then routes updates to a main server and queries to a potentially unlimited number of read-only copies. The system guarantees that all transactions see a consistent data state (snapshot isolation). In the paper we describe the scheduling algorithm, the architecture of Ganymed, and present an extensive performance evaluation that proves the potential of the system.

1 Introduction

Traditionally used in predictable and static environments like ERP (Enterprise Resource Planning), data-base management systems had to face new challenges in the last few years. Web services, application service providing and grid computing require higher scalability and availability. Database replication is widely used to achieve those goals. The problem with replication is that existing commercial solutions do not behave like single instance databases. Often, a choice must be made between scalability and consistency. If full consistency is required, the price is a loss in scalability [1].

Recent research in the area of Transactional Web Applications has led to many alternative proposals, but they all suffer from a variety of problems. Systems that put data on the edge of the network, [2,3,4], are able to reduce response times but give up consistency. Other approaches, [5, 6, 7], work on the middleware layer and need a predeclaration of the access pattern of all transactions to

H.-A. Jacobsen (Ed.): Middleware 2004, LNCS 3231, pp. 155–174, 2004.

enable efficient scheduling. [8] offers both scalability and consistency, however the database designer is forced to partition the data statically. This forbids certain queries and restricts the free evolution of the application. In this system, a reasonable scale-out is possible only if the load conforms exactly to the chosen data partition.

This paper describes Ganymed, a middleware based system designed to address such problems. The system is able to offer both scalability and consistency without having to partition the data or declaring/extracting the transaction access pattern. Ganymed does not impose any restrictions on the queries submitted and does not duplicate work of the underlying database engines. The main component of Ganymed is a lightweight scheduler that routes transactions to a set of snapshot isolation [9, 10, 11] based replicas by using RSI-PC, a novel scheduling algorithm. The key idea behind RSI-PC is the separation of update and read-only transactions. Updates will always be routed to a main replica, whereas the remaining transactions are handled by any of the remaining replicas, which act as read-only copies. The RSI-PC approach is tailored to dynamic content generation (as modelled in the TPC-W benchmark) and database service providing, where a vast amount of complex reads is conducted together with a small number of short update transactions. RSI-PC makes sure that all transactions see a consistent data state, inconsistencies between the replicas are hidden from the clients. A JDBC driver enables client applications to be connected to the Ganymed scheduler, thereby offering a standardized interface to the system.

The evaluation presented in the paper shows that Ganymed offers almost linear scalability. The scalability manifests itself both as increased throughput as well as reduced response times. In addition, Ganymed significantly increases the availability of the system. In the experiments we show the graceful degradation properties of Ganymed as well as the ability to migrate the main replica as needed.

The paper is structured as follows: first, we describe the RSI-PC scheduling algorithm and the middleware architecture of Ganymed. The system overview is followed by an evaluation of our working Java based prototype. The paper concludes with a discussion of related and future work.

2   Motivation

Database replication is the process of maintaining multiple copies of data items on different locations called replicas. As already noted, the motivation for doing this is twofold. First, the availability can be increased since the database system can better tolerate failures. Second, the systems's throughput can be increased and response times can be lowered by distributing the transaction load across the replicas.

Traditionally, there are two types of replication system: *eager* and *lazy* [1]. Eager (or *synchronous*) systems keep the replicas synchronized within transaction boundaries. They conform to *1-copy-serializability* [12]: the resulting schedules are equivalent to a serial schedule on a single database. Although eager systems offer the same correctness guarantees as single-database installations, the concept is rarely used in commercial replication products. This stems from the fact that conventional eager protocols have significant drawbacks regarding performance and scalability [1, 12, 13, 14]: first, the communication overhead between the replicas is very high, leading to long response times, and second, the probability of deadlocks is proportional to the third power of number of replicas. Such traditional eager implementations are not able to scale beyond a few replicas. To circumvent these problems, database designers started creating lazy systems, in which replicas can be updated outside the transaction boundaries. As already noted, lazy replication scales very well, but leads to new problems: transactions can read stale data and conflicts between updating transactions are possibly detected very late, introducing the need for conflict resolution. Unfortunately, these problems cannot easily be hidden from the user, and must often be resolved by the client application.

The unsatisfactory properties of lazy protocols have led to a continuation in the research on eager protocols [5, 6, 15, 16]. An important result [15] is the insight that the distribution of full SQL update statements, as often done in eager update-everywhere approaches, is not optimal. Performance can be significantly improved by executing SQL statements only once and then propagating the resulting database changes (so called *writesets*) to other replicas.

The approach in Ganymed tries to combine the advantages of lazy and eager strategies. Ganymed uses a set of fully replicated databases. Internally, Ganymed works in a lazy way, not all replicas are updated inside transaction boundaries. For efficiency, the replication process is writeset based. Nevertheless, by working at the middleware layer the system is able to offer an eager service. In addition, Ganymed transparently takes care of configuration changes, failing replicas, migration of nodes, etc.

3   The RSI-PC Scheduling Algorithm

In this section we present our novel RSI-PC scheduling algorithm. RSI-PC stands for *Replicated Snapshot Isolation with Primary Copy*. It can be used to schedule transactions over a set of *Snapshot Isolation* based database replicas. RSI-PC works by separating read-only and update transactions and sending them to different replicas: updates are sent to a master replica (the primary copy), reads are sent to any of the other replicas, which act as caches. To the clients, the scheduler looks like a snapshot isolation database. Temporary inconsistencies between the replicas are hidden from the client by the scheduler, all synchronization is done transparently. The RSI-PC approach fits exactly the needs of typical dynamic content generation, where a vast amount of complex reads is conducted by a small number of short update transactions.

3.1   Snapshot Isolation

Snapshot Isolation (SI) [9, 10] is a multiversion concurrency control mechanism used in databases. Popular database engines that use SI include Oracle [17] and

PostgreSQL [18]. One of the most important properties of SI is the fact that readers are never blocked by writers, similar to the multiversion protocol in [12]. This property is a big win in comparison to systems that use two *two phase locking* (2PL), where many non-conflicting updaters may be blocked by as simply as one reader. SI completely avoids the four extended ANSI SQL phenomenas P0-P3 described in [9], nevertheless it does not guarantee serializability. As shown in [19, 20] this is not a problem in real applications, since transaction programs can be arranged in ways so that any concurrent execution of the resulting transactions is equivalent to a serialized execution.

For the purposes of this paper, we will work with the following definition of SI (slightly more formalized than the description in [9]):

SI: A transaction T_i that is executed under snapshot isolation gets assigned a start timestamp $start(T_i)$ which reflects the starting time. This timestamp is used to define a snapshot S_i for transaction T_i. The snapshot S_i consists of the latest committed values of all objects of the database at the time $start(T_i)$. Every read operation issued by transaction T_i on a database object x is mapped to a read of the version of x which is included in the snapshot S_i. Updated values by write operations of T_i (which make up the *writeset* WS_i of T_i) are also integrated into the snapshot S_i, so that they can be read again if the transaction accesses updated data. Updates issued by transactions that did not commit before $start(T_i)$ are invisible to the transaction T_i. When transaction T_i tries to commit, it gets assigned a commit timestamp $commit(T_i)$, which has to be larger than any other existing start timestamp or commit timestamp. Transaction T_i can only successfully commit if there exists no other committed transaction T_k having a commit timestamp $commit(T_k)$ in the interval $\{start(T_i), commit(T_i)\}$ and $WS_k \cap WS_i \neq \{\}$. If such a committed transaction T_k exists, then T_i has to be aborted (this is called the *first-commiter-wins* rule, which is used to prevent lost updates). If no such transaction exists, then T_i can commit (WS_i gets applied to the database) and its updates are visible to transactions which have a start timestamp which is larger than $commit(T_i)$.

A sample execution of transactions running on a database offering SI is given in 1. The symbols B, C and A refer to the *begin, commit* and *abort* of a transaction. The long running transaction T_1 is of type $read - only$, i.e., its writeset is empty: $WS_1 = \{\}$. T_1 will never be blocked by any other other transaction, nor will it block other transactions. Updates from concurrent updaters (like T_2, T_3, T_4 and T_6) are invisible to T_1. T_2 will update the database element X, it does not conflict with any other transaction. T_3 updates Y, it does not see the changes made by T_2, since it started while T_2 was still running. T_4 updates X and Y. Conforming to the first-committer-wins rule it cannot commit, since its writeset overlaps with that from T_3 and T_3 committed while T_4 was running. The transaction manager has therefore to abort T_4. T_5 is read-only and sees the changes made by T_2 and T_3. T_6 can successfully update Y. Due to the fact

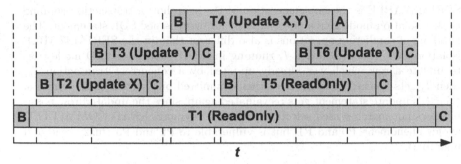

Fig. 1. An example of transactions running under SI.

that T_4 did not commit, the overlapping writesets of T_6 and T_4 do not impose a conflict.

As will be shown in the next section, practical systems handle the comparison of writesets and the first-committer-wins rule in a different, more efficient way. Both, Oracle and PostgreSQL, offer two different ANSI SQL isolation levels for transactions: SERIALIZABLE and READ COMMITTED. An extended discussion regarding ANSI SQL isolation levels is given in [9].

3.2 The SERIALIZABLE Isolation Level

Oracle and PostgreSQL implement a variant of the SI algorithm for transactions that run in the isolation level SERIALIZABLE. Writesets are not compared at the commit time of transactions, instead this process is done progressively by using row level write locks. When a transaction T_i running in isolation level SERIALIZABLE tries to modify a row in a table that was modified by a concurrent transaction T_k which has already committed, then the current update operation of T_i gets aborted immediately. Unlike PostgreSQL, which then aborts the whole transaction T_i, Oracle is a little bit more flexible: it allows the user to decide if he wants to commit the work done so far or if he wants to proceed with other operations in T_i. If T_k is concurrent but not committed yet, then both products behave the same: they block transaction T_i until T_k commits or aborts. If T_k commits, then the same procedure gets involved as described before, if however T_k aborts, then the update operation of T_i can proceed. The blocking of a transaction due to a potential update conflict is of course not unproblematic since it can lead to deadlocks, which must be resolved by the database by aborting transactions.

3.3 The READ COMMITTED Isolation Level

Both databases offer also a slightly less strict isolation level called READ COMMITTED, which is based on a variant of snapshot isolation. READ COMMITTED is the default isolation level for both products. The main difference to

SERIALIZABLE is the implementation of the snapshot: a transaction running in this isolation mode gets a new snapshot for every issued SQL statement. The handling of conflicting operations is also different than in the SERIALIZABLE isolation level. If a transaction T_i running in READ COMMITTED mode tries to update a row which was already updated by a concurrent transaction T_k, then T_i gets blocked until T_k has either committed or aborted. If T_k commits, then T_i's update statement gets reevaluated again, since the updated row possibly does not match a used selection predicate anymore. READ COMMITTED avoids phenomena P0 and P1, but is vulnerable to P2 and P3 (fuzzy read and phantom).

3.4   RSI-PC Definition

Schedulers implementing the RSI-PC algorithm can be used with SI based replicas that offer the transaction isolation levels SERIALIZABLE and READ COMMITTED as defined above. For incoming update transactions, RSI-PC is able to support the SERIALIZABLE and READ COMMITTED transaction isolation levels. Read-only transactions always have to be run in isolation mode SERIALIZABLE, therefore they the see the same snapshot during the whole transaction.

> **RSI-PC:** A RSI-PC scheduler is responsible for a set of n SI-based replicas. One of the replicas is used as *master*, the other $n - 1$ replicas are the *slaves*. The scheduler makes a clear distinction between *read-only* and *update* transactions, which have to be marked by the client application in advance.
>
> **Update transactions:** b_i, $r_j(x)$, $w_j(x)$ and c_i statements of any arriving update transaction are directly forwarded to the master (including their mode, SERIALIZABLE or READ COMMITTED), they are never delayed. The scheduler takes notice of the order in which update transactions commit on the master. After a successful commit of an update transaction, the scheduler makes sure that the corresponding write set is sent to the $n - 1$ slaves and that every slave applies the write sets of different transactions in the same order as the corresponding commit occurred on the master replica. The scheduler uses also the notation of a global database version number. Whenever an update transaction commits on the master, the global database version number is increased by one and the client gets notified about the commit. Write sets get tagged by the version number which was created by the corresponding update transaction.
>
> **Read-only transactions:** read-only transactions can be processed by any replica in SERIALIZABLE mode. The scheduler is free to decide on which replica to execute such a transaction. If on a chosen replica the latest produced global database version is not yet available, the scheduler must delay the creation of the read-only snapshot until all needed write sets have been applied to the replica. For clients that are not willing to accept any delays for read-only transactions there are two choices:

either their queries are sent to the master replica, therefore reducing the available capacity for updates, or the client can set a staleness threshold. A staleness threshold is for example a maximum age of the requested snapshot in seconds (similar as proposed in [21]) or the condition that the client sees its own updates. The scheduler can then use this threshold to choose a replica. Once the scheduler has chosen a replica and the replica created a snapshot, all consecutive operations of the read-only transaction will be performed using that snapshot. Due to the nature of SI, the application of further write sets on this replica will not conflict with this or any other running read-only transaction.

Due to its simplicity, there is no risk of a RSI-PC scheduler becoming the bottleneck in the system. In contrast to other middleware based schedulers, like the ones used in [5,8], this scheduling algorithm does not involve any SQL statement parsing or concurrency control operations. Also, no row or table level locking is done at the scheduler level. The detection of conflicts, which by definition of SI can only happen during updates, is left to the SI database running on the master replica. Moreover, (unlike [7,8]), RSI-PC does not make any assumptions about the transactional load, the data partition, organization of the schema, or answerable and unanswerable queries.

Since only a small amount of state information must be kept by a RSI-PC scheduler, it is even possible to construct parallel working schedulers. This helps to improve the overall fault tolerance. In contrast to traditional eager systems, where every replica has its own scheduler that is aware of the global state, the exchange of status information between a small number of RSI-PC schedulers can be done very efficiently. Even in the case that all schedulers fail, it is possible to reconstruct the overall database state: a replacement scheduler can be used and its state initialized by inspecting all available replicas.

In the case of failing slave replicas, the scheduler simply ignores them until they have been repaired by an administrator. However, in the case of a failing master, things are a little bit more complicated. By just electing a new master the problem is only halfway solved. The scheduler must also make sure that no updates from committed transactions get lost, thereby guaranteeing ACID durability. This goal can be achieved by only sending commit notifications to clients after the writesets of update transactions have successfully been applied on a certain, user defined amount of replicas.

4   Ganymed Middleware Architecture

The main component of Ganymed is a lightweight middleware scheduler which balances transactions from clients over a set of SI based database replicas. Clients are typically application servers in e-commerce environments. From the viewpoint of such clients, the Ganymed scheduler behaves like a single SI based database. We have implemented a working prototype of the system using Java. Figure 2 shows the main components of the architecture. Applications servers connect to the Ganymed scheduler through a custom JDBC driver. The Ganymed

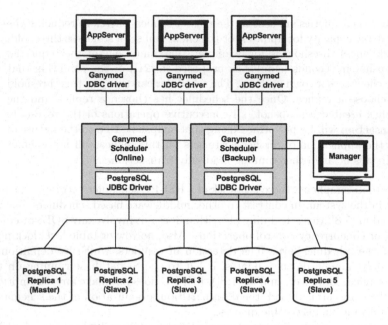

Fig. 2. Ganymed Prototype Architecture.

scheduler, implementing the RSI-PC algorithm, then distributes incoming transactions over the master and slave replicas. Replicas can be added and removed
from the system at runtime. The master role can be assigned dynamically, for
example when the master replica fails. The current prototype does not support
parallel working schedulers, yet it is not vulnerable to failures of the scheduler. If
a Ganymed scheduler fails, it will immediately be replaced by a standby scheduler. The decision for a scheduler to be replaced by a backup has to be made
by the manager component. The manager component, running on a dedicated
machine, constantly monitors the system. The manager component is also responsible for reconfigurations. It is used, e.g., by the database administrator to
add and remove replicas. Interaction with the manager component takes place
through a graphical interface. In the following sections we describe each component in more detail.

4.1   Client Interface

Clients connect to the scheduler through the Ganymed JDBC database driver.
The availability of such a standard database interface makes it straightforward
to connect Java based application servers (like BEA Weblogic[1] or JBoss[2]) to
Ganymed. The migration from a centralized database to a Ganymed environment

---

[1] http://www.bea.com
[2] http://www.jboss.org

is very simple, only the JDBC driver component in the application server has to be reconfigured, there is no change in the application code. Our driver also supports a certain level of fault tolerance. If a configured Ganymed scheduler is not reachable, the driver automatically tries to connect to an alternate scheduler by using a client side configurable list of possible schedulers.

Since the scheduler needs to know if a transaction is an update or read-only, the application code has to communicate this to the Ganymed JDBC driver. This mechanism is already included in the JDBC standard. Application code that wants to start a read-only transaction simply calls the *Connection.setReadonly()* method. If an application programmer forgets to insert such a call, consistency is still guaranteed, but reduced performance will result due to the increased load on the master replica.

4.2   Replica Support and Writeset Handling

On the replica side, Ganymed currently supports PostgreSQL and Oracle database engines. This allows to build heterogenous setups, where replicas run different engines. Also, our approach is not limited to a specific operating system. As in the client side, the communication with the replicas is done through JDBC drivers. In a heterogenous configuration, the Ganymed scheduler has therefore to load for every different type of replica the corresponding JDBC driver. Since this can be done dynamically at run time, on startup the scheduler does not need to be aware of the type of replicas added at runtime.

Unfortunately, the JDBC interface has no support for writeset extraction, which is needed on the master replica. In the case of PostgreSQL, we implemented an extension of the database software. PostgreSQL is very flexible, it supports the loading of additional functionality during runtime. Our extension consists of a shared library which holds the necessary logic to collect changes of update transactions in the database. Internally, the tracking of updates is done using triggers. To avoid another interface especially for the writeset handling, the extension was designed to be controlled over the normal JDBC interface. For instance, the extraction of a writeset can be performed with a *"SELECT writeset()"* SQL query. The extracted writesets are table row based, they do not contain full disk blocks. This ensures that they can be applied on a replica which uses another low level disk block layout than the master replica.

In the case of Oracle, such an extension can be built in a similar manner.

4.3   RSI-PC Implementation

The Ganymed scheduler implements the RSI-PC algorithm. Although feasible, loose consistency models (like those in [21]) are not supported in the current version. The scheduler always provides strong consistency. Read-only transactions will always see the latest snapshot of the database. The scheduler also makes a strict distinction between the master and the slave replicas. Even if there is free capacity on the master, read-only transactions are always assigned to a slave

replica. This ensures that the master is not loaded by complex read-only transactions and that there is always enough capacity on the master for sudden bursts
of updates. If there is no slave replica present, the scheduler is forced to assign
all transactions to the master replica, acting as a relay.

As already noted, implementing RSI-PC does not involve any SQL parsing
and table locking at the middleware layer. In some regards, Ganymed resembles
more a router than a scheduler. Incoming transactions result in a decisions step:
to which replica they must be sent. In the case of updates, this is always the
master. Read-only transactions are assigned to a valid replica according to the
LPRF (*least pending requests first*) rule. Valid means in this context, that the
replica must contain the latest produced writeset. If no such replica exists, the
start of the transaction is delayed.

For every replica, Ganymed keeps a pool of open connections. After an incoming transaction has been assigned to a replica, the scheduler uses a connection
from the replica's pool to forward the SQL statements of that transaction. Every
connection is used for a single transaction, connections are never shared. Also,
once a transaction is assigned to a connection, this assignment will not change. If
a pool is exhausted, Ganymed opens new connections until a per replica limit is
reached, at that point arriving transaction are blocked. After a transaction commits or aborts, the assigned connection is returned to the pool of the respective
replica. Unlike solutions using group communication [7, 15] Ganymed does not
require that transactions are submitted as a block, i.e., the entire transaction
must be present for it to be scheduled. In Ganymed different SQL statements of
the same transaction are progressively scheduled as they arrive, with the scheduler ensuring that the result is always consistent.

To achieve a consistent state between all replicas, the scheduler must make
sure that writesets of update transactions get applied on all replicas in the same
order. This already imposes a problem when writesets are generated on the
master, since the scheduler must be sure about the correct commit order of
transactions. Ganymed solves this problem by sending COMMIT operations to
the master in a serialized fashion. The distribution of writesets is handled by
having a FIFO update queue for every replica. There is also for every replica
a thread in the scheduler software that applies constantly the contents of that
queue to its assigned replica. Clearly, the distribution of writesets for a large set
of replicas in a star configuration is not optimal. A concrete optimization would
be to have the replicas directly receiving writesets from the master, e.g. similar
to the Oracle STREAMS [22] feature.

4.4   Manager Console

The manager console is responsible for monitoring the Ganymed system. On the
one hand, it includes a permanently running process which monitors the load of
the system and the failure of components. On the other hand it is used by the
administrator to perform configuration changes.

While the failure of replicas can directly be handled by the scheduler (failed
replicas are just discarded, failed masters are replaced by a slave replica), the

failure of a scheduler is more critical. In the event that a scheduler fails, the monitor process in the manager console will detect this and is responsible for starting a backup scheduler. Client side Ganymed JDBC drivers will also detect the failure and try to find a working scheduler according to their configuration. Assuming fail stop behavior, the connections between the failing scheduler and all replicas will be closed, all running transactions will be aborted by the assigned replicas. The manager will then inspect all replicas, elect a master and configure the new scheduler so that transaction processing can continue. The inspection of a replica involves the detection of the last applied writeset, which can be done by the same software implementing the writeset extraction.

The manager console is also used by administrators that need to change the set of attached replicas to a scheduler, or need to reactivate disable replicas. While the removal of a replica is a relatively simple task, the attachment or re-enabling of a replica is a more challenging task. Syncing-in a replica is actually performed by copying the state of a running replica to the new one. At the scheduler level, the writeset queue of the source replica is also duplicated and assigned to the destination replica. Since the copying process uses a SERIALIZABLE read-only transaction on the source replica, there is no need for shutting it down during the duplicating process. The new replica cannot be used to serve transactions until the whole copying process is over. Its writeset queue, which grows during the copy process, will be applied as soon as the copying has finished. Although from the viewpoint of performance this is not optimal, in the current prototype the whole copying process is done by the scheduler under the control of the manager console.

5   Experimental Evaluation

To verify the validity of our approach we performed several tests. First, we did extensive scalability measurements by comparing the performance of different Ganymed configurations with a single PostgreSQL instance. We used a load generator that simulates the transaction traffic of a TPC-W application server. Second, we tested the behavior of Ganymed in scenarios where replicas are failing. The failure of both, slaves and masters, was investigated.

5.1   TPC-W Traces

The TPC benchmark W (TPC-W) is a transactional web benchmark from the Transaction Processing Council [23]. TPC-W defines an internet commerce environment that resembles real world, business oriented, transactional web applications. The benchmark also defines different types of workloads which are intended to stress different components in such applications (namely multiple on-line browser sessions, dynamic page generation with database access, update of consistent web objects, simultaneous execution of multiple transaction types, a backend database with many tables with a variety of sizes and relationships, transaction integrity (ACID) and contention on data access and update). The workloads are as follows: primarily shopping (WIPS), browsing (WIPSb) and web-based ordering (WIPSo). The difference between the different workloads is the ratio of browse to buy: WIPSb consists of 95% read-only interactions, for WIPS the ratio is 80% and for WIPSo the ratio is 50%. WIPS, being the primary workload, it is considered the most representative one.

For the evaluation of Ganymed we generated database transaction traces with a running TPC-W installation. We used an open source implementation [24] that had to be changed to support a PostgreSQL backend database. Although the specification allows the use of loose consistency models, we did not make use of that. Our implementation is based on strong consistency. The TPC-W scaling parameters were chosen as follows: 10.000 items, 288.000 customers and the number of EB's was set to 100.

Traces were then generated for the three different TPC-W workloads: *shopping mix* (a trace file based on the WIPS workload), *browsing mix* (based on WIPSb) and *ordering mix* (based on WIPSo). Each trace consists of 50'000 consecutive transactions.

5.2   The Load Generator

The load generator is Java based. Once started, it loads a trace file into memory and starts parallel database connections using the configured JDBC driver. After all connections are established, transactions are read from the in-memory tracefile and then fed into the database. Once a transaction has finished on a connection, the load generator assigns the next available transaction from the trace to the connection.

For the length of the given measurement interval, the number of processed transactions and the average response time of transactions are measured. Also, to enable the creation of histograms, every second the current number of processed transactions and their status (committed/aborted) is recorded.

5.3   Experimental Setup

For the experiments, a pool of machines had to be used to host the different parts of the Ganymed system. For every component (load generator, scheduler, database replicas) of the system, a dedicated machine was used. All machines had the same configuration (Dual AMD Athlon 1400 MHz CPU, 1 GB RAM, 80 GB IBM Deskstar harddisk, Linux kernel 2.4.20, PostgreSQL 7.4.1, Blackdown-1.4.2-rc1 Java 2 Platform). All machines were connected through a 100 MBit Ethernet LAN.

Before starting any experiment, all databases were always reset to an initial state. Also, the PostgreSQL *VACUUM FULL ANALYZE* command was executed. This ensured that every experiment started from the same state.

In the experiments, we did not use a manager console or a backup Ganymed scheduler. The scheduler was always configured with automatic generated configuration scripts. Also, for update transactions, the Ganymed scheduler was always configured to report a transaction as committed to the client as soon as

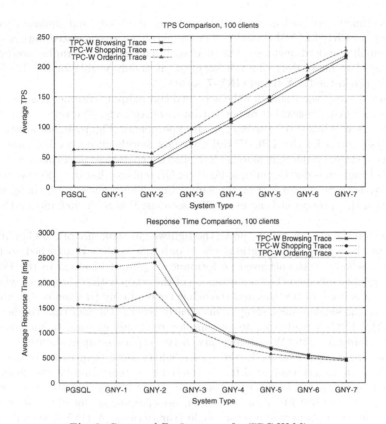

Fig. 3. Ganymed Performance for TPC-W Mixes.

the commit was successful on the master replica. In theory, this could rise the small possibility of a lost update in case the scheduler fails. The detection of a failed scheduler is outside of the scope of this evaluation.

5.4 Part 1: Performance and Scalability

The first part of the evaluation analyzes performance and scalability. The Ganymed prototype was compared with a reference system consisting of a single PostgreSQL instance. We measured the performance of the Ganymed scheduler in different configurations, from 1 up to 7 replicas. This gives a total of 8 experimental setups (called PGSQL and GNY-n, $1 \leq n \leq 7$), each setup was tested with the three different TPC-W traces.

The load generator was then attached to the database (either the single instance database or the scheduler, depending on the experiment). During a measurement interval of 100 seconds, a trace was then fed into the system over 100 parallel client connections and at the same time average throughput and response times were measured. All transactions, read-only and updates, were executed in SERIALIZABLE mode. Every experiment was repeated until a sufficient, small standard deviation was reached (included in the graphs, however, the attained standard deviation was very low, it is only visible for the TPC-W ordering mix in the GNY-6 and GNY-7 setups.).

Figure 3 shows the results for the achieved throughput (transactions per second) and average transaction response times, respectively. The rate of aborted transactions was below 0.5 percent for all experiments. Figure 4 shows two example histograms for the TPC-W ordering mix workload: on the left side the reference system, on the right side GNY-7. The sharp drop in performance in the GNY-7 histogram is due to multiple PostgreSQL replicas that did checkpointing of the WAL (*write ahead log*) at the same time. The replicas were configured to perform this process at least every 300 seconds, this is the default for PostgreSQL.

Based on the graphs, we can prove the lightweight structure of the Ganymed prototype. In a relay configuration, where only one replica is attached to the Ganymed scheduler, the achieved performance is almost identical to the PostgreSQL reference system. The performance of the setup with two replicas, where one replica is used for updates and the other for read-only transactions, is comparable to the single replica setup. This clearly reflects the fact that the heavy part of the TPC-W loads consists of complex read-only queries. In the case of the write intensive TPC-W ordering mix, a two replica setup is slightly slower than the single replica setup. In the setups where more than two replicas are used, the performance compared to the reference system could be significantly improved. A close look at the response times chart shows that they converge. This is due to the RSI-PC algorithm which uses parallelism for different transactions, but no intra-parallelism for single transactions. A GNY-7 system, for example, would have the same performance as a GNY-1 system when used only by a single client.

One can summarize that in almost all cases a nearly linear scale-out was achieved. These experiments show that the Ganymed scheduler was able to attain an impressive increase in throughput and reduction of transaction latency while maintaining the strongest possible consistency level.

It must be noted that in our setup all replicas were identical. By having more specialized index structures on the non-master replicas the execution of read-only transactions could be optimized even more. We are exploiting this option as part of future work.

5.5   Part 2: Reaction to a Failing Slave Replica

In this experiment, the schedulers reaction to a failing slave replica was investigated. A GNY-4 system was configured and the load generator was attached with the TPC-W shopping mix trace.

After the experiment run for a while, one of the the slave replicas was stopped, by killing the PostgreSQL processes with a kill (*SIGKILL*) signal. It must be emphasized that this is different from the usage of a *SIGTERM* signal, since in

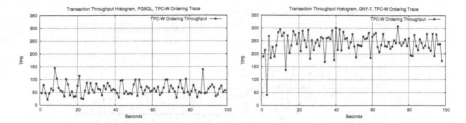

Fig. 4. Example histograms for the TPC-W Ordering Mix.

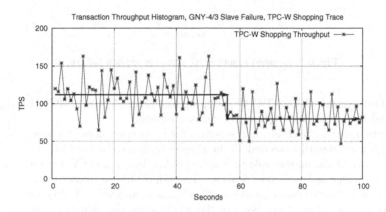

Fig. 5. Ganymed reacting to a slave replica failure.

that case the PostgreSQL software would have had a chance to catch the signal and shutdown gracefully.

Figure 5 shows the generated histogram for this experiment. In second 56, a slave replica was killed as described above. The failure of the slave replica led to an abort rate of 39 read-only transactions in second 56, otherwise no transaction was aborted in this run. The arrows in the graph show the change of the average transaction throughput per second. Clearly, the system's performance degraded to that of a GNY-3 setup. As can be seen from the graph, the system recovered immediately. Transactions running on the failing replica were aborted, but otherwise the system continued working normally. This is a consequence of the lightweight structure of the Ganymed scheduler approach: if a replica fails, no costly consensus protocols have to be executed. The system just continues working with the remaining replicas.

5.6   Part 3: Reaction to a Failing Master Replica

In the last experiment, the schedulers behavior in case of a failing master replica was investigated. As in the previous experiment, the basic configuration was a

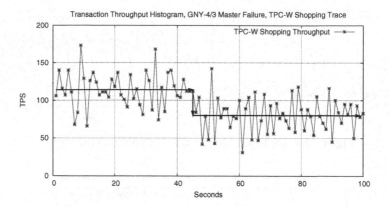

Fig. 6. Ganymed reacting to a master replica failure.

GNY-4 system fed with a TPC-W shopping mix trace. Again, a SIGKILL signal
was used to stop PostgreSQL on the master replica.

Figure 6 shows the resulting histogram for this experiment. Transaction processing is normal until in second 45 the master replica stops working. The immediately move of the master role to a slave replica leaves a GNY-3 configuration
with one master and two slave replicas. The failure of the master replica led to
an abort of 2 update transactions, no other transactions were aborted during the
experiment. As before, the arrows in the graph show the change of the average
transaction throughput per second.

This experiment shows that Ganymed is also capable of handling failing master replicas. The system reacts by reassigning the master role to a different, still
working slave replica. It is important to note that the reaction to failing replicas
can be done by the scheduler without intervention from the manager console.
Even with a failed or otherwise unavailable manager console the scheduler can
still disable failed replicas and, if needed, move the master role autonomously.

6   Related Work

Work in Ganymed has been mainly influenced by C-JDBC [8], an open source
database cluster middleware that can be accessed by any Java application that
uses the supplied JDBC driver. C-JDBC is a general replication tool, the only
assumption it makes about the database replicas is accessibility through a vendor
supplied JDBC driver. The downside of this approach is the need for duplicating
logic from the backend databases into the middleware, since JDBC does not
supply mechanisms to achieve a fine grained control over a replica. An example
for this is *locking*, which has to be done at the middleware level by parsing
the incoming statements and then doing table-level locking. Another example
are writesets, since these are not supported by JDBC, the middleware has to
broadcast SQL update statements to all replicas. When encountering peaks of

updates, this leads to a situation where every replica has to evaluate the same update statements. Ganymed behaves differently under such loads: all update statements go to the master, freeing capacity on the read-only replicas since these install only the resulting writesets. To circumvent these scalability problems, C-JDBC offers also the partition of the data on the backend replicas in various ways (called *RAIDb-levels*, in analogy to the RAID concept). As already noted, static partitions of data restrict the queries that can be executed.

Distributed versioning is an approach introduced in [5]. Again, the key idea is to use a middleware based scheduler which accepts transactions from clients and routes them to a set of replicas. The main idea is the bookkeeping of *versions* of tables in all the replicas. Every transaction that updates a table increases the corresponding version number. At the beginning of every transaction, clients have to inform the scheduler about the tables they are going to access. The scheduler then uses this information to assign versions of tables to the transactions. Similar to the C-JDBC approach, SQL statements have to be parsed to be able to do locking at the scheduler level. Also, replicas are kept in sync by sending the full SQL update statements. Since table level locking reduces concurrency, distributed versioning also introduces the concept of *early version releases*. This allows clients to notify the scheduler when they have used a table for the last time in a transaction.

Group communication has been proposed for use in replicated database systems [16, 25, 26], however only a few working prototypes are available. Postgres-R [15] is an implementation of such a system, based on a modified version of PostgreSQL (v. 6.4.2). The clear advantage of these approaches is the avoidance of centralized components. Unfortunately, in case of bursts of update traffic, this becomes a disadvantage, since the system is busy resolving conflicts between the replicas. In the worst case, such systems are slower than a single instance database and throughput increases at the cost of a higher response time. A solution to the problem of high conflict rates in group communication systems is the partition of the load [7]. In this approach, although all replicas hold the complete data set, update transaction cannot be executed on every replica. For every transaction it has to be predeclared which elements in the database it is going to update (so called *conflict classes*). Depending on this set of conflict classes, a so called *compound conflict class* can be deduced. Every possible compound conflict class is statically assigned to a replica, replicas are said to act as *master site* for assigned compound conflict classes. Incoming update transactions are broadcasted to all replicas using group communication, leading to a total order. Each replica decides then if it is the master site for a given transaction. Master sites execute transactions, other sites just install the resulting writesets, using the derived total order. Recently, the work has been extended to deal with autonomous adaption to changing workloads [27].

IBM and Microsoft [2,3,4] have recently proposed solutions for systems where web applications are distributed over the network. The main idea is to do caching at the edge of the network, which leads to improved response times. Of course, full consistency has to be given up. To the application servers, the caches look like an ordinary database system. Some of these approaches are not limited to static cache structures, they can react to changes in the load and adapt the amount of data kept in the cache.

7 Conclusions and Further Work

This paper has presented a novel algorithm for the replication of databases at the middleware level (RSI-PC) as well as the the design, implementation and evaluation of a replication platform (Ganymed) based on this algorithm. Although the algorithm may appear to be conceptually simple, it combines subtle insights in how real databases work and several optimizations that make it extremely efficient. The resulting system is light weight and avoids the limitations of existing solutions. For instance, the fact that Ganymed does not use group communication helps both with scalability and fast reaction to failures. It also reduces the footprint of the system and the overall response time. Ganymed does not duplicate database functionality either. It performs neither high level concurrency control (which typically implies a significant reduction in concurrency since it is done at the level of table locking) nor SQL parsing (which is a very expensive operation for real loads). This is an issue that needs to be emphasized as the redundancy is not just a matter of footprint or efficiency. We are not aware of any proposed solution that duplicates database functionality (be it locking, concurrency control, or SQL parsing) that can support real database engines. The problem of these designs is that they assume the middleware layer can control everything which happens on a database engine. This is, however, not a correct assumption as concurrency control affects more than just tables (e.g., recovery procedures, indexes) and, to work correctly, important database functionality such as triggers would have to be disabled or the concurrency control at the middleware level had to work at an extremely conservative level, thereby slowing down the system. In the same spirit, Ganymed imposes no data organization, structuring of the load, or particular arrangements of the schema. Finally, applications that want to make use of Ganymed do not have to be modified, the JDBC driver approach guarantees the generality of the interface that Ganymed offers. Since all existing solution suffer from one or more of these problems, Ganymed represents a significant step forward in database replication.

Thanks to the minimal infrastructure needed, Ganymed provides excellent scalability and reliability. We have shown that for typical benchmarks Ganymed scales almost linearly. Even if replicas fail, Ganymed is able to continue working with proper performance levels thanks to the simple mechanisms involved in recovery. It is also important to note that the results provided are a lower bound in terms of scalability. There are many optimizations possible that will increase scalability even further. As part of future work, we are exploring the use of specialized indexes in the read-only replicas to speed up query processing. We are also studying the possibility of autonomic behavior in the creation of such indexes. For instance, the manager console could adapt these indexes dynamically as a result of inspecting the current load. Given the low overhead of the infrastructure, we can invest in such optimizations without worrying about the impact of the extra computations on performance. In the medium term, the implementation of complete autonomous behavior is an important goal. This would affect the automatic creation of read-only copies as needed, supporting several database instances in a cluster setting, etc. One can think of scenarios with multiple, independent schedulers responsible for different logical databases and large sets of replicas. The replicas could then be automatically assigned to schedulers, e.g., based on load observations, charging schemas (e.g., *pay per TPS*) or business rules. Such a system would enable the creation of large scale database provisioning services. Again, the fact that the infrastructure has a very low overhead makes many of these ideas feasible.

References

1. Jim Gray, Pat Helland, Patrick O'Neil, and Dennis Shasha. The Dangers of Replication and a Solution. In *Proceedings of the 1996 ACM SIGMOD International Conference on Management of Data*, pages 173–182, June 1996.
2. Mehmet Altinel, Christof Bornhövd, Sailesh Krishnamurthy, C. Mohan, Hamid Pirahesh, and Berthold Reinwald. Cache Tables: Paving the Way for an Adaptive Database Cache. In *Proceedings of the 29th International Conference on Very Large Data Bases, September 9-12, 2003, Berlin, Germany.*
3. K. Amiri, S. Park, R. Tewari, and S. Padmanabhan. DBProxy: A Dynamic Data Cache for Web Applications. In *Proceedings of the 19th International Conference on Data Engineering, March 5-8, 2003, Bangalore, India.*
4. Per-Åke Larson, Jonathan Goldstein, and Jingren Zhou. Transparent Mid-tier Database Caching in SQL Server. In *Proceedings of the 2003 ACM SIGMOD International Conference on Management of Data*, pages 661–661. ACM Press, 2003.
5. Cristiana Amza, Alan L. Cox, and Willy Zwaenepoel. Distributed Versioning: Consistent Replication for Scaling Back-End Databases of Dynamic Content Web Sites. In *Middleware 2003, ACM/IFIP/USENIX International Middleware Conference, Rio de Janeiro, Brazil, June 16-20, Proceedings*, 2003.
6. Cristiana Amza, Alan L. Cox, and Willy Zwaenepoel. Conflict-Aware Scheduling for Dynamic Content Applications. In *Proceedings of the 4th USENIX Symposium on Internet Technologies and Systems (USITS)*, March 2003.
7. R. Jiménez-Peris, M. Patiño-Martínez, B. Kemme, and G. Alonso. Improving the Scalability of Fault-Tolerant Database Clusters. In *IEEE 22nd Int. Conf. on Distributed Computing Systems, ICDCS'02, Vienna, Austria*, pages 477–484, July 2002.
8. Emmanuel Cecchet. C-JDBC: a Middleware Framework for Database Clustering. IEEE Data Engineering Bulletin, Vol. 27, No. 2, June 2004.
9. Hal Berenson, Phil Bernstein, Jim Gray, Jim Melton, Elizabeth O'Neil, and Patrick O'Neil. A Critique of ANSI SQL Isolation Levels. In *Proceedings of the SIGMOD International Conference on Management of Data*, pages 1–10, May 1995.
10. Ralf Schenkel and Gerhard Weikum. Integrating Snapshot Isolation into Transactional Federation. In Opher Etzion and Peter Scheuermann, editors, *Cooperative Information Systems, 7th International Conference, CoopIS 2000, Eilat, Israel, September 6-8, 2000, Proceedings*, volume 1901 of *Lecture Notes in Computer Science*, pages 90–101. Springer, 2000.

174   Christian Plattner and Gustavo Alonso

11. Sameh Elnikety, Fernando Pedone, and Willy Zwaenepoel. Generalized Snapshot Isolation and a Prefix-Consistent Implementation. EPFL Technical Report IC/2004/21, March 2004, http://ic.epfl.ch/.
12. P. A. Bernstein, V. Hadzilacos, and N. Goodman. *Concurrency Control and Recovery in Database Systems*. Addison-Wesley, 1987.
13. Gerhard Weikum and Gottfried Vossen. *Transactional Information Systems*. Morgan Kaufmann Publishers, 2002.
14. R. Jiménez-Peris and M. Patiño-Martínez and G. Alonso and B. Kemme. Are Quorums an Alternative for Data Replication? *ACM Transactions on Database Systems*, 2003.
15. Bettina Kemme and Gustavo Alonso. Don't be lazy, be consistent: Postgres-R, a new way to implement Database Replication. In *Proceedings of the 26th International Conference on Very Large Databases*.
16. Bettina Kemme. Implementing Database Replication based on Group Communication. In *Proc. of the International Workshop on Future Directions in Distributed Computing (FuDiCo 2002), Bertinoro, Italy*, June 2002.
17. Concurrency Control, Transaction Isolation and Serializability in SQL92 and Oracle7. Oracle White Paper, July 1995.
18. PostgreSQL Global Development Group. PostgreSQL: The most advanced Open Source Database System in the World. http://www.postgresql.org.
19. Alan Fekete, Dimitros Liarokapis, Elizabeth O'Neil, Patrick O'Neil, and Dennis Sasha. Making Snapshot Isolation Serializable, http://www.cs.umb.edu/~isotest/snaptest/snaptest.pdf.
20. Alan D. Fekete. Serialisability and Snapshot Isolation. In *Proceedings of the Australian Database Conference*, pages 210–210, January 1999.
21. Uwe Röhm, Klemens Böhm, Hans-Jörg Schek, and Heiko Schuldt. FAS - A Freshness-Sensitive Coordination Middleware for a Cluster of OLAP Components. In *Proceedings of the 28th International Conference on Very Large Data Bases (VLDB 2002), Hong Kong, China*, pages 754–765, August 2002.
22. Oracle Streams Concepts and Administration, Oracle Database Advanced Replication, 10g Release 1 (10.1). Oracle Database Documentation Library, 2003.
23. The Transaction Processing Performance Council. TPC-W, a Transactional Web E-Commerce Benchmark. http://www.tpc.org/tpcw/.
24. Mikko H. Lipasti. Java TPC-W Implementation Distribution of Prof. Lipasti's Fall 1999 ECE 902 Course, http://www.ece.wisc.edu/~pharm/.
25. Y. Amir and C. Tutu. From Total Order to Database Replication. Technical report, CNDS, 2002.
26. Y. Amir, L. E. Moser, P. M. Melliar-Smith, D. A. Agarwal, and P. Ciarfella. The Totem Single-Ring Ordering and Membership Protocol. *ACM Transactions on Computer Systems*, 13(4):311–342, 1995.
27. J. M. Milan-Franco, R. Jiménez-Peris, M. Patiño-Martínez, and B. Kemme. Adaptive Distributed Middleware for Data Replication. In *Middleware 2004, ACM/IFIP/USENIX 5th International Middleware Conference, Toronto, Canada, October 18-22, Proceedings*, 2004.

Adaptive Middleware for Data Replication*

Jesús M. Milan-Franco[1], Ricardo Jiménez-Peris[1],
Marta Patiño-Martínez[1], and Bettina Kemme[2]

[1] Facultad de Informática, Universidad Politécnica de Madrid (UPM), Spain
milanjm@sip.ucm.es, {rjimenez,mpatino}@fi.upm.es
[2] McGill University, School of Computer Science, Montreal, Quebec, Canada
kemme@cs.mcgill.ca

Abstract. Dynamically adaptive systems sense their environment and adjust themselves to accommodate to changes in order to maximize performance. Depending on the type of change (e.g., modifications of the load, the type of workload, the available resources, the client distribution, etc.), different adjustments have to be made. Coordinating them is already difficult in a centralized system. Doing so in the currently prevalent component-based distributed systems is even more challenging. In this paper, we present an adaptive distributed middleware for data replication that is able to adjust to changes in the amount of load submitted to the different replicas and to the type of workload submitted. Its novelty lies in combining load-balancing techniques with feedback driven adjustments of multiprogramming levels (number of transactions that are allowed to execute concurrently). An extensive performance analysis shows that the proposed adaptive replication solution can provide high throughput, good scalability, and low response times for changing loads and workloads with little overhead.

1 Introduction

Tuning an information system in order to provide optimal performance for a specific application is a challenging task. So far, human administrators have traditionally outperformed software based solutions due to their in-depth knowledge of the application. However, more and more applications cannot be described anymore with static characteristics but are dynamic in nature. For instance, depending on the time of the day, the workload submitted to a database can be sometimes update intensive, sometimes read intensive. Also, the type of users connected to the database at a given time, or the current state of the application (e.g., in workflows) will have an influence on which parts of a database are accessed more frequently. This dynamic behavior requires prompt and frequent adjustments of the underlying information system. This, however, will be difficult to achieve when relying on humans to turn the right knobs in the system configuration. Instead, dynamic applications require an adaptive infrastructure. Adaptive systems use context awareness to perceive the surrounding context and the effect of its

---

* This work has been partially funded by the European Commission under the Adapt project, IST-2001-37126, and by the Spanish Research Council, MCyT, under project TIC-2001-1586-C03.

H.-A. Jacobsen (Ed.): Middleware 2004, LNCS 3231, pp. 175–194, 2004.
© IFIP International Federation for Information Processing 2004

reactions on it. Based on this monitoring information, the system modifies itself to accommodate to the new conditions in the computing environment in which it operates, and thus, behaves in an optimal fashion according to some target performance metrics. The most ambitious goal of an adaptive system is autonomy, in which a system adapts itself automatically to ambient changes [18].

In this paper, we focus on the automatic adaptation of a replicated database. Database replication is used for scalability (read-only queries can be executed at any replica; hence, the more replicas the more queries can be served), fast response times (adding new replicas reduces the resource consumption on each replica), and fault-tolerance (the data is available as long as one replica is accessible). Hence, replicating databases over a cluster of workstations has become attractive for current web-based information systems that are used for read-intensive applications like online bookstores or auction systems (more than 50% reads). The challenge is replica control, i.e., changes of update transactions have to be applied at all replicas in a consistent way. Database replication at the middleware level has received considerable attention in the last years [14, 1, 2, 26, 27, 19], since it can be developed without the need to change the underlying database system. In such systems, transactions are submitted to the middleware which then forwards it to the appropriate database replica(s) (both to provide replica control as for load-balancing). For locality and fault-tolerance, the middleware is usually also replicated. Transactions can then be submitted to any middleware replica.

Target performance metrics for database systems are throughput (rate of executed transactions) and response time. These metrics depend on the workload (mix of transaction types), load (rate of submitted transactions), cache hit ratio, etc. In order to have optimal resource utilization in a replicated database, transactions have to be equally distributed among all replicas. Another important aspect of the database system to work well under a given workload is the *multiprogramming level* (MPL), i.e., the number of transactions that are allowed to run concurrently within the database system. Initially, when resources are freely available, then a high MPL boosts throughput. Also, if some transactions are I/O bound, concurrent transactions might keep the CPU busy while I/O takes place. However, when resources are highly utilized or a single resource becomes the bottleneck (e.g., the log), increasing the MPL will only increase context switches, and hence, put even more restraint on the resources. Performance is then lower than in a system with less concurrent transactions. Also, if conflict rates are high, additional transactions will only lead to higher abort rates, and hence, wasted execution time.

In dynamic environments, workload and/or the load can change over time. As a result, the system configuration has to be adapted dynamically, i.e., the MPL and the distribution of transactions across replicas must be adjusted. An additional dynamic behavior is the crash of individual components. If a node fails, the other nodes must not only be able to continue execution but should also take over the load of the failed node.

The contribution of this paper lies in providing a hierarchical approach with two levels of adaptation for a replicated database. At the local level, the focus is on maximizing the performance of each individual replica by adjusting the MPL to changes in the load and workload. At the global level, the system tries to maximize the performance of the system as a whole by deciding how to share the load among the different replicas. The challenge of performing these kinds of adaptation at the middleware level is the reduced information that is available about the changes in behavior and internals of the database making it hard to detect bottlenecks.

At the local level, each middleware instance has a pool of active connections to the local database replica. This determines the MPL since each transaction requires its own connection. If there are more transaction requests than active connections, transactions are enqueued at the middleware. In this way, each local replica is able to handle interme- diate periods of high load. In order to adapt to changes in workload and load, the num- ber of active connections has to be adjusted dynamically. We use an approach adapted from [11] that only requires to monitor the database load and the achieved throughput in order to adapt the MPL appropriately. Other approaches that we are aware of [20, 6] require a deeper knowledge of the database internals, and hence are not appropriate. But even [11] is designed for database internal adaptation. Hence, we had to extend their approach to work at the middleware level. Using this local approach, each replica adapts its MPL individually so that it can execute its load in the most efficient way without any specific knowledge of the workload nor of the database internals.

However, if the number of transactions to be executed at a replica continuously ex- ceeds the optimal MPL, the set of transactions enqueued at the middleware becomes bigger and bigger, and the response time for those transactions deteriorates. Increasing the MPL would only worsen the situation. Instead, some of the load assigned to this replica should be redirected to other replicas with free capacity. In order to detect repli- cas that are overloaded or have free capacity, the local load of each replica has to be monitored. Our approach achieves this by keeping track of the number of transactions enqueued at each middleware server. If a significant imbalance is detected, the load will be redistributed. Load balancing takes place continuously as a background process in order to capture workload changes. In order to not consume too many resources, we use a greedy-algorithm with little computation overhead. Other load-balancing algorithms we are aware of (e.g., [22, 3, 2]) have a quite different transaction execution model (i.e. only deal with queries), and hence, result in different solutions.

We have evaluated our approach extensively for local and global adaptation, both in isolation and combined, in a cluster of workstations under various workloads and loads. Our results show that hierarchical adaptation provides evenly loaded replicas, avoids deterioration of individual database replicas, and is able to handle intermediate periods of overload. Furthermore, it is able to handle various workloads and database sizes, and adapts smoothly to changes in the environment.

The rest of the paper is structured as follows. Section 2 introduces the architecture of Middle-R [14] that was used as our base system. Section 3 discusses the local adaptation of MPL, and Section 4 is devoted to global load balancing adaptation. In Section 5 we show some of the results of our extensive performance evaluation. Related approaches are compared in Section 6. We conclude in Section 7.

2   Middleware-Based Database Replication

Middle-R is a cluster based database replication tool that serves as target and base sys- tem for our adaptability analysis. [14] describes the system in more detail. The system consists of N nodes (machines), each node hosts a database system and a Middle-R server. Each database system stores a full copy of the database (replica).

The database application programs are written in the usual way, using one of the standard database interfaces to interact with the database (the current system is based on C programs with Embedded SQL). Given a transaction in form of an application program, Middle-R can identify which data objects are accessed by the transaction. Object granularity can be a table, or any application specific granularity level.

Middle-R is responsible for concurrency and replica control. It uses a group communication system to disseminate information among the replicas. The group communication system, Ensemble [10], provides support for group maintenance and reliable multicast. One of the available multicast primitives provides total order delivery, i.e., although different servers might multicast messages concurrently, the group communication system will deliver to each server all messages in exactly the same order (a sending server will also receive its own message in total order). This order is used as execution order for conflicting transactions that want to access the same objects. In order to achieve this, Middle-R servers maintain a lock table, and requests locks in the total order in which transactions are received.

The system applies asymmetric transaction processing to boost scalability [16, 15]. Each update transaction (consisting of at least one update operation) is only executed at one replica. The other replicas do not re-execute the transaction (neither read nor write operations) but simply change the affected records in an efficient manner. This spare capacity can be used to process additional transactions. Several analyses have shown that asymmetric processing can outperform symmetric processing [16, 14, 15]. Furthermore, symmetric processing is not feasible for database systems with triggers or non-deterministic behavior. Hence, most commercial systems use asymmetric replication approaches. In order to use asymmetric processing at the middleware layer, the underlying database system has to provide a function to get the changes performed by a transaction (the *write set*), and a second that takes the write set as input and applies it without re-executing the entire SQL statements. Such an extension was implemented for PostgreSQL and is currently being implemented for MySQL and Microsoft SQL Server. Oracle uses such mechanism for its own replication protocol [21].

In order to share the load among all the replicas, we follow a primary copy approach. Each set of data objects that can be accessed within a single transaction is assigned a primary replica that will be in charge of executing programs that access this specific set. For instance, replica $N1$ might be primary of object set $\{O1\}$ and replica $N2$ of object sets $\{O2\}, \{O1, O2\}$. That is, overlapping sets might be assigned to different replicas. With this we allow transactions to access arbitrary object sets. Disallowing overlapping object sets to be assigned to different replicas means that we partition the data among the replicas, each replica being responsible for transactions accessing object sets within its partition. As a result, we would disallow object sets spanning two or more partitions, and hence disallow transaction to access arbitrary objects. The primary of a multiple object set (for transactions spanning multiple object sets) is selected by selecting one of the primaries of the basic object sets. This is done through a deterministic function (e.g. a hash function such as SHA-1) applied to the basic object sets of a transaction. In this way, each transaction has a primary and it is only needed to assign primaries to each basic object set (instead of selecting a primary for every possible combination of basic object sets). The conflict-aware scheduling algorithm and its correctness can be found at [24].

Assigning object sets to primary nodes determines which transactions are executed at which nodes. Given a static workload, an optimal distribution of object sets can easily be found. However, when the workload characteristics change over time, a reassignment is necessary. This is the task of our global adaptation (dynamic load balancing).

Let us first have a look at *update transactions* that perform at least one update operation. The client can submit an *update request* to any Middle-R server which multicasts it to all middleware servers using total order multicast. Upon receiving a request to execute transaction T delivered in total order, all servers append the lock requests for objects accessed by T into the corresponding queues of the lock table (a form of conservative 2PL locking). The primary executes T when T's locks are the first in all queues. It starts a database transaction, executes T's code, and retrieves the write set from the database. Then it commits T locally and multicasts (without ordering requirement) the write set to the other Middle-R servers which apply it at their databases. The Middle-R server which originally received the client request returns the commit confirmation once it receives the write set (or after local commit if it was the primary of the transaction).

For queries (read-only transactions), there exist several alternatives. Firstly, they could always be executed locally at the server they are submitted avoiding communication. However, this disallows any form of load balancing, and if all requests are submitted to one server, this server will quickly become a bottleneck. Since communication in a local area network is usually not the bottleneck, an alternative is to also execute queries at the primary. Apart of load balancing issues this might lead to a better use of the main memory of the database system since each replica is primary only of a subset of the data. Hence, we can expect higher cache hit ratios at each replica [3] than if each replica executes any type of query. In the primary approach, a query request is forwarded to all replicas; the primary then executes the query, returns the result to the submitting Middle-R server and notifies the end of the query to all replicas. In this paper, we assume a primary approach for queries. Independently of whether a local or primary approach is used the executing Middle-R server might not need to acquire locks for queries but immediately submit them for execution if the database uses snapshots for queries (as is done by PostgreSQL or Oracle). The approach provides 1-copy-serializability because all replicas decide on the same execution order of conflicting transactions due to the total order multicast. Even if the primary fails after committing but before sending the changes, a new primary will take over and re-execute the transaction in the same order due to the total order multicast.

At the start of Middle-R, a pool of connections to the database is created as common for application servers (since connection creation is very expensive). Initially all connections are marked as free. Whenever a transaction is able to execute or a write set can be applied, the system looks for a free connection. If there is none, execution is delayed. Otherwise the system takes one of the free connections, marks it as busy, and submits the necessary statements over this connection to the database. Once the transaction terminates, the connection is again marked as free, and waiting requests are activated. Dynamically adjusting the size of the connection pool to the workload characteristics is the task of our local adaptation protocol.

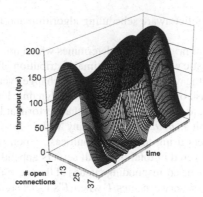

Fig. 1. Throughput as a function of the MPL over time

3   Local Level Adaptation

At the local level, each middleware server is configured to maximize the performance of its local database replica. Measurements have shown that Middle-R servers are light-weight while the database servers are the first to be the bottleneck [14]. Hence, controlling the MPL is an important step in dynamic performance optimization, and is done by limiting the connection pool to the database replica.

Our solution to control the MPL is based on the feedback control approach proposed in [11]. Since it does not require database internal information like conflict rate, memory and other resource consumption, etc. it is suitable for a middleware-based system. In a feedback system, one uses the output of the system as an indicator whether the input of the system should be changed. [11] proposes to take the transaction throughput as output parameter. In a system without control on the number of concurrent transactions, the throughput of the database system usually rises with increasing the number of transactions until the system saturates at a throughput peak. If the number of concurrent transactions increases further, the database enters the thrashing region in which the throughput falls very fast until it stabilizes at some low residual value. Fig. 1, adjusted from [11], illustrates this behavior. The x-axis depicts the MPL, the y-axis depicts the throughput achieved by the system with it, and the z-axis shows how the curve changes over time (assuming the workload changes over time). For instance, the percentage of update transactions has a significant influence on the maximum throughput since all update transactions must access the log. This means, e.g., that a read-only workload could have a high throughput peak at a high number of concurrent transactions, while update transactions could have a considerably smaller peak at a smaller number of concurrent transactions. When now the workload moves from a read intensive workload to a write intensive workload, so does the dependency between MPL and throughput.

Hence, we have two goals. Firstly, at any given time with a given workload, we have to determine the optimal MPL, i.e., to deny newly submitted transactions to execute whenever this would lead to a load that cannot be handled anymore by the database. That is, we should set a MPL such that the database system is never in the thrashing region. The *optimal MPL* is now defined as the MPL allowing for the maximum achievable throughput. The second goal is to provide dynamic adaptability, that is, to adjust the MPL when the workload changes such that it is never higher than the optimal MPL. [11] approximates the relationship between concurrent transactions and throughput at each time point with a parabola. In order to estimate the coefficients, the system periodically measures the number of concurrent transactions and the throughput. In order to capture the time dependency of the parabola, more recent measurements are given a higher weight than older measurements[1]. After each measurement period, the optimal MPL is set to the number of concurrent transactions achieving the highest throughput. The approach also addresses some stability problems. If the load is very stable, too few different data points are collected to correctly estimate the parabola. If results are imprecise one can get phenomena like inverted parabolas. Finally, if the workload changes too fast, adaptation can lead to a ping-pong effect. For all of them, [11] proposes several counter-measures which are all implemented in our system.

3.1   Adaptive MPL Implementation

Middle-R implements this approach with all proposed optimizations at the middleware layer by controlling the connection pool. Each Middle-R server creates a pool of $cmax$ open connections to the database at startup. We assume that $cmax$ is chosen big enough to be at least as large as the largest optimal MPL for any given workload (otherwise $cmax$ could be increased at runtime). At any time, out of the $cmax$ connections, at most $mplmax \leq cmax$ connections can be used. Additionally, Middle-R keeps track of $mplcurrent$, the number of connections that are currently used to execute transactions. $mplcurrent$ is always smaller or equal to $mplmax$. If $mplcurrent < mplmax$, then there are less requests available for execution than Middle-R would allow to execute. If $mplcurrent = mplmax$, then all allowed connections are used, and Middle-R will queue any further requests until a currently active transaction has terminated. r depicts the number of waiting requests. If r is zero, then $mplcurrent$ reflects the current load submitted to the replica. If r is greater than zero, then the middleware is reducing the load of the database by queuing requests.

Middle-R now periodically measures $mplcurrent$, and the database load and throughput. From there, it estimates the load/throughput parabola, and $mplopt$, the optimal MPL for the given workload. $mplmax$ is now constantly adjusted. However, $mplmax$ is not simply set to $mplopt$ but takes into account that during the last period the load submitted to the system might have been smaller than the maximum achievable throughput. This is the case if, for the last period, $mplcurrent$ was smaller than the estimated $mplopt$. In such case, it is better to keep $mplmax$ closer to the actual load, $mplcurrent$, in order to guarantee that once $mplmax$ is changed it will actually have the desired effect. As an example why this is needed, assume the type of workload has changed (e.g., many more updates) requiring to decrease the MPL. A decrease in $mplmax$ will not have an immediate effect if $mplmax$ is bigger than $mplcurrent$. As such, we can distinguish the following cases.

---

[1] Parabola coefficients are estimated using a recursive least-square estimator with exponentially fading memory.

- The system is in underload (the system is in the increasing slope of parabola).
  - If $mplcurrent = mplmax$, then $mplmax$ is increased. It is set to a value between its current value and the newly calculated $mplopt$. The larger r (waiting requests), the closer the new value will be to $mplopt$.
  - If $mplcurrent < mplmax$, then $mplmax$ is decreased to $mplcurrent$.
  - If $mplcurrent \geq mplmax$, nothing is done.
- The system is at peak throughput ($mplmax$ equals the newly calculated $mplopt$)
  - If $mplcurrent \geq mplmax$, nothing is done.
  - If $mplcurrent < mplmax$, then $mplmax$ is decreased to $mplcurrent \geq mplmax$.
- The system is in thrashing region ($mplmax > mplopt$)
  - If $mplcurrent = mplmax$, $mplmax$ is decreased by one whenever an active transaction terminates and as long as $mplmax > mplopt$.
  - The case $mplcurrent < mplmax$ cannot occur in thrashing region.

If the number of submitted requests is consistently higher than the throughput that can be handled by the database, the queues at the Middle-R server will become longer and longer. Middle-R can handle this for a certain time period. After this, the system performance degrades. The solution is to perform a global adaptation in order to redistribute some of the load of the overloaded replica to other nodes. If all replicas are overloaded, the system should disallow new client requests until active transactions have terminated.

4   Global Level Adaptation

A replicated database might potentially improve its throughput as more replicas are added to the system [15]. However, this potential throughput is only reached under an even load in which all replicas receive the same amount of work (assuming a homogeneous setting), which in practice might never happen. If the load is concentrated at one replica, the throughput will be the throughput of a single replica or even worse due to the overhead of the replication protocol to ensure consistency among replicas. Load balancing is aimed to correct situations in which some replicas are overloaded, while others have still execution capacity. This is done by redistributing the load as evenly as possible among the replicas. Therefore, any load balancing algorithm requires a means to estimate the current load at each replica.

Each Middle-R server knows the total number of concurrent active transactions in the system, since requests are multicast to all servers. All servers acquire locks for the objects accessed by transactions that are kept until the transaction terminates locally. Hence, looking at its lock table, each server has a good estimate of the total number of active transactions. For some of them the server is the primary copy. We call these the local transactions of the server. Local transactions might either be executing or waiting for locks or waiting for a free connection. For others, the server is not the primary. We call them remote transactions. If it is an update transaction the server is waiting for the write set (it is still active at the primary), or currently applying the write set or waiting for a free connection (the transaction is committed at the primary). If it is a query, the write set message is empty and used as an indication of the end of the query.

Each server can estimate the number of local active transactions of any other server S by looking at its lock table and the active transactions for which S is primary and for which it has not yet received the write set message. This calculation can be done without any additional communication overhead.

The number of local active transactions at a server is a good estimate of the load at this server. The higher this number, the higher the load of this server. If it is known that different transaction types have different execution times, then this load metrics can be made more precise by weighting the number of local active transactions with the observed average execution time [2]. The degree of balance (or imbalance) is captured by the variance among the number of local active transactions at each node. A variance with a value of zero means that the load is evenly distributed (balanced) among all replicas. On the other extreme, the maximum variance is achieved when the entire load is concentrated on a single replica.

4.1 Dynamic Load Balancing Implementation

The load balancing algorithm is in charge of finding a primary assignment of object sets to servers that minimizes the variance. Our first algorithm uses a branch-and-bound mechanism. For each object set it defines the load of this object set as the number of active transactions that want to access this set. For each replica it defines the current load as the sum of the loads of object sets for which that replica is the primary. At the start all object sets have to be assigned and the load of each replica is zero. Object sets are now assigned to primaries in the following way. At each step the algorithm selects the most loaded object set and assigns it to all servers yielding a set of partial solutions. The algorithm then traverses all partial solutions and prunes those that will not yield in a better solution than the current one (initially there are no computed solutions, hence all partial solutions are explored). The pruning in branch & bound algorithms is based on an estimation function. This function is applied to a partial solution and provides a lower bound of the variance of the optimal solution that might be found searching from this partial solution. The input of the estimation function is the total load of all object sets that have not yet been assigned, and a partial solution. The function assigns the transactions in that unassigned load to the less loaded servers in the partial solution in order to minimize the variance. This assignment, however, does not take into consideration the object sets accessed by these transactions. That is, two transactions accessing the same object set might be assigned to different servers. Hence, the function provides a lower bound of the actual possible variance. The algorithm provides an optimal assignment due to it performs an exhaustive search in the solution space. However, its use is limited to small number of object sets and replicas since its computation time grows exponentially.

Our alternative is an inexpensive greedy algorithm. It uses the same definitions of object set load and current replica load as the branch-and-bound algorithm. The greedy algorithm assigns at each step an object set to a replica. It selects the unassigned object set with the highest load and assigns it to the replica with the smallest current load. It proceeds recursively until all object sets are assigned to a replica.

The cost of both algorithms in terms of CPU time as a function of the number of replicas and the number of object sets is shown in Fig. 2. The branch-and-bound algo-

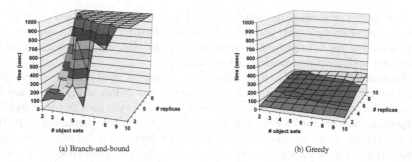

(a) Branch-and-bound   (b) Greedy

Fig. 2. Computation time of the two load balancing algorithms

rithm goes beyond 1 ms of computing time with a number of object-sets and replicas higher than 5. The greedy algorithm takes a tenth of millisecond to compute a primary assignment for 10 replicas and 10 object sets. It is worth to note that the number of object sets is usually higher than the number of replicas. Fortunately, as can be seen in the graph, the computational cost of the greedy algorithm grows at a lower pace with the number of object sets than with the number of replicas.

A Middle-R server S responsible for load balancing periodically calculates the load variance. If the variance exceeds a given threshold, the load balancing algorithm calculates a new primary assignment to balance the load. The new primary assignment is not applied immediately. Instead S checks whether the current imbalance will be improved by the new configuration by a significant percentage. This prevents performing redistribution when the system performance cannot be improved appreciably. If the new configuration is better than the previous one, S multicasts a load balancing message m_l in total order to all Middle-R servers to inform about the new primary assignment. Transaction requests that are received after m_l are executed according to the new configuration. Reconfiguration for each object set takes place once all transaction requests accessing that object set that were received before m_l have been executed. For object sets that are not currently accessed by any transaction, reconfiguration can take place immediately. The time of the switch is different for each object set, depending on the number of transactions requesting access to it.

5   Experimental Results

5.1   Experiment Setup

The experiments were run in a cluster of 10 homogeneous machines. Each machine is equipped with two processors AMD Athlon 2GHz, 512 MB of RAM, and a 60 GB disk (with a 30 GB partition used for the experiments). The nodes were interconnected through a 100-MBit switch. The database used is PostgreSQL 7.2 enriched with a couple of services that enable asymmetric processing at the middleware level [14].

We used two different database sizes in the experiments. One is very small and easily fits into main memory (a 10MB database). After the warm-up it was guaranteed that all data was kept in the database cache and that no access to disk was needed to read data. The other is a medium-sized database (1 GB) that was set up very scattered forcing I/O on every access with a high probability. In any case, the database consisted of 36 tables with equal number of tuples (3,000 and 300,000 tuples, respectively).

Three workloads have been chosen to evaluate the adaptation. UPD8 is a pure update transaction that performs 8 SQL update statements on the same table. Each statement changes one tuple that is determined by indicating the value of its primary key. Hence, access to this tuple is through the B+-tree of the primary key without reading any other tuples of the table. SELUPD is an update statement that queries a table in order to perform a single update. It represents a mixed workload of read and write accesses. LQ1 is a read only query that queries a full table. That is, each transaction accesses a single table, and there exist 36 object sets each containing one table[2]. The first three experiments analyze local adaptation, and hence, are run on a single server. The remaining experiments use up to 9 machines to evaluate global adaptation. In all experiments an additional machine was used to run the client simulator.

All experiments (except the temporal ones, 1.3 and 2.1) consisted of three phases: 1) A warm-up phase (500 transactions), during which the load was injected but no measures were taken; 2) a measurement phase (1000 transactions) in which the end-to-end throughput and response time are measured; 3) and finally, a cold-down phase (500 transactions) in which the load was kept without taking any measurements. Each experiment was repeated at least 3 times.

5.2   Local Adaptation

Experiment 1.1: Optimal MPL. This experiment aims to motivate that there is an optimal value for $mplmax$, i.e., the number of connections that are made available at the middleware server, and this optimal is different under different workloads.

In these experiments, no adaptive algorithm was run. Instead in each test run, $mplmax$ was set to a specific value. Then a given load (in transactions per second) was submitted to the system, and the throughput measured. If the throughput was smaller than the load, the system was overloaded. Each of the Fig. 3(a-d) present the throughput of the system (y-axis) given different values for $mplmax$ (x-axis) for different loads submitted to the system (different curves). For each curve the maximum value represents the maximum achievable throughput. We can observe that this peak is achieved at different values for $mplmax$, and hence, illustrates the need to adjust $mplmax$ according to the application type.

Fig. 3(a-b) show results on a small database where computation is CPU bound, whereby (a) uses update transactions while (b) uses queries. In both figures, we can see the throughput behavior as described in Fig. 1. In (a), at low loads the maximum throughput is equal to the load submitted to the system. At 100 transactions per second (tps), a single connection can already easily handle the load, and any additional connections will probably never be used. At 200 tps, two connections help to increase the

---

[2] We conducted experiments with transactions that accessed several tables. Response times of such workloads are generally higher due to the conflict behavior. The relative behavior of the adaptive system, however, was similar, and hence, we focus our discussion on transactions accessing a single table.

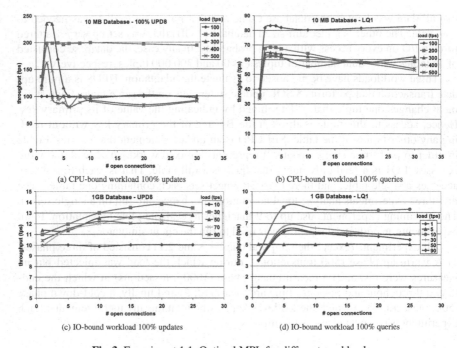

(a) CPU-bound workload 100% updates

(b) CPU-bound workload 100% queries

(c) IO-bound workload 100% updates

(d) IO-bound workload 100% queries

Fig. 3. Experiment 1.1: Optimal MPL for different workloads

throughput over one (which only can handle around 140 tps), and any additional connection is probably never used. Starting at 300 tps, the system is not able anymore to handle the entire submitted load. Two connections are able to achieve around 240 tps, but moving to three connections the system starts to deteriorate and allow a throughput of only 100 tps. All higher loads show similar behavior, however the maximum achievable throughput is even smaller, probably due to the fast growth of enqueued transactions at the middleware layer. The optimal MPL of 2 is the same as the number of CPUs available on the test machine. This means, it is optimal for the database that each CPU executes exclusively one transaction. Any increase in concurrent update transactions deteriorates performance. We assume that the reason is that all update transactions access the log to write the redo information. As far as we know, PostgreSQL does not perform any group commit (committing several transactions at the same time to reduce log induced I/O). Writing the log can easily take as long as executing the entire transaction in memory, hence, the degree of parallelism is limited by the time to flush the log to disk. For query workloads (b), the maximum throughput of 85 tps is achieved at an optimal MPL of 3-5. This MPL is higher than for update workloads. Queries do not have the log as single bottleneck. The reason that it is worth to execute more than one query on each CPU is probably due to the communication delay between application program and the database server. For queries, the query result has to be returned to the application program. The program uses complex data structures to retrieve the result, and the interaction between program and database can be quite complex. Hence, while the response is transferred from the database to the program and processed by the program, the server is free to execute additional queries.

When we now move to an I/O bound configuration (Fig. 3.c-d), the system is less vulnerable to thrashing and the optimal degree of concurrency is very different. Generally, maximum achievable throughputs are much smaller than with small database sizes, since each transaction needs longer to finish. Write intensive workloads (Fig. 3.c) require a substantially larger connection number (around 20) to maximize throughput. Each transaction takes now considerable time to retrieve the 8 tuples to be updated since each operation probably requires I/O. Hence, the log is no more the bottleneck and we can take advantage of more concurrency in the system. For read intensive workloads (Fig. 3.d), once the system works at saturation (load of 10 tps), the optimal MPL is at around 5 concurrent transactions. We assume the reason why an increase in MPL does not lead to higher throughput is due to the fact that queries have higher main memory requirements in the database. The chosen query performs aggregation, and hence, some temporary results have to be stored in the database before results are returned to the application program. Hence, if too many queries run concurrently they compete for main memory and some intermediate results might be swapped to disk leading to thrashing [6].

The conclusion from this experiment is that there is no single optimal MPL that holds for every workload, but instead, each workload has a different optimal MPL. What is more, depending whether the workload is CPU-bound or IO-bound the optimal degree of concurrency is substantially different. Therefore, to attain an optimal performance on a continuous basis, an adaptive control of the number of active connections is required. Note that although the database size might be relatively fixed in a given application, the portion of the database that is accessed might change over time. For instance, in an online bookstore, during daytime there will be a lot of queries scanning huge data sets. During night, update intensive batch processing on subset of the data might be performed. When this change in workload occurs, the system should automatically adjust the number of active connections.

Experiment 1.2: Local Adaptation Under Constant Load. This experiment is targeted to show the behavior of the local adaptation under a constant load. Although it might appear surprising at first glance, a constant load is one of worst case scenarios for adaptive algorithms. This is due to the fact that a constant load provides little information to the adaptive system [11]. In each setting of the experiment we measured the throughput for different values of $mplmax$ and compared it with the one obtained using the adaptive algorithm (local adaptation). Fig. 4 (a-d) show the achieved throughput (y-axis) when we increase the load in the system (x-axis) for different numbers of active connections (curves)[3]. Additionally, one curve indicates the throughput achieved by our adaptive algorithm.

The adaptive control exhibits a near-optimal throughput both for CPU and IO-bound workloads as well as in read and write intensive workloads. That is, for each given workload and load it dynamically determines the optimal value for $mplmax$. We want to emphasize that this adaptation is achieved without having any knowledge of the work-

---

[3] The different data points can be extrapolated from Fig. 3, except for the adaptive curve.

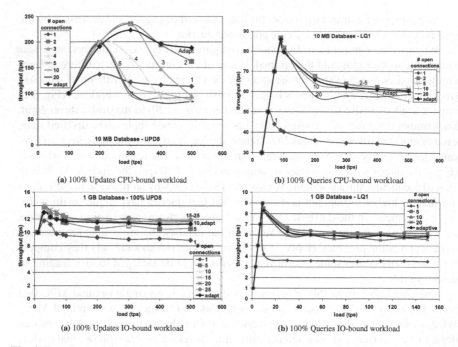

(a) 100% Updates CPU-bound workload

(b) 100% Queries CPU-bound workload

(a) 100% Updates IO-bound workload

(b) 100% Queries IO-bound workload

Fig. 4. Experiment 1.2: Adaptive number of connections vs. fixed number of connection under constant load

load or database size but is based solely on the observed throughput. It also does not need to know the reasons that might lead to the need for low or high MPLs ($mplmax$), as analyzed in the previous experiment. Hence, while manual tuning (increasing or decreasing the MPL) will require the database administrator to have knowledge of the current workload characteristics and their possible effects on concurrent transactions, the local adaptation algorithm chooses a nearly optimal concurrency level without any application or domain specific knowledge. Hence, it can be a general module of a middleware without any application specific adjustments.

Experiment 1.3: Temporal Evolution of Local Adaptation. The goal of this experiment is to show how long the local adaptation needs to determine the optimal MPL when the workload characteristics change. The workload chosen for the experiment is SELUPD and a 10MB database. In this case the maximum throughput was achieved with an MPL of 2. Since we want to show how long the system needs to adapt to this MPL, the experiment starts with an MPL of 20, i.e., far of being optimal. Fig. 5 shows the throughput achieved over time in intervals of 5 seconds and at a load of 200 tps. During the first two seconds of runtime, the system collects the historical information needed to adapt the MPL. Then, it increases the MPL only to determine that this does not improve the behavior. However, it helps to build a parabola shaped transaction/throughput curve. The system now detects that it is in the downwards part of the

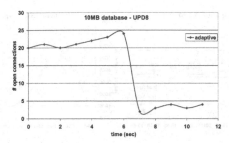

Fig. 5. Experiment 1.3: Temporal evolution of local adaptation

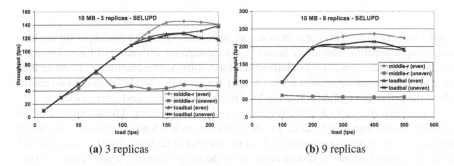

(a) 3 replicas   (b) 9 replicas

Fig. 6. Experiment 2.1: Global Adaptation vs. No Adaptation at 3 and 9 replicas

parabola and realizes that it is in the thrashing region. At this point, the system starts to reduce drastically the MPL until it finds itself in the upwards part of the parabola. Then, the MPL stabilizes in a quasi-optimal interval, between 2-4. The adaptation of the MPL takes around 5 seconds (subtracting the 2 seconds it takes to collect the historical information). That is, in a system where workload changes do not appear every couple of seconds, our approach should not lead to any ping-pong behavior. It should be noticed that this experiment stress tests the system by imposing a very extreme change in the optimal MPL. Less extreme workload changes should lead to a quasi-optimal MPL in shorter time.

5.3 Global Adaptation

Experiment 2.1: Performance of Global Adaptation. This experiment is aimed to measure the improvement in throughput provided by the load balancing algorithm. The experiment compares the performance of Middle-R with and without global adaptation for different workloads and number of replicas. Fig. 6 shows the throughput achieved with increasing loads for 3 and 9 replicas respectively. The workload consists of transactions of type SELUPD. Each graph includes four curves. One curve corresponds to the best achievable throughput. This optimal throughput is achieved by Middle-R without load balancing with a totally even load that is, each replica is the primary of the same amount of objects (tables) and submitted transactions access these objects in a

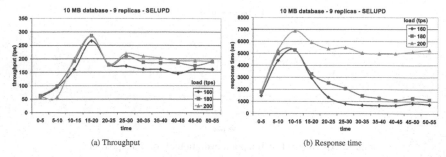

(a) Throughput

(b) Response time

Fig. 7. Experiment 2.2: Temporal evolution of the performance with dynamic load balancing

round-robin fashion. This curve provides an upper bound of the throughput for the load balancing algorithm. The lower bound is the throughput without load balancing for a totally imbalanced load. This imbalanced load consists in concentrating the entire load in a single replica (one replica is the primary for all object sets). The other two curves show the behavior of Middle-R using load balancing for even and uneven loads.

Let us first have a look at the results without load balancing. The throughput of the middleware without load balancing with the totally uneven load (lowest curve) is nearly the same (around 50 tps) independently of the number of replicas. This is a logical result since the throughput of the system is precisely the throughput of a single replica. Therefore, the number of replicas does not have any influence in the throughput. With an even load the 9 replicas achieve a higher maximum throughput than 3 replicas. This holds despite SELUPD is a pure update workload. The reason is the asymmetric processing of transactions where non-primary replicas only apply updates which require fewer resources. Hence, the maximum achievable throughput is higher. The performance gain is due to the fact that the primary performs many read operations that are not executed at non-primaries. As a result, for 3 replicas, the maximum throughput achievable is around 140 tps, whilst with 9 replicas it reaches 200 tps. That is, a 43% higher throughput.

When we now look at Middle-R with load balancing, we see that for an even load the achievable throughput is basically the same as without load balancing. This shows that the overhead introduced by the load balancing algorithm is negligible. When the system starts with an uneven load, we can see that the maximum achievable throughput is nearly as good as when the system starts with a balanced load. This is achieved by the global adaptation through redistribution of object sets (tables) to different primaries such that all replicas are primary of some of the accessed tables. The final distribution leads to an even load at all replicas yielding a quasi-optimal throughput.

Experiment 2.2: Temporal Evolution of the Global Adaptation. The previous experiment showed that the load balancing algorithm achieves a better performance than any of them in isolation. This experiment complements the previous one by showing how long the system needs to balance the load starting from a totally imbalanced situation (all the load is concentrated in a single replica). The experiment is run on 9 replicas and with a SELUPD workload. A configuration with 9 replicas is more sensitive to load imbalances and therefore, will better show how good the load balancing is. Three different loads have been used in the experiment. The load with which the optimal throughput is obtained (180 tps, the maximum load at which the throughput equals the load), a lower load (160 tps, underload), and a higher load (200 tps, thrashing)[4]. For all the loads, a single run of the load balancing algorithm achieved the optimal throughput. That happened in second 4 for 160 tps, and in second 2 for the other loads.

Fig.7.a and Fig.7.b exhibit the average throughput and response time as seen by clients. Fig.7.a shows that at the beginning the system provides low throughput due to the imbalance. Once the load balancing algorithm was triggered, the throughput increases very fast until it peaks at around 250 tps. This is more than the submitted load. The reason is that the achieved throughput (60 tps) was far lower at the beginning of the experiment than the submitted load what forces Middle-R servers to enqueue many transactions. Hence, once reconfiguration has taken place, the actual load submitted to the database is higher than the submitted load to Middle-R until all waiting transactions have been executed. Finally, the throughput levels off at the actually submitted load.

The response time (Fig.7.b) takes longer to reach the optimal (around 25 sec.). The reason is again that the system starts from a totally imbalanced situation which enqueues transactions at the middleware. Once the system has reconfigured itself to attain an optimal configuration in the first 2-4 seconds, there are many queued transactions. These pending transactions have high average response times (due to the long queues created by the initial imbalanced assignment) even with an optimal configuration till the system is able to catch up.

Experiment 2.3: Combining Local and Global Adaptation. This experiment aims to show that the combination of local and global adaptation exhibits a performance close to the optimal. The experiment was run on six nodes and the workload used was SELUPD. Initially, for all curves, a replica is primary of all object sets (i.e. a totally imbalanced assignment). The initial number of connections in the adaptive curve is 20.

Fig. 8.a b presents the (a) throughput and (b) response time with increasing load. Two curves are presented for comparison purposes: one with the optimal MPL (2) and one with the worst MPL (1). Then, a third curve is presented for the middleware with both dynamic load balancing and adaptive MPL. As can be seen in Fig. 8.a, the combination of local and global adaptation outperforms the load balancing with the worst fixed MPL and is very close to throughput of a fixed MPL of 2. Fig. 8.b shows that this quasi-optimal throughput is achieved without degrading the response time. The response time of the combined global and local adaptation is the same as the one of global adaptation with a fixed MPL of 2.

6 Related Work

Jim Gray's paper [9] stated that traditional textbook database replication algorithms providing 1-copy-serializabilty, were not scalable. This paper, instead of closing down

---

[4] Notice that with a load of 200 tps the system is thrashing since the achieved throughput is slightly below 200 tps. See Fig. 6.b.

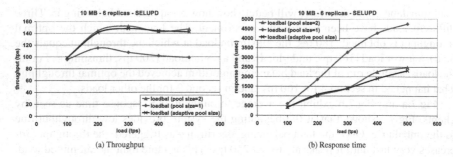

(a) Throughput   (b) Response time

Fig. 8. Experiment 2.3: Local+Global Adaptation vs. Global adaptation

the area of consistent replication, opened new lines of research. The idea was to reduce the communication to the minimum needed to enforce 1-copy-serializability. Some of these efforts can be found in [1, 2, 4, 5, 7, 8, 12, 13, 16, 17, 23, 25, 27, 19, 26]. Most of the approaches implement eager replication, although a few are based on lazy replication [23, 26]. However, both of these works address the problem of inconsistencies in lazy replication. [23] provides freshness guarantees whilst [26] enforces a level of consistency similar to eager replication. Replication at the middleware level can perform symmetric processing of updates [1, 2, 7, 27, 19] or asymmetric processing [14, 26] depending on whether update transactions are run at all replicas or they are run at a single replica while the rest of them just install the resulting updates. If an update transaction performs many reads in order to update a few tuples, the amount of work saved at the rest of the replicas can be considerable. Symmetric processing can work with any database but at the cost of an inherent limited scalability. The asymmetric processing approach requires two services to get the updates from a transaction and to install them at a different replica. These services can be implemented on top of the functionality provided by commercial databases (black box approach) such as Microsoft SQL Server (such as triggers or specialized APIs) or they can be implemented within the database (gray box approach) as it has been done with PostgreSQL for this paper.

Adaptation is receiving a growing attention since the autonomic computing vision from IBM [18]. [22] uses adaptation at different levels in a distributed middleware supporting web services. The system administrator can define utility functions that are used by the adaptive middleware to guide its decisions. This middleware provides load control, connection load balancing, and admission control. A lot of attention is paid to service differentiation that provides some QoS guarantees for different kinds of clients.

In the area of databases most work has concentrated on implementing adaptation within databases. [28] summarizes the work performed in the last years around self-tuning of memory management for data servers. Advances in this area include predictive local caching and distributed caching.

Load control has been traditionally static requiring tuning by an experienced administrator [20]. Adaptation can be used to perform this tuning automatically. In [20] adaptive load control is used to prevent data contention thrashing. The undertaken approach is enacted by monitoring the transaction conflict rate and reducing the degree of concurrency when conflicts go beyond a given threshold.

[11] uses feedback control to determine the optimal MPL independently of its nature, data or memory contention. A simulation is performed to study different strategies to provide load control. Their conclusion is that adaptation can improve notably the performance of a centralized database system under overloads. Our approach for load control extends the parabola approximation method presented in [11] in that it is able to work at the middleware level, and provides performance results of a real implementation. [6] also analyzes a feedback driven approach for determining the optimal MPL. At the same time the authors attempt to find the optimal main memory allocation for a transaction type within the database system. As such, the approach can only be applied within the database kernel.

[29] introduces a dynamic replication scheme in which the location and number of object replicas is changed dynamically depending on the access pattern. The algorithms minimize the communication overhead introduced by remote accesses by locating replicas of the accessed objects close to clients. C-JDBC [7] and [3] present a database replication middleware that performs symmetric replication. They assign incoming new queries to replicas according to three different policies: round-robin, weighted round-robin, the replica with the fewest pending queries, or the replica that recently answered a query accessing the same tables.

7 Conclusions

Database replication at the middleware level has attracted a lot of attention in the last years. One of the goals of replication is to increase the system throughput. That is, the more replicas the system has, the higher the throughput. However, if the system is not carefully tuned, the expected throughput increase will not occur.

In this paper we have shown that there are a number of factors to take into account in order to tune a replicated database. These factors include the load and workload in the system. Since these parameters typically change dynamically, the system should be able to adapt itself to the new configuration in order to maximize its throughput. We combine automatic adaptation at two levels. Local adaptation limits the number of concurrent transactions according to the workload type (but without knowing the workload type). Global adaptation performs load balancing to distribute evenly the load (queries and updates) among replicas. The conducted performance evaluation has shown that the proposed dynamic adaptation is able to achieve a throughput close to the optimal without disrupting response time.

References

1. Y. Amir and C. Tutu. From Total Order to Database Replication. In *Proc. of Int. Conf. on Distr. Comp. Systems (ICDCS)*, July 2002.
2. C. Amza, A. L. Cox, and W. Zwaenepoel. Distributed Versioning: Consistent Replication for Scaling Back-End Databases of Dynamic Content Web Sites. In *Proc. of Middleware 03*.
3. C. Amza, A. L. Cox, and W. Zwaenepoel. Scaling and Availability for Dynamic Content Web Sites. Technical Report TR-02-395, Rice University, 2002.
4. T. Anderson, Y. Breitbart, H. F. Korth, and A. Wool. Replication, Consistency, and Practicality: Are These Mutually Exclusive? In *ACM SIGMOD Conference*, 1998.

5. Y. Breitbart and H. F. Korth. Replication and Consistency: Being Lazy Helps Sometimes. In *Proc. of the Principles of Database Systems Conf.*, pages 173–184, 1997.
6. K. P. Brown, M. Mehta, M. J. Carey, and M. Livny. Towards Automated Performance Tuning For Complex Workloads. In *Proc. of 20th VLDB*, 1994.
7. E. Cecchet, J. Marguerite, and W. Zwaenepoel. RAIDb: Redundant Array of Inexpensive Databases. Technical Report Technical Report 4921, Inria, 2003.
8. S. Gancarski, H. Naacke, E. Pacitti, and P. Valduriez. Parallel Processing with Autonomous Databases in a Cluster System. In *Proc. of CoopIS/DOA/ODBASE*, pages 410–428, 2002.
9. J. Gray, P. Helland, P. O'Neil, and D. Shasha. The Dangers of Replication and a Solution. In *Proc. of the SIGMOD*, pages 173–182, Montreal, 1996.
10. M. Hayden. The Ensemble System. Technical Report TR-98-1662, Department of Computer Science. Cornell University, Jan. 1998.
11. H. Heiss and R. Wagner. Adaptive Load Control in Transaction Processing Systems. In *Proc. of 17th VLDB*, 1991.
12. J. Holliday, D. Agrawal, and A. E. Abbadi. The Performance of Database Replication with Group Communication. In *Int. Symp. on Fault-tolerant Computing Systems*, 1999.
13. R. Jiménez-Peris, M. Patiño-Martínez, and G. Alonso. Non-Intrusive, Parallel Recovery of Replicated Data. In *IEEE Symp. on Reliable Distributed Systems (SRDS)*, 2002.
14. R. Jiménez-Peris, M. Patiño-Martínez, G. Alonso, and B. Kemme. Scalable Database Replication Middleware. In *Proc. of IEEE Int. Conf. on Distributed Computing Systems*, 2002.
15. R. Jiménez-Peris, M. Patiño-Martínez, G. Alonso, and B. Kemme. Are Quorums an Alternative for Data Replication. *ACM Transactions on Databases*, 28(3):257–294, Sept. 2003.
16. B. Kemme and G. Alonso. Don't be lazy, be consistent: Postgres-R, A new way to implement Database Replication. In *Proc. of the Int. Conf. on Very Large Databases (VLDB)*, 2000.
17. B. Kemme and G. Alonso. A new approach to developing and implementing eager database replication protocols. *ACM TODS*, 25(3):333–379, Sept. 2000.
18. J. Kephart and D. Chess. The vision of autonomic computing. *IEEE Computer*, Jan. 2003.
19. A. Kistijantoro, G. Morgan, S. K. Shrivastava, and M. Little. Component Replication in Distributed Systems: A Case Study Using Enterprise Java Beans. In *Proc. of SRDS*, 2003.
20. A. Moenkeberg and G. Weikum. Performance Evaluation of an Adaptive and Robust Load Control Method for the Avoidance of Data – Contention Trashing. In *Proc. of VLDB*, 1992.
21. Oracle. *Oracle 8 (tm) Server Replication*. 1997.
22. G. Pacifici, M. Spreitzer, A. Tantawi, and A. Youssef. Performance Management for Cluster Based Web Services. Technical report, IBM Technical Report, 2003.
23. E. Pacitti, P. Minet, and E. Simon. Replica Consistency in Lazy Master Replicated Databases. *Distributed and Parallel Databases*, 9(3):237–267, 2001.
24. M. Patiño-Martínez, R. Jiménez-Peris, B. Kemme, and G. Alonso. Scalable Replication in Database Clusters. In *Proc. of Distributed Computing Conf.(DISC)*, 2000.
25. F. Pedone, R. Guerraoui, and A. Schiper. Exploiting Atomic Broadcast in Replicated Databases. Technical report, Département d'Informatique, EPFL, 1996.
26. C. Plattner and G. Alonso. Ganymed: Scalable Replication for Transactional Web Applications. In *Proc. of Middleware*, 2004.
27. L. Rodrigues, H. Miranda, R. Almeida, J. Martins, and P. Vicente. Strong Replication in the GlobData Middleware. In *Proc. Work. on Dependable Middleware-Based Systems*, 2002.
28. G. Weikum, A. Christian, A. Kraiss, and M. Sinnwell. Integrating Snapshot Isolation into Transactional Federations. *Data Engineering Bulletin*, 22(2), 1999.
29. O. Wolfson, S. Jajodia, and Y. Huang. An adaptive data replication algorithm. *ACM Transactions on Database Systems*, 22(2):255–314, 1997.

Alternative Edge-Server Architectures for Enterprise JavaBeans Applications

Avraham Leff and James T. Rayfield

IBM T. J. Watson Research Center, P. O. Box 704 Yorktown Heights, NY 10598
{avraham,jtray}@us.ibm.com

Abstract. Edge-server architectures are widely used to improve web-application performance for non-transactional data. However, their use with transactional data is complicated by the need to maintain a common database that is shared among different edge-servers. In this paper we examine the performance characteristics of alternative edge-server architectures for transactional Enterprise JavaBeans (EJBs) applications. In one architecture, a remote database is shared among a number of edge-servers; in another, edge-servers maintain cached copies of transactionally-consistent EJBs. Importantly, the caching function is transparent to applications that use it.

We have built a prototype system in which edge-servers are enhanced with an EJB caching capability. The prototype enables a realistic comparison of these architectural alternatives. We use a benchmark EJB application to drive a performance analysis of the architectures. We also compare these edge-server architectures to a classic clustered datacenter architecture.

1 Introduction

1.1 Edge-Server Architectures

Edge-server architectures [16][6][2][5] are widely used to improve web-application performance by moving web-content from back-end servers to the edge of the network (e.g., internet service providers). By caching data at the "edge", edge-servers increase throughput (by offloading traffic from back-end servers), and reduce application latency (by moving data closer to the client).

Unfortunately, the data replication and update algorithms used in current edge-server architectures are severely limited. First, updates take place at a single central server (the master copy of the database). Updates to shared data cannot be made at the edge servers. Second, updates are pushed (or pulled) from the central server to the edge servers in a non-transactional fashion. Thus different edge servers will receive the updates at different times (i.e. the data as seen across all edge servers is not consistent).

For many web applications, these are reasonable compromises which are made in order to achieve high performance and scalability. In a typical ecommerce

H.-A. Jacobsen (Ed.): Middleware 2004, LNCS 3231, pp. 195–211, 2004.

application, it is not critical to have all the edge-cached catalogs updated transactionally. Similarly, it is not necessary to allow applications running at the edge to update the shared catalog database.

However, for transactional data (e.g. bank accounts), this is not sufficient. Bank accounts must show the same balance at every edge server, and update (e.g. debit) operations must happen in an ACID[11] fashion. The simple approach is to centralize transactional data, and not to replicate or cache it. Unfortunately this brings back the latency and bandwidth problems that were addressed by edge servers for non-transactional data.

This paper explores whether the benefits of edge-server technology can be extended to applications requiring the use of transactional data. Specifically, we examine whether *Enterprise JavaBeans*[4] (EJBs) applications can be deployed to edge-server architectures. EJBs are an example of a transactional component model; and, while this paper is focused on EJB technology, it applies more generally to any framework for distributed enterprise components[13].

1.2   Enterprise JavaBeans Component Model

EJBs are a component model for enterprise applications. (We refer here to the *entity bean* flavor of EJBs, in contrast to the *session bean* flavor.) Like CORBA[3] and RMI[17], EJBs are a distributed component model, and, as such, encapsulate both "data" (the component's state) and "code" (business logic in the component's methods). In addition, EJBs automatically supply common requirements of enterprise applications such as persistence, concurrency, transactional integrity, and security. Bean developers focus on the business logic of their application; when deployed to an EJB *container*, the components are embedded in an infrastructure that automatically supplies the above requirements. For example, a deployer might specify that an *Employee* entity bean's state is backed by persistent storage in the *HR* relational database, specifically in its *Employees* table. EJBs use declarative transaction management on a per-method basis, so that the `incrementSalary` method might be declared to require a transactional scope.

1.3   Edge-Servers and EJBs

While edge-servers currently cache both dynamic and static web-content, the cached data are not transactional. Static data are especially easy to cache because they are infrequently updated. Even when dynamic data are cached, updates typically do not need to be propagated atomically throughout the web cluster, since no transactional model is provided. Web-servers can therefore use algorithms which are expensive for write operations, and which do not provide a traditional *ACID*[11] transaction model[12]. Such applications and environments differ greatly from that of EJBs in which writes are frequent and strong transactional guarantees must be provided.

Specifically, edge-server caching of EJBs faces the following challenges:

- EJB caching must deal with read/write data as well as read-only data.
- As a stronger requirement than read/write capability, EJB caching must provide transactional consistency among the cached replicas.
- "Cache-enabling" existing applications and J2EE application servers must involve little effort. Customers should not be forced to modify existing applications in order to improve performance. Customers will also not want to maintain two programming models: one, for non-cache-enabled applications, and one for cache-enabled applications. Specifically, an EJB caching framework should have the following features:
  - It should not inject a new application component model, but instead use the EJB model of session and entity beans.
  - Although the runtime of cache-enabled application servers differs from standard J2EE application servers, the application developer should not be forced to write new code to access the runtime. Instead, tooling should take standard EJBs as input and produces cache-enabled EJB implementations with the same Java interface as output.
  - The cache-enabled version of the EJBs should support the same transactional model as described in the EJB specification: i.e., it must provide concurrency and transactional isolation.

While EJB caching has been successfully applied [14] to improve throughput in low-latency, clustered, environments, it does not necessarily follow that caching will be useful for high-latency (several hundred milliseconds per interaction) edge-server environments. The key issue is that transactional consistency requires that the EJB state at each of the edge-servers be synchronized with the persistent state of the remote database. This implies that whenever a transaction commits, at least one high-latency round trip must be performed between an edge-server and the remote database. First, the edge-server must transmit its transactional state (e.g., the set of EJBs modified during the transaction) to the remote database. In contrast to non-transactional data, an edge-server cannot independently commit local modifications to the EJBs because it must ensure that these changes do not conflict with the actions of other edge-servers. Second, after receiving the transaction state, the remote database must determine whether the transaction can be committed or whether it must be aborted; it then informs the edge-server of the transaction's outcome. The duration of this round-trip may be sufficiently long as to counter one of the basic motivations for edge-server architectures: namely, to use cached data to reduce application latency

1.4   Relationship to Other Caching Work

We have already explained that the key difference between classic web-caching and edge-server caching of EJBs involves the fundamental requirements of transactional data. EJB-caching more closely resembles distributed client-server database systems. Typically, such systems use one of two approaches: function (query) shipping or data shipping. In function-shipping systems, operations applied to shared data are propagated to the shared server. In data-shipping systems such as ours, the database clients cache a portion of the database, and operations are executed against the cached data on the client. Data-shipping systems require the use of a transactional cache-consistency algorithm in order to maintain ACID properties among the different client applications. A common approach is to designate one copy of the database as the "master" copy, and use algorithms which synchronize access (and recovery) against this copy.

Many such algorithms have been proposed and studied for distributed client-server database systems[8]. In terms of this taxonomy, we use a detection-based algorithm, with deferred validity checking, and invalidation when notified by the server about an update. Our system is somewhat different, using a component-server model rather than page-based models. In our work, we have extended the transactional consistency algorithm to include predicate-based queries, rather than simply direct access. This forces us to deal with more complex isolation issues such as the "phantom-read" problem.

Most importantly, our work addresses the issue of transparently cache-enabling an existing, high-level component API such as the EJB model.

More recent work in distributed client-server caching attacks performance issues by relaxing the consistency requirements. For example, DBCache[15] uses the federated features of DB2 to maintain a partial copy of a database that is weakly synchronized with the database server. Application queries are then executed against the cached database. DBProxy[1] retains the results of previously executed queries in a cache; this cache is then used to satisfy subsequent queries or subsets of the original query. Both of these approaches improve performance at the cost of replacing the traditional transactional guarantees with "time-based" guarantees: the data are only guaranteed to be up-to-date within some specified time period. In contrast to some of this database caching work, we assume that cached-enabled applications will expect the same transactional model as non-cached-enabled applications (i.e. strict ACID semantics). Furthermore, we examine the caching of transactional data to high-latency environments such as edge-servers.

1.5 Key Contributions

One contribution of this work is to advance the "state of the art" of edge-server architecture by demonstrating that edge-servers can successfully cache transactional, as well as non-transactional, data. We quantify the benefits of this approach by comparing the performance of a benchmark EJB application when deployed to (1) a cache-enabled edge-server architecture and (2) a "vanilla" edge-server architecture that must access a remote EJB application server whenever an application accesses EJBs. Further, we examine which of two alternate EJB caching architectures are best suited to an edge-server environment.

Another contribution of this work is to question whether edge-servers should cache transactional data at all. As explained above, transactional requirements imply that at least one high-latency round-trip be performed whenever a transaction commits. This raises a intriguing question: perhaps a classic, clustered (non-edge) data-center architecture is best suited for high-latency transaction environments. Rather than clients running application on edge-servers, clients may be better served by directly accessing a remote EJB application server. This paper quantifies the benefits of the clustered data-center for transactional applications deployed to high-latency environments, and shows that the (cache-enabled) edge-server architecture is a valid architecture even for transactional applications.

1.6   Paper Organization

The rest of this paper is organized as follows. First, we describe the EJB caching in some detail; then, we describe a set of alternative high-latency architectures for EJB (transactional) applications. The remainder of the paper is a performance evaluation of these architectures based on a benchmark EJB application.

2   Caching Framework

2.1   Application Components

Our caching framework [14] substitutes *Single Logical Image* (or *SLI*) Home and bean implementations for the standard JDBC Home and bean implementations used in the non-cache-enabled application. The caching runtime copies the state of the relevant persistent EJBs into *transient* EJBs as necessary, and then transparently delegates to them. The SLI bean introduces no business logic of its own; it simply delegates all method invocations to the transient bean. Because the transient bean implements the same interface as the original, JDBC, bean and differs only in the way it accesses its datastore, the *business logic* of the application is unchanged.

Since the EJB specification requires that EJBs cannot be serialized (rather, they are passed by reference), we must provide "value objects" that can be passed between address spaces. We term these value objects *mementos*[10]. Mementos have the same notion of "identity" as EJBs, as they support the getPrimaryKey method. Transient EJBs introduce two memento-related methods: create(Memento) (on the EJB home) so that they can be created from persistent state; and Memento getMemento() (on the Remote interface) so that the caching runtime can update the persistent state from the client's cached state. The memento containing the state at the beginning of a transaction is called the *before-image*; the memento containing the state at the transaction's end is called the *after-image*. The cache-enhanced application server maintains a transient datastore of memento instances.

The EJB container that manages the transient and SLI Homes is a standard container. The SLI and transient beans are fully compliant EJBs with Remote and Home interfaces and a Bean implementation. They differ from the familiar persistent, jdbc, beans only in that they use a transient datastore when loading and storing bean state. A SLI and associated transient bean share a common identity because `getPrimaryKey` returns the same value; this value is identical to that returned by persistent bean in the original application.

2.2   Populating the Cache

The EJB cache is populated in one of the following ways:

1. Direct application access through the bean's primary key, via an `ejbLoad` or `findByPrimaryKey` invocation.
   In this case, the cache runtime first determines whether the bean is already cached. If a cache miss occurs, the cache runtime fetches the before-image directly from the persistent datastore and caches it for subsequent use.
2. Indirect application access, when the bean is part of the result set returned by a custom finder method invocation.
   Unlike a direct access, the cache runtime must first run the query against the persistent datastore because only that datastore is guaranteed to have the entire (potential) result set available. The result set returned by the persistent datastore is then used to populate the cache. However, in order to guarantee that the application sees its prior updates, the runtime ensures that result set elements that were cached prior to the custom finder invocation are not overlaid with the current persistent state. Finally, with the finder's entire result set available in the cache, the custom finder is run against the transient Home, and that result is returned to the application.
   Other transactions may commit their state to the persistent datastore while a given transaction executes on a cache-enhanced application server. This implies that the algorithm used to implement custom finders can add members to the result set if the application executes the finder multiple times in a single transaction. The isolation model supplied by the framework is therefore slightly less powerful than *serializable* isolation, and corresponds instead to *repeatable-read* isolation[11].
3. Explicit bean creation by the application.
   In this case, the appropriate `create` method is invoked on the SLI home, delegated to the transient Home, and the resulting bean is cached.

2.3   Implementing Transactions

Populating a transient EJB cache is only one part of an EJB caching framework. The system must also provide transactional semantics identical to that provided by a non-cache-enabled runtime to a J2EE application. Because we want to allow inter-transaction caching (i.e., to allow EJBs cached by one transaction to be available to other, concurrent and subsequent, transactions) the system uses *optimistic* rather than *pessimistic* concurrency control[11] (or *detection based* rather than *prevention based*[8]). Under the pessimistic approach, one transaction cannot use data cached on behalf of another transaction because cached data must be locked throughout the period that it's accessed. The long duration of the lock period implied by inter-transaction caching makes the pessimistic approach much less feasible than the optimistic approach.

In our approach, a common transient store (not EJB-based) is maintained alongside a per-transaction transient store. When a direct-access operation results in a cache miss on the per-transaction store, the common store is checked for a copy of the EJB data before an attempt is made to access the persistent EJB. The disadvantage of this approach is that, since each cache-enabled application server maintains its own common transient store, the "conflict window" (i.e., the period of time in which an application's persistent state can be concurrently modified by some other transaction) widens. Just as we replace the original application's JDBC Homes and beans with their SLI equivalents, we replace the original pessimistic JDBC Resource Manager with an optimistic SLI Resource Manager.

Whenever the cache runtime must access the persistent EJBs (in any of the "populate" scenarios discussed above), it creates a separate (non-nested) short transaction for the duration of the access. This transaction is committed immediately after the access completes so that locks are released quickly by the persistent store. The application-generated transactions are thus decoupled from the datastore transactions used to provide data to the cache and update data from the cache. A single application transaction thus typically brackets multiple persistent datastore transactions. Finally, when the application transaction running on the cache-enabled application server commits, a persistent datastore transaction is run to commit the application's state changes.

The isolation semantics provided to the application are the following. If another transaction, t_2, modifies the persistent datastore's data from the state that existed at the beginning of the application's transaction t_1, t_1 will be aborted. We implement this behavior by comparing the before-image of every bean accessed in the transaction to the current corresponding image in the datastore at commit time. Only if no conflicts exist are t_1's EJBs committed to the datastore. During a successful commit, the transaction's set of after-image mementos are written to the datastore in a single datastore transaction. More subtly, if the application creates an EJB, the system must also verify that no EJB with the same key exists at commit time. Similarly, if the application removes an EJB, the system must also verify that the current-image still exists before deleting it and committing the transaction.

2.4 EJB Caching Architectures

Two EJB-caching configurations are discussed in this paper. In the *split-servers* configurations, the cache-enhanced application server requires a *back-end* application server that is one deployment "tier" removed from the client. The logic that handles cache misses and the logic that implements the optimistic concurrency control algorithm reside on the back-end server (see Figure 1). In the *combined servers* configuration, the back-end-server function is merged in the cache-enhanced application server (see Figure 2). This has the advantage of removing cross-address-space communication between the application servers, which improves performance under some scenarios. The disadvantage of the combined-servers approach is that the communication protocol between the cache-enabled application server and the database is whatever the JDBC driver uses to communicate with the database. Such protocols are typically not suitable for internet or Grid[9] usage due to firewall and security issues. In contrast, the back-end server approach introduces a known interface between the application server and back-end server. The protocol used to bridge this gap can be customized appropriately to the environment.

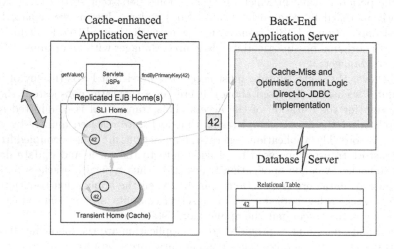

Fig. 1. Split-Server Configuration

3   High-Latency Architectures for EJB Applications

High-latency communication is a principal characteristic of internet environments. In order to better evaluate the benefits of edge-server use of EJB-caching, we characterize three architectures in terms of the location of the high-latency communication path.

1. An architecture in which a remote database is shared by a number of edge-servers. We term this an *ES/RDB* architecture. The edge-servers can be optionally enhanced with an EJB-caching capability. In that case, the ES/RDB configuration corresponds to the "combined-servers" EJB-caching configuration (Figure 2).
   In the ES/RDB architecture, the high-latency communication path lies between the application servers and the database (see Figure 3).
2. An architecture in which cache-enhanced application servers coordinate transactional activity using a common, remote, back-end server. The remote back-end server is closely clustered with a database. We term this an *ES/RBES* architecture.

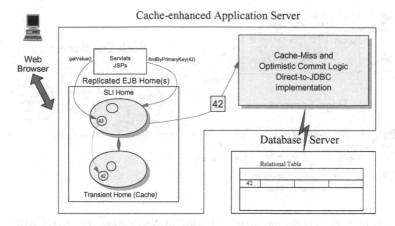

Fig. 2. Combined-Server Configuration

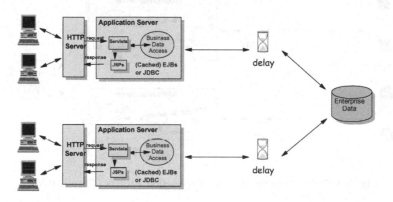

Fig. 3. Edge-Servers Sharing a Remote Database (ES/RDB)

In the ES/RBES architecture, the high-latency communication path lies between the cache-enhanced application servers and the back-end server that provides the cache-miss and transaction commit logic (see Figure 4). This architecture is meaningless to anything but a EJB-caching architecture, and corresponds, specifically, to the "split-servers" configuration (Figure 1).

3. A classic clustered datacenter architecture, in which clients do not interact with edge-servers but instead communicate directly with remote application servers. We term this a *Clients/RAS* architecture.

In the Clients/RAS architecture, the high-latency communication path lies between the web-clients and the remote application servers (Figure 5). As explained previously, in a transactional high-latency environment, this is a plausible alternative to an edge-server architecture.

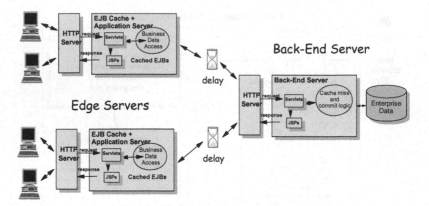

Fig. 4. Edge-Servers Sharing Remote Back-End Application Server (ES/RBES)

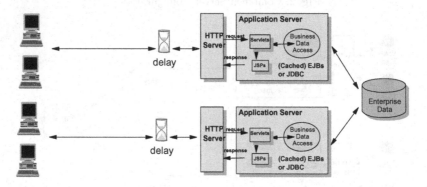

Fig. 5. Clients Accessing Remote Application Servers (Clients/RAS)

4   Performance Evaluation

In this section we evaluate:

1. Whether, and to what degree, Cache-enabled edge-servers improve the performance of EJB applications as compared to "vanilla" edge-servers.
2. Which version of the EJB-caching architecture is best suited for an edge-server environment.
3. Whether edge-servers – even when cache-enabled – are in fact suitable for transactional applications.

We do this by running cache-enabled and non-cache-enabled versions of a sample application in each of the three latency configurations discussed in Section 3. Before describing the test application, we describe the test configuration.

4.1 Test Configuration

System Components. The application server, *delay-proxy* server, back-end server, and database server run on four separate machines. Each is a uniprocessor, Pentium III, 1266MHz Intel machine with 256MB physical memory and 1GB paging space. The machines run RedHat Linux 7.1 (kernel 2.4.2-2), and are connected with a 100 Mbit Ethernet. DB2, version 7.2 provides the persistent datastore. The JVM is IBM's JDK Version 1.3.1; and the J2SDKEE version is 1.2.1. Tomcat, version 4.1.12 is used as the servlet engine. A prototype J2EE container is used for the SLI, persistent, and transient containers.

Delay Proxy. Our machines are deployed in a LAN environment with latency of, at most, several milliseconds. Because the performance evaluation requires that the application be deployed in an environment with latency of tens of milliseconds, we use a proprietary delay proxy to emulate a high-latency communication path. The delay proxy process runs on a dedicated machine. Depending on which communication path has high-latency, all communication between the specified endpoints (e.g., application servers and the database server) is intercepted by the delay proxy listening at a specific port. The proxy reads the incoming data, interposes a specified amount of delay, and only then writes the incoming data to the original destination. The data interception is functionally transparent to both the load generation program and the application. Performance results were generated by varying the delay injected by the proxy and determining the resulting application client latency.

4.2 Test Application

Trade2 is a publicly available application developed by IBM that "models an online brokerage firm providing web-based services such as login, buy, sell, get quote and more". Table 1, extracted from the application's documentation, describes the Trade2 runtime and database usage characteristics. A client interaction with the application involves a random sequence of the "trade actions" listed in the Table, bracketed by a "login" and "logout". The client web-browser sends a trade action request to a servlet; the servlet invokes the appropriate session bean method; the method, in turn, drives methods on or more entity beans. Finally, the result of the "trade action" is constructed in a JSP and returned to the client browser. On average, a single session consists of about 11 individual trade actions. We consider Trade2 to be a sufficiently complex application to make it a suitable J2EE benchmark. We downloaded version 2.531, cache-enabled it, and then evaluated its performance.

4.3 Results Roadmap

To evaluate the effectiveness of a given architecture, we focus on two statistics: the latency of a client/server interaction, and the bandwidth required to service

Table 1. Trade Runtime and Database Usage Characteristics

Trade Action	Description	CMP Bean Operation	HTTP Session	DB Activity $(C/R/U/D)$
Login	User sign in, session creation	Update	Create, Update	Registry R, U Account R
Logout	User sign-off, session destroy	Update	Read, Destroy	Registry R, U
Register	Create a new user profile and account	Multi-Bean Create	Create, Update	Account C, R, Profile C, Registry C
Home	Personalized home page including current market conditions	Read	Read	Account R
Account	Review current user profile information	Read	Read	Profile R
Account Update	"Account" followed by user profile update	Read/Update	Read	Profile R, U
Portfolio	View users current security holdings	Read	Read	Holding R
Quote	View a current security quote	Read	Read	Quote R
Buy	"Quote" followed buy a security purchase	Multi-Bean Read/Update	Read	Quote R, Account R, U Holding C, R
Sell	"Portfolio" followed by the sell of a holding	Multi-Bean Read/Update	Read	Quote R Account R, U Holding D, R

the client's request. These results are presented for the performance of the Trade2 benchmark in the three architectures discussed above.

Within a specific architecture, the effectiveness of EJB caching is evaluated by comparing its performance against two, non-cached-enabled, versions of the application.

- *JDBC*: a pure JDBC [7] implementation, included in Trade2. We include this algorithm because JDBC implementations are commonly understood to provide better performance than "higher-level" implementations such as EJBs.
- *Vanilla EJBs*: an implementation using non-cached EJBs with bean-managed-persistence (BMP), with persistence provided by DB2. This corresponds to the EJB-ALT mode in Trade2.

Results were obtained in a "low-load" situation so as to factor out queuing delay effects: specifically, one virtual client makes repeated requests to the Trade2 running on a single application server. The latency metric represents average latency of a round-trip interaction between the client and the application as a function of the (*one-way*) delay injected by the delay proxy at the specified

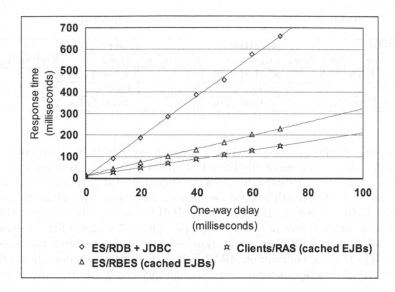

Fig. 6. Comparison of High-Latency Architectures

communication path. The set of possible trade actions are those listed in Table 1. (Both latency and the delay are specified in milliseconds.) In addition to individual data points, we show a linear curve extrapolating the data with an R^2 (quality of fit) of 99%. Client requests are driven by a load generator program on a dedicated machine. Reported latency is the batched (over 20 batches) average of a run consisting of 300 sessions. Each session consists, on average, of about 11 client/server interactions. A warmup period, consisting of 400 sessions, preceded each run.

4.4 Results

Figure 6 shows the latency behavior of the application when deployed to the three architectures; Figure 8 shows the bandwidth required to service client requests for the architectures.

We first observe that the non-edge-server architecture (Clients/RAS, "stars") has lower latency than either of the two edge-server architectures. We also observe that, of the two edge-server configurations, EJB-caching enables the ES/RBES architecture ("triangles") to perform far better than the best algorithm of the ES/RDB ("diamonds") architecture.

One way to understand these results is to examine *latency sensitivity* (Table 2), defined as the increase in the latency of a single client interaction for each unit increase in communication delay.

We see that the non-edge-server architecture is the least sensitive to increases in latency: every increase in *one-way* latency causes a *two-fold* increase in round-trip latency. This is because once the request is received by the application server,

Table 2. Algorithm Sensitivity to Communication Latency

ES/RDB		ES/RBES		Clients/RAS	
Algorithm	*Sensitivity*	*Algorithm*	*Sensitivity*	*Algorithm*	*Sensitivity*
Cached EJBs	13.0	Cached EJBs	3.1	Cached EJBs	2.0
JDBC	9.4	JDBC	N/A	JDBC	2.0
Vanilla EJBs	23.6	Vanilla EJBs	N/A	Vanilla EJBs	2.0

latency does not affect processing of the request in any way. In contrast, even the
best performing algorithm of the ES/RDB architecture is much more affected
by latency (9.4) since it incurs this penalty every time that a database access is
performed. Note that multiple database requests are required per client request.
Also, the JDBC implementation in the ES/RDB architecture is less affected by
latency than either vanilla or cached EJBs (see Figure 7). This is likely because
the (hand-crafted) JDBC implementation is better optimized than the tooled
EJB implementation. For example, BMP EJBs have difficulty caching the results
of a `findByPrimaryKey` operation, even though such results are typically reused
immediately.

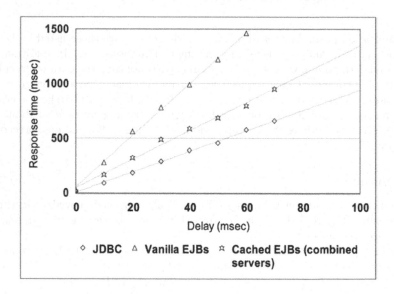

Fig. 7. Edge-Servers Accessing Remote Database

Compared to vanilla EJBs, EJB-caching is quite effective in reducing latency
sensitivity. In the ES/RDB architecture (Figure 7), sensitivity is reduced from
23.6 to 13.0; in the ES/RBES architecture, sensitivity is reduced to 3.1. Caching
is effective because fewer calls have to be made to access data across the high-
latency path. Why is caching more effective in the ES/RBES architecture than

in ES/RDB? The reason has to do with the way that the combined-servers (ES/RDB using cached EJBs) and split-server (ES/RBES) architectures commit a transaction. The combined-servers configuration requires multiple database server accesses, one per memento image. Assuming no cache misses, the split-server configuration requires only a single access to the back-end server. This access is done at commit time in order to transmit the set of memento images involved in the transaction. Of course, the back-end server will, in turn, perform multiple accesses to the database server. However, these occur over a low-latency path. In contrast, the combined-servers configuration has large delays between the cache-enhanced application server and the database server. In consequence, the extra round-trips incurred when a transaction commits dominates the extra address-space crossing required by the split-server configuration.

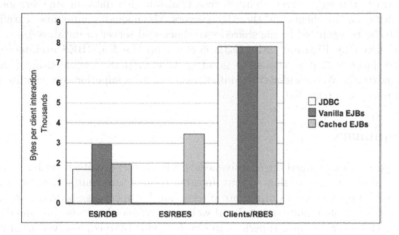

Fig. 8. Bandwidth

Why do the edge-server architectures, even using EJB caching, have greater latency than the remote data-center architecture? With the transactional caching algorithms that we have examined, at least one call to the database or back-end server is required for each commit operation. In Trade2, each client request involves at least one commit operation, because all client requests require access to some transactional data. Therefore, each client request involves at least one round-trip call to the back-end server, and possibly more calls to handle cache misses. These transactional caching algorithms cannot yield an edge-server with lower latency than a non-edge-server configuration. Although we use optimistic concurrency control (Section 2), the use of pessimistic concurrency-control algorithms will not improve the situation. Pessimistic concurrency control requires at least as many calls to acquire and release locks at the back-end server.

We do not claim that non-edge-servers will always supply lower-latency than edge-servers for transactional applications. Other applications may not require

210 Avraham Leff and James T. Rayfield

access to transactional data on every request. For example, workflow techniques could batch the commit of multiple client requests as a single transaction.

Although latency performance suggests that the non-edge-server architecture is best suited for transactional applications, Figure 8 shows the weakness of this architecture. We see that every client/server round-trip transmits more than 7000 bytes to the back-end server, while the edge-server architectures transmit far fewer bytes. ES/RBES transmits 3000 bytes and ES/RDB transmits 2000 bytes. These differences relate to one of the basic motivations for edge-servers: to reduce the amount of bandwidth that must be provisioned for the back-end server. In the Clients/RAS architecture, the presentation portion (HTML, images, JavaScript) of an application must all be transmitted on connections to the back-end server. (Because Trade2 does not contain images or static HTML, we expect that other applications would show an even greater "bandwidth effect".) In contrast, the edge-server architectures transmit this data on smaller, local pipes, between the clients and the edge-servers. Much smaller amounts of traffic needs to be transmitted to the shared site (back-end server or database).

As shown by Figure 6, using EJB caching on the ES/RBES architecture provides latency that is almost as good as Clients/RAS – while using much less bandwidth. We consider this configuration to be a superior compromise to optimize these two goals.

5 Summary

In this paper we examined the effectiveness of edge-server architectures for transactional applications. We showed that, in order to maintain transactional consistency, such applications require more interaction between edge-servers and the back-end server than non-transactional web-data. While this causes a non-edge-server architecture to have superior latency behavior than edge-server architectures, we showed that EJB-caching allows edge-servers to provide almost the same latency performance as the non-edge-server architecture, while providing much better bandwidth behavior.

Acknowledgements

We would like to thank Vikaram Desai, Jiwu Tao, and Michael Young (IBM Pittsburgh Lab) for their help in architecting and implementing an earlier version of the ejb caching framework.

References

1. K. Amiri, R. Tewari, S. Park, and S. Padmanabhan. On Space Management in a Dynamic Edge Data Cache . Fifth International Workshop on the Web and Databases (WebDB 2002). 2002.
http://www.db.ucsd.edu/webdb2002/papers/42.pdf

2. A Distributed Infrastructure for e-Business.
   http://www.akamai.com/en/html/services/white_paper_library.html. 2002.
3. OMG Specifications and Process. http://www.omg.org/gettingstarted, 2002.
4. Enterprise JavaBeans Specifications.
   http://java.sun.com/products/ejb/docs.html, 2002.
5. Edge Side Includes (ESI). http://www.esi.org/index.html, 2002.
6. WebSphere Edge Server.
   http://www-3.ibm.com/software/webservers/edgeserver/, 2002.
7. JDBC Data Access API http://java.sun.com/products/jdbc/, 2002.
8. M. J. Franklin, M. J. Carey, and M. Livny. Transactional Client-Server Cache Consistency: Alternatives and Performance. ACM Transactions on Database Systems. Vol. 22, No. 3. September 1997. 315-363.
9. I. Foster, C. Kesselman, and S. Tuecke. The Anatomy of the Grid: Enabling Scalable Virtual Organizations. International Journal of High Performance Computing Applications. 15(3). 2001. www.globus.org/research/papers/anatomy.pdf. 200-222.
10. E. Gamma et al. Design Patterns. Addison Wesley Longman, Inc. 1995.
11. J. Gray. A. Reuter. Transaction Processing: Concepts and Techniques. Morgan Kaufmann. 1993.
12. J. Gwertzman and M. I. Seltzer. World Wide Web Cache Consistency. USENIX Annual Technical Conference. 1996. 141-152.
13. A. Leff, P. Prokopek, J. T. Rayfield, and I. Silva-Lepe. Enterprise JavaBeans and Microsoft Transaction Server: Frameworks for Distributed Enterprise Components. Advances in Computers, Academic Press. Vol. 54. 2001. 99-152.
14. A. Leff and J. T. Rayfield. Improving Application Throughput with Enterprise JavaBeans Caching. May 2003. 23rd International Conference on Distributed Computing Systems.
15. Q. et al Luo. Middle-tier Database Caching for e-Business. Proc. ACM SIGMOD International Conference on Management of Data, 2002.
16. M. Rabinovich. O. Spatscheck. Web Caching and Replication. Addison Wesley Professional, 2002.
17. Java Remote Method Invocation (RMI).
    http://java.sun.com/docs/books/tutorial/rmi/, 2002.

Transparent Information Dissemination*

Amol Nayate[1], Mike Dahlin[1], and Arun Iyengar[2]

[1] University of Texas at Austin, Austin TX 78712, USA
{nayate,dahlin}@cs.utexas.edu
[2] IBM TJ Watson Research Center, Yorktown Heights, NY 10598, USA
aruni@us.ibm.com

Abstract. This paper describes Transparent Replication through Invalidation and Prefetching (*TRIP*), a self tuning data replication middleware system that enables transparent replication of large-scale information dissemination services. The TRIP middleware is a key building block for constructing *information dissemination* services, a class of services where updates occur at an origin server and reads occur at a number of replicas; examples information dissemination services include content distribution networks such as Akamai [1] and IBM's Sport and Event replication system [2]. Furthermore, the TRIP middleware can be used to build key parts of general applications that distribute content such as file systems, distributed databases, and publish-subscribe systems.
Our data replication middleware supports *transparent* replication by providing two crucial properties: (1) sequential consistency to avoid introducing anomalous behavior to increasingly complex services and (2) self-tuning transmission of updates to maximize performance and availability given available system resources. Our analysis of simulations and our evaluation of a prototype support the hypothesis that it is feasible to provide transparent replication for dissemination services. For example, in simulations, our system's performance is a factor of three to four faster than a demand-based middleware system for a wide range of configurations.

1 Introduction

This paper explores integrating self-tuning updates and sequential consistency to provide middleware support for replication of large-scale information dissemination services. We pursue the aggressive goal of supporting *transparent* service replication by providing two key properties.

1. The middleware provides *self-tuning updates* to maximize performance and availability given the system resources available at any moment. Self-tuning updates are crucial for transparent replication because static replication policies are more complex to maintain, less able to benefit from spare system resources, and more prone to catastrophic overload if they are mis-tuned or during periods of high system load [3].

---

* This work was supported in part by the Texas Advanced Technology Program, the National Science Foundation (CNS-0411026), and an IBM Faculty Partnership Award.

H.-A. Jacobsen (Ed.): Middleware 2004, LNCS 3231, pp. 212–231, 2004.

2. The middleware provides *sequential consistency* [4] with a tunable maximum-staleness parameter to reduce application complexity. Weaker consistency guarantees can introduce subtle bugs [5], and as Internet-scale applications become more widespread, ambitious, and complex, simplifying the programming model becomes increasingly desirable [6]. If we can provide sequential consistency, then we can take a single machine's or LAN cluster's service threads that access shared state via a file system or database and distribute these threads across WAN edge servers without re-writing the service and without introducing new bugs.

Not only is each of these properties important, but their combination is vital. Sequential consistency prevents the use of stale data, which could hurt performance and availability, but prefetching replaces stale data with valid data. Conversely, prefetching means that data are no longer fetched when they are used, so a prefetching system must rely on its consistency protocol for correct operation.

Providing sequential consistency in a large scale system while providing good availability [7] and performance [8] is fundamentally difficult. We therefore restrict our attention to replicated *dissemination services*, in which updates occur at one origin server and multiple edge server replicas treat the underlying replicated data as read-only and perform data caching, fragment assembly, per-user customization, and advertising insertion. Although this case is restrictive, it represents an important class of services. For example, Akamai's Edge Side Include [1] and IBM's Sport and Event replication system [2] both focus on improving the performance, availability, and scale of dissemination services.

In this paper, we describe the TRIP (Transparent Replication through Invalidation and Prefetching) middleware that integrates self tuning updates with sequential consistency to enable transparent replication for dissemination services. We define the node where updates originate to be the *origin server* and the receiving nodes the *replicas* of the system. Although we focus on dissemination services, more general services can make use of dissemination for subsets of their workloads. We therefore believe that TRIP can be used as a building block for services such as file systems, distributed databases, publisher/subscriber systems, and applications that use per-object-customized consistency [9].

This paper evaluates the TRIP middleware using both trace-based simulation and evaluation of an implementation. Our simulations use access/update traces obtained for a highly accessed sporting and event web site [10]. We build an NFS loopback interface [11] to emulate a smaller version of this web service on our TRIP middleware. Our configuration allows us to run unmodified edge servers that provide both static HTML files and dynamic responses generated by programs (e.g., CGI, Servelets, Server Side Include, or Edge Side Include), and that share data through the file system. Although our implementation exports a file system interface, a similar approach could be used to support a database or publisher/subscriber interface to the shared state.

This paper makes three contributions. First, it provides evidence that systems can maintain sequential consistency for some key WAN distributed services despite the CAP dilemma, which states that systems cannot get strong

Consistency and high Availability for systems vulnerable to Partitions [7]. The replication middleware circumvents this dilemma by (a) restricting the workload it considers and (b) integrating consistency with prefetching. Second, it presents a novel middleware component that integrates prefetching and consistency by (a) using a new self-tuning push-based prefetching algorithm and (b) carefully ordering and delaying the application of messages at replicas. Third, it provides a systematic evaluation and a working prototype of such a middleware component to provide evidence for the effectiveness and practicality of the approach.

2   System Model

Figure 1 provides a high level view of the environment we assume. An *origin server* and several *replicas* (also called content distribution nodes or edge servers) share data, and logical *clients* – either on the same machine or another – access the service via the replicas, which run service-specific code to dynamically generate responses to requests [1, 12–14]. The system typically uses some application-specific mechanism [2] to direct client requests to a good (e.g., nearby, lightly loaded, or available) replica. The design of such a redirection infrastructure is outside the scope of the paper; instead, we focus on the *data replication middleware* that provides shared state across the origin server and replicas. We focus on supporting on the order of 10 to 100 long-lived replicas that each have sufficient local storage to maintain a local copy of the full set of their service's shared data. Although our protocol remains correct under other assumptions about the number of replicas, replica lifetimes, and whether replicas replicate all shared data or only a subset, optimizing performance in other environments may require different trade-offs.

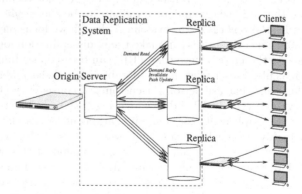

Fig. 1. High level system architecture.

2.1   Consistency and Timeliness

Evaluating the semantic guarantees of large-scale replication systems requires careful distinctions between *consistency*, which constrains the order that updates across multiple memory locations become *observable* [5] to nodes in the system, *coherence*, which constrains the order that updates to a single location become observable but does not additionally constrain the ordering of updates across different locations, and *staleness*, which constrains the real-time delay between when an update completes and when it becomes observable. Adve discusses the distinction between consistency and coherence in more detail [15].

To support transparency, we focus on providing sequential consistency. As defined by Lamport, "The result of any execution is the same as if the [read and write] operations by all processes were executed in some sequential order and the operations of each individual processor appear in this sequence in the order specified by its program." [4] Sequential consistency is attractive for transparent replication because the results of all read and write operations are consistent with an order that could legally occur in a centralized system, so – absent time or other communication channels outside of the shared state – a program that is correct for all executions under a local model with a centralized storage system is also correct for a distributed storage system.

Typically, providing sequential consistency is expensive in terms of latency [8, 16] or availability [7]. However, we restrict our study to *dissemination services* that have one writer and many readers, and we enforce *FIFO consistency* [8] under which writes by a process appear to all other processes in the order they were issued, but different processes can observe different interleavings between the writes issued by one process and the writes issued by another. Note that for applications that include only a single writer, FIFO consistency is identical to sequential consistency or the weaker causal consistency.

Although sequential consistency provides strong semantic guarantees at replicas, clients of those replicas may observe unexpected behaviors in at least two ways due to communication channels outside of the shared state.

First, because sequential consistency does not specify any real-time requirement, a client may observe stale (but consistent) data. For example, a network partition between the origin server and replica could cause the client of a stock ticker service to observe the anomalous behavior of a stock price not changing for several minutes. We note that in this scenario, physical time acts as a communications channel outside of the control of the data replication middleware that allows a user to observe anomalous behavior from the replication system. Hence, we allow systems to enforce timeliness constraints on data updates by providing Δ-*coherence*, which requires that any read reflect at least all writes that occurred before the current time minus Δ. By combining Δ-coherence with sequential consistency, TRIP enforces a tunable staleness limit on the sequentially consistent view. The Δ parameter reflects a per-service trade-off between availability and worst case staleness: reducing Δ improves timeliness guarantees but may hurt availability because disconnected edge servers may need to refuse a request rather than serve overly stale data.

Second, some redirection infrastructures [2] may cause a client to switch between replicas, allowing it to observe inconsistent state. For example, consider two replicas r_1 and r_2 where r_2 processes messages more slowly than r_1, and updates u_1 and u_2 such that u_1 *happens before* [17] u_2. If a client of r_1 sees update u_2, switches to r_2 (which has not seen u_1 yet) and sees data that should have been modified by u_1 but is not, it observes an inconsistency. In [18] we discuss how to adapt Bayou's session consistency protocol [19] to our system to ensure that each client observes a sequentially consistent view regardless of how often the redirection infrastructure switches the client among replicas.

3   Algorithm

TRIP is based on a novel replication algorithm that revolves around two simple parts: (1) the origin's self-tuning efforts to send updates in priority order without interfering with other network users and (2) each replica's efforts to buffer messages it receives, to apply them in an order that meets consistency constraints, and to delay applying some of these messages to improve availability and performance. We describe the algorithm in the rest of the section.

Algorithm 1 Origin server.

State
> $seqNo$; // Global sequence number
> $storage$; // Seq number + body of each object
> $nReplicas$; // Number of replicas
> $updtChnl[]$; // Lossy, prior. order, low prior. link
> $invDemChnl[]$; // Lossless, FIFO channels

On local call to write(objID, body, priority, timestamp):
> $seqNo$++;
> $storage.update(objId, body, seqNo)$;
> **for** $(i = 0;\ i < nReplicas;\ i$++$)$ **do**
>> $invDemChnl[i].send(INVAL, objId, seqNo, timestamp)$;
>> $updtChnl[i].insert(UPDATE, objId, body, seqNo, priority)$;

On receiving (READ, objId) from replica:
> $(body, objSeqNo) = storage.get(objId)$;
> $invDemChnl[replica].send(REPLY, objId, body, objSeqNo)$;
> $updtChnl[replica].cancel(objId)$;

3.1   Origin Server

As we show in the pseudocode in Algorithm 1, the origin server maintains a global monotonically increasing sequence number *seqNo*, local *storage* with the body and sequence number of each object, per-replica channels *invDemChnl[]* for sending invalidations and demand replies, and per-replica channels *updtChnl[]* for pushing updates. Each *invDemChnl* is a FIFO ordered, lossless network channel, and each *updtChnl* is a priority ordered, low-priority channel.

The algorithm proceeds as follows. To write an object, an origin server increments *seqNo*, updates *storage* with *seqNo* and the object's new body, sends invalidations on each replica's *invDemChnl*, and enqueues updates on each replica's *updtChnl*. Each enqueued update includes a *priority* that specifies the update's relative ranking to other pending updates. These priorities can be calculated using existing mechanisms [20–23], or using application-specific knowledge. By adding a *replicaID* parameter to our *write* method, our algorithm can be extended to accommodate per-replica priorities as well.

When the origin server receives a demand *read(objId)* from a replica, it retrieves from its local store the object's body and per-object sequence number, and it sends on the replica's *invDemChnl* a demand reply message. Notice that this reply includes the sequence number stored with the object when it was last updated, which may be smaller than the current global *seqNo*. Upon sending a demand reply to a client, the origin server also cancels any push of the object to that client still pending in the *updtChnl* for the receiving replica.

Each *updtChnl* provides an abstraction suited for self-tuning push-based prefetching by (1) buffering updates in a priority queue and (2) sending them across the network using a lossless, blocking, low priority network protocol. Three actions manipulate each per-replica priority queue. First, an *insert* adds an update with a specified priority, replacing any other update to the same *objId*. Second a *cancel(objId)* call removes any pending update for *objId*. Third, a worker thread loops, removing the highest priority update from the queue and then doing a low-priority network send of a push-update message containing the *objId*, *body*, and *seqNo* of the item. The low priority network protocol should ensure that low priority traffic does not delay, inflict losses on, or take bandwidth from normal-priority traffic; a number of such protocols have been proposed [24]. Thus, when sufficient bandwidth is available, an *updtChnl* behaves like a lossless FIFO channel and delivers all updates to its replica. When less bandwidth is available, however, (1) it only allows valuable updates to be sent, and (2) it allows unsent updates to the same object to be merged and sent later either when requested by a replica or during a lull in network traffic.

3.2   Replica

The core of each replica is a novel *scheduler* that coordinates the application of invalidations, updates, and demand read replies to the replica's local state. The scheduler has two conflicting goals. On one hand, it would like to delay applying invalidations for as long as possible to minimize the amount of invalid data and thereby maximize local hit rate, maximize availability, and minimize response time. On the other hand, it must enforce sequential consistency and Δ-coherence, so it must enforce two constraints:

C1 A replica must apply all invalidations with sequence numbers less than N to its storage before it can apply an invalidation, update, or demand reply with sequence number N.[1]

C2 A replica must apply an invalidation with timestamp t to its storage no later than $t + \Delta - maxSkew$.

Δ specifies the maximum staleness allowed between when an update is applied at the origin server and when the update affects subsequent reads, and *maxSkew* bounds the clock skew between the origin server and the replica.

---

[1] We show in [18] that enforcing condition C1 yields sequential consistency

---

Algorithm 2 Replica.

State

    storage; // *Validity, sequence number, and body of each object*
    pendingInval; // *Received but unprocessed invalidation*
    pendingUpdate; // *Received but unprocessed updates*
    delta; // *Max staleness between server and replica*
    maxSkew; // *Max clock skew between server and replica*

On receiving (INVAL, objId, seqNo, timestamp) on invDemChnl:

    pendingInval.put(objId, seqNo, timestamp);

On receiving (UPDATE, objId, body, seqNo) on updtChnl:

    pendingUpdate.put(objId, body, seqNo);

If pendingUpdate.head.seqNo≤pendingInval.nextSeqToProcess():

    // *Scheduler applies an update*
    (objId, body, seqNo) = pendingUpdate.removeHead();
    if *(seqNo ≥ storage.getSeqNo(objId))* **then**
      storage.update(objId, VALID, seqNo, body);
    if *(seqNo == pendingInval.nextSeqToProcess())* **then**
      pendingInval.doneProcessing(seqNo);

If currentTime() ≤ pendingInval.head.timestamp+delta-maxSkew:

    Scheduler applies an invalidate
    applyNextInval(); // *See below*

On local call to read(objId):

    if *(VALID == storage.getState(objId))* **then**
      return storage.getBody(objId);
    send(READ, objId) to origin server;
    storage.waitUntilValid(objId);
    return storage.getBody(objId);

On receiving (REPLY, objId, body, seqNo) on invDemChnl:

    while *(pendingInval.nextSeqToProcess() ≤ seqNo)* **do**
      applyNextInval(); // *See below*
    storage.update(objId, VALID, seqNo, body); // *Unblock read*

applyNextInval() // Internal private method called from above

    (objId, seqNo, timestamp) = pendingInval.readHead();
    if *(seqNo ≥ storage.getSeqNo(objId))* // '*At least once*' *chnl* **then**
      storage.update(objId, INVALID, seqNo);
    pendingInval.doneProcessing(seqNo);

Algorithm Details. The pseudocode in Algorithm 2 describes the behavior of a replica. Each replica maintains five main data structures. First, a replica maintains a local data store *storage* that maps each object ID for the shared state to either the tuple *(INVALID, seqNo)* if the local copy of the object is in the invalid state or the tuple *(VALID, seqNo, body)* if the local copy of the object is in the valid state. Second, a replica maintains *pendingInval*, a list of pending invalidation messages that have been received over the network but not yet applied to *storage*; these invalidation messages are sorted by sequence number. Third, a replica maintains *pendingUpdate*, a list of pending pushed updates that have been received over the network but not yet applied to the local data store; notice that although the origin server sorts and sends these update messages by priority, each replica sorts its list of pending updates by *sequence number*. Finally, Δ specifies the maximum staleness allowed between when an update is applied at the origin server and when the update affects subsequent reads, and *maxSkew* bounds the clock skew between the origin server and the replica.

Scheduler Actions. After *INVAL* and *UPDATE* messages arrive and are enqueued in *pendingInval* and *pendingUpdate*, a scheduler applies these buffered messages in a careful order to meet the two constraints above and to minimize the amount of invalid data.

The scheduler removes the update message with the lowest sequence number from its *pendingUpdates* and applies it to its *storage* as soon as it knows it has applied all invalidations with lower sequence numbers from *pendingInvals*. Applying a prefetched update normally entails updating the local sequence number and body for the object, but if the locally stored sequence number already exceeds the update's sequence number, the replica must discard the update because a newer demand reply or invalidation has already been processed.

The scheduler removes the invalidation message with the lowest sequence number from *pendingInval* and applies it to its *storage* when the invalidation's deadline arrives at *timestamp* + Δ − *maxSkew*. The *pendingInval* queue and network channel normally provide FIFO message delivery, and they guarantee at least once delivery of each invalidation when crashes occur. To support end-to-end at-least-once semantics, before applying an invalidation, a replica verifies that it is a new one, and after applying an invalidation a replica calls *pendingInval.doneProcessing(seqNo)* to allow garbage collection of the message and to acknowlege processing of invalidation *seqNo* to the origin server.

Processing Requests from Clients. When servicing a client request that reads object *objId* (either as input to a dynamic content-generation program or as the reply to a request for a static data file), a replica uses the locally stored body if *objId* is in the *VALID* state. But, if the object is in the *INVALID* state, the replica sends a demand request message to the server and then waits for the demand reply message. Note that by sending demand replies and invalidations on the same FIFO network channel, the origin server guarantees that when a demand reply with sequence number N arrives at a replica, the replica has already received all invalidations with sequence numbers less than N, though some of these invalidations may still be buffered in *pendingInval*. So when a demand reply arrives, the replica enforces condition C1 by simply applying all invalidation messages whose sequence numbers are at most the reply's sequenceNumber before applying the reply's update to the local state and returning the reply's value to the read request.

Our protocol implements an additional optimization (not shown in the pseudo-code for simplicity) by maintaining an index of pending updates searchable by object ID. Then, when a read request encounters an invalid object, before sending a demand request to the origin server, the replica checks the pending update list. If a pending update for the requested object is in this list, the system applies all invalidations whose sequence numbers are no larger than the pending update's sequence number, applies that pending update, and returns the value to the read request.

A remaining design choice is how to handle a second read request r_2 for object o_2 that arrives when a first read request r_1 for object o_1 is blocked and waiting to receive a demand reply from the origin server. Allowing r_2 to proceed and potentially access a cached copy of o_2 risks violating sequential consistency [15] if program order specifies that r_1 *happens before* r_2. On the other hand, if r_1 and r_2 are issued by independent threads of computation that are not synchronized, then the threads are logically concurrent and it would be legal to allow read r_2 to "pass" read r_1 in the cache [4,5]. TRIP therefore provides two options. *Conservative* mode preserves transparancy but requires a read issued while an earlier read is blocking on a miss to block. *Aggressive* mode compromises transparancy because it requires knowledge of application internals, but it allows a cached read to pass a pending read miss. Our experiments examine this trade-off in more detail.

Operating during Disconnection. When a replica becomes disconnected from the server due to a network partition or server failure, the replica attempts to service requests from its local store as long as possible. However, to enforce Δ-coherence, a replica must block all reads if it has not communicated with the origin server for Δ seconds. In a web service environment, blocking a client indefinitely is an undesirable behavior. Therefore, TRIP provides three ways for services to give up some transparancy in order to gain control of recovery in the case where a replica blocks because it is disconnected from the origin server. First, TRIP can reply to read requests from the calling edge server program by returning an error code. Because this approach requires that the edge server program be designed to expect such an error code, it prevents the replication layer from being fully transparent. Second, TRIP can (1) signal the redirection layer [2] to stop sending requests to this replica and (2) signal the local web server infrastructure to close all existing client connections and to respond to subsequent client requests with HTTP redirects [25] to different replicas. Although this approach requires web servers to be augmented with the ability to handle signals from the replication layer, we do not expect these changes to be invasive. Third, TRIP can increase Δ (and thus increase observable data staleness) when it detects a disconnection from the server. Increasing Δ allows the system to further delay applying pending invalidations and thus maximize the amount of valid local data and maximize the amount of time the replica can operate before suffering a miss.

3.3   Limitations and Optimizations

Our current protocol faces two limitations that could be addressed with future optimizations. First, as described in Section 2.1 our current protocol can allow a client that switches between replicas to observe violations of sequential consistency. We speculate in [18] that a system could shield a client from inconsistency by adapting Bayou's session guarantees protocol [19]. Second, our protocol sends each invalidation to all replicas even if a replica does not currently have a valid copy of the object being invalidated. We take this approach for simplicity, although our protocols could be extended to more traditional caching environments where replicas maintain small subsets of data by adding callback state [26].

4 Prototype

We have developed a prototype that implements the *conservative* version (Section 3.2) of the algorithm described in Section 3. Deployment depends on two subsystems that are outside the scope of this project: a protocol for limiting the clock skew between each replica and the origin server [27] and a policy for prioritizing which documents to push to which replicas [21,23], which may, in turn, require some facility for gathering read frequency information from replicas [28]. We discuss limitations of our prototype in more detail in [18].

Our prototype is implemented in Java, C, and C++ on a Linux platform, but we expect the server code to be readily portable to any standard operating system and the replica code to be portable to any system that supports mounting an NFS server. The code is available for download from http://www.cs.utexas.edu/users/nayate/TRIP.

The rest of this section discusses internal details and design decisions in the server and replica implementations.

Origin Server. The origin server uses the local file system for file storage. Note that rather than store per-file sequence numbers, which the protocol sends with demand read replies, our prototype only maintains a global sequence number. The algorithm operates as described in Section 3, except the server includes the current global sequence number when sending a demand reply rather than the sequence number of the object's most recent update. This simplification can force a replica to process more invalidation messages before processing a demand reply; the resulting protocol thus continues to provide sequential consistency, but its performance and availability may be reduced compared to the full protocol.

To simplify handing failures, the origin server uses a custom persistent message queue [29] for sending updates and invalidations to each replica. Because our protocol only uses the update channel to push update data, the origin server does not store out-bound updates to persistent storage and considers it permissible to lose these updates across crashes. To provide a low-priority network channel for updates that does not interfere with other network traffic, we use an implementation of TCP-Nice [24].

Replica. The replica implements a single *read* method to access shared data. The simplicity of this interface allows us to use TRIP as a building block for a variety of replicated applications that require sophisticated interfaces. For example, publish/subscribe systems can be implemented by having the publisher perform write calls to publish data to the matching service, and the matching service can later make read calls to request data to serve to clients. Chen et al. [30] shows an approach that can be adopted to compute priorities for pages in a publisher/subscriber model. For our prototype, however, we build TRIP to export a subset of the interface used by the NFS file system via a local user-level NFS file server [11], allowing the replica to mount this local file server as if it were a normal NFS server. Shared objects are accessed as if they are stored in a standard file system. For simplicity, we respond to reads to invalidated data during disconnections by returning an NFS IO error code to the calling program.

5   Evaluation

We evaluate our traces using two approaches: by employing a trace-driven simulator and evaluating a prototype.

5.1   Simulation Methodology

Our trace-driven simulator models an origin server and twenty replicas and assumes that the primary bottleneck in the system is the network bandwidth from the origin server. To simplify analysis and comparisons among algorithms, we assume that the bandwidth available to the system does not change throughout a simulation. We also assume that bandwidth consumed by control information (invalidate messages, message queue acknowledgments, meta data, etc.) is insignificant compared to the bandwidth consumed transferring objects; we confirm using our prototype that control messages account for less than 1% of the data transferred by the system. Transferring an object over the network thus consumes a link for $objectsize/bandwidth$ seconds, and the delay from when a message is sent to when it is received is given by $nwLatency+messageSize/bandwidth$. By default we simulate a round-trip time (or 2 * $nwLatency$) of 200ms +/- 90% between the origin server and a replica.

We compare TRIP's *FIFO-Delayed-Invalidation/Priority-Delayed-Update* algorithm with two algorithms: *Demand Only*, which delivers invalidates eagerly in FIFO order but does no prefetching, and *Push All* which eagerly pushes all updates to all replicas in FIFO order. We initially assume that the system requires (1) sequential consistency, which all of these algorithms provide, and (2) a Δ-coherence guarantee of $\Delta = 60$ seconds, which Demand Only naturally meets, TRIP consciously enforces, and Push All may or may not meet depending on available bandwidth. We will later modify these assumptions.

We evaluate our algorithms using a trace-based workload of the Web site of a major sporting event [10] hosted at several geographically distributed locations. In order to simplify simulations we ignore those entries in our trace files that contain dynamic/malformed requests, result in invalid server return codes, or that appear out of order.

Prediction Policy. Our interface allows a server to use any algorithm to choose the priority of an update, and this paper does not attempt to extend the state of the art in prefetch prediction. A number of standard prefetching prediction algorithms exist [20–23] or the server may make use of application-specific knowledge to prioritize an item. Our simple default heuristic for estimating the benefit/cost ratio of one update compared to another is to first approximate the probability that the new version of an object will be read before it is written as the observed read frequency of the object divided by the observed write frequency of the object and then to set the relative priority of the object to be this probability divided by the object's size [23]. This algorithm appears to be a reasonable heuristic for server push-update protocols: it favors read-often objects over write-often objects and it favors small objects over large ones.

5.2   Simulation Results

Our primary simulation results are that (1) self-tuning prefetching can dramatically improve the response time of serving requests at replicas compared to demand-based strategies, (2) although a Push All strategy enjoys excellent response times by serving all requests directly from replicas' local storage, this strategy is fragile in that if update rates exceed available bandwidth for an extended period of time, the service must either violate its Δ-consistency guarantee or become unavailable, (3) when prefetching is used, delaying application of invalidation messages by up to 60 seconds provides a modest additional improvement in response times, and (4) by maximizing the amount of valid data at replicas, prefetching can improve availability by masking disconnections between a replica and the origin server.

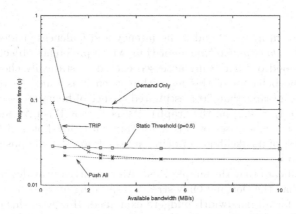

Fig. 2. The effect of bandwidth availability on response times.

Response Times and Staleness. In Figure 2 we quantify the effects of different replication strategies on client-perceived response times as we vary available bandwidth. We assume that client requests for valid objects at the replica are satisfied in 20ms, whereas requests for invalidated objects are forwarded from the replica to the origin over a network with an average round-trip latency of 200ms as noted above. To put these results in perspective, Figure 3 plots the average *staleness* observed by a request. We define staleness as follows. If a replica serves version k of an object after the origin site has already (in simulated time) written version j ($j > k$), we define the staleness of a request to be the difference between when the request arrived at the replica and when version $k + 1$ was written. To facilitate comparison across algorithms, this average staleness figure includes non-stale requests in the calculations. We omit due to space constraints a second graph that shows the (higher) average staleness observed by the subset of reads under each algorithm that receives stale data.

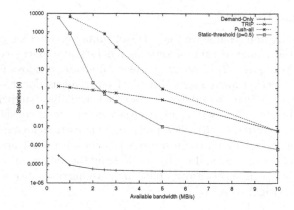

Fig. 3. Average staleness of data served by replicas.

We also show in figures 2 and 3 the latency and staleness yielded when using the *static-threshold-prefetching* algorithm, which prefetches objects when the predicted likelihood of their being accessed exceeds a statically chosen threshold. We plot the behavior of this algorithm when it is tuned to prefetch objects that have a greater than 50% estimated chance of being accessed (denoted *Static Threhold* ($p = 0.5$) on the graph). We note that Push All and Demand Only represent extreme cases of this algorithm with thresholds of 0 (push an update regardless of its likelihood of being accessed) and 1 (only push an update if it is certain to be accessed), respectively.

The data indicate that the simple Push All algorithm provides much better response time than the Demand Only strategy, speeding up responses by a factor of at least four for all bandwidth budgets examined. However, this comparison is a bit misleading as Figure 3 indicates: for bandwidth budgets below 2.1MB/s, Push All fails to deliver all of the updates and serves data that becomes increasingly stale as the simulation progresses. If the system enforces Δ-coherence with $\Delta = 60$ seconds, Push All replicas would be forced to either violate this freshness guarantee or become unavailable when the available bandwidth falls below about 5MB/s.

The static-threshold line illustrates precisely the problem with static thresholds. When the system has less than 2MB/s available bandwidth, the static-threshold algorithm yields lower response times than the TRIP algorithm. However, we note that for this bandwidth range the static-threshold algorithm also violates staleness guarantees. Similarly, when the system has more than 2MB/s bandwidth available, the static-threshold algorithm fails to utilize it to reduce response times.

Even at low bandwidths, TRIP gets significantly better response times than the Demand Only algorithm because (a) the self-tuning network scheduler allows prefetching to occur during lulls in demand traffic even for a heavily loaded system [3] and (b) the priority queue at the origin server ensures that the prefetching that occurs is of high benefit/cost items. TRIP's ability to exploit lulls in demand bandwidth also constitutes the reason that when the system has 2MB/s available bandwidth TRIP can outperform static-threshold while still retaining its timeliness guarantees.

Variations of TRIP. Due to space constraints, we omit a graph that plots response times for two variations of TRIP. In the first variation, we reduce the Δ parameter to 0 to evaluate the behavior of TRIP when we require replicas to apply all invalidate messages immediately. Under this scenario we find that values of Δ below 60s inflict a modest cost on response times, but this cost falls as available bandwidth increases. For example, at 1MB/s of available bandwidth, the $\Delta = 60s$ case yields 12.6% lower response times than the $\Delta = 0s$ case. However, our second variation of TRIP, *TRIP-aggressive*, which sacrifices some transparency and assumes that parallel read requests are independent, can result in substantial benefits. For example, for a system with 500KB/s of available bandwidth, this optimization improves response time by a factor of 2.5. But, this benefit falls as available bandwidth increases, suggesting that this optimization may become less valuable as network costs fall relative to the cost of requiring programmers to carefully analyze applications to rule out the possibility of unexpected interactions [6].

5.3 Availability

We measure the replication policies' effect on availability as follows. For each of 50 runs of our simulator for a given set of parameters, we randomly choose a point in time when we assume that the origin server becomes unreachable to replicas. We simulate a failure at that moment and measure the length of time before any replica receives a request that it cannot mask due to disconnection. We refer to this duration as the *mask duration*. We assume that systems enforce Δ-coherence

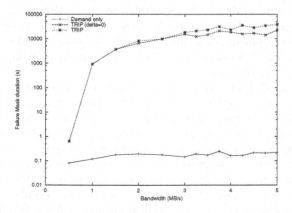

Fig. 4. Dependence of mask duration on bandwidth.

with $\Delta = 60$ seconds before the disconnection but that disconnected replicas maximize their mask duration by stopping their processing of invalidations and updates during disconnections and extending Δ as long as they can continue to service requests. Thus, during periods of disconnectivity, our system chooses to provide stale data rather than failing to satisfy client requests. Note that given these data, the impact of enforcing shorter Δs during disconnections can be estimated as the minimum of the time reported here and the Δ limit enforced.

Figure 4 shows how the average mask duration varies with bandwidth for the TRIP, TRIP ($\Delta = 0$), and Demand Only algorithms. Because mask duration is highly sensitive to the timing of a failure, different trials show high variability. We quantify this variability in more detail in an extended technical report [18].

Note that the traditional Demand Only algorithm performs poorly. In Figure 4, the line closely follow $y = 0$, indicating virtually no ability to mask failures. This poor behavior arises because the first request for an object after that object is modified causes a disconnected replica to experience an unmaskable failure. On the other hand, the Push All algorithm can mask all failures due to the fact that at any point in time, the entries in a replica's cache form a sequentially consistent (though potentially stale) view of data.

The TRIP algorithm outperforms the Demand Only algorithm in the graph by maximizing the amount of local valid data. We note that both TRIP variations provide average masking times of thousands of seconds for bandwidth of 1.5MB/s and above and that providing additional bandwidth allows these systems to prefetch more data and hence mask a failure for a longer duration. As noted in Section 3, systems may choose to relax their Δ-coherence time bound to some longer Δ' value during periods of disconnection to improve availability. These data suggest that systems may often be able to completely mask failures that last the maximum maskable duration even for relatively large Δ' limits.

5.4   Prototype Measurements

We evaluate our prototype on the Emulab testbed [31]. We configure the network to consist of an origin server and 4 replicas that receive 5MBps of bandwidth and 200ms round-trip times. We mount the local user-level file server using NFS with attribute caching disabled. For simplicity, we do not monitor object replication priorities in real time but instead pre-calculate them using each object's average read rate, write rate, and size [23].

Since the goal of the prototype is to evaluate how our system performs in practice, we use a more realistic evaluation methodology from the one we use for our simulator. In particular, when evaluating our prototype we do not remove any entries from our traces and make no simplifying assumptions about the size of invalidate messages or the behavior of network links. However, due to the lack of data on which resources or objects get accessed to handle dynamic requests, our system incorrectly treats dynamic requests as accesses to static objects.

Figure 5 shows the response times as seen at each of the 4 replicas. We collect these data by replaying at the origin and at each replica the first hour of our update trace and web traces in real time. The response time for a given request

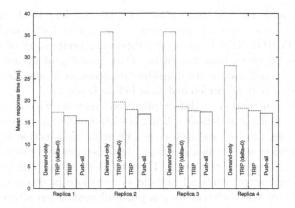

Fig. 5. Replica-perceived response times yielded by the Demand-fetch-only, FIFO-push-all, and the TRIP algorithms.

is calculated as the difference between when the request arrives at a replica and when its reply is generated. Note that these response times do not represent the end-to-end delay experienced by clients because they do not include the network delays between clients and replicas. However, one can easily compute total end-to-end delays by adding client-replica network delays to this data.

As we see in the graph, the Push All algorithm yields the best response time. For example, it outperforms the Demand Only algorithm by a factor of 2 for 3 of the 4 replicas. We note that at 5MBps bandwidth available to the system, TRIP incurs only minor increases in response times over Push All: 7.5%, 6.2%, 1.4%, and 3.4% overhead for each replica respectively. We also note that by delaying the application of invalidate messages, TRIP with $\Delta = 60s$ reduces response times compared to $\Delta = 0$ by 4.4%, 8.7%, 5.0%, and 3.0% respectively. Because we use real traces instead of simulated workloads, we notice that our response times vary greatly between replicas. However, our TRIP algorithms consistently outperform the Demand Only algorithm on each replica.

6 Related Work

In contrast with TRIP, most existing and proposed replication systems provide neither self-tuning replication nor sequential consistency with tunable staleness.

In particular, most replication systems use static replication policies such as always-conservative demand fetching [1, 32], always-aggressive push-all [2, 33], or hand-tuned threshold-based prefetching [20–22]. Davison et al. [34] propose using a connectionless transport protocol and using low priority datagrams (the infrastructure for which is assumed) to reduce network interference. Chen et al. [30] study content delivery and caching in publish/subscribe systems and discuss methods to estimate the benefit of caching pages that are directly applicable in computing update priorities in our system. In earlier work, we describe a threshold-free prefetching system called NPS [3] that like TRIP makes use of TCP-Nice [24] to avoid network interference. The rest of NPS's design is quite different than TRIP's: NPS focuses on supporting prefetching of soon-to-be-accessed objects by client browsers rather than pushing of updates by origin servers to replicas, and it does not consider the problem of maintaining consistency for data that may be prefetched long before being used.

Most proposed Internet-scale data replication systems focus on ensuring various levels of coherence or staleness or both [35–38], but few provide explicit consistency guarantees. Bradley and Bestavros [39] argue that increasingly complex Internet-scale services will demand sequential consistency and propose a vector-clock-based algorithm for achieving it. They focus on developing a backwards-compatible browser-server protocol and do not explore prefetching. The IBM Sporting and Event CDN system uses a push-all replication strategy and enforces delta coherence via invalidations [40]. Akamai's EdgeSuite [1] primarily relies on demand reads and enforces delta coherence via polling with stronger consistency available via object renaming. Most of these systems use demand reads, but several strategies for mixing updates and invalidates have been explored for multicast networks [41, 35] or broadcast media [42]. These proposals all use static thresholds to control prefetching and provide best-effort consistency, coherence, and timeliness semantics by sending and applying all messages eagerly. A potential avenue for future work is to develop a way for TRIP to make use of multicast or hierarchies to scale to larger numbers of replicas.

In replicated databases, several systems have explored ways to allow different updates to specify different consistency requirements. Lazy Replication [43] allows an update to enforce causal, sequential, or linearizable consistency. Bayou [33] maintains causal consistency at all times and asynchronously reorders operations to eventually reach a global sequentially-consistent ordering of updates. These systems both focus on multi-writer environments and eventually propagate all updates to all replicas. Yu and Vahdat [44] show that in such systems minimizing the time between when an update occurs and when it propagates maximizes system availability for any given consistency constraint. Our protocol exploits this observation for dissemination workloads by integrating consistency and self-tuning prefetch.

Our argument for sequential consistency is similar in spirit to Hill's position that multiprocessors should support simple memory consistency models like sequential consistency rather than weaker models [6]. Hill argues that speculative execution reduces the performance benefit that weaker models provide to the point that their additional complexity is not worth it. We similarly argue that for dissemination workloads, as technology trends reduce the cost of bandwidth, prefetching can reduce the cost of sequential consistency so that little additional benefit is gained by using a weaker model and exposing more complexity to the programmer.

7   Conclusion

This paper explores integrating self-tuning updates and sequential consistency to enable transparent replication of large-scale dissemination services. Our novel architecture succeeds in this goal by (1) providing self-tuning push-based prefetch from the server and (2) buffering and carefully scheduling the application of invalidations and updates at replicas to maximize the amount of valid data – and thus maximize the hit rate, minimize the response time, and maximize availability – at a replica. Our analysis of simulations and our evaluation of a prototype support the hypothesis that it is feasible to provide transparent replication for dissemination applications by integrating consistency and prefetching.

A limitation of this work is its focus on information dissemination applications. This class of applications is important, but in the future we hope to apply our protocol as part of a more general system where one subset of the data is read-only at the replicas, where another subset is read/write at the replicas, and where different subsets use different consistency algorithms [9].

Acknowledgments

We thank Paul Dantzig for his help in obtaining access and update logs, Arun Venkataramani for his crucial help in the design of the algorithm, and Jian Yin for his helpful comments on the presentation.

References

1. Turbo-charging dynamic web data with akamai edgesuite. Akamai White Paper (2001)
2. Challenger, J., Dantzig, P., Iyengar, A.: A scalable and highly available system for serving dynamic data at frequently accessed web sites. In: ACM/IEEE, Supercomputing '98. (1998)
3. Kokku, R., Yalagandula, P., Venkataramani, A., Dahlin, M.: Nps: A non-interfering deployable web prefetching system. In: 4th USENIX Symposium on Internet Technologies and Systems. (2003)
4. Lamport, L.: How to make a multiprocessor computer that correctly executes multiprocess programs. IEEE Transactions on Computers C-28 (1979) 690–691
5. Frigo, M., Luchangco, V.: Computation-Centric Memory Models. In: Tenth Annual ACM Symposium on Parallel Algorithms and Architectures. (1998)
6. Hill, M.: Multiprocessors should support simple memory consistency models,. In: IEEE Computer. (1998)
7. Brewer, E.: Lessons from giant-scale services. IEEE Internet Computing (2001)
8. Lipton, R., Sandberg, J.: PRAM: A scalable shared memory. Technical Report CS-TR-180-88, Princeton (1988)
9. Gao, L., Dahlin, M., Nayate, A., Zheng, J., Iyengar, A.: Application specific data replication for edge services. In: International World Wide Web Conference. (2003)
10. Sydney olympic games web site. http://www.olympic.com – site is no longer available (2000)

11. Mazières, D.: A toolkit for user-level file systems. In: 2001 USENIX Technical Conference. (2001) 261–274
12. Awadallah, A., Rosenblum, M.: The vMatrix: A network of virtual machine monitors for dynamic content distribution. In: Internat. Workshop on Web Caching and Content Distribution. (2002)
13. Vahdat, A., Dahlin, M., Anderson, T., Aggarwal, A.: Active Naming: Flexible Location and Transport of Wide-Area Resources. In: 2nd USENIX Symposium on Internet Technologies and Systems. (1999)
14. Whitaker, A., Shaw, M., Gribble, S.: Denali: Lightweight virtual machines for distributed and networked applications. In: 2002 USENIX Technical Conference. (2002)
15. Adve, S., Gharachorloo, K.: Shared memory consistency models: A tutorial. IEEE Computer **29** (1996) 66–76
16. Burns, R., Rees, R., Long, D.: Consistency and locking for distributing updates to web servers using a file system. In: Workshop on Performance and Architecture of Web Servers. (2000)
17. Lamport, L.: Time, clocks, and the ordering of events in a distributed system. Comm. of the ACM **21** (1978)
18. Nayate, A., Dahlin, M., Iyengar, A.: Integrating Prefetching and Invalidation for Transparent Replication of Dissemination Services. Technical Report TR-03-44, University of Texas at Austin (2003)
19. Terry, B., Demers, A., Petersen, K., Spreitzer, M.J., Theimer, M., Welch, B.: Session guarantees for weakly consistent replicated data. In: International Conference on Parallel and Distributed Information Systems. (1994) 140–149
20. Duchamp, D.: Prefetching Hyperlinks. In: 2nd USENIX Symposium on Internet Technologies and Systems. (1999)
21. Gwertzman, J., Seltzer, M.: The case for geographical pushcaching. In: HOTOS95. (1995) 51–55
22. Padmanabhan, V., Mogul, J.: Using Predictive Prefetching to Improve World Wide Web Latency. In: ACM SIGCOMM Conference. (1996) 22–36
23. Venkataramani, A., Yalagandula, P., Kokku, R., Sharif, S., Dahlin, M.: Potential costs and benefits of long-term prefetching for content-distribution. In: Web Caching and Content Distribution Workshop. (2001)
24. Venkataramani, A., Kokku, R., Dahlin, M.: TCP-Nice: A mechanism for background transfers. In: OSDI02. (2002)
25. Fielding, R., Gettys, J., Mogul, J., Frystyk, H., Misinter, L., Leach, P., Berners-Lee, T.: Hypertext Transfer Protocol – HTTP/1.1. RFC 2616, IETF (1999)
26. Howard, J., Kazar, M., Menees, S., Nichols, D., Satyanarayanan, M., Sidebotham, R., West, M.: Scale and Performance in a Distributed File System. ACM Trans. on Computer Systems **6** (1988) 51–81
27. Mills, D.: Network time protocol (version 3) specification, implementation and analysis. Technical report, IETF (1992)
28. Yalagandula, P., Dahlin, M.: SDIMS: A scalable distributed information management system. Technical Report TR-03-47, University of Texas Dept. of CS (2003)
29. MQSeries: An introduction to messaging and queueing. IBM Corporation GC33-0805-01 (1995)
30. Chen, M., LaPaugh, A., Singh, J.P.: Content distribution for publish/subscribe services. In: Proceedings of the International Middleware Conference. (2003)
31. White, B., Lepreau, J., Stoller, L., Ricci, R., Guruprasad, S., Newbold, M., Hibler, M., Barb, C., Joglekar, A.: An integrated experimental environment for distributed systems and networks. In: 5th Symp on Operating Systems Design and Impl. (2002)

32. Chankhunthod, A., Danzig, P., Neerdaels, C., Schwartz, M., Worrell, K.: A Hierarchical Internet Object Cache. In: 1996 USENIX Technical Conference. (1996)
33. Petersen, K., Spreitzer, M., Terry, D., Theimer, M., Demers, A.: Flexible Update Propagation for Weakly Consistent Replication. In: 16th ACM Symposium on Operating Systems Principles. (1997)
34. Davison, B.D., Liberatore, V.: Pushing politely: Improving Web responsiveness one packet at a time (extended abstract). Performance Evaluation Review **28** (2000) 43–49
35. Li, D., Cheriton, D.R.: Scalable web caching of frequently updated objects using reliable multicast. In: Proceedings of the 1999 Usenix Symposium on Internet Technologies and Systems (USITS'99). (1999)
36. Worrell, K.: Invalidation in Large Scale Network Object Caches. Master's thesis, University of Colorado, Boulder (1994)
37. Yin, J., Alvisi, L., Dahlin, M., Lin, C.: Volume Leases to Support Consistency in Large-Scale Systems. IEEE Transactions on Knowledge and Data Engineering **11** (1999) 563–576
38. Yin, J., Alvisi, L., Dahlin, M., Iyengar, A.: Engineering web cache consistency. ACM Transactions on Internet Technologies **2** (2002)
39. Bradley, A., Bestavros, A.: Basis token consistency: Supporting strong web cache consistency. In: GLOBECOMM. (2003)
40. Challenger, J., Dantzig, P., Iyengar, A., Squillante, M., Zhang, L.: Efficiently serving dynamic data at highly accessed web sites. IEEE/ACM Transactions on Networking **12** (2004) 233–246
41. Fei, Z.: A novel approach to managing consistency in content distribution networks. In: Internat. Workshop on Web Caching and Content Distribution. (2001)
42. Acharya, S., Franklin, M., Zdonik, S.: Balancing push and pull for data broadcast. In: Proceedings of the 1997 ACM SIGMOD international conference on Management of data, ACM Press (1997) 183–194
43. Ladin, R., Liskov, B., Shrira, L., Ghemawat, S.: Providing high availability using lazy replication. ACM Trans. on Computer Systems **10** (1992) 360–361
44. Yu, H., Vahdat, A.: The costs and limits of availability for replicated services. In: 18th ACM Symposium on Operating Systems Principles. (2001)

An Ontology-Based Publish/Subscribe System*

Jinling Wang[1,2], Beihong Jin[1], and Jing Li[1]

[1] Institute of Software, Chinese Academy of Sciences, Beijing, China
{jlwang,jbh,lij}@otcaix.iscas.ac.cn
[2] Graduate School of the Chinese Academy of Sciences, Beijing, China

Abstract. Expressiveness and matching efficiency are two key design goals of publish/subscribe systems. In this paper, we introduce the Semantic Web technologies into the publish/subscribe system and propose an ontology-based publish/subscribe (OPS) system. The system can make use of the semantic of events to match events with subscriptions, and can support events with complex data structure (such as graph structure). An efficient matching algorithm is proposed for the OPS system, which can match events with subscriptions in a speed much higher than conventional graph matching algorithms. Therefore, the main contribution of our work is that it greatly improves the expressiveness of the publish/subscribe system without the sacrifice of matching efficiency.

1 Introduction

Publish/subscribe (pub/sub) is a loosely coupled communication paradigm for distributed computing environments. In the pub/sub systems, *publishers* publish information to *event brokers* in the form of *events*, *subscribers* subscribe to a particular category of events within the system, and event brokers ensures the timely delivery of published events to all interested subscribers. The advantage of pub/sub paradigm is that publishers and subscribers are full decoupled in time, space and flow [1], so it is well suitable for the large-scale and highly dynamic distributed systems.

In different distributed systems, the information exchanged between participants differs greatly in formats and semantics. If the pub/sub system is to become a general infrastructure for distributed computing and support different applications, it should have strong expressiveness, i.e.:

- It should support events in different formats and semantics;
- It should provide a powerful subscription language, so that information consumers can easily express their interest in certain events.

For each published event, the pub/sub system should match it with subscriptions to find out the interested subscribers. A large-scale distributed system may have millions of subscribers, and events may be published frequently. Therefore, the efficiency of the matching algorithm significantly affects the performance and scalability of a pub/sub system.

---

* This work was supported by the National Grand Fundamental Research 973 Program of China under Grant No. 2002CB312005; the National Hi-Tech Research and Development 863 Program of China under Grant No. 2001AA113010; and the National Natural Science Foundation of China under Grant No. 60173023.

H.-A. Jacobsen (Ed.): Middleware 2004, LNCS 3231, pp. 232–253, 2004.
© IFIP International Federation for Information Processing 2004

There is a close relation between the expressiveness and the efficiency of matching algorithm for a pub/sub system. Generally speaking, the more expressive a pub/sub system is, the more difficult it is to design an efficient matching algorithm, and vice versa. On the one hand, the pub/sub system should have strong expressiveness to support more applications; on the other hand, the system should keep a high matching efficiency to ensure the scalability of the system. Therefore, expressiveness and scalability are two key goals of a pub/sub system that needs trade-off [2].

Although much work has been done on the research of pub/sub systems, there are still some problems in the expressiveness of existing pub/sub systems, such as:

1. The existing systems mainly use the structural information of events to match them with subscriptions, and they generally have no sense of the semantic of events. If the pub/sub system could match events with subscriptions based on both the semantic and the structure of events, it would be more intelligent and could better serve the distributed applications.
2. The existing systems can only support events with relational data structure (such as "attribute=value" pairs) or tree data structure (such as XML), but some distributed systems may require events to have more complex format (such as graph structure). Furthermore, events from different publishers may be in different formats. Therefore, a unified mechanism is needed to process events with different formats at the same time.

To solve the above problems, we introduce the Semantic Web technologies into the pub/sub system and propose an Ontology-based Publish/Subscribe (OPS) system. In the OPS system, the domain concepts involved in all events are integrated together to form a concept model, and the system matches events with subscriptions both semantically and syntactically. Inside the OPS system, each event is represented as a Resource Description Framework (RDF) [3] graph, which is a kind of directed labeled graph. As Tim Berners-Lee has stated [4], data in almost any form can be broken down into a representation as a directed labeled graph, and then be represented as RDF graph. Therefore, the OPS can support events in almost any complex format. When an event is published, it is firstly converted into a RDF graph before further processing. For subscribers, the received events are always in RDF format.

In the OPS system, subscriptions are represented as graph patterns, so the matching algorithm is in fact a kind of graph matching algorithm. Based on the characteristic of the RDF graph and a few constraints on the graphs and graph patterns, we designed a highly efficient matching algorithm for the OPS system. Experimental results show that under the same environment and workload, the matching time of our algorithm is much lower than existing graph matching algorithms. While there are 10,000 graph patterns in the system, the matching time for an input graph is just 1-2 seconds.

The remainder of the paper is organized as follows. In Section 2, we discuss related work. In Section 3, we introduce the data model of the OPS system. In Section 4, we introduce the subscription language supported by the OPS system. In Section 5, we give the matching algorithm. In Section 6, we present and analyze the experimental results. Finally, in Section 7, we conclude the paper with a summary.

2   Related Work

Pub/sub systems are generally divided into two categories: *subject-based* and *content-based*. In subject-based systems (such as IBM MQSeries [5]), each event belongs to one of a fixed set of *subjects* (also called *topics*, *channels*, or *groups*). Publishers are required to label each event with a subject name; subscribers subscribe to all events under a particular subject. In content-based systems, each subscriber defines a subscription according to the internal structure of events; all events that meet the constraints of the subscription will be sent to the subscriber. The content-based systems are more expressive and flexible than the subject-based pub/sub systems; they enable subscribers to express their interests in a finer level of granularity.

Existing content-based pub/sub systems can be further divided into two sub-categories: *Map-based* and *XML-based*. In Map-based systems, each event is a set of "attribute=value" pairs, and subscriptions are usually conjunctions of simple predicates on data attributes, which are called *flat patterns*. Known prototype systems include SIENA [6], Gryphon [7], JEDI [8], etc. In XML-based pub/sub systems, each event is an XML document, and subscriptions are usually XPath expression or its variations, which contain not only constraints on the structure of the XML documents but also constraints on certain elements and attributes. Such subscriptions are called *tree patterns*. Known prototype systems include XFilter [9], XTrie [10], WebFilter [11], etc.

Our OPS system differs from the existing content-based pub/sub systems in the following ways:

1. Most existing systems are not aware of the semantic of events, whereas the OPS system can match events with subscriptions based on both the semantic and the structure of events.
2. Events in the OPS system are represented as graphs rather than "attribute=value" pairs or XML, so the system can support events with more complex formats.
3. Subscriptions in the OPS system are *graph patterns*, which are more expressive than flat patterns and tree patterns.

In recent years, there are also some works on the research of semantic matching for pub/sub systems, such as S-ToPSS [12] and CREAM [13]. Our work differs from their works in that events are represented as RDF graphs and subscriptions are represented as graph patterns. Furthermore, our work is focused on designing an efficient matching algorithm for the system, while the matching efficiency issues are seldom touched in their works.

On the other hand, there have been a lot of algorithms for graph matching by the graph theory community. In this community, graph matching is divided into two types: exact matching and approximate matching; the matching problem in the OPS system belongs to the first one. The exact graph-matching problem is in fact the subgraph isomorphism problem. The classical algorithms for subgraph isomorphism are based on backtracking in a search tree, and using refinement procedures to prevent the search tree from growing unnecessarily large. Common refinement procedures include Ullman algorithm [14], forward checking [15], graph partition [16], etc. These algorithms can only work on the matching of one input graph and one graph pattern at a time. In [17, 18, 19], algorithms were proposed for applications where an input graph should be matched with a database of graph patterns. In the algorithms proposed in [17, 18], all graph patterns are organized into a hierarchical index structure, and the system traverses the hierarchical structure to find the matched graph patterns for a given input graph. However, these algorithms cannot find all matched graph patterns for an input graph. In the algorithm proposed in [19], every graph pattern is continuously decomposed into sub-graphs, until each sub-graph contains only one vertex. On the arrival of an input graph, the system first matches it with the smallest sub-graphs, and then assembles the matched sub-graphs into larger sub-graphs; finally get all matched graph patterns. But the algorithm can only support a database of tens or hundreds of graph patterns, and cannot serve the large-scale pub/sub systems where there are thousands or millions of subscriptions.

Compared with existing graph matching algorithms, the algorithm in the OPS system makes use of the characteristic of the RDF graph and adds a few constraints on the graphs and graph patterns, so it can achieve a matching efficiency much higher than existing ones. Furthermore, conventional graph matching algorithms are mainly focus on the matching efficiency when there are numerous vertexes and edges in graphs, while our algorithms are mainly focus on the matching efficiency when there are numerous graph patterns that need to be matched.

3   Data Model

In the OPS system, we use RDF and DAML+OIL [20] in the Semantic Web to describe the data model. The data model consists of following two parts:

1. Event model, which specifies the organization of data inside events. It is described with RDF.
2. Concept model, which specifies the concepts involved in the events, the relations between them, and the constraints on them. It is described with DAML+OIL.

Since RDF and DAML+OIL are mainly used to represent information on the Web, they use URI as the identifiers of different entities. However, an event-based system mainly cares about the events that are being exchanged, which usually don't have a URI. Therefore, when we represent events with RDF, they (and most entities inside them) are represented as *blank nodes* (nodes without URI). According to the RDF specification, a blank node can be assigned an identifier prefixed with "_:".

For the sake of clarification, we call nodes in a graph as *vertexes* and call nodes in a tree as *nodes* in the remainder of the paper.

3.1   Event Model

Inside the OPS system, each event is represented as a RDF graph. RDF is a way to represent fact using the (*subject, property, object*) triples. Each triple is called a *statement*, in which *subject* and *property* are URI, and *object* can be URI or literals. RDF data can be represented as a directed labeled graph, in which vertexes represent subjects and objects of statements, and arcs represent properties of statements. We call the RDF graph of an event as an *event graph*.

For example, in a pub/sub style Internet auction system, suppose Jinling Wang wants to sell an IBM Desktop PC at the price of $450, and the PC contains a 40G-size hard disk that was also produced by IBM, then the corresponding event graph is shown in Figure 1. For the sake of simplicity, we omit the "daml:Thing" vertex, the "rdf:Literal" vertex, and the arcs pointing to them in the Figure.

In the OPS system, we add the following restrictions on event graphs:

1. There is one and only one vertex in the graph that is called the *home vertex*, which describes the global information about the event (such as the type and the creation time of the event). We specify that the identifier of the home vertex is "_:H".

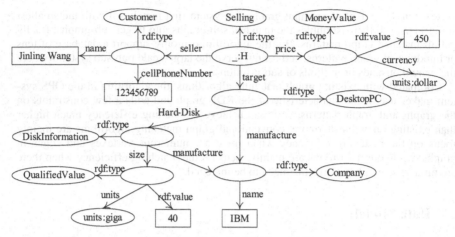

Fig. 1. An example of event graph.

2. There are paths from the home vertex to any other vertexes in the RDF graph.
3. Each vertex in the graph is a *typed vertex*, i.e., the graph specifies the class of each vertex. The publisher can specify multiple classes for a vertex, meaning that the entity simultaneously belongs to multiple classes.

3.2   Concept Model

The OPS system uses ontologies to represent the concept model of events, which describe not only the structural information but also the semantic information of events.

Ontology can be considered as a specification of a conceptualization [21]. It describes the concepts in a domain, the relations between them and the constraints on them. In the area of the Semantic Web technologies, one of the most influential ontology languages is DAML+OIL, which is used in the OPS system.

In the OPS system, the concept model of events is composed of the following three parts:

1. The description of classes and their hierarchical structure. An entity can belong to multiple classes. A class can have multiple parent classes, but the subclass-relations between classes must be acyclic (although there is no such restriction in DAML+OIL). For example, a part of the hierarchical structure of classes in an Internet auction system is shown in Figure 2(a).

   In this paper, we use two symbol $\sqsupseteq$ and $\sqsubseteq$ to represent the *containing* relations between two concepts. $X \sqsupseteq Y$ means X contains Y, and $X \sqsubseteq Y$ means X is contained by Y. The $\sqsupseteq$ and $\sqsubseteq$ relations are both reflexive and transitive.

   For two class A and B, predicate "A rdfs:subClassOf B" can be represented as "$A \sqsubseteq B$".

   Suppose A is the class specified in a subscription and B is the class of an entity in an event, A can match with B if A is the ancestor of B. For example, in the Internet auction system, if someone is interested in all computer-selling events with price lower than $400, he can use the *Computer* class to define his subscription, and all computer-selling events (no matter selling Desktop PCs or Notebook PCs) with price lower than $400 will be sent to him. However, most existing content-based pub/sub systems can just support the hierarchy of event types, but cannot support the class hierarchy for entities inside the events.

2. The description of properties and their hierarchical structure. A property can have multiple parent properties, and the sub-property-relations between properties must be acyclic. For example, a part of the hierarchical structure of properties in an Internet auction system is shown in Figure 2(b).

For two properties p_1 and p_2, predicate "p_1 rdfs:subPropertyOf p_2" can be represented as "$p_1 \sqsubseteq p_2$".

Suppose p_1 is the property specified in a subscription and p_2 is the property appearing in an event, p_1 can match with p_2 if p_1 is the ancestor of p_2. For example, if there is a subscription "*telephoneNumber*=123456789" and an event that contains "*cellPhoneNumber*= 123456789", then the event can match with the subscription.

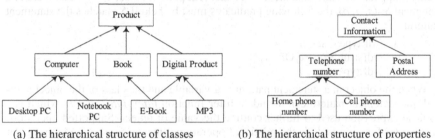

(a) The hierarchical structure of classes   (b) The hierarchical structure of properties

Fig. 2. A part of classes and properties in an online auction system.

3. Meta-statement. We called the triple (*subject-class, property, object-class*) as a *meta-statement*. It specifies the allowed properties for a given class (*subject-class*), and the classes (*object-class*) that the values of these properties belong to.

For example, an Internet auction system may have the following meta-statements:

  (Selling, seller, Customer)
  (Selling, target, Product)
  (Product, manufacture, Company)
  (Customer, name, xsd:string)
  ...

There is also a hierarchical structure for the meta-statements. For two meta-statement $ms_1=(sc_1, p_1, oc_1)$ and $ms_2=(sc_2, p_2, oc_2)$, we say ms_2 is the *ancestor* of ms_1 (denoted as $ms_1 \sqsubseteq ms_2$) if the following predicate is held:

$$(sc_1 \sqsubseteq sc_2) \wedge (p_1 \sqsubseteq p_2) \wedge (oc_1 \sqsubseteq oc_2)$$

It means that if a statement satisfies the type constraints of ms_1, it also satisfies the type constraints of ms_2.

4   Subscription Language

Since events are represented as RDF graphs in the OPS system, the subscription is in fact a graph pattern built on the RDF graph syntax, which specifies the shape of the graph as well as the constraints on some vertexes and arcs in the graph. Based on a number of RDF query languages such as SquishQL [22], RDQL [23] and RQL [24], we design a subscription language for the OPS system.

In the OPS system, a subscription is the conjunction of a number of *statement patterns*; each statement pattern specifies a statement in event graphs. The format of a statement pattern is as follows:

(*subject, object, meta-statement,* [*filter_func(object)*])

The subject and object in the statement pattern specify the subject and object of a statement in the event graph. They can be variables or specific values, and variables can match with any values. The variable names always begin with "?", such as ?1 and ?2.

The meta-statement in the statement pattern specifies the type constraints of statements. Suppose the meta-statement in a statement pattern is (*sc, sp, oc*) and there is a statement $S=(s, p, o)$, the following predicates must be held if S matches the statement pattern:

s   rdf:type   sc
p   rdfs:subPropertyOf   sp
o   rdf:type   oc

When the object in a statement pattern is a variable and the class of the object is literal, the statement pattern can include a filter function *filter_func(object)*, which is a boolean expression used to further confine the value of object. Supported operations in the filter function include the relational operations such as >, <, = and the regular expression operations.

For example, in the Internet auction system, if someone is interested in all computer-selling events with price lower than $400, he can define the following subscription:

(_:H, ?1, (Selling, target, Computer))
(_:H, ?2, (Selling, price, MoneyValue))
(?2, units:dollar, (MoneyValue, currency, daml:Thing))
(?2, ?3, (MoneyValue, rdf:value, xsd:decimal), ?3<400.00)

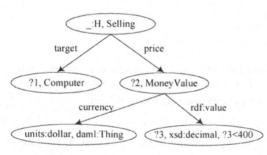

Fig. 3. An example of subscrition graph.

Inside the OPS system, each subscription is represented as a graph (called *subscription graph*), in which each vertex corresponds to a vertex in the event graph and each arc corresponds to an arc in the event graph. For example, the preceding subscription can be represented as a graph shown in Figure 3.

Each vertex in the subscription graph has a label (*id, class,* [*filter_func(id)*]), in which *id* is the *subject* or *object* in statement patterns, *class* is the class of *id*, and *filter_func(id)* is the filter function on the value of *id* if *id* is a variable and the class of *id* is literal. Each vertex has a unique *id* in the graph.

The label on the arc in the subscription graph is the property name, which forms a meta-statement together with the class of the starting vertex and the class of the end vertex. Each arc plus its starting vertex and ending vertex forms a statement pattern.

In the OPS system, we add the following restrictions on a subscription:

1. There is at least one statement pattern in which the subject is "_:H". We call the vertex with *id*="_:H" in the subscription graph as the *home vertex* of the subscription graph.
2. There are paths from the home vertex to any other vertexes in the subscription graph.

5   Matching Algorithm

The key points of our algorithm are as follows:

1) Each subscription is decomposed into a set of statement patterns, which are the basic units of matching;
2) The index structure of statement patterns is built on the basis of the concept model;
3) Statement patterns with same contents are matched only once;
4) The decomposition of subscription is gradually performed to avoid the creation of unnecessary statement patterns;
5) The event graph and subscription graphs are all traversed in broad-first order to form BFS trees, the matching of two BFS trees resulting in an AND-OR tree.

5.1   Formal Definition of the Matching Problem

Suppose there is an arc a^G in a graph G. We use function $SV(a^G)$ to denote the starting vertex of the arc, function $EV(a^G)$ to denote the ending vertex of the arc, and function $label(a^G)$ to denote the label of the arc.

Suppose the ith vertex of an event graph EG is v_i^{EG}. We denote the *id* of the vertex as id_i^{EG} and the set of classes of the vertex as $classes_i^{EG}$.

Suppose the ith vertex of a subscription graph SG is v_i^{SG}. We denote the *id* of the vertex as id_i^{SG}, the class of the vertex as $class_i^{SG}$, and the filter function of the vertex as $filter\_func_i^{SG}$. If the vertex does not have a filter function, then $filter\_func_i^{SG}$ always returns *true*.

We use function $isVariable(id)$ to denote the predicate "*id* is a variable".

Since the *id* of each vertex is unique in subscription graphs and event graphs, we do not strictly distinguish a vertex and its *id* in the following discussion.

Definition 1. An event graph *EG* matches a subscription graph *SG* if and only if the following conditions are held:

1) For each vertex v_i^{SG} in *SG*, there is a corresponding vertex v_j^{EG} in *EG*, and

$$\exists c: c \in classes_j^{EG} \wedge (c \sqsubseteq class_i^{SG}) \wedge (id_i^{SG}=id_j^{EG} \vee isVariable(id_i^{SG})) \wedge$$
$$filter\_func_i^{SG}(id_j^{EG})$$

We denote the mapping between v_i^{SG} and v_j^{EG} as $v_i^{SG} \leftrightarrow v_j^{EG}$.

2) For two vertexes v_i^{SG}, v_j^{SG} in SG and two vertexes v_x^{EG}, v_y^{EG} in EG:

$$v_i^{SG} \leftrightarrow v_x^{EG} \wedge v_j^{SG} \leftrightarrow v_y^{EG} \wedge v_i^{SG} \neq v_j^{SG} \Rightarrow v_x^{EG} \neq v_y^{EG}$$

3) For each arc a_i^{SG} in SG, there is a corresponding arc a_j^{EG} in EG, and

$$SV(a_i^{SG}) \leftrightarrow SV(a_j^{EG}) \wedge EV(a_i^{SG}) \leftrightarrow EV(a_j^{EG}) \wedge (label(a_j^{EG}) \sqsubseteq label(a_i^{SG}))$$

We denote the mapping between a_i^{SG} and a_j^{EG} as $a_i^{SG} \leftrightarrow a_j^{EG}$.

5.2   Index Structure

Based on the hierarchical structure of classes, the hierarchical structure of properties and the user-defined meta-statements in the concept model, we can figure out all valid meta-statements in the system. We store all these valid meta-statements in an array (called *Extended Meta-Statement array*, abbreviated as *EMS array*), which is the basis of the index structure of the OPS system. The items in the EMS array are sorted in alphabetical order, so that the binary-search algorithm can be used when we look up an item.

Each item in the EMS array contains two lists: the *ancestor list* and the *waiting-pattern list*. The ancestor list records the sequence numbers of all ancestors of the meta-statement. The waiting-pattern list includes the corresponding statement patterns that are waiting for matching. In the initial state, the waiting-pattern lists just include the statement patterns with *subject*="_:H". For example, suppose a system just contains one subscription as shown in Figure 4(a), the initial state of the EMS array can be shown in Figure 4(b). The first list of each item in Figure 4(b) is the ancestor list (drawn in real lines), and the second list of each item is the waiting-pattern list (drawn in broken lines). *Nil* means the null pointer.

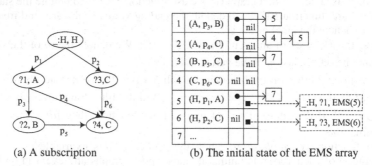

(a) A subscription   (b) The initial state of the EMS array

Fig. 4. A subscription and the initial state of the EMS array.

For the sake of simplicity, in Figure 4 and the following examples, we use capital letters (such as A, B) to denote classes, p_i (such as p_1, p_2) to denote properties except "rdf:type", and EMS(i) to denote the meta-statement in the ith item of the EMS array.

5.3 Traversal of RDF Graphs

When an event arrives, the OPS system will traverse the event graph from the home vertex in a breadth-first order, so that every arc with label≠"rdf:type" is traversed once and only once. For each traversed arc, the system will generate one or several triples with the following format:

$$(subject, object, meta\text{-}statement)$$

We call the triples as *typed-statements*, in which *subject* is the identifier of the starting vertex of the arc, *object* is the identifier of the ending vertex of the arc, and *meta-statement* is the corresponding meta-statement of the statement. The rule for creating meta-statements for a given statement is as follows: suppose the statement is (s, p, o) and the created meta-statement is (ts, tp, to), then ts is the class of s specified in the event graph, tp equals p, and to is the class of o specified in the event graph. One statement can generate multiple typed-statements.

The traversal of an event graph results in a tree structure, in which all nodes except the root node are typed-statements. We call the tree as the *BFS tree* of the event. For example, Figure 5(a) shows an event graph, and Figure 5(b) shows the corresponding BFS tree.

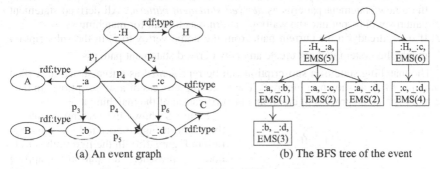

(a) An event graph   (b) The BFS tree of the event

Fig. 5. The RDF graph and the BFS tree of an event.

5.4 Matching Process and the Matching Tree

For each generated typed-statement during the traversal of the event graph, the OPS system will find the corresponding item in the EMS array according to its meta-statement, and matches it with the waiting-pattern list of the item. After that, the system will find all ancestors of the meta-statement (according to the ancestor list of the item), and then matches the typed-statement with the waiting-pattern lists of those ancestors.

For a statement pattern $sp=(s_1, o_1, ms_1, filter\_func_1)$ and a typed-statement $ts=(s_2, o_2, ms_2)$, the necessary and sufficient condition for sp matching with ts is as follows:

$$(s_1=s_2 \lor isVariable(s_1)) \land (o_1=o_2 \lor isVariable(o_1)) \land (ms_1 \sqsupseteq ms_2) \land filter\_func_1(o_2)$$

The matching results in the mapping of two pairs of vertexes: $s_1 \leftrightarrow s_2$ and $o_1 \leftrightarrow o_2$.

For example, the typed-statement (_:H, _:a, EMS(5)) in Figure 5(b) can match with the statement pattern (_:H, ?1, EMS(5)) in Figure 4(a) with vertex pairs {"_:H"↔"_:H", ?1↔"_:a"}. To accept these vertex pairs, other statement patterns should also be matched, such as (_:a, ?2, EMS(1)) and (_:a, ?4, EMS(2)). Therefore, the matching process of a subscription and an event is actually the process of trying and evaluating different mapping solutions between the vertexes of the two graphs.

Now we study the matching process of a single subscription and an event. At the beginning, all statement patterns with *subject*="_:H" have already been put into the waiting-pattern lists in the EMS array. For each typed-statement in the event, the system will match it with the statement patterns in the corresponding waiting-pattern lists in the EMS array. For each matched statement pattern, a *partial mapping solution* is created, which records all vertex pairs resulting from the current matching and previous matchings. Suppose a statement pattern $sp=(s_1, o_1, ms_1, filter\_func_1)$ has matched with a typed-statement $ts=(s_2, o_2, ms_2)$, the system will act as follows:

1) If o_1 is not in the current path from the home vertex to s_1 in the subscription graph, the system will find out all statement patterns in the subscription graph with *subject*=o_1, and then create new statement patterns based on them, in which variables are replaced with the specific values according to the known vertex pairs. We call these new statement patterns as *derived statement patterns*. All derived statement patterns will be put into the waiting-pattern lists to wait for matching.

2) If o_1 is already in the current path from the home vertex to s_1 in the subscription graph, the system will not create any new derived statement patterns.

The matching state of a subscription can be represented as a tree structure (called *matching tree*), as shown in Figure 6. The matching process of a subscription can then be regarded as the process of creation and verification of the matching tree.

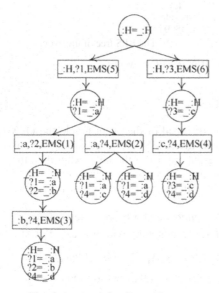

Fig. 6. An example of matching tree.

Figure 6 shows the matching state of the event in Figure 5(a) and the subscription in Figure 4(a). In the figure, the circle node represents a partial mapping solution, and the rectangle node represents a statement pattern. The root node is a circle node with vertex pair "_:H"↔"_:H" (we use symbol "=" to represent "↔" in the figure), and the children of the root node are statement patterns with *subject*="_:H" in the subscription graph. A circle node can have multiple rectangle nodes as its children, meaning the derived statement patterns of the partial mapping solution. Only after all its children being successfully matched, can a circle node be accepted as successful. A rectangle node can also have multiple circle nodes as its children, meaning the multiple matching solutions for the same statement pattern. As long as any one of its children succeeds, the rectangle node also succeeds. Therefore, the circle node implies the "and" relation of its children and the rectangle node implies the "or" relation of its children, so the whole matching tree is actually an AND-OR tree.

During the matching process, the system may generate multiple statement patterns with same contents. If the system put all these statement patterns into the waiting-pattern lists, a typed-statement would match with identical statement patterns for multiple times, which is undesirable. To avoid this phenomenon, a straightforward idea is to let a statement pattern be shared by multiple matching trees. However, since different statement patterns imply different path information in matching trees, it is very difficult for a statement pattern to be shared by multiple matching trees. To solve this problem, we use an approach similar to the *Observer* design pattern [25]. When the system put a statement pattern (suppose it to be A) into a waiting-pattern list, it first examine whether there is an existing statement pattern with the same contents in the list. If there exists such a statement pattern (suppose it to be B), then A will not be put into the list, but be registered to B. In the future, whenever B successfully matches with a typed-statement, it will notify all the statement patterns that have been registered to it. In this way, statement patterns with same contents will be matched only once.

5.5 Verification of Matching Trees

After the traversal of an event graph, the OPS system has created the matching trees for all subscriptions. Then the system will judge from the matching trees whether a subscription is successfully matched. We call the process as the *verification* of the matching trees. The OPS system uses two methods to verify the matching trees: Boolean Expression Based Verification (BEBV) and State Based Partial Verification (SBPV).

In the BEBV method, each leaf node in a matching tree is given a boolean expression, and the system calculates the expression for the root node to judge the result of matching. The calculation rules are as follows:

1) If a leaf node is circle node with vertex pairs $\{v_1^{SG} \leftrightarrow v_{x1}^{EG}, v_2^{SG} \leftrightarrow v_{x2}^{EG}, \ldots, v_k^{SG} \leftrightarrow v_{xk}^{EG}\}$, its boolean expression is $(v_1^{SG} \leftrightarrow v_{x1}^{EG}) \wedge (v_2^{SG} \leftrightarrow v_{x2}^{EG}) \wedge \ldots \wedge (v_k^{SG} \leftrightarrow v_{xk}^{EG})$.

2) If a leaf node is rectangle node, its expression is *false*.

3) The expression of a non-leaf circle node is the conjunction of the expressions for its children, and the expression of a non-leaf rectangle node is the disjunction of the expressions for its children.

4) For any vertex v_i^{SG} in the subscription graph and two vertex v_x^{EG} and v_y^{EG} in the event graph:

$$(v_i^{SG} \leftrightarrow v_x^{EG}) \wedge (v_i^{SG} \leftrightarrow v_y^{EG}) \wedge (v_x^{EG} \neq v_y^{EG}) = false.$$

It means that one vertex in the subscription graph cannot simultaneously maps to two different vertexes in the event graph.

5) For any vertex v_x^{EG} in the event graph and two vertex v_i^{SG} and v_j^{SG} in the subscription graph:

$$(v_i^{SG} \leftrightarrow v_x^{EG}) \wedge (v_j^{SG} \leftrightarrow v_x^{EG}) \wedge (v_i^{SG} \neq v_j^{SG}) = false.$$

It means that one vertex in the event graph cannot simultaneously maps to two different vertexes in the subscription graph.

According to the above rules we can calculate the boolean expression of the root node for all matching trees. If the expression of the root node in a matching tree is *false*, then the matching fails. Otherwise the matching is successful.

However, it would be very inefficient if the system calculates boolean expressions for every matching tree. To improve the matching efficiency, we design another verification method – SBPV method, which can check out most unmatched subscriptions with very low cost, but cannot tell whether a subscription is successfully matched. Only after a subscription has passed the SBPV check should it perform the time-consuming BEBV check.

In the SBPV method, each node in the matching trees has two possible states: *unchecked* and *checked*. The *checked* state means that the node has passed the SBPV check, and the *unchecked* state means that the node has not passed the check. The initial state of every node is *unchecked*. For a rectangle node, its state turns to *checked* as long as the state of one of its children turns to *checked*. For a circle node, its state turns to *checked* only after the states of all its children turn to *checked*.

In the SBPV method, each circle node has an *unCheckedChildren* field, recording the number of its children whose states are *unchecked*.

During the creation of a matching tree, when a partial mapping solution cannot create new statement patterns as its children, the system begins to backtrack on the matching tree. The backtracking procedure is as follows:

1) Set the state of the current node as *checked*.
2) If the current node is a circle node:
   a) If the current node is the root node, the procedure finishes.
   b) If the current node is not the root node, examine whether the state of its parent is *checked*. If it is already *checked*, the procedure finishes, otherwise set the parent node of the current node as the current node and execute the procedure recursively.
3) If the current node is a rectangle node, subtract 1 from the value of *unCheckedChildren* field of its parent node. If the value turns to 0, set the parent node as the current node and execute the procedure recursively, otherwise the procedure finishes.

The backtracking procedure of the SBPV check is shown in Figure 7. There is a label *id(state, unCheckedChildren)* besides each circle node and a label *id(state)* besides each rectangle node. In the labels, *id* means the identifier of the

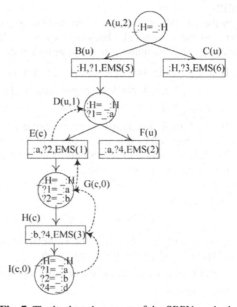

Fig. 7. The backtrack process of the SBPV method.

node, and the *state* field has two possible values: *c* and *u*, meaning *checked* and *unchecked* respectively. The broken lines in Figure 7 show the backtracking process. When node *I* cannot create new statement patterns, The states of node *I*, *H*, *G*, *E* are set to *checked*, and the value of the *unCheckedChildren* field in node *D* turns to 1 from 2.

When the SBPV check finishes, if the state of the root node in a matching tree is *unchecked*, then the subscription cannot match with the event. Since the SBPV check can be performed simultaneously with the creation of the matching tree, the system just needs to do the BEBV check for the matching trees in which the state of the root node is *checked* after the traversal of an event graph. Therefore, the performance of the system can be greatly improved.

5.6 Correctness Proof of the Algorithm

In the following discussion, we call the expression of a node in the matching tree calculated with the BEBV method as the *BEBV expression* of the node, and the state of a node in the matching tree calculated with the SBPV method as the *SBPV state* of the node.

When the BEBV expression of the root node in a matching tree is not *false*, we can cut some unnecessary branches out from the tree to create a *reduced matching tree*. The rules for creating a reduced matching tree are as follows:

1) Transform the BEBV expressions of all nodes into the simplest disjunctive normal form, i.e., the disjunction of non-false conjunction expressions.
2) Cut some branches off from the tree layer by layer from top to bottom:
   a) For the root node, randomly select one of the disjuncts from the disjunction as its new expression, and delete other disjuncts.
   b) For any non-leaf circle node (including the root node): Let the new expression is P, and P must be a conjunction expression. Suppose the node has n children and the expression of the kth child is $p_{x1}^k \vee p_{x2}^k \vee \ldots \vee p_{xm}^k$, in which p_{xi}^k ($i=1..m$) is a conjunction expression. Each child must have a disjunct (suppose it to be p_{xk}^k for the kth child), so that $p_{x1}^1 \wedge p_{x2}^2 \wedge \ldots \wedge p_{xn}^n = P$. Therefore, we can set these disjuncts as the new expressions for the children; i.e., the new expression of the kth child is p_{xk}^k.
   c) For any rectangle node: Since the expression of its parent is not *false*, the expression of itself is not *false* too, so it must be a non-leaf node. Let the new expression is P, and P must be a conjunction expression. Suppose the node has n children and the expression of the kth child is $p_{x1}^k \vee p_{x2}^k \vee \ldots \vee p_{xm}^k$, in which p_{xi}^k ($i=1..m$) is a conjunction expression. P must be equal to a conjunction expression in one of its children, supposing $P = p_{xk}^k$. Then we can keep this child and delete all other children and the corresponding sub-trees. The new expression of the remaining child is set to p_{xk}^k.

Obviously, the reduced matching tree has the following features:

1) It is still an AND-OR tree;
2) Each rectangle node has only one child;
3) All leaf nodes are circle nodes;
4) The expression of every node is a non-false conjunction expression.

Lemma 1. For each statement pattern sp^{SG} in the subscription graph SG, there is a rectangle node sp^T in the reduced matching tree T, so that sp^T equals sp^{SG} or sp^T is the derived pattern of sp^{SG}.

Proof. Suppose there is a statement pattern $sp_i^{SG}=(s_i, o_i, ms_i, filter\_func_i)$ in SG. There must be at least one acyclic path $sp_1^{SG}{\circ}sp_2^{SG}{\circ}...{\circ}sp_i^{SG}$ from the home vertex to s_i in SG, in which each item is a statement pattern. The subject of sp_1^{SG} is the home vertex. We can use the mathematical induction to prove sp_i^{SG} has a corresponding rectangle node in T.

1) The statement pattern sp_1^{SG} is put into the matching tree as the child of the root node at the beginning of the matching process. When we cut branches from the matching tree to form a reduced matching tree, we will not delete the children of the root node, so sp_1^{SG} is also in the reduced matching tree T.

2) For $2 \leq k \leq i$, suppose sp_{k-1}^{SG} has a corresponding rectangle node in T, and let it be sp_{k-1}^T. Suppose the object of sp_{k-1}^{SG} is v_k^{SG}. Since v_k^{SG} is not in the path of $sp_1^{SG}{\circ}sp_2^{SG}{\circ}...{\circ}sp_i^{SG}$, the object of sp_{k-1}^T is also v_k^{SG}. The node sp_{k-1}^T must have a child (let it be pm_k) in T, i.e., it can match with a typed-statement in the event graph and form a partial mapping solution. Since v_k^{SG} is not in the path of $sp_1^{SG}{\circ}sp_2^{SG}{\circ}...{\circ}sp_i^{SG}$, the system should create derived patterns for all statement patterns with $subject=v_k^{SG}$ in SG and put them into the waiting-pattern lists. Since the subject of sp_k^{SG} is v_k^{SG}, it must have a derived pattern (let it be sp_k^T) in the matching tree as the child of pm_k. Since pm_k is in T, so are all its children (including sp_k^T). Therefore, sp_k^{SG} also has a corresponding rectangle node in T.

Lemma 2. For each vertex v_i^{SG} in the subscription graph SG, there is at least one leaf node in the reduced matching tree T that includes the mapping from v_i^{SG} to a vertex in the event graph.

Proof. For the home vertex of SG, its mapping pair exists in every leaf nodes of T. For any other vertex v_i^{SG} in SG, since there is at least one path from the home vertex to v_i^{SG}, there is at least one statement pattern sp_i^{SG} with $object= v_i^{SG}$. From Lemma 1 we can know there is a corresponding rectangle node (let it be sp_i^T) for sp_i^{SG} in T. The node sp_i^T must have a child (let it be pm_i), i.e., it can match with a typed-statement in the event graph and form a partial mapping solution, so pm_i include a mapping pair from v_i^{SG} to a vertex in the event graph. The mapping pair must exist in all leaf nodes that are descendants of pm_i.

Lemma 3. If the expression of a node in the reduced matching tree includes a vertex pair, then the expressions of all its ancestor nodes also include the vertex pair.

Proof. Suppose there is a node n_i in the reduced matching tree, the expression of which include a vertex pair $v_i^{SG}{\leftrightarrow}v_j^{EG}$. There are two possible cases:

1) Node n_i is a circle node. Since n_i is the only child of its parent, the expression of its parent is equal to the expression of n_i, which certainly includes $v_i^{SG}{\leftrightarrow}v_j^{EG}$.

2) Node n_i is a rectangle node. The expression of its parent is the conjunction of the expressions of n_i and its siblings, and all these expressions are non-false conjunction expressions, so the expression of the parent node must include $v_i^{SG} \leftrightarrow v_j^{EG}$.

Therefore, the expression of the parent node of n_i must include $v_i^{SG} \leftrightarrow v_j^{EG}$. By repeating the process recursively, we can know that all ancestors of n_i include $v_i^{SG} \leftrightarrow v_j^{EG}$.

Lemma 4. The expression of the root node in the reduced matching tree includes the mapping pairs for all vertexes in the subscription graph.

Proof. From Lemma 2 we know that for each vertex in the subscription graph, there is at least one leaf node in the reduced matching tree that includes the mapping pair for it. According to Lemma 3, we can know that the expression of the root node includes the mapping pairs of all vertexes in the subscription graph.

Lemma 5. Suppose the BEBV expression of the root node in a matching tree is not *false*. It cannot become *false* if we add sub-trees under any rectangle node of the tree.

Proof. Suppose we add a sub-tree under a rectangle node n_a in the matching tree, and the root of the sub-tree is n_b. Suppose the expression of n_b is P_b, and the original expression of n_a is P_a. After the addition of n_b, the expression of n_a becomes $P_a \vee P_b$.

Now we will prove that for any node n_k in a matching tree, when its expression changes from P_k to $P_k \vee P_x$, the expression its parent n_p changes from P_p to $P_p \vee P_y$, in which P_x and P_y are boolean expressions. Suppose the node n_p has m children $n_1, \ldots,$ $n_k, \ldots, n_m$ $(k \le m)$.

1) Suppose n_k is a rectangle node. Then n_p is a circle node, and the original expression of n_p is:

$$P_p = P_1 \wedge \ldots \wedge P_k \wedge \ldots \wedge P_m$$
The new expression of n_p is:
$$
\begin{aligned}
P_p' &= P_1 \wedge \ldots \wedge (P_k \vee P_x) \wedge \ldots \wedge P_m \\
&= P_1 \wedge \ldots \wedge P_k \wedge \ldots \wedge P_m \vee P_1 \wedge \ldots \wedge P_x \wedge \ldots \wedge P_m \\
&= P_p \vee P_1 \wedge \ldots \wedge P_x \wedge \ldots \wedge P_m \\
&= P_p \vee P_y \quad (\text{Let } P_y = P_1 \wedge \ldots \wedge P_x \wedge \ldots \wedge P_m)
\end{aligned}
$$

2) Suppose n_k is a circle node. Then n_p is a rectangle node, and the original expression of n_p is:

$$P_p = P_1 \vee \ldots \vee P_k \vee \ldots \vee P_m$$
The new expression of n_p is:
$$
\begin{aligned}
P_p' &= P_1 \vee \ldots \vee (P_k \vee P_x) \vee \ldots \vee P_m \\
&= P_1 \vee \ldots \vee P_k \vee \ldots \vee P_m \vee P_x \\
&= P_p \vee P_x
\end{aligned}
$$

We can calculate the expressions of the ancestors of n_a from bottom to top until the root node. Suppose the original expression of the root node is P_r, then the new expression of the root node is $P_r'=P_r \vee P_y$. Since P_r is not *false*, P_r' is not *false* too.

Theorem 1. For any subscription S and event e in the OPS system, suppose the resulting matching tree is MT, and the BEBV expression of the root node in MT is P_{root}, then:

$$(P_{root} \neq false) \Leftrightarrow (e \text{ matches } S)$$

Proof. We first prove $(P_{root} \neq false) \Rightarrow (e \text{ matches } S)$.

1) Since the expression of the root node of the matching tree is not *false*, we can create a reduced matching tree based on it. From Lemma 4 we know that the expression of the root node of the reduced matching tree includes the mapping pairs for all vertexes in the subscription graph, so we can get the vertex mappings from the subscription graph to the event graph.

2) Suppose there is a statement pattern $sp_i^{SG}=(s_i, o_i, ms_i, filter\_func_i)$ for arc a_i^{SG} in the subscription graph. According to Lemma 1, it must have a corresponding rectangle node (let it be sp_i^T) in the reduced matching tree, and sp_i^T has a child (let it be pm_i). Suppose pm_i is the result of the matching between sp_i^T and a typed-statement $ts_j=(s_j, o_j, ms_j)$ in the event graph, then pm_i must includes the vertex pairs $\{s_i \leftrightarrow s_j, o_i \leftrightarrow o_j\}$. According to Lemma 3, the vertex pairs are consistent with the mapping solution in the root node of the reduced matching tree. Suppose the arc for ts_j in the event graph is a_j^{EG}, then we can get an arc mapping from a_i^{SG} to a_j^{EG}. In this way, we can get all arc mappings from the subscription graph to the event graph.

According to Definition 1, we can conclude that the event matches with the subscription.

Now we prove $(e \text{ matches } S) \Rightarrow (P_{root} \neq false)$.

Suppose there is a known mapping from the vertexes and arcs of the subscription graph to those of the event graph. Since the event graph is traversed in a breadth-first order, after the traversing of the first-layer type-statement in the BFS tree of the event, there is at least one circle node under every first-layer rectangle node in the matching tree, in which the vertex pairs are consistent with the known vertex mapping. We keep these circle nodes and delete all other circle nodes (and their corresponding sub-trees) in this layer.

The remaining circle nodes may have created new rectangle nodes (the second-layer rectangle nodes) in the matching tree. Since there is a know mapping from the arcs of the subscription graph to those of the event graph, after the traversing of the second-layer typed-statement in the BFS tree of the event, every second-layer rectangle node in the matching tree can match with at least one typed-statement and form a circle node, in which the vertex pairs are consistent with the known vertex mapping. We keep these circle nodes and delete all other circle nodes (and their corresponding sub-trees) in this layer.

According to the above rules we can cut some branches out from the matching tree from top to bottom, and the resulting tree is a reduced matching tree. The expression of the root node of the reduced matching tree is the known vertex mapping solution, which is certainly not *false*. Then we can add the deleted sub-trees into the reduced matching tree and return it to the original matching tree. According to Lemma 5, the expression of the root node of the resulting matching tree is also not *false*.

Lemma 6. The SBPV state of every node in the reduced matching tree is *checked*.

Proof. We can use the mathematical induction to prove it. Suppose the depth of the reduced matching tree is n.

1) The nodes in layer n of the tree are all leaf nodes. As all leaf nodes in the reduced matching tree are circle nodes, the state of the nodes are *checked*.
2) For $1 \leq i < n$, suppose the states of nodes in layer $i+1$ are all *checked*. For the leaf nodes in layer i, since they are circle nodes, their state are *checked*. For the non-leaf nodes in layer i, since the states of all of their children are *checked*, their states are also *checked*. Therefore, the state of every node in layer i is *checked*.

Lemma 7. If we add sub-trees under any rectangle node of the reduced matching tree, the SBPV state of the root node will not become *unchecked*.

Proof. Suppose we add a sub-tree under a rectangle node n_i in the reduced matching tree, and the root of the sub-tree is n_j. Since n_i already has a child whose state is *checked*, the state of n_i remains *checked* no matter what the state of n_j is, so the state of all ancestor nodes (including the root node) of n_i also remain *checked*.

Theorem 2. For any subscription S and event e in the OPS system, suppose the resulting matching tree is MT, and the SBPV state of the root node in MT is $State_{root}$, then:

$$(State_{root} = unchecked) \Rightarrow (\ e \text{ doesn't match } S)$$

Proof. We can prove its inverse and negative proposition, i.e., $(e$ matches $S) \Rightarrow (State_{root} = checked)$.

If an event can match with a subscription, we can know from Theorem 1 that the BEBV expression of the root node in the matching tree is not *false*, so we can build a reduced matching tree based on the matching tree. According to Lemma 6, the state of the root node in the reduced matching tree is *checked*. Then we can add the deleted sub-trees into the reduced matching tree and return it to the original matching tree. According to Lemma 7, the state of the root node in the resulting matching tree is also *checked*.

6   Experimental Evaluation

In this section we evaluate the performance of the OPS system with a variety of simulated workloads. The prototype system was implemented in Java, and the performance tests discussed below were performed on a common Notebook PC with an Intel Pentium IV CPU at 1.6GHz and 512MB RAM running Windows 2000 Sever and JDK 1.4.1.

To demonstrate the efficiency of our algorithm, we also implemented a recently proposed graph-matching algorithm in [19], and compared the performance of the two algorithms under the same environment and workloads. For the sake of simplicity, we call our algorithm as the *OPS* algorithm and their algorithm as the *Decomposition* algorithm in the follows.

Suppose the concept model contains C numbers of classes and P numbers of properties. There are no sub-class relations among classes and no sub-property relations among properties. In the following experiments, the value of P is fixed to be 10, and each class has exactly 2 properties.

Suppose there are S numbers of subscriptions in the system. Every subscription has 10 vertexes and 11 arcs. The *id* of the home vertex was "_:H", and the *id* of all other vertexes were variables. The *class* of every vertex was randomly selected from the total classes, and there were no filter functions in any vertexes.

Every generated event had 50 blank nodes, and there were 55 arcs among the blank nodes.

We define a parameter *matching rate*, meaning the ratio of matched subscriptions to total subscriptions for a given event. The value of matching rate considerably affects the performance of graph matching algorithms.

Figure 8(a) shows the matching times of the OPS algorithm under different numbers of subscriptions. In the experiments, the value of C is 10, and the value of S varies from 500 to 10,000. The resulting matching rates are always around 3%. From the figure we can see that the matching time is just 1.2 seconds when the number of subscriptions is 10,000.

Figure 8(b) shows the comparison of the matching times of the two algorithms. In the experiments, the value of C is 10, and the value of S varies from 1 to 20. From the figure we can see the OPS algorithm is much faster in event matching than the Decomposition algorithm. When the there are just 20 subscriptions, the matching time of the Decomposition algorithm reaches 500ms, while the matching time of the OPS algorithm is merely 1ms. Therefore, the conventional graph matching algorithms are not suitable for the pub/sub systems where there are large numbers of subscriptions.

Figure 8(c) shows the matching times of the OPS algorithm under different numbers of classes. In the experiments, the value of S is 1,000, and the value of C varies from 2 to 20. From the figure we can see that the matching time decreases dramatically from 2500ms to about 50ms. We believe the real reason is the changing of the matching rate, i.e., the matching rate decreases greatly when the number of classes increases, which leads to the decrease of matching time. Figure 8(d) shows the same experimental results, in which the x-axis represents the matching rate rather than the number of classes. From the figure we can see that the matching time is almost linear in the value of matching rate.

Now we evaluate the space usage of the OPS algorithm. In the OPS algorithm, the space is mainly used in the creation of matching trees for subscriptions. Figure 8(e) shows the average number of nodes in each matching tree under different numbers of subscriptions. In the experiments, the value of C is 10, and the number of subscriptions varies from 500 to 10,000. From the figure we can see that the average number of nodes in each matching tree is always around 5. Therefore, the space usage in the OPS algorithm is linear in the number of subscriptions.

Figure 8(f) shows the average number of nodes in each matching tree under different values of matching rates. In the experiments, the value of S is 1,000, and the value of C decreases from 20 to 2, so the matching rate increases from 1.3% to 23.8%. From the figure we can see that the average number of nodes in each matching tree increases just a little while the matching rate increases a great deal. Therefore, the space usage in the OPS algorithm is sub-linear in the value of matching rate.

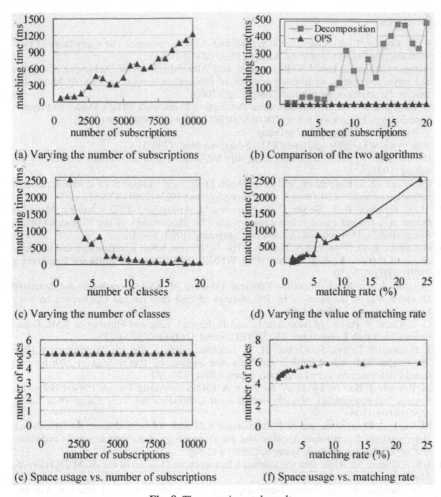

Fig. 8. The experimental results.

7   Conclusions

In this paper, we described the data model, subscription language and matching algorithm of an ontology-based publish/subscribe system. Through the combination of the publish/subscriber technologies and the Semantic Web technologies, the system can make use of the semantic of events to match events with subscriptions, and can support events with complex data structure (such as graph structure). Furthermore, we design a highly efficient matching algorithm for the OPS system, which can match RDF graphs with graph patterns in a speed much higher than the conventional graph matching algorithms. Therefore, the main contribution of our work is that it greatly improves the expressiveness of the pub/sub system and at the same time it keeps a high matching efficiency.

References

1. P. Th. Eugster, P. A. Felber, R. Guerraoui, and A.-M. Kermarrec: The many faces of publish/subscribe. ACM Computing Surveys 35(2) (2003) 114-131
2. Antonio Carzaniga, David S. Rosenblum, and Alexander L: Wolf. Achieving scalability and expressiveness in an Internet-scale event notification service. In 19th ACM Symposium on Principles of Distributed Computing. (2000)
3. O. Lassila and R. R. Swick: Resource Description Framework (RDF) Model and Syntax Specification. http://www.w3.org/TR/1999/REC-rdf-syntax-19990222/ (1999)
4. T. Berners-Lee: Using XML for Data. http://www.w3.org/DesignIssues/XML-Semantics.html. (2001)
5. IBM: Internet Application Development with MQSeries and Java. Vervante Corporate Publishing (1997)
6. Carzaniga, D. S. Rosenblum, and A. L. Wolf: Design and evaluation of a wide-area event notication service. ACM Trans. on Computer Systems 19(3) (2001) 332-383
7. M. K. Aguilera, R. E. Strom, D. C. Sturman, M. Astley, and T. D. Chandra: Matching events in a content-based subscription system. In: Proceedings of the Eighteenth ACM Symposium on Principles of Distributed Computing (1999) 53-61
8. G. Cugola, E. D. Nitto, and A. Fuggetta: The JEDI event-based infrastructure and its application to the development of the OPSS WFMS. IEEE Trans. on Software Engineering 27(9) (2001) 827-850
9. M. Altinel and M. J. Franklin: Efficient Filtering of XML Documents for Selective Dissemination of Information. In: Proceedings of 26th International Conference on Very Large Data Bases. (2000) 53-64
10. C.-Y. Chan, P. Felber, M. Garofalakis, and R. Rastogi: Efficient Filtering of XML Documents with XPath Expressions. The VLDB Journal 11(4) (2002) 354-379
11. J. Pereira, F. Fabret, F. Llirbat, H.-A. Jacobsen, and D. Shasha: WebFilter: A High Throughput XML-based Publish and Subscribe System. In: Proceedings of 27th International Conference on Very Large Data Bases. (2001) 723-724
12. M. Petrovic, I. Burcea, and H.-A. Jacobsen: S-ToPSS: Semantic Toronto Publish/Subscribe System. In: Proceedings of 29th International Conference on Very Large Data Bases. (2003) 1101-1104
13. M. Cilia, C. Bornhoevd, and A. P. Buchmann: CREAM: An Infrastructure for Distributed, Heterogeneous Event-based Applications. In: Proceedings of the International Conference on Cooperative Information Systems. (2003) 482-502
14. J. R. Ullmann: An Algorithm for Subgraph Isomorphism. Journal of the ACM 23(1) (1976) 31-42
15. R.M. Haralick and G.L. Elliot: Increasing Tree Search Efficiency for Constraint Satisfaction Problems. Artificial Intelligence 14 (1980) 263-313
16. R.E. Blake: Partitioning Graph Matching with Constraints. Pattern Recognition 27(3) (1994) 439-446
17. H. Sossa and R. Horaud: Model Indexing: The Graph-Hashing Approach. In: Proceedings of IEEE Conference on Computer Vision and Pattern Recognition. (1992) 811-814
18. K. Sengupta and K.L. Boyer: Organizing Large Structural Modelbases. IEEE Trans. on Pattern Analysis and Machine Intelligence 17(4) (1995)
19. B. T. Messmer and H. Bunke: Efficient Subgraph Isomorphism Detection: A Decomposition Approach. IEEE Trans. on Knowledge and Data Engineering 12(2) (2000) 307-323
20. F. V. Harmelen, P. F. Patel-Schneider and I. Horrocks: Reference description of the DAML+OIL (March 2001) ontology markup language. http://www.daml.org/2001/03/reference. (2001)
21. T. R. Gruber: A translation approach to portable ontologies. Knowledge Acquisition 5(2) (1993) 199-220

22. L. Miller, A. Seaborne, and A. Reggiori: Three Implementations of SquishQL, a simple RDF Query Language. In: Proceedings of the First International Semantic Web Conference. (2002) 423-435
23. HP Labs: RDQL: RDF Data Query Language. http://www.hpl.hp.com/semweb/rdql.htm
24. G. Karvounarakis, S. Alexaki, V. Christophides, D. Plexousakis, and M. Scholl: RQL: A Declarative Query Language for RDF, In: Proceedings of the Eleventh International World Wide Web Conference. (2002) 592-603
25. E. Gamma, R. Helm, R. Johnson, and J. Vlissides: Design pattern, elements of reusable object-oriented software. Addison-Wesley (1994)

Meghdoot: Content-Based Publish/Subscribe over P2P Networks*

Abhishek Gupta, Ozgur D. Sahin, Divyakant Agrawal, and Amr El Abbadi

Department of Computer Science
University of California at Santa Barbara
{abhishek,odsahin,agrawal,amr}@cs.ucsb.edu

Abstract. Publish/Subscribe systems have become a prevalent model for delivering data from producers (publishers) to consumers (subscribers) distributed across wide-area networks while decoupling the publishers and the subscribers from each other. In this paper we present Meghdoot, which adapts content-based publish/subscribe systems to Distributed Hash Table based P2P networks in order to provide scalable content delivery mechanisms while maintaining the decoupling between the publishers and the subscribers. Meghdoot is designed to adapt to highly skewed data sets, which is typical of real applications. The experimental results demonstrate that Meghdoot balances the load among the peers and the design scales well with increasing number of peers, subscriptions and events.

1 Introduction

Publish/Subscribe systems are used to deliver data events from *publishers* (data/event producers) to *subscribers* (data/event consumers) in a decoupled fashion. Publishers can be completely unaware of the subscribers and simply introduce data events into the system. A data event specifies values for a set of attributes associated with the event. Subscribers can register their interests with the system in the form of *subscriptions* which act as filters that are used by the system to deliver relevant events to the subscribers. Content-based subscriptions specify the subscription based on attribute properties of the data events. The publish/subscribe system, or equivalently the publish/subscribe middleware, manages the subscriptions and delivers the events to the matching subscriptions.

Publish/subscribe systems arise in many applications including online stock quotes, Internet games, and sensor networks. In the stock quote application, for example, the events are generated by various stock exchanges where trading occurs. The events contain information about the open, close, low, and high values of companies' stocks at various times. The subscribers are clients interested in trading, and they are usually interested in the values of the stocks they trade. Another interesting example is IBM's web service for information on events in

---

* This research was supported in parts by NSF grants EIA00-80134, IIS-0220152, and IIS-0223022.

H.-A. Jacobsen (Ed.): Middleware 2004, LNCS 3231, pp. 254–273, 2004.

the 2000 Olympics at Sydney. Users could query events in sports of their interest or events relating to their countries by contacting the web service. According to IBM [13], there were 11.3 billion hits to the web server. This number is expected to grow higher in upcoming events. Users are interested in a notification service that can allow them to track events of interest. The information for such events can be distributed to users by utilizing a distributed publish/subscribe system.

Current solutions are either centralized or distributed. Centralized solutions based on a DBMS use triggers [11, 6], which have an inherent scalability problem as the number of events in the system increase. Specialized data structures have been proposed to overcome these scalability problems [7]. However, to ensure efficient processing, restrictions are placed on the types of subscriptions that the system can support. Distributed solutions are usually restricted to specific subject-based subscriptions [5, 31, 19] and hence do not support general content-based subscriptions. Alternatively, routing trees [4, 2] are used to support multicast to prevent communication bottlenecks.

Peer-to-peer systems are particularly attractive for supporting publish/ subscribe systems since they are flexible, modular, and scalable. In such systems, peers are used both to store subscriptions and to route events to other peers with relevant subscriptions. Peer-to-peer systems are very scalable since additional peers can contribute their machines, thus increasing the computational and storage resources in the system. Traditionally, peer-to-peer systems were designed to answer exact match queries. In this paper we present Meghdoot[1], a P2P based publish/subscribe system. Meghdoot uses a structured distributed hash table [1] to determine where subscriptions are stored and how to route the events to the subscriptions. Meghdoot is a scalable architecture for publish/subscribe systems that applies a flexible model of content-based publish/subscribe systems to structured P2P systems.

A particular challenge in peer-to-peer systems involves ensuring a uniform distribution of load among the different peers in the system. Traditional peer-to-peer systems are oblivious to the content of the data and hence use a uniform hash function to distribute the data among the different peers. However, in a content-based publish/subscribe system, we distribute the subscriptions and events based on their content. Most real world datasets tend to be skewed and hence will cause a non-uniform distribution of load on the peers. One important innovation of Meghdoot is the alternative methods it uses to balance the load among peers. Our experimental results clearly demonstrate that even when using highly skewed real world datasets, the system ensures that no peer is unduly loaded.

The rest of the paper is structured as follows. Section 2 presents a survey of related work. Section 3 presents the basic design of our proposed approach. This is followed by Section 4 which presents strategies for employing peers in the system in a load balanced manner, and presents some optimizations. Section 5 presents the experimental setup and results. Section 6 concludes the paper.

---

[1] The name Meghdoot originates from an ancient epic where clouds were used as messengers.

2   Related Work

Publish-subscribe systems are designed for disseminating information (events) to a subset of the clients (subscribers) who are actually interested in this information. The designs for publish/subscribe systems can be classified into two categories: *Subject-based* and *Content-based*. Subject-based publish/subscribe systems assign each event to one of a set of pre-defined subjects (also referred to as topics, channels, or groups). The events themselves specify the topics that are relevant to the event. A client subscribes to a set of subjects it is interested in and is notified of all the events that are associated with these subjects. Examples of these systems include research proposals ISIS [3], iBus [16] and commercial products Tibco [26], and Vitria [28].

Content-based publish/subscribe systems allow more complex subscriptions by enabling restrictions on the event content. A subscriber can specify multiple predicates as a subscription and only those events whose content satisfies all the predicates are notified to the subscriber. Subscriptions in these systems are more expressive, but the systems are harder to implement. Examples of distributed content-based systems include Elvin [22], Siena [4], and Gryphon [2]. Elvin uses a central server which stores all the subscriptions and evaluates the subscriptions affected by the events. Fabret et al. [7] proposed novel data structures and application-specific caching policies and query processing in centralized systems to support high rates of subscriptions and events in a content-based system. For scalability purposes, subscriptions in this system must contain at least one equality predicate. Other centralized approaches have been proposed for scalable matching of predicates in the context of database trigger processing [11] and continuous queries [6]. Siena and Gryphon are distributed systems, in which a network of broker nodes is created and the events are distributed within the network.

P2P systems have emerged as a popular technique for exchanging information among a set of distributed peers. Initial approaches used a centralized index and/or flooding for locating objects in the system (e.g. Gnutella [9], Napster [15], KaZaA [14]). Advanced P2P systems provide more efficient lookups using structure in the logical overlay network formed by the peers. They implement a hash table functionality distributed over the peers, and are referred to as *Distributed Hash Tables* (DHT's). CAN [18], Chord [23], Pastry [20], and Tapestry [30] are different examples of DHT's. Most P2P systems were designed for locating information based on exact names, e.g. names of files. However, recently several proposals have been made to extend P2P functionality to more complex queries, e.g., range queries [10, 21], joins [12], SQL [27], XML [8], etc.

Several application level multicast systems have been proposed employing an underlying DHT, and can be easily adapted for subject-based publish/subscribe. These systems inherit the scalability and fault tolerance properties from the underlying DHT structure. Scribe [5] is built on top of Pastry [20]. Scribe assigns a unique groupId to each topic and the node whose nodeId is numerically closest to the groupId becomes the rendezvous point for this topic. For each topic, a multicast tree, that is rooted at the rendezvous point, is created by combining the paths from each subscriber to the rendezvous point. The messages (events) associated with the group (subject) are disseminated along the corresponding multicast tree starting from the root. A Pastry [20] based P2P overlay is used in [17] to provide support for a type based publish/subscribe system using similar rendezvous mechanism as Scribe [5]. The P2P overlay is also used by [17] for installing content based filters close to the publishers. Bayeux [31] uses Tapestry [30] as the underlying structure. Similar to Scribe, each group is associated with a root node based on its unique ID and a multicast tree rooted at that node is used for data dissemination. CAN-based multicast [19] is an application level multicast system based on CAN. Unlike the approaches above, CAN multicast does not build a distribution tree for each group. Instead, the members of a group form a separate group specific CAN and the multicasting is achieved by flooding over this separate CAN.

Our work implements a content-based publish-subscribe system over a DHT based on CAN [18]. There are several similar efforts [25, 24]. Terpstra et al. [25] partition the event space among the peers in the system. Chord [23] is used to broadcast events and subscriptions to all nodes in the system. These broadcasts are attenuated by filters installed at peer nodes due to the subscriptions stored in the system. This approach may require all peers in the system to be contacted to install a subscription. Unlike Terpstra et al., in our solution subscriptions are installed by routing through $O(dN^{\frac{1}{d}})$ peers, where N is the number of peers in the system and d is the dimensionality of the logical DHT space. Tam et al. [24] extend an existing subject-based system (Scribe [5]). Ordered collections of a set of selected attributes are used for indexing subscriptions into a subject-based publish/subscribe system. Thus a subscription can be submitted into the system only if it specifies all attribute values for at least one of the indices. The domains of attribute values are partitioned into intervals. If a subscription specifies a range over some attribute, it is decomposed into subparts according to the domain intervals. Meghdoot is a content-based publish/subscribe system that imposes no restrictions on the subscriptions or the events. It provides scalability by leveraging the P2P design, thus allowing flexible addition of peers into the system to match the demand. It uses innovative load distribution techniques to maintain the load balance in presence of highly skewed real world data.

3 Meghdoot Design

In this section, we start with a description of the schema and the representation of the events and the subscriptions in the system. Next, we describe the storage model for subscriptions and the event delivery mechanism.

3.1 Publish/Subscribe Model in Meghdoot

We consider a content-based publish/subscribe system with multiple attributes. The model and definitions are based on the model proposed by Fabret et al. [7]. The schema for the system can be described as: $\mathbb{S} = \{A_1, A_2, \ldots, A_n\}$, where each A_i corresponds to an attribute. Each attribute has a name, type and domain, and can be described by the tuple {Name: Type, Min, Max}. The attributes are identified by their unique names. The data types we consider are integer, floating point and character strings. The values Min and Max describe the range of domain values taken by the given attribute. All the peers participating in the publish/subscribe system use the same schema $\mathbb{S}$.

A *subscription* is a conjunction of predicates over one or more attributes. Each predicate specifies a constant value (using $=$) or a range (using $<, >, \leq, \geq$) for an attribute. If a subscription needs to specify multiple predicates over the same attribute, we can model such a subscription as a combination of multiple subscriptions, each of which specifies one continuous range over the attribute. For simplicity of presentation, henceforth, we assume each subscription specifies a continuous range over an attribute. An example subscription is $S = (A_1 \geq v_1) \wedge (v_2 \leq A_3 \leq v_3)$. An *event* is a set of equalities over the attributes in the schema. Therefore, an event can be represented as $e = \{A_1 = c_1, A_2 = c_2, \ldots, A_n = c_n\}$. In general, events may specify values for a subset of the attributes.

An event e matches a subscription S if each predicate of S is satisfied by the value of the corresponding attribute specified by the event e. The publish/subscribe system is required to store the subscriptions specified by the users and given an event, find all subscriptions matching the event and deliver the event to the subscribers.

The schema based clustering algorithms in [7] require that there be at least one equality predicate in each subscription. Applications may be interested in range predicates over all attributes specified in a subscription. For example, a subscription in the case of a stock quotes application can ask for all quotes where the volume of trade is greater than 100,000 on any day, without specifying any equality predicate. An event at the end of a day needs to specify values for stock name, its open, high, low and close values, and the volume of trade in that day. Our model is general and does not restrict the subscriptions and allows them to specify ranges over all attributes or a subset.

3.2   Logical Space Construction

In this section, we describe the construction of the logical space used for maintaining the distributed hash table. Given a schema $\mathbb{S} = \{A_1, A_2, \ldots, A_n\}$ with n attributes, we create a cartesian space with $2n$ dimensions. The mapping for the construction of the logical space as described below has been adapted from Sahin et al. [21]. Attribute A_i with domain range $[L_i, H_i]$ corresponds to dimensions $2i - 1$ and $2i$ of the cartesian space. Intuitively, the predicates of a subscription specify ranges of interest over the attributes, and the ranges are represented by a point in the logical space. The start of the range over the ith attribute is mapped to dimension $2i - 1$ corresponding to attribute A_i, and the end of the range is mapped to the dimension $2i$. Therefore the domain of the $2i - 1$ and $2i$ axes in the cartesian space is bounded by $[L_i, H_i]$. This logical space is partitioned among the peers present in the system, and each peer is responsible for one of the partitions. The partitions are referred to as *zones*, and if a peer is responsible for a partition, we say the peer *owns* the zone.

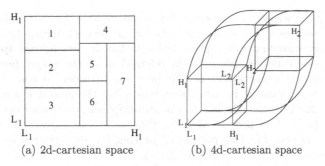

(a) 2d-cartesian space   (b) 4d-cartesian space

Fig. 1. Logical space construction.

The peers maintain a multidimensional Distributed Hash Table (DIIT) as described in CAN [18]. Each peer maintains information about the coordinates of its own zone. In addition, the peers store coordinate information of their neighboring zones as well as the IP addresses of the peers owning those zones. This information is used for the purposes of routing in the overlay network formed by the peers.

Figure 1 shows examples of the cartesian space. Figure 1(a) is the logical cartesian space for the case when the schema has only one attribute. The bounds of both axes in this case correspond to the bounds $[L_1, H_1]$ of the attribute. The rectangular regions form a partitioning of the space. Each rectangle is a zone and is owned by a peer in the system. Figure 1(b) is an example logical cartesian space when the schema has two attributes. The first two dimensions in the figure are bounded by the domain $[L_1, H_1]$ of the first attribute, whereas the next two dimensions are bounded by the domain $[L_2, H_2]$ of the second attribute.

3.3 Subscription Installation

A user can specify a subscription S by defining the ranges or values over one or more attributes in the schema. A subscription S can be expressed in the following format:

$S = (l_1 \leq A_1 \leq h_1) \wedge (l_2 \leq A_2 \leq h_2) \wedge \ldots \wedge (l_n \leq A_n \leq h_n)$.

If the subscription is interested in a specific value v of an attribute A_i then both l_i and h_i are set to v. If the subscription S does not specify any range over an attribute A_i then l_i and h_i are considered to be the boundaries L_i and H_i of the domain of A_i. The subscription S is mapped to the point $\langle l_1, h_1, l_2, h_2, \ldots, l_n, h_n \rangle$ in the $2n$-dimensional space which is referred to as the *subscription point*. Note that all subscriptions are stored in the upper left side of the diagonal hyperplane. This is due to the fact that the coordinate value of the $(2i-1)$th dimension is smaller than or equal to the $(2i)$th dimension for a subscription point since they correspond to the start and end values of the range over the ith attribute. The zones in the bottom right of the diagonal hyperplane are primarily used for routing purposes. Later, we utilize these zones for fault tolerance.

When a user wishes to subscribe for some events, the user submits the subscription to a peer in the system. The origin peer P_o maps the subscription to its corresponding subscription point in the $2n$-dimensional space. The peer whose *zone* contains this point is referred to as the target peer P_t. P_o needs to route the subscription to the peer P_t. In order to route the subscription, P_o selects one of its neighbors, which has the closest Euclidean distance in the $2n$-dimensional space to the subscription point, and forwards the subscription to it. This process of forwarding is repeated until the subscription reaches the peer P_t. This process of routing the subscription to the peer responsible for managing it takes $O(dN^{\frac{1}{d}})$ overlay hops [18] on average, where N is the number of peers in the system and d is the dimensionality of the cartesian space. When P_t receives the subscription, it stores the subscription along with an identifier (e.g. IP address, user name, e-mail, etc.). Figure 2 shows an example routing path for a subscription in the case of a single attribute schema. The subscription is finally stored in the target zone and the subscription point is marked S.

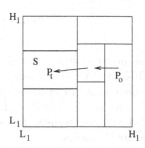

Fig. 2. Routing a subscription to its destination for installation.

3.4   Event Delivery

When an event is introduced into the system, Meghdoot is required to find all the matching subscriptions installed in the system, and deliver the event to the subscribers. Consider an event $e = \{A_1 = c_1, A_2 = c_2, \ldots, A_n = c_n\}$. The event e is mapped to the point $\langle c_{11}, c_{12}, c_{21}, c_{22}, \ldots, c_{n1}, c_{n2} \rangle$ in the $2n$-dimensional space, and is referred to as an *event point*. If the event specifies a value v for the ith attribute then $c_{i1} = c_{i2} = v$, otherwise $c_{i1} = L_i$ and $c_{i2} = H_i$. Note that the event points lie on the diagonal hyperplane of the space if all the attribute values are specified. A subscription $S = (l_1 \leq A_1 \leq h_1) \wedge (l_2 \leq A_2 \leq h_2) \wedge \ldots \wedge (l_n \leq A_n \leq h_n)$ is affected by the event e if the following property holds:
$$\forall i \in \{1, 2, \ldots, n\} \quad l_i \leq c_{i1} \wedge c_{i2} \leq h_i$$
The shaded area in Figure 3 shows the region of event points in a $2d$ cartesian space corresponding to a single attribute schema that can affect a subscription S, because all the event points in the shaded region will satisfy the above property.

The shaded region in Figure 4 shows the region of subscription points of all subscriptions affected by an event e. In the $2n$-dimensional space, event e mapping to the point $\langle c_{11}, c_{12}, c_{21}, c_{22}, \ldots, c_{n1}, c_{n2} \rangle$ affects the hyper rectangular region defined by the following points:
$$\langle L_1, c_{11}, L_2, c_{21}, \ldots, L_n, c_{n1} \rangle \text{ and } \langle c_{12}, H_1, c_{22}, H_2, \ldots, c_{n2}, H_n \rangle.$$
When an event is introduced in the system at a peer P_o, it maps the event to the corresponding *event point* and routes the event to the peer P_t which contains the event point. Figure 4 shows the routing path of an event e from P_o to P_t and the region of affected subscriptions of e in a $2d$ space. The event is then propagated starting from P_t to all peers which are in the region affected by

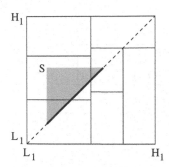

Fig. 3. Region of events affecting a subscription $S = \langle l_1, h_1 \rangle$.

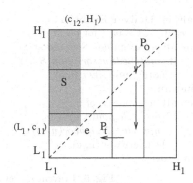

Fig. 4. Region of subscriptions affected by an event $e = \langle c_1, c_1 \rangle$.

the event. P_t sends the event to its immediate neighbors in the affected region, which in turn propagate the event to their neighbors in the affected region. This process repeats until all peers in the affected region have been notified of the event. The basic algorithm for event delivery is given below.

The algorithm **Deliver Event** is initiated at event e's target peer, P_t, which owns zone z. Lines 1-4 check for all affected subscriptions that are stored at zone z and deliver the event to those subscriptions. Predicate $matchedSubscription(S, e)$ is true if the subscription point corresponding to subscription S is contained in the affected region of event e within zone z. Lines 5-8 find all neighbors, n, of zone z that are affected by event e and are in the upper left region of the zone z itself. The predicate $eventRegion(n, e)$ is true if the region of zone n intersects with the affected region of event e. The predicate $upperleftNeighbor(n, z)$ evaluates to true if neighbor n lies in the upper left region of zone z. We use the bottom right point of zone z as the reference point for the upper left region of z to ensure that none of the affected neighbors are missed. For example, in Figure 1(a) zones 1, 2, and 4 are in the upper left of zone 5, but zones 3, 6, and 7 are not. This predicate is required to prevent back propagation of events. In Figure 5, all (dashed and solid) arrows represent the propagation of the event. Predicate $upperleftNeighbor(n, z)$ prevents messages from propagating in the reverse order of the arrows. For example, it prevents zone z_4 from sending a message back to zones $z_1, z_2,$ and z_3.

The event propagation algorithm can be further optimized to prevent the same event from being delivered to a zone by multiple neighbors. Figure 5 shows only zones of interest for illustration and the dashed region is the region of subscription points affected by event e. In the figure, zones z_2 and z_3 do not need to send the event message to the zone z_4 because zone z_1 sends the message to z_4. These messages can be prevented in the following way. When propagating an event to a neighbor z_n, a zone z checks if any of its bottom right neighbors could have already delivered the message to that neighbor, in which case it would not propagate the event to that neighbor. In our implementation we also use this optimization. Dashed arrows in Figure 5 are the duplicate messages that can be avoided by this optimization.

Algorithm: **Deliver Event**(z, e)
/* Executed at zone z for event e. */
1. **for all** subscriptions S stored at z
2.   **if** $(matchedSubscription(S, e))$
3.   notifySubscriber(S, e)
4. **end for**
5. **for all** neighbors n of z
6.   **if** $(eventRegion(n, e)\ \wedge$
7. $upperleftNeighbor(n, z))$
8.   DeliverEvent(n, e)
9. **end for**

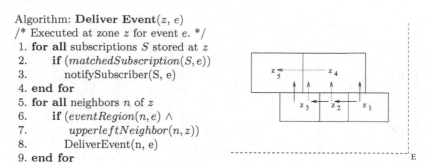

Fig. 5. Preventing repetitive propagation.

3.5 Example Applications

In this section, we present some examples of applications that can be implemented using Meghdoot. As an example consider an application where distributed sensors are used for gathering environmental parameters such as temperature, humidity, illumination, etc. The sensors in various geographical locations send the measured data to their local base stations. Users can specify continuous queries over the data, and these queries are stored at the base stations. This application can be modeled using Meghdoot where the base stations form a P2P network. The user queries are stored as subscriptions on the base stations and the sensor readings can be directed to all the affected queries using the event delivery mechanism.

Meghdoot can also be utilized in critical systems for event monitoring applications, for example power distribution system. The power distribution system consists of *Power Stations* which generate power which is sent to *Transmission Substations*. These transmission substations use high voltage transmission lines to convey power to various *Power Substations* which are located in different geographical areas. The power substations step down the power voltage and distribute it to the residential locations. The power system has sensors that measure the amount of power generated (in MW), transmitted and consumed (in KW) at various points in the system. Sensors also measure the voltage in the transmission lines. Monitoring agents can specify continuous queries that detect anomalies, like sudden drop in voltage over transmission lines or a trip in power generation. This enables early detection of events that can lead to serious problems, e.g. power outages. According to a recent report, the August 14th 2003 blackout in the North East USA and Canada, the cause of the large scale failure was due to lack of timely information about individual failures.

4   Peer Management in Meghdoot

In this section we discuss the mechanisms used by peers to join and leave the system. We start with a description of how a peer joins the system. In the simplest case, a new peer P_n can use the algorithm described in CAN [18] for joining the system. Peer P_n contacts some existing node P_e in the system and requests P_e to locate a randomly generated point in the logical space. Once the peer P_t whose zone contains the random point is located, P_n submits a join request to P_t. The peer P_t then divides its zone space into two halves and assigns one half to P_n. The two peers then update their neighbor information and also inform the neighbors of the new zone coordinates. The CAN system [18] was originally designed for storing files and multimedia objects with syntactic identifiers. To distribute this information uniformly in the multidimensional identifier space, a uniform hash function was used, thus ensuring a balanced load among the peers. However, in a data-driven environment, as in our approach, the distribution of the data among the peers is content-based. Hence, if a set of events are popular, then the subscription distribution will be skewed in that region of the space. This is due to the fact that Meghdoot uses the content of the subscriptions, rather than a uniform hash function to place data on peers. Furthermore, unlike a standard DHT based P2P system, in a publish/subscribe setting a data event needs to be forwarded to all subscriptions interested in this event. Hence, a direct application of the original CAN join procedure to a publish/subscribe setting can lead to significant load imbalance among the peers. In this section, we study the characteristics of load and develop strategies for load balancing.

4.1   Load Characteristics

The peers in the system need to store subscriptions associated with the subscribers. In addition, they need to propagate the events to all peers in the affected region. Therefore, load on a peer is due to both subscriptions and events, and they have different characteristics, which we described below. Our proposed strategies for admitting new peers in the system exploit these varying characteristics.

Subscription Load. When a user installs a subscription, the subscription is mapped to its corresponding point, and is stored at the peer which owns the zone containing the subscription point. Thus a zone owned by a peer can contain various subscription points. Since the peer owning the zone is responsible for delivering the events it receives to the affected subscriptions it stores, the load on the peer due to subscriptions is proportional to the number of stored subscriptions in the zone. In particular, the load is reduced on a peer, if the subscriptions in its zone are reduced. Therefore, the load due to subscriptions on a peer can be reduced by dividing the spatial extent of a zone so that the number of stored subscriptions is evenly divided with the joining peer. Figure 6 shows an example in 2d space.

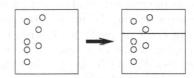

Fig. 6. Splitting a zone divides subscription load.

Event Load. An event generates load because it needs to be propagated to all zones that are in the affected region of the zone. If a zone is loaded because it falls in the propagation path of too many events, splitting the zone in two will not help, because the zone will still remain in the path of those events. For example, in Figure 7(a), lets say that the zones owned by peer nodes N_1, N_2, and N_3 are in some event propagation path, and node N_2 is overloaded due to event propagation. If a new peer N_4 joins the system and splits the zone owned by N_2, now both N_2 and N_4 are in the propagation path, and hence this splitting does not reduce the load on N_2. In order to reduce the load due to event propagation, we need to create alternate propagation paths and select one of the available paths to propagate each event. Thus, not every event will propagate through the same set of nodes, and overload them. This can be achieved by replicating a zone that is overloaded due to event propagation. In the context of P2P systems partitioning is typically used for load distribution. Our approach is different, in that, we are proposing replication for load distribution.

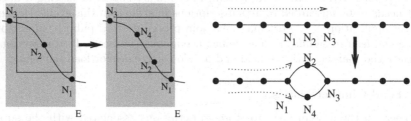

(a) Splitting does not divide event propagation load.

(b) Replicating a zone divides propagation load.

Fig. 7. Event propagation load.

Figure 7(b) shows how this will be implemented. The straight line on top represents the original situation along a propagation path. The black dots represent the peers owning the zones in the path. Peer N_2 in the center was overloaded due to event propagation. When a new peer N_4 wishes to join the system, it can replicate the exact zone as peer N_2 along with all its subscriptions. The neighbors N_1 and N_3 need to store the IP addresses of both peers N_2 and N_4 associated with the zone coordinates. Effectively the neighbors have two paths to propagate the event through the replicated zone. When a neighbor needs to propagate an event to the zone, it picks one replica peer out of the list of replicas for the zone in a round robin fashion. This will distribute the propagation load on the old peer responsible for the zone.

4.2 Peer Join

When a new peer P_n wishes to join the system, it contacts a known peer P_e in the system. P_e tries to locate a heavily loaded peer in the system. After P_e finds a heavily loaded peer P_h, it forwards P_n to P_h. In order to locate a heavily loaded peer, each peer in the system maintains information about its current load as well as its neighbors' load when it last heard from them. In addition, each peer maintains an estimated list called *loadedPeerList* of k most heavily loaded peers in the system that they ever heard about. The peers can decide a local value of k depending on available memory.

Peers in the system periodically update their neighbors about their load statistics. The peers also propagate their *loadedPeerList* to their neighbors. A peer merges its *loadedPeerList* with the received list. When required to locate a heavily loaded peer, the load information about the neighbors is utilized by the peers to perform a distributed hill climbing algorithm to locate a local maxima. The initiating peer sends a probe for a heavily loaded node to one of its neighbors that has the heaviest load. The probe is forwarded to the heaviest loaded neighbor by each receiving peer until it reaches a peer which has a load higher than any of its neighbors. This peer is referred to as a local maxima. The new peer is notified of the heavily loaded peer.

When contacted by the new peer, the heavily loaded peer chooses to either split its zone or replicate it based on its load conditions. If the peer is loaded due to event propagation it hands over a copy of its zone to the new peer, thus creating a replica of the zone. The neighbors are informed of the existence of this new replica. If the peer is loaded because it is managing too many subscriptions, it splits its zone in such a way that the two partitions have even distribution of subscriptions between them, and hands over one partition to the new peer.

4.3   Peer Departure or Failure

When a peer wishes to depart from the system, it first checks if there are any replicas for its zone. If one or more replicas exist, it simply informs its replicas as well as the neighbors of its decision to leave, and leaves the system. The neighbors and replicas update their information. If there are no available replicas for a peer leaving the system, it contacts its neighbors and finds a neighbor willing to take over its zone. Then it transfers all its subscriptions to this neighbor and leaves the system.

Since peers periodically send load messages to their neighbors, a neighbor that discovers a failed peer needs to either take up the zone of the failed peer or find some other peer to hand over the zone. In the case of failure, the information about the subscriptions stored at the failed peer can be lost, unless replicas exist due to event load balancing. To avoid this problem, we use the following replication scheme. As described in Section 3.3, all subscriptions are stored in the upper left side of the diagonal hyperplane. We exploit this property of

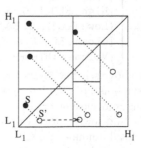

Fig. 8. Replicating subscriptions at mirror image.

our design for fault tolerance. When installing a subscription at subscription point $\langle l_1, h_1, l_2, h_2, \ldots, l_n, h_n \rangle$, we also store a copy of the subscription at point

$\langle h_1, l_1, h_2, l_2, \ldots, h_n, l_n \rangle$. This point is the reflection of the subscription point in the diagonal hyperplane of the $2n$-dimensional cartesian space. This is illustrated by Figure 8 for a $2d$ space. The filled dots represent the subscription points and the circles are their reflections in the diagonal. Therefore, if a peer fails and there are no replicas for the zone, then the lost subscriptions can be recovered by querying the reflection of the zone's coordinates in the diagonal hyperplane.

If the reflection of a subscription point falls into the same zone, for example subscription S in Figure 8 has its reflection S' in the same zone, we move along the increasing values of all odd dimensions until we find a neighbor zone with higher odd dimensional coordinates, and store the copy at this zone. For example S' is actually stored in the zone to its right in the Figure 8. In case any of the odd dimensional coordinates wrap around before reaching a neighboring zone, we start again with the reflection point and move towards the decreasing even dimensional coordinate values until we find a neighboring zone, and store the copy there. In 2 dimensions, this is equivalent to first moving right and if no neighbor is found, then moving down from the reflection point. If a zone splits, it has to accordingly move the reflection subscriptions to the left or top neighbors.

5 Experimental Evaluation

In this section we evaluate Meghdoot using a model of stock quotes application. We start the discussion by explaining the schema for the stock quotes application and the datasets used for evaluation. Next, we present the evaluation results for various metrics.

5.1 Experimental Setup

We developed a simulator of Meghdoot in C++. We used the simulator in conjunction with a model of the stock quotes application with the following schema:

$$\mathbb{S} = \left\{ \begin{array}{l} \{\text{Date}: \text{STRING}, \text{ 2/Jan/98}, \text{ 31/Dec/02}\}, \\ \{\text{Symbol}: \text{STRING}, \text{ aaa}, \text{ zzzzz}\}, \\ \{\text{Open}: \text{FLOAT}, 0, 500\}, \\ \{\text{High}: \text{FLOAT}, 0, 500\}, \\ \{\text{Low}: \text{FLOAT}, 0, 500\}, \\ \{\text{Close}: \text{FLOAT}, 0, 500\}, \\ \{\text{Volume}: \text{INTEGER}, 0, 310000000\} \end{array} \right\}$$

In the above schema, Symbol is the stock symbol for the corresponding company. The symbols are character strings of lengths 3 to 5. Open and Close are the opening and closing prices of the stock on a given day. High and Low are the highest and lowest price values attained by the stock in the given day. Volume is the total amount of trade in this stock on that day.

An example subscription in the stock market publish/subscribe system with the above schema is: $\{\text{Symbol} = aapl \wedge \text{High} \geq 45\}$, which subscribes for any events for the stock of Apple when the high value of the stock is greater than or equal to \$45. An example event is $\{\text{Date} = 30/Jan/98, \text{Symbol} = aapl, \text{Open} = 18.31, \text{High} = 18.87, \text{Low} = 18.25, \text{Close} = 18.31, \text{Volume} = 1450600\}$.

The input sets for the simulations consist of subscriptions and events drawn randomly. The subscriptions were generated using five template subscriptions. A template was picked at random with probability p and parameterized to generate a subscription. We assign general subscriptions low probabilities of occurrence. The reason for this choice is that in a real application subscribers are usually interested in specific events relevant to their narrow interests. Our standard subscription set included 14,029 subscriptions, however, in some of the experiments we increased the number of subscriptions to study the scalability of the system. The templates along with their probability of occurrence are described below:

- $\{(\texttt{Symbol} = P1) \wedge (P2 \leq \texttt{Open} \leq P3)\}$. Notify events for stock $P1$ when its open value is between $P2$ and $P3$. Probability = 20%.
- $\{(\texttt{Symbol} = P1) \wedge (\texttt{Low} \leq P2)\}$. Notify events where a certain stock $P1$'s value is less than or equal to $P2$. Probability = 35%.
- $\{(\texttt{Symbol} = P1) \wedge (\texttt{High} \geq P2)\}$. Notify events where a certain stock $P1$'s value is higher than or equal to $P2$. Probability = 35%.
- $\{(\texttt{Symbol} = P1) \wedge (\texttt{Volume} \geq P2)\}$. Notify events where a certain stock $P1$ was traded more than or equal to $P2$. Probability = 5%.
- $\{\texttt{Volume} \geq P1\}$. Notify if a stock is traded more than $P1$. Probability = 5%.

We have used two different sets of events. One of the event sets was created synthetically by generating uniformly random values in the domains of the attributes. This event set consists of 115,000 events (again in the scalability experiments we varied the number of events). The other event set is the real stock event data for 100 stocks. The data was obtained from Yahoo! Finance [29] by downloading the stock events on a daily basis starting from 2/Jan/ 1998 to 31/Dec/2002. This event set contains 115,353 events. The real event set is highly skewed because most of the stock prices ranged between the values of $10 to $30. This is typical of real world datasets.

We evaluated the scalability of the system by running the simulation with varying number of peers in the system. We performed measurements for 100, 1000 and 10,000 peers in the system. The simulations were initialized with one peer in the system. A new peer joins the system after each simulation event with a probability of 10%, until the total number of peers reaches the bound. We measured the number of peers contacted to deliver each event. To evaluate the load on the peers, we measured the total number of messages received by each peer during the run of the simulation. This includes messages due to routing of events and subscriptions, as well as messages due to propagation of events. These experiments do not include peer failure.

In the following sections we present the results of the evaluation. First we present the evaluation results for the scalability and load balancing of the system for the synthetic and real event sets. Later, we analyze the effectiveness of zone replication in the system.

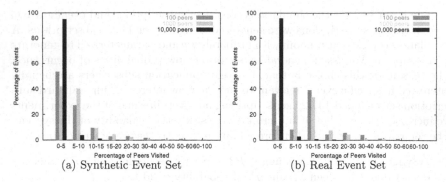

(a) Synthetic Event Set   (b) Real Event Set

Fig. 9. Scalability Performance of the System.

5.2   System Scalability

In this section we present the evaluation results for the scalability of the system
when the number of peers in the system is varied. We also analyzed the effect of
varying the number of subscriptions and the number of events on the system.

Figure 9 shows the distribution of the number of peers that were contacted in
order to deliver events to relevant subscriptions. The x-axis in the plot represents
the percentage of peers contacted to deliver an event out of the total number
of peers that were present in the system when the event was generated. The
buckets on the x-axis have been recalibrated because the values 60-100 on x-axis
had no data points, and the range 0-20 has been expanded.

Figure 9(a) shows the scalability of the system for the synthetic event set,
where the events are distributed uniformly in the domain. In the case of 100
peers, more than half of the events were delivered to all the relevant subscriptions
by contacting at most upto 5% of the peers only. For the case of 10,000 peers 95%
of the events were delivered to all affected subscriptions by contacting less than
5% of the peers. In fact, almost all the events were delivered by contacting less
than 10% of the peers. Overall, as the number of peers in the system increases,
the peers needed to be contacted for delivering events scales very well.

Figure 9(b) shows the results for the simulations with the real event set
which is highly skewed. Because of the skewed distribution of the event data,
more zones are created in the vicinity of event points which leads to a small
increase in the number of peers contacted to deliver events. Even with skewed
events, in the cases of 100 and 1000 peers, 85%-90% are delivered by contacting
at most 15% of the peers. For the experiment with 10,000 peers, almost all
events are delivered by contacting less than 10% of the peers and 97% of those
events contact less than 5% of the peers. This strengthens our conclusion that
Meghdoot scales very well as the number of peers in the system increase.

We performed an experiment with 10,000 peers in the system by varying
the number of subscriptions installed in the system from 25,000 to 150,000.
We used the synthetic event set for this experiment which contained 115,000
events. Figure 10 shows the results. In all cases more than 95% of the events are

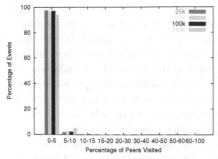

Fig. 10. Effect of Varying the Number of Subscriptions.

Fig. 11. Effect of Varying the Number of Events.

delivered by contacting less than 5% of the peers in the system. There is only a marginal degradation in performance even as the number of subscriptions stored in the system increases from 25,000 to 150,000 over 10,000 peers. This shows that Meghdoot scales well as the number of installed subscriptions increases.

In another experiment we varied the number of events from 200,000 to 500,000. These simulations had 10,000 peers in the system and 50,000 subscriptions. The events sets contained uniformly distributed events. Figure 11 shows the results of the experiment. With 200,000 events in the system more than 75% of the events are delivered by contacting at most 5% of the peers. For all cases, at most 15% of the peers are contacted to deliver the events. The results are very similar in all cases demonstrating that the system scales very well with the number of events.

5.3   Load Distribution

We measure the load on a peer as the ratio of messages the peer receives to the total number of messages processed in the system since the peer joined the system. Figure 12 shows the load distribution on the peers in the system. The peers were sorted in decreasing order of the load, and were grouped by their rank into groups of size 10% each. The plot shows the average load on each group.

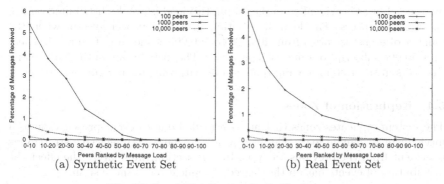

(a) Synthetic Event Set   (b) Real Event Set

Fig. 12. Load Distribution in the System.

Figure 12(a) shows the load distribution in the system for the synthetic event set where the events are distributed uniformly. Even in the case of 100 peers the maximum load is only 5.35% of the messages, which is very good. In the case of 10,000 peers the load is very evenly distributed among all the peers in the system. As the number of peers increase in the system, the load is evenly shared by the new peers. This shows that our load balancing schemes are quite effective.

Figure 12(b) shows the load distribution over the peers for the real event set which is highly skewed. In the case of 100 peers, the maximally loaded peers handle less than 5% of the total messages. As the number of peers increases, the load is well distributed among the new joining peers. The trend of load distribution is very similar to the case of uniformly distributed events. Therefore, our load balancing strategies are very effective and adapt very well dynamically to the distribution of subscriptions and events.

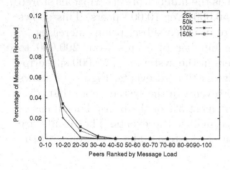 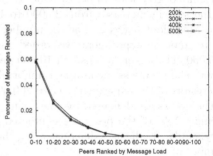

Fig. 13. Effect of Varying the Number of Subscriptions on Load Distribution.   **Fig. 14.** Effect of Varying the Number of Events on Load Distribution.

Figure 13 shows the load distribution in the system when we varied the number of stored subscriptions. This experiment had 10,000 peers and used the synthetic event set with 115,000 events. Even the most heavily loaded peers received only about 0.123% of the total messages generated in the system. When the number of stored subscriptions increases, the number of messages generated increases, but as is evident from the graph, this load is evenly distributed among the available peers. The load distribution in a 10,000 peer system when the number of events is varied from 200,000 to 500,000 is shown in Figure 14. There were 50,000 subscriptions in this experiment. The distribution of the load among the peers in the system remains quite stable with the growing number of events.

5.4   Replication of Zones

The system replicates zones that are overloaded due to event propagation as a mechanism to handle load. This has proved to be a very effective strategy as is evident from the previous analysis. In this section, we analyze the effect the distribution of events has on the degree of replication in the system.

Table 1. Number of Unique Zones.

#peers	Synthetic Events	Real Events
100	76	73
1000	652	470
10,000	9622	9323

Table 1 summarizes the number of unique zones that were created during the simulations with real and synthetic event sets with 14,029 subscriptions. Each zone in the system has at least one peer associated with it. The remaining peers are used for replication. Note that the number of peer nodes used for the replication of existing zones is higher in all cases when the real event set is used. This is the case because the real event set, as is typical of many real world datasets, is very skewed and a lot of events are propagated through the same zones which overloads them. Therefore, new joining peers are directed to those zones and they are replicated to reduce the propagation load.

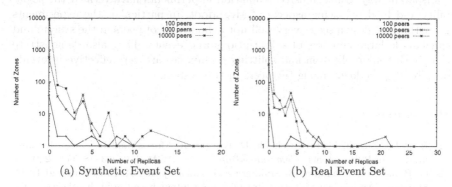

(a) Synthetic Event Set   (b) Real Event Set

Fig. 15. Replication of zones.

Figure 15 presents the distribution of the degree of replication in the system. The x-axis is the degree of replication and the y-axis is the number of unique zones that were replicated with that degree. The y-axis has been plotted on logscale because of the large variation in the number of non-replicated zones in the cases of different number of peers in the simulations. In Figure 15(a) for 10,000 peers, there was a zone which was replicated 20 times. From Figure 15(b), we can see that one of the zones was replicated to a high degree of 27. As mentioned earlier, in the real event set, most stock events had price values in the range of \$10-\$30. Thus a large subset of the events map to the event points that fall in a small number of zones. These zones therefore have a high degree of replication to overcome the load generated by these events.

6   Conclusions

We presented Meghdoot, a middleware for a content-based publish/subscribe system, which leverages peer-to-peer based Distributed Hash Tables for scalable dissemination of data events to subscribers distributed across the network. P2P design offers the flexibility of incorporating additional resources, thus providing performance scalability. Meghdoot imposes no restrictions over subscriptions and allows them to be specified in terms of range predicates over all attributes in a schema. Unlike most other P2P approaches, Meghdoot uses the semantics of the subscriptions and the events to store subscriptions and deliver matching events to them. Since real world datasets tend to be skewed, existing peer management techniques fail to distribute load well among the peers. Hence, unlike previous work, we use the characteristics of the load to determine how to distribute the load. Subscription load leads to zone splitting, while event propagation load leads to zone replication. We also exploit the underlying distributed hash structure to replicate subscriptions for fault tolerance in an innovative and systematically transparent way. Our extensive simulation experiments have verified the scalability and load balancing aspects of Meghdoot. In particular, the experiments show that the design scales very well upto thousands of peers in the system and can handle large numbers of subscriptions and events. They also demonstrate that both zone replication and splitting techniques are very effective in evenly distributing the load among the peers in the system.

References

1. H. Balakrishnan, M. F. Kaashoek, D. Karger, R. Morris, and I. Stoica. Looking up data in P2P systems. *Communications of the ACM*, 46(2):43–48, Feb. 2003.
2. G. Banavar, T. Chandra, B. Mukherjee, J. Nagarajarao, R. E. Strom, and D. C. Sturman. An efficient multicast protocol for content-based publish-subscribe systems. In *Proceedings of the 19th ICDCS*, pages 262–272, 1999.
3. K. P. Birman. The process group approach to reliable distributed computing. *Communications of the ACM*, 36(12):36–53, Dec. 1993.
4. A. Carzaniga, D. S. Rosenblum, and A. L. Wolf. Design and evaluation of a wide-area event notification service. *ACM Transactions on Computer Systems*, 19(3):332–383, 2001.
5. M. Castro, P. Druschel, A. Kermarrec, and A. Rowstron. SCRIBE: A large-scale and decentralized application-level multicast infrastructure. *IEEE Journal on Selected Areas in Communications*, 20(8):100–110, 2002.
6. J. Chen, D. J. DeWitt, F. Tian, and Y. Wang. NiagaraCQ: A scalable continuous query system for internet databases. In *Proceedings of the 2000 ACM SIGMOD*, pages 379–390, 2000.
7. F. Fabret, H. A. Jacobsen, F. Llirbat, J. Pereira, K. A. Ross, and D. Shasha. Filtering algorithms and implementation for very fast publish/subscribe systems. *SIGMOD Record*, 30(2):115–126, 2001.
8. L. Galanis, Y. Wang, S. R. Jeffery, and D. J. DeWitt. Locating data sources in large distributed systems. In *Proceedings of the 29th VLDB*, pages 874–885, 2003.
9. Gnutella. http://gnutella.wego.com/.

10. A. Gupta, D. Agrawal, and A. El Abbadi. Approximate range selection queries in peer-to-peer systems. In *Proceedings of the 1st CIDR*, pages 141–151, 2003.

11. E. N. Hanson, C. Carnes, L. Huang, M. Konyala, L. Noronha, S. Parthasarathy, J. B. Park, and A. Vernon. Scalable trigger processing. In *Proceedings of the 15th ICDE*, pages 266–275, 1999.

12. M. Harren, J. M. Hellerstein, R. Huebsch, B. T. Loo, S. Shenker, and I. Stoica. Complex queries in DHT-based peer-to-peer networks. In *Proceedings of the first International Workshop on Peer-to-Peer Systems*, pages 242–250, 2002.

13. IBM News. http://www.ibm.com/ibm/history/history/year_2000.html.

14. KaZaA. http://www.kazaa.com/.

15. Napster. http://www.napster.com/.

16. B. Oki, M. Pfluegl, A. Siegel, and D. Skeen. The information bus: an architecture for extensible distributed systems. In *Proceedings of the fourteenth ACM SOSP*, pages 58–68, 1993.

17. P. R. Pietzuch and J. Bacon. Peer-to-peer overlay broker networks in an event-based middleware. In *Proceedings of the 2nd DEBS*, pages 1–8, 2003.

18. S. Ratnasamy, P. Francis, M. Handley, R. Karp, and S. Shenker. A scalable content-addressable network. In *Proceedings of the 2001 ACM SIGCOMM*, pages 161–172.

19. S. Ratnasamy, M. Handley, R. Karp, and S. Shenker. Application-level multi-cast using content-addressable networks. In *Proceedings of the 3rd International Workshop of NGC*, volume 2233, pages 14–29. LNCS, Springer, 2001.

20. A. Rowstron and P. Druschel. Pastry: Scalable, distributed object location and routing for large-scale peer-to-peer systems. In *IFIP/ACM Middleware 2001*.

21. O. D. Sahin, A. Gupta, D. Agrawal, and A. El Abbadi. A peer-to-peer framework for caching range queries. In *Proceedings of the 20th ICDE*, pages 165–176, 2004.

22. B. Segall and D. Arnold. Elvin has left the building: A publish/subscribe notification service with quenching. In *Proceedings of AUUG*, 1997.

23. I. Stoica, R. Morris, D. Karger, M. F. Kaashoek, and H. Balakrishnan. Chord: A scalable peer-to-peer lookup service for internet applications. In *Proceedings of the 2001 ACM SIGCOMM*, pages 149–160.

24. D. Tam, R. Azimi, and H.-A. Jacobsen. Building content-based publish/subscribe systems with distributed hash tables. In *Proceedings of International Workshop on Databases, Information Systems and Peer-to-Peer Computing*, 2003.

25. W. W. Terpstra, S. Behnel, L. Fiege, A. Zeidler, and A. P. Buchmann. A peer-to-peer approach to content-based publish/subscribe. In *Proceeding of the Second DEBS*, 2003.

26. Tibco. http://www.tibco.com/.

27. P. Triantafillou and T. Pitoura. Towards a unifying framework for complex query processing over structured peer-to-peer data networks. In *Fist International workshop DBISP2P 2003*, pages 169–183.

28. Vitria. http://www.vitria.com/.

29. Yahoo! Finance. http://finance.yahoo.com/.

30. Y. B. Zhao, J. Kubiatowicz, and A. Joseph. Tapestry: An infrastructure for fault-tolerant wide-area location and routing. Technical Report UCB/CSD-01-1141, University of California at Berkeley, 2001.

31. S. Q. Zhuang, B. Y. Zhao, A. D. Joseph, R. H. Katz, and J. D. Kubiatowicz. Bayeux: an architecture for scalable and fault-tolerant wide-area data dissemination. In *Proceedings of the 11th ACM NOSSDAV*, pages 11–20, 2001.

Subscription Propagation in Highly-Available Publish/Subscribe Middleware

Yuanyuan Zhao, Daniel Sturman, and Sumeer Bhola

IBM T.J.Watson Research Center,
Hawthorne, NY 10532, USA
{yuanyuan,sturman,sbhola}@us.ibm.com

Abstract. Achieving availability and scalability while providing service guarantees such as in-order, gapless delivery is essential for deploying publish/subscribe messaging middleware in wide area networks. Scalability often requires a publish/subscribe system to propagate subscription information and perform content matching across the network. Existing subscription propagation algorithms do not support in-order, gapless delivery in a redundant overlay network.

This paper presents a novel approach that utilizes virtual time (VT) vectors to convey temporal consistency in propagating incremental and consolidated subscription information. The VT vectors provide a means of testing sufficiency of filtering information, by comparing a broker's VT vector with that of a message. When the test fails, indicating insufficient broker subscription information, safety may be preserved by 'flooding' the message to all neighbors on a routing tree. This approach does not require subscription state agreement across redundant paths and hence is highly available. We present a detailed evaluation of the approach.

Keywords: publish/subscribe middleware, subscription propagation, high availability

1 Introduction

Content-based publish/subscribe(pub/sub) messaging is a popular paradigm for building asynchronous distributed applications. A content-based pub/sub system consists of *publishers* that generate messages and *subscribers* that register interest in messages. The interest is usually expressed through content filters in the form of Boolean expressions. The system ensures timely delivery of published messages to all interested subscribers, and typically contains *routing brokers* for this purpose. Publishers and subscribers obtain service by connecting to brokers and are decoupled with each other.

In many cases, publishers and subscribers also want strong service guarantees, such as in-order, gapless delivery [3, 4] (referred to as reliable delivery in the rest of the paper). These services are usually provided by the broker network and made available to clients through standard messaging interfaces, like the Java Message Service (JMS) [1]. Reliable delivery guarantees that for every subscription s and a published message stream, the system finds a starting message

H.-A. Jacobsen (Ed.): Middleware 2004, LNCS 3231, pp. 274–293, 2004.

m_0 and from m_0, delivers all and only those messages matching s in an order conforming to the original stream.

In addition to providing reliable delivery guarantees, commercial deployment over wide-area networks requires a pub/sub system to be scalable, highly available and utilize network bandwidth efficiently. In order to efficiently utilize network bandwidth, a pub/sub system usually propagates information about subscriptions across the broker network. A broker stores, for each of its neighboring part of the network, the information on what messages are needed by subscribers from the network. When a new message is published and routed, a broker filters out and does not send the message to parts of the network where no subscriber is interested. However, the amount of subscription information could get very large as it approaches the publishers. A scalable pub/sub systems should aggregate and only maintain a subset of subscription information for each routing direction of a broker as long as the subset of information is sufficient to match all messages that are needed by subscribers from that routing direction.

The combination of content-based routing and reliable delivery provides some unique challenges. Unlike in topic or group-based pub/sub systems, reliability cannot be based only on detecting gaps in publisher-assigned sequence numbers as each content subscriber may request a completely unique set of messages to be delivered. Reliable delivery protocols typically rely on brokers on the routing path to assist on detecting gaps. A routing broker with incorrect subscription information may decide not to forward on a message. Given that gaps cannot be detected by checking publisher-assigned sequence numbers, an end subscriber may never discover that a message was missed.

Numerous studies have shown that loss of connectivity is common in wide-area networks, due to hardware and software failures and network misconfigurations. Hence, pub/sub systems should be built on networks with redundant links. This further complicates subscription propagation as alternative routes with different subscription information may filter out messages matching subscriptions that are unknown to a route.

In this paper, we present a subscription propagation algorithm that supports reliable delivery in redundant overlay networks. Using this algorithm, a pub/sub system is able to (1) propagate and aggregate subscriptions; (2) support reliable delivery; (3) choose freely (based on other criteria such as traffic load, system faults) among multiple redundant links for data message routing; and (4) not require heavy consensus protocols among brokers that serve as alternatives or backups of each other. Our approach deals with link failure, message losses and re-ordering and broker crash failures. Byzantine failures are outside the scope of this work.

We have implemented our algorithm in the Gryphon system. Gryphon is a content-based pub/sub system designed for high-volume, low latency, Internet-scale distribution. Gryphon can be deployed using multiple geographically-distributed application-level routers (called brokers), with tens of thousands of clients and with tens of thousands of messages being delivered across the system each second. Our algorithm, however, applies to a wide range of messaging systems.

Previous pub/sub systems have mainly focused on efficiently utilizing network bandwidth and on scalability issues concerning propagating and aggregating subscriptions. However, few of these systems efficiently exploit the network redundancy and recover from failures in a timely fashion. Indeed, existing pub/sub systems are usually unable to utilize the redundant links or do not support reliable delivery. Simply extending existing work that utilizes only a single path requires consensus between multiple brokers on alternative paths and will incur a lot of overhead.

The remainder of this paper is organized as follows: Section 2 presents a redundant overlay network model. Section 3 describes the basic algorithm, and then discusses a number of variants. Section 4 discusses liveness and failure recovery, and Section 5 describes our implementation and experimental results. Section 6 is an overview of related work and we conclude in Section 7.

2   Context: Redundant Overlay Network

In this section, we describe a simplified topology model of a redundant overlay network of messaging brokers. We assume a redundant routing tree where each tree node may contain more than one broker/server(Figure 1). We further restrict the edge nodes (e.g. N_{11}, N_{12}, N_{13}, and N_{31}) to contain only one broker. We assume there are bi-directional links between any two brokers in neighboring nodes. Furthermore, we assume brokers residing in the same tree nodes are fully connected when there is no failure. The algorithm, however, does not depend on the full connectivity.

As we describe the protocol from the standpoint of a single publisher connecting broker, we arbitrarily designate an edge node as the root of the tree and other edge nodes as the leaves. Publishers connect at the root broker (also called *publisher connecting broker*) and subscribers at leaf brokers (*subscriber connecting brokers*). The full algorithm with publishers/subscribers connecting at any edge node is a repetition of this simplified description with repetitive information avoided. As a convenience, we refer to where the root node resides as upstream, and leaf nodes as downstream.

The singleton broker in an edge node can be replicated but requires strong consistency to ensure client connection and failover from one replica to another does not cause message loss or duplication.

Figure 1 shows a redundant routing tree that contains: 2 non-edge nodes N_{21} and N_{22} each with two brokers; 1 root node N_{31} with broker PB_1 for publisher connections; and 3 leaf nodes N_{11}, N_{12} and N_{13} each with one broker (SB_1, SB_2 and SB_3, respectively) for subscriber connections.

This model may seem a bit restrictive at first glance. However, the brokers referred here are logical brokers. A broker process may represent multiple logical brokers and hence participate in more than one node and have virtual links between its multiple presence in neighboring tree nodes. Furthermore, publishers

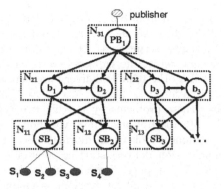

Fig. 1. A Redundant Routing Tree.

and subscribers can connect to any physical brokers. The physical broker in this case implements a logical leaf broker. Thus we abstract the topology to have publishers and subscribers connecting only at the edge nodes. How to map physical brokers to logical brokers, and what brokers reside in which tree nodes is an important part of the Gryphon technology. We do not describe it here.

3   Algorithms

3.1   Solution Intuition

To properly introduce the intuition behind our algorithm, we revisit in detail the challenges facing subscription propagation. We use the example network shown in Figure 1 to illustrate.

One challenge is to decide the delivery starting point of a subscription, that is, to find a position in a published message stream from which the system can deliver messages in order and without gaps. This problem is complicated because the new subscriptions may partially overlap with existing subscriptions. Suppose in the network in Figure 1, subscriber/subscription s_1 of $stock = nyse : ibm$ has been propagated to all brokers in the tree nodes on the path from N_{11} to N_{31}, that is, broker SB_1, b_1, b_2 and PB_1. When subscriber s_2 submits subscription $stock = nyse : *$ (which matches all messages matching s_1 and more), broker SB_1 propagates this information toward PB_1. However, when message m_1 with content $(nyse : ibm, 92)$ arrives, broker SB_1 does not know whether it should deliver it to subscription s_2 as well. It might be an error to deliver m_1 because m_1 arrives only as a result of matching subscription s_1. If this is the case, there is no guarantee that a later message m_2 of $(nyse : t, 19)$ will be routed by the system and thus result in a gap in the messages delivered to subscription s_2.

Another challenge arises when messages that are part of the same ordered stream travel along different paths. This might be a result of a load sharing decision or a failed link. Furthermore, the message delivery path could be different from the path subscription has been propagated. For example, subscription

s_2 might have been propagated from SB_1 to b_1 and PB_1 but not yet to b_2. If message m_1 is routed through broker b_1 and m_2 through b_2, b_2 would not send m_2 to SB_1 without knowing subscription s_2. Delivery for s_2 might have already started and SB_1 would not detect the gap created by missing m_2. This kind of gap can not be detected by the reliable delivery protocol because it relies on *correct* subscription information.

Our algorithm solves these problems by making two types of information explicit, i.e., the set S_m of subscriptions a message should be matched against and the set S_b of subscriptions a broker has information of and uses for message matching. Using this information, delivery starting point of a subscription can be detected by choosing the first message whose S_m set contains the subscription. In addition, the system guarantee that for every message published in the same stream after the first message, its S_m set (eventually) includes the subscription until it is unsubscribed. How and when the S_m set of a message is assigned and changed is a dimension in which an algorithm can vary.

To prevent a broker (e.g. b_2) to filter out a message by mistake, the broker compares its S_b set with the S_m set of the message. The broker contains information of the subtree where a subscription in S_b set is connected and thus can project/partition the S_b set onto each subtree rooted at the tree node where the broker resides. The broker can also project the S_m set onto each subtree but only partially because the S_m set may contain subscriptions that is not in the broker's S_b set. The comparison of S_m and S_b is thus performed for each subtree rooted at a child node (e.g. N_{11}). It is possible that in subtree N_{11} there is a subscription that is contained in S_m but not in S_b, and the subscription matches the message. However, since the broker does not have information about the subscription, its filtering result will probaby indicate that the message does not need to be sent to subtree N_{11}. Our algorithm takes the comparison result of S_m and S_b as an indicator that whether the broker matching/filtering result should be used. If S_b is the same or a superset of S_m for a subtree, the broker contains *sufficient* information to perform matching and can decide whether or not to send the message to a subtree based on the existence of matching subscriptions. Otherwise, as a conservative measure, the message should be sent to the subtree regardless of the matching result. We call this comparison of S_b and S_m sets the *sufficiency test*.

With this type of algorithm, there is no need to maintain consistent states of subscription information between redundant path brokers. As a result, the solution is light-weight and highly available.

3.2   Solution Overview

Obviously, concise representation of S_m and S_b sets and efficient computation of the sufficiency tests are crucial for system performance. In our approach, each leaf broker maintains a virtual time clock. We assign each subscription a virtual start time (vst) at its subscribing time and a virtual end time (vet) at its unsubscribing time using the current value (VT) of the virtual clock at the leaf broker to which the subscription connects. We call a subscription that has not unsubscribed *active*. Such a subscription has a *vet* that is greater than the VT of the leaf broker to which the subscriber is connected. The virtual clock advances whenever necessary and more than one subscription/unsubscription can occur in a single virtual time tick.

Thus, we can represent the set S_m of a message as a vector V_m, with one element per leaf broker. Assume a V_m vector $(SB_1 : v_1, \cdots, SB_n : v_n)$, the set S_m of the message is "any active subscription at broker SB_1 with *vst* no later than v_1 and *vet* later than the current virtual time VT_1 , $\cdots$, plus any active subscription at broker SB_n with *vst* no later than v_n and *vet* later than the current virtual time VT_n".

Similarly, we represent the set S_b of a broker as a vector V_b, with one element per leaf broker. Assume a V_b vector $(SB_1 : v_1', \cdots, SB_n : v_n')$, the set S_b of the broker is " subscriptions at broker SB_1 with *vst* no later than v_1' and *vet* later than v_1', $\cdots$, plus subscriptions at broker SB_n with *vst* no later than v_n' and *vet* greater than v_n'".

Because virtual time is generated from a leaf broker's virtual clock, $v_i' \leq VT_i$ $(i = 1..n)$. If $v_i' \geq v_i$ $(i = 1..n)$, $S_b \supseteq S_m$. Thus, the sufficiency test can be efficiently implemented as comparison of V_b and V_m on the relevant elements. That is, for a downstream where certain subscriber-connecting/leaf brokers exist, the sufficiency test succeeds when V_b is element-wise no less than V_m for those brokers. In Figure 1, when broker b_1 or b_2 routes a message to tree node N_{11}, the sufficiency test succeeds when its V_b is no less than V_m for the element of SB_1. When broker PB_1 in node N_{31} routes a message toward N_{21}, the sufficiency test succeeds when its V_b is no less than V_m for the elements of both SB_1 and SB_2.

In the remainder of this section, we describe in detail how subscriptions are assigned virtual start and end times, how subscription information is propagated, how messages are routed and how the system decides a message delivery starting point for a subscription. We discuss in Section 5.1 the optimization techniques to avoid sending full V_m vectors in messages and to cache sufficiency test results.

3.3   Assigning Subscription Virtual Start/End Times

Clients submit subscriptions to a pub/sub system through their connecting brokers. A broker assigns a virtual start time to a subscription during its subscribing process. As mentioned in Section 2, these brokers are in the leaf nodes of the redundant routing tree. A leaf broker usually aggregates subscriptions and only propagates to upstream the aggregated results.

A client subscription/unsubscription may or may not change the aggregated subscriptions of its connecting broker, depending on existing subscriptions. Whenever a leaf broker's subscriptions change and the broker decides to propagate the change to upstream, the broker advances its virtual time clock by 1. The virtual clock is maintained in an integer counter and is also used to assign virtual start/end times to subscriptions.

The leaf broker ensures the monotonicity of its virtual clock, despite crash recovery. There are many possible techniques to achieve this, such as using a monotonic system clock, or persisting an upper bound on the highest clock value.

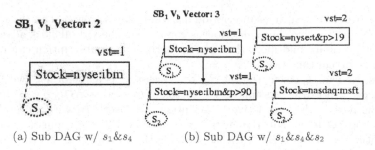

(a) Sub DAG w/ s_1&s_4 (b) Sub DAG w/ s_1&s_4&s_2

Fig. 2. Broker SB_1 Subscription DAGs.

We assume that the clock time never overflows, which is reasonable for a value that is 64 bits.

We assume that a client subscription is in the form of a set of Boolean conjunctions. Any other form of Boolean expression can be transformed into disjunctive normal form (DNF). We define the following "covering" relationship of conjunctions similar to that of [5].

Definition 1. *Conjunction c_1 covers c_2, denoted as $c_1 \succeq_c c_2$, if and only if all messages matching c_2 also match c_1. That is*
$$c_1 \succeq_c c_2 \Leftrightarrow \{M(c_1) \supseteq M(c_2)\}$$
where $M(c)$ is the set of all messages matching conjunction c.

Conversely, c_2 is said to be "covered by" c_1.

Subscribing Process. To assign a virtual start time to a new subscription, we analyze the covering relationship of its conjunctions with the existing subscription conjunctions. We use a directed acyclic graph (DAG) by modeling conjunctions as nodes and drawing a directed edge from a covering conjunction to a covered conjunction. As the covering relationship is transitive, we omit the transitive edges. Initially, broker conjunction DAGs are empty. Examples of conjunction DAGs are shown in Figure 2 and 3. Each conjunction is represented as a rectangle, with a virtual start time and an oval representing the list (called *subscriber list*) of subscribers or downstream routing tree nodes whose subscriptions contain the conjunction.

For each conjunction c of the new subscription, the broker finds existing conjunctions that cover c and set $c.vst$ to the minimum of these conjunctions. If no covering conjunction exists, $c.vst$ is set to the broker's current virtual time.

To ensure reliable delivery, message delivery for a new subscription cannot start until matching messages for all its conjunctions start to arrive, hence vst of the new subscription is set to the maximum of its conjunctions'. The new conjunction nodes are added into the conjunction DAG.

Example 1. Suppose clients in Figure 1 submit the following subscriptions:
1. s_1:*stock* $= nyse : ibm$ (submitted at SB_1)
2. s_4:*stock* $= nyse : *$ (submitted at SB_2)
3. s_2:*stock* $= nyse : ibm$&$p > 90$ *or stock* $= nyse : t$&$p > 19$ *or stock* $= nasdaq : msft$ (submitted at SB_1)

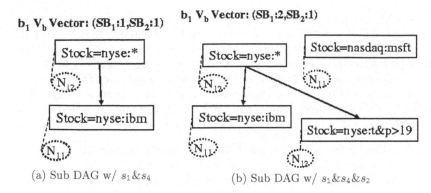

(a) Sub DAG w/ $s_1 \& s_4$ (b) Sub DAG w/ $s_1 \& s_4 \& s_2$

Fig. 3. Broker b_1 Subscription DAGs.

The conjunction DAGs and V_b vectors of broker SB_1 and b_1 after subscription s_1 and s_4 are shown in Figure 2(a) and 3(a). When s_2 is subscribed, its first conjunction is covered by the only node in the conjunction DAG (Figure 2(a)) and thus has a *vst* of 1. The other two conjunctions are not covered and thus have *vst* of 2. Hence $s_2.vst = 2$. SB_1 increments its VT to 3 and changes the conjunction DAG to Figure 2(b).   □

It is interesting to observe that the nodes in the conjunction DAG are assigned non-increasing *vst*'s as one travels from a root node to the covered nodes. Thus computing *vst* of a new conjunction only takes into consideration the immediate covering nodes. As a reminder, transitive arcs are omitted from the conjunction DAG.

Unsubscribing Process. During client's unsubscription of its conjunctions, the client is removed from the subscriber lists of the nodes in the conjunction DAG. Conjunctions with empty lists are removed from the DAG. The subscription is assigned a virtual end time using the broker's current virtual time. Note that since a subscription is removed, there is no need to store information for it. The *vet* is not really assigned and is never maintained in the system. We only use it for convenience in describing the subscription sets S_m and S_b.

At the end of the client subscribing/unsubscribing process, if any roots are added or removed, the leaf node broker advances its virtual clock by one. In addition, an incremental update is generated and propagated to upstream brokers in the redundant routing tree.

We should note that although we have discussed the subscribing and unsubscribing process as if there is only one request at a time, the algorithm actually processes requests in batches. The broker only advances its virtual clock at the end of the batch process if the set of root nodes is changed.

3.4   Propagating Subscription Changes

As described previously, if client subscription/unsubscription results in changes in the set of root nodes of a conjunction DAG, the leaf broker generates and propagates incremental changes. An incremental change contains the name of the originating leaf broker SB_1, the virtual time v_1 of SB_1 when the change occurred, a list of additive/subtractive conjunctions $\{+c_1, +c_2, \cdots, -c_i, -c_{i+1}, \cdots\}$, the subscribing tree node, and a constraint vector on receiving broker's V_b vector. c_1 and c_2 are the new root DAG nodes. c_i and c_{i+1} are the old roots that were just removed from the DAG. The constraint vector is initially $(SB_1, v_1 - 1)$. That is, we require a broker have information of all subscriptions connected at leaf broker SB_1 with $vst < v_1$.

Example 2. Continuing with Example 1, the incremental change SB_1 generated as a result of s_2 subscription is:
$SB_1, 2, \{+(stock = nyse : t\&p > 19), +(stock = nasdaq : msft)\}, N_{11}, cons = (SB_1 : 1)$. □

The leaf broker sends the incremental change to a broker in its parent node, e.g., broker b_1 in N_{21} in Figure 1. As brokers in the same tree node are usually fully connected, b_1 forwards the incremental change to other brokers (b_2) in N_{21}. How this incremental change is propagated to all brokers in the parent node is not fixed and a specific algorithm may adapt if the topology assumptions are different.

Upon receiving an incremental change, a broker checks whether its V_b vector satisfies the constraint. If so, it updates its V_b vector and applies the additive/subtractive conjunctions by adding/removing the tree node (e.g., N_{11}) to/from the subscriber lists of conjunction nodes and inserting new conjunctions or removing conjunctions with empty subscriber lists from the DAG. A non-leaf node broker's conjunction DAG (e.g., Figure 3(a) and (b)) is similar to that of a leaf node broker's, except that vst's are not recorded for conjunctions. Same as in a leaf broker, the additive/subtractive conjunctions in the new incremental change are computed as a result of the root node changes in the DAG. If the incremental change is a pure additive change and no aggregation happened in the current broker, the constraint vector of the new change is unchanged. Otherwise, the constraint vector is set to the old V_b vector of the broker. The subscribing tree node of the new incremental change is set to the tree node where the current broker resides. The original receiving broker of the incremental change then forwards the new incremental change to a broker in its parent tree node.

If the constraint is not satisfied, the broker cannot apply the incremental change. Furthermore, if some elements of the broker's V_b vector are smaller than that of the constraint vector, the broker detects its subscription information is lagging behind, and initiates liveness mechanism to get up-to-date (described in Section 4).

Example 3. In our example, broker b_1 satisfies the constraint vector of the incremental change. As conjunction $stock = nyse : t\&p > 19$ is covered by an existing conjunction $stock = nyse : *$, it is aggregated away. Hence the new incremental change is:
$SB_1, 2, \{+(stock = nasdaq : msft)\}, N_{21}, cons = (SB_1 : 1, SB_2 : 1)$
b_1's V_b vector is set to $(SB_1 : 2, SB_2 : 1)$. □

In our examples below, we use a vector such as $(1, 1, 1)$ to represent V_m or V_b vectors without mentioning the leaf broker names SB_1, SB_2 and SB_3.

Similar things happen at the root broker in the routing tree. Continuing with our example, broker PB_1 updates its V_b vector from $(1, 1, 1)$ to $(2, 1, 1)$.

3.5   Data Message Routing

Data messages are published through the root broker (e.g., PB_1) of the routing tree. Before sending a newly published message, PB_1 assigns to it a V_m vector. How this V_m vector is assigned is a dimension in which the algorithm could vary and is further discussed in Section 3.7. For now, we assume PB_1 keeps a persistent record of the highest V_m vector it has ever assigned and ensures non-decreasing V_m's for new messages. When $V_b \geq$ highest V_m, V_b is used.

For an incoming message, a broker performs matching to decide which downstream routing tree nodes it should send the message to. Many efficient matching algorithms exist such as [2] [8]. Our algorithm works with any of them.

Furthermore, the broker compares its V_b vector with the V_m vector of the message for each child node. It does so by slicing both vectors with only the elements for the leaf brokers in the subtree rooted at the child node. If the V_b vector is no less than the V_m for the slicing, the broker sends the message if and only if the matching results show a match for the downstream. Otherwise, the broker conservatively sends the message down, regardless of the matching result. This is the *sufficiency test* we have mentioned in Section 3.1.

As we can see, it is possible for the broker to send down messages that do not match any subscription. This only happens at non-leaf brokers. In the leaf broker, as it always has the latest subscription information, its V_b vector (containing only one element for itself) always satisfies the sufficiency test and only the matching messages will be delivered to subscribers.

Example 4. Suppose PB_1 assigns V_m vector $(1, 1, 1)$ to message $m_1(nyse : ibm, 95)$ and $m_2(nyse : t, 20)$. m_1 is sent to b_1 and m_2 to b_2. Suppose V_b vectors of b_1 and b_2 are $(2, 1, 0)$ and $(1, 1, 0)$. Both messages will be sent to SB_1 as the sufficiency tests are satisfied for SB_1 and there is a match from node N_{11}.

Suppose now PB_1 processes an incremental change and advances its V_b vector to $(2, 1, 1)$. On the other hand, b_2 does not receive the incremental change and thus its V_b vector stays at $(1, 1, 0)$. PB_1 assigns V_m vector $(2, 1, 1)$ to $m_3(nyse : ibm, 98)$ and $m_4(nyse : t, 22)$ and sends m_3 to b_1 and m_4 to b_2. Both broker b_1 and b_2 send the messages to SB_1 because b_1 has a match and b_2, even though without a match for N_{11}, detects its sufficiency test fails.   □

Justification of Correctness. The sufficiency test is satisfied when a broker's V_b vector is equal to or greater than V_m with regard to the relevant leaf brokers. When it is greater, the broker can have *wider* (matching more messages) conjunctions as new subscriptions may have happened. It can also have *narrower* conjunctions as unsubscriptions may have happened. When the conjunctions are wider, the broker obviously passes all messages matching the subscriptions required by the V_m vectors plus more that match the new subscriptions. In the narrower case, a broker drops messages matching only unsubscribed subscriptions at a leaf broker sb. Those subscriptions have $vet \leq V_b(sb) \leq VT_{sb}$ and hence are not in the S_m set.

3.6 Detecting Subscription Delivery Starting Point

For a new subscription, its connecting leaf broker must decide a safe point from which the system can deliver a gapless, in-order stream of published messages. The actual protocol for reliable delivery is a complicated scheme and has been discussed in our work in [3] [4]. We do not deal with that problem here, rather we deal with how subscription propagation will not produce subscription information that is wrong for reliable delivery. Our solution can work with any reliable delivery protocol.

Detecting delivery starting point is accomplished by comparing a message's V_m vector element with the vst of the subscription s. As soon as the leaf broker sb sees a message with $V_m(sb) \geq s.vst$, it starts to deliver matching messages for s.

Example 5. Broker SB_1 receives m_1. Even if m_1 matches subscription s_2, this is not a delivery starting point for s_2 as m_1's $V_m(SB_1) == 1$ and is less than $s_2.vst == 2$. This is correct because there is no guarantee a later message ($nyse : t, 20$) will not be filtered out if it is routed through broker b_2. Broker SB_1, instead, starts delivery for s_2 from message m_3.   □

3.7 Algorithm Variants

We have extended our basic algorithm with two variants. These extensions continue to support reliable delivery. Due to space restriction, we only provide brief description of these extensions:

- Non-monotonic assignment of V_m vectors to messages in a published stream;
- Non-fixed V_m vector for a message m.

Our basic algorithm stores persistently the highest V_m assigned and assigns monotonically non-decreasing V_m vectors to messages at the publisher connecting brokers. Our extension does not require persistent storage and allows non-monotonic V_m vector assignments to messages. This could happen due to a publisher connecting broker crash/recovery.

In the basic algorithm, a message's V_m vector is fixed once assigned. In some cases, the aggregation of subscriptions may result in incremental updates with empty lists of additive/subtractive conjunctions. The basic algorithm requires such *empty* updates to propagate to the root broker as a means of conveying the latest V_m the broker could use. Our extension does not require propagation of this kind of update, rather we record the fact that a V_m vector could be automatically changed to V_m' due to the empty incremental update. This is recorded at the last broker where such an empty update occurred.

In both extensions, not only are published messages assigned V_m vectors, so are the silence periods between them. In addition, the leaf brokers hosting subscribers perform monotonicity checking on message/silence V_m vectors and initiate negative-acknowledgments if monotonicity is violated.

4   Liveness and Failure Handling

Our solution intrinsically supports pub/sub message delivery with high availability and light failover. The solution itself has to deal with failures as incremental subscription updates can be lost and arrive out-of-order. This section describes the failure handling with regard to the subscription propagation protocol. This is an important part of our work, however, due to space restriction, we only describe it briefly.

Broker Crash Recovery. Upon recovery from a crash, a leaf broker sets its virtual clock time VT to be greater than all previous values it has assigned. The leaf broker initializes its conjunction DAG to contain conjunctions for the durable subscriptions ([1][4]) it maintains. All conjunctions are then propagated by sending a full state update and the current VT. The broker then advances its VT by one.

Non-leaf brokers recover from a crash by initializing an empty conjunction DAG and resetting its V_b vector to all 0's.

Leaf Broker Driven Liveness. As the sources of subscription changes and virtual times, leaf brokers ensure all publisher connecting brokers receive up-to-date subscription information and assign latest V_m vectors to messages. For subscription/unsubscription received during virtual time vt and propagated, a leaf broker SB maintains an expected starting time from which data messages should have V_m vector with an element vt' for SB such that $vt' \geq vt$. This expected time can be dynamically adjusted through similar techniques that estimates TCP round trip times. Messages received after the elapsed time with $vt' < vt$ trigger a full subscription state update with SB's latest propagated VT. Alternatively, SB can repeat the incremental updates sent from vt' to vt. This requires a cache for the latest incremental updates at SB.

Non-leaf Broker Driven Liveness. A non-leaf broker (including publisher connecting brokers) b detects that its subscription information is lagging behind in two ways: (1) receives a data message with V_m vector that is greater than V_b vector for the elements of downstream leaf brokers; (2) receives incremental updates with constraint vectors $\nleq V_b$. Broker b initiates a negative acknowledgment message toward the leaf broker SB for whom b's V_b vector is lagging behind. Such negative acknowledgment may be satisfied by SB or a broker on the route from b to SB with the required subscription information.

5   Implementation and Experimental Results

5.1   Implementation

Our implementation performs monotonic and fixed V_m vector assignment at the publisher connecting brokers. These brokers persist the highest V_m vector assigned. The liveness and failure handling utilizes full-update messages.

Subscription aggregation is based on covering relations (Section 3). Our current covering relation is restricted to identical conjunctions. Since the covering test is a black-box component in our implementation, a sophisticated covering relation can be plugged in to replace this simple one.

The number of leaf brokers affects system performance and scalability, since it directly impacts the length of V_m and V_b vectors and computations involving them. In our implementation, we utilize the property that links are usually FIFO. This is true of links implemented as TCP connections such as in Gryphon.

Instead of full V_m vectors, we use fixed-length vector digests. When a new V_m is first assigned to a message, the publisher connecting broker assigns a digest to V_m by taking a snapshot of a monotonically increasing value. This can be implemented in many ways, such as using the system clock. As publisher connecting broker assigns monotonically non-decreasing V_m vectors and digests are monotonic, the system satisfies the following monotonicity – $d < d'$ if $V_m < V_m'$ with regard to the same assigning broker. A broker does not persist the digests, therefore it can assign two different digests to one V_m at different times. Thus $d < d' \Rightarrow V_m \leq V_m'$.

In this scheme, the first message with a new V_m vector going down each link carries the original V_m and its digest. Later messages only need to carry the digest until the V_m changes or the link fails and recovers.

In addition, each broker maintains a cache of the sufficiency test results. This cache is indexed by the digest and the assigning broker. It only maintains an entry for the highest digest it has seen from a publisher connecting broker. From the digest monotonicity, any message originated from the same broker with a digest no greater than the cache entry can reuse the cache result. Otherwise, the broker conservatively computes $false$ as the sufficiency test result for the message. The cache entry is updated when the broker advances its V_b vector or when it receives a message with higher V_m vector and digest. We omit the details of a negative-acknowledgement scheme that is used to retrieve the original V_m vector for a digest if the message carrying the mapping was lost.

5.2   Experiment Results

The testbed for our experiments is a set of RS6000 F80 machines with six 500MHz processors and 1G RAM. Each machine has dual network interfaces and is connected through a 100Mbps Ethernet network and a gigabit switch to other machines.

We focus primarily on metrics that are impacted by the specifics of our solution. Metrics such as routing table (conjunction DAG) size and subscription incremental update message size are common to subscription propagation algorithms and have been investigated in previous work such as [12, 5].

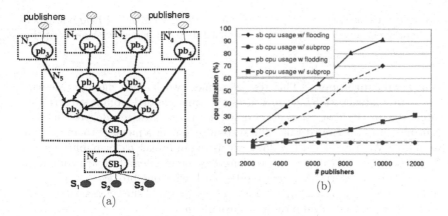

Fig. 4. System Load(CPU) Comparisons.

System Load Comparison in Selective Subscription Tests. This test compares the system overhead of using subscription propagation with that of using flooding when client subscriptions are selective. The workload is motivated by sensor networks where there are many publishers collecting and publishing various kinds of data and relatively few subscribers that selectively subscribe to data of interest.

The test is set up as Figure 4(a) with 4 publisher connecting brokers pb_{1-4} and 1 subscriber connecting broker sb, each in its own tree node. These brokers also reside in an intermediate tree node N_5 and thus each implements two virtual brokers. Four redundant routing trees can be defined by taking each of pb_{1-4} as root node.

We fix the number of subscriptions at 2000 and vary the number of publishers from 2000 to 12000. The message rate per publisher is fixed at 2 messages/second. Each subscription is distinct and to the messages published by 1 publisher. Hence, the total receiving message rate of subscribers is 4000 messages/second throughout the test. The publishers are evenly distributed among pb_{1-4}. Figure 4(b) shows the CPU utilization of sb and pb_{1-4} (averaged) in both schemes.

With 2000 publishers, all published messages are subscribed. This case is not favorable to subscription propagation. However, CPU utilization difference at sb in flooding and subscription propagation schemes are negligible due to the use of efficient matching algorithm [2]. In addition, when the number of publishers increases, sb CPU utilization stays constant in the subscription propagation scheme but increases linearly in flooding scheme even though the number of *useful* messages does not change.

In both schemes, CPU utilization at pb_{1-4} increases linearly with the number of publishers. However, the flooding scheme shows a much steeper slope because each of pb_{1-4} not only accepts messages from publishers but also sends these messages to other pb's and receives all messages published through other pb's.

As a result, CPU utilization at pb_{1-4} reaches $> 90\%$ with only 10000 publishers in the flooding scheme compared to 31% with 12000 publishers with subscription propagation.

Latency Measurements. This test examines two latency metrics. Message delivery start latency ($DSLat$) measures the time elapsed from a subscription is submitted to the first message is delivered to it. Message delivery latency ($DLat$) measures the time it takes the system to deliver a message to an existing subscription. We use a linear topology consisting of broker pb for publishers and sb for subscribers each in its own routing tree node. pb and sb are connected through n hops of intermediate tree nodes, each with one broker.

$DLat$ is measured by a latency sampler(LS) that publishes messages through pb and subscribes to its own messages through sb.

$DSLat$ for a new subscription is measured at the subscriber by taking the difference between time of subscription and time of first message delivery. We further distinguish $DSLat$ for subscriptions that are covered locally in sb and subscriptions that are not covered hence must propagate to pb. We call the first $DSLat$ *local* and the latter *global*. Global $DSLat$ is the sum of the following times: (1) time taken to send subscription to sb; (2) processing time at sb; (3) processing time at other brokers; (4) network delays(bi-directional) at each hop; (5) expected interval till next message published that matches the subscription. If messages that match the subscription are published at a steady rate every t milliseconds (ms), this time is $t/2$ on average; (6) time taken to send the message from sb to the subscriber. Similarly, local $DSLat$ is the sum of (1),(2),(5),(6).

We make time (5) negligible by using a high publishing rate (200 messages/second/topic) but on few (16) topics. The aggregated publishing rate is 3200 messages/second. In addition, since we are mainly interested in measuring processing overhead (2) and (3), we do not inject additional latency on the links. Since we are running in a LAN environment, (1), (4) and (6) are small. We impose load on sb by connecting 60 steady subscribers to 8 topics. Local $DSLat$ is measured by subscribers that dynamically subscribe and unsubscribe to the same 8 topics as the steady subscribers and global $DSLat$ is measured by subscribers that dynamically subscribe to the remaining 8 topics. We take the median of all measurements. Figure 5 shows $DLat$, local and global $DSLat$ when there are 1,4 and 7 hops from pb to sb.

Message delivery latency $DLat$ increases linearly from 3 to 6 to 9 ms. Local $DSLat$ – delivery start latency for covered subscriptions – stays roughly constant at $17ms$. Global $DSLat$ increases linearly from $26.5ms$ to $36ms$ to $45ms$. The differences of global and local $DSLat$, which shows the network latency and broker (other than sb) processing overhead also increases from $9.5ms$ to $20ms$ to $28ms$, which shows that subscription processing overhead is small.

Scalability Measurements. This test examines the system scalability with regard to the V_m and V_b vector sizes, i.e., number of subscriber connecting brokers. The test is set up with a broker pb for publishers and a broker ib connecting

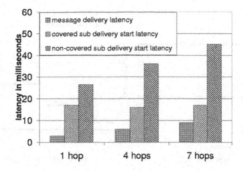

Fig. 5. Subscription Delivery Start Latency & Message Delivery Latency.

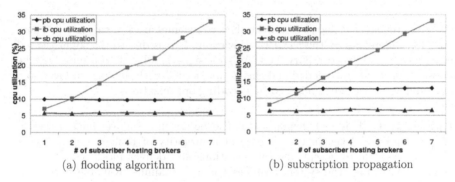

Fig. 6. Scalability: Broker CPU Utilization Versus Number of Brokers.

pb to a number of brokers sb_{1-n} for subscribers. Each of these brokers is in a separate routing tree node. We vary the number n of sb's.

Messages are published through pb at a fixed rate of 2000 messages/second throughout the test. We demonstrate the result in a setup that is not favorable to subscription propagation to show the low overhead incurred by it compared with the flooding scheme. We set up each published message to be subscribed by some subscriber at each sb. Subscribers are evenly distributed onto sb's. Each sb has two groups of subscribers with each group receiving 10000 messages/second. One group is steady and the other is dynamic with periodic unsubscriptions followed immediately by re-subscriptions. Every 2 seconds on average, an unsubscription/subscription occurs at a sb and causes the sb virtual time to advance by 2. Thus, this simulates the situation where the broker virtual time advances by one every second at each sb. In situations where subscription/unsubscription occurs more frequently, they could be batched to reduce the rate at which the sb virtual times advance. Figure 6 shows the CPU utilization at pb, ib and sb_{1-n}(averaged).

In both the flooding scheme and with subscription propagation (Figure 6(a) & (b)), CPU utilization at pb and sb_{1-n} stays constant with n changing from $1 - 7$. This is due to the Vector-Digest and caching scheme we described. The

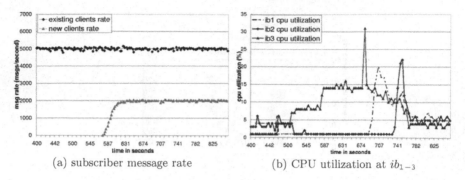

(a) subscriber message rate   (b) CPU utilization at ib_{1-3}

Fig. 7. Client message rate and intermediate broker CPU utilization with crash failure.

CPU differences at ib and sb's between the two schemes are also very small. There are (3%) differences on the pb CPU utilization. This is due to the sophisticated message encoding used in Gryphon. As pb assigns V_m digest to a message, the message has to be re-encoded and this is not needed with flooding in Gryphon. Such difference can be eliminated by encoding optimizations.

Failure Test. This test demonstrates the lightweight failover characteristics of our approach. Even in the absence of a majority of brokers in a cell, our algorithm is able to accept new subscriptions and deliver messages for them. When a path fails, the system switches to the remaining available paths and provides continuing service.

The test is set up as a redundant routing tree of 4 nodes and 6 brokers: broker pb for publishers and sb_{1-2} for subscribers, each in a separate node N_{pb}, N_{sb_1} and N_{sb_2}. Broker ib_{1-3} are all in one node N_{ib}. Node N_{pb} is connected to N_{ib}, which further connects to N_{sb_1} and N_{sb_2}.

In this test, traffic from pb to sb_{1-2} is shared among ib_{1-3}. Messages are published through pb at a rate of 2000 messages per second on 100 topics. Initially, there are 2 groups of clients connected to sb_1 and 1 group to sb_2, each group with 250 subscribers evenly distributed among the first 50 topics. Thus, the aggregated message rate per group is 5000. A fourth group of 100 clients to the remaining 50 topics connect at a later time. The aggregated message rate for this group is 2000. Figure 7(a) shows the message rates for one of the first 3 groups and the fourth group. Figure 7(b) shows the CPU utilization at ib_{1-3}.

At time 400, since only the first 50 topics are subscribed to, the messages are routed through ib_1 and ib_2. Broker ib_3 is not used because of the simple hashing scheme used for load balancing. At time 475, ib_1 crashes, the system fails over to ib_3, and CPU utilization at ib_3 increases to 4% to the same as ib_2. About 30 seconds later, at time 505, ib_2 crashes, and all messages on the first 50 topics are routed through ib_3. CPU utilization at ib_3 doubles to 8%. During these routing changes the client message rate is not affected. At time 565, a new group of 100 subscribers to the latter 50 topics starts to connect. Even though only ib_3 is available, our approach is able to make progress and starts to deliver messages for the new clients. When ib_1 and ib_2 recover about 130 and 160 seconds later at time 691 and 731, traffic is once again shared among the available paths. During this process, service to clients is not affected as their message rate stays constant.

6   Related Work

In this section we survey previous work on subscription propagation and aggregation in publish/subscribe systems. Techniques for subscription aggregation ([12]) are complimentary to our work.

Siena [5] and XNet [6] support subscription propagation and aggregation to achieve scalability. Their topology has redundancy, with multiple routes between servers. However, the subscriptions are only propagated along a single selected "best route" in a spanning tree. If a failure occurs on the selected path, the system must select another path and subscription information need to be set up for the new path before message routing can be resumed. As a result, recovery from a spanning tree link failure is slow. In addition, these works do not address the support of reliable delivery.

Elvin [17] is mainly designed around a single server that filters and forwards producer messages directly to consumers. It doesn't have a scalable solution for multiple servers.

Snoeren et. al [18] propose an approach for improving reliability and low latency by sending simultaneously over redundant links in a mesh-based overlay networks. The protocol does content-based routing and provides high level of availability. However, there is no guarantee of reliable delivery when subscriptions are dynamically added and removed.

REBECA [12, 13] supports subscription propagation and aggregation over a network constructed as a tree of brokers. Their subscription aggregation techniques, such as filter merging, are applicable to our work. The system has a self-stabilization component that uses time based leases to validate routing entries in brokers. This is a viable technique for best-effort delivery, but does not support reliable delivery since it is possible for a broker to filter a message that is relevant for a downstream subscriber.

JEDI [7] guarantees causal ordering of events. Their distributed version of event dispatcher constitutes of a set of dispatching servers interconnected into a tree structure. This distributed version, while addressing part of the need of Internet-wide distributed applications engaging in an intense communication, does not accommodate and utilize redundant links between dispatching servers and hence is not highly available and easy for load sharing.

Tapestry [20] provides fault tolerant routing by dynamically switching traffic onto precomputed alternate routes. Messages in Tapestry can be duplicated and multicast "around" network congestion and failure hotspots with rapid reconvergence to drop duplicates. However, it does not support content routing.

Scribe [15] is a large-scale and fully decentralized event notification system built on top of Pastry – a peer-to-peer object location and routing substrate overlayed on the Internet. It leverages the scalability, locality, fault-resilience and self-organization properties of Pastry. However, Scribe does not support content-based routing and wild card topic subscriptions . The system builds separate multicast trees for individual topics using a scheme similar to reverse path forwarding and inverts the subscription message path for later event distribution. This makes it impossible to add a node to the multicast tree for load sharing. The system recovers from multicast node failures by building new trees. It does not support reliable delivery, and unsubscription has to be delayed until the first event is received.

Triantafillou et. al [19] proposed an approach to propagating subscription summaries and performing event matching and routing. Their subscription propagation algorithm, which affects the way events are routed, requires each broker to have global knowledge on the broker network topology. In addition, the approach does not support reliable delivery.

Since Lamport's work on logical time and clocks [11], significant work has been done using logical time such as virtual time [9], version vectors [14], vector times [16] and multipart timestamps [10]. Our work shares the property that logical time vectors are used as a concise form for representing large information. However, these works are focused on detecting state inconsistencies or causal relationships, which is only part of the problem subscription propagation is facing in pub/sub systems.

7 Conclusions

We have developed algorithms supporting subscription propagation with high availability, easy load-sharing and light failover in a content-based pub/sub system over a redundant overlay network. The algorithm does not require agreements or quorum among redundant brokers. We also presented the experiment results that show the high performance, scalability, low latency and availability. Future work includes investigation into support for event advertisement ([5]), adaptively applying subscription propagation according to different subscription profile and locality.

References

1. Java (tm) message service. In *http://java.sun.com/products/jms/*.
2. M. K. Aguilera, R. E. Strom, D. C. Sturman, M. Astley, and T. D. Chandra. Matching events in a content-based subscription system. In *Proceedings of the Principles of Distributed Computing, 1999*, pages 53–61, May 1999.
3. S. Bhola, R. Strom, S. Bagchi, Y. Zhao, and J. Auerbach. Exactly-once delivery in a content-based publish-subscribe system. In *Proceedings of the International Conference on Dependable Systems and Networks (DSN'2002)*, pages 7–16, 2002.

4. S. Bhola, Y. Zhao, and J. Auerbach. Scalably supporting durable subscriptions in a publish/subscribe system. In *Proceedings of the International Conference on Dependable Systems and Networks (DSN'2003)*, pages 57–66, 2003.

5. A. Carzaniga, D. Rosenblum, and A. Wolf. Design and evaluation of a wide-area event notification service. *ACM Transactions on Computer Systems*, 19(3):332–383, August 2001.

6. R. Chand and P. Felber. A scalable protocol for content-based routing in overlay networks. In *Proceedings of the IEEE International Symposium on Network Computing and Applications (NCA'03)*, Cambridge, MA, April 2003.

7. G. Cugola, E. D. Nitto, and A. Fuggetta. The jedi event-based infrastructure and its application to the development of the opss wfms. *IEEE Transactions on Software Engineering*, 27(9):827–850, September 2001.

8. F. Fabret and et. al. Filtering algorithms and implementation for very fast publish/subscribe systems. *SIGMOD Record (ACM Special Interest Group on Management of Data)*, 30(2):115–126, 2001.

9. D. Jefferson. Virtual time. *ACM Transactions on Programming Languages and Systems*, 7(3):404–425, 1985.

10. R. Ladin, B. Liskov, and L. Shrira. Lazy replication: Exploiting the semantics of distributed services. In *ACM Symposium on Principles of Distributed Computing*, 1990.

11. L. Lamport. Time, clock, and the ordering of events in a distributed system. *Communications of the ACM*, 21:558–565, 1978.

12. G. Mühl. *Large-Scale Content-Based Publish/Subscribe Systems*. PhD thesis, Darmstadt University of Technology, September 2002.

13. G. Mühl, L. Fiege, and A. P. Buchmann. Filter similarities in content-based publish/subscribe systems. In *Proceedings of International Conference on Architecture of Computing Systems (ARCS'02)*, 2002.

14. D. Parker and et.al. Detection of mutual inconsistency in distributed systems. *IEEE Transactions on Software Engineering*, SE-9(3):240–247, 1983.

15. A. Rowstron, A. Kermarrec, M. Castro, and P. Druschel. Scribe: The design of a large-scale event notification infrastructure. In *Proceedings of 3rd International Workshop on Networked Group Communication (NGC 2001)*, UCL, London, UK, November 2001.

16. R. Schwarz and F. Mattern. Detecting causal relationships in distributed computations: In search of the holy grail. *Distributed Computing*, pages 149–174, 1994.

17. B. Segall, D. Arnold, J. Boot, M. Henderson, and T. Phelps. Content based routing with elvin4. In *Proceedings of AUUG2K, Canberra, Australia*, April 2000.

18. A. Snoeren, K. Conley, and D. Gifford. Mesh-based content routing using xml. In *Proceedings of the 18th ACM Symposium on Operating System Principles*, 2001.

19. P. Triantafillou and A. Economides. Subscription summarization: A new paradigm for efficient publish/subscribe systems. In *Proceedings of the 24th International Conference on Distributed Computing Systems (ICDCS'04)*, 2004.

20. B. Zhao, L. Huang, A. Joseph, and J. Kubiatowicz. Exploiting routing redundancy using a wide-area overlay. Technical Report UCB/CSD-02-1215, University of California, Berkeley, 2002.

Composition of Coordinated Web Services

Stefan Tai, Rania Khalaf, and Thomas Mikalsen

IBM T.J. Watson Research Center, Hawthorne, New York, USA
{stai,rkhalaf,tommi}@us.ibm.com

Abstract. The Web services architecture defines separate specifications for the composition and the coordination of Web services. BPEL is a language for creating service compositions in the form of business processes, whereas the WS-Coordination framework defines coordination protocols for distributed activities. In this paper, we investigate the combination of these two aspects to compose coordinated Web services. We argue for a policy-based approach to address this problem and introduce a new model and middleware that enables the flexible integration of diverse coordination types into (existing) process-based Web services compositions.

1 Introduction

The landscape of business technology today is shifting. Traditional integrated enterprises with centralized control are giving way to loosely-coupled networks of applications owned and managed by diverse business partners. *Service-oriented computing* is a distributed computing paradigm that treats the distributed, loosely-coupled, heterogeneous nature of this trend in a first-class manner. Its approach is centered on standards and the pervasiveness of Internet technologies.

The *Web services architecture* defines a set of specifications that provide an open XML-based platform for the description, discovery, and interoperability of distributed, heterogeneous applications as services. Included are specifications for business process management and various quality-of-service protocols supporting, for example, transactions, reliable messaging, and security [29] [15] [1].

Figure 1 illustrates the Web services architecture. The various Web services specifications are designed to complement each other, serving as building blocks that can be combined to provide interoperability at different software layers, from low-level transport protocols to high-level application interactions. The combined usage of some specifications is well-understood, such as WSDL [31] for description, SOAP [30] bindings in the WSDL for interaction, and UDDI [25] registries holding WSDL descriptions. However, this is not the case for all specifications, in particular, where the integration of respective middleware implementations supporting the individual Web services specifications is required.

In this paper, we look at the combined use of the Web services specifications for service composition and service coordination: the *Business Process Execution Language (BPEL)* for Web Services [27], and the specifications that use the *Web Services Coordination (WS-C)* framework [19]. These include *Web Services Atomic Transaction (WS-AT)* [20] and *Web Services Business Activity (WS-BA)* [21].

These specifications can be used in combination to support production workflows for Web services. In [6], we provided an overview of these specifications and a high level view of how they conceptually fit together. However, we did not propose a full

H.-A. Jacobsen (Ed.): Middleware 2004, LNCS 3231, pp. 294–310, 2004.
© IFIP International Federation for Information Processing 2004

solution or detailed strategy for how this may be done. In this paper, we argue for the use of declarative policies to address this problem, and introduce an approach that utilizes the *Web Services Policy Framework (WS-Policy)* [12].

Thus, the paper has two main objectives.

1. To provide a process-based Web services composition model that supports the integration of a variety of coordination protocols; current approaches to Web services composition have limited or no support for the external coordination of Web services.
2. To achieve the composition of coordinated activities using existing Web Services specifications. Rather than proposing a new service composition language, we define WS-Policy-based assertions that integrate the existing BPEL language and the WS-C framework (specifically, WS-AT and WS-BA).

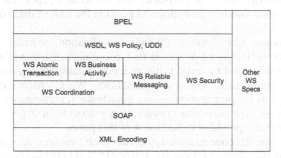

Fig. 1. Web Services Architecture.

2 Background

Web services are software applications that support open, Internet and XML standards-based interfaces and protocols [29]. In this section, we provide a brief summary of the Web services specifications relevant to our discussion. We refer the reader to the published specifications and diverse Web services literature for further details [1] [14] [24].

The functional description of a Web service is provided by the *Web Services Description Language (WSDL)* [31]. WSDL separates the abstract functionality of a service from its mappings to available deployed implementations. The abstract description consists of the operations supported by a service and the definition of their input and output messages. A *portType* groups a set of operations.

The concrete aspects of a WSDL definition include *bindings* that map operations and messages of a portType to specific protocol and data encoding formats (such as SOAP), *ports* that provide the location of physical *endpoints* implementing a specific portType using a specific binding, and *services* definitions as collections of ports.

The *Web services Addressing (WS-Addressing)* specification has been developed to provide transport-neutral mechanisms to identify Web services endpoints through *endpoint references* and to address messages through *message information headers* [3].

The *Business Process Execution Language (BPEL)* is a language for creating compositions of Web services in the form of business processes [27]. Compositions are created by defining control semantics around a set of interactions with the services being composed. The BPEL composition model is recursive: a BPEL process, like any Web service, supports a set of WSDL interfaces that enable it to be exposed and invoked as a regular Web service.

A BPEL process contains a set of typed connectors known as *partnerLinks*, each specifying the portType required from the party being connected along that link and the portType provided by the process to that party in return. The composition model explicitly stays away from binding these to actual service endpoints, leaving the door open for flexible binding schemes and selection algorithms. The "activity" is the unit of composition. Primitive activities provide such actions as Web services invocations, waiting, and throwing faults. Structured activities impose predefined control semantics on the activities nested within them, such as sequence or parallel execution. Additional control may also be defined using explicit conditional control links. We mention one BPEL activity that is of particular interest to this paper: the *scope*. BPEL scopes contain a set of (nested) activities and provide the unit of data, fault, and compensation handling.

The *Web Services Coordination (WS-C)* specification provides an extensible framework for the definition of protocols that coordinate distributed activities [19]. The framework can be used to support different coordination types, including atomic transactions and long-running business transactions. WS-C enables the creation of coordination contexts for propagation among coordination participants, and the registration of participants for particular coordination protocols of a given coordination type. Further details are provided in Section 4 of this paper.

Examples of specific coordination types are *Web Services Atomic Transaction (WS-AT)* [20] and *Web Services Business Activity (WS-BA)* [21]. These specifications define agreement coordination protocols, such as a durable two-phase commit protocol (WS-AT) or a participant-driven completion protocol for business transactions (WS-BA). Other coordination types and protocols can be defined using WS-C.

The *Web Services Policy Framework (WS-Policy)* defines a general-purpose model and syntax for expressing functional or non-functional properties of a Web service in a declarative manner [12]. A policy is an XML-expression that logically combines one or more assertions which specify concrete or abstract service characteristics such as a required security authentication scheme or a desired quality of service. Policies can flexibly be attached to various Web services definitions, including WSDL type definitions, as described in the *Web Services Policy Attachment* specification [13].

3   Motivation: Composing Coordinated Activities

In service-oriented computing, services are the basic building blocks out of which new applications can be created. With a plethora of services in-place and accessible in a standardized way, composition languages such as BPEL are needed to weave those services together and subsequently expose the resulting artifact itself as a Web service.

Composition and coordination and, correspondingly, composition middleware and coordination middleware, are two complementary aspects and techniques. The schema for a service composition is an aspect that is mostly internal to the implementation of the service that composes other Web services, whereas the protocols for service coordination are required properties of the external interactions between Web services [1].

A composition of Web services may not always require additional external coordination protocols. However, in order to develop *production workflows* [22] any functional composition of a set of Web services must be combined with the non-functional (reliability, transactions, security, and other) coordination properties required for process partner interactions. Production workflows are processes that define and implement the business logic and the quality-of-service necessary to integrate distributed heterogeneous applications. The overall motivating objective for our work is to enable production workflows using Web services.

Consider a workflow process that must interact with a partner using a reliable messaging protocol (such as *Web Services Reliable Messaging, WS-RM* [9]). The workflow (BPEL process) and the service provider each need to advertise their support for a reliable messaging protocol as a capability and/or requirement for interaction. In a dynamic service-oriented computing environment, such advertisement must be part of the WSDL service descriptions. The process and partner service use such information to agree on a particular protocol, which must then be supported by the middleware implementations of both workflow client and service provider.

Another example concerns declaring a (sub-) set of activities within a business process to be atomic using the WS-AT atomic coordination type. The service partners that are part of this atomic scope must correspondingly support the required WS-AT coordination protocols.

Additionally, another set of activities within the same business process may need to be coordinated with partners using a loosely-coupled business transaction model. A transaction coordination type such as WS-BA is required here.

The requirement for different coordination types and their protocols in a single service composition is illustrated in Figure 2. Here, activity *1* interacts with Web service *A* using the WS-RM protocol. Activity *2* and activity *3* are coordinated with Web service *B* and *C* using the WS-AT coordination type. Activity *4* is coordinated with Web service *D* using the WS-BA coordination type.

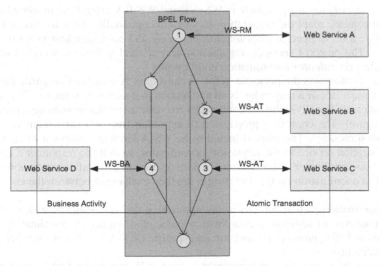

Fig. 2. Coordination requirements for service composition.

In this paper, we investigate a policy-based approach and middleware for composing coordinated activities as illustrated in Figure 2. The objective is to integrate the use of external coordination protocols (specifically, WS-AT and WS-BA) for different activities of a BPEL process composition, where BPEL defines the scope of the coordination. We propose a generic approach that can be applied for various defined coordination types.

It is not our objective to investigate the integration of all Web services interoperability protocols (like WS-RM) and of ad-hoc combinations of diverse protocols (such as a combination of WS-AT and WS-RM). We focus attention on the integration of (transactional) coordination types that are based on WS-C. Our approach aims to support any coordination type that is defined using WS-C.

4 Coordination Policies for BPEL

We propose a model for integrating WS-C coordination types and BPEL definitions using declarative policies attached to selected Web services constructs. The model does not introduce a new language or Web service specification, but integrates existing specifications through policy assertions.

4.1 Coordination Model

The WS-C specification defines three main elements that are commonly required for different kinds of coordination:

- A *coordination context*: the context that is shared and propagated among the participants in the coordinated activity
- An *activation service*: the Web service used to create a coordination context
- A *registration service*: the service used by participants to register for inclusion in specific coordination protocols

WS-C *coordination types* such as WS-AT and WS-BA extend the proposed coordination context, adapt the registration service (and optionally, the activation service) and define a set of specific *coordination protocols* and corresponding protocol Web services. The protocol services, registration service, and activation service together constitute a *coordinator* (coordination middleware).

Figure 3 illustrates the principle WS-C architecture. A coordination participant, in role of a requestor or a responder, is an application that uses a coordinator. The application interacts (locally) with the coordinator to create a coordination context (omitted in the figure). The context is propagated to any other (remote) participant(s) via an application message. The context includes the WS-Addressing endpoint reference of the registration service of the requestor's coordinator, so that the responder's coordinator ("sub-coordinator") can register for participation in a specific coordination protocol. The coordination protocol messages are then exchanged between the coordinators.

A coordination participant thus is any application that is capable of understanding WS-C contexts. In addition, a coordination participant requires a coordination middleware for WS-C protocol registration and specific (WS-AT, WS-BA, or other) protocol interactions.

Technically, a coordination participant is a set of Web services that support application-specific and coordination-middleware interfaces (port types) that may result in

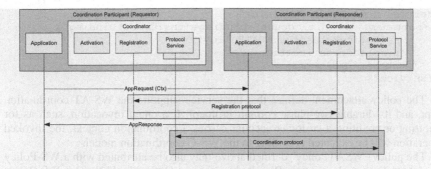

Fig. 3. WS-Coordination Architecture.

multiple endpoints at runtime. In this paper, we use both "coordinated (Web) service" and coordination participant to refer to the same concept.

4.2 Coordination Policies

The capability (of a Web service or BPEL process) to participate in WS-C coordination can easily be communicated using a declarative policy assertion. We define a *coordination policy* as an XML element referencing a WS-C coordination type and specific protocols of that type.

An example policy for the WS-AT coordination type and its durable two-phase commit protocol is given below. The policy uses the XML syntax defined in the WS-Policy framework [12] and the XML element <wsce:CoordinatedService> for coordination policies as proposed in [26].

```
<wsp:Policy wsu:Name="tns:WSATPolicy"
  <wsce:CoordinatedService
    CoordinationType=
      "http://schemas.xmlsoap.org/ws/2003/09/wsat">
    <wsce:Protocol
      ProtocolIdentifier=
        http://schemas.xmlsoap.org/ws/2003/09/wsat#Durable2PC
    />
  </wsce:CoordinatedService>
</wsp:Policy>
```

The policy references a (transaction) coordination type that is defined in a published XML schema. Authoring such policies is a matter of selecting a published WS-C coordination type and including in the <wsce:CoordinatedService> element the links that hold the XML schema.

These policies can then be flexibly and meaningfully attached to various Web services definitions [13]. To declare a coordination capability of a deployed Web service provider, we attach coordination policies to Web services port bindings. For example, a banking Web service "ABCBankService" may declare its support for WS-AT as follows.

```
<service name="ABCBankService"
  <port name="creditAccount" binding="tns:CreditBinding"
     wsp:PolicyRefs="tns:WSATPolicy">
     <soap:address location=…/>
  </port>
</service>
```

The policy attachment defines that the service supports the WS-AT coordination type and its durable two-phase commit protocol. If a client invocation, such as for debiting or crediting a customer account carries a coordination context, the invoked operation will be executed according to the WS-C coordination model.

The policy "WSATPolicy" defined above may also be attributed with a WS-Policy usage attribute such as <wsp:Required> or <wsp:Optional> [12]. The WS-Policy usage attributes, if specified for a coordination type, define the processing semantics of the policy. In this example, the WS-AT coordination type may be declared to be required or optional for any invocation on the port that the policy is attached to. If a required attribute is specified and an invocation on the port does not carry a proper coordination context, a fault will be raised.

Different coordination (and other) policies may also be combined using WS-Policy operators corresponding to the logical operators AND, OR, XOR. For example, a service that alternatively supports two coordination types would create a policy for each and combine them with an XOR. The WS-Policy operators corresponding to AND, OR, and XOR are <wsp:All/>, <wsp:OneOrMore/>, and <wsp:ExactlyOne/>, respectively.

4.3 BPEL Coordinated Partner Links and Coordinated Scopes

Through the attachment of coordination policies coordination semantics are introduced to (existing) BPEL compositions. We propose to attach coordination policies to BPEL *partner links* and to BPEL *scopes*. As noted earlier, a BPEL partner link is a typed connector along which a conversation with another party occurs. A BPEL scope is the demarcation of a group of activities of the process. Scopes are the units of fault handling and compensation in BPEL.

A partner link with an attached coordination policy is a *coordinated partner link*. Such a link describes the (abstract) requirement on any (concrete) deployed Web service that aims to provide the partner functionality at process execution time. The interpretation is similar to the attachment of a policy to a WSDL port type definition; it is a requirement for every deployed service to satisfy the policy [13].

If a coordinated partner link is used within a regular BPEL scope, for the duration of the scope the conversation with that partner is carried out using the declared coordination protocol. That is, a coordination context will be created for the conversation with that specific deployed service. Interactions with other (non-coordinated) partners in the same scope will not share the coordination context. This is illustrated in Figure 4.

In addition to partner links, however, coordination policies can also be attached to BPEL scopes to define *coordinated scopes*. The semantics of a policy attachment to a scope is that a coordination context is created for the scope by the BPEL middleware and that the context will be propagated to all the partners that are part of the scope.

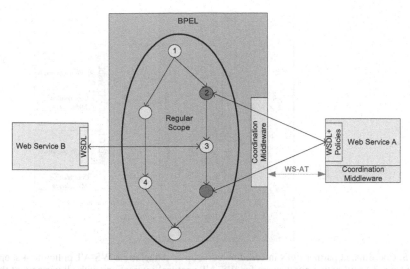

Fig. 4. Coordinated partner links in regular scopes: Attaching a WS-AT policy on a Partner-Link connecting the process with Web Service A and required coordination middleware for WS-AT protocol interactions.

Using a WS-AT coordination policy, for example, an *atomic scope* [22] can be modeled. Using a WS-BA coordination policy, a compensation-based *business activity scope* can be modeled.

WS-BA coordinated scopes are not to be confused with the concept of *compensation scopes* [22], which are the units of compensation handling that are already present in BPEL. WS-BA coordinated scopes establish a coordination context for distributed partners that engage in compensation-based business transaction protocols; WS-BA defines the messages and message exchange order for driving compensation. BPEL compensation scopes define actual compensation flows to be executed.

If coordination policies are attached to both scopes and partner links, the policies of the scope dictate the required policy for each partner. For example, if a scope is declared to be atomic using a WS-AT coordination policy, each coordinated partner in the scope must be compatible and support the WS-AT coordination type. The scope's policy defines a requirement on all partner links of the scope, and establishes a shared context for all partners in the scope. This is illustrated in Figure 5.

In either case of using a coordination context for a specific partner conversation (in a regular scope), or for conversation with multiple partners (in a coordinated scope), the BPEL scope demarcates the coordination. The context is created when entering the scope and the coordination is completed when closing the scope.

Notice that with coordinated scopes, BPEL is in the role of the initiator (requestor) of the coordination. Coordinated scopes do not model BPEL as a participant (responder) that registers with coordination contexts that have been created outside the process and propagated to the BPEL process through receive operations. Also, coordinated scopes do not allow nesting. External coordination and nesting of coordinated scopes is discussed in Section 6.3.

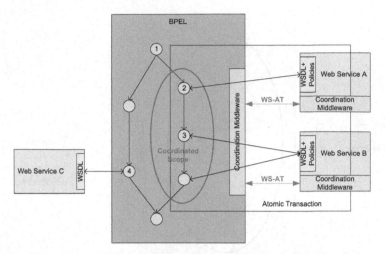

Fig. 5. Coordinated partner links in coordinated scopes: Attaching a WS-AT policy to a scope and required coordination middleware for WS-AT protocol interactions with all partners of the scope.

Using coordination policies, a scope defines a WS-C coordinator that provides the required registration and coordination type-specific protocol service port types. Coordination middleware on both sides can then engage in protocol interactions.

The programming complexity of authoring and attaching coordination policies to BPEL compares to the complexity associated with (declarative) transaction processing in general. A transaction model (for atomic transactions, long-running business transactions, or other) must be carefully selected for a given coordination problem, and the desired transaction semantics of the process must be carefully analyzed. Our policy-based approach does not simplify the task of understanding transactional semantics, but allows for a simple and effective way to extend BPEL to support (different) transaction coordination models.

4.4 Policy Matchmaking

The above proposed model of coordinated partner links and coordinated scopes introduces the need for two kinds of policy matchmaking:

- A static check on the compliance of coordinated scope and coordinated partner link policies within the BPEL definition
- Deployment-time and/or runtime policy matchmaking of coordinated partner links and deployed services

4.4.1 Static Verification
Static verification takes place to ensure that all coordinated partner links support at least the policies needed by the coordinated scope. For each coordinated scope, all BPEL constructs that make use of an abstract partner (such as an invoke statement) are verified: The coordination policy of the partner must satisfy the policies of the scope. Static verification ensures a correct BPEL process flow before instantiating the

abstract partners; it ensures the ability of a single coordination context of a particular coordination type to be shared among all partners of the scope.

4.4.2 Dynamic Matchmaking

After static verification is successfully completed, all coordinated partner links, within regular scopes or within coordinated scopes, describe valid requirements for the interaction with deployed services that aim to fulfill the partner role at process execution time.

The partner links can be instantiated at BPEL deployment time or dynamically through the exchange of endpoint references at runtime. When instantiation occurs, the coordination policies of the partner links must be matched with the coordination policies declared by the deployed services. The policies must be evaluated for compliance of their coordination type and protocols, and they must not conflict with one another.

Policy matchmaking determines if the BPEL requirements on coordination can be fulfilled by the deployed service under investigation. Matchmaking is required only once for each partner link, as long as the effective policy and the physical endpoint reference of the partner do not change.

The policy matchmaking algorithm [32] first calculates for each (potentially complex) WS-Policy expression the acceptable assertion set in terms of Boolean algebra. Each assertion, such as support for a coordination protocol, is interpreted as a unique Boolean variable. The acceptable assertion set is the set that consist of a list of assertions that when set to true reduce the entire policy to true. For each set, all assertions that are not on the list are set to false.

Next, the acceptable policy sets are compared to find matching sets that contain exactly the same list of assertions. A matching set is then selected by the middleware. If no matching set is found then the requestor and responder are incompatible and a BPEL runtime exception will be raised. (In future work, a mismatch may be resolved through dynamic policy negotiation or other application logic.)

4.5 Policy Mediation Meta-protocol

To compare policies for matchmaking, a policy mediation meta-protocol such as the GPP described in [32] can be used. The GPP proposes the steps of *policy request* to initiate a policy exchange, *policy promise* as the reply by the responder, and *policy confirmation* as the notification of a successful match. The protocol must be executed for any partner conversation for which no matching policy is in effect.

Alternatively, the recently published *Web Services Metadata Exchange (WS-MetadataExchange)* specification may be used [8]. WS-MetadataExchange defines three request-response message pairs to retrieve the policies, WSDL, or the XML schema of a Web services endpoint and/or given target namespace. WS-MetadataExchange replaces a proprietary solution like the GPP.

4.6 Programming Model

The programming model for composing coordinated activities is standard BPEL. Coordination policies, which may be defined separately, are attached to selected partner links and/or scopes. Coordinated partner links are interpreted depending on the declaration of coordinated scopes, as described above. The required coordination policy for a partner interaction is determined using static verification. Policy match-making, possibly using a policy mediation meta-protocol, is performed when needed at deployment and/or runtime. Policy mediation and matchmaking, as well as all co-ordination protocol interactions are the responsibility of the supporting middleware.

5   Middleware Prototype

We have implemented a middleware research prototype that demonstrates and vali-dates the approach described. This prototype provides a *BPEL compiler*, a *policy middleware*, and a *Web services transaction processing middleware (WSTPM)* that supports the WS-AT and WS-BA coordination types.

5.1   Components

Using our prototype, a BPEL definition with coordinated scopes and coordinated partner links is parsed and processed, together with the WSDL definitions of deployed partners (those available at deployment time), to generate a Java implementation. During code generation, the policy middleware is consulted for policy matchmaking.

The resulting code is then deployed as a regular Web service. For those abstract partners that did not have a concrete service at deployment time, the GPP policy me-diation meta-protocol and dynamic policy matchmaking is executed at runtime. The generated BPEL Web service interacts with the policy middleware for this purpose. The generated Web service further interacts with the WSTPM to begin, end, and manage transactional coordination. Standard J2EE and proprietary APIs are used for the generated service to interact with the policy and WSTPM middleware. Figure 6 illustrates a sample deployment architecture that utilizes our policy and WSTPM middleware on all nodes.

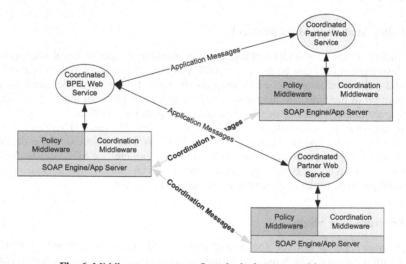

Fig. 6. Middleware prototype: Sample deployment architecture.

5.2 Process Execution

The coordination policies describe external interaction properties required for process execution. When entering a scope, a WS-C coordination context is created using the coordination middleware. In our prototype, the context is created by the generated service implementation executing the process. Alternatively, the context may be created by a BPEL middleware (a process runtime engine) or by any other coordination middleware client.

The context is then propagated to the partner as part of an application message, and the partner's coordination middleware in turn registers with the requestor's coordination middleware as previously described in Section 4. Subsequent application messages will carry the coordination context. The context is the means based on which the coordination middleware on both sides can identify the coordination to handle messages appropriately.

When the BPEL scope is about to close, the process implementation (the generated Web service or a process runtime) initiates any completion necessary according to the chosen coordination type. In case of WS-AT, a commit request is made to the local coordination middleware, which in turn will drive the two-phase commit protocol with all registered remote coordinators. In case of WS-BA, a completion request is made and the local coordinator will send WS-BA completion messages to all registered participants.

Failures can either be communicated using the defined coordination protocol messages (such as an "abort" message), in which case they will be handled by the coordination middleware. Failures may also be detected and handled by the BPEL middleware, and then communicated by the BPEL middleware to the coordination middleware.

Notice that heterogeneous middleware systems can be used on either end, as long as they support the Web services specifications. That is, (transactional) coordination can be implemented in different ways, with diverse internal options for registering (local and remote WS-C) resources and handling recovery from failures, as long as the external messages conform to the WS-C coordination types. For example, a coordination middleware may use a proprietary transaction service such as the J2EE Java transaction service. Java transaction contexts must then be mapped to WS-C XML contexts for all external interaction, and the messages and protocols defined in the WS-AT and WS-BA specifications must be understood and supported for interoperability.

6 Discussion and Related Work

In this paper, we presented an approach to composing coordinated Web services by means of declarative policy attachments to Web services definitions.

We previously reported on our work from the viewpoint of transaction processing [26] and software engineering [32], independent of the BPEL-related issues presented in this paper.

Although the use of policies for combining BPEL with WS-C coordination types has been mentioned as a desirable approach before [27] [16], we are not aware of prior work that has concretely combined the composition and coordination of Web services using policies. In this section, we discuss our approach and study related work.

6.1 Other Coordination Protocols

This paper provides a solution in which the supported coordination models for BPEL are WS-C coordination types. Other Web services transaction and coordination specifications have been proposed, however, including the Business Transaction Protocol (BTP) [5] and the Web Services Composite Application Framework (WS-CAF) [4]. Both define coordination types that are similar to WS-AT and WS-BA, but also feature subtle semantic differences.

In order to support these alternative coordination models with our approach, the coordination models would need to be represented as WS-C coordination types. Then, corresponding policies can be defined and attached as described in this paper. We do not see any reason why a definition of these alternative models as WS-C coordination types would not be possible. WS-C is a generic framework providing only the very fundamental coordination mechanisms.

Other, non-transactional coordination protocols have also been proposed. These include a service availability tracker [28], previously published as WS-Membership. Since it utilizes the same WS-C coordination model, we believe this coordination type to also be readily applicable to our approach. In this way, a BPEL process may also support group membership coordination for selected partners.

In all cases of BTP, WS-CAF, and the service tracker, however, corresponding middleware systems must also be integrated.

Non-WS-C coordination types, such as the reliable messaging protocol WS-RM, may also be applicable. This depends however on the extent that the coordination protocol interactions are (or can be) separated from the application messages. For example, message acknowledgments of receipt may be communicated via the reliable messaging middleware. The WS-RM message ordering and sequencing constructs for application messaging, however, may conflict with the BPEL message sequencing and flow definition. The composition of WS-RM and BPEL may therefore require additional integration and preference rules beyond the attachment of policies.

6.2 Other Coordination-Aware Composition Models

The most directly related approach to solving part of the problem addressed in this paper is presented in [10]. In that work, transaction management capabilities are added directly to BPEL as language extensions. New syntax is proposed to add support for a subset overlapping with specific business coordination models (WS-BA, BTP Cohesions).

In contrast, our work uses policies to non-intrusively attach coordination capabilities to parts of BPEL process definitions. Our approach enables an extensible variety of coordination protocols to be used, the potential of dynamically choosing from a set of supported protocols based on the environment, and the separation of concerns between the business process logic and the available/required coordination protocols. While extending the language directly may provide for a more integrated BPEL (middleware) implementation, we believe our approach using policy attachments to be more aligned with the dynamic nature of the service-oriented computing landscape. It is this dynamic nature that has led to the modularity of the Web services stack of specifications.

In our approach, coordination models are represented as policies that complement the workflow definition. In this way, a business process may interact with different services using the diverse coordination protocols that they require without the need to redefine the business logic or to port it to another language or system. Implementations executing the business process can then make use of modules that support the different parts of the Web service stack to make the execution happen. In this way, our approach introduces a dynamic aspect-oriented programming model for BPEL.

A large number of existing workflow systems also has built-in, proprietary support for transactional coordination. This has been a major requirement of workflow since many years. For example, [22] defines compensating actions on activities and a default coordination model for the set of compensable activities. The transaction literature has also proposed many ways to do (extended) transactions, some of which essentially are coordination-based workflows. The Sagas model, for example, defines a long-running process to consist of a set of atomic transactions and corresponding compensating transactions [11]. Some of these extended transactions models have also been adapted to support Web services, for example [18]. These approaches are similar to the approach of extending the BPEL language as discussed above in that they do not provide for an open, dynamic integration of diverse coordination models.

Even BPEL itself defines a built-in compensation mechanism that operates at the level of scopes. However, as described earlier in Section 4.3, BPEL compensation scopes differ from (WS-AT or WS-BA) coordinated scopes. BPEL and related workflow systems have considered the transactions governing the process model's activities directly and do not consider the interactions with services in a first class manner or how their coordination requirements may be composed. This is where the combination of BPEL and such specifications as WS-C comes into play. Additionally, these approaches are not adaptable to different coordination requirements of service providers.

The basic idea of attaching declarative policies to business process definitions is not new either. However, prior work on policy-based composition has been mainly used for selecting which service provider(s) to bind to at runtime, using measurable parameters. [2] devise a global planning approach to optimizing service selection during execution based on a set of measurable quality of services properties that can be objectively compared (such as price, reputation, and reliability). This is in contrast to our work on coordination interoperability protocols. Also, [23] suggests semantic annotations on BPEL processes that can be used at runtime to perform matchmaking and possible service chaining. However, our work is unique to our knowledge in that policies are used to describe and choose from a set of coordination protocols which require a middleware for runtime interoperability.

6.3 Future Work

In this paper, we address the problem of composing coordinated Web services independent of how the services are implemented. It may be that the coordinated services are themselves compositions, in which case the question of "composing coordinated compositions" arises. For example, a BPEL process coordinates services which are implemented as BPEL processes.

In this case, there are two "levels" of composition and coordination. The first level is the BPEL process that initiates coordinated activities (as presented in this paper); the second level concerns the BPEL processes that join those coordinated activities.

The first level does not need to differentiate between simple and composed services, since the composed services appear as regular Web services. This paper so far has only addressed first level composition of coordinated services.

In order to address the second level, our approach would need to be extended to allow the coordinated scopes (of the second level) to be coordinated by the first level composition. This includes the ability to accept and register with incoming coordination contexts (on receives) in addition to creating new coordination contexts as described earlier in this paper. Also, the compatibility of a coordinated scope with the coordination policy declared on the receiving partner link within that scope must be verified. The propagation of an incoming coordination context to other partners within coordinated scopes must be guided by policies.

There are also some special cases in the composition of diverse coordination protocols in BPEL that need to be addressed. The semantics of nested coordinated scopes requires careful attention. If a coordination type does not support nesting, BPEL scopes should not be used to introduce nesting into the coordination type. For example, a WS-BA coordinated scope within a WS-AT coordinated scope is undefined. One solution is to raise an error during the static process verification, and to only allow nested coordinated scopes for those coordination types that define nesting themselves.

Other future work relates to the generation of a Java implementation (to be deployed as a Web service) for executing the BPEL composition. Our current prototype does not support code generation for all possible BPEL constructs; for example, complex partner conversations using asynchronous messaging are not supported. While the prototype could be extended to fully support all BPEL constructs, the generated code may become increasingly complex and require sophisticated support mechanisms. These include support for parallelism, the conversational nature of BPEL [17], correlation and the handling of faults and conditional links/joins. The use of a first-class, separate BPEL runtime such as [7] may therefore be advantageous. The BPEL runtime however would need to be integrated with a policy and coordination middleware, as described in Section 5.

7 Conclusion

The Web services architecture intends to provide a standards-based platform for service-oriented computing. Various specifications supporting the integration of distributed heterogeneous applications as Web services are proposed. These include the Business Process Execution Language (BPEL) for service composition and the Web services Coordination (WS-C), Atomic Transaction (WS-AT), and Business Activity (WS-BA) specifications for (transactional) service coordination.

Additionally, the descriptive capabilities of WSDL are enhanced by the Web services Policy Framework (WS-Policy), which extends WSDL to allow the encoding and attachment of quality-of-service information in the form of reusable declarative policies.

In this paper, we investigated the combination of BPEL with WS-C, WS-AT and WS-BA using WS-Policy to support the definition of production workflows for Web services. We introduced coordination policies and specific BPEL coordination policy attachments to compose Web services that require coordination protocols for interaction. We defined the semantics of the proposed policy-based composition model and discussed methods, programming model, and middleware support needed for defining and executing composed coordinated services.

Revisiting the two objectives of the paper stated in the beginning, we have (1) introduced a process-based Web services composition model that supports a flexible, dynamic integration of diverse coordination protocols, and (2) demonstrated the feasibility of combining the existing Web services specifications of BPEL and WS-C using WS-Policy.

We discussed the advantages of our approach, which include the ability to support an extensible variety of coordination types in BPEL, to dynamically choose among the types, and to allow for a clear separation of concerns between business process logic and (different) coordination protocols. The flexibility comes at the expense of a potentially more complex middleware infrastructure, which must integrate the various implementations of the individual (BPEL, policy, and coordination) specifications supported.

Acknowledgements

The research presented is based on joint work with Isabelle Rouvellou, Eric Wohlstadter, and Nirmit Desai. We gratefully acknowledge their invaluable contributions.

References

1. G. Alonso, F. Casati, H. Kuno, V. Machiraju. *Web Services*. Springer-Verlag, 2004
2. B. Benatallah, M. Dumas, Z. Maamar. Definition and Execution of Composite Web Services: The Self-Serv Project. *Data Engineering Bulletin, 25(4)*, 2002
3. D. Box, F. Curbera (Eds). *Web Services Addressing (WS-Addressing)*. Published online at http://www.ibm.com/developerworks/library/ws-add, 2004
4. D. Bunting, M. Chapman, O. Hurley, M. Little, J. Mischkinsky, E. Newcomer, J. Webber, K. Swenson. *Web Services Composite Application Framework (WS-CAF)*. Published online at http://developers.sun.com/techtopics/webservices/wscaf/, 2003
5. A. Ceponkus, S. Dalal, T. Fletcher, P. Furniss, A. Green, B. Pope. *Business Transaction Protocol*. Published online at http://www.oasis-open.org/committees/download.php/1184/2002-06-03.BTP_cttee_spec_1.0.pdf, 2003
6. F. Curbera, R. Khalaf, N. Mukhi, S. Tai, S. Weerawarana. The Next Step in Web Services. *Communications of the ACM, 46(10):29–34*, 2003
7. F. Curbera, M. Duftler, R. Khalaf, N. Mukhi, W. Nagy, S. Weerawarana. *BPWS4J*. Published online at http://www.alphaworks.ibm.com/tech/bpws4j, 2003
8. F. Curbera, J. Schlimmer (eds.) *Web Services Metadata Exchange (WS-MetadaExchange)*. Published online at http://www-106.ibm.com/developerworks/ library/specification/ws-mex/, 2004
9. C. Ferris, D. Langworthy (eds.) *Web Services Reliable Messaging (WS-ReliableMessaging)*. Published online at http://www-106.ibm.com/developerworks/ webservices/library/ws-rm/, 2004
10. T. Fletcher, P. Furniss, A. Green, R. Haugen. *BPEL and Business Transaction Management*. Published online at http://www.choreology.com/standards/BPEL.and. Business.Transaction.Management.Choreology.Submission.html, 2003
11. H. Garcia-Molina, K. Salem. Sagas. *Proceedings ACM SIGMOD*, 1987
12. M. Hondo, C. Kaler. *Web Services Policy Framework (WS-Policy)*. Published online at http://www-106.ibm.com/developerworks/library/ws-polfram/, 2003

13. M. Hondo, C. Kaler. *Web Services Policy Attachment (WS-PolicyAttachment)*. Published online at http://www-106.ibm.com/developerworks/library/ws-polatt/, 2003
14. IBM Corporation. http://www-136.ibm.com/developerworks/webservices/
15. R. Khalaf, F. Curbera, W. Nagy, S. Tai, N. Mukhi, M. Duftler. Understanding Web Services. In M.P. Singh (ed.), *Practical Handbook of Internet Computing*, CRC Press, 2004 (to appear)
16. R. Khalaf, F. Leymann. On Web Services Aggregation. *Proceedings of the VLDB Technologies for e-Services Workshop*, Springer LNCS, 2003
17. R. Khalaf, N. Mukhi, and S. Weerawarana. Service-Oriented Composition in BPEL4WS. *Proceedings of the 2003 World Wide Web Conference, Web Services Track*, 2003
18. N. B. Lakhal, T. Kobayashi, H. Yokota. THROWS: An Architecture for Highly Available Distributed Execution of Web Services Compositions. *Proceedings of the 14th International Workshop on Research Issues on Data Engineering Web Services for E-Commerce and E-Government Applications*, 2004
19. D. Langworthy (ed.) *Web Services Coordination (WS-Coordination)*. Published online at http://www-106.ibm.com/developerworks/library/ws-coor/, 2003
20. D. Langworthy (ed.) *Web Services Atomic Transaction (WS-AtomicTransaction)*. Published online at http://www-106.ibm.com/developerworks/library/ws-atomtran/, 2003
21. D. Langworthy (ed.) *Web Services Business Activity Framework (WS-BusinessActivity)*. Published online at http://www-106.ibm.com/developerworks/webservices/library/ws-busact/, 2004
22. F. Leymann, D. Roller. *Production Workflow*. Prentice-Hall, 2000
23. D. J. Mandell, S. A. McIlraith. A bottom-up Approach to Automating Web Service Discovery, Customization, and Semantic Translation. *Proceedings of the 2003 WWW Conference Workshop on E-Services and the Semantic Web*, 2003
24. Microsoft Corporation. http://msdn.microsoft.com/webservices/
25. OASIS. *UDDI*. Specifications published at http://www.oasis-open.org/committees/ uddi-spec/doc/tcspecs.htm
26. S. Tai, T. Mikalsen, E. Wohlstadter, N. Desai, I. Rouvellou. Transaction Policies for Service-Oriented Computing. In *Data and Knowledge Engineering Journal*, Special Issue on Contract-based Coordination and Collaboration, 2004 (in press)
27. S. Thatte (ed.) *Business Process Execution Language for Web Services Version 1.1*. Published online at http://www-106.ibm.com/developerworks/library/ws-bpel/, 2003
28. W. Vogels. Tracking Service Availability in Long Running Business Activities. In *Proceedings 1st International Conference on Service-oriented Computing*, 2003
29. W3C. *Web Services Architecture Requirements*. Published online at http://www.w3.org/TR/wsa-reqs, 2002
30. W3C. *SOAP*. Specifications published at http://www.w3.org/2000/xp/Group/
31. W3C. *Web Services Description Language (WSDL)*. Specifications published at http://www.w3.org/2002/ws/desc/
32. E. Wohlstadter, S. Tai, T. Mikalsen, I. Rouvellou, P. Devanbu. GlueQoS: Middleware to Sweeten Quality-of-Service Policy Interactions. In *Proceedings of the 26th International Conference on Software Engineering*, 2004

Adaptive Resource Sharing in a Web Services Environment

Vijay K. Naik[1], Swaminathan Sivasubramanian[2], and Sriram Krishnan[3]

[1] IBM T. J. Watson Research Center, Yorktown Heights, NY 10598
vkn@us.ibm.com
[2] Vrije Universiteit, Amsterdam, The Netherlands
swami@cs.vu.nl
[3] Indiana University, Bloomington, IN 47405
srikrish@cs.indiana.edu

Abstract. One effect of the push towards business process automation and IT consolidation is that low-level resources from multiple administrative domains are shared among multiple workloads and the middleware is called upon to bring about the integration while masking the details of sharing such resources. Web services and grid based technologies hold promise for developing such middleware. However, existing solutions do not extend well when resources to be shared belong to multiple administrative domains and when resource sharing is governed by local policies. In this paper, we describe an architecture for adaptive resource sharing among two types of workloads: (i) local resource specific workload and (ii) global web services based grid workload. Each resource can set its own policies regarding how the resource is to be shared. Our approach leverages both the grid and the web services based technologies and overcomes the limitations of existing solutions by providing an additional layer of middleware. This layer provides services for dynamic discovery and aggregation of resources, policy based and transparent management of resources, and dynamic workload scheduling using the concept of virtualized resources. We discuss some of the design choices we made and present performance results to show the effects of policy-based resource sharing on the throughput delivered to the grid workload.

1 Introduction

In an Enterprise many different types of applications are used to deliver IT services (e.g., financial, accounting, supply-chain management, e-commerce, billing, customer relations). Each serves its own workload and typically each service is run on servers dedicated to provide that service. One drawback of using a dedicated set of servers is that sufficient server capacity must be allocated to handle peak workloads in order to meet the response time and throughput guarantees. Since not all workloads are correlated, when one service is dealing with peak workload, demand on other services may be at or below average. Therefore, if resources can be shared by two or more non-correlated services, average utilization of the resources can be raised and higher workload demands can be met without provisioning resources for the worst case scenarios.

H.-A. Jacobsen (Ed.): Middleware 2004, LNCS 3231, pp. 311–330, 2004.

While resource sharing is beneficial from IT consolidation point of view, sharing of resources by different types of applications and their workload is not straightforward even when resource capacity is not an issue. This can be because of application-legacy reasons, workload-resource affinity issues, unpredictability in the workload arrival patterns, security and isolation needs, and so on. Obviously, applications that require special hardware or non-generic platform configurations cannot easily share their resources with other applications. Workloads that have affinity to specific resources (e.g., desktop users sending their interactive workload to their own desktops) cannot be sent over to other resources, but it may be possible to share the underlying resources with other types of workloads. In this paper, one of our workloads is of this type. Unpredictability in the demand leads application and system administrators to take conservative approaches and to over-provision resources. However, even limited predictability about the demand can help administrators in setting policies so the underlying resources can be shared adaptively and dynamically in anticipation of the predicted demand. We use such an approach in our present work. Security and isolation are real concerns even when all workloads are generated within the same organization. Resource sharing can lead to security related compromises. In this paper, we describe an approach that uses hypervisor-based virtual machines. This is an extension of our earlier work described in [11]. Specifically, we make use of the VMWare Workstation product [4] to isolate the two types of workloads. Hypervisor-based virtual machines such as these address OS and application level security concerns and thus facilitate resource sharing without compromising isolation.

In this work, we describe a middleware that enables resource sharing among two classes of workloads that characterize a typical enterprise environment: (i) resource specific workload, in particular, the interactive workload submitted by users to their desktops and (ii) workload for applications that conform to the J2EE programming model and, in particular, to the Web Services programming model. In an enterprise environment, desktops, in aggregate, represent one of the largest set of underutilized resources and their raw capacities are increasingly matching server capacities. Secondly, the Web Services programming model is increasing being adopted by enterprises to automate many of their business processes and many different types of workloads can be handled by Web Services [5]. The Web Services abstraction allows development of general purpose containers that can be supported by a variety of platforms. General availability of such containers makes it possible to deploy and process Web Service requests on a variety of platforms.

Although desktop systems are resource rich and they are highly underutilized, harnessing the available cycles from desktop based resources and applying them in an aggregate manner for supporting business processes is a hard problem. The problems are primarily related to the conflicting requirements placed by the desktop users and by the workload for the Web Services. For the desktop users, interactivity, responsiveness, and security are of prime concern. From the point of view of the business process clients, discovery, responsiveness, and security are of prime concern. While the desktop users want the entire system at their disposal when they want to use it, for the Web Services clients it is important that a sufficient number of resources be available at all times to handle the workload. As we discuss in Section 2.3, desktop users may set policies, independent of other users, that determine how their desktop system is to be shared with some other workload. It is impractical for the Web Services clients to go hunting for resources that may be idle at that instance. Because of the unpredictability in the desktop resource availability, a mechanism is needed to identify resources available for processing the Web Services dynamically and to route the requests to the appropriate resources transparent to the client(s) generating the workload. It is also equally important to mask the changes in the resource pool available for sharing.

Transparent management of resources that belong to multiple administrative domains is at the core of grid computing architecture. The Open Grid Services Architecture (OGSA) defines a uniform service semantics (the *Grid service*) and standardized basic mechanisms required for creating and composing distributed computing systems [8]. With this service oriented approach of OGSA, Grid computing has become an attractive platform for deploying business applications and for supporting commercial workload. OGSA makes it possible to manage and administer large scale systems, in a standardized manner, across multiple administrative domains. Using the Grid architecture, it is possible to associate individual policies with each participating Grid resource and to determine the manner in which a resource is to be shared by grid and non-grid workload. Thus, grid based technologies, and OGSA in particular, are ideal candidates for enabling desktop (and in general, any resource) sharing among multiple types of workloads. However, existing grid enabling toolkits such as Globus (versions 2.x and 3.0) do not adequately address the business application requirements, which we explain in more detail in Section 2.2.

In this paper, we describe a middleware architecture that overcomes the above discussed resource sharing difficulties. In our architecture, a virtual service layer is created that provides an additional layer of indirection. This helps to mask the actual changes in the physical resource layer from the workload for the Web Services. To reduce the overhead of this additional layer of indirection, the dynamic effects of the policies governing the physical resources (in this case the desktop systems) transcend the multiple layers and make their effect visible to the request scheduling layer without reducing the transparency or the administrative independence of the individual resources.

The rest of the paper is organized as follows. In the next section, we first briefly discuss the J2EE programming model and describe the characteristics of the transactional business oriented workload. In Section 2.3, we discuss the requirements of desktop systems, when used as shared resources. In Section 3, we describe the highlights of our middleware architecture. In Section 4, we discuss the design and implementation of the Gateway that acts as the coordinator between the deployed Web Services and the Grid clients. Performance results from an implementation of our architecture are described in Section 5. In Section 6, we discuss how our work relates to other work in the literature. Finally, we present our conclusions in Section 7.

2   Preliminaries

2.1   J2EE Programming Model

Java 2 Enterprise Edition (J2EE) is a standard for developing enterprise applications in a composable manner using reusable Java components, called Enterprise Java Beans (EJBs). The standard spells out programming interfaces that the EJB components conform to. The EJBs provide services to local and remote clients. The EJB components and their life cycle are managed within a special container provided by an application server such as IBM's WebSphere Application Server [3]. The J2EE standard makes it possible so that EJBs can be developed in a container independent manner and the a J2EE compliant application server can handle its life cycle by providing a set of standard runtime services specified by J2EE. These services include naming and directory services, authentication and authorization, state management, interfacing with a Web server, and so on. The application server handles all the platform and vendor specific details such as those involved initializing and maintaining interactions with the OS, databases, and network subsystems. The J2EE programming model provides an abstraction for the multi-tier architecture implicit in many business processes. The persistent state is maintained in the database tier, processing of this state is performed in the business logic tier, and the results of which may be rendered in a presentation tier before being sent to a remote client. The remote client itself could be an application. This makes it possible to integrate multiple business processes using standard technologies.

For more information on the J2EE standards and the associated programming models, we refer interested readers to [10]. In the context of our work, Web Services are specialized EJB components. Web Services further standardize the distributed interactions by conforming to Web based technologies. Complex business processes can be modeled and deployed using reusable components. However, application servers such as IBM WebSphere Application Servers need to be deployed in order to run the Web Services and handle their workload.

2.2   Characteristics of Transactional Applications

In the following, we highlight the requirements posed by the transactional business applications and services. We contrast these against the requirements posed by the scientific and engineering applications, which have motivated the development of the classical grid related middleware work.

Transactional business services exhibit *high degree of interactivity* with human operators and/or with databases where business state information is held in a persistent manner. The time spent interacting with the external environment is typically comparable to the time spent in performing local computations. Moreover, the frequency of interactions with the external environment is relatively high. On the other hand, typical scientific and engineering applications start with a state encapsulated in a small number of static files or other objects and evolve that state over a period of time and/or space. Such computations can continue in batch mode without significant interactions with a database or with a human operator. The time spent in batch mode can be order of magnitude higher than the time spent interacting with the external environment.

One effect of the interactivity is that business services need to be much more sensitive to *response time constraints* posed by the users. This is not only because of the human factors involved (e.g., on-line shoppers may not have patience for long response time delays), but also because of the role played by these applications in time sensitive business processes. In such cases, any processing delays can result in financial losses and/or competitive disadvantages. Typical response times are of the order of seconds or minutes.

The flip side of response time is the throughput, which is a measure of the number of transactions performed per unit time. Although many types of business interactions tend to be bursty (i.e., low activity followed by sudden rise in the demand, which is again followed by weak demand), they also require that the service throughput should rise with demand, without deteriorating the response time. Unless enough resources are allocated at all times to handle the peak demand, necessary resources must be allocated dynamically and on demand. Moreover, the resource management mechanisms must be sensitive to the changes in the workload and must respond rapidly so the response time and overall throughput do not deteriorate.

Finally, many of the business processes are mission critical. This means the business services and the state information they process, must be available to corporate customers at all times – 24 hours a day and 7 days a week. This results *in the high availability* requirements on the on-line business services. At the minimum, services need to recover gracefully from failures and user data is not to be lost.

In contrast, typical scientific and engineering applications have low response time requirements and no availability requirements to speak of, but they do have reliability and service time requirements. This means users of such applications, who many times are also the application developers, are more flexible about the turnaround time as long as their applications run to completion in a reliable manner. The job arrival patterns are much less bursty and demand on resources fluctuates within a narrow range. Because of these characteristics, Grid systems catering to users of scientific applications emphasize services related to reservation mechanisms, job queuing, launching, checkpointing, migration, file transfers, and so on.

In short, typical Grid systems used for scientific computing workloads provide services that focus on maintaining high utilization of Grid resources. But such systems provide inadequate or no support for response time guarantees, continuous availability of applications, work-flow type of application setup, or for dynamic provisioning of resources in response to changes in the request arrival patterns. To provide these functionalities, middleware services are needed to provide monitoring mechanisms to evaluate the rate at which different types of requests are processed, analytic capabilities to determine if these processing rates are adequate, prediction capabilities to anticipate future demand and resources needed to satisfy the demand. Such a middleware also needs to provide support for deploying services that can persist and remain available even if the underlying resources become unavailable for some reason.

In Section 3 we describe our architecture that responds to response time, throughput, and availability requirements.

2.3   Sharing Desktop-Based Resources

The primary objective of desktop systems is to provide a high degree of interactivity to desktop users and to create an environment that is conducive to high-levels of productivity in a collaborative environment. The nature of the desktop-based interactive applications is such that the demand on the desktop resources occurs in frequent, but short bursts and the load dissipates rapidly. On a desktop system, there are many unused cycles, but their frequency and duration are highly unpredictable. Moreover, desktop users (or administrators) may set policies that enforce conditions under which desktop resources may be used for processing other workload. Each desktop may have a unique local policy, which may change over time. Examples of local desktop policies include: (i) interactive workload always has the highest priority, (ii) allocate no more than a certain percent of the desktop resources to Web Services at any given time, (iii) allow processing of grid workload only when the interactive workload is below a certain threshold, (iv) allow participation in the Grid computations only during certain time of the day or on certain days of the week, and so on. Thus, policy enforcement requires evaluation of certain conditions, which may be static and predictable or dynamic and unpredictable such as the current interactive workload. Moreover, policies may be defined using a combination of static and dynamic conditions. The architecture needs to take into account individual policies and the heterogeneity in the capacities associated with each desktop resource while addressing the availability, throughput, and responsiveness requirements associated with the transactional services.

Clearly, for effective utilization of desktop systems in a Grid like environment, one needs to take into account the following requirements: (i) Utilize the desktop system whenever conditions allow it to be used in Grid computations, and (ii) not to schedule any computations on a desktop system, beyond its available capacity.

The first requirement implies that a mechanism is needed to accurately predict when a desktop system becomes available for Grid computations. The second requirement implies that the Grid workload assigned to a desktop should match the available capacity. Note that desktop policies may not allow full utilization of the maximum available capacity of a desktop system. For example, a policy may specify the maximum fraction of the CPU, memory, and network bandwidth that a particular Web Service may use at any given time.

Clearly, the desktop resource availability and capability is more predictable when the desktop user is away from the system (e.g., in the evening and night hours). This information can be gathered and analyzed by running a monitoring agent on the desktop to understand the daily, weekly, monthly and seasonal patterns in "macro" usage of the system. Even when the desktop system is being used by the desktop user, there are many opportunities for running Grid workload on the system under the specified policies. However, because of the unpredictable nature of the interactive usage, only short term predictions about the future usage by interactive applications can be made with a given level of confidence.

Thus, to effectively utilize desktop-based resources, the middleware architecture needs to provide support for monitoring desktop resource usage patterns, both for the interactive workload as well as for the Grid workload. It needs to incorporate analytical mechanisms to predict resource availability and capabilities at various time intervals in the future. Furthermore, the system needs to be able to bound the uncertainties in the predictions. We now describe our architecture that takes into account these requirements.

3 Architecture Overview

3.1 Requirements

Availability and responsiveness to the changes in the client demands are the key criteria that a transactional service provider must meet. The primary figure-of-merit is throughput and response time. This means the architecture should be able to deliver a service requested by the clients on demand and it should be able to adjust the capacity of the underlying resource so as to meet the intensity of the demand. The client requests can be complex (e.g., requests resulting in a work-flow), request arrival rates can be unpredictable, and clients may have multiple levels of service-level-agreements (SLA) with the service provider. The architecture needs to address these requirements.

Intuitively, the desired architecture needs to facilitate (i) deployment of appropriate Web Services on the desktop resources, and (ii) route client requests to appropriate Web Service instances. These tasks are made challenging because of (i) the uncertainties in the resource availability for deploying a Web Service at any given instance in time and (ii) the uncertainties in the client demand on a Web Service at any instance in time. If we assume that there are *enough* idle desktop-based resources available to meet demand at any given time, then the task of the architecture is (i) to deploy Web Service instances on appropriate desktop resources so as to empower them with the desired capacity just-in-time for delivering the service, and (ii) to identify and match Grid client requests with Web Service instances with appropriate capacity (i.e., with ability to respond within prescribed time limits).

Even when sufficient desktop resources are available on an aggregate basis, efficient identification of the once that can provide the desired capabilities at any given time requires good prediction mechanisms. Given the ability to discover, monitor, and predict resource availability and demand, the architecture is basically reduced to scheduling appropriate number of service instances, mapping the service instances on to the physical resources, and routing client requests to appropriate service instances. Note that the predictions need to be only reasonably accurate and not highly accurate.

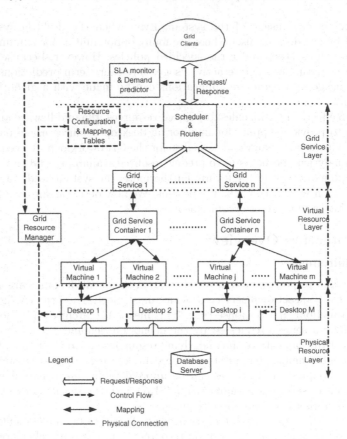

Fig. 1. Layered architecture for the enabling policy-based resource sharing. The interactive workload for the desktops is not shown.

3.2   Highlights of Our Architecture

The architecture is defined using a layered approach. This allows addressing the requirements of the transactional workload separately from the requirements of interactive workload and desktop related policies. The architecture, as shown in Figure 1, has three layers: (i) The Grid Service Layer, (ii) The Logical Resource Layer, and (iii) The Physical Resource Layer. In the following, we describe the salient features and functionality of each layer.

Each layer is associated with Control and Management Components (CMCs). The interactions among the CMCs and the functionality they provide largely define the architecture. The SLA Monitor and Demand Predictor, shown in Figure 1 is one such CMC. This component monitors request arrivals per Web Service type and per Grid client class basis. It also monitors SLA violations on a per client basis. In addition, predictions on future arrival rates are made for each Web Service type. Based on the predicted arrivals and available Web Service capabilities, a scheduling strategy for request processing is adopted to meet the SLA requirements. This process is repeated frequently as arrival patterns change and/or as the Web Service capabilities change. Some of examples of scheduling strategies are weighted round robin, priority based scheduling (with priorities derived from SLAs), one-to-many scheduling (i.e., simultaneous processing of a request on multiple Web Service instance to overcome uncertainties in service capabilities), and so on.

The CMCs in the Physical Resource Layer enforce desktop related policies, monitor and analyze the interactive workload, and predict the short range availability and capability of the desktop system for a particular Web Service. This are described in more detail in [11]. The CMCs in the Logical Resource Layer act as coordinators between the Grid Service Layer and Physical Resource Layer.

The Grid Resource Manager (GRM) shown in Figure 1 acts as a facilitator across all three layers. One function provided by GRM is to discover desktop resources that are available and are capable of deploying one or more Web Services. This is accomplished by coordinating and heart-beating with a CMC known as a Virtual Machine Manager (VMM). One instance of VMM runs on each physical desktop resource as long as that resource is participating as a grid resource. It controls and monitors all virtual machines on that resource. Using the same mechanisms, it also detects when a desktop resource is no longer provisioning a particular Web Service or is no longer available as grid resource. A second key function provided by GRM is to allocate the predicted capacities of each participating desktop resource to Web Services requiring the resource during that future time interval. It tries to locate and allocate as many resources to each Web Service as possible making sure that the conflicts caused by sharing are minimized. To perform this task, GRM collects from each VMM the usage and policy related data for its resource and predicted availabilities. The VMM in turn uses a platform specific CMC known as the Host Agent for monitoring, gathering, and aggregation of performance and usage related data. GRM normalizes the raw capacity of each desktop against a standard platform. In case the desktop node is to be shared among multiple Web Services, it further reduces the available capacity in proportion to the share made available for other Web Services. This represents the maximum normalized capacity available to a particular Web Service. It then takes into account the predicted available capacity as a fraction of the total capacity and uses that to compute the predicted available capacity from a desktop resource for each Web Service. This forms the basis for the allocation of resources to the expected workload. This information is represented in the Resource Configuration & Mapping Tables shown in Figure 1 and is dynamically updated by GRM.

The Scheduler uses this information to determine the number of service instances to deploy for each Web Service for which it anticipates demand. The number of instances deployed is proportional to the allocated capacity and to the expected demand. When requests arrive, the Router routes those requests to the physical resources where the service instance is actually deployed. The

Scheduler also takes into account the uncertainty in the predicted allocations. When the uncertainty is high, it may decide to schedule a request on more than one service instance simultaneously, making sure that the service instances are mapped on-to distinct physical resources. In such cases, the Router replicates a request and multicasts it to multiple instances of the same Web Service.

4 Gateway Architecture and Design

4.1 Gateway Requirements

An important component of our architecture is the *request scheduler* responsible for scheduling requests from Grid clients, based on the relative priorities of the requests and their SLA requirements. Another essential component is the *request router*, which routes the client request to an appropriate end point resource (also referred to as a Grid node), where the request is processed. Recall that this may be a shared resource. The request router monitors the execution status of each request it has dispatched. It is capable of restarting a request, if a request fails (possibly due to a Grid node failure, network failure etc.) to ensure that the request is not dropped.

The request scheduler and router components together form a single logical component referred to as the *Gateway*, which serves as the entry point for the requests from Grid clients. It is a logically centralized component. However, if necessary (for reasons of scalability), it can be implemented as a federation of gateways, as described in section 4.2.

In addition to scheduling and request tracking, Gateway must be capable of handling the variability in resource availability and smoothen it so that Grid clients do not see the effects of variability. In our system, this is handled by the Grid Resource Manager, which coordinates with various CMCs of physical and Grid layers, and smoothes the variability in the resource availability of the desktops. As noted before, the process of handling this variability can be done in two ways: (i) predicting the resource availability in a Grid node and scheduling based on that prediction or (ii) schedule assuming they are available all the time and migrate the request, if they become unavailable during the course of execution of a request. In our system we adopt the first approach, since for transactional workloads the execution times are much smaller compared to those of the batch-computing applications. The overhead introduced in migrating an active transaction can be comparable to the service time of a transaction itself. However, the success of the first approach design relies on the accuracy of the prediction mechanisms.

4.2 Gateway Design and Implementation

In our design, we make a clear demarcation of resource prediction models from on-line allocation and scheduling components. Such a demarcation is required for the following two reasons:

i. The availability of each Grid node is governed not only by its (interactive workload) usage pattern but also by the local policy set by the desktop user.

ii. Separation of resource prediction components from allocation and scheduling components allows the system to use different resource prediction algorithms without affecting other system behavior.

In our system, the scheduling and resource allocation components are also separated. Thus, the Gateway schedules the request onto logical resource pools and routes it to the actual Grid nodes based on the routing and mapping tables populated by the GRM. The GRM (resource allocator) is responsible for allocating the Grid nodes onto these logical resource pools such that the overall Grid throughput is maximized. The advantage of this approach is that the Gateway can schedule client requests independent of the changes in the participating Grid nodes. However, as noted in the preceding section, the Gateway (through the SLA monitor) must communicate with GRM and inform the expected demand for a particular Web Service, to ensure that enough resources are allocated for provisioning each type of Web Service requested by clients.

Design Choices. The design of Gateway can be done in several ways: For example, Gateway can be built using network-level redirector such as IBM Network Dispatcher [2]. The other way to build the Gateway is by modifying the application-level transaction scheduler. In the following, we discuss the relative merits and demerits of these two approaches:

- *Network-level solution:* Gateway Router can be built using network-level redirectors that cluster together the available servers into a logical resource pool and route requests to the cluster [9]. APIs are provided to allocate or deallocate servers from the pool. The primary advantage of this approach is its performance. Since all the routing is done in network level, it does not suffer the overhead of call marshaling and unmarshaling. However, it has the following disadvantages: It assumes that all the servers are equally capable of serving all Web Services. If not, then it requires the use of one network-level redirector for each Web Service. Thus, this approach lacks flexibility in adding new Web Services dynamically. Further, network redirectors are built for server clusters and is not suitable for our desktop pools, where the maximum number of desktop nodes in a pool can be relatively high, with dynamic change in their availability.

- *Application-level solution:* Gateway can also be built using application level redirector. In this approach, the Gateway receives service requests from clients, unmarshals them and, based on the type of service required, it schedules the requests using the routing table populated by the GRM for that service. GRM, by populating a per-service routing table, essentially creates a per-service resource pool, based on which the Gateway Router schedules the service requests. The primary advantage of this approach is that this design can support different types of Web Services, without any changes or addition of new hardware. Further, this design can possibly manage a larger resource pool. However, this approach introduces some processing overhead as it needs to marshal and unmarshal a service request.

In our system, we adopt the application-level solution as it is more flexible to add/remove more Web Services dynamically. We have also observed that the overhead introduced by processing the request at application-level is negligible compared to the overall service execution time.

Gateway Implementation. In our system, we have implemented GRM as a Web Service and is deployed in IBM WebSphere Application Server [3]. Similarly, Gateway Router is also implemented and deployed as a Web Service. The Grid clients submit their requests with Web Service calls to the Gateway Router. However, since the Grid clients make Web Service calls as if the service is running on the gateway, we have to implement our router in such a way that forwarding of request from the Gateway to the Grid node is transparent to the client.

In WebSphere Application Server (versions 4.x and 5.x), every Web Service call is being trapped by its appropriate RPCProvider, as defined in Apache SOAP [1]. This provider is responsible for locating the actual class and method that needs to be invoked to make a (Web Service based) transaction. In our system, we implemented a new provider (which is in conformance with regulations of Apache SOAP specifications) that similarly receives this request at the Gateway. However instead of finding a method to invoke, it makes a call to a *forward* method of Gateway Router Service. This method receives the call object and consults the routing table for that service request, and forwards requests to different Grid nodes on a weighted round robin fashion.

By implementing a new provider, we have made no changes to WebSphere or its SOAP implementation and have just added a new plug-in to support our new provider. Thus, Grid clients make service requests as normal Web Service calls with no change in their code. The GRM Web Service populates the routing tables of the Gateway Router by making a standard Web Service call.

4.3   Design Scalability

The design described above assumes a centralized Gateway and a centralized GRM. Such a system will have scalability problems as the number of desktop nodes increases and/or the number of Grid clients rises. However, this scalability issue can be addressed in several different ways. In the following, we briefly describe some of these concepts.

Federated Gateways. One way to alleviate the Gateway congestion is to provide multiple Gateways, each responsible for serving a subset of Grid clients using a subset of Grid nodes. The problem to address here is that of load balancing among the Gateways. One possibility is to use DNS servers and another possibility is to use a network dispatcher type of mechanism in front of the Gateways. Both of these approaches suffer the shortcomings described above and in [6]. We now describe third approach which is more appropriate when Grid clients perform many transactions within a session. When a new session is to begin, a Grid client registers for that session with a single well known Grid

Registry. As a part of the registration the client receives address to one of the multiple Gateways that is capable of serving the client requests. The Registry keeps track of the current load on multiple Gateways and randomizes new client requests among lightly loaded possible Gateways.

Similarly, GRM allocates Grid nodes among multiple Gateways by knowing the current load among the Gateways. If it detects that some of the Gateways are not able to keep up with their demand, then it readjusts the current allocations among the Gateways and resets the Mapping Tables provided to each Scheduler & Router.

Hierarchical Control Structure. Another potential source of bottleneck in scaling up the system is the GRM and associated control structure. Here again the answer is to provide an hierarchy of GRMs. At the lowest level, each GRM looks after a manageable number of Grid nodes and then it forwards the allocation information to the GRM at the next higher level. The GRM at the top level has the consolidated information from all GRMs. This is then forwarded to the one or more Gateways in the system.

Databases. In case of commercial applications, client state is typically stored in backend database servers. This information may be accessed multiple times when a single transaction is being processed. Thus, in a large Grid system, a single backend database server can be a source of bottleneck. If the database is mostly used for retrieving information (e.g., content distribution or page serving), then the bottleneck problem can be alleviated by replication and periodic refresh. However, when transactions result in database update, the backend databases need to consistent with one another. While the database community has developed solutions to provide concurrent database systems, we admit that for a large scale system, the database subsystem may prove to be the true source of bottleneck for certain class of applications.

As we noted earlier, a Grid request can be executed in multiple Grid nodes for reasons of fault-tolerance. Replicating a transaction is straightforward if the transaction does not update the backend database. However if the transaction modifies the database, then the system must commit only one of the replicated transactions. Such scenarios warrant a database middleware that identifies such replicated transactions (using an unique transaction identifier) and commits only one of them. Our current implementation supports only replication of read-only transactions. For update transactions, we plan to build such database middleware for replicated transactions in the future.

5 Performance Evaluation

5.1 Performance Modeling

We now describe a model for quantifying the variability in the capabilities of the resources that are used to form the resource grid. From our model, we try to infer the maximum throughput that is deliverable to a Grid client by our system, and compare it with our observations.

Assuming that a set of resources $0..m$ are available to be utilized, we associate a normalization factor, f_i, with each resource i. This factor quantifies the capabilities of a computing resource, and is the ratio of the capability of a particular resource with that of the best one available. Thus f_i varies in the set $(0..1]$.

We assume a set of types of requests from Grid clients $0..n$. For each request, we define the normalized service time, s_j, which is the time required by a Grid node with $f_i = 1$ to service a request of type j. In addition, we define the node service time, s_{ij}, as the time required by the node i to service a request of type j. It follows from the definition that $s_{ij} = s_j/f_i$. We note here that both s_j and s_{ij} are defined assuming that the nodes on which they are running are fully available for the Grid workload, without any timesharing or multitasking.

The availabilities of each resource are predicted at regular intervals, δt. This availability is a function of time (which varies from 0 to T). We define $p_i(t)$ as the fraction of the ith resource available at time t. $p_i(t)$ varies from 0 (when the machine is not available to the Grid) to 1 (when the machine can be fully dedicated to the Grid workload).

If $a_i(t)$ is the actual fraction of resource i available at time t, and δa is the time interval between our observations of resource availability (note that δa need not necessarily be the same as δt), $A_{ij}(q)$, the maximum number of requests for service j that can potentially be processed by node i over time $0..q$ is equal to $\sum_{t=0}^{q/\delta a} a_i(t*\delta a)*f_i*\delta a/s_j$. The maximum number of requests that can potentially be processed by the Grid, $A_j(q)$, equals $\sum_{i=0}^{m} A_{ij}(q)$.

If $O_j(q)$ is the observed number of requests for service j that are processed in our implementation during time $0..q$, we can define the observed efficiency of our system, $o_j(q)$, as $O_j(q)/A_j(q)$.

It is worth noting that our model has a few limitations. In particular, it assumes no latencies between the Grid client and the Gateway, and between the Gateway and the Grid node. In addition, we neglect the scheduling overhead at the Gateway.

5.2   Experiment Setup

We tested the performance of our system on a small scale with a set of five Grid nodes. We logged the CPU utilization of the interactive workloads of desktops used by the administrative personnel in our lab. These logs were used to simulate the interactive workloads on three of our Grid nodes. By doing this, we are able to simulate a real world situation where idle cycles can be used from desktops serving common users. These desktops will typically be highly available for Grid users as compared to the ones serving as development and production machines. We assumed two of our Grid nodes to be available all the time.

From our experiments, we compare the observed throughput ($O_j(q)$) with the maximum available throughput ($A_j(q)$) and determine the efficiency of our system. This efficiency depends on the accuracy of our predictions, and the associated overheads (as noted in the preceding subsection). Also, we verify that our predictions are reasonably accurate for the type of workloads we used in our experiments.

In order to measure the maximum observed throughput, we had to generate enough requests to keep the Grid nodes busy at all times they were available. To do so, we created a traffic generator that would generate a request as soon as it would receive a response to its prior call. In addition, this traffic generator is multi-threaded ensuring that multiple requests can be made in parallel, in order to keep all the Grid nodes busy at all available times.

5.3   Performance Analysis

The individual service times for our transaction on different Grid nodes is as shown in Table 1. We calculate the normalization factors f_i for each of the Grid nodes from the individual service times. We computed the actual availabilities of the individual Grid nodes, $a_i(t)$, from the utilization logs used for simulating the interactive workload on the desktops and is given in Table 2. The average availability of the three non-dedicated Grid nodes is close to 100%. This is because the CPU utilization of interactive workload is bursty in nature and lasts for a short period, thereby providing a high *average* availability. For example, the actual availability of Node 3 can be seen in Figure 2, and its bursty usage pattern is apparent from it.

<table>
<tr><td colspan="2" align="center">Table 1.</td><td colspan="3" align="center">Table 2.</td></tr>
<tr><th>Node</th><th>Service Times (ms)</th><th>Node</th><th>Availability</th><th>Prediction Accuracy</th></tr>
<tr><td>Node 1</td><td align="center">914</td><td>Node 1</td><td>100%</td><td>-</td></tr>
<tr><td>Node 2</td><td align="center">912</td><td>Node 2</td><td>100%</td><td>-</td></tr>
<tr><td>Node 3</td><td align="center">1060</td><td>Node 3</td><td>99%</td><td>90%</td></tr>
<tr><td>Node 4</td><td align="center">1384</td><td>Node 4</td><td>99%</td><td>89%</td></tr>
<tr><td>Node 5</td><td align="center">1652</td><td>Node 5</td><td>99%</td><td>93%</td></tr>
</table>

From Tables 1 and 2, we computed the maximum number of requests that can be potentially served $A_j(q)$, where q, the duration of the experiment, is 3570 seconds. $A_j(q)$ is found to be equal to 15872. We observed that our system was able to service 14594 requests during the same time $(O_j(q))$. Thus, the efficiency of our system, $o_j(q)$, is 0.92. Apart from the overheads in the system, a potential factor that can cause a decrease in the efficiency is a faulty prediction scheme. From Table 2, we can see that our predictions are accurate for around 90% of the times for each of the Grid nodes.

Thus, from our experiments, we observe an efficiency factor of 0.92, which implies that the system is able to utilize over 90% of the unutilized desktop resources for running transactional workloads. This also implies that (i) the overheads introduced by request redirection at the Gateway is minimal, and (ii) the prediction algorithm is effective enough to handle the bursty desktop

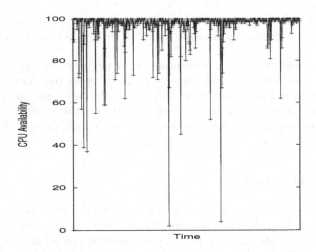

Fig. 2. The actual usage pattern for Node 3.

workloads with minimal overhead. We note that our studies are simple in nature as they were conducted with a relatively small number of desktops. We are planning to extend this study to include a larger number of desktops with more comprehensive workload scenarios. We are also planning to develop a simulator to analyze our model with a large set of parameters.

6 Related Work

There are several groups working on resource management in the context of grid and peer computing, although their motivations and approaches differ from ours.

One of the leading projects addressing scheduling for the Grid is Condor. Condor is a specialized workload management system for compute-intensive jobs [14]. It provides mechanisms for job queuing, scheduling, resource monitoring and resource management. The *ClassAd* mechanism provides a way of matching job requirements with resource offers. A central manager is responsible for scheduling the jobs on resources by matching these ClassAds. Certain types of jobs can also be checkpointed and migrated if the availability of the resources change during the course of execution of the job. Our target workloads are not the typical long-running scientific workloads that Condor targets, but are instead transactional workloads that have shorter turn-around times. Hence, migration does not make much sense in our case. In addition, evaluation of complicated ClassAds may be too much of an overhead for transactional workloads. In our case, requests from Grid clients for these transactions may arrive at a high rate. This necessitates replication of services so that requests from Grid clients can be processed in parallel. Condor is not based on such a request-response model, and does not need to replicate any jobs explicitly. To ensure higher throughput, it is also imperative that we predict the availability of our resources. Condor does not do any prediction of resource availability, and this makes sense in the case of long-running computational workloads, since the availability of resources can not be accurately predicted over long lengths of time. However, in our case, each request from a Grid client can be serviced in a short period of time, and predictions can be made reasonably accurately for shorter time intervals.

Another class of applications that are related to our work are the several projects dealing with *Volunteer Computing*, viz. Bayanihan [13], SETI@home, `distributed.net`, Entropia [7], etc. Typically, all such applications try to leverage cycles from voluntary underutilized resources on the Internet, and deal with applications that are embarrassingly parallel. In general, no guarantees are provided for the performance that can be obtained from such a set of resources. The scheduling policies of most such systems are not very complicated, since the participating resources *pull* work from a centralized *Work Manager* as and when they run out of work to execute. There is generally enough work to be pulled from such Work Managers to keep all the resources busy when they would otherwise be idle. In our case, we don't have a pool of work to keep distributing among the grid resources. Instead, the amount of work to be done depends on the outstanding requests from the Grid clients. Thus, our work differs from traditional Volunteer Computing in the type of workloads that we target.

Leff et al [9] try to address delivering Service Level Agreements (SLAs) for commercial (transactional) workloads. However, their emphasis is not on leveraging idle cycles from resources, but reconfiguring resources inside a resource pool so that the number of resources that are currently serving customer requests are optimal for the SLAs agreed upon. They provide the scheduling of requests using a Network Dispatcher (ND) [2], which is a load-balancing switch that distributes requests across a server cluster. Hence, it is not very suitable to deal with requests to multiple services in the same resource pool. Currently, there is no prediction information being used, although it is part of their long term goals. Crawford et al [6] have also discussed a Grid using dedicated set of servers for deploying financial and content distribution type of applications. They describe a Topology Aware Grid Services Scheduler (TAGSS) for dynamic creation and deployment of Grid services.

7   Concluding Remarks

In this paper, we have described a middleware architecture that enables policy based sharing of enterprise resources by two types of workloads: (i) a resource specific workload and (ii) a Web Services based grid workload. We have designed and implemented the system where desktop based resources are the shared resources. These type of resources represent a rich source of underutilized resources in many organizations and also because the resource specific workload (in this case, the interactive workload submitted by desktop users) is more likely to be non-correlated with any external grid workload. We address the key concerns of desktop users for responsiveness, privacy and protection by isolating the grid workload in a virtual machine in the desktop. The proposed architecture and its key design concepts are equally applicable to other types of resources in an enterprise, e.g., they can be the servers that are primarily used for running backend applications that can be shared by their primary workload and the grid workload.

The salient components of our middleware architecture are: (i) Grid Resource Manager, (ii) End-point resource agents, and (iii) Scheduler and Router. Together, these components enable dynamic discovery of resources, identification of services offered to grid workload on the resources, predicted capacity available to grid workload, policy management, deployment and provisioning of services, and transparent scheduling and routing of the grid workload. With this middleware, individual resources are free to join and disconnect, based on their local policies, from the pool of resources available to the grid workload. The middleware manages these changes transparently from the grid clients as well as from the other resources in the pool. The scheduling of grid workload adapts dynamically to the availability and sharing capabilities of the individual resources.

To deploy and process Web Services, we use IBM WebSphere Application Server – a J2EE container – on each shared resource. Use of such a container has advantages and disadvantages. The container masks the heterogeneity in the underlying resources and creates a homogeneous environment so a request can be processed on any one of resources. For Web Services based workload this choice works out very well. However, for any workload that is not supported by the current container technology, the middleware discussed here may not be readily suitable. We also note that in the current release of WebSphere Network Deployment Edition (Release 5), multiple application servers can be configured to form a cell and requests can be processed on any one of the members of such a cell, transparent to the client making the request [3]. Such a cell is essentially a static cluster of application servers that cannot dynamically join and disconnect from the cell without affecting the operations in the rest of the cell. In our approach, we do not use WebSphere's network deployment mechanisms. Our middleware is designed specifically to handle dynamic changes in the resource availability. The main difference between our system and a statically configured system is that in our system the actual resources providing a service may enter and exit the resource pool, but the system continues to service client requests and clients are unaware of the low level dynamic changes taking place in the system. However, many of the reliability issues are handled in a manner similar to those in a statically configured system. In addition, the Gateway maintains the client request state until a response is sent back. By continuously monitoring the availability of the underlying resources providing a service and by discovering and provisioning additional resources the system tries to masks the changes from the clients of the service.

One disadvantage of using managed container such as that provided by Web-Sphere is that configuring and deploying such a container is not trivial and requires some domain specific expertise. In our approach, we deploy virtual machines that are pre-configured with the WebSphere Application Server. This reduces some of the system management complexities and improves the degree to which the resource configuration can be automated. However, because of the bandwidth requirements, our solution is well suited for resources in an intranet environment and not over a wide area network. Recently efficient mechanisms have been proposed for migrating virtual machine states [12] and we are investigating the applicability of such approaches to our work. Similarly, in the three-tier distributed computing model (i.e., client logic, business logic, and data logic) that is inherent to most business processes and is supported by the J2EE technology, a Web Service providing the business logic may require access to a database for state information. In this work, we assume that a Web Service can access the necessary state information from any of the resources where it may be deployed. Again for this reason, the solution discussed here is better suited for an intranet environment. Note that resources over the intranet can belong to multiple administrative domains.

Another point to note here is that in our approach, the request to a Web Service is trapped in the Gateway before it is routed to the most suitable resource available at that time. This requires partial processing of the request at the "Network Layer 7" and this may introduce significant overhead especially when the service time of the request is relatively short. However, the advantages of processing requests at Layer 7 are obvious as reflected in our architecture.

Resource sharing across multiple workloads, as described in this paper, is effective when the capacity prediction mechanisms are accurate. Primarily, we rely on predictions about the available capacity on each shared resource for the grid workload. When a resource is to be shared with an interactive workload, as we do in this work, the prediction mechanisms have certain limitations. By sampling over a long period of time and by using techniques based on time series analysis, one can identify daily, weekly, and seasonal patterns in the utilization for each type of resource for a specific workload. For example, desktop utilization during evening and night hours is mostly zero while during the day time on a weekdays it is significantly higher. In the case of interactive workload, for the intervals where there are no long term patterns, fairly accurate short term predictions may be possible. We discuss one such mechanism in [11] that we found to perform reasonably well. However, the effectiveness of such an approach diminishes for large time intervals (e.g., larger than tens of minutes) and intervals that are further away in the future. We note that in case of many business application that run on backend servers, the workload is more predictable than the interactive workloads on the desktops. In such cases, the resource sharing can be more straightforward. Similarly, predictions about workload arrival patterns can improve the effectiveness of dynamic resource provisioning. We note that the predictions need not be highly accurate, but higher accuracy can result in better performance (i.e., response time or throughput) using a smaller number of resources.

Our results and experience so far with the system we have developed have been encouraging and lead us believe that our middleware provides a flexible design for sharing enterprise resources by a resource specific workload and a global Web Services based workload. In an enterprise environment, such a system can be used for off-loading peak demands at data centers and backend servers, for testing and deploying new releases of backend applications or for improving the availability of existing mission critical backend infrastructure, by sharing underutilized resources across an organization.

In the future, we plan to expand the scope of this word along the following dimensions: (i) to share a resource across multiple types workloads, (ii) use of a light weight virtual machine, (iii) development and testing of other prediction algorithms, and (iv) affinity based request routing.

References

1. Apache SOAP, as of July 2004. http://ws.apache.org/soap/.
2. IBM Network Dispatcher User's Guide, as of July 2004. ftp://ftp.software.ibm.com/software/websphere/info/edgeserver/ndugv3-us.pdf.
3. IBM WebSphere, as of July 2004. http://www.ibm.com/websphere/.
4. VMWare, as of July 2004. http://www.vmware.com/.
5. J. Chung, K. Lin, and R. Mathieu. Guest Editor's Introduction–Web Services Computing: Advancing Software Interoperability. *Computer 36(10)*, 2003.
6. C. H. Crawford, D. M. Dias, A. K. Iyengar, M. Novaes, and L. Zhang. Commercial Applications of Grid Computing, Jan. 2003. IBM Research Report, RC22702, IBM T. J. Watson Research Center, Yorktown Heights, NY, USA.
7. Entropia PC Grid Computing. DCGrid Platform, as of July 2004. http://www.entropia.com/dcgrid_platform.asp.
8. I. Foster, C. Kesselman, J. Nick, and S. Tuecke. Grid Services for Distributed System Integration. *Computer 35(6)*, 2002.
9. A. Leff, J. T. Rayfield, and D. M. Dias. Service-Level Agreements and Commercial Grids. In *IEEE Internet Computing, Special Issue on Grid Computing*, July 2003.
10. S. Microsystems. J2EE Platform Specification, 2002. http://java.sun.com/j2ee/.
11. V. K. Naik, S. Sivasubramanian, D. F. Bantz, and S. Krishnan. Harmony: A Desktop Grid for Delivering Enterprise Computations. November 2003.
12. C. P. Sapuntzakis, R. Chandra, B. Pfaff, J. Chow, M. S. Lam, and M. Rosenblum. Optimizing the migration of virtual computers. In *Proceedings of the 5th Symposium on Operating Systems Design and Implementation*, December 2002.
13. L. Sarmenta. Web-based Volunteer Computing using Java. In *Proc. 2nd Intl. Conference on Worldwide Computing and its Applications*, 1998.
14. T. Tannenbaum, D. Wright, K. Miller, and M. Livny. *Beowulf Cluster Computing with Linux*, chapter 15, Condor - A Distributed Job Scheduler. MIT Press, 2002.

Interoperability Among Independently Evolving Web Services

Shankar R. Ponnekanti and Armando Fox

Stanford University

Abstract. The increasing popularity of XML Web services motivates us to examine if it is feasible to substitute one vendor service for another when using a Web-based application, assuming that these services are "derived from" a common base. If such substitution were possible, end users could use the same application with a variety of back-end vendor services, and the vendors themselves could compete on price, quality, availability, etc. Interoperability with substituted services is non-trivial, however, and four types of incompatibilities may arise during such interoperation – *structural, value, encoding* and *semantic*. We address these incompatibilities three-fold: (1) static and dynamic analysis tools to infer whether an application is compatible with a substituted service, (2) semi-automatically generated middleware components called *cross-stubs* that actually resolve incompatibilities and enable interoperation with substituted services, and (3) a lightweight mechanism called *multi-option types* to enable applications to be written from the ground up in an interoperation-friendly manner. Using real applications and services as examples, we both demonstrate and evaluate our tools and techniques for enabling interoperation with substituted services.

1 Introduction

Maintaining interoperability among independently evolving components is an important but challenging problem in distributed systems (e.g., Vinoski [1]). We address a variant of this problem in the context of SOAP/WSDL based XML Web services. Multiple Web service vendors (e.g., Google, Hotbot and Altavista) may offer services with substantially similar functionality, and this leads to two scenarios: (1) *autonomous services*, where each vendor independently defines his WSDL service, or (2) *derived services*, where once a vendor becomes popular, other vendors adopt and extend the popular vendor's service. This paper shows that if vendors cooperate and espouse the derived services model, cross-vendor interoperability can be achieved. (While our techniques also apply to the autonomous services case, it is much more difficult, as explained in section 8.)

The derived services case, illustrated in figure 1, is a variant of the independent evolution problem, since each of the derived vendor services represents an independent extension of the base service. Our goal is to facilitate interoperation with *non-native services*, i.e., services other than the one the application was originally written to. (See the figure for more details.) E.g., a Google application

H.-A. Jacobsen (Ed.): Middleware 2004, LNCS 3231, pp. 331–351, 2004.

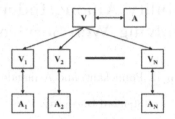

Fig. 1. Vendors $V_1, V_2, \ldots, V_N$ derive their services from base service V. Applications $A_1, A_2, \ldots, A_N$ are written to services $V_1, V_2, \ldots, V_N$ respectively. We refer to the service V_i as the *native* or *source* service of A_i, while all other services $V_j, j \neq i$ and V are considered *non-native* services for A_i. For an application A written to base service V, all of the derived services $V_1, V_2, \ldots, V_N$ are non-native services. Only a sibling, parent or a child of the source service – and not any unrelated service – qualifies as a non-native service. We only consider one level of derivation in this paper.

should ideally interoperate with other search engines also, a driving directions application written to an existing provider (e.g., Arcweb) should be switchable to a future provider that offers traffic-sensitive driving directions. Much like other services in the economy such as credit-cards and insurance services, the choice of a Web service depends on many factors (cost, reputation, quality, speed, etc.), all of which vary over time, apart from the fact that some vendors may shut down and others may come online. E.g., Inktomi was once the dominant search provider, today it is Google, and it might be Microsoft or Yahoo in the future. Lack of interoperability with non-native vendors can significantly undermine the "revolution" promised by Web service proponents. An analogy is being unable to switch credit card, cellphone, insurance or mortgage providers.

Non-native service interoperability is challenging however – in section 2, we identify four types of incompatibilities it may entail: *structural, value, encoding* and *semantic*. We address this problem with static/dynamic analysis and middleware based tools and techniques, and the results obtained with existing Web services and applications are summarized below:

- Static analysis reveals that many Web service applications only use a fraction of a service's functionality, making the proposition of interoperation with non-native services a reasonable one.
- For existing applications and services we have studied, a combination of static and dynamic analysis is sufficient to make automated determinations of compatibility with non-native services.
- Actual interoperation with the non-native service can be realized through semi-automatically generated *cross-stubs*. Cross-stub generation involves incompatibility resolution when the application is not fully compatible with the non-native service, and is done using a GUI-based tool.
- A number of incompatible application-service pairs we studied indicates that incompatibilities often arise due to *non-critical* reasons – reasons that do not hamper the basic functioning of the application.

- If applications are authored using our proposed *multi-option types*, it is possible to automatically determine whether incompatibilities with a non-native service are non-critical, and if so, automatically resolve the incompatibilities.

To summarize, an application owner (i.e., a developer or a user/administrator) can (1) auto-determine which non-native services are fully compatible, (2) set up interoperation even with incompatible services, provided the incompatibilities are (manually) determined to be non-critical, and (3) for applications written with multi-option types, even auto-determine whether the incompatibilities with a non-native service are non-critical, and if so, auto-resolve them.

In the context of XML applications and services, HydroJ [2] has recently addressed the evolution problem by building upon "XML pattern languages" [3]. While HydroJ proposes new kinds of language types and paradigms, we address the problem using the *static host types* approach, in which WSDL specifications are statically mapped to language types in the client application. The static host types approach is already widely adopted through Web service toolkits such as AXIS, Glue, Wasp and .NET, making our approach easier to deploy and also applicable to legacy applications. Furthermore, we go beyond HydroJ by providing a mechanism for resolving incompatibilities if a desired non-native service is not fully compatible, and we also propose multi-option types to further enhance interoperability. Vinoski [1] observes that the static host types approach is convenient but sacrifices XML flexibility, a limitation we address in this paper.

Although our work is implemented in the context of Web services due to the current interest in these technologies, our techniques are more generally applicable. Also, while our focus is on *cross-vendor* interoperability, our techniques can also be applied to the (simpler) *cross-version* interoperability problem, where an application needs to interoperate with multiple versions of the same vendor service. The rest of the paper proceeds as follows. Section 2 describes service derivations and the types of incompatibilities that may arise with non-native services. Section 3 describes the static and dynamic analysis algorithms and tools we use to identify compatibility between applications and non-native services. Section 4 describes incompatibility resolution and cross-stubs. Section 5 reports experiments with existing Web services (Google, Mappoint and Arcweb) and existing client applications. Section 6 describes our proposal for authoring future client applications in an interoperation-friendly manner. We discuss semantic issues in section 7, related work in section 8 and conclude in section 9.

2   Service Derivations and Incompatibilities

2.1   Background

A WSDL *service* (see figure 2 for an example) is a collection of *porttypes* (which roughly correspond to RPC interfaces, although Web services are *not* equivalent to traditional distributed objects [4–6]), each of which supports a set of *operations*. An operation has input and output *messages*. The types of input and output messages are specified using XML schema. (We sometimes use the terms parameters and returns to denote inputs and outputs respectively.) XML schema defines built-in *simple types* (int, float, string, etc.) and allows *complex types* to be built up from them. Unlike most traditional type systems, type derivation in XML schema allows for both *extension* and *restriction*. Thus, a complex type can be extended by adding new mandatory or optional elements, and also restricted by removing optional (but not mandatory) elements. In addition, the value space of simple types can be restricted (but not extended) by applying one or more *facets* such as enumeration, regular expression pattern, minimum/maximum value, etc.

Limitations: For the reader familiar with XML schema, we only consider complex types with element-only content, and do not consider identity constraints, wildcards or substitution groups. For a reader familiar with WSDL, we deal with document style and RPC-style operations in this paper, but not the other lesser known and used operation styles. Finally, we only consider one level of service derivation. (Service derivation is explained below.) Some of these excluded features may not raise any new issues, and none are used by the services we have experimented with so far, but we plan to consider them in future work when services using them become available.

2.2   WSDL Service Derivation

The WSDL specification does not yet define service derivation. One might imagine two types of derivations: add/remove an operation or extend/restrict the input and output message types of an operation. As an example, two vendors etailer1 and etailer2 could independently derive from vendor etailer's service of figure 2 as follows:

- etailer1 adds customer ratings. Accordingly, etailer1 extends `KSRequest` to `KSRequest1` by adding an optional `minRating` field. Similarly, `Product` is extended to `Product1` by adding an optional `rating` field.
- etailer2 does not sell books, and does not maintain sales ranks. So, etailer2 restricts `Category` to `Category2`, which only allows "All", "Music" and "Movies". Also, `Product` is restricted to derived type `Product2`, which removes the optional `salesrank` field.

Independent extensions (but not restrictions) can lead to semantic conflicts if two vendors each add a field with the same name but different "meanings". This problem is avoided in XML schema if each vendor defines his extensions in his own namespace. Thus, the `minRating` field added by etailer1 belongs to namespace "etailer1", and our techniques (conservatively) consider it as different from a `minRating` field added by another vendor. If, on the other hand, a vendor wishes to reuse a field with the same semantics added by another vendor, there is a mechanism to import an element from another namespace in XML schema.

While XML schema allows both extension/restriction for complex types by adding/removing fields, it only allows restriction of the value spaces of simple

```
<definitions targetNamespace="etailer">
  <portType name="EShop">
    <operation name="keywordSearch">
      <inputpart name="request" type="KSRequest"/>
      <outputpart name="product" type="Product"/>
    </operation>
  </portType>
  <complexType name="KSRequest">
    <element name="keyword" type="string"/>
    <element name="category" type="Category" minOccurs="0"/>
  </complexType>
  <complexType name="Product">
    <element name="id" type="string"/>
    <element name="category" type="Category"/>
    <element name="salesrank" type="int" minOccurs="0"/>
  </complexType>
  <simpleType name="Category">
    <restriction base="string">
      <enumeration values="All, Books, Music, Movies"/>
    </restriction>
  </simpleType>
</definitions>
```

Fig. 2. A vendor named etailer defines a WSDL service in the "etailer" namespace containing a porttype EShop with a single operation keywordSearch with input type KSRequest and output type Product. KSRequest has two fields: a keyword and an optional category that can take one of four values "All", "Books", "Music" or "Movies". The output type Product has three fields: id, category and salesrank. (We use some notational shortcuts here, e.g., inputpart and outputpart are not legal WSDL elements.)

types. Value space extension, while useful for deriving services, raises the same semantic issues as adding fields. Unlike fields, values have no namespaces, but we can address this problem with facets, as discussed in section 7.

2.3 Types of Incompatibility

Given the service derivation scheme of the previous section, four types of incompatibilities may arise between applications and non-native services: *structural*, *value*, *encoding* and *semantic*. A structural incompatibility is a mismatch in the structure of the (XML) message sent by the sender and expected by the receiver, while a value incompatibility arises when the structure is as expected, but the filled-in values are unexpected. The bulk of the paper deals with structural and value incompatibilities (together referred to as *SV-incompatibilities*), and they are explained in more detail below. Encoding incompatibilities, illustrated and addressed in section 4, arise because instances belonging to different schema types are not identical even if they have the same structure and identical values. As explained in the previous section, semantic incompatibilities arise when different vendors introduce extensions with identical syntax (i.e., same structure and value) but differing meanings, and the problem can be alleviated by namespaces and facets as further discussed in section 7.

Considering applications written to a given source service S, a non-native target service T may differ from S in the following ways, each of which represents a kind of SV-incompatibility:

- Missing methods: If T removes a method from the base service, or if S adds a method, S-applications may use this method and hence be incompatible with T. The converse case of extra methods in T does not cause an incompatibility.
- Extra fields: If T adds a field f to the base service, or if S removes f, S-applications do not use f, but T expects a value for f if it is mandatory (minOccurs > 0). No incompatibility occurs for optional extra fields, or for extra T fields in method outputs (as opposed to method inputs).
- Missing fields: If T removes (or S adds) a field f, S-applications using this field are incompatible with T. Incompatibility occurs even if f is optional (minOccurs=0) – if an S-application uses an optional field, it may be important to the application, and cannot be ignored.
- Facet mismatches: If S and T have different facets for an input field f, where the value space for $S.f \nsubseteq$ the value space for $T.f$, values passed by S-applications may be disallowed for T resulting in incompatibility. For output fields, incompatibility occurs when value space of $T.f \nsubseteq$ value space of $S.f$.
- Cardinality mismatches: If S and T have different cardinality requirement for a field f, as when T declares minOccurs=3 and S declares minOccurs=2, incompatibility may result.

In the first case, we refer to the offending method m as the *causal method*, while in other cases the offending field is called the *causal field*. In the last four cases, we further distinguish whether the causal field is an input/output field. These incompatibility categories are summarized in figure 3. In the examples we have experimented with so far, $I_1 - I_5$ (missing methods, missing/extra fields and input facet mismatches) are prevalent, while the others are rare. Finally, note that all the SV-incompatibilities can be detected automatically given the source and target service WSDL specifications.

3   Application Usage Behavior and Compatibility

While the incompatibilities of figure 3 represent *all* the potential SV-incompatibilities between S and T, many of them are irrelevant for a given S-application A, e.g., an I_1-category incompatibility is irrelevant for A if A never calls the causal method. In this section, we discuss how we gather the method and field usage information from the application.

3.1   Usage Inference with Static Analysis

As noted earlier, our approach is primarily intended for applications written using static host types. In the static host types approach, the WSDL specification

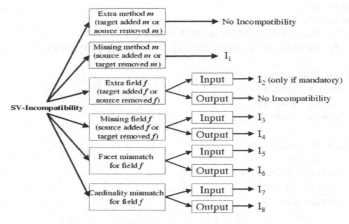

Fig. 3. The possible SV-incompatibilities (i.e., structural and value incompatibilities) when applications written to service S interoperate with a non-native service T. T may differ from S in having extra/missing methods, extra/missing fields or cardinality/facet mismatches. The I_2 incompatibility occurs only if the causal field is mandatory i.e., minOccurs>0. (Other incompatibilities can occur even with optional fields).

and XML schema types are mapped to Java classes, and applications are written using these classes. The Java classes generated for etailer1's service, and sample application code using this service is shown in figure 4.

Our static analysis tool, called UAT-S (usage analysis tool-static) identifies which fields of the inputs are filled in by the application, and for leaf-level fields UAT-S also determines which values they are set to. Similarly, UAT-S also identifies which output fields of the service result are actually consumed by the application. To do this, UAT-S performs an interprocedural points-to analysis [7] on the application code. For each call site of every method in the service interface, UAT-S determines which allocation sites the parameters and returns (and their subfields) can point to. Based on these points-to sets, UAT-S generates *usage tuples*, such as shown below for the application code in figure 4:

```
T1   <method, keywordSearch>
T2   <method, alsoBought>
T3   <input, keywordSearch@param1.category, known, "Music", appCode>
T4   <input, keywordSearch@param1.keyword, unknown>
T5   <input, alsoBought@param1, return, keywordSearch@return.id>
T6   <input, alsoBought@param2, return, keywordSearch@return.category>
T7   <output, keywordSearch@return.id>
T8   <output, keywordSearch@return.salesrank>
     . . . . .
```

The first component indicates whether the tuple refers to a method or an input/output field. The second component identifies the method or the input/output field. A method tuple identifies that the specified method is invoked

```
package etailer1;
public interface JEShop1 {
  public JProduct1 keywordSearch(JKSRequest1 x);
  public JProduct1[] alsoBought(String id, String category);
}
public class JKSRequest1 {
  public String keyword;
  public String category;
  public Integer minRating;
}
public class JProduct1 {
  public String id;
  public String category;
  public Integer salesrank;
  public Integer rating;
}
public class JEShop1Stub implements JEShop1 { .. }
// Sample application code
L1   JEShop1Stub stub = new JEShop1Stub();
L2   JKSRequest1 req = new JKSRequest1();
L3   req.category = "Music";
L4   req.keyword = infile.read(..);
L5   JProduct1 prod = stub.keywordSearch(req);
L6   outfile.write(prod.id, prod.salesrank);
L7   JProduct1[] others = stub.alsoBought(prod.id, prod.category);
```

Fig. 4. Java classes generated for the etailer1 service of section 2. We add an extra method "alsoBought" here, which returns other products purchased by customers who bought a given product. Notice how the code "pipes back" the id and category fields of the keywordSearch return from line L5 to the alsoBought method on line L7.

at some call site in the application. For input tuples, the third component can be known, unknown or return as explained below:

- known: This means at some service callsite, the application passes a known value for this field. For example, T3 was derived from line L3 of the sample code. For known input tuples, the final component indicates the source of this value, i.e., application or library code.
- unknown: This means at some service callsite, the value passed to this field cannot be statically determined. T4 and line L4 illustrate this case.
- return: This means that at some callsite, the value passed to this field was obtained as a return from another callsite. For example, T5 indicates that prod.id obtained as return from keywordSearch on line L5 is piped back to alsoBought on line L7.

The output tuples record which output fields are consumed by the application. For example, T7,T8 indicate that output fields id and salesrank were consumed (line L6). The input field minRating is never used by the application, and the output field rating is never consumed, so no tuples are generated for them.

Input tuples of type "known" and "unknown" are only generated for leaf level input fields. Values are not recorded for outputs (unlike for inputs), and we assume that services can generate any legal output value (i.e., any value allowed by the facets declared in the specification).

3.2 Compatibility Based on Statically Inferred Usage Behavior

We provide a tool CAT-S (compatibility analysis tool-static) that uses the usage tuples to eliminate irrelevant SV-incompatibilities between the source and target interfaces. Each incompatibility i is processed by CAT-S as follows depending on which category (among $I_1 - I_8$ from figure 3) it belongs to:

- I_1: If the causal missing method m is never invoked, i.e., there is no method usage tuple for m, i is irrelevant.
- I_2: If the causal extra field belongs to method m, and there is no usage tuple for m, i is irrelevant, because the method to which the extra field belongs to is never invoked.
- I_3-I_4: If there is no usage tuple for the causal missing field f, i is irrelevant because the missing field is never used.
- I_5: If there is no input tuple for the causal field f, i is irrelevant. Otherwise, set RELEVANT to false and iterate through each input usage tuple t involving f:
  - If t's type is unknown, set RELEVANT to true. This is because if the value for f at some call site is unknown, we assume (conservatively) that it can be the worst case value – one that causes the incompatibility.
  - If t's type is known, and the known value is disallowed by the target service's facets for f, set RELEVANT to true, else leave RELEVANT unchanged.
  - If t's type is return, and if the piped return field is r (for example, in tuple T6, $r =$ keywordSearch@return.category and $f =$ alsoBought @param2), if the target service's value space for $r \not\subseteq$ the target service's value space for f, we set RELEVANT to true, else leave RELEVANT unchanged. (This is because the value returned by the target service for r is being sent back to the target service as f, so there is no incompatibility if the value space for $r \subseteq$ the value space for f.)

  Once we have iterated through all tuples involving f, if RELEVANT is false, i cannot occur and is irrelevant.
- I_6-I_8: If there is no usage tuple for the causal field f, i is irrelevant.

First, the asymmetry in handling inputs vs. outputs in rules I_5 and I_6 arises because, as noted earlier, we assume that services can generate any legal value allowed by the declared facets. Second, the above rules are correct, but not optimal as elaborated below:

Correctness: The points-to analysis we perform as part of UAT-S can escape assignments when the application code uses native methods, dynamically loaded code (using URLClassLoader) or reflection. In these cases, the above rules only declare incompatibilities as "likely irrelevant" rather than irrelevant. In other cases, the above rules are always conservative.

Optimality: The above rules for $I_5 - I_8$ are not optimal – unlike missing method and missing/extra field incompatibilities, exact constraint and facet compatibility cannot always be determined statically for applications written in general-purpose languages such as Java, so we err on the conservative side. For example, it is possible that an application always passes values allowed by the target service facets, but if the values passed cannot be statically determined (i.e., there is an unknown input usage tuple for this field), the above rule for I_5 (conservatively) does *not* rule the incompatibility as irrelevant. Similarly, fields that can occur multiple times are typically modeled as arrays in the static host types approach, and optimal detection of cardinality incompatibilities requires that the array lengths be determined statically, which is not always possible.

We have rarely encountered $I_6 - I_8$ incompatibilities in the examples we have dealt with so far, although I_5 incompatibilities are quite frequent. Dynamic analysis (discussed in the next section) partially addresses the sub-optimality of the rules in this case.

3.3 Dynamic Analysis

Dynamic analysis complements static analysis, especially when an application can theoretically generate an incompatible message, but never does so in practice. To enable dynamic analysis, we track the input messages sent by the application to the service at runtime in normal operation. Message interception can be performed at the stubs if they are suitably instrumented, or using a network-level proxy otherwise. Since we control stub generation, we use the former approach. CAT-D (compatibility analysis tool-dynamic) simply checks if all the past input messages sent by the application are compatible for the target service. Clearly, the effectiveness of CAT-D increases as time of capture increases. Dynamic message tracking and compatibility checking is technically straightforward, so we do not discuss further mechanical details.

Summary of compatibility determination: When it is desired to switch an S-application A to one of several non-native target services, say available at a registry, we do the following for each target service T:

- Generate all SV-incompatibilities between S and T from their specifications.
- Using the usage tuples for A and the CAT-S rules, filter out irrelevant incompatibilities.
- Among the remaining incompatibilities (if any), mark the ones that do not occur in practice (as determined by CAT-D) as likely irrelevant.

The target services are ranked based on the remaining incompatibilities, referred to as *relevant incompatibilities*. While fully compatible target services (if any) are best from an interoperability standpoint, the application owner may still choose a not fully compatible target service for other reasons (cost, reputation, quality, etc), and the next section explains incompatibility resolution.

4   Cross-Stubs

Instead of a regular stub, the interaction between an application and a non-native target service is mediated at runtime by a semi-automatically generated middleware component called *cross-stub*. A cross-stub is link-compatible with a regular-stub, allowing the unmodified application to be run against the non-native service. When generating a cross-stub, the application owner must resolve the relevant incompatibilities (if any). The available resolution choices are:

1. Runtime exception: Here, the cross-stub throws a runtime exception when this incompatibility is detected at runtime. As indicated by JEShop1Stub, a network service application is already expected to handle an exception, for other reasons such as service and network failures. This choice is applicable for all incompatibility categories.
2. Ignore: For missing fields and for cardinality/facet mismatches involving optional fields, the owner may choose this option if it is acceptable for the causal field to be dropped.
3. Supply a value: For extra fields (category I_2), the owner can supply a value that should be used for this field.
4. Alternative value: For facet mismatch incompatibilities, the owner can provide a substitute value to be used when the value supplied by the application is disallowed by the target service facets. The substitutes can be tailored to the target service facets, as the following examples indicate:
   - Enumeration facet: A fixed substitute value is specified.
   - Range facet: The owner may choose to use the closest legal value.
   - Pattern facet: A search and replace substitute pattern (similar to the "s/../../" expressions of **sed** and **perl**) may be specified, and is applied when the original value is disallowed by the target service facets.

As an example for the pattern facet case, in both their Web UI and WSDL API, the Google query parameter allows special operators in queries, such as "foo file:pdf" and "foo site:cnn.com". If the target service specifies a pattern facet disallowing "file:" queries, the application owner can provide a substitute pattern that removes the "file:" terms from the query.

In all the above four options, the owner can optionally specify a *notify message*, to be displayed to the user (with a pop-up window) at runtime when the incompatibility occurs and the resolution action is taken. Once the owner resolves all the relevant incompatibilities, the cross-stub is auto-generated from the source and target service specifications and incorporates the resolution code.

For some incompatibilities, resolution may require more complex handling than selecting one of the standard resolution choices. (E.g., a missing method incompatibility may be better handled by invoking a third-party service.) Modifying the application sources (if at all available) is not desirable from a maintenance standpoint, because the core application logic should ideally be kept separate from the incompatibility handling code. For this purpose, we allow the application developer to optionally provide a *custom handler* (written to well-defined conventions) that is interposed between the application and the cross-stub. The custom handler may use arbitrary code to handle the incompatibility.

Another advantage of custom handlers is that they can be used to handle new types of incompatibilities. For example, extending the service derivation scheme of section 2 to allow derived services to add new fault types (i.e., exceptions) to existing operations results in a new type of incompatibility – mismatch in thrown fault types. Additional fault types introduced by the target non-native service can be handled in the custom handler.

During the resolution process, an application owner may determine that an incompatibility can not be handled and critically affects the functioning of the application, and thus abort the cross-stub generation process. In section 6, we examine how such aborts can be avoided by automatically determining beforehand whether the incompatibilities with a non-native service are critical.

In addition to implementing SV-incompatibility resolution, cross-stubs also handle *encoding incompatibilities* that arise because, as shown below, instances of different XML schema types (such as etailer1's KSRequest1 and etailer2's KSRequest2) derived from a common base type are not identical even if they contain the same (non-null) elements and values.

```
<KSRequest xsi:type="KSRequest1">
  <keyword xsi:type="string">foo</keyword>
  <category xsi:type="Category1">Music</category>
  <minRating xsi:type="int" xsi:nil="true"/>
</KSRequest>
<KSRequest xsi:type="KSRequest2">
  <keyword xsi:type="string">foo</keyword>
  <category xsi:type="Category2">Music</category>
</KSRequest>
```

Depending on how etailer2 service is implemented, it may expect the type attribute to be set to "KSRequest2", and hence not recognize even an SV-compatible KSRequest1 instance. To address this, a cross-stub from services S to T is link-compatible with an S stub, but generates messages on the wire identical to those generated by a T stub.

5   Experimental Results

Our implementation was primarily done within AXIS, an open source toolkit from Apache that implements static Java host types for WSDL services. Dynamic analysis and cross-stub generation was implemented by modifying the AXIS stub generators. UAT-S was implemented using joeq [8], which allows us to perform context-sensitive (but flow-insensitive) inter-procedural points-to analysis. We implemented an optional extension that allows the analysis to include primitives, i.e. an instruction that assigns the value 10 to a primitive int is considered as an allocation site that creates a `java.lang.Integer` object with value 10. In some cases, UAT-S declares a primitive value "unknown" even if a more detailed analysis could have ascertained a known value, e.g. static evaluation (or partial evaluation) of arithmetic expressions; but we have found that this does not significantly reduce the effectiveness of the analysis.

Table 1. Usage statistics extracted by UAT-S for several applications. These results indicate that the applications only exercise a fraction of the service functionality. For example, JDLS only accessed 4 out of 11 methods, and even among these 4 methods, filled in only 98/446 input fields and consumed only 58/380 output fields. (The 446 inputs/380 outputs belong to the 4 accessed methods only, not all the 11 methods.) The Google applications filled in all inputs because they were forced to – the 10 inputs are simple type parameters rather than fields of a single structure – but they exercise only a small fraction of the input value space for these parameters. E.g., the language and country restricts parameters permit search customized to hundreds of language and countries, but these applications only use a few of these options.

Application	Service	#meths	#used	#i/p	#filled	#o/p	#consumed
ORG #60	Google SearchService	3	1	10	10	27	6
ORG #69	Google SearchService	3	1	10	10	27	6
ORG #78	Google SearchService	3	1	10	10	27	6
ComparePop	Google SearchService	3	1	10	10	27	2
JDLS	Mappoint FindService	5	1	17	9	51	16
JDLS	Mappoint RenderService	4	2	327	39	48	17
JDLS	Mappoint RouteService	2	1	102	50	281	25
JDLS	All Mappoint Services	11	4	446	98	380	58
StoreLocator	All Mappoint Services	11	5	414	62	446	44
AW-apps	All Arcweb Services	45	13	446	134	210	83

We perform three sets of experiments. (1) Application usage behavior experiments, where we study what fraction of service functionality typical applications exercise. Non-native service interoperability is more likely to be successful if applications typically exercise only a small subset of the service functionality, because this small subset is likely also supported by non-native services. (2) Compatibility and integration experiments, where we demonstrate our tools and techniques in action. (3) Nature of incompatibilities experiments, where we study how often incompatibilities occur due to non-critical reasons. If incompatibilities frequently arise due to non-critical reasons, then non-native service interoperability can be further automated by employing *multi-option types* (to be described in section 6).

5.1   Application Usage Behavior

We examine several existing applications. The first three are taken from the O'Reilly book "Google Hacks", although we reimplemented them in Java. ComparePop is a Google application we wrote that compares relative popularity of search phrases across different languages (English, French, etc) based on the number of matches and where the words occur in the matching Web pages (title, URL or link). JDLS (Java Desktop Location Suite, a desktop application that provides maps, routes, panning/zooming, etc), StoreLocator (a JSP-based application created by a third-party vendor SpatialPoint) and AW-apps (collection of JSP applications accessing Arcweb location services) are available from the Mappoint and Arcweb web sites. Mappoint is a collection of three document style services (Find, Route and Render), while Arcweb, provided by the leading GIS software vendor ESRI, is RPC-style and consists of six different services. Both are quite complicated – for example, AXIS generates over 125 classes for Mappoint.

Table 1 shows the results produced by UAT-S on these applications. The results indicate that applications often only exercise a subset of features of the backend service they are written to, implying they can be compatible with non-native services even if the latter do not support all the features of the source service. (Also, the results of the next section show that most inputs/outputs used by these applications are supported by other services.) Thus, interoperation with non-native services is a reasonable proposition.

Table 2. Compatibility of search applications with different vendors. (TC indicates trivially compatible, $\sqrt{}$ means compatible, i.e., all incompatibilities removed by CAT-S, while a blank indicates one or more relevant incompatibilities.) The row ComparePop-AltaVista is missing because ComparePop cannot be implemented using AltaVista, since one or more features needed by ComparePop is not provided by AltaVista. The same applies to other missing rows. These results show that when an application owner has a choice of several non-native services to use, (s)he can automatically determine which among them are compatible using our techniques.

Application	Google	AltaVista	AllTheWeb	Hotbot	Teoma
ORG#60-Google	TC				
ORG#60-AltaVista	$\sqrt{}$	TC			
ORG#60-AllTheWeb	$\sqrt{}$		TC		
ORG#60-Hotbot	$\sqrt{}$	$\sqrt{}$	$\sqrt{}$	TC	
ORG#60-Teoma	$\sqrt{}$	$\sqrt{}$	$\sqrt{}$		TC
ORG#69-Google	TC				
ORG#69-AltaVista	$\sqrt{}$	TC			
ORG#69-AllTheWeb	$\sqrt{}$		TC		
ORG#69-Hotbot	$\sqrt{}$	$\sqrt{}$	$\sqrt{}$	TC	
ORG#78-Google	TC	$\sqrt{}$	$\sqrt{}$		$\sqrt{}$
ORG#78-AltaVista	$\sqrt{}$	TC	$\sqrt{}$		$\sqrt{}$
ORG#78-AllTheWeb	$\sqrt{}$	$\sqrt{}$	TC		$\sqrt{}$
ORG#78-Teoma	$\sqrt{}$	$\sqrt{}$	$\sqrt{}$		TC
ComparePop-Google	TC		$\sqrt{}$	$\sqrt{}$	
ComparePop-AllTheWeb	$\sqrt{}$		TC	$\sqrt{}$	
ComparePop-Hotbot	$\sqrt{}$		$\sqrt{}$	TC	

5.2   Compatibility and Integration

We first consider the scenario where an application owner needs to choose a suitable target service from among several non-native services available at a registry. In particular, we study compatibility of several search applications with five different search vendors: Google, AltaVista, AllTheWeb, Hotbot and Teoma. The Google WSDL service is considered the base service; we created WSDL services for the other vendors based on the features supported in each vendor's "advanced search" Web pages. We paired each of four search-based applications – ORG#60, ORG#69, ORG#78 and ComparePop – with each of the five search services. Each application-service pair only makes calls that are legal for its native service. For example, ORG#60-AltaVista, an interactive application, allows a user to enter only queries containing operators supported by AltaVista. As shown in table 2, the owner can use CAT-S to automatically determine which among the potential target non-native services are compatible with the application at hand. For a compatible service, no resolution step is needed, and the owner can auto-generate the needed cross-stub.

We next consider a scenario where an application owner has pre-decided on a specific (possibly incompatible) target service, and the goal is to enable rapid integration. We consider two Mappoint applications and four Google applications and target services Arcweb and AltaVista respectively. Table 3 shows the effectiveness of automatic application usage inference during the integration process. Using the usage tuples inferred by UAT-S, CAT-S eliminates most of the incompatibilities, so the owner is only left with a few incompatibilities to resolve using the GUI tool.

Table 3. Number of incompatibilities (total and relevant) for two Mappoint and four Google applications with the non-native Arcweb and AltaVista services respectively. These results are based on CAT-S alone (i.e, CAT-D was not used here.) and demonstrate the effectiveness of application usage behavior inference in the integration process. Using the usage behavior data gathered by UAT-S, CAT-S is able to weed out most incompatibilities. Without CAT-S/UAT-S, the owner has to manually determine the relevance of each incompatibility.

Application	Service	#Total	#Relevant	Application	Service	#Total	#Relevant
JDLS	Find	25	1	ORG#60	Google	13	1
JDLS	Render	44	10	ORG#69	Google	13	1
JDLS	Route	50	2	ORG#78	Google	13	1
StoreLocator	Find	25	4	ComparePop	Google	13	2
StoreLocator	Render	44	10	-	-	-	-
StoreLocator	Route	50	0	-	-	-	-

5.3 Nature of Incompatibilities

Here, we study a number of incompatible application-service pairs to determine how often incompatibilities occur due to non-critical vs critical reasons. To maximize incompatibility cases, we study compatibility of Google applications with other vendors, since Google supports more features than others. Figure 5 shows that in as many as 33 out of the 56 incompatible pairs, the incompatibilities do not affect the basic functioning of the application. This result is significant for two reasons. (1) the results of section 5.1 show that applications typically exercise only a fraction of the service functionality. Figure 5 suggests that even among the features exercised, many are not critically needed for the functioning of the application, further suggesting that interoperability with non-native

App	AltaVista	AllTheWeb	Hotbot	Teoma
60	SO	SO, F	D	SO, F
61	SC	SC	SC	SC
62		F	F	F
63	SO	SO, F	D	SO, F
65		R	R	R
67	SO	SO, F	SO, F	SO, F
68	SO	SO, F	D	SO, F
69	SO	SO, F	SO, F	SO, U, F
70		F	F	F
73	SO	SO, F	SO, F	SO, F
74-77	SO	SO, F	SO, F	SO, F
78		F	D, F	F
81	SS	SS	F	SS
83	T	T	T	T
84	CS	CS	CS	CS

Fig. 5. Compatibility of various O'Reilly Google applications with non-native vendors. Black indicates compatible, white indicates incompatibility due to a critical feature, and grey indicates incompatibility due to a non-critical feature. Each label identifies an incompatibility, e.g., SO = special operators (i.e., "file:pdf", "site:cnn.com", etc) F = filter (indicates if multiple results from same host should be filtered out). For legacy applications, the white vs. grey determination requires manual effort, whereas it can be automated for multi-option types.

services is practical. (2) the figure indicates that a mechanism for automated "white vs grey" determination is desirable, since this allows the "white" cases (i.e., critically incompatible cases) to be auto-filtered out without manual effort.

6   Interoperation-Friendly Applications

In this section, we examine how applications can be written ground-up for better interoperability. Specifically, if an application were explicitly authored to indicate *which* features are critical, then our algorithms could use this information to automatically resolve non-critical incompatibilities. Non-critical should not be confused with optional. (Recall that the service specification can declare a certain field as optional, e.g., `minRating` was declared optional in the schema definition of `KSRequest1`.) Whether a field is non-critical depends on application semantics. Much like WSDL, RPC systems in the past have often allowed *services* to specify (in their interface specifications) whether certain parameters are optional, but few systems allow a *client* to specify that a particular parameter or field that it supplies is non-critical.

Our goal is to specify the critical/non-critical information manually only once at application authoring time, and to use it automatically every time integration with a non-native service is desired. (An application is written once, but integrated multiple times during its lifetime.) To enable this goal, we propose *multi-option host types*.

6.1 Multi-option Host Types

Example multi-option types for the KSRequest1 input message are shown below. (A different design based on generic types is possible in Java 1.5.)

```
public class M_JKSRequest1 {
  boolean non_critical = false; // ok to ignore?
  boolean ignored = false; // was it ignored?
  M_String category;
  M_String keyword;
  M_String minRating;
}
public class M_String {
  boolean non_critical = false;  // ok to ignore?
  boolean ignored = false; // was it ignored?
  String suppliedValue; // value supplied by app
  Object substitutes;  // other values to use if suppliedValue
    is disallowed
  String usedValue; // value that was actually sent to the service
  public M_String(String val) {
    suppliedValue = val;
  }
}
```

A multi-option simple type (such as M_String) is similar to the corresponding plain simple type (such as java.lang.String) except that in addition to supplying a value, a multi-option type provides a boolean non_critical indicating whether it is OK for the application if this field were altogether ignored, and an optional substitutes object providing a set of alternative values to use if the supplied value is not allowed by the service. A multi-option complex type (M_JKSRequest1) is similar to the corresponding ordinary complex type, except each of its fields is replaced by the corresponding multi-option type, and the boolean non_critical indicates if the whole subtree corresponding to this complex type can be ignored. Multi-option types are used as shown below:

```
M_String m_cat = new M_String("Books");
m_cat.substitutes = {''All''};

M_Integer m_rating = new M_Integer(4);
m_rating.non_critical = true;

M_JKSRequest1 req = new M_JKSRequest1();
req.category = m_cat;
req.rating = m_rating;
```

Instead of specifying values, the substitutes object can also specify *substitute patterns* (like the "s/../.." patterns in sed and perl) or *substitute ranges*. The former specifies that the value can be transformed using the specified pattern if need be. A substitute range indicates that any value in the range is acceptable. For applications using multi-option types, the cross-stub generator generates *best-effort cross-stubs* automatically from the source and target non-native service specifications. A best-effort cross-stub behaves similarly to a regular cross-stub, except (1) if it detects a missing field incompatibility, but the causal field is `non_critical`, it simply sets `ignored` to `true` and ignores the incompatibility, and (2) if it detects a facet mismatch incompatibility, but the causal field specifies substitute values one of which is compatible with the target service facets, `usedValue` is set to the compatible substitute value, and the incompatibility is ignored. (Substitute patterns and ranges are similarly handled.) Once the call is made, the application can determine if the value was ignored or substituted by the cross-stub, and (perhaps) notify the user:

```
stub.keywordSearch(req); // see req in previous code snippet
// we've called the service. were the values changed by the stub?
if (m_cat.usedValue != "Books" or m_rating.ignored) {
  // if need be, notify the user or log somewhere
}
```

The philosophical essence of multi-option types is to build substitutability from ground up – fine-grained field-level substitutability is an atomic building block for higher-level service substitutability.

6.2   Multi-option Types in Use

Here, we discuss real examples of multi-option types in use. First, Mappoint applications such as JDLS and StoreLocator specify fonts and styles, and colors for routes/zones, which could be made `non_critical` and/or substitutable. Second, the O'Reilly Google applications specify `filter` and `safesearch`, but do not critically rely on them, so these can be made `non_critical`. (These parameters respectively indicate if multiple results from the same host and adult content should be excluded.) Finally, many O'Reilly Google applications allow special operators to be entered by the user, but can usefully function with services that disallow some special operators. So, a substitute pattern can be specified that removes the special operators.

For applications written using multi-option types, UAT-S records which fields were indicated as `non_critical`, and the provided substitute values/patterns/ ranges (if any). The CAT-S rules of section 3.2 are updated as follows. If a missing field incompatibility i is considered relevant by the rules of section 3.2, but the field is always declared `non_critical`, declare i as non-critical. If a facet mismatch incompatibility i is considered relevant by the rules of section 3.2, but substitute values or ranges are available, we check if any of the specified substitute values or any value in the substitute range is legal for the target service facets. If so, i is declared non-critical. The case when substitute patterns are available is a bit involved, and not implemented yet, but is theoretically tractable. Substitute patterns are finite state transducers, and since regular languages are closed under FST's, we can check if the regular language obtained by applying a substitute pattern to the source value space is a subset of the target value space.

If the Google applications of figure 5 were written using multi-option types, the new CAT-S rules would automate the "white vs. grey" classification, and non-critical incompatibilities will be automatically resolved by the cross-stubs.

7 Semantics and SV-Compatibility

The bigger picture is that we have facilitated automatic detection of SV-compatibility, but this does not assure semantic compatibility, i.e. it does not guarantee the service will "do what you want." Ideally, we want an application and service to be SV-compatible if and only if they are semantically compatible. We can approach this ideal if service creators follow these guidelines:

1. If a vendor restricts some base interface construct (method, type, type field or valuespace) or keeps it the same, he should keep its semantics the same as those of the corresponding base interface construct.
2. If a vendor extends by adding a method, type or type field, he should do so in his own namespace, unless he wants to reuse an extension already done by someone else, in which case he should import the construct from that party's namespace.
3. If a vendor extends the value space of some type/field, and uses facets to specify this, the system would know which values carried over from the base and which are added by each vendor. So, even if two vendors add the same value with different semantics, the system can infer that the value is not part of the base type and hence can conservatively assume that this value might have different semantics for each vendor.

The above conventions are similar to the *re-use namespace names* and the *new namespaces to break* rules of Orchard [9], and if adhered to will ensure that:

1. For methods, types and type fields, (a) SV-compatibility implies semantic compatibility, and (b) semantic compatibility implies SV-compatibility to the extent vendors reuse existing extensions from other namespaces;
2. For values, SV-compatibility will imply semantic compatibility, though not necessarily the converse.

8 Related Work

We urge that vendors cooperate and derive their services from existing WSDL services. This may make economic sense even for competing vendors, since a derived service may help them draw traffic. However, we recognize that a competing vendor may (e.g., for political reasons) choose to define a completely different autonomous WSDL specification. Building upon [10, 11], we have partially addressed autonomous services interoperability before [12] by employing *adapters*. In future work, we combine UAT-S/CAT-S/CAT-D with adapters to better address the autonomous services case. However, unlike the semi-automatically generated cross-stubs, adapters must be completely handwritten, and thus autonomous services interoperability requires much more effort.

Referring back to the derived services case, service interface subtyping has been used for evolution, but with a base service V and two derivatives V_1 and V_2, traditional subtyping only handles two (namely $V \rightarrow V_1$ and $V \rightarrow V_2$) out of the six non-native service interoperation scenarios ($V \rightarrow V_1$, $V \rightarrow V_2$,

$V_2 \rightarrow V$, $V_1 \rightarrow V$, $V_1 \rightarrow V_2$ and $V_2 \rightarrow V_1$). Also, traditional subtyping does not consider restriction. Compared to systems that address cross version/vendor substitutability without relying on subtyping [13–16], we leverage application usage behavior and multi-option types to customize the integration behavior to the application with minimal effort from the application developer/owner.

Schmidt et al. [17] explain the lack of practical versioning support in CORBA, while Vinoski [1] and Vogels [4] point out some of the interoperability/versioning issues with XML Web services. XDuce [3] provides static type checking for programs processing XML data, but does not target compatibility of applications exchanging XML messages over the network. Debugging tools such as SOAP-scope [18] can check differences in WSDL documents, but UAT-S/CAT-S/cross-stubs go much further. David Orchard's guidelines [9] for XML schema versioning emphasize the need to provide *processing models* to deal with unrecognized schema components/extensions (i.e., incompatibilities). Our contribution is in allowing automated detection of which unrecognized components/extensions can break a *given application* and to specify a processing model (i.e., resolution choice) in an application-specific manner.

Multi-option types are most similar to Spreitzer's flexible types [19]), Orchard's "mustUnderstand" model [9] and the HTTP extension framework's non-ignorable bits [20]. These mechanisms at best only provide the equivalent of the non-critical flag, but not the substitute patterns, ranges or values. Furthermore, they rely on both client and server side support, while our multi-option types are entirely client-side and require no changes to wire protocols or server-side implementations. Schema evolution [21] and data integration [22] are well-researched, but do not leverage application usage behavior or provide multi-option types. Schema matching systems [23] attempt to auto-derive semantic relationships between different schemas; we rely on simple conventions, and perform no non-trivial semantics inference. Unlike semantic Web services [24], our approach does not require development of or global agreement on semantic markup languages.

9   Conclusions

Interoperability with non-native services is an enabling technology, because it assures application developers that their applications will stay relevant and usable across vendors, and hence promotes Web services adoption and application development. Our foray into this problem space reveals that many applications only access a fraction of the service functionality, and even among the features accessed only a subset is critically needed. Leveraging these observations, we address the problem threefold: (1) static and dynamic analysis tools that automatically infer application behavior and determine compatibility with non-native services, (2) a GUI tool for resolving incompatibilities and generating cross-stubs, middleware components that actually enable the interoperation to occur, and (3) a lightweight mechanism called multi-option types that enables applications to be authored from ground up for better interoperability. We presented a set of experiments that, although by no means exhaustive, provide initial support for our claims and demonstrate the workings of our techniques.

Acknowledgements

We thank Godmar Back and John Whaley for implementation tips, and George Candea, Andy Huang, Emre Kiciman, John Mitchell, Terry Winograd and the anonymous reviewers for their feedback on prior drafts.

References

1. Vinoski, S.: The More Things Change... IEEE Distributed Systems Online **5** (2004)
2. Lee, K., et al.: Hydroj: object-oriented pattern matching for evolvable distributed systems. In: OOPSLA 2003, ACM Press (2003) 205–223
3. Hosoya, H., Pierce, B.C.: Xduce: A statically typed xml processing language. ACM Transactions on Internet Technology **3** (2003) 117–148
4. Vogels, W.: Web Services Are Not Distributed Objects. IEEE Internet Computing **7** (2003) 59–66
5. Stal, M.: Web services: beyond component-based computing. Commun. ACM **45** (2002) 71–76
6. Mikalsen, T., et al.: Reliability of Composed Web Services–From Object Transactions to Web Transactions. In: Workshop on Object-oriented Web Services, OOPSLA. (2001)
7. Berndl, M., et al.: Points-to Analysis using BDDs. In: PLDI, San Diego, CA (2003)
8. Whaley, J.: The joeq project pages (1999) http://joeq.sourceforge.net.
9. Orchard, D.: Versioning XML Vocabularies (2003) http://www.xml.com/pub/a/2003/12/03/versioning.html.
10. Gribble, S.D., et al.: The ninja architecture for robust internet-scale systems and services. Special Issue of Computer Networks on Pervasive Computing **35** (2001)
11. Vayssiere, J.: Transparent Dissemination of Adapters in Jini. In: DOA 2001, (Italy)
12. Ponnekanti, S.R., Fox, A.: Application Service Interoperation without Standardized Interfaces. In: IEEE Percom '03, Dallas-Fort Worth, TX (2003)
13. Senivongse, T.: Enabling flexible cross-version interoperability from distributed services. In: DOA 1999, IEEE (1999) 201–210
14. Evans, H., Dickman, P.: Drastic: A run-time architecture for evolving, distributed, persistent systems. In: ECOOP'97. Volume 1241 of LNCS., Springer (1997)
15. Ajmani, S., Liskov, B., Shrira, L.: Scheduling and simulation: How to upgrade distributed systems. In: Proc. of Ninth HotOS, Lihue, III (2003)
16. Melloul, L., et al.: Reusable Functional Composition Patterns for Web Services. In: To Appear, IEEE ICWS. (2004)
17. Schmidt, D.C., Vinoski, S.: CORBA and XML, Part 1: Versioning (2001) http://www.cuj.com/documents/s=7995/cujcexp1905vinoski/.
18. Mindreef: (SOAPscope) http://www.mindreef.com.
19. Spreitzer, M., et al.: More Flexible Data Types. (In: Eighth IEEE WET-ICE 1999)
20. Nielsen, H.F., et al.: HTTP Extension Framework (1999) Internet draft.
21. Skarra, A.H., Zdonik, S.B.: The management of changing types in an object-oriented database. In: OOPSLA '86, ACM Press (1986) 483–495
22. Levy, A.Y.: Answering Queries using Views: A Survey. www.cs.washington.edu/homes/alon/views.ps (1999)
23. Rahm, E., Bernstein, P.: On Matching Schemas Automatically. Technical Report MSR-TR-2001-17, Microsoft Research, Redmond, WA (2001)
24. McIlraith, S.A., Son, T.C., Zeng, H.: Semantic Web Services. IEEE Intelligent Systems (Special Issue on Semantic Web) **16** (2001) 46–53

SyD: A Middleware Testbed for Collaborative Applications over Small Heterogeneous Devices and Data Stores*

Sushil K. Prasad[1], Vijay Madisetti[2], Shamkant B. Navathe[3],
Raj Sunderraman[1], Erdogan Dogdu[1], Anu Bourgeois[1], Michael Weeks[1],
Bing Liu[1], Janaka Balasooriya[1], Arthi Hariharan[1], Wanxia Xie[3],
Praveen Madiraju[1], Srilaxmi Malladi[1], Raghupathy Sivakumar[2],
Alex Zelikovsky[1], Yanqing Zhang[1], Yi Pan[1], and Saied Belkasim[1]

[1] Computer Science Department, Georgia State University
[2] School of Electrical and Computer Engineering, Georgia Institute of Technology
[3] College of Computing, Georgia Institute of Technology

Abstract. Developing a collaborative application running on a collection of heterogeneous, possibly mobile, devices, each potentially hosting data stores, using existing middleware technologies such as JXTA, BREW, compact .NET and J2ME requires too many ad-hoc techniques as well as cumbersome and time-consuming programming. Our System on Mobile Devices (SyD) middleware, on the other hand, has a modular architecture that makes such application development very systematic and streamlined. The architecture supports transactions over mobile data stores, with a range of remote group invocation options and embedded interdependencies among such data store objects. The architecture further provides a persistent uniform object view, group transaction with Quality of Service (QoS) specifications, and XML vocabulary for inter-device communication. This paper presents the basic SyD concepts and introduces the architecture and the design of the SyD middleware and its components. We also provide guidelines for SyD application development and deployment process. We include the basic performance figures of SyD components and a few SyD applications on Personal Digital Assistant (PDA) platforms. We believe that SyD is the first comprehensive working prototype of its kind, with a small code footprint of 112 KB with 76 KB being device-resident, and has a good potential for incorporating many ideas for performance extensions, scalability, QoS, workflows and security.

Keywords: Mobile Servers, SyD Coordination Bonds, Object and Web Service Coordination, Atomic Transactions, Application-Level QoS.

* This Research was partially supported by Georgia Research Alliance's Yamacraw Embedded Software Contract #CLH49 and #DLN01. The SyD middleware and demo application codes can be downloaded from www.cs.gsu.edu/~yes.

H.-A. Jacobsen (Ed.): Middleware 2004, LNCS 3231, pp. 352–371, 2004.
© IFIP International Federation for Information Processing 2004

1   Introduction

Requirements for a Middleware Platform: There is an emerging need for a comprehensive middleware technology to enable development and deployment of collaborative distributed applications over a collection of mobile (as well as wired) devices. This has been earlier identified as one of the key research challenges [3, 14]. Our work is an ongoing effort to address this challenge, and this paper reports our first prototype design and its implementation. We seek to enable group applications over a collection of heterogeneous, autonomous, and mobile data stores, interconnected through wired or wireless networks of various characteristics, and running on devices of varying capabilities (pagers, cell phones, PDAs, PCs, etc.). The key requirements for such a middleware platform are to allow:

1. Uniform Connected View: Present a uniform view of device, data and network to ease programmer's burden. Provide a device-independent and a persistent (always connected) object-view of data and services, so as to mask mobility and heterogeneity. Allow multiple data models and representations on device data stores.
2. Distributed Server Applications on Small Devices: Enable developing and deploying distributed server applications possibly hosted on mobile devices. Support atomic transactions across multiple, independent, and heterogeneous device-applications.
3. High-Level Development and Deployment Environment: Enable rapid development of reliable and portable collaborative applications over heterogeneous devices, networks and data stores. Provide a general-purpose high-level programming environment that uses existing sever applications and composes them to create, possibly ad-hoc, integrated applications rapidly.

Limitations of Current Technology: The current technology for the development of such collaborative applications over a set of wired or wireless devices and networks has several limitations. It requires explicit and tedious programming on each kind of device, both for data access and for inter-device and inter-application communication. The application code is specific to the type of device, data format, and the network. The data store provides only a fixed set of services disallowing dynamic reconfiguration. Applications running across mobile devices become complex due to lack of persistence and weak connectivity. A few existing middlewares have addressed the stated requirements in a piecemeal fashion. Limitations include only client-side programming on mobile devices, a restricted domain of applications, or limited in group or transaction functionalities or mobility support, as further elaborated in Section 8.

SyD Solution: System on Mobile Devices (SyD) is a new platform technology that addresses the key problems of heterogeneity of device, data format and network, and mobility. SyD combines ease of application development, mobility of code, application, data and users, independence from network and geographical location, and the scalability required of large enterprise applications concurrently with the small footprint required by hand held devices. SyD separates device management from management of groups of users and/or data stores. Each device is managed by a SyD deviceware that encapsulates it to present a uniform and persistent object view of the device data and methods. Groups of SyD devices are managed by the SyD groupware that brokers all inter-device activities, and presents a uniform world-view to the SyD application. The SyD groupware directory service enables SyD applications to dynamically form groups of objects hosted by devices. The SyD groupware enables group communication and other functionalities across multiple devices. Section 2 presents the detailed SyD architecture.

Contributions and Significance: The primary contributions of our work presented here are broadly two-fold [10, 16, 17, 20–22, 26].

1. A proof-of-concept, working middleware, unique of its kind, that enables distributed server and collaborative applications over multiple small mobile devices, possibly hosting data stores. This is as much an engineering feat as is a middleware design. The foot-print of the entire SyD kernel code is 112 KB, out of which only 76 KB is currently device-resident; the rest is for directory and global event handling. For even smaller devices, this can be further reduced to 42 KB. The execution time work space used by SyD is 4-8 MB, exclusive of JVM and OS.
2. A methodology to rapidly develop and deploy robust distributed collaborative applications, and an execution platform to deploy such applications, while masking mobility and heterogeneity from application programmers, and allowing inter-device constraints and atomic transactions.

Hardware/Software Platform: Various technologies employed to prototype SyD kernel testbed are as follows:

1. HP's iPAQ models 3600 and 3700 with 32 and 64 MB storage running Windows CE/Pocket PC OS interconnected through IEEE 802.11 adapter cards and a 11 MB/s Wireless LAN.
2. Jeode EVM personal Java 1.2 compatible, implementing Java Virtual Machine; KVM/MIDP for cellphone emulator.
3. Instant DB version 3.26 on iPAQ for databases for various applications; Oracle 8i DBMS on PC as a directory server.
4. TCP Sockets for remote method invocation and JAVA RMI for local method execution through reflection.
5. μCode [15] version 1.03 as the mobile agent frame work on the iPAQ.
6. XML standard for all inter-device communication.

We will not be able to provide in-depth description of all aspects of SyD middleware, but will attempt to be complete while highlighting our key contributions. This paper is organized as follows. Section 2 provides a broad overview of SyD and presents the SyD prototype implementation and the current implementation architecture of SyD and SyD-based applications. The next three sections describe the three key aspects of SyD: Section 3 describes the SyD Listener module, which enables data hosting and serving capability in small, mobile, devices. Section 4 describes a range of options available in SyD for invoking individual and group remote methods. Section 5 then describes one key innovation, namely SyD coordination links/bonds which enable distributed object coordination and rapid ad-hoc application prototyping. Section 6 summarizes how SyD-based applications are developed in our framework, and mentions a few sample SyD applications. In Section 7, we attempt to place SyD middleware among the emerging middleware technologies and assess the level by which SyD currently meets its design goals. Section 8 presents the related work. Section 9 contains a summary and future work.

2   SyD Architecture Overview

In this section, we describe the design of SyD and related issues, and highlight the important features of its architecture. Each individual device in SyD may be a traditional database such as relational or object-oriented database, or may be an ad-hoc data store such as a flat file, an EXCEL worksheet or a list repository. These may be located in traditional computers, in personal digital assistants (PDAs) or even in devices such as a utility meter or a set-top box. These devices are assumed to be independent in that they do not share a global schema. The devices in SyD cooperate with each other to perform interesting tasks and we envision a new generation of applications to be built using the SyD framework. The SyD architecture is shown in Fig. 1.

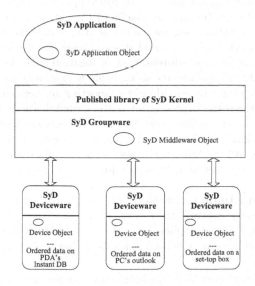

Fig. 1. SyD Framework.

The SyD framework has three layers.

1. At the lowest layer, individual data stores are represented by device objects that encapsulate methods/operations for access, and manipulation of this data. The SyD Deviceware consists of a listener module to register objects and to execute local methods in response to remote invocations, and an engine module to invoke methods on remote objects. Object composition and execution of atomic transactions over multiple objects are provided by a bonding module.
2. At the middle layer, there is SyD groupware, a logically coherent collection of services, APIs, and objects to facilitates the execution of application programs. Specifically, SyD groupware consists of a directory service module, group transactions and global event support, with application-level Quality of Service (QoS).
3. At the highest level are the applications themselves. They rely only on these groupware and deviceware SyD services, and are independent of device, data and network. These applications include instantiations of server objects that are aggregations of the device objects and SyD middleware objects.

The three-tier architecture of SyD enables applications to be developed in a flexible manner without knowledge of device, database and network details. SyD groupware is responsible for making software applications (anywhere) aware of the named objects and their methods/services, executing these methods on behalf of applications, allowing the construction of SyD Application Objects (SyDAppOs) that are built on the device objects. SyD groupware provides the communications infrastructure between SyD Applications (SyDApps), in addition to providing QoS support services for SyDApps. SyDApps are applications written for the end users (human or machine) that operate on the SyDAppOs alone and are able to define their own services that utilize the SyDAppOs. The SyD groupware provides only a named device object for use by the SyDApps, without revealing the physical address, type or location of the information store.

SyDApps are able to operate across multiple networks and multiple devices, relying on the middleware to provide the supporting services that translate the SyDApps code to the correct drivers, for both communications and computing. SyDApps can also decide on their own features and services they offer, without depending on individual databases residing on remote computing devices to offer those services. The SyD architecture, thus, is compatible with and extends the currently emerging Web services paradigm for Internet applications.

Current Prototype Implementation: We have developed a prototype testbed of SyD middleware that captures the essential features of the SyD's overall framework and several SyD-based applications. We have designed and implemented a modular SyD kernel in Java, which includes the following five modules (Fig. 2):

1. The SyDDirectory provides publishing, management, and lookup services to SyD device objects and their proxies, and users.

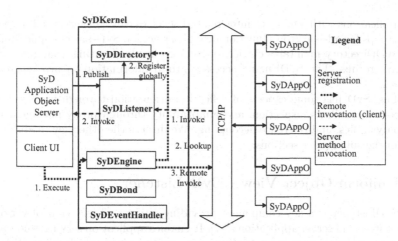

Fig. 2. SyD kernel architecture, and interactions among modules and SyD application objects (SyDAppO).

2. The SyDListener enables SyD device objects to publish their services (server functionalities) as "listeners" locally on the device and globally via the directory services. It responds to invocations of server methods by the users and other application objects on SyD network.
3. The SyDEngine allows users to execute single or group services remotely and aggregate results. Its sub-modules extend it with transactions with QoS.
4. The SyDBond module enables a SyD entity to link to other entities for automatic updates and to create and enforce interdependencies.
5. The SyDEventHandler module handles local and global event registration, monitoring, and triggering.

Disconnection Tolerance via Proxy: The SyDDirectory keeps track of application objects and their associated devices via location information (IP plus port number). Server applications can register their proxies, too. SyDDirectory actively maintains the availability of applications hosted on mobile devices versus their proxies via a "live bit" in the directory entries; this bit can be set/reset by an application on power-on/power-off or by SyDEngine on time-outs. The device's location is also tracked and kept current in the SyD directory. If the device is inaccessible, due perhaps to an intermittent disconnection or battery discharge, then, after a timeout, the SyDEngine invokes the proxy application to complete the requested service and resets the "live-bit" of the application with the SyD Directory. The application on the mobile device, when online, synchronizes intelligently with its proxy updates and sets its "live-bit". The assumption here is that an application running on a mobile device is most up-to-date. (Thus, a user calendar's proxy allows a meeting to be only tentatively scheduled, which after synchronization with the mobile calendar may get converted into a permanent meeting; on the other hand, if mobile calendar is online, permanent meeting can be setup in real time). A detailed implementation of a proxy module incorporating and extending these functionalities is underway.

Applications with similar or inter-related services can be aggregated to form SyD groups for ad-hoc group functionality of services in SyD-based applications. The SyDDirectory maintains entries for SyD groups by creating, changing, and deleting groups. The SyDEngine accesses group information to invoke group services.

Thus, SyD has some aspects of reflection-orientation through its directory service, which allows inspection, and adaptability through proxy management, group dynamics, and reference decoupling. We discuss the other key modules of SyD in the subsequent sections.

3   Uniform Object View – SyD Listener

Our SyDListener is a key component providing uniform object view of various data sources and server applications [17]. It enables application serving, and data store and web service hosting capabilities in small devices, which are traditionally thought of as mere client devices. It is effectively a stand-alone lightweight extended SOAP server enabling XML-based inter-device interactions. SyDListener is implemented as a multi-threaded application enabler with simple persistence management and asynchronous invocation functionality for (i) Personal Profile on Connected Device Configuration (CDC) devices, suitable for high-end PDAs [11], and (ii) J2ME Mobile Information Device Profile (MIDP) on Connected Limited Device Configuration(CLDC) devices, such as mobile phones [12].

The SyDListener module has dual responsibilities: (1) registering server applications for remote method invocations, and (2) performing local method execution and responding with results when remote requests are received [17]. Service registration is done locally to local object repository, and globally to SyDDirectory. There are three important classes in SyDListener module: SyDRegistrar, SyDListener, and SyDDelegate (Fig. 3). SyDRegistrar performs registration of server and its proxy, initially upon application deployment and after each reconnection or power-on of the device, ensuring that subsequent invocations are directed to the server object, not to its proxy. As part of the initialization of the server object, it typically should have a synchronization mechanism, possibly application-specific, with its proxy. The SyDListener class is instantiated at server side and performs listening for, parsing and invoking local methods in response to remote invocations. The SyDListenerDelegate is at the client side and performs communication with SyDListener, including transmission of request messages and receiving of results. The SyDListenerDelegate acts as an adaptor for SyDListener and hides all the communication details from clients. This means that the communication method, TCP sockets in this case, can also be changed without any influence on clients.

CDC/JVM Version: The first version of SyDListener is built upon TCP sockets and Java RMI. SyDListenerDelegate and SyDListener communicate through TCP sockets. SyDListener locally accesses active service objects from RMI registry (Fig. 3). Inside the SyDListener, we integrate Java reflection mechanism with RMI. This implementation is single-threaded and only provides syn-

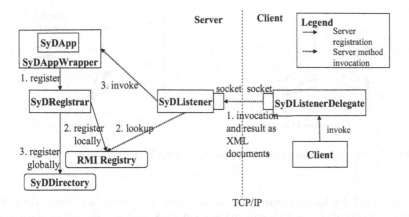

Fig. 3. SyDListener module architecture using TCP sockets.

chronous invocation. The footprint of this implementation of the whole listener module is 10.3 KB.

CLDC/KVM Version: The listener architecture provides flexibility in that we could replace RMI with other technologies, and limit the change within SyDListener and the service application. This was employed to yield a second version of listener for CLDC devices, and is built upon J2ME Mobile Information Device Profile (MIDP). It utilizes the limited programming APIs available on MIDP and acts as a multi-threaded application server, which manages the lifecycle of SyD applications without using Java RMI. It provides simple persistence management to service objects and asynchronous method invocation to service clients. The footprint of the CLDC/KVM version is 19.5 KB, an increase when compared to that of CDC/JVM version because of the missing base functionalities in CLDC and the new functionalities such as multi-threading.

Figures 4 and 5, respectively, present the total connection time for round-trip response time from SyDListener using synchronous requests (on iPAQs) and asynchronous requests (on cell-phone emulator). We employ varying (i) exponentially distributed inter-arrival times of invocation from clients, and (ii) normally distributed service times (grain-size of method execution) at the SyDListener. There is a good amount of saving in air time, as well as opportunities for concurrency in client application with asynchronous invocation, but that does entail more programming burden.

4   Remote Methods and Transactions – SyD Engine and Its Extensions

SyD recognizes the need for simplicity in method invocation on individual and groups of objects as well as the need for sophistication in light of mobility and heterogeneity of clients and servers. Therefore, it provides a range of mechanisms

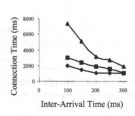

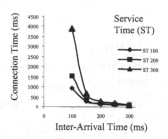

Fig. 4. Synchronous Invocation Model.   **Fig. 5.** Async. Invocation Model.

with sub-modules for tracking group invocations with real-time constraints, for adaptive transactions with application-level QoS and for on-server data processing with mobile capabilities. At the minimum, (i) language independence is enforced through a generic "invoke" method to SyDEngine, (ii) reference decoupling and group dynamicity are ensured through dynamic object/group IDs to address mapping via SyDDirectory, and (iii) XML vocabulary is employed to mask communication heterogeneity.

SyDEngine: The two major components of the SyDEngine are: the SyD-Dispatcher and the SyDAggregator. The SyDDispatcher module is responsible for dispatching method calls either on the local device or on to the remote device. At runtime, the SyDEngine looks up the SyD directory for current device location or proxy information and makes calls to the methods accordingly. The average round-trip time between SyDEngine on an iPAQ to SyD directory hosted on wireless LAN laptop is 218 ms out of which internal processing time of SyDEngine is only 7 ms. A local directory cache can cut this time further. The SyDAggregator module is responsible for aggregating multiple SyDDoC objects obtained from the SyDDispatcher. The possible operations currently implemented are: append, max, min and intersection, primarily over database tables. The SyDDoC utility provides a uniform data exchange capability throughout the SyD middleware and SyD-enabled modules. It is based on XML and is lightweight compared to DOM and SAX models of XML.

The three modules, SyDDirectory, SyDListener and SyDEngine, along with the document utility module SyDDoc form the essential core of the SyD middleware, and account for a foot-print of only 60 KB with 42 KB being device-resident (the auxiliary technologies such as Jeode or Instant DB are not accounted for in this). The basic capabilities of SyDEngine are being enhanced by several extension sub-modules. For example, a client application can employ a Transaction-Tracker sub-module, residing off-device (possibly as a Web service object), which supports sophisticated asynchronous group invocations with real-time deadlines with timeouts [5]. Two additional sub-modules are as follows.

QoS-Aware Transactions: An extended architecture [25, 26] for the development and runtime support of QoS-aware transaction service is shown in Fig. 6.

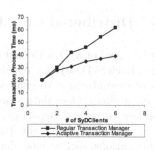

Fig. 7. Transaction Quality.

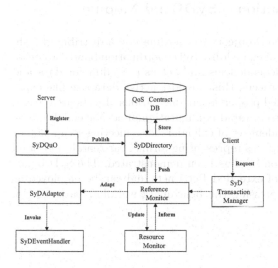

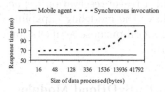

Fig. 6. QoS-aware Transaction.

Fig. 8. Mobile agent vs Sync. invocation.

SyDQuO is the core component that describes and represents QoS contracts for transaction services. SyDDirectory provides QoS contract publish and lookup services for transactions. Reference Monitor watches all valid QoS contracts of currently running transactions and sends the updated resource thresholds to the resource monitor. Resource Monitor monitors the changes of resources such as CPU and memory. SyDAdapter manages the intra-transaction adaptation process while the Transaction Manager supports inter-transaction QoS. Fig. 7 shows preliminary performance results of the adaptive transaction manager, which sends load feedbacks to SyD clients whose transactions have the least priority to reduce the transaction transmission rates, thereby achieving better transaction rate overall. A detailed implementation of this sub-module is underway.

Agent-Based Transactions: Mobile agent sub-module exploits the agent capability of on-server processing to save communication bandwidth. This sub-module replaces the SyDEngine-SyDListener pair with μCode's Client and Server pair [15]. We have conducted preliminary experiments comparing the synchronous remote invocation (SI) through SyDEngine-SyDListener pair with the mobile agent (MA) [9]. Fig. 8 gives the comparison of SI with MA based on the size of the data processed. In the MA approach, data is processed at server sites and processed data is sent across the network. In the SI approach, data is collected from multiple devices and then processing takes place on the gathered data at the client and therefore results in higher response time. Effort is underway for SyDEngine to seamlessly switch to MA approach based on data size on agent-enabled SyD servers.

5   Distributed Coordination – SyDBond Module

A key goal of SyD is to enable SyD objects to coordinate in a distributed fashion. Each SyD object is capable of embedding SyD coordination bonds[1] to other entities enabling it to enforce dependencies and act as a conduit for data and control flows. Over data store objects, this provides active database like capabilities; in general, aspect-oriented properties among various objects are created and enforced dynamically. Its use in rapid configuration of ad-hoc collaborative applications, such as inter-dependent set of calendars for a meeting setup [20], or a set of inter-dependent Web services representing airline, car rental, and hotel in a travel reservation application [4], has been demonstrated. The SyD bonds have the modeling capabilities of extended Petri nets and can be employed as general-purpose artifacts for expressing the benchmark workflow patterns [18, 19].

5.1   SyDBond Module

Coordination bonds enable applications to create contracts between entities and enforce interdependencies and constraints, and carry out atomic transactions spanning over a group of entities/processes. While it is convenient to think of an entity as a row, a column, a table, or a set of tables in a data-store, the concept transcends these to any SyD object or its component. There are two types of bonds: subscription bonds and negotiation bonds. Subscription bonds allow automatic flow of information from a source entity to other entities that subscribe to it. This can be employed for synchronization as well as more complex changes, needing data or event flows. Negotiation bonds enforce dependencies and constraints across entities and trigger changes based on constraint satisfaction.

A SyD bond is specified by its type (subscription/negotiation), its status (certain/tentative), references to one or more entities, triggers associated with each reference (event-condition-action rules), a priority, a constraint (and, or, xor), bond creation and expiry times, and a waiting list of tentative bonds (a priority queue). A tentative bond may become certain if the awaited certain bond is destroyed. Let an entity A be bonded to entities B and C, which may in turn be bonded to other entities. A change in A may trigger changes in B and C, or A can change only if B and C can be successfully changed. In the following, the phrase "Change X" is employed to refer to an action on X (action usually is a particular method invocation on SyD object X with specified set of parameters); "Mark X" refers to an attempted change, which triggers any associated bond without an actual change on X.

- Subscription-and Bond: Mark A; If successful Change A then Try: Change B and Change C. A "try" may not succeed.
- Negotiation-and Bond: Change A only if B and C can be successfully changed.

---

[1] Alternatively called "coordination links" [21, 22], or "Web bonds" in the context of Web services [18].

Similar semantics can be defined with "or" and "xor" logic. A subscription bond from A to B is denoted as a dashed directed arrow from A to B. A negotiation bond from A to B is denoted as a solid directed arrow from A to B. A negotiation-and bond from A to B and C is denoted by two solid arrows, one each to B and C, with a "*" in between the arrows. Similarly, a "+" and a "∧" depict "or" and "xor" logic, respectively. A tentative bond, which is a negotiation bond in a waiting list, is shown as a solid arrow with cuts.

5.2   Modeling Dependencies Using Coordination Bonds

The modeling and execution capabilities of SyD bonds can be illustrated through typical scenarios of dependencies.

Producer-Consumer Dependencies: Fig. 9 shows how a classic relationship of a producer and consumer object can be bonded using two negotiation bonds. The *Place Order* method at a consumer object needs to ensure that the producer has enough inventories such that the corresponding *Accept Order* method will get executed successfully. Before guaranteeing this, the *Accept Order* probably will check the current and projected inventory. A negotiation bond is created from consumer to producer. This is the basic situation for deploying a negotiation bond. Once an order has been placed by the consumer and accepted by the producer, a subscription bond serves notice to *Dispatch Goods* method. Note that the bonds are useful within an object as well. Again before *Dispatch Goods* executes, it needs to ensure that consumers *Accept Delivery* method can be completed successfully (ensuring that enough space is available, for example) [18].

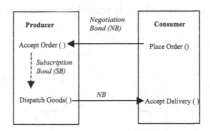

Fig. 9. Coordinating Producer-Consumer Objects.

A Meeting Example: The potential of SyD bonds and their utility in modeling and enforcing contracts among coordinating objects can be further illustrated by a calendar of meeting example. For this application, we demonstrate here how an empty time slot is found, how a meeting is setup (tentative and confirmed), and how voluntary and involuntary changes are automatically handled. A simple scenario is as follows: A wants to call a meeting between dates d_1 and d_2 involving B, C, D and himself. The first step is to find the empty slots in everybody's calendar. *A* then clicks the desired empty slot. This causes a series of steps. A negotiation-and bond is created from *A*'s slot to the specific slot in each calendar table (Fig. 10). Choosing the desired slot attempts to write and reserve that slot in *A*'s calendar, triggering the negotiation-and bond. The "action" of this bond is as follows:

1. Query each table for this desired slot, ensure that it is not reserved, and reserve this slot.
2. If all succeed, then each corresponding slot at *A*, *B*, *C* and *D* creates a negotiation bond back to *A*'s slot.

Else, for those folks who could not be reserved, a tentative bond back to *A* is queued up at the corresponding slots to be triggered whenever the status of the slot changes. The forward negotiation-and bond to *A*, *B*, *C* and *D* are left in place. Back subscription bonds to *A* from others are created to inform *A* of subsequent changes in the other participants and to help *A* decide to cancel this tentative meeting or try another time slot. Assume that *C* could not be reserved. Thus, *C* has a tentative back bond to *A*, and others have subscription bonds to *A* (Fig. 11). Whenever *C* becomes available, if the tentative bond back to A is of highest priority, it will get triggered, informing *A* of *C*'s availability, and will attempt to change *A*'s slot to be reserved. This triggers the negotiation-and bond from *A* to *A*, *B*, *C* and *D*, resulting in another round of negotiation. If all succeed, then corresponding slots are reserved, and the target slots at *A*, *B*, *C* and *D* create negotiation bonds back to *A*'s slot (Fig. 10). Thus, a tentative meeting has been converted to committed. Now suppose *D* wants to change the schedule for this meeting. This would trigger its bond to *A*, triggering the forward negotiation-and bond from *A* to *A*, *B*, *C* and *D*. If all succeed, then a new duration is reserved at each calendar with all forward and back bonds established. If not all can agree, then *D* would be unable to change the schedule of the meeting.

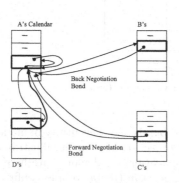

Fig. 10. A Scheduled Meeting.

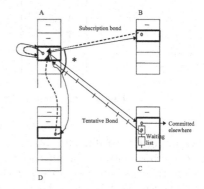

Fig. 11. A Tentative Meeting.

5.3   Modeling Workflow Control Patterns

SyD bonds are being applied in distributed coordination among Web services, in particular, to express workflows (therefore, renamed Web coordination bonds). We illustrate the implementation of a few selected workflow patterns [1] using Web bonds. Further details are in [19].

Exclusive Choice (Xor-Split): Xor-Split is a point in a workflow where only one of possible paths is selected. Almost all the workflow modeling frameworks (except Petri net based) require considerable designer involvement to enforce XOR-Split. Web bonds eliminate this requirement by embedding *xor* logic among subscription bonds (Fig 12). If both paths get evaluated to true, only one will be selected. Negotiation bonds from B and C to A ensure that B and C could be executed only after A is completed.

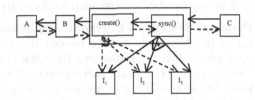

Fig. 12. Xor-Split.

Fig. 13. Multiple instances with prior runtime knowledge.

Multiple Instances with Prior Runtime Knowledge: As number of instances is not known at the design time, most of the workflow models cannot enforce this construct. Due to the dynamic creation and deletion facility of Web bonds, this can easily be enforced. Activity B passes the control to *create* sub-activity with instance creation parameters. Subscription bonds with *and* logic will be created with each instance (Fig. 13). At the same time, it makes sure that the sub-activity *Sync* creates negotiation bond with each instance. Having negotiation bonds to each instance, *Sync* activity ensures that it waits for all instances to be finished before passing the control to C.

6   Guidelines for Developing Collaborative Applications

SyD Methodology: SyD allows rapid development of a range of portable and reliable applications. The three-tier architecture of SyD enables development of applications in a flexible manner without explicit dependence on device, database, and network details. The steps involved in developing a SyD application are as follows.

Step 1: Model the application using SyD device objects, the device-based predefined or new objects, SyDMWOs, the available middleware objects, and SyDAppOs, new or previously designed application objects developed by an application platform developer. SyD directory aids in this search. Create, deploy and publish those server objects that are unavailable, by specifying their data and methods.

Step 2: Develop high level application server code by employing the objects/methods in Step 1. If new, composite server functionalities need to be published. Additionally, develop a separate client code, which typically is like a browser/GUI page.

Sample SyD Applications: Currently there are two key SyD applications, one each in the personal and enterprise domains. We implemented these using various technologies, including JDBC, SOAP, and SyD. The initial database programming using JDBC, and subsequently using SOAP, were carried out as student projects. These highlighted the cumbersome programming, lack of support for small devices, and the desired SyD-like features. The SyD-based development was by far the quickest, with more functionalities, due to high-level APIs of SyD (2-3 weeks each by 3-4 students), with comparable execution efficiencies.

Personal System of Calendar Application: The first is a calendar application in which each user has his own database that is either stored locally or on a proxy. The application can be logically divided into two parts, the server and the client. The server part includes all the methods that interact with the local data store and can be invoked remotely. The client part consists of the user interface which enables the user to interact with the application. One example of the SyD functionality is that the calendar application uses the SyDBond module to logically bond all members of a particular meeting together. A meeting can be rescheduled in real-time for all attendees by invoking the corresponding SyD Bonds by anyone participant [20, 21]. The time to setup a meeting between two iPAQs is about 1-2 secs, and increases slightly for larger groups. Automatic rescheduling and cancellation also have similar timing characteristics.

Enterprise Fleet Application: The second application is a truck fleet that operates an automated package delivery system. In this system, a user may connect through the Internet to the Web and Data Center (WDC), request delivery of a package, and give information pertaining to the package. The WDC passes this information to a depot, which schedules a pick-up [16, 23]. Average execution time for truck-to-truck communication querying about location using SyD is 885 ms, where as using JDBC is 1150 ms. Thus, the various abstraction layers (SyDEngine, Directory and Listener) are efficient and comparable to the older technology.

Developing Ad-Hoc Applications and Travel Application: SyD bonds can be employed to compose Web services (non-SyD-enabled) with an ad-hoc SyD application acting as a centralized coordinator. In [4], we demonstrate a travel application which allows for automatic rescheduling and cancellation of itineraries involving reservations for airline, hotel and car. Once an itinerary is decided and the trip is planned for the user, bonds are created and maintained in the user's SyDBond database. If the flight is canceled, then automatic cancellation of car and hotel reservations is triggered, thus easing the burden on the user to manually cancel all associated reservations. An ad-hoc application developer's nook provides a simple GUI-based interface for the application developer to initially set up and develop SyDBond-enabled coordinator applications.

7 Discussion

SyD has been driven by the current practical necessity to contribute fundamentally on certain aspects of middleware, database, Internet, mobile computing and related arenas. We briefly discuss SyD's place among the emerging middleware and distributed computing technologies, as well as where it is in terms of its goals. SyD as a middleware has a varying degree of flavors of object orientation (to mask heterogeneity), coordination orientation (for distributed coordination and ad-hoc group applications), and aspect orientation (distributed coordination among SyD objects with dynamic restructuring of embedded SyD bonds among coordinating objects). Additionally, it presents a reflection orientation with inspection, reference decoupling and dynamicity of groups through SyD-Directory, and adaptation through smart proxy management, real-time tracking and scheduling of sub-invocations and application level QoS.

The overriding philosophy of SyD has been to be simple and modular, from middleware design and implementation to application development and execution. The main goal has been to mask heterogeneity of device, data, language/OS, network and mobility for rapid collaborative application development. These have been achieved to the following extent: (i) device and data store through listener, (ii) language and OS through generic remote invocation semantics, (iii) network by XML vocabulary for all inter-device communication, (iv) mobility by (a) reference decoupling and replication/proxy through combined workings of SyD engine, directory service and registrar, (b) temporal decoupling through asynchronous invocation with various remote invocation options for mobile clients, and (c) an always connected object view through persistence/proxy mechanism for mobile hosts. A secondary goal has been to develop coordination mechanisms among objects to enable rapid ad-hoc application development, which has yielded SyD bond artifacts.

SyD's object model is persistent, is replicated with proxies, and encapsulates its distribution and replication policies, security, transaction support, etc. The object interface is generic XML/SOAP based for interoperability. Object reference is via XML strings dynamically bound through the directory service. Other aspects are as follows: (i) communication types are both synchronous and asynchronous; (ii) process model - listener is the object server, ensuring registration of objects and its proxies initially and after each disconnect; (iii) naming - object reference is generic XML using global id, id-to-address mapping is dynamic and location independent; (iv) synchronization - object implements its own synchronization mechanism for transaction support or for locking; SyD bonds are employed for inter-object coordination to enforce dependencies; (v) replication - proxy containing actively-managed replica or a functional substitute, object responsible for synchronization with proxy; used for persistence in connectivity for mobile objects; coordination bonds can be employed for coordination among object and its proxies; (vi) fault tolerance - faults/disconnections are supported through seamless switching between object and its proxies; varying level of transaction support and adaptive QoS properties are supported by SyDEngine and its sub-modules; (vii) security - objects encapsulate their own authentication mechanism; SyD relies on underlying network model for communication security.

8   Related Work

In this section we review several related middleware systems for mobile intelligent devices. Generally, these systems can be classified into P2P-protocol oriented systems and dynamic distributed applications (e.g. JXTA) or IP-based client-server applications (Jini, Microsoft .NET, IBM WebSphere Everyplace Suite). A large body of work in the heterogeneous database integration area has largely remained in the research domain without any specific products that can be named.

JXTA [2] is a set of open, generalized P2P protocols that allows any connected device on the network – from cell phone to PDA, from PC to server – to communicate and to collaborate as peers. Currently, JXTA provides a way of peer-to-peer communication at the level of socket programming. Proem [8, 7] is another mobile peer-to-peer platform supports developing and deploying mobile peer-to-peer applications. Compared to JXTA, Proem is geared more toward supporting mobile applications characterized by immediate physically proximal peers. SyD goes further in this arena by focusing on general collaborative applications involving intensive database operations and complex business logic. In contrast to Proem, SyD relies on proxies and provides mechanisms for reusing existing SyD applications and services. Jini [13], a more mature system compared to JXTA, uses Java's remote method invocation. Jini's limitations include the lack of scalability – Jini was originally designed for resource sharing within groups of about 10 to 100 – and that at least one machine on the network is required to run a full Java technology-enabled environment. Qualcomm's Binary Runtime Environment for Wireless (BREW) allows development of a wide variety of handset applications that users can download over carrier networks onto any enabled phone. Microsoft's .Net is a platform based on Web Services built using open, Internet-based standards such as XML, SOAP and HTTP. Communication among .NET Web Services is achieved through SOAP message passing. IBM WebSphere provides the core software needed to deploy, integrate and manage e-business applications. Web Sphere Everyplace Suite extends them to PDA's and Internet appliances. It supports client-side programming through WAP and allows the creation of discrete groups of users.

SyD supersedes the above technologies in terms of unique features such as orientation on mobile-specific applications, easy application to mobile devices, heterogeneity of data, simple middleware API, heterogeneous software/hardware, etc. Only SyD supports a normal database transaction model. Table 1 summarizes the important differences and similarities between SyD and above major related technologies.

Table 1. SyD Comparison to existing middleware systems.

Middlewares	Mobile Domain	Server on Mobile Host	Atomic Tranx	Workflow Modeling	Disconnection Tolerated	Platform Independence
SyD	Y	Y	Y	Y	Y	Y
.NET compact framework	Y	N	N	N	N	N
Jini	N	Y	N	N	N	Y
BREW	Y	N	N	N	N	Y
JXTA	X	Y	N	N	Y	Y
Proem	Y	Y	N	N	Y	Y
WebSphere Everyplace Suite	Y	N	N	Y	N	N

Among research projects and experimental systems, the ICEBERG Project at U. C. Berkeley [24] is based on an open and composite service architecture based on Internet standards for flow routing and agent deployment. Cooltown is HP's vision of a technology future where people, places, and things are first class citizens of the connected world, wired and wireless [6]. The Wireless Messaging API (WMA) 1.0 extends the J2ME platform by providing application developers device-independent access to "short message service" and "cell broadcast service". MicroChai VM is a Java application environment that allows customers to download Java applications to mobile intelligent devices.

9   Conclusions

We have described the System on Mobile Devices (SyD) which is the first working middleware prototype supporting an efficient collaborative application development for deployment on a collection of mobile devices. Our prototype also supports peer-to-peer and server applications. One of the main advantages of SyD is a modular architecture which hides inherent heterogeneity among devices (their OS and languages), data stores (their format and access mechanism) and networks (protocols, wired or wireless) by presenting a uniform and persistent object view of mobile server applications and data-stores interacting through XML/SOAP requests and responses.

The paper has demonstrated the systematic and streamlined application development and deployment capability of SyD on three representative applications from disparate domains: a system of mobile fleet vehicles, a system of calendars, and a travel application.

The device-resident portion of our system has a small code footprint to be accommodated within mobile devices (76 KB). SyD employs seamless switching between a hosted application and its stable proxy to tolerate temporary disconnections and provide persistence.

370 Sushil K. Prasad et al.

The ongoing and future work involves porting SyD to devices other than iPAQs such as Palm Pilots and cell phones, obtaining a pure peer-to-peer version, possibly leveraging off JXTA's directory service, providing more robust QoS functionalities, and addressing dynamic group security issues.

Acknowledgments

To current and past students who contributed at various stages: S. Bhagavati, P. Bhatia, T. Chang, W. Chen, X. Chen, S. Desetty, B. Gamulkiewicz, J. Gong, J. He, Y. He, P. Jayanthi, W. Johnson, H. Liu, F. Tan, Y. Tang, and W. Zhong.

References

1. W. M. P. Aalst van der. Workflow patterns. 2003. http://tmitwww.tm.tue.nl/research/patterns,.
2. D. Brookshier. *JXTA: Java P2P Programming.* Sams, 2002.
3. Keith W. Edwards, Mark W. Newman, et al. Challenge:: recombinant computing and the speakeasy approach. In *Procs. of the 8th annual Intl. conference on Mobile computing and networking,* pages 279–286, Atlanta, Georgia, USA, 2002.
4. Arthi Hariharan, Sushil K. Prasad, et al. A framework for constraint-based collaborative web service applications and a travel application case study. In *Intl. Symposium on Web Services and Applications (ISWS),* Las Vegas, June 21-24, 2004.
5. William G. Johnson. *Relaxed Transaction Model for Composite Web Services Using XML.* MS thesis, Computer Science Department, Georgia State University, Atlanta, 2004. http://konya.cs.gsu.edu/~wjohnson6.
6. T. Kindberg, J. Barton, et al. People, places, things: Web presence for the real world. In *Procs. 3rd Annual Wireless and Mobile Computer Systems and Applications,* page 19, Monterey, Dec, 2000.
7. G. Kortuem. Proem: A peer-to-peer computing platform for mobile ad-hoc networks. In *Advanced Topic Workshop Middleware for Mobile Computing,* Heidelberg, Nov 2001.
8. G. Kortuem, J. Schneider, et al. When peer-to-peer comes face-to-face: Collaborative peer-to-peer computing in mobile ad-hoc networks. In *First Intl. Conf. on Peer-to-Peer Computing (P2P2),* pages 75–91, Sweden, Aug 2001.
9. Praveen Madiraju, Sushil K. Prasad, et al. An agent module for a system of mobile devices. In *Procs. of the 3rd Intl. Workshop on Agents and Peer-to-Peer Computing (AP2PC) in conjunction with Third Intl. Joint Conf. on Autonomous Agents and Multi Agent Systems (AAMAS).* LNCS, New York, July, 2004.
10. Vijay Madisetti. SyD: A middleware infrastructure for mobile iAppliance devices. EE Times Network, Nov 5, 2002.
11. Sun Microsystems. *Connected Device Configuration (CDC) and the Foundation Profile.* Technical White Paper, 2001.
12. Sun Microsystems. *Connected Limited Device Configuration (CLDC).* JSR-000139, May, 2000.
13. Jan Newmarch. *A Programmer's Guide to Jini Technology.* A Press, 2000.

14. Thomas Phan, Lloyd Huang, and Chris Dulan. Integrating mobile wireless devices into the computational grid. In *MobiCom*, pages 271 – 278, Atlanta, Sep, 2002.

15. Gian Pietro Picco. μcode: A lightweight and flexible mobile code toolkit. In *Mobile Agents, Procs. of the 2nd Intl. Workshop on Mobile Agents (MA)*, volume 1477, pages 160–171. Springer, LNCS, Stuggart, 1998.

16. S. K. Prasad, M. Weeks, et al. Mobile fleet application using SOAP and system on devices (SyD) middleware technologies. In *Communications, Internet and Information Technology (CIIT)*, pages 426–431, St. Thomas, Nov 18-20, 2002.

17. Sushil Prasad, Erdogan Dogdu, et al. Design and implementation of a listener module for handheld mobile devices. In *ACM Southeast Conf.*, Savannah, Mar 7-8, 2003.

18. Sushil K. Prasad and Janaka Balasooriya. Web coordination bonds: A simple enhancement to web services infrastructure for effective collaboration. In *37th Hawaii Intl. Conf. on System Sciences*, Big Island, Jan 5-8, 2004.

19. Sushil K. Prasad and Janaka Balasooriya. Web coordination bonds: A simple and theoretically sound framework for effective collaboration among web services. Technical report, CS-TR-04-01, Department of Computer Science, Georgia State University, June, 2004. http://www.cs.gsu.edu/~cscskp/Pub/PB04TR.pdf.

20. Sushil K. Prasad et al. Implementation of a calendar application based on SyD coordination links. In *3rd Intl. Workshop Internet Computing and E-Commerce in conjunction with the 17th Annual Intl. Parallel & Distributed Processing Symposium (IPDPS)*, page 242. IEEE Computer Society Press, Nice, April 22-26, 2003.

21. Sushil K. Prasad et al. Enforcing interdependencies and executing transactions atomically over autonomous mobile data stores using SyD link technology. In *Mobile Wireless Network Workshop held in conjunction with The 23rd Intl. Conf. on Distributed Computing Systems (ICDCS)*, pages 803–811, Providence, May.

22. Sushil K. Prasad, V. Madisetti, et al. System on mobile devices (SyD): Kernel design and implementation. In *First Intl. Conf. on Mobile Systems, Applications, and Services (MobiSys), Poster and Demo Presentation*, San Francisco, May 5-8, 2003.

23. Sushil K. Prasad, M. Weeks, et al. Toward an easy programming environment for implementing mobile applications: A fleet application case study using SyD middleware. In *IEEE Intl Workshop on Web Based Systems and Applications, at 27th Annual Intl. Computational Software and Applications Conf. (COMPSAC)*, pages 696 – 703, Dallas, Nov 3-6, 2003.

24. Helen Wang et al. Iceberg: An internet-core network architecture for integrated communications. In *IEEE Personal Communications : Special Issue on IP-based Mobile Telecommunication Networks*, pages 10–19, 2000.

25. Wanxia Xie and S. B. Navathe. Transaction adaptation in system on mobile devices (SyD): Techniques and languages. In *Symposium of Database Management in Wireless Network Environments in the 58th IEEE Vehicular Technology Conf. (VTC)*, Orlando, Oct 7-10, 2003.

26. Wanxia Xie, Shamkant B. Navathe, and Sushil K. Prasad. Supporting QoS-aware transaction in the middleware for a system of mobile devices (SyD). In *1st Intl. Workshop on Mobile Distributed Computing held in conjunction with The 23rd Intl. Conf. on Distributed Computing Systems (ICDCS)*, pages 498–502, Providence, May 19-22, 2003.

Dynamically Programmable
and Reconfigurable Middleware Services

Manuel Roman and Nayeem Islam

DoCoMo Communications Labs
181 Metro Drive
San Jose, CA 95110
{roman,islam}@docomolabs-usa.com

Abstract. The increasing software complexity and proliferation of distributed applications for cell phones demand the introduction of middleware services to assist in the development of advanced applications. However, from the user perspective, it is essential that these new phones provide a smooth error-free experience. Despite of the complexity underlying a cell phone, placing a phone call remains a simple task that can be performed by most users regardless of their technical background. Furthermore, cell phones rarely crash (especially compared to PCs) and carriers are able to correct certain problems remotely without user intervention.
We advocate for a middleware infrastructure that allows carriers and developers to correct middleware behavior, configure it, and upgrade it, without requiring user intervention and without stopping the execution of applications. We introduce a new technique we refer to as externalization. This technique explicitly externalizes the state, the logic, and the internal component structure of middleware services. As a result, carriers and developers have full control over these middleware services. They can access, inspect, and modify the state, logic, and structure of middleware services at runtime while preserving the execution of existing applications and providing an error-free experience to users. We claim that externalization is the key for the future evolution of cell phones' middleware infrastructure.

1 Introduction

Cell phone functionality has evolved tremendously over the last 10 years. First, there was just voice transmission. Then, short messages (SMS) and web browsing (WAP and iMode) were added. Later, interactions with vending machines (cMode [1]) and multimedia messaging (MMS) became available. Most recently, video conferencing, Internet access, and interaction with the surrounding physical environment (iArea [2]) became possible. The evolution of cell phones and wireless-enabled handheld devices as well as the increasing proliferation of wireless networks are changing our traditional understanding of computers. The notion of desktop computing is slowly evolving into a more dynamic model. Cell phones do not sit on a desktop, are not disconnected from the surrounding environment, and are not immobile anymore. These devices are capable of connecting to wireless networks, they have enough processing power to perform tasks previously reserved for servers and workstations, and they are carried by users on a regular basis. Phones are poised to replace our keys [3], identification cards, and money with digital counterparts. Furthermore, increasing data

H.-A. Jacobsen (Ed.): Middleware 2004, LNCS 3231, pp. 372–396, 2004.

transmission rates (2Mbps with UMTS or 14.4Mbps with Japan's FOMA networks[4]) enable the development of applications that allow cell phones to interact with distributed services (e.g., Web Services) and access and share rich multimedia contents.

The increasing number and sophistication of cell phone applications demands a cell phone middleware infrastructure to assist in the development and execution of applications. Examples of middleware are: RPC, discovery, security, QoS, group management, event distribution, and publish subscriber.

Due to the cell phone constraints (for example, limited resources and reliability) these services must meet the following requirements:

1. They must be configurable, both statically and dynamically, to accommodate the requirements of applications (e.g., transactions, QoS, and security) and to meet the requirements of heterogeneous devices and execution environments[5].
2. They must be dynamically updateable to correct errors and therefore provide users with an error-free and zero maintenance execution model [6]. According to existing studies [7], 10% cell phones are returned due to software problems. With over 1200 million subscribers worldwide, it means that over 120 million phones are returned every year. Requesting cell phone users to take their device to a customer support center to correct the software errors is too costly for carriers and frustrating for cell phone users.
3. They must provide support for run-time upgrades to incorporate new functionality (for example, new interfaces, new protocols, and new policies)[8].

We refer to the previous issues as configurability (1), updateability (2), and upgradeability (3). Reflective middleware services[9, 10] provide functionality for configurability. They support replacement and assembly of certain components to adapt to changes and create certain device dependent configurations. However, most reflective systems assume a basic skeleton where only certain pre-defined changes and configurations are allowed. We seek a mechanism that allows modifying every aspect of the system (including the static skeleton), and enables fine-grained customizations.

Bitfone[7], Redbend [11], and DoOnGo[12] support updateability and upgradeability. They provide functionality to update the cell phone's firmware at runtime. They calculate the binary differences between the new and old images and update the differences. However, none of these products allows updating the software without stopping the system. They require restarting the devices, require user intervention, and do not provide fine-grained updating capabilities, that is, it is not possible to change certain logic or structural properties. The whole software image has to be replaced. Our goal is to avoid or minimize user intervention and preserve the normal execution of the system.

In this paper, we present a new middleware construction approach that assists in the development of configurable, updateable, and upgradeable middleware services. These services are assembled dynamically from small execution units (micro building blocks) and can be reconfigured at runtime. Our approach externalizes three key middleware execution elements: state, structure, and logic. As a result, we have fine-grained control over running middleware services in terms of configurability, updateability, and upgradeability. We have used the construction technique to build an efficient communication middleware service that we can configure, update, and upgrade at runtime. Despite of this flexibility, the service provides performance equivalent to non-reconfigurable services.

The paper is structured as follows: Section 2 motivates middleware externalization as a key technique for middleware configuration, updating, and upgrading. Section 3 describes Dynamically Programmable and Reconfigurable Software (DPRS), our approach to construct flexible middleware services. Section 4 describes in detail a communication middleware service (ExORB) that we have built using a Java prototype of DPRS. Section 5 provides a performance evaluation of ExORB. We present related work in Section 6 and conclude in Section 7.

2   Motivation for Middleware Architecture Externalization

Middleware architecture externalization relies on three key aspects: state externalization, structure externalization, and logic externalization. State externalization exports the internal middleware state attributes so they can be inspected and modified. Structure externalization exports the list of components that compose the middleware service and supports inspection and modification. Finally, logic externalization exports the interaction rules among the structural components (logic of the middleware service), thus providing support to inspect and modify the logic.

The main benefit of architecture externalization is the ability to learn, reason, and modify every aspect of a middleware service. The notion of architecture externalization is similar to computational reflection[13], which is a technique that allows a system to maintain information about itself (meta-information) and use this information to change its behavior (adapt). However, the key difference between computational reflection and architecture externalization is the scope of information maintained by the software, and the scope of the changes allowed. Existing computational reflection middleware services [14, 15], explicitly define the internal aspects they export, and the changes they accept. However, middleware services based on architecture externalization export every detail in terms of structure, logic, and state, and accept arbitrary changes in any of the three categories. Building an externalized middleware service requires identifying the functional units of the service (we call them micro building blocks) and using the techniques described in Section 3 to define their composition and interaction rules. The resulting middleware service can be inspected and modified. Figure 1 depicts an architecture browser tool we have built that connects to a device and extracts the structure, logic, and state of the software it hosts. The figure illustrates the structure and part of the logic of the externalized communication middleware service running in the device (RemoteInvocationSupport).

Externalized middleware services are assembled at runtime using an architecture descriptor that contains information about the components that compose the system (structure), the interaction rules for these components (logic), and a descriptor with detailed information about each structural component (input parameters, output parameters, and state attributes). The collection of all state attributes corresponds to the global middleware service state. These descriptors are the service blueprints and provide the information required to assemble the service at runtime. We use the descriptors to configure middleware services to different devices. Furthermore, these blueprints constitute a valuable formalism to understand the composition and behavior of existing middleware services. Developers can access these descriptors (or extract them directly from a running system), understand the internal details of the system, and introduce changes to customize the service without reading a single line of source code.

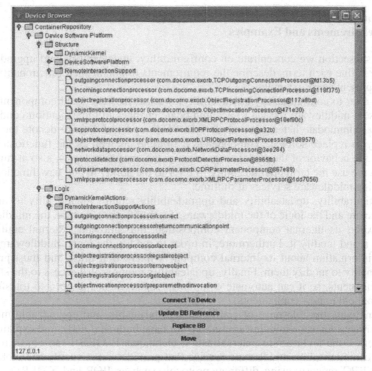

Fig. 1. Middleware architecture browser.

Another benefit of architecture externalization is that it exports the execution state of the system, which includes information about the currently executed internal component. This information becomes essential in determining safe reconfiguration points, which correspond to execution states where it is safe to replace components, modify the logic, and modify state attributes. The system can determine these safe points without requiring any support from the software developers.

Finally, a benefit of architecture externalization is the ability to virtualize the software infrastructure and create snapshots of the running system. This functionality is particularly useful to suspend, resume, and migrate software automatically. Furthermore, heterogeneous systems can exchange architecture definitions and reconfigure themselves to enable interoperability.

We have built a software construction mechanism that relies on architecture externalization. We refer to this type of software as Dynamically Programmable and Reconfigurable Software (DPRS). Programmable because similarly to hardware FPGAs (Field Programmable Gate-Arrays) that allow programming the behavior of the hardware, our technique allows programming the behavior of the software by defining the structure and logic of the software. Reconfigurable, because it is possible to access and alter the structure, logic, and state of the middleware. Finally, the adverb dynamically specifies that changes to the middleware architecture can be performed at runtime. In this paper we describe our experience using DPRS to build middleware services.

2.1 Configurability, Updateability, and Upgradeability: Requirements and Examples

In this subsection we concentrate on configurability, updateability, and upgradeability. We define each term, describe the requirements to obtain such functionality, and finally present some examples.

We refer to configurability as the ability to select the functional components that compose a middleware service to accommodate changes in the execution conditions and to accommodate heterogeneous devices. With updateability we denote the functionality to replace software components at runtime, as well as the functionality to modify the behavior of the middleware (that is, the execution logic), also at runtime. Finally, we use the term upgradeability to refer to the ability to add new functionality to existing middleware services at runtime.

Configurability, updateability and upgradeability require functionality to modify the structure and the logic of the middleware. To modify the structure, the middleware must export its internal component composition, thus allowing external entities to inspect it and modify it. Furthermore, in order to modify the logic, middleware must export information about its internal component interaction rules, and must provide functionality to modify them. Finally, updateability requires also access to the state of the components, so it can automate component replacement (no need to transfer the state from old to new components).

To motivate the relevance of configurable, updateable, and upgradeable middleware services we use a middleware service we have built (ExORB), and explain how we leverage the architecture externalization technique. ExORB is an object request broker communication middleware service that provides functionality to invoke and receive RPC requests using different protocols such as IIOP and XMLRPC. As a DPRS-enabled service, ExORB can be configured, updated, and upgraded. We present an example for each feature next and leave the detailed description of the design of ExORB for Section 4.

As an example of **configurability** assume the following two cases:

- Customizing ExORB for client-side only functionality (sending requests only) or client and server side functionality (sending and receiving requests) depending on the role of the devices and available resources
- Replacing an existing protocol encoding component with a new one that implements an algorithm optimized to the new execution conditions (for example, reduced bandwidth).

Regarding **updateability**, consider the two following examples:

- Assume that the component that encodes IIOP requests has an error and adds wrong information to the request header. Developers can correct the component code and replace the existing component with the new one without stopping the system and without requiring user intervention.
- Consider the case where developers find a more efficient way to send requests. The new approach invokes ExORB's internal components in a different order (connects first to the remote object and generates the IIOP messages only upon successfully connecting) and reduces the time required to send remote invocations. Due to the logic externalization property, we can dynamically modify the component invocation order.

Finally, regarding **upgradeability**, we describe four examples next:

- The first example is about interceptors, which allow adding functionality to object request brokers. An interceptor is an object that is invoked before and after sending a request to customize the behavior of the request broker. Interceptors are used, for example, to encrypt and decrypt the buffer before it is sent. Building interceptors in ExORB is simple. We create a new component, register it with ExORB's externalized structure, and modify the logic of ExORB so it invokes the new component before sending the request data over the network. The key difference with traditional interceptors is that with ExORB we can leverage the structure and logic externalization to insert interceptors in arbitrary positions. With existing ORBs, interceptors are installed at predefined points. Furthermore, most existing ORBs do not accept installing or modifying interceptors at runtime.
- The second example extends ExORB with functionality to broadcast information about its registered objects, which is functionality commonly implemented by discovery services. In order to provide the functionality, we create and register a new component that accesses the state attribute that stores the list of registered objects and broadcasts their references. Then, we modify the logic of ExORB so we invoke this new component periodically.
- The third example adds a new protocol to ExORB at runtime (for example, SOAP). We develop components to marshal and demarshal SOAP parameters, encode and decode SOAP messages, and leverage the rest of ExORB's infrastructure. To add the new functionality, we leverage structure externalization to register the new components, and the logic externalization to modify the logic of the system. Once the functionality is installed, existing applications can receive and send requests over SOAP without any change in their code.
- Finally, the last example adds new functionality to ExORB to support object migration. The new migration functionality removes the target object from the source ExORB, instantiates a copy of the object in the remote location, transfers the state, and registers the object with the target ExORB. Furthermore, we insert a component that maintains a list of migrated objects so it can redirect incoming requests. We can install the new functionality at runtime without affecting the execution of the existing ExORB. Adding the migration functionality leverages the logic externalization to add new logic to ExORB, structure externalization to add new components that implement the migration functionality, and state externalization to access and modify the list of registered objects both at the source and target ExORBs.

Based on our experience building ExORB and an event distribution middleware service, architecture externalization is a key mechanism to achieve configurability, updateability, and upgradeability. Externalization gives full control over running middleware services and allows tuning and correcting their behavior without requiring user intervention. Furthermore, with architecture externalization, the scope of reconfiguration of middleware services is open ended. The ability to manipulate the structure, logic, and state, allows programming the behavior of the middleware services at runtime.

3 Dynamically Programmable and Reconfigurable Software (DPRS)

This section provides a detailed description of DPRS. The description includes information about the abstractions and the execution model. Furthermore, in this section we explain how the different components of DPRS contribute to the middleware configurability, updateability, and upgradeability.

3.1 DPRS Abstractions

DPRS relies on three abstractions to build dynamically reconfigurable software: Micro Building Block (MBB), Action, and Domain. An MBB is the smallest functional unit in the system, an action defines the logic of the system, and a domain represents a collection of related MBBs. DPRS relies on name and value tuples as an indirection mechanism to address system entities. This indirection simplifies the introduction of changes in the system at runtime and has proved effective to build decoupled and manageable systems.

3.1.1 Micro-building Block

An MBB is the smallest addressable functional unit in the system. An MBB receives a collection of input parameters, executes an action that might affect its state, and generates a collection of output parameters. An example of an MBB is "registerObject", which receives two input parameters, a name and an object reference, updates a list (its state) with the new entry, and returns the number of registered objects.

MBBs store their state attributes as name and value tuples in a system provided storage area. This mechanism avoids implementing state transfer protocols to replace MBBs. Replacing an MBB requires registering the new MBB instance and providing it with a pointer to the existing state storage area. Accessing the attributes by name enables also external attribute manipulation. External services operate on the existing state and the MBBs obtain the new values when they resolve them by name during the execution of their algorithm. Furthermore, storing the state as a collection of name and value tuples simplifies state suspension, resumption, and migration. We provide services that implement this functionality transparent to MBBs. Figure 2 illustrates the structure of an MBB.

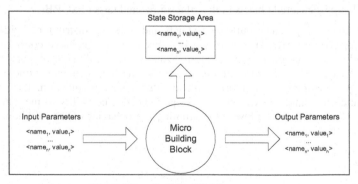

Fig. 2. Micro Building Block structure.

The execution model of DPRS invokes a collection of MBBs in a specific order (the exact mechanism is described in section 3.2). However, MBBs do not store references to the next MBB in the chain. This mechanism implies that no MBB in the system stores references to any other MBB. This approach allows replacing MBBs easily. There is no need to notify any MBB about the replacement because no MBB knows about any other MBB.

3.1.2 Action

Actions specify the MBB execution order and therefore define the logic of the system. DPRS defines two types of actions: interpreted actions, and compiled actions.

An **interpreted action** is a deterministic directed graph where nodes are MBBs that denote execution states, and edges define the transition order. Every edge has an associated conditional statement that is evaluated at runtime to determine the next transition. Conditional statements can refer to parameters generated by MBBs (output parameters). Finally, for nodes with multiple out edges, only one of edge can evaluate true at runtime (deterministic graph). By default, the value of this conditional statement is true. Action graphs have one start node, intermediate nodes, and one end node. The start and end nodes (the end node denotes the action graph terminates) are part of every graph traversal. The intermediate nodes depend on the traversal of the graph according to the conditional statements assigned to the edges and their runtime evaluation. Action graphs include additional nodes and edges that specify the transitions in case of errors. That is, if no errors are detected, the system uses the default action graph (for example, the one depicted in Figure 3). However, if execution errors are detected, then the system uses the error nodes and edges. For example, Figure 3 has an additional edge that goes from each node to the end state (not included in the figure). That is, if an error is detected, the action simply terminates. Note, however, that it is possible to define more sophisticated behaviors. Action graphs allow cycles to support loop statements, such as "while", "for", and "repeat".

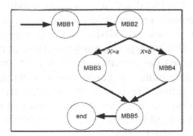

Fig. 3. Interpreted Action example.

Executing an interpreted action corresponds to traversing the graph. Figure 3 depicts an action example where MBB1 is the start node. The action starts with the invocation of MBB1, continues with the invocation of MBB2, then, depending on the value of 'X' it invokes MBB3 or MBB4, and finally, it invokes MBB5. The value of the variable 'X' is either provided by the client invoking the action or it is an output parameter generated by MBB1 or MBB2. This value is stored as part of the action execution state, which is described in detail in the execution model (Section 3.2).

Interpreted actions provide reflection at the execution level by exporting information about the current execution state, and by providing support to modify the action graph at runtime. Furthermore, the explicit representation simplifies reasoning about the logic of the system, supports static analysis, and allows third parties to modify the behavior of the system by adding or removing states and configuring the graph.

A **compiled action** is a code fragment that specifies the MBB invocation order. Compiled actions invoke MBBs using a DPRS library. This library receives an MBB name and a collection of input tuples, and invokes the specified MBB with the provided input parameters. This mechanism allows DPRS to take control over MBB invocation, which allows DPRS to replace MBBs safely. Figure 4 illustrates an example of a compiled action, which corresponds to the interpreted action depicted in Figure 3.

```
action Test
{
    outputParams = InvokeMBB(MBB1, inputParams);
    outputParams = InvokeMBB(MBB2, outputParams);
    char X = outputParams.get("X");
    if (X=='a')
        outputParams = InvokeMBB(MBB3, outputParams);
    if (X=='b')
        outputParams = InvokeMBB(MBB4,outputParams);
    outputParams = InvokeMBB(MBB5, outputParams);
}
```

Fig. 4. Compiled action example.

The compiled actions' code is provided as an MBB that is registered with the system. Therefore, invoking the action corresponds to invoking the MBB. This approach allows us to replace action definitions at runtime.

The key difference between interpreted and compiled actions is the runtime manipulation granularity. Compiled actions cannot be modified at runtime, that is, it is not possible to add, remove, or modify transition states. Changing their behavior requires replacing their associated MBB, that is, replacing the action code. Furthermore, it is not possible to inspect compiled actions at runtime, and therefore it is not possible to learn about the current execution state, or learn about the action behavior. With interpreted actions, the graph provides enough information to learn about the behavior of the action. The benefit of compiled actions is that they execute faster than interpreted actions because they do not require an interpreter to drive their execution. Furthermore, a compiled action gives more control to the programmer over the programming of the software behavior.

Both interpreted and compiled actions contribute to MBB replacement. One of the key requirements to automate runtime MBB replacement is detecting the system has reached a safe execution state. With DPRS actions, these safe states can be determined automatically. The safe reconfiguration states correspond to MBB invocations. With interpreted actions, the interpreter explicitly invokes the MBBs. Compiled actions use a DPRS library to invoke MBBs. In both cases, the supporting system controls MBB invocation and therefore can safely replace MBBs.

Finally, both interpreted and compiled actions contribute to updateability and upgradeability of the systems. Updating an action corresponds to replacing an existing action, or in the case of interpreted actions, modifying the execution graph. Upgrading the system implies adding new actions, or in the case of interpreted actions, modifying the action graph to incorporate or modify states.

3.1.3 Domain

A domain is an abstraction that aggregates collections of related MBBs. It provides a storage area to store the structure of the domain (list of MBBs), the logic of the domain (list of actions), and the state of the domain (MBBs state attributes and execution state values). Domains can be composed hierarchically, and they provide a useful mechanism to manipulate collections of MBBs as a single unit (for example, move, suspend, and resume).

Figure 5 illustrates the components and structure of a domain. All three memories (structure, logic, and state) store name and value tuples. The **structure memory** maintains a collection of tuples that correspond to MBBs registered in the domain. The tuple name refers to the name of the MBB (every MBB is assigned a name at registration time), and the value stores the reference to the MBB. Note that the reference can be a local pointer or a pointer to a remote MBB. The DPRS execution model makes local or remote invocation transparent to developers. The **logic memory** stores a list of actions exported by the domain. Similarly to the structure memory, the logic memory refers to actions by name. Finally, the **state memory** stores the state attributes for the MBBs registered in the domain. During the MBB registration, the system assigns a pointer to the state memory to the MBB. MBBs belonging to the same domain share the same state memory. We refer to the three memories as the *domain memory*.

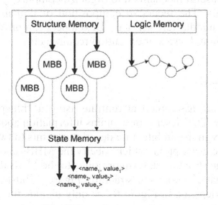

Fig. 5. Domain components.

Domains can be composed hierarchically, which provides a useful mechanism to organize large collections of MBBs. Domain memories store a reference (name and value tuple) to the domain memories of the registered sub-domains, and they also store a reference to the root domain memory. Figure 6 illustrates an example of a hierarchical composition of domains. Root domain has two sub-domains (domain 1 and domain 2) and domain 1 has three sub-domains (domain 3, domain 4, and domain 5).

The default visibility policies dictate that a domain has access to the sub-domain memories. For example, the root domain has access to all the domain memories of the system (that is, domains 1, 2, 3, 4, and 5), while domain 5 has access to its own domain memory only. However, it is possible to modify the visibility policies and allow sub-domains to access their parents or siblings' domain memories.

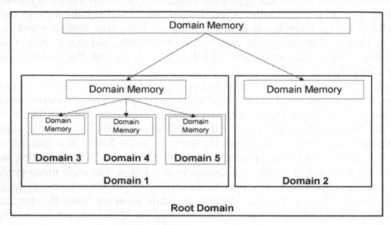

Fig. 6. Hierarchical composition of domains.

Domains provide a useful mechanism to organize complex systems consisting of a large number of MBBs. The recursive composition of domains contributes to the static configuration of middleware services. Developers can provide different domain compositions for different devices or execution requirements.

3.2 Instantiation Model

DPRS-based systems are assembled at runtime using a "blueprint" we refer to as *architecture descriptor*. This descriptor contains information about the domain hierarchy. Each domain entry in the architecture descriptor points to two additional descriptors, structure and logic descriptors, which specify the MBBs and actions registered in the domain. Finally, the structure descriptor points to the MBB descriptors that correspond to the MBBs that compose the structure. Figure 7 illustrates a descriptor diagram for the example depicted in Figure 6 (we only include the root domain descriptors' hierarchy for clarity).

DPRS relies on a runtime infrastructure that provides functionality to parse the architecture descriptor, instantiate the required MBBs, introduce changes at runtime, and parse interpreted actions. Figure 8 illustrates the runtime infrastructure. It consists of two key components: Static Kernel and Dynamic Kernel. The static kernel provides functionality to parse the architecture descriptor, functionality to generate an architecture descriptor for the running system, and functionality to instantiate micro building blocks (for example, Java objects, .NET object, or DLLs). The static kernel is the minimum functionality required to assemble a system based on micro building blocks and it is the only non-reconfigurable non-MBB based component in the system. The layers on top of the static kernel are recursively built using micro building blocks. The dynamic kernel consists of a domain called Domain Manager, which provides micro building blocks to manage the domain. The dynamic kernel provides also the Micro Building Block Scheduler, which provides functionality to execute interpreted actions. Finally, on top of the dynamic kernel are the dynamically programmable and reconfigurable middleware services.

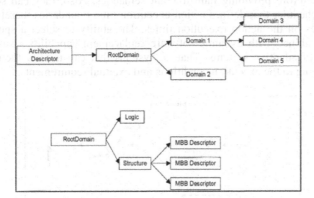

Fig. 7. DPRS architecture description.

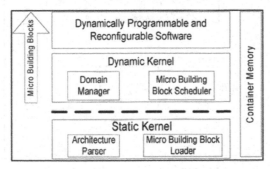

Fig. 8. DPRS Runtime Infrastructure.

3.3 DPRS Execution Model

DPRS interpreted actions externalize the logic of the system. They provide information about the MBB invocation sequence required to execute a functional aspect of the system. The DPRS execution model relies on a component called *MBB scheduler*, which drives the execution of the system using the action's graph as an MBB invocation schedule. The MBB scheduler maintains and exports information about the execution state of the system. This information consists of:

1. Currently executed action
2. Currently executed MBB
3. Action associated parameters, that is, parameters provided by the action invoker, plus parameters generated by the action's MBBs.

The MBB scheduler is implemented as an MBB. Therefore, its state is accessible, and it can be modified at runtime as any other MBB. The ability to replace the MBB scheduler allows developers to provide different execution semantics. For example, they can choose an MBB scheduler that supports transparent local or remote MBB invocation, therefore simplifying runtime software partitioning. Furthermore, they can choose an MBB scheduler that checkpoints the parameters and state after every MBB invocation therefore providing fault tolerant semantics. Also, they can select a real time MBB scheduler that defines action execution time boundaries therefore providing guarantees on the action execution times. The ability to select a specific MBB scheduler combined with dynamic software replacement capabilities simplifies the construction of adaptive systems. That is, systems that can modify their execution model according to the execution conditions and external requirements.

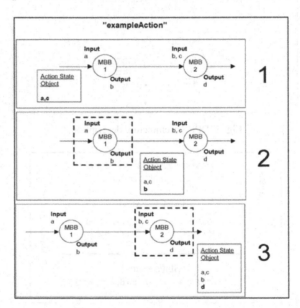

Fig. 9. Action execution example.

The DPRS execution model associates an object called *action state object* to each action execution. Actions use this object to store the input and output parameters associated to the action execution. Parameters are provided by the clients invoking the action and are also generated by MBBs as the result of their invocation. MBBs consume parameters stored in the action state object to implement their algorithm. Saving the parameters generated during the action invocation and synchronizing the MBB access to their state attributes allows clients to invoke actions concurrently. Figure 9 illustrates an interpreted action execution example. The name of the action is "exampleAction" and it consists of two MBBs. To simplify the explanation we assume an action with no conditional transitions or loops. The execution model remains the same. The difference is that the MBB scheduler evaluates an expression to obtain the name of the next state. We describe the execution model algorithm next:

1. The MBB scheduler receives a request to execute an action called "exampleAction". The request includes an action state object that contains two parameters, a, and c (Step 1 in Figure 9).
2. The MBB scheduler uses the action name to access the logic memory and obtains a pointer to the action graph's first node.
3. The MBB scheduler obtains the name of the MBB from the action graph's node, and uses the name (MBB1) to resolve the MBB from the structure memory.
4. After resolving MBB1, the MBB scheduler invokes the MBB passing the action state object. MBB1 requires an input parameter named a, which it obtains from the action state object. MBB1 executes its algorithm and generates an output parameter called b, which it stores in the action state object (Step 2 in Figure 9).
5. Next, the MBB scheduler obtains the name of the next state from the current actions graph's node, obtains the name of the MBB (MBB2), and resolves MBB2 from the structure memory.
6. The MBB scheduler invokes MBB2 with the action state object as a parameter. MBB2 requires two parameters, b and c, which it obtains from the action state object. MBB2 executes its algorithm, generates an output parameter called d, and stores the parameter in the action state object (Step 3 in Figure 9).
7. Finally, the MBB scheduler returns the action state object to the caller.

The main contribution of the DPRS' execution model is the ability to detect safe software reconfiguration points automatically. The basic rule is that the system allows reconfiguring the system between MBB invocations only. MBBs are allowed to access and modify the externalized structure, logic, and state. Therefore, modifying these parameters might affect the execution of the MBBs and could lead to an inconsistent software state. The system waits until the MBB completes its execution to avoid undesirable results. Note that this behavior applies to both interpreted and compiled actions. Compiled actions use a DPRS library to invoke MBBs and therefore give control to the system to implement reconfiguration.

The main concern about the interpreted execution model is performance. Invoking an action requires accessing the domain memory to resolve the nodes of the action graph, the MBBs, and accessing the parameters stored in the action state object. In Section 5, we present experimental results that illustrate the performance penalty incurred by DPRS. The results indicate that the penalty can be considered negligible in most cases.

4 ExORB: A Dynamically Reconfigurable Communication Middleware Service

In this section we present a multi-protocol Object Request Broker (ORB) communication middleware service that we have built using DPRS. The service provides client and server functionality independently of wire protocols. That is, the server object's methods can be invoked over different protocols, such as IIOP or XML-RPC. Similarly, client requests use the same interface and semantics regardless the underlying protocol. Although our implementation supports IIOP and XML-RPC, it is possible to add additional protocols by developing and deploying additional micro building blocks at runtime. As a DPRS system, ExORB's architecture (state, structure, and logic) is externalized, and therefore, it is possible to inspect it and manipulate it at runtime. ExORB has been built using a Java implementation of the DPRS supporting infrastructure, and we use it extensively as a basic component of our infrastructure to enable transparent remote MBB invocation. In the following section, we present the architecture of ExORB including a list of micro building blocks, domains, and actions.

4.1 Structure of ExORB

ExORB is composed of 28 micro building blocks grouped into 11 domains. Figure 10 depicts the structure of ExORB. Next we explain the functional goal of each domain and the MBBs that compose each of the domains.

The CDR Parameter Management domain provides functionality to marshal and demarshal parameters according to the Common Data Representation (CDR) format (CORBA default representation). It contains two MBBs: CDR Marshal Parameters and CDR Demarshal Parameters.

The XMLRPC Parameter Management domain is similar to the CDR Parameter Management Domain but provides functionality to marshal and demarshal parameters encoded according to the XMLRPC protocol.

The IIOP Protocol Processing domain aggregates micro building blocks that export functionality to encode and decode messages that conform to the IIOP protocol. It contains five MBBs: IIOP Encode Request, IIOP Decode Request, IIOP Encode Reply, IIOP Decode Reply, and IIOP Decode Header.

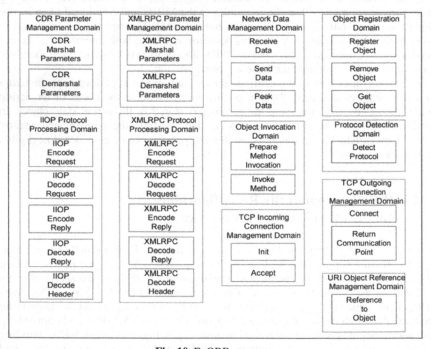

Fig. 10. ExORB structure.

The XMLRPC Protocol Processing domain is equivalent to the IIOP Protocol Processing Domain and provides functionality to handle XMLRPC requests and replies.

The Network Data Management domain is responsible for handling incoming and outgoing network traffic. It is composed of three micro building blocks: Send Data, Receive Data, and Peek Data.

The Object Invocation domain contains two micro building blocks: Prepare Method Invocation and Invoke Method. These MBBs automate server method invocation using the Java language reflection capabilities. Developers do not need to build skeletons for their server objects; they simply register them and the system automatically obtains all the information it requires.

The TCP Incoming Connection Management domain provides functionality to handle incoming TCP network connections. It exports two MBBs: Init and Accept.

The TCP Outgoing Connection Management domain handles TCP connection establishment with remote peers. The domain includes two micro building blocks: Connect and Return Communication Point.

The Object Registration domain is responsible for the management of server objects. It contains three MBBs: Register Object, Remove Object, and Get Object.

Table 1. ExORB size.

Domain	Size
CDR Parameter Management	16KB
XMLRPC Parameter Management	20KB
IIOP Protocol Processing	7KB
XMLRPC Protocol Processing	8KB
Network Data Management	3KB
Object Invocation	2KB
TCP Incoming Connection Management	5KB
TCP Outgoing Connection Management	4KB
Object Registration	2KB
Protocol Detection	1KB
URI Object Reference Management	2KB

The Protocol Detection domain exports functionality to identify the communication middleware protocol of incoming requests. This functionality is required to support the multi-protocol behavior of ExORB. It exports one MBB only: Detect Protocol. Current implementation of the MBB detects two types of protocols: XMLPRC and IIOP.

Finally, the URI Object Reference Management domain provides functionality to parse a remote object URI reference and extract all required information to send requests to the remote object. This domain contains a single micro building block called Reference to Object, which receives a URI and a protocol type, and returns a host name, a port number, and the object id.

Table 1 lists the size of each ExORB domain (Java version). The total size, without debugging information is 70KB. For the current implementation, each domain statically aggregates the micro building blocks. That is, micro building blocks are not installed individually but as a group. The numbers in Table 1 correspond to the size of the code of the domain.

4.2   Logic of ExORB

ExORB exports four actions: send request, receive request, init, and register object. The first one is intended for client-side functionality, while the remaining three (receive request, init, and register object) are intended for server-side functionality. Init and register object are single node interpreted actions, which simply invoke the init MBB and register object MBB described in section 4.1. In this section we provide a detailed description of send request.

Figure 11 illustrates the action graph for the *send request* action. To simplify the figure, we have removed the error states. When the client object invokes the action, it provides an action state object (the one storing the parameters generated during the execution of the action) containing the name of the action, the remote object's reference, the method to invoke, the required parameters, and the protocol to use (that is, XMLRPC or IIOP). The action starts invoking the *reference to object* micro building block, which parses the remote object's reference and extracts the hostname, object id, and port. These parameters are stored in the action state object.

Next, the action invokes *connect*, which obtains the hostname and port from the action state object, establishes a connection with the remote host (or reuses an existing connection), and stores an object that encapsulates the TCP socket (TCP Communication Point) in the action state object. The transition to the next state is conditional. It depends on the value of the "protocol" variable stored in the action state object. If the value of the variable is "iiop", the action invokes *CDR Marshal Parameters* to marshal the parameters, and then it invokes *IIOP Encode Request* micro building block to create the request message. If the value of the variable is "xmlrpc", the action invokes *XMLRPC Marshal Parameters* and then *XMLRPC Encode Request*. Both *IIOP Encode Request* and *XMLRPC Encode Request* micro building blocks generate a byte buffer with the request formatted according to the appropriate protocol. The next state in the action graph is *Send Data*, which retrieves the buffer from the action state object and sends it to the remote object using the TCP Communication Point object stored in the action state object. After invoking *Send Data*, the action retrieves a tuple named "oneway" from the action state object. If the value is "true", the action invokes *Return Communication Point*, which disposes the TCP communication point object from the action state object, and finishes, returning the action state object to the action invoker.

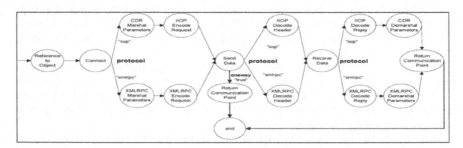

Fig. 11. Send Request action graph.

If the value of "oneway" is "false", the action continues with the decoding of the reply. First, depending on the value of the "protocol" tuple, the action decodes an

IIOP header, or an XMLRPC header. Both micro building blocks parse the message header and store information about the request in the action state object. One compulsory field for both micro building blocks is the length of the remaining of the reply. The action invokes *Receive Data*, which requires the length tuple to determine the amount of data that it has to read from the network. Next, the action proceeds with the decoding of the reply and the demarshaling of the parameters. Again, the action interpreter uses the value of "protocol" to decide what path to follow in the graph. Finally, the action invokes the *Return Communication Point* micro building block (disposes the TCP communication point) and terminates, returning the actions state object to the action invoker. The action state object contains the result parameters.

4.3 State of ExORB

A key feature of DPRS is the ability to manipulate the software state as a first class object. Every micro building block explicitly specifies its state dependencies, which are defined in terms of name and value pairs. These tuples are stored in a storage area provided by the micro building block domain. The state of the software is the union of all the micro building blocks' state attributes. The state of ExORB consists of all the state attributes defined by the 28 micro building blocks. Table 2 lists the state attributes associated to ExORB. The table includes the name of the attribute, its purpose, and the name of the domain that stores it.

Table 2. ExORB state attributes.

	Domain	Purpose
Sent Data (long)	Network Data Management	Stores the total amount of bytes sent by ExORB.
Received Data (long)	Network Data Management	Stores the total amount of bytes received by ExORB.
Send Timeout (long)	Network Data Management	Value in milliseconds the send MBB waits before timing out.
Receive Timeout (long)	Network Data Management	Value in milliseconds the receive MBB waits before timing out.
Server Object Registry (hash table)	Object Registration	Stores the list of registered server objects.
Server Communication Point Cache (list)	TCP Incoming Connection Management	Stores a list of connected communication points.
Client Communication Point Cache (list)	TCP Outgoing Connection Management	Stores a list of connected communication points.

5 DPRS Evaluation

In this section, we use ExORB to provide a quantitative and a qualitative evaluation of DPRS. For the quantitative evaluation, we present performance numbers and compare ExORB with a non-reconfigurable communication middleware. For the qualitative evaluation, we explain how we have successfully configured, updated, and upgraded ExORB using the functionality provided by DPRMS.

5.1 Quantitative Evaluation

The goal of this section is to examine the overhead incurred by DPRS. According to our experiments, this overhead is mostly due to domain memory accesses (currently implemented as a hash table). When an action is invoked, the MBB Scheduler parses the graph and accesses the logic memory to resolve each of the nodes of the graph. For each graph node, the scheduler obtains the MBB from the structure memory, and finally, during the MBB execution, the MBB might access the state memory and action state object to obtain and store state variables and input and output parameters. Note that the MBB execution is atomic and the MBB resolves any required state variable and input and output parameters at the beginning of its execution, and stores the values before completing its execution. That is, the MBB does not resolve the state variables and input and output parameters each time it needs to use them during an invocation; it caches their references until the end of its execution. For every action state, there is one access to the logic memory to obtain the action graph node, and another access to the structure memory to resolve the MBB. Then, each MBB accesses input (*input*) and output (*output*) parameters from the action state object, and state (*state*) variables from the state memory. Equation 1 illustrates the total number of memory accesses for an action with "n" states.

$$MemoryAccesses = 2 * n + \sum_{i=n}^{i=1}(input_{\underline{i}} + output_{\underline{i}} + state_i) \qquad (1)$$

To measure the performance overhead of the Java implementation of DPRS (Java 1.4), we built a static version of the IIOP configuration of ExORB. We took the IIOP related MBBs' code, modified it, and created a collection of non-MBB Java objects. These objects have internal state (they do not access a hash table), use standard interfaces (instead of a generic "process" method), keep references to other objects, and are assembled statically. As a result, the new IIOP-based ORB does not incur any of the DPRS overhead but it cannot be reconfigured). We used this ORB as the performance baseline for our experiments. For the experiments, we created two objects that communicate using IIOP, a server that receives an integer, calculates its cube, and returns the result, and a client that invokes the remote method 10000 times and outputs the average requests per second value. We repeated the test 10 times and generated an average value, as well as the standard deviation. For the experiment, we used two machines connected to a 100Mbps Ethernet LAN. The server was a Pentium IV at 2.2GHz, with 512MB of RAM. The client was a Pentium M at 1.7GHz with 1GB of RAM. We run the experiment using the static ExORB implementation first, and then we repeated the experiment using the DPRS version of ExORB, followed by three optimized DPRS versions (we explain these optimizations next). Figure 12 illustrates the results of the experiments.

The left-most bar corresponds to the static version of ExORB with 4260 requests per second. The next bar to the right illustrates the performance of the unoptimized version of DPRS ExORB, which handles 1937 requests per second (45% of the static version's performance). The unoptimized version uses interpreted actions, and a hash table to implement the state memory and the action state object. The next bars on Figure 12 correspond to the performance of DPRS ExORB with a number of optimizations. The third bar from the left shows a version of DPRS ExORB that uses compiled actions. With compiled actions, we do not need to obtain each action graph node from the logic memory and therefore, for an action of "n" states we eliminate "n" logic memory accesses. As illustrated in figure 12, the improvement is not too significant (around 300 requests per second more, or 52.4% of the static ExORB performance). For the next optimization, we replace the state memory and the action state object hash table with an array of references, and use an index to access each variable. For this optimization, we need to process the logic and MBB descriptors to assign an index to each variable. We are currently creating a tool that parses the descriptors and generates the additional information automatically. This approach maintains the full flexibility of DPRS ExORB (we can reconfigure every aspect of the system at runtime) but requires additional steps when installing, removing, and reconfiguring the system (which can be automated). With this optimization we obtain 3126 requests per second, which corresponds to 73.3% of the performance of the static ExORB implementation. When using indices, we do not reduce the number of accesses to the domain memory; instead, we reduce the lookup time by avoiding the hash table. The last optimization uses indices and replaces the interpreted actions with compiled actions. As before, the improvement is not significant, we get an additional 112 requests per second.

Although the optimizations presented in this section are still work in progress initial results are promising. The architecture externalizing technique provides detailed information about the system that we leverage to build optimization tools that reduce the overhead of the system.

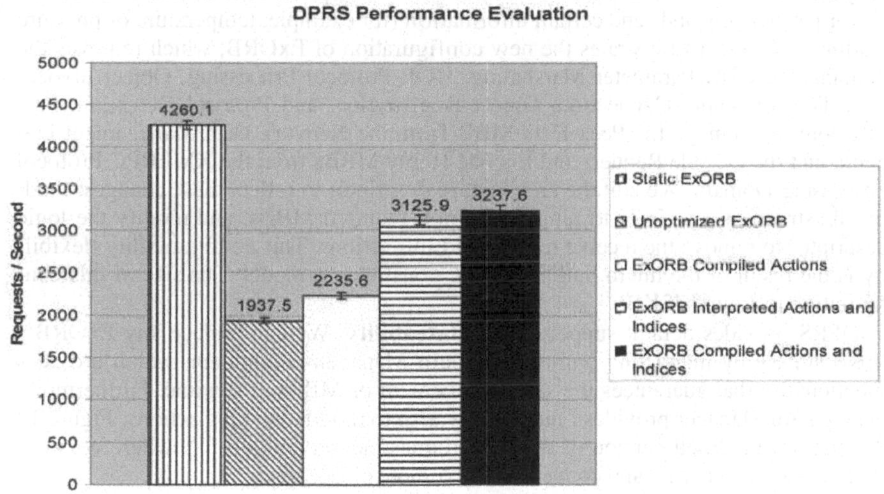

DPRS Performance Evaluation

Fig. 12. DPRS Performance Evaluation.

5.2 Qualitative Evaluation

In this section, we show examples of ExORB configurability, updateability, and upgradeability. These examples leverage the basic functionality provided by DPRS and sustain the claims made in Section 2.1.

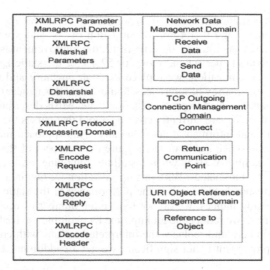

Fig. 13. ExORB configuration for client-side and XMLRPC only functionality.

For the **configurability** evaluation, we modify ExORB to provide client-side functionality and support for the XMLRPC protocol only. This configuration is particularly useful for resource constrained devices (for example, a sensor) that connect to a server periodically and send certain information (for example, temperature or pressure readings). Figure 13 illustrates the new configuration of ExORB, which removes the domains for CDR Parameter Marshaling, IIOP Protocol Processing, Object Invocation, TCP Incoming Connection, Object Registration, and Protocol Detection. Furthermore, we remove the Peek Data MBB from the Network Data Management Domain, and the Decode Request and Encode Reply MBBs from the XMLRPC Protocol Processing Domain. We edit the architecture descriptor to reflect these changes: modify the structure descriptor to remove the non-required MBBs, and modify the logic descriptor to remove the receive request and init actions. This configurability flexibility is the result of the micro building block construction model. The size of this configuration is around 43KB.

DPRS provides default support for **updateability**. We can replace any ExORB's MBB simply by interacting with the Domain Management domain, which provides functionality that guarantees the safe replacement of MBBs at runtime. Furthermore, the Domain Manager provides functionality also to modify existing actions. Figure 14 illustrates a modified version of the send request action (Figure 11), where we marshal the parameters first and connect to the remote object later.

Finally, **upgradeability** is also an integral part of DPRS. We have upgraded ExORB with functionality to encrypt and decrypt the data buffer before sending and receiving it. The upgrade requires adding an encrypting MBB, a decrypting MBB, and modifying the send request and receive request actions. The new actions invoke the encrypting/decrypting MBBs before and after sending data over the network. Figure 15 illustrates the changes to the send request action. The dashed circle corresponds to the encryption MBB, which is invoked after coding the request and before sending it over the network. Another example of upgradeability corresponds to the evolution of

ExORB. Our initial implementation provided IIOP functionality only. Later, we added XMLRPC capabilities by introducing new MBBs and modifying the existing actions.

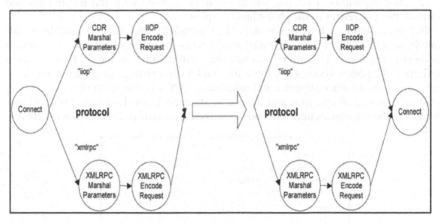

Fig. 14. Updating an interpreted action.

6 Related Work

For the related work, we compare DPRS with reflective middleware systems and dynamic software updating systems.

Reflective middleware [14, 15] refers to the capability of a service to reason about and act upon itself. Reflective middleware services provide a representation of their own behavior that can be inspected and modified at runtime. This representation is known as causally connected self representation (CCSR). Causally-connected implies that changes in the representation affect the underlying system and vice-versa. DPRS is a fully reflective (structural and behavioral) system. It provides a methodology to construct fully reflective middleware services. This approach contrasts with existing reflective middleware services that have to be designed having reflection in mind. That is, developers must decide beforehand those aspects of their services they plan to make reflective. DPRS supports structural reflection (supported interfaces) by means of action listing (actions correspond to interfaces). DPRS also provides architectural behavior by exporting the list of components and their interactions rules. Finally, DPRS provides behavioral reflection; it provides information about invocations' arrivals, and provides functionality to modify the behavior.

There is abundant work in the area of dynamic software updating systems [16]. These projects support executable code replacement at runtime. For example Hicks et al [6] describe a mechanism that relies on the OS linker to introduce code changes at runtime. Their work does not require a special software construction mechanism but they require developers to specify when it is safe to replace code. DPRS does not require developers to specify when it is safe to replace code. Its execution model can detect safe reconfiguration states automatically. Furthermore, DPRS provides information about the composition and execution state of the system. None of the traditional updating systems provides such functionality. Bitfone[7], Redbend [11], and

DoOnGo [12] are commercial products that support over-the-air cell phone firmware updates. Their approach is different from previous work on dynamic updates because they do not support partial image updates. They replace the whole cell phone firmware. Their algorithms calculate the differences between new and old images and transmit the differences to the phone update agent.

Finally, systems such as Ensemble[17] , Cactus[18], and the Dynamically Loadable Protocol Stacks[19] provide functionality to create updateable network protocols using state machines. The latter generates the protocol stack on the fly from a formal definition. The other systems assemble the stack from existing components but allow for changes in the stack (updates and upgrades). DPRS is similar to these systems in terms of dynamic composition and the use of state machines. However, DPRS allows inspecting the internal architecture and supports the construction of arbitrary software.

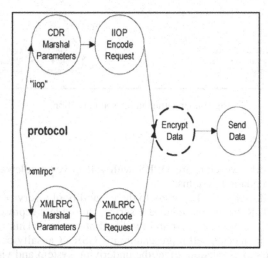

Fig. 15. Upgraded send request action that uses encryption and decryption.

Petri Nets [20] are a formalism to model concurrent asynchronous processes. Petri Nets consist of places (conditions), transitions (events or processes), arcs connecting places and transitions, and markings consisting of a number of tokens associated to each place. Unlike our system, Petri Nets do not directly address state, and structure externalization. Furthermore, Petri Nets do not define mechanisms for safe replacement of components. Finally, our system uses a scheduler that drives the execution of the system. With Petri Nets, state transitions are modeled asynchronously based on the firing of conditions. Note however, that we can leverage Petri Nets theory to model our systems.

7   Conclusions

In this paper, we present a technique to build dynamically programmable and reconfigurable middleware services. This technique relies on three abstractions: micro building blocks, actions, and domains. A micro building block (MBB) is the smallest functional unit in the system that can be composed with additional MBBs to implement software functionality. An MBB receives input parameters, implements an algorithm that affects state attributes, and generates output parameters. An action is responsible for the coordination of MBBs and defines the logic of the system. Finally, a domain aggregates related MBBs and provides a storage area to save the state, the structure, and the logic of the system. DPRS supports the construction of configurable, updateable, and upgradeable middleware services that suit the requirements of next generation mobile handsets.

The architecture externalization technique gives software administrators and developers full control over middleware services. This supports phone evolution by allowing different software configurations, runtime updates, and runtime upgrades. The result is remotely managed cell phones that minimize or eliminate crashes and maximize user satisfaction by avoiding users from participating in maintenance tasks.

Our key assumption is that the individuals that benefit from architecture externalization are experts that know well their domain. For example, we assume that someone modifying ExORB will not insert an MP3 decoder micro building block between the parameter marshaler and the connector micro building blocks. Using the different system descriptors (logic, structure, and state) we implement static analysis to detect syntactic errors, such as mismatching number or type of input and output parameters. However, we do not provide any functionality to check for structural and logic semantic errors. Parlavantzas et al. [5] use component frameworks to address this issue. We leave the topic as future research work.

The architecture externalization technique has proven useful not only for configuring, updating, and upgrading software, but also for simplifying the suspension, resumption, migration, and partitioning of software. Accessing the externalized architecture allows services to automate these tasks without requiring any code from the original software developer.

One of the main concerns about DPRMS is the programming model. MBBs can be built using existing languages such as C, C++, Java, or C#. However, software development requires developers to think in terms of MBBs and actions. A solution to this problem is to provide tools that hide these extra steps. For example, it is possible to provide an IDE environment where users can define the actions visually and the system generates their XML representation (or even compiled code) automatically.

Finally, DPRS introduces a performance overhead, which we have been able to reduce to 25% with initial optimizations. We are currently working on additional optimizations and expect to reduce the current overhead even further.

References

1. http://www.nttdocomo.com/corebiz/imode/alliances/cmode.html.
2. http://www.nttdocomo.com/corebiz/imode/services/iarea.html.
3. A. Beaufour and P. Bonnet, "Personal Servers as Digital Keys," presented at International Conference on Pervasive Computing and Communications, Orlando, Florida, 2004.
4. http://www.3gnewsroom.com/3g_news/dec_02/news_2861.shtml.
5. N. Parlavantzas, G. Blair, and G. Coulson, "An Approach to Building Reflective Component-Based Middleware Platforms," presented at MSRC Summer Research Workshop, Cambridge, U.K., 2002.

6. M. Hicks, J. T. Moore, and S. Nettles, "Dynamic Software Updating," presented at (SIGPLAN) Conference on Programming Language Design and Implementation, Snowbird, Utah, United States, 2001.
7. Biftone, "http://www.bitfone.com/usa/index.html."
8. A. Andersen, G. Blair, V. Goebel, R. Karlsen, T. Stabell-Kulo, and W. Yu, "Artic Beans: Configurable and Reconfigurable Enterprise Component Architectures," *IEEE Distributed Systems Online*, 2001.
9. F. Kon, F. Costa, G. Blair, and R. H. Campbell, "The Case for Reflective Middleware," *Communications of the ACM*, vol. 45, pp. 33-38, 2002.
10. L. Capra, G. Blair, C. Mascolo, and W. Emmerich, "Exploiting Reflection in Mobile Computing Middleware," *Mobile Computing and Communications Review*, vol. 6, pp. 34-44, 2002.
11. Redbend, "http://www.redbend.com/."
12. DoOnGo, "http://www.doongo.com/us_web/."
13. P. Maes, "Concepts and Experiments in Computational Reflection," presented at Conference on Object Oriented Programming Systems Languages and Applications, Orlando, Florida, USA, 1987.
14. M. Roman, F. Kon, and R. H. Campbell, "Design and Implementation of Runtime Reflection in Communication Middleware: the dynamicTAO case," presented at ICDCS, Austin, Texas, 1999.
15. G. Blair, G. Coulson, A. Andersen, L. Blair, M. Clarke, F. Costa, H. Duran-Limon, T. Fitzpatrick, L. Johnston, R. Moreira, N. Parlavantzas, and K. Saikoski, "The Design and Implementation of Open ORB v2," *IEEE Distributed Systems Online. Special Issue on Reflective Middleware*, vol. 2, 2001.
16. M. E. Segal and O. Frieder, "On-the-fly Program Modification: Systems for Dynamic Updating," in *IEEE Software*, vol. 10: IEEE, 1993, pp. 53-65.
17. R. v. Renesse, K. P. Birman, M. Hayden, A. Vaysburd, and D. Karr, "Building Adaptive Systems Using Ensemble," *Software - Practice and Experience*, vol. 28, pp. 963-979, 1998.
18. M. A. Hiltunen, R. D. Schlichting, C. A. Ugarte, and G. T. Wong, "Survivability through Customization and Adaptability: The Cactus Approach," presented at DARPA Information Survivability Conference and Exposition (DISCEX 2000), 2000.
19. S. K. Tan, Y. Ge, K. S. Tan, C. W. Ang, and N. Ghosh, "Dynamically Loadable Protocol Stacks. A Message Parser-Generator Implementation," in *IEEE Internet Computing*, vol. 8, 2004, pp. 19-25.
20. C.A. Petri, "Kommunikation mit Automaten" Bonn: Institut für Instrumentelle Mathematik, Schriften des IIM Nr. 2, 1962

MiddleWhere: A Middleware for Location Awareness in Ubiquitous Computing Applications

Anand Ranganathan, Jalal Al-Muhtadi, Shiva Chetan,
Roy Campbell, and M. Dennis Mickunas

Department of Computer Science, University of Illinois at Urbana Champaign,
1304 W. Springfield Ave., Urbana, IL 61801
{ranganat,almuhtad,chetan,rhc,mickunas}@cs.uiuc.edu

Abstract. Location awareness significantly enhances the functionality of ubiquitous computing services and applications, and enriches the way they interact with users and resources in the environment. Many different alternative or complementary location sensing technologies are available. However, these technologies give location information in different formats and with different resolution and confidence. In this paper we introduce "MiddleWhere" a distributed middleware infrastructure for location that separates applications from location detection technologies. MiddleWhere enables the fusion of different location sensing technologies and facilitates the incorporation of additional location technologies on the fly as they become available. MiddleWhere utilizes probabilistic reasoning techniques to resolve conflicts and deduce the location of people given different sensor data. Besides, it allows applications to determine various kinds of spatial relationships between mobile objects and their environment, which is key in enabling a strong coupling between the physical and virtual world, as emphasized by ubiquitous computing. We have integrated MiddleWhere with our ubiquitous computing infrastructure, and have verified its flexibility and usefulness by incorporating various location sensing technologies and building a number of location-sensitive applications on top of it.

1 Introduction

Ubiquitous computing has inspired the construction of active, information-rich physical spaces that encompass large numbers of interconnected computer devices and embedded processors. This dust of computing machinery will be providing new functionality, offering personalized services, and supporting omnipresent applications. Location awareness enables significant functionality to ubiquitous computing applications, users, resources and the ways they interact. It allows ubiquitous computing environments to tailor themselves according to users' preferences and expectations, and reconfigure the available resources in the most efficient way to meet users' demands and provide seamless interaction. For example, applications and data can follow users as they roam around, content can be customized based on users' location, and physical surroundings can be customized according to their inhabitants.

A plethora of different alternative or complementary location technologies and sensors are available. The different technologies have different capabilities and assumptions and provide assorted levels of location accuracy. No single location sensing technology has emerged as a clear winner in all kinds of environments. For exam-

H.-A. Jacobsen (Ed.): Middleware 2004, LNCS 3231, pp. 397–416, 2004.

ple, GPS is the de facto location technology for wide outdoor areas; however it does not work in covered areas or indoors. For indoor environments, many technologies have been proposed based on badges, wireless devices, etc. We expect different location sensing technologies to be deployed in different environments depending on the specific requirements of the environment. Some environments may even have multiple location technologies deployed.

We believe that ubiquitous computing environments must provide middleware support for fusing data from different location technologies to get a more complete picture of the physical environment and its contents, and to determine location with higher accuracy. Further, a middleware-based solution enables the separation of applications from the location detection and sensing technologies. This makes it possible to extend the infrastructure with new location technologies on the fly, as they become available, without any change to existing applications and services.

In this paper, we propose a middleware for location-awareness called "Middle-Where." MiddleWhere integrates multiple location technologies and presents applications with a consolidated view of the location of mobile objects (which may be persons or the devices they carry). It handles conflicting information from different sensors based on the confidence of their readings. MiddleWhere maintains a model of the physical layout of the environment and allows deriving various spatial relationships between mobile objects and their physical environment. Since no sensor can accurately sense location, MiddleWhere associates a probability value with location information and spatial relationships. Ubiquitous applications or services using this middleware can utilize these probability values, and choose to act upon location information only if it is accurate "enough" for their purposes.

We have integrated MiddleWhere in our prototype ubiquitous computing environment. It currently fuses location information from four different technologies, and has allowed the rapid development of many location aware applications.

1.1 Features of MiddleWhere

MiddleWhere offers a number of advantages in the development of location-aware applications and the deployment of location sensing technologies in ubiquitous computing environments:

1. *Incorporation of multiple location sensing technologies.* MiddleWhere allows the deployment of different kinds of location detection or tracking technologies with different characteristics. Location information can be got from RF-based badges, Ubisense™ tags [1], card swipes, login information on desktops, fingerprint recognizers, Bluetooth, etc. These different technologies give location data with different resolutions and different levels of confidence. MiddleWhere fuses location data from multiple sensors to get a spatial probability distribution of the location of the mobile object. It can also handle conflicting data obtained from different sensors.

2. *Handling the temporal nature of location information.* The quality of location data depends on how fresh it is. As time goes on, the quality of location data reduces. MiddleWhere handles this temporal degradation of the quality of location data by reducing the confidence of location data with time. For example, people in our building have to swipe their ID cards on a card reader whenever they enter certain rooms. Hence, at the time of swiping their card, their location is known with high

confidence. With the passage of time, however, this location data becomes less reliable, since they might have left the room.

3. *Hybrid location model.* MiddleWhere employs a hybrid location model that uses both coordinate as well as symbolic models of location. Location-sensitive applications can express locations either in terms of coordinates with respect to a certain axis of reference, or in terms of symbolic names (such as floor or room numbers, etc.) MiddleWhere also allows easy conversion between the two forms of location data. This gives application developers maximum flexibility in expressing locations in a manner suitable to their applications.

4. *Push and pull modes of interaction.* Location-sensitive applications can interact with the Location Service using either a push or a pull mode. They can ask queries about the current location of objects or they can ask to be notified whenever a certain location-based condition becomes true.

5. *Handles region-based and object-based locations.* There are two kinds of location information that most applications are interested in. (a) Object-based location – this relates to the location of objects, e.g. "where is person X?" (b) Region-based location – this relates to the objects found within a region, e.g. "who are the people in room 3105?"

6. *Model of the world.* MiddleWhere uses a spatial database to model the physical world. The physical layout of the environment (such as position of various rooms and corridors) as well as relevant physical objects (like displays and tables) are represented in the spatial database.

7. *Spatial relationships between objects.* An important feature that distinguishes MiddleWhere from other location middleware is its ability to deduce spatial relationships between mobile objects and their physical environment (which includes other mobile objects, static objects like tables and displays, and physical locations like rooms and corridors). Examples of spatial relationships that are deduced by MiddleWhere include proximity to another object, collocation of two objects in a certain region, containment of an object within a region and so on. MiddleWhere also associates probabilities with these spatial relationships. This allows Middle-Where to be especially suited to the requirements of ubiquitous computing environments. These environments emphasize a strong coupling between the physical and virtual worlds, and MiddleWhere provides functions to relate the two.

The remainder of the paper is divided as follows. Section 2 gives a brief overview of MiddleWhere architecture. Section 3 describes MiddleWhere's location model. Section 4 talks about the location service and reasoning engine components of MiddleWhere. Section 5 explains the spatial database. Section 6 describes the sensor technologies we used. Section 7 gives a brief explanation of our implementation. Section 8 briefly mentions some applications that use the system. Finally, we conclude the paper with evaluations, related work, and future work.

2 Architecture

MiddleWhere uses a layered architecture for collecting sensor information, representing it in a spatial database and reasoning about it. Figure 1 shows the architecture of MiddleWhere.

Location sensors send information to the spatial database through the MiddleWhere system. Adapters map raw sensor information into a common representation to

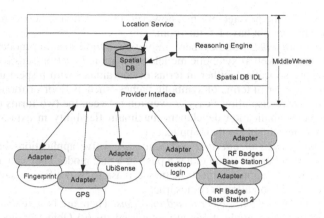

Fig. 1. MiddleWhere Architecture.

be stored in the spatial database. Adapters can be programmed to filter certain events or send information to the MiddleWhere system at varying rates.

The spatial database stores a representation of the physical space as a collection of basic geometric types such as points, lines and polygons. Sensor information is also stored as a separate table in the database. The database provides geometric functions such as distance, containment and intersection that are used for spatial reasoning.

The reasoning engine uses sensor and spatial model information in the database to determine an object's location with a certain probability. It fuses data from different sensors and reasons about relationships between mobile objects and regions. In the next sections we describe the different components of MiddleWhere in more detail.

3 Location Model

MiddleWhere uses a hybrid location model, which includes both coordinate as well as symbolic location information. A coordinate location model expresses location data in the form of an (x,y,z) coordinate with respect to certain reference axes. A symbolic location model gives names to various location regions (such as rooms or floors).

MiddleWhere views location in a hierarchical manner, which makes it suitable for both outdoor and indoor environments. Outdoor environments can be hierarchically divided into countries, states, cities, boroughs, blocks and so on. Indoor locations consist of buildings, floors and rooms. In this paper, we focus on indoor environments, though the middleware can be extended to outdoor environments as well. The coordinate model of location also follows a hierarchical organization. Each building, floor and room has its own coordinate axes and a point of origin. Locations within a room can be expressed with respect to the coordinate system of the room, the floor or the building. MiddleWhere stores the relationships between the different coordinate axes, and hence coordinates can be easily converted from one system to another.

Having multiple coordinate axes for different levels of granularity within a building allows easier specification of location information. For example, if a location-sensitive application is being developed for a specific room, the application developer can specify locations with respect to the room's coordinate system. He does not have to worry about the coordinate system of the floor or the building. Forcing developers to adhere to a single coordinate system would make their applications unwieldy and difficult to change.

MiddleWhere allows defining symbolic locations by giving names to specific regions. Each symbolic location is associated with a coordinate location in a certain coordinate system. For example, names of rooms are associated with the vertices of a polygon representing the room. These vertices are expressed with respect to the coordinate system of the floor.

The location model defines three types of locations: points, lines and polygons. Symbolic locations can be defined for points, lines or polygons. For example, a symbolic point location can be defined for a light-switch by giving its (x, y, z) position with respect to the rooms or floors coordinate system. A symbolic line location can be defined for a door, and a polygon for a table or the floor-space next to a wall mounted screen.

3.1 GLOB

MiddleWhere represents a location in a hierarchical format called a GLOB (Gaia LOcation Byte-string). A GLOB can represent both coordinate as well as symbolic locations. Also, GLOBs can represent point, line or polygon regions. In the case of a coordinate location, the GLOB contains information about the axes with respect to which the coordinates are expressed. A GLOB uses a hierarchical representation of location similar to a directory structure. Some examples of GLOBs are:

- *SC/3/3216/lightswitch1* represents a point location The same location may also be represented in a coordinate format as *SC/3/3216/(12,3,4)* . This means that the *lightswitch1* is located at the coordinate (12,3,4) with respect to the coordinate system of room 3216 in floor 3 of building SC (Siebel Center for Computer Science).
- *SC/3/3216/Door2* or *SC/3/3216/(1,3),(4,5)* represents a door
- *SC/3/3216* or *SC/3/(45,12),(45,40),(65,40),(65,12)* represents the room 3216

3.2 Quality of Location Information

A ubiquitous computing environment provides many different ways of sensing the location of a mobile object (such as a person or a mobile device). Each sensing technology provides location information with different quality. We measure the quality of location information according to three metrics:

1. *Resolution*, which is the region that the sensor says the mobile object is in. Resolution can be expressed either as a distance or as a symbolic location, depending on the kind of sensor. Sensors like RF badges or GPS devices give resolution in terms of distance. For example, some GPS devices have a resolution of 50 feet, which means that the object lies within a circle of 50 feet from the location given. Other sensors such as card-readers give resolution in terms of a symbolic location, like a room. For example, a card reader says that a person is somewhere inside a room.

2. *Confidence*, which is measured as the probability that the person is actually within a certain area returned by the sensor. This probability is calculated based on which sensors can detect the person in the area of interest.
3. *Freshness*, which is measured based on the time that has elapsed since the sensor reading. All sensor readings have an expiry time, beyond which the reading is no longer valid. Besides, our location model employs a temporal degradation function (tdf) that reduces the confidence of the location information from a particular sensor with time,

$$\text{tdf}_{\text{sensor-type}} : \text{conf x time} \rightarrow \text{conf}$$

The tdf may degrade the confidence in a continuous or in a discrete manner with time. Each location sensing technology (or sensor-type) in MiddleWhere is associated with a resolution, a confidence level and a temporal degradation function.

4   The Location Service

The Location Service is the source of location information for all location-sensitive applications. It reasons about location information from different sensors and provides a consolidated view to all location-sensitive applications. It performs the following tasks. (1) Fuses data from multiple sensors and resolves conflicts. (2) Answers object-based and region-based queries. (3) Accepts subscriptions for location-based conditions and notifies applications when the conditions become true. (4) Supports the creation of spatial regions and the association of different kinds of properties with these regions. (5) Supports the addition of static objects, along with spatial properties of these objects. (6) Deduces a number of higher-level spatial relationship functions.

4.1   Multi-sensor Location Information Fusion

MiddleWhere allows the use of different kinds of sensors. Different sensors give location information in different formats (either as coordinate or as symbolic locations), and with different resolution, confidence and freshness. Multi-sensor fusion uses data from different sensors to derive a spatial probability distribution of the location of the person, which is the probability that the person is in different regions of space.

4.1.1   Sensor Errors
Before we describe our algorithm, we first characterize the kinds of errors sensors can have. There are in general two kinds of errors that sensor readings can have for a certain region A. (1) The sensor says a person is not in A when he is actually in A. (2) The sensor says a person is in A when he is actually not in A.

All location sensing technologies rely on the person carrying a certain device (like a badge, a laptop or even a finger). Hence the technology only works if the person is carrying the device. Let the probability that he is carrying the device be x. The value of x can be assumed to be 1 for biometric authentication devices, like fingerprint readers. For devices like badges, the value of x can be determined by observing user behavior.

Most product specifications of location sensing technologies give the conditional probability that the device is correctly detected when and where it is present:

P(sensor says device is in A | device is in A) = y .

In addition, location technologies also have a probability of misidentification,

i.e. P(sensor says device is in A | device is not in A) = z

Such an event occurs if a different person was in the region and the sensor incorrectly identified him. For example, a fingerprint recognizer can wrongly match the fingerprint of a person to someone else.

We shall now derive an expression for the probability, p, of the first kind of error:

p = P(sensor says person is not in A | person is actually in A)

= P(sensor says person is not in A | person is carrying device, person is in A)*P(person is carrying device) + P(sensor says person is not in A | person is not carrying device, person is in A)*P(person is not carrying device)

= $(1-y)*x + (1-z)*(1-x)$

The probability, q, of the second kind of error is:

q = P(sensor says person is in A | person is actually not in A)

= P(sensor says person is in A | person is carrying device, person is not in A)*P(person is carrying device) + P(sensor says person is in A | person is not carrying device, person is not in A)*P(person is not carrying device)

= $z*x + (y+z)*(1-x)$ = $z + y*(1-x)$

Thus, each sensor has 2 confidence values associated with it : p and q (which in turn are derived from x, y and z). These values are used when we combine multiple sensor readings. For example, the Ubisense UWB technology deployed in our building can detect the location of a badge within 6 inches 95% of the time. Thus, for Ubisense, the area A is a circle of radius 6" centered at the location returned by Ubisense. The various sensor probabilities are: y =0.95 and z = 0.05 * area(A)/area(U) , where U is the area of coverage of Ubisense. This value comes about because the device wrongly detects the person's location with probability 0.05 and the probability that it says that the person is in A is proportional to the area of A. x is calculated from user studies which measure what percentage of time the user carries his badge with him.

4.1.2 Algorithm for Multi-sensor Location Fusion

The input to our algorithm is sensor data about the location of people. This data can either be in a coordinate format (i.e. an (x,y,z) coordinate with an error radius) or as a symbolic location (like a room).

The first step in our algorithm is to get all the sensor data in a common format. All locations are converted to a common coordinate format (such as the building's) and are expressed as minimum bounding rectangles. While approximating sensor regions with minimum bounding rectangles decreases the accuracy of location detection, the advantages in terms of performance and simplicity far outweigh the loss in accuracy. Many operations like finding intersection regions, area and containment properties are very easy and fast to perform on rectangles (as opposed to circles or arbitrary polygons).

Various sensor rectangles are then combined with the intuition that different sensors reinforce one another if their rectangles intersect, and are in conflict if their rectangles are disjoint. In order to explain this intuition, we take the case of two different sensor rectangles. There are 3 cases: when one rectangle contains the other, when they intersect and when they are disjoint.

Case 1: One rectangle contains the other
In Figure 2, sensor s_1 says that the person is in the inner rectangle A, and sensor s_2 says that the person is in the outer rectangle B. The sensors are also associated with probability specs, p_1, q_1, p_2 and q_2 (as obtained from the previous section).

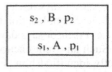

Fig. 2.

These two sensor readings partition the world into 3 different regions, rectangle A, rectangle B and the region outside B. Hence, we can calculate the probability that the person is actually within these regions using the data from the two sensors. Let the event that the person is in rectangle j be represented as $person_j$ and let the event that sensor s_i says he is in rectangle j be represented as $s_{i,j}$ (where i is 1 or 2 and j is A or B). We use Bayes theorem to get the conditional probability that the person is in various regions given the sensor readings.

$$P(person_B \mid s_{1,A}, s_{2,B}) =$$

$$\frac{P(s_{1,A}, s_{2,B} \mid person_B) * P(person_B)}{P(s_{1,A}, s_{2,B} \mid person_B) * P(person_B) + P(s_{1,A}, s_{2,B} \mid \neg person_B) * P(\neg person_B)} =$$

$$\frac{P(s_{1,A} \mid person_B) * P(s_{2,B} \mid person_B) * P(person_B)}{P(s_{1,A}, s_{2,B} \mid person_B) * P(person_B) + P(s_{1,A}, s_{2,B} \mid \neg person_B) * P(\neg person_B)}. \quad (1)$$

(Since sensors s_1 and s_2 are conditionally independent given $person_B$)

Now, $P(person_B)$ is the probability that the person is in the rectangle B. The value of this depends on the movement patterns of B. In order to calculate this, we would need to measure how much time a person spends in different regions. However, in the absence of such data, we assume that the person is equally likely to be in any region. In that case, the probability that the person is in rectangle B is $area_B/area_U$, where U represents the whole universe under consideration and $area_i$ is the area of region i (where i is U or B). In our setting, U is the floor-area of the entire building.

Now, $P(s_{1,A} \mid person_B) =$

$$P(s_{1,A} \mid person_A, person_B) * P(person_A \mid person_B) + P(s_{1,A} \mid \neg person_A, person_B) * P(\neg person_A \mid person_B)$$

$$= p_1 * area_A / area_B + q_1 * (1 - area_A/area_B) \quad (2)$$

Similarly, $P(s_{1,A} \mid \neg person_B) =$

$$P(s_{1,A} \mid person_A, \neg person_B) * P(person_A \mid \neg person_B) + P(s_{1,A} \mid \neg person_A, \neg person_B) * P(\neg person_A \mid \neg person_B)$$

$$= 0 + q_1 * 1 = q_1 \quad (3)$$

From Equations (1), (2) and (3),

$$P(person_B \mid s_{1,A}, s_{2,B}) =$$

$$\frac{[p_1 * area_A / area_B + q_1 * (1 - area_A/area_B)] * p_2 * area_B/area_U}{[p_1 * area_A / area_B + q_1 * (1 - area_A/area_B)] * p_2 * area_B/area_U + q_1 * q_2 * (1 - area_B/area_U)}$$

$$= \frac{[p_1 * area_A + q_1 * (area_B - area_A)] * p_2}{[p_1 * area_A + q_1 * (area_B - area_A)] * p_2 + q_1 * q_2 * (area_U - area_B)} \quad (4)$$

If only a single sensor (say sensor s_2) detected the person, then, using a similar process,

$$P(\text{person}_B | s_{2,B}) = \frac{[\text{area}_B] * p_2}{[\text{area}_B] * p_2 + q_2 * (\text{area}_U - \text{area}_B)} \qquad (5)$$

It can be verified that that $P(\text{person}_B | s_{1,A}, s_{2,B}) > P(\text{person}_B | s_{2,B})$ if $p_1 > q_1$, which will be true if there is a greater chance of the sensor giving the correct reading than a wrong reading. This implies that the two sensor readings reinforce each other and increase the probability of the person being in the region.

Similarly, we calculate the probability that the person is in area A. Note that all p_i's are net probabilities obtained after applying the temporal degradation function.

Case 2: The rectangles intersect
In Fig 2, the rectangles A and B intersect and a new intersection rectangle is formed - C. In this case, too, we can calculate the probability that the person is in the various areas. We just show one of the areas due to space constraints:

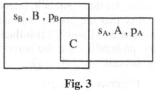

Fig. 3

$$P(\text{person}_C | s_{1,A}, s_{2,B}) =$$

$$\frac{p_1 * p_2 * \text{area}_C}{p_1 * p_2 * \text{area}_C + [p_1 * (\text{area}_A - \text{area}_C) + q_1 * (\text{area}_U - \text{area}_A)] * [p_2 * (\text{area}_B - \text{area}_C) + q_2 * (\text{area}_U - \text{area}_B)]}$$

$$(6)$$

Case 3: The rectangles are disjoint
Disjoint rectangles imply that the sensors are giving conflicting information. This means that one of the sensor readings is wrong and should be discarded. We use a set of rules to decide which the wrong reading is. An example set of rules is shown below:

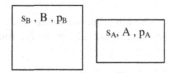

Fig. 4.

1. If either of the rectangles is moving with time, then take that reading and discard the other one. A moving rectangle implies that the person is carrying a location device (such as a badge) and thus has a greater chance of being valid than a stationary rectangle (which may occur if the person has left his badge in his office).
2. else, if $P(\text{person}_B | s_{2,B}) < P(\text{person}_A | s_{1,A})$, then discard reading B (or vice-versa).

In order to efficiently combine different sensor readings, we construct a lattice of rectangles, where the lattice relationship is containment. The rectangles in the lattice are both sensor rectangles as well as any new rectangle regions that are formed due to the intersection of two rectangles. The children of any node in the lattice are all rectangles that are contained by the node.

For example, assume that there were 5 different sensors that detected the location of a person. Their sensor rectangles (S1, S2, S3, S4, S5) are as shown in Fig 5. Besides, the various rectangles create many new intersection regions (D, E, F, G). These regions form a lattice as shown in Fig 6.

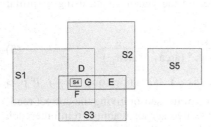

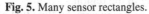

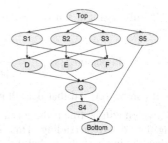

Fig. 5. Many sensor rectangles.

Fig. 6. Lattice of rectangles.

The probability associated with any node in the lattice is influenced by all sensor rectangles that contain it, intersect it or are contained within it. For example, the probability that the person is actually within the region D (which is the intersection of rectangles S1 and S2) is influenced by sensors s_1, s_2, s_3 and s_4. The general formula for the probability that the person is in any region R given n sensor readings $s_{i,Ai}$ with probabilities p_i, $i=1,\ldots n$ is

$$P(\text{person}_R \mid s_{i,Ai}) =$$

$$\frac{\prod_{i=1}^{n}\left[p_i * \text{area}_{\text{int}(Ai,R)} + q_i*(\text{area}_R - \text{area}_{\text{int}(Ai,R)})\right]}{\prod_{i=1}^{n}\left[p_i * \text{area}_{\text{int}(Ai,R)} + q_i*(\text{area}_R - \text{area}_{\text{int}(Ai,R)})\right] + \prod_{i=1}^{n}\left[p_i *(\text{area}_{Ai} - \text{area}_{\text{int}(Ai,R)}) + q_i*(\text{area}_U - \text{area}_R - \text{area}_{Ai} + \text{area}_{\text{int}(Ai,R)})\right]}$$

$$(7)$$

The *int()* function in the above equation returns the intersection of two regions. The probabilities of all regions are finally normalized.

4.2 Queries

The Location Service handles both object-based and region-based queries. The lattice obtained before gives a spatial probability distribution of the location of the person. However, most location-sensitive applications just require a single value for the location of a person and do not want to deal with a spatial probability distribution. Hence, we need to infer a single value for the location of the person from the lattice. To do this, we compare all the parents of the "Bottom" node (since these give the smallest areas). If "Bottom" has just one parent, then the rectangle corresponding to that parent is returned to the application. If there are many parents, then it means that the various sensors report two or more disjoint rectangles. Hence, there is a conflict and just one of the parents must be chosen and the rest discarded. To choose the most likely parent, we use the rules for conflict resolution mentioned earlier. For example, if S4 or one of its parent rectangles is moving with time and S5 is stationary, then S4 is chosen as the actual location of the person. S5 is removed from the lattice. The probability that the person is in S4 is the probability associated with the node.

Applications can also make region-based queries, e.g. what is the probability that a person is located within a certain region. To calculate this, we approximate the region with a minimum bounding rectangle and insert this into the lattice. We find the probability of this rectangle (using Eq. 7) and return it to the application.

4.3 Region-Based Notifications

The other common kind of location-based interaction required by applications is a notification when a person enters a certain region of interest. We have an efficient algorithm to determine if a person entered a certain region with a certain probability. All regions of interest required by various applications are organized into a lattice, just as before. All sensor rectangles are inserted into the lattice as well. The probabilities of all rectangles are now calculated (in a manner similar to what was shown before for rectangle D). Conflicting sensors are removed. Finally, if the probability that the person is within a notification rectangle exceeds a certain threshold, the application is notified.

4.4 Classifying the Probability Space

The lattice described above gives the probability that the person is in various regions. Applications can get the probability and handle it, if they choose it. However, most application developers, in our experience, do not want to deal with actual probability values. For example, it is difficult for application developers to specify different behaviors for the application if the probability that the person is in a region is known with a probability of 0.91, as opposed to 0.93, for instance. Hence, to make it more convenient for application developers, we divide the probability space into various regions. Our current implementation divides the probability space into 4 regions based on the accuracy of various sensors:

> $(0, min(p_i$'s of all sensors$)]$: low probability
> $(min(p_i$'s of all sensors$)$, median of all p_i's$]$: medium probability
> $(median of all p_i$'s , highest of all p_i's$]$: high probability
> $(highest of all pi$'s, $1]$: very high probability

Applications can, thus, choose to be notified if the location of the person is known with low, medium, high or very high probability. Alternatively, an application can explicitly ask for the probability and interpret it as it sees fit.

4.5 Symbolic Regions

Many location-sensitive applications prefer getting location information as a symbolic region rather than a coordinate. For example, when somebody queries for a person's location, he would prefer getting the location as a room number or floor number rather than as a coordinate In order to give location information as a symbolic region, the Location Service maintains a lattice of all symbolic regions. This includes rooms, corridors and other building structures. In addition, other symbolic locations can be defined such as "East wing of the building" or "work region inside a room", etc. The lattice representation also allows incorporating privacy constraints that specify that a user's location can only be revealed upto a certain granularity (like a room or a floor).

4.6 Spatial Relationship Functions

So far we have only talked about single objects and regions. However, the richness of ubiquitous computing interactions arises from the relationships between objects and regions. The Location Service calculates different kinds of commonly used spatial relationships between objects and regions. The availability of these functions in the Location Service simplifies the development of location sensitive applications since application developers do not have to re-write these functions. We also associate probabilities with spatial relations, which are derived from the probabilities of locations of the objects in the relation. There are 3 types of spatial relationships: (a) Relations between two regions. (b) Relations between an object and a region. (c) Relations between two objects.

4.6.1 Relations Between Two Regions

We define several relations between regions based on the Region Connection Calculus (RCC) [2]. RCC is a first order theory of spatial regions. RCC-8 defines various topological relationships: Dis-Connection (DC), External Connection (EC), Partial Overlap (PO), Tangential Proper Part (TPP), Non-Tangential Proper Part (NTPP) and Equality (EQ). Any two regions are related by exactly one of these relations.

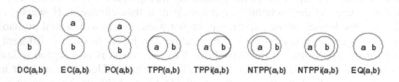

Fig. 7. Different relations between regions, as explained in [2].

A key relation is that of external connectedness (EC). If two regions are externally connected, it means that it may be possible to go from one region to another. An example of this is two rooms that are connected by a door. However two adjacent rooms that just have a wall (with no door) in between are also externally connected. To make this distinction, we define three additional relations:

   ECFP(a,b) is true if EC(a,b) and there is a free passage to go from a to b.
   ECRP(a,b) is true if EC(a,b) and there is a restricted passage to go from a to b.
   ECNP(a,b) is true if EC(a,b) and there is a no passage to go from a to b.

An example of a restricted passage is a door that is normally locked and which requires either a card swipe or a key to open. The various relations between regions are useful for a number of applications such as route-finding applications.

Evaluating the relation between 2 regions is just O(1) given the vertices of the two regions. The vertices of all the rooms and corridors in the building are obtained from the blueprints of the building. The vertices of application defined regions are given by the application. Finally, the relations ECFP, ECRP and ECNP are evaluated by checking if there is a door or an obstruction like a wall between the regions. The Location Service reasons further about these relations using XSB Prolog [3].

Another relation between regions is distance. Two kinds of distance measures are used: Euclidean, which is the shortest straight line distance between the centers of the regions, and path-distance, which is the length of a path from the center of one region to the center of the other region.

4.6.2 Relations Between an Object and a Region

MiddleWhere defines various relations between an object and a region. These relations are probabilistic if the location of the object is only known with some probability. Some of the main relations defined are: (a) *Containment*: whether an object is within a certain region. (b) *Usage*: Usage Regions are defined for certain objects (like displays or tables) such that if a person has to use these objects for some purpose, he has to be within the usage region of the object. (c) *Distance*: the distance from an object to a region (Euclidean or path-based).

4.6.3 Relations Between Two Objects

The main relations between two objects are (a) *Proximity*: whether the two objects are closer than a pre-defined distance. (b) *Co-location*: whether the two objects are located in the same symbolic region (of a specified granularity such as room, floor or building). (c) *Distance*: the Euclidean or path-based distance between the two objects.

5 Spatial Database

MiddleWhere uses a spatial database for modeling the physical space and storing location information from various sensors. The spatial database also supports operations on geometric data types such as intersection, union, disjoint and so on. These operations are used by the Location Service for reasoning about spatial relationships between objects and regions.

5.1 Modeling the Physical Space

The physical space consists of objects and regions. Objects are represented as points, lines or polygons while regions are represented using minimum bounding rectangles (MBR). An MBR of a region is a rectangle of minimum area that fully encloses the region. This approximation enables ease of representation and reasoning [4]. The concept of minimum bounding rectangles is used heavily by the spatial data mining community [5]. Minimum bounding rectangles provide approximate boundaries to objects of interest to enable efficient processing of operations such as checking for certain spatial characteristics, verifying proximity of an object to another object and so on. Once a certain condition is satisfied by a MBR, more accurate processing of the operation is performed taking the actual region boundaries. Figure 8 and Table 1 show the graphical and spatial representation of our floor.

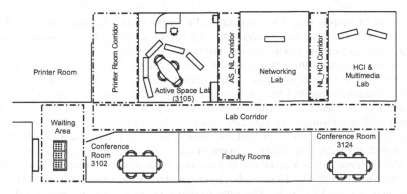

Fig. 8. Graphical Layout of floor.

Table 1. Database table representing the floor.

Object Identifier	Glob Prefix	Object Type	Geometry Type	Points
Floor3	CS	Floor	Polygon	(0, 0), (0,500), (500, 100), (0,100)
3105	CS/Floor3	Room	Polygon	(330, 0), (350, 0), (350,30), (330,30)
NetLab	CS/Floor3	Room	Polygon	(360, 0), (380,0), (380, 30), (360,30)
HCILab	CS/Floor3	Room	Polygon	...
LabCorridor	CS/Floor3	Corridor	Polygon	(310,0), (330,0), (330,30), (310,30)

Table 2. Sensor Information Table Schema and sample sensor readings.

Sensor Id	Glob Prefix	Sensor Type	MObject Id	Obj Location	Detection Radius	Detection Time
RF-12	SC/Floor3/3105	RF	tom-pda	(5, 22,9)	30	11:52:35
Ubi-18	SC/Floor3/3102	Ubisense	ralph-bat	(41,3,9)	6	11:51:22

The *ObjectIdentifier* is a unique name in the name space of *GlobPrefix*. The *GlobPrefix* field specifies the identity of the enclosing space for an object. For example, NetLab is located in Floor3 of the CS department. *GlobPrefix* and *ObjectIdentifier* make up the combined key for the spatial table. The *ObjectType* field assigns semantic information to the object such as *Room, Corridor, Floor, chair, table,* etc. The *GeometryType* field specifies the geometry type used to represent the object. Though we use bounding rectangles to represent objects in our model, certain entities such as non-enclosing walls, light switches, etc are more conveniently represented with other geometry types such as lines and points. Finally, the Points field represents a sequence of points describing the geometry. In addition to the information mentioned above, the database also stores spatial properties of objects, like location, dimension, orientation, etc. Furthermore, modeling the physical space allows SQL queries on objects and regions. An example query is 'Where is the nearest region that has power outlets and high Bluetooth signal?'

5.2   Representing Sensor Information

Sensor information is stored in a separate table in the spatial database. Sensor information from various sensors is converted, by sensor adapters, to a common sensor schema before inserting it in the sensor information table. The table contains temporal information indicating the time when the sensor reading was obtained. The sensor information table schema and some sample sensor readings are shown in Table 2.

We maintain a separate table for storing information about each sensor. This table contains the confidence with which a sensor can detect the location of an object and the time-to-live information of the sensor data. Each sensor is associated with a confidence value that measures the uncertainty that is associated with a sensor's reading. This confidence value is found through empirical means. The time-to-live information indicates the time before a certain sensor reading expires. For example, a card reader has a time-to-live value of 10 seconds. A card reader location value that is older than 10 seconds is considered stale. The sensor table schema and sample data are shown below.

SensorId	Confidence(%)	Time-to-live(s)
RF-12 72	60	
Ubisense-18	93	3

5.3 Location Triggers

Location triggers are events that are generated when a certain spatial condition is satisfied. These conditions include mobile object entering a certain region, mobile object at a certain distance from another object and so on. MiddleWhere uses the spatial database to generate location triggers. Applications can subscribe to receive triggers by specifying spatial conditions. MiddleWhere interprets these conditions into appropriate database triggers and creates these triggers in the database. When a condition is satisfied, the spatial database generates the corresponding trigger. MiddleWhere maintains an internal list of subscribers and trigger identifiers and when it receives a trigger it redirects it to the subscribed application.

6 Location Sensors and Adapters

In order to facilitate plug-and-play support for new location technologies, at the lowest layer of MiddleWhere (Figure 1), we define an object called a *location adapter*. The location adapter is a CORBA client wrapper for the specific location technology at hand. The adapter communicates natively to the interface exposed by the location technology, and acts as a device driver that allows the location sensor to work with MiddleWhere seamlessly.

Upon installing a new location technology, a calibration process needs to be undertaken. This process involves using the characteristics and specifications of the location sensor to convert the location readings to symbolic and/or coordinate location information that matches the location model and coordinate system that MiddleWhere uses. In addition, the two confidence values p and q (as mentioned in Section 4) are estimated. In essence, the adapter translates the location readings into a GLOB that is fed into MiddleWhere through the provider interface.

Every adapter has an *adapter ID* and an *adapter type*. The adapter ID uniquely identifies a particular adapter. The adapter type classifies adapter objects based on the location technology they wrap. Different instances of the same adapter type can be created to wrap multiple sensors of the same type. For instance, we are running RF badge base stations in three different locations. In each location, an RF badge adapter is instantiated with the correct information.

At this time, we implemented adapters for four different location technologies:

1. *Ubisense™*. Ubisense consists of tags and base stations that utilize Ultra Wide-Band technology. The base stations are able to pinpoint the location of a tag within 6 inches 95% of the time. As described in Section 4, we estimate the confidence values of Ubiense as follows. Area A is a circle of radius 6" centered at the location returned by Ubiense, where y = 0.95, and z = 0.05 * area(A)/area(U), where U is the area of coverage of Ubisense.
2. *RFID Badges* [6]. These are RF-based active badges that can transmit identification information. This identification information is in the form of a 32 byte string. This string can be written into the badge. The transmitted ID is received by base

stations that can be positioned in different locations. The base stations can detect badges within a range of approx. 15 ft. This system cannot give exact coordinates of the badge; instead, it is capable of capturing the IDs of the badges in its vicinity. In our experiments, we found that different obstacles can weaken the signal significantly, thus, the best set up for the RF badges is to define an area of interest, A, and set up a base station in the center of A. No error rates are documented for this device, but we found out that there are good chances that it is not picked up due to the system's inaccuracy. So we set $y = 0.75$, and $z = 0.25 *$ area(A)/ area(U), where U is the area of coverage as documented in RF badges hardware specs.

3. *Fingerprint devices and other biometric logins.* In many scenarios, users of our system are required to authenticate to access some data or perform some tasks. Most biometric authentication technologies require physical presence. We exploit this information to get short-lived but relatively accurate readings of a person's location. Unlike the previous technologies, these devices do not transmit continuous signals when users are in the vicinity. In addition, we assume that these devices are secure, i.e., it is very unlikely that a fingerprint device would detect a positive fingerprint match of a user without that user being there physically! Once a user is identified, there is a good possibility that the user may leave the vicinity. In many cases, users are encouraged to manually logout for security reasons. However, in reality, people often forget to logout before leaving the vicinity. For this reason, a biometric authentication adapter provides two different location readings to MiddleWhere: a short-term reading, and a longer-term reading. For short-term reading, we set the expiration time to 30 seconds, define a small area (in our case, a circle centered at the device position with a radius of 2 feet), set $y = 0.99$, $z=0.01$ and $x=1$ (because of our assumptions). In the second reading, we set the expiration time to T minutes, where T can be estimated based on user studies for finding how long a person is likely to stay in the room after authenticating. For our purposes we found that $T = 15$ minutes is reasonable, given the fact that confidence will degrade with time anyway. In this reading, the area is set to the whole room, and z is set to the probability of a user leaving the room before T and without manual logout. If a user elects to logout manually, then this is a clear indication that the user is in the room now, but he is leaving soon. So, the adapter feeds the system with a short-term location reading, where expiration time is 15 seconds, radius is 2 feet, $y = 0.99$, $z=0.01$, and $x=1$. The adapter also forces all location information relating to that user and obtained from the same device to expire immediately.

4. *GPS.* The GPS adapter works as follows. The GPS device tries to achieve a satellite lock. If successful, the adapter should be able to translate longitude, latitude, and altitude information into a coordinate location that matches MiddleWhere's coordinate system. Unlike the above technologies, GPS can give an estimation of its accuracy; therefore, the adapter uses this value for calculating the confidence values. If the GPS receiver estimates an accuracy of 15 feet, we set area A to a sphere with a radius of 15 feet. We can set $y=0.99$ and $z=0.01$ (assuming that the accuracy estimate of the GPS is correct), however, x, will still equal the probability of a person not carrying his GPS device.

7 Implementation

In this section, we provide a brief description of MiddleWhere implementation. We use CORBA to enable distributed communication between MiddleWhere components, Applications, and adapters (that wrap the location technologies). To implement the spatial database, we use PostGIS with the PostgreSQL object-relational database. PostGIS adds support for geographic objects and provide basic spatial support.

While MiddleWhere can run as a standalone service in any distributed computing environment, our objective was to develop a general-purpose location middleware that can be integrated into Gaia. Gaia [7] is a generic computational environment that integrates physical spaces and their ubiquitous computing devices into a programmable computing and communication system. Gaia provides the infrastructure and core services necessary for constructing ubiquitous computing environments. We implement MiddleWhere as an extended Gaia service. Gaia applications can discover the location service component of MiddleWhere by querying the Gaia Space Repository service, which provides a list of available services. Gaia applications can then talk directly to the location service. To access location information, we provide push and pull models. An application can choose to query the location service for location information for a particular object or person, or it can define one or more location triggers for regions of interest, where it is notified when an object of interest is detected inside that region. Additionally, applications can choose to query about confidence levels. We integrated four different location technologies in the system (as mentioned in Section 6), at this time, the location sensors cover four different rooms, that includes a lab, a conference room, and two offices.

8 Example Applications

To demonstrate our system, we have developed several location-aware applications. We briefly mention some of them here:
1. *Follow Me Application.* In this application, we define a user session as a set of applications and files that a user interacts with. The session also includes state information and customization options chosen by the user. If a user moves out of the vicinity of the display he is using, the application will automatically suspend the session. When a user is detected in the vicinity of any other display or workstation, the session is automatically migrated and resumed at that machine. In effect, users can resume their work anywhere and anytime without having to remember to save the latest changes or to worry about copying their data to a removable disk. To implement this application, we create a "user proxy," which manages the sessions of a certain user. The proxy then uses MiddleWhere to discover the location of the user. If the location of the user is obtained, the proxy queries the Location Service for nearby displays or workstations that are suitable for resuming the session; if found, the session can be resumed immediately on the new display. The user can customize the behavior of the *Follow Me* application by changing the settings in the user proxy to accommodate privacy preferences.
2. *Anywhere Instant Messaging.* This application allows a user to receive instant messages from a designated list of "buddies" on whichever display is closest to him. A user can customize the application by choosing to block particular users at

certain locations, or by configuring the system to display private messages only if the location accuracy is 'high' and other users are not in the immediate vicinity!
3. *Location-Based Notifications.* In this application, notifications are sent to people located in a particular geographical boundary (which could be a region or a sphere, etc.) The notification may be a message like "The store is closing in five minutes," for example. This application is implemented by setting up location triggers in the target area, and maintaining a list of users in the region.
4. *Vocal Personnel Locator:* This application combines voice recognition with location-awareness. A user asks the computer to locate a person or an object using a speech interface. The application then queries the spatial database for the required info, and replies verbally.

9 Evaluation

We have evaluated the performance of MiddleWhere on a 4 CPU 3.06 GHz machine with 3.6 GB RAM. The spatial database used was PostGIS 0.8.1 with PostgreSQL 7.3.4 and the communication middleware was Orbacus. Figure 9 shows the time taken for a trigger to be notified by MiddleWhere. The graph shows the trigger response times for 10 different updates to the location service. The various curves indicate the number of trigger notifications programmed into the location service. We expected the response time to increase with the number of programmed triggers but we found that the response time was almost independent of it. This indicates that MiddleWhere scales well with number of programmed triggers. It can be noticed from the figure that the first update requires a higher trigger response time than subsequent updates. This is due to the initial setup time taken by MiddleWhere.

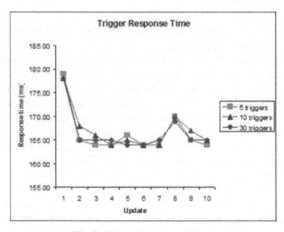

Fig. 9. Trigger Response Time.

10 Related Work

Location-aware computing has been an active area of research. Most projects on location-tracking focus on accurately reasoning an object's location or sensor fusion. In our work, we also focus on designing a middleware that caters to the requirements of location-aware applications.

The Location Stack [8] defines a layered modeled for fusing location information from multiple sensors and reasoning about an object's location. It, however, does not incorporate a spatial model of the physical world. It does not support representations of immobile objects and so does not support spatial reasoning relative to stationary entities such as rooms, corridors and so on.

The NEXUS project [9] uses a spatial database to model the physical world. It supports toplogical and topographic models similar to the symbolic and coordinate systems supported by our system. The focus of NEXUS is on modeling the physical world – it does not address location determination issues. It does not support multi-sensor probabilistic fusion of location information and reasoning with a spatial model as supported by MiddleWhere.

The Aura Space Service [10] provides spatial models for context-aware applications. It combines coordinate and hierarchical location models into a single hybrid model, which supports spatial queries. MiddleWhere uses the hybrid location model introduced by the Aura Space Service. The focus of the Aura Space Service is only on modeling the physical space and supporting spatial queries. It does not address location inferencing issues and does not provide a framework for spatial reasoning like MiddleWhere.

Sematic Spaces [11] has developed spatial models to represent rooms, buildings and other objects. It uses a topological model for representing relationships among various objects. The topological model is similar to the symbolic model supported by MiddleWhere. The project does not integrate the spatial model with a location system and supports no probabilistic reasoning techniques like MiddleWhere. Further, the spatial model of Semantic Spaces does not seem to support a coordinate system like MiddleWhere.

Location-based Spatial Queries [12] project addresses ways of indexing and caching spatial data for location-based queries. The focus of this project is on developing database techniques for queries with location constraints. It does not support sensor fusion and reasoning.

11 Conclusion

We presented the design and implementation of MiddleWhere, a distributed middleware system that fuses various location technologies, resolves conflicts, and combines multi-sensor readings to get more accurate location readings for people and objects. The system facilitates the separation between applications and location technologies to enable dynamic add-on of new technologies, without changing existing applications. We demonstrated the potential of the system by integrating four different location technologies, and developing several location-aware applications.

In the future, we plan to incorporate more devices and deploy the middleware widely. We also plan to conduct user studies to get accurate values of various parameters of our system like the probability of carrying location devices and the temporal degradation function. These probability values can then be used by the middleware and location-aware applications to improve their reliability and accuracy.

References

1. UbiSense, "Local position system and sentient computing." http://www.ubisense.net/.
2. A. G. Cohn, B. Bennett, J. M. Gooday, and N. Gotts, "RCC: a calculus for Region based Qualitative Spatial Reasoning," presented at GeoInformatica, 1997.
3. "XSB Prolog." http://xsb.sourceforge.net.
4. A. Guttman, "R-trees: a dynamic index structure for spatial searching," presented at 1984 ACM SIGMOD international conference on Management of data, 1984.
5. K. Koperski, J. Adhikary, and J. Han, "Spatial Data Mining: Progress and Challenges," presented at SIGMOD'96 Workshop on Research Issues on Data Mining and Knowledge Discovery, Montreal, Canada, 1996.
6. RFId, "Radio Frequency Identification, (RFID)," http://www.aimglobal.org/technologies/rfid/.
7. M. Román, C. K. Hess, R. Cerqueira, A. Ranganathan, R. H. Campbell, and K. Nahrstedt, "Gaia: A Middleware Infrastructure to Enable Active Spaces," *IEEE Pervasive Computing (accepted)*, 2002.
8. D. Graumann, W. Lara, J. Hightower, and G. Borriello, "Real-world implementation of the Location Stack: The Universal Location Framework," presented at 5th IEEE Workshop on Mobile Computing Systems & Applications, 2003.
9. O. Lehmann, M. Bauer, C. Becker, and D. Nicklas, "From Home to World - Supporting Context-aware Applications through World Models," presented at the Second IEEE International Conference on Pervasive Computing and Communications, Orlando, FL, 2004.
10. C. Jiang and P. Steenkiste, "A hybrid location model with a computable location identifier for ubiquitous computing," presented at Lecture Notes in Computer Science, 2498, Ubi-Comp, 2002.
11. B. Brumitt and S. Shafer, "Topological World Modeling Using Semantic Spaces," presented at Workshop on Location Modeling for Ubiquitous, UbiCom, 2001.
12. B. Zheng, W.-C. Lee, and D. Lee, "Spatial Index on Air," presented at IEEE International Conference on Pervasive Computing and Communications (PerCom'03), 2003.

A Game Theoretic Approach
for Power Aware Middleware*

Shivajit Mohapatra and Nalini Venkatasubramanian

School of Information and Computer Science
University of California, Irvine
mopy,nalini@ics.uci.edu

Abstract. In this paper, we propose a dynamic game theoretic approach for choosing power optimization strategies for various components(e.g. cpu, network interface etc.) of a low-power device operating in a distributed environment. Specifically, we model the energy consumption problem as a dynamic non-cooperative game theoretic problem, where the various components of the device are modelled as the players in the game that simultaneously consume a common resource(device battery power). An analysis for the Nash and social optima of the game is presented. We then introduce an adaptive distributed power-aware middleware framework, called "Dynamo", that incorporates the game theoretic approach for determining optimal power optimization strategies. We simulate the distributed game environment for proxy-based video streaming to a mobile handheld device. Our performance results indicate that significant energy savings are achievable for the device when the energy usage of the individual components achieve a social optima than when the energy usage achieves the strategic Nash equilibria. The overall utility of the system is measured both in terms of energy gains and the quality of video playback. Our results indicate that the device lifetime was increased by almost 50%-90% when compared to the case where no power optimization strategies were used, and 30-40% over device lifetime when Nash equilibrium is achieved; the overall utility of system for both types of equilibria were similar(utilities differ by ≤ .5%), indicating that the Nash equilibrium strategies tend to overuse the battery energy consumption.

Keywords: power optimization, game theory, power-aware middleware

1 Motivation

Limiting the energy consumption of low-power mobile devices has become an important research objective in recent years. The capabilities of these devices are limited by their modest sizes and the finite lifetimes of the batteries that power them. As a result, minimizing the energy usage of every component (e.g. CPU, network card, display, architecture etc.) in such devices remains an important

* This work was supported by funding from ONR MURI Grant N00014-02-1-0715 and NSF Career Grant ANI-9875988.

H.-A. Jacobsen (Ed.): Middleware 2004, LNCS 3231, pp. 417–438, 2004.
© IFIP International Federation for Information Processing 2004

design goal and continues to pose significant challenges. These issues have been aggressively pursued by researchers and numerous interesting power optimization solutions have been proposed at various cross computational levels – system cache and external memory access optimizations [18], dynamic voltage scaling(DVS) [9, 7] of the CPU, dynamic power management of disks and network interfaces(NICs) [10, 4, 5], efficient compilers and application/middleware [20, 19] based adaptations for power management. Consequently, future generations of these low-power mobile devices will represent a new class of *"power-aware"* systems. These power-aware systems will be able to make the best use of the available battery power by adapting their behavior to the constraints imposed by their operating environments (users, network topology etc.). Additionally, components of these systems will be capable of multiple modes of operation for power management. Already, current wireless network cards have various power modes (sleep, transmit, idle etc.) and some CPUs (e.g. Transmeta's Crusoe) can be operated at various lower voltages(or frequencies). Moreover, the selection of the modes would be accomplished through various strategies that would control the aggressiveness of the power management for that component.

Interestingly, power optimization techniques developed for individual components of a device have remained seemingly incognizant of the strategies employed for other components. Therefore, increased research effort needs to be devoted to study the important issues involved in the interplay between the power management [25, 18] of the various components. While focussing their attention to a single component, researchers make a general assumption that no other power optimization schemes are operational for other components. Consequently, only the most aggressive forms of power management for individual components are investigated. We contend that unless a study is made of the trade-offs involved in the joint operation of the various components and the customizations/adaptations therein, the power gains (or performance) may turn out to be reductive instead of cumulative. For example, a cache optimization strategy for power optimization might adversely affect the performance of an aggressive DVS based algorithm, as the execution times of the tasks might be affected. Therefore, when multiple components are co-operating to effect power savings, the most aggressive strategies may not necessarily be the best ones. At a very high level, we view the system as a collection of components, that draw power from a common shared energy source (battery) and provide some utility in return. The overall utility of the system can be considered to be a function(e.g. sum, product etc. and is usually defined by the system designer) of the individual utilities of the components. We now need to solve the following problem: *how can we maximize the cumulative user experience (e.g. quality of video for multimedia applications) of the system while ensuring that the low-power device is operational for the longest time?* Fortunately, this problem is amenable to game theoretic analysis, which provides powerful tools for analyzing precisely such interactions.

Game Theory [1, 21] provides a set of tools to model interactions between agents with conflicting interests. For decades, game theoretic tools have been used by economists and others to model economic agents such as firms and stock markets. Game theory typically assumes that all players seek to maximize their utilities in a perfectly rational manner. Economists have a hard time as human players are seldom perfectly rational. However, as in our case, when players are computational entities, it is reasonable to assume some notion of strong rationality (at least as far as computationally possible). Therefore, game theoretic analysis has also been widely used in the study of power control [17], flow control [3] and routing problems [23] in wireless networks. The purpose of our study is to use game theoretic analysis to tailor aggressiveness of power optimization techniques (for individual components), such that both the battery lifetime as well as the cumulative system utility are optimized.

2   Modelling Power Optimization as a Dynamic Game

To model a joint management strategy for power optimization, we must first identify the sources of power consumption. In modern mobile systems, there are three primary sources of power consumption: the CPU, the network interface and the display. At the architectural level, components such as caches, memory and logic gates are also driven by battery power. In this section, we present our view of the system and model the power management problem as a dynamic game. A basic introduction to game theory and some preliminary definitions are posted at *http://www.ics.uci.edu/~dsm/dyn/prelim.pdf*. In a typical low-power system, we have multiple components jointly utilizing a resource (the battery) to which they all have access. In exchange for the extraction of some fraction of the resource, they provide some utility to the user of the system. As an example, for streaming media applications a measure of utility could be both the battery lifetime of the device and the application output quality as perceived by the user. The actual representation of the utility is in itself a rather hard research issue as it might contain both objective and subjective elements. We will revisit this topic in a later section. Moreover, in this case, the residual power of the device (battery) evolves through time according to the pattern of past component usage; note that the overall utility of a set of power management strategies is impacted as the residual power vanishes.

  We can characterize the conjunctive operation of the various components of a low-power device as a non-cooperative dynamic game(Γ). We denote the primary power consuming components of the system as the set of players (P) in the game. Therefore $P = \{P_{cpu}, P_{net}, P_{display}, ...\}$ and let P_N denote the number of such players. Note that all the players concurrently draw energy from a common exhaustible resource(battery). We define the "*game environment*" at a period T as the current residual energy of the device(or battery) $= E_R^T \geq 0$, which evolves over time depending on the energy consumptions of the individual components of the system. The period identifies the frequency at which a sub-game is played and identifies the points in time at which the strategies can be re-evaluated. The strategy space S of each player is represented by an aggregation of all the power management strategies that are available for that player. For example, the strategy space for the processor can be denoted as $S_{cpu} = \{S_{cpu}^0, S_{cpu}^1, S_{cpu}^2, ..., S_{cpu}^N\}$, where there are "N+1" independent power optimization strategies available for the cpu. These strategies could represent the various dynamic voltage scaling (DVS) algorithms suggested for slowing down the cpu under various conditions for energy gains. In general, this strategy space would include all power management strategies available for cpu slowdown. Additionally, we define a basic strategy denoted by S_{cpu}^0, which denotes a strategy that does not employ any power optimization technique for the cpu. Consequently, the power consumed by a basic strategy would be the maximum of all the strategies in the strategy space of that player. Similarly, the strategy spaces are defined for other players(components) in the game. We denote player P_i's ($P_i \in P$) energy consumption during a period T by C_{iT} (for strategy S_i^k); C_{0T} is assumed to be the energy consumed by the player under its "basic strategy", i.e. S_i^0, where $i = cpu, net, display, etc..$ It is natural to consider $C_{iT} \geq 0$ and that consumption gives player P_i a payoff or utility. The value of E_R (residual energy of battery) constraints the total amount of energy that can be consumed by the players, i.e. at every period T, it must be the case that

$$\sum_{i=1..P_N} C_{iT} \leq E_R^T \tag{1}$$

The amount of residual energy that would remain when each player plays its basic strategy (no power optimization) is given by $X_T = E_R^T - \sum C_{0T}$, However, when power optimization strategies are employed, each player generates an energy saving over the energy consumed by its basic strategy. We denote these energy savings as $\triangle_i^k$, where i is the player index {cpu, disk etc.} and k is the strategy used by the player. Therefore, the residual energy available in the period $T + 1$ is ($E_R^{(T+1)} \geq X_T$) and is given by

$$E_R^{(T+1)} = E_R^T - \sum C_{0T} + \sum \triangle_i^k \tag{2}$$

Now if energy gain was the only measure of the utility, then maximizing $\triangle_i^k$ would maximize the utility. However in practice, the payoffs for power management strategies are influenced by a number of factors beyond the control of the players. The form factor of the device, the number and type of executing applications, energy gains, perceived user satisfaction, QoS guarantees, application response times etc. are all factors that could define the utility of a particular strategy. This makes defining an ideal utility function a very hard research problem. For our purpose, we define the utility for a particular strategy as a function of the energy savings from the strategy (can be measured) and the perceived user satisfaction (determined subjectively). From experience, we know that these two factors are somewhat in conflict. For example, if we slowdown the cpu for power savings, the response times of the applications will increase thereby reducing the perceived user satisfaction. In multimedia applications, a slower processing of video frames might cause a jitter. In general, a more aggressive power saving strategy tends to save more power, but might have a greater negative impact on the user perception. Consequently, higher $\triangle_i^k$ may not directly translate to a higher utility. Our objective is to determine a value for $\triangle_i$ such that both the device lifetime and the overall utility of the device is maximized. A logarithmic function closely depicts such an utility function. In Sec. 4.2, we study the utility functions for the CPU and the network card and show that they can be approximated using logarithmic functions. We therefore define player i's utility function when it employs strategy S_i^j as $log(C_{iT})$. Moreover, the amount of power saved by any strategy can be expressed as a function of the residual energy of the device at the time the strategy is employed; therefore we can define $\triangle_i^k = f(E_R^T)$ for each player. We can say that the power optimization strategies regenerate(in some sense) some of the energy that would otherwise be used up with the basic strategies. We therefore assume that the residual energy for the next period can be expressed as $E_R^{(T+1)} = f(X_T)$. This characterization lends the game to be analyzed as a classical game theory problem called the tragedy of the commons [2, 15]. Note that duration of this potentially infinite game can be restricted by setting a threshold battery energy level until which the game is played. This level can be selected such that minimum energy requirements for the device components are reserved.

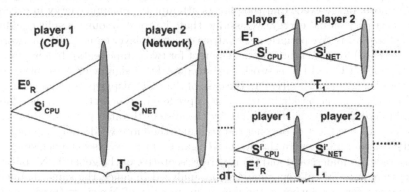

Fig. 1. Extensive form for a 2 player game(CPU,Network)

The extensive form of the game (with 2 players) is shown in Fig. 1. Initially, the residual energy of the low-power device is assumed to be E_R^0. At this point, both the CPU and the network interface card(NIC) choose their power management strategies indicated by S_{CPU}^i and S_{NET}^i. The game is played in accordance with these strategies for the period T_0. At the end of the period the strategies are again re-evaluated depending on the residual device power. We assume that the evaluation takes a small time δT as shown in the figure. At this point, both players decide on the new strategies and the game continues over period T_1. Note however, that depending on the initial strategies chosen the game could take one of many courses (2 of them are depicted in the figure). The oval represents the range of the strategies that can be employed by the players. This game continues indefinitely until either the battery drains out of power (inevitable) or the device is stopped.

2.1 Game Analysis

By designing the conjunctive component power management for low-power devices as a non-cooperative dynamic game (as above) makes it amenable to several different types of game theoretic analysis. In this section, we investigate the game from the perspective of Markovian strategies that provide Nash equilibrium for each period. This is representative of the current research approaches, where each player(component) unilaterally chooses its strategies with the objective of maximizing its own utility. We also present a social optimality analysis wherein the objective is to maximize the conjunctive utility of the system. This is representative of the approach we suggest. A brief comparison of the analytical results is made and its implications to our overall problem is discussed. Using our analysis, we can answer the following questions – how does the residual energy of the device y_t evolve over time? Does strategic interaction of the components lead to persistent overuse of the battery resource?

Before we present the analysis, we redefine some of the notations presented in the last section for easier readability. Let the "game environment" (residual energy of device) at the beginning of period t be $y_t \geq 0$. We denote player i's energy consumption due to the adopted strategy in period t as $c_{it} \geq 0$. Furthermore, in the event that the players attempt to consume energy in excess of the current residual energy, we assume that the total amount is split equally among the players. We perform our analysis on a two player game (CPU, network interface card) for power/utility management for two components). In low-power devices, the CPU and the network card account for a significant percentage of the overall energy consumption. In the case of the LCD displayo, the main energy drain comes from the backlight, which has a predefined user setting and therefore has a limited degree of controllability by the system through various strategies. This remains a subject of ongoing research and therefore we do not include the backlight in our analysis. In the two player game: i) the analysis is much simpler and is easier to understand and (ii) it is representative of the general "N" player game, that is a "N" player game can be analyzed in much the same manner. Fortunately, for our purposes, the maximum number of players is three (N=3) (considering the LCD display and the fact that most handhelds do not have disks).

Furthermore, as the analysis is quite complex for a two player game [2, 15], we show the analysis for specific forms of the utility function and the energy regeneration functions. An analogous analysis is possible for other types of functions. Without loss of generality, we assume that player i's utility from consuming c_i amount of energy in any period is given by $Blog(c_i)+C$, and that $y_{t+1} = A.X_t{}^D$, where A,B,C and D are constants. We simply denote the players by subscripts 1 and 2. More specifically, we use the functions $log(c_i)$ (B=1,C=0) for the utility function and $y_{t+1} = A.\sqrt{X_t}$ ($D = \frac{1}{2}$) to improve readability of the analysis.

2.2 Social Optimum Analysis

From an analogous economic game theory standpoint, social optimality is defined as: In a society of two individuals having simultaneous unrestricted access to a common resource, how should each player extract the common resource such that this society of two individuals remain as "happy" as they can be. In our case, the "happiness" is represented by the joint utility of the players with the common resource being the battery energy. Therefore to derive the social optimality solution we need to consider the sum of the two players' utilities – and maximize it. This can be achieved through analysis by backward induction. Suppose to begin with, there are exactly 2 periods (as shown in Fig. 1). If we are in the last period with residual energy y, then we need to solve

$$Max \ \{log(c_1) + log(c_2)\} \tag{3}$$

where $c_1 + c_2 \leq y$. In order to maximize utility, all the available residual energy should be used up at this period; that is it must be that $c_1 + c_2 = y$. Hence, the maximization problem can be written as

$$Max_{c_1} \ \{log(c_1) + log(y - c_1)\} \tag{4}$$

Using the first order condition for maximization (1st order derivative $= 0$) we get $\frac{1}{c_1} = \frac{1}{y-c_1}$; that is consumption by both the components should be equal ($c_1 = c_2$ and equal to $\frac{y}{2}$). Consequently, each components socially optimal utility when there is one period left and the residual energy is y, is given by $V^1(y) = log\frac{y}{2} = log(y) - log(2)$. This can be written as $log(y) + B(1)$, where B(1) stands for the constant -log(2). Let us now consider the penultimate period (i.e fold back the tree in Fig. 1). Clearly, when there are 2 periods left the socially optimum energy consumption is found from solving the following problem:

$$Max \ \{log(c_1) + log(c_2) + 2\delta V^1[A(y - c_1 - c_2)^{0.5}]\} \tag{5}$$

where $c_1 + c_2 \leq y$ and δ is the discount factor. In our case the discount factor is important because as the device runs out of power, the energy resource gets more valuable, and therefore so do the utilities. Since, $V^1[A(y - c_1 - c_2)^{0.5}] = log[A(y - c_1 - c_2)^{0.5}] = log(A) + \frac{1}{2}log(y - c_1 - c_2) + B(2)$; we can write the problem as

$$Max \ \{log(c_1) + log(c_2) + \delta log(y - c_1 - c_2)\} \tag{6}$$

where $c_1 + c_2 \leq y$, where we have suppressed the additive constants log(A) and B(2), as they do not affect the optimal choice. Again, the first-order conditions for maxima are obtained by equating the derivative of the above equation to zero. We have $\frac{1}{c_1} = \delta[y - c_1 - c_2]^{-1}$ and $\frac{1}{c_2} = \delta[y - c_1 - c_2]^{-1}$. Since, the expressions are identical, it must be that the two consumptions are equal. Using the above equations it follows that the common consumption is $\frac{y}{2+\delta}$. Note that the energy consumption is less than it is when there is only one period left. After collecting the terms, the socially optimal utility for a component can be written as $(1 + \frac{\delta}{2})log(y) + B(3)$, where B(3) is a compilation of constants.

Now we consider the case when there are more than 2 periods. Instead of solving the general case right away, let us do one more step of induction to see if there is a solution pattern. Now, suppose there are three periods of resource usage. In the first period we have the following problem to solve:

$$Max \ \{log(c_1) + log(c_2) + 2\delta V^2[A(y - c_1 - c_2)^{0.5}]\} \tag{7}$$

where $c_1 + c_2 \leq y$. Now, by substituting for V^2 and by suppressing all the (irrelevant) constants we can rewrite the last expression as

$$Max \; \{log(c_1) + log(c_2) + \delta(1 + \frac{\delta}{2})log(y - c_1 - c_2)\} \qquad (8)$$

where $c_1 + c_2 \leq y$. Proceeding similarly as before we can get the first-order conditions for this problem as $\frac{1}{c_1} = \delta(1 + \frac{\delta}{2})[y - c_1 - c_2]^{-1}$ and an identical expression for c_2. It can be shown that the socially optimal consumption equals $\frac{y}{2}(1 + \frac{\delta}{2} + \frac{\delta^2}{4})^{-1}$ and the socially optimal utility for each player is of the form $(1 + \frac{\delta}{2} + \frac{\delta^2}{4})log(y) + A(3)$, where A(3) is a compilation of the constants. At this stage a pattern is clearly observed. Similarly, the analysis for "T" remaining periods is present in Table 1.

Table 1. Energy consumption for various remaining periods

periods remaining	consumption (fraction of y)
1	$\frac{1}{2}$
2	$\frac{1}{2(1+\frac{\delta}{2})}$
3	$\frac{1}{2(1+\frac{\delta}{2}+\frac{\delta^2}{4})}$
T (conjecture)	$\frac{1}{2[1+\frac{\delta}{2}+...+(\frac{\delta}{2})^{T-1}]}$

Using the above conjecture, we now know the equilibrium consumptions for the game for T periods. Note that in an infinite period model, we can get this identical consumption function (call it $c(y)$) by taking the limit of the optimal consumption as T$\rightarrow \infty$. Since, $1 + \frac{\delta}{2} + ... + \frac{\delta}{2}^{T-1} + ... = \frac{1}{1-\frac{\delta}{2}}$, we can say that

$$c(y) = \frac{1 - \frac{\delta}{2}}{2}y \qquad (9)$$

Based on this optimal energy consumption rule an optimal power management strategy can be executed for each component. In a later section, we will discuss some component based power management strategies and how we profile such strategies for various components.

2.3   Best-Response(Nash) Equilibrium Analysis

We now present a parallel analysis in a strategic (rather than social) setting. Here the assumption is that the players are consuming the battery resource unilaterally. Therefore, each player (component) will only consider its own utility and seek the strategy that maximizes this utility. Much like the social optimality analysis, the game equilibrium can be solved by backward induction. We present a similar analysis for a two player game. As before, suppose we are in the last period with residual energy y. At this point, all the energy can be consumed. Hence, the stage sub-game equilibrium is one where each player's actual consumption is $\frac{y}{2}$. Consequently, each components equilibrium utility is given by $W^1(y) = log(\frac{y}{2}) = log(y) + B(1)$, where B(1) is a constant (= -log(2)). Let us now fold the tree back to consider the penultimate period. When there are two periods left, player 1 faces the following best-response problem:

$$Max \; log(c_1) + \delta W^1[A(y - c_1 - \theta y)^{0.5}] \tag{10}$$

where $c_1 \leq (1 - \theta)y$, δ is the discount factor and θ is the fraction of the resource that player 2 is expected to consume in the first period . Note that we have assumed that the consumption of player 1, $c_1 \leq (1 - \theta)y$. Otherwise, we know that there will be no consumption for either player in the last period. Since, $W^1\{A(y - c_1 - \theta y)^{0.5}\} = log(A) + \frac{1}{2}log[(1 - \theta)y - c_1] + B(2)$, we can rewrite the problem as

$$Max \; log(c_1) + \frac{\delta}{2}log[(1 - \theta)y - c_1] \tag{11}$$

where $c_1 \leq (1 - \theta)y$ and the constants are suppressed. Applying the first order condition we have $\frac{1}{c_1} = \frac{\frac{\delta}{2}}{(1-\theta)y-c_1}$. Therefore, the best response consumption is given by $(1 + \frac{\delta}{2})c_1 = (1 - \theta)y$. If we write the consumption as a fraction of the residual energy at that time - that is, if we write it as $b(\theta)y$ - then it follows that

$$b(\theta) = \frac{1 - \theta}{1 + \frac{\delta}{2}} \tag{12}$$

If we do a similar analysis for player 2, we get the symmetric equilibrium condition, wherein each player has the same consumption, and the rate is such that it is the best response to itself. Therefore, $b(\theta) = \theta$. Put differently, the extraction rate $\frac{1}{2+\frac{\delta}{2}}$ is a symmetric equilibrium. As before, after collecting the terms, the equilibrium utility when there are two remaining periods, W^2, can be written as $(1 + \frac{\delta}{2})log(y) + B(3)$, where B(3) is a constant. After substituting the formula for W^2, it can be shown that the first period best response problem for player 1 is

$$Max \; log(c_1) + \frac{\delta}{2}(1 + \frac{\delta}{2})log[(1 - \theta)y - c_1] \tag{13}$$

where the previous conditions for the variables hold. Solving for the first order condition we get $\frac{1}{c_1} = \frac{\frac{\delta}{2}(1+\frac{\delta}{2})}{(1-\theta)y-c_1}$. We get the symmetric consumption level for each player equal to $\frac{1}{2+\frac{\delta}{2}+\frac{\delta^2}{4}}$. As with social optimality we can generalize the solution for T periods as follows: when there are "T" remaining periods, the energy consumption fraction of each player is given by $\frac{1}{2+\frac{\delta}{2}+...+(\frac{\delta}{2})^{T-1}}$. In the infinite period model, the equilibrium consumption function (call it $c^*(y)$), will be given by the limit of the equilibrium consumption as $T \to \infty$. Since $2 + \frac{\delta}{2} + ... + (\frac{\delta}{2})^T + ... = 1 + \frac{1}{1-\frac{\delta}{2}}$, we can say that

$$c^*(y) = \frac{1 - \frac{\delta}{2}}{2 - \frac{\delta}{2}}y \tag{14}$$

Using the above equilibrium consumption, a best response strategy can be chosen for each component.

Discussion: From the above analysis we observe that when each component (player) employs its power optimization strategies unilaterally, there is a possibility of overuse of the battery resource. As mentioned earlier, such one-sided decisions do not necessarily translate to the highest overall utility for the system. Comparing the two consumption functions: the socially optimal function $c(y)$ (eqn 9) and the strategically optimal function c_y^*(eqn 14), we see that

$$c(y) = \frac{1 - \frac{\delta}{2}}{2}y \; < \; \frac{1 - \frac{\delta}{2}}{2 - \frac{\delta}{2}}y = c^*(y) \tag{15}$$

The equation holds as $(2 - \frac{\delta}{2}) < 2$. It can be concluded that the strategic equilibrium are suboptimal. While theoretically it has been proved that the social optimal is better than the strategic optimal, it is a challenge to design a system that can facilitate such optimal battery usage. In the next section, we present a middleware framework that can be effectively used for optimal use of the system battery resource.

3   The Dynamo Middleware Framework

In the previous section, we presented a theoretical analysis for optimized power consumption for a generic set of components and their power management strategies. However, in practice, the options available for power optimization are limited by type of low-power devices used and the context of the applications. For example, a cpu slowdown strategy that slows down the cpu by 70%(say) may not be feasible for multimedia applications(as frames cannot be decoded in time); again a handheld without a network card need not be optimized for that component. Therefore, we need to conduct a case-specific analysis for a given environment and device context. Furthermore, in our case, it is important to reevaluate the strategies used for various components as the game environment evolves (network/device conditions dynamically change). A distributed adaptive middleware framework designed for cross-level power optimization is a natural choice for performing such an optimality analysis. The system architecture for such an adaptive middleware framework (called Dynamo) is depicted in Fig. 2. A prototype implementation of the framework is presented in section 5.

In Fig. 2, the lowest level shows the various hardware components targeted for power optimization. The driver interfaces and the power optimization strategies for the various components are available at the operating system layer. A battery monitor provides higher layers with realtime information on the current residual battery level of the low-power device. Dynamo consists of a lightweight middleware runtime layer that executes on the device and provides an API interface for dynamically deploying power management strategies for the various components. Additionally, the framework contains a more heavy weight component that can execute on a network node (e.g. a proxy server) and performs

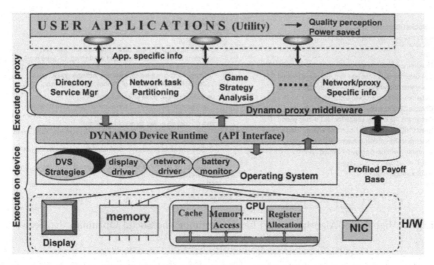

Fig. 2. The Dynamo middleware architecture

the game theoretic analysis remotely using a distributed protocol; As the more computationally expensive game theoretic analysis is shifted onto a distributed proxy, the middleware on the low-power devices can have a lightweight footprint. By using this model, the middleware can exploit knowledge of the local device state (e.g. residual power levels stored & updated at a directory service) and global state (e.g. network congestion, node mobility etc.) that can be available at the proxy to dynamically select optimal power optimization strategies for the components. We assume that the middleware has at its disposal a knowledge base of the strategy space and corresponding utility functions for each of the components. Such a knowledge base can be created by extensively profiling (or using research literature) each component and its various strategies under different operating conditions. Additionally, the middleware can implement various policies that affect the analysis of the strategic interaction of the components. For example, the middleware can fix the number of periods for which the game is played (or if the game is infinite) using various policies(e.g. constant,infinite etc.); dynamically modify the game environment incase there is a sudden drift in the battery energy level, assign value of the discount factor(δ) and set the threshold energy level before the start of the game. By using a distributed approach, much of the computationally expensive analysis is moved away from the low-power device to a network entity (proxy). Furthermore, the proxy is better suited to make dynamic global adaptations because it has information of the global state that would be unavailable at the device. The communication overheads in this approach are minimal as the proxy communicates with the device only when power management strategies for individual devices need to change.

The high level algorithm employed by the middleware for determining the socially optimal energy strategies are presented in Fig. 3. Fig. 3(a) presents the

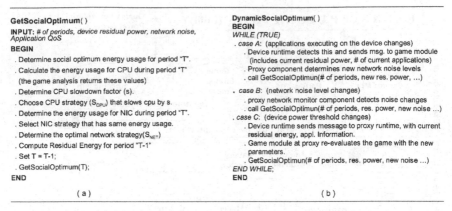

GetSocialOptimum( )
INPUT: # of periods, device residual power, network noise, Application QoS
BEGIN
. Determine social optimum energy usage for period "T".
. Calculate the energy usage for CPU during period "T" (the game analysis returns these values)
. Determine CPU slowdown factor (s).
. Choose CPU strategy (S_{CPU}) that slows cpu by s.
. Determine the energy usage for NIC during period "T".
. Select NIC strategy that has same energy usage.
. Determine the optimal network strategy(S_{NET})
. Compute Residual Energy for period "T-1"
. Set T = T-1;
. GetSocialOptimum(T);
END

(a)

DynamicSocialOptimum( )
BEGIN
WHILE (TRUE)
. case A: (applications executing on the device changes)
  . Device runtime detects this and sends msg. to game module (includes current residual power, # of current applications)
  . Proxy component determines new network noise levels
  . call GetSocialOptimun(# of periods, new res. power, ...)
. case B: (network noise level changes)
  . proxy network monitor component detects noise changes
  . call GetSocialOptimun(# of periods, res. power, new noise ...)
. case C: (device power threshold changes)
  . Device runtime sends message to proxy runtime, with current residual energy, appl. Information.
  . Game module at proxy re-evaluates the game with the new parameters.
  . GetSocialOptimun(# of periods, res. power, new noise ...)
END WHILE;
END

(b)

Fig. 3. High-Level Algorithm used for determining the Social Optimum Strategies

algorithm for a static scenario where parameters of the power management game are fixed. Given a residual power of the device, the number of applications and application QoS requirements and a constant network noise level, the algorithm can be used to determine strategies that achieve a social energy consumption equilibria. In a dynamic scenario, some or all of the game parameters can change randomly. The middleware can implement a dynamic algorithm(Fig. 3(b)) that detects these changes in application load, network noise levels and diminishing device power levels and repeatedly executes the static equilibrium algorithm continuous adaptation.

4 Performance Evaluation

We adopt a two pronged approach to evaluate the performance of our framework. First, we use profiled results to simulate the game environment and compare the performance of the game strategies. In Sec. 5, we present a prototype implementation of the middleware framework on a Linux based system. In this section, we focus on the results of our simulations in the context of video applications.

In our simulations, we consider two system components(CPU & NIC) for power optimization. We measure the energy consumption and overall utility of the system and the individual components, when the components consume energy according to "social" and "best-response" equilibria conditions. A comparison is made with the energy consumption of the baseline condition in which no optimizations are made for either the CPU or the NIC. We use a streaming video player as the user application executing on the device. Streaming video applications are ideal for our simulation, as they heavily use both the cpu and the network. The values used in our simulations are based on our extensive work [18] in profiling the power consumption characteristics of streaming video onto handheld computers. The next section presents the details of the simulation environment and a discussion on the strategy spaces used for both components.

Table 2. CPU and Video burst length configurations for ideal energy and performance gains

Video Quality	Cache (Size,Assoc)	Voltage	Original Energy	Optimized Energy	Savings	Video Bursts (in secs)	Power Saved (Watts)
Q1(Highest)	8,8	1	1.29	0.76	47.5%	2.3	0.925
Q2	8,8	1	1.09	0.64	47.8%	3.5	1.0
Q3	8,8	1	0.95	0.56	48.0%	4.6	1.04
Q4	32,2	0.9	0.54	0.26	57.6%	4.85	1.05
Q5	32,2	0.9	0.48	0.23	57.8%	6.8	1.08
Q6	32,2	0.9	0.42	0.20	58.0%	14.5	1.12
Q7	8,8	0.9	0.29	0.14	57.3%	17.5	1.13
Q8(Lowest)	8,8	0.9	0.24	0.11	57.5%	17.0	1.12

4.1   Simulation Environment

We model our low-power device after a Compaq iPAQ 3650, with a 206Mhz Intel StrongArm processor, with 16MB ROM, 32MB SDRAM. The iPAQ is equipped with a Cisco 350 Series Aironet 11Mbps wireless PCMCIA network interface card for communication. The streaming video application is modelled after the Pocket Video Player available for Windows CE. Table. 2 present sample values for optimized network and cpu operating points for videos of different qualities. We then identify the strategy spaces for the CPU and the NIC for the above device.

CPU: Instead of identifying individual CPU strategies for power optimization, we assumed that the speed of the processor can be varied continuously from the minimum(S_{min}) to the maximum(S_{max}) supported CPU speeds for the device, and normalize the values such that the operating range varies from $[\nu_{min}, 1]$, where $\nu_{min} = \frac{S_{min}}{S_{max}}$. We then use the commonly used energy model presented in [14] to calculate the power P as a function of "*slowdown factor*(ν)".
$P = f(\nu) = 0.284 \cdot \nu^3 + 0.225 \cdot \nu^2 + 0.0256 \cdot \nu + \sqrt{311.16 \cdot \nu^2 + 282.24 \cdot \nu} \times (0.0064 \cdot \nu + 0.014112 \cdot \nu^2)$
We assume that the strategy space for the CPU is the set of strategies that can can vary the CPU speed between the minimum and maximum supported speeds. However in practice, these values will be discrete slowdown factors supported by the CPU, so an approximation to the closest theoretical slowdown factor needs to be chosen. This can be achieved through an operating system API interface available to the middleware. Also using the above model, we can determine a CPU slowdown factor that corresponds to a particular energy consumption level.

NIC: In [4, 18, 22], it is demonstrated that if video packets are buffered and sent to the device in bursts, then the NIC card on the device can be transitioned from the "*active*" to the "*sleep*" mode, thereby saving significant power. As the energy saved for a network card is proportional to the amount of time it spends in the "*sleep*" mode, the energy consumption of the NIC is dependent on the burst sizes used for transmitting packets [18]. Note here that "burst size" refers to the number of seconds of video payload that can be buffered and sent to the device in one burst over the network. While large bursts sizes can cause significant savings in power, they cause higher packet drop rates and buffer overflows at the wireless access point resulting in a significant drop in perceived video quality. We assume the strategy space for the network card as the set of strategies that set the burst sizes of video transmissions (in secs) to continuous values in the range between 1 second to 150 seconds. Note that for each burst size chosen there is a unique value for the energy consumed by the NIC. In the next section, we use our empirical studies from [18] to derive the utility functions for the CPU and the network card.

4.2   Utility Functions

In this section, we describe how we identify the utility functions for the various strategies used for the power management of the CPU and the NIC. Recall that we define the utility function for a strategy as a function of both the power consumed (essentially equal to power saved) and the satisfaction as perceived by the user. For video applications, we assume that the user perception is directly related to the quality of the video(described by frame rate, frame resolution and bit rate of the stream) as in [18]. Fig. 4 shows how the normalized power savings and the perceived video quality varies with the cpu slowdown factor. Clearly the power savings increase as the cpu is slowed. However, the user perception remains at the highest level till the cpu is slowed by about 48%. Subsequent reduction in cpu speeds causes a drop in the video quality, due to frame deadline misses. Fig. 5 shows the actual utility curve for the video as the sum of the curves in Fig. 4, plotted against the cpu energy usage. A curve fitting technique is then used to determine an approximation of this curve. We determine that the utility for the video application can be specified as a function of the power consumption as follows: $Utility = 0.0408Log(Power) + 1.369$, with a R^2 value of 0.0197. Fig. 6 demonstrates how video quality(based on % of pkts dropped) and the power savings of the network card vary with the packet burst sizes in seconds. Clearly, the power savings improve when the burst sizes increase. However, as the burst size becomes larger than 1.48 seconds, packets start getting dropped at the wireless access point. As a result, there is a perceived drop in the user perceived video quality. Fig. 7 shows the actual utility curve for the video against the burst size. Fig. 8 plots the power savings of the NIC versus the video burst size used. Using a curve fitting method can specify the network card power savings as a function of the packet burst size as follows: $y = 0.1909Log(x) + 0.4139$. Using the above strategy spaces and utility functions for the CPU and the NIC, we now present the results for the overall energy savings achieved when the CPU and the NIC operate under conditions of "social" and "best-response" equilibria.

4.3   Experimental Results

We used our simulator to determine the energy consumption of the device under both static and dynamic application loads and network noise levels. In both

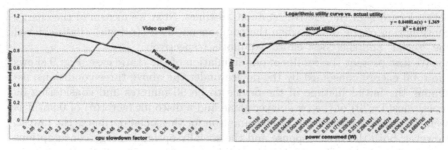

Fig. 4. power & video quality (cpu)   **Fig. 5.** cpu power vs. utility

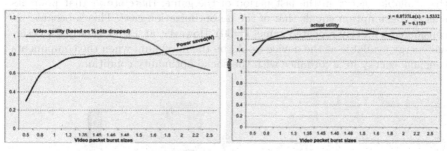

Fig. 6. power & video quality (NIC)   **Fig. 7.** video burst size vs. utility

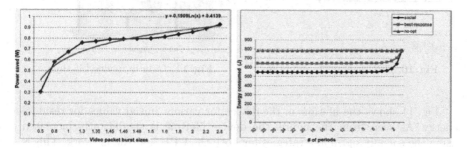

Fig. 8. burst size vs. power saved   **Fig. 9.** total energy consumption

cases, we estimated the energy consumption characteristics of the device under three different operating (social,nash and no-optimization) conditions of the CPU and the NIC. For the static measurements, we assumed that a multimedia application (video player) playing streaming video on the device with a static network noise level. The energy consumptions were calculated assuming a fixed number of repetitions of the game while a single application executed on the device. In the dynamic case, we randomly started and stopped a set of applications as well as varied the network noise levels randomly. As a baseline condition, we estimated the energy consumption when no power optimization strategies were used. Under this assumption,the CPU operates at its maximum speed and the network card is in the "active" state at all times. Next we measured the energy consumption of the device when the components used strategies that achieved the "social" and the "best-effort" equilibria respectively.

We first present the results of our simulation of the static case. Fig. 9 shows the total energy consumed by the device under the above three conditions, assuming the initial lifetime of the device to be 90 minutes and considering 30 repetitions(T=30) of the two-player game and a discount factor(δ) of 0.95. It is seen that the the overall energy consumption for the social optima is the lowest. However, both the best-response and the socially optimal energy consumptions are significantly less than the energy used when no power optimizations are in place. As seen in the analysis earlier, the social equilibrium tends to consume all the available energy in the last period of the game, therefore at that point its energy consumption equals that of the no optimization case. This is because we considered a finitely repeated game(T=30). However, at T=30, clearly the residual energy available at the device would be the maximum when the components consume energy in accordance with the social optimality condition.

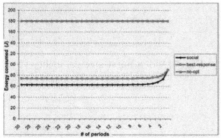

Fig. 10. CPU energy consumption

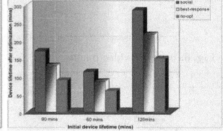

Fig. 11. Gain in device Lifetime

Fig. 11 shows the lifetime of the device for various initial values for residual energy. As seen from the figure, the device lifetime is significantly increased using the socially optimal strategies for both the CPU and the network. This is expected as less battery energy is drawn under this condition. Fig. 10 compares the energy consumed by only the CPU under the two equilibria. It is seen that the CPU consumes 13% less energy when it operates at a social equilibrium than when it operates under the best-response equilibrium. Fig. 12 compares the normalized video quality levels achieved by the strategies used for the CPU. Clearly, there is very little difference($\leq$ 0.1) in the normalized quality of video attained by the two equilibrium conditions for the cpu. However, much lower energy consumption levels are attained for the social equilibrium strategies. Note that the utility for the no-optimization case is much less than either of the above techniques as it consumes significantly more energy with possibly a slight increase in the user perceived quality.

In the dynamic case, we used a set of 6 applications and randomly started and stopped the applications and randomly varied the network noise levels. Fig. 13

shows the energy consumption characteristics of the CPU as the dynamic adaptation is performed for both social and Nash equilibrium conditions. The small frequent spikes in the graph indicate the points at which the application load (no. of applications) on the device changes. Fig. 15 shows the corresponding energy consumption plot for the NIC. For both the CPU and the NIC, the social equilibrium strategy tends to consume lesser energy than the Nash equilibrium strategy. The overall energy consumed over time for both the equilibrium conditions and the baseline case is shown in Fig. 14. The total energy consumption is much lesser for the socially optimal strategy.

Finally, in order to compare the dynamic adaptation with the static case, we started out by executing eight applications on the device and computed the static social and Nash equilibrium energy consumptions. Then we randomly stopped applications one by one and performed dynamic adaptation for the new application load. Intuitively, as the number of applications are reduced we should be able to reduce the equilibrium energy consumption dynamically, while still maintaining the same perceived quality. Fig. 16 shows the residual energy of the device over time for static and dynamic social equilibria. Clearly, significant amount of residual energy is saved over time when dynamic adaptation is performed. In conclusion, as the number of applications decrease randomly, dynamic adaptation can increase the overall lifetime of the device. On the other hand, as the number of tasks increase, dynamic adaptation can provide a better quality.

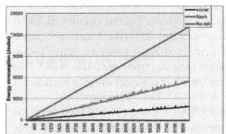

Fig. 12. Quality Comparison (cpu)

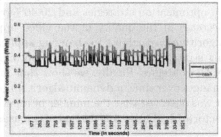

Fig. 13. CPU power vs. time

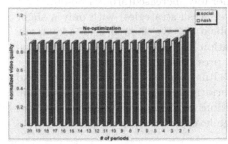

Fig. 14. Total Energy over time

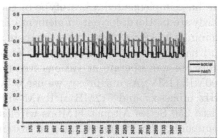

Fig. 15. Network power vs. time

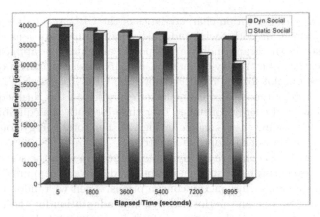

Fig. 16. Dynamic vs. Static Adaptation

4.4   Summary of Results

We compared the performance of socially optimal power consumption strategies
with the strategies that achieve strategic equilibrium and the ones that implement no energy optimization under both static and dynamic load conditions.
Under static conditions, the energy consumed for the socially optimal strategies
was lesser(about 20J for every repeated game) than the energy used by the Nash
strategies. The device lifetime was considerably increased(around 80-90% over
no optimization strategies and 20-40% over Nash strategies) with only a slight
decrease in the quality of the video application. We showed that a dynamic
algorithm that adapts to changing application load and network noise levels using strategies that provide social optima provide significant energy gains over
Nash strategies. Finally, we show that in situations where the application load
changes over time, a dynamic algorithm performs better than a static algorithm.
It was observed that the number of repetitions of the game(T) and the discount
factor(δ) had little impact on energy usage levels of the components.

5   Prototype Implementation

We have implemented a prototype of the Dynamo middleware framework. The
hardware platform for our implementation is the Sharp Zaurus (model SL5600)
running the Linux operating system. It uses an Intel 400MHz Xscale processor
and has 32MB of SDRAM and 64MB of protected flash memory. The Xscale
processor can operate at various frequencies ranging from 100MHz(0.85V) to
400MHz(1.3V).As our proxy, we use a Windows XP desktop system with a 2.4
GHz processor and 512MB of RAM and a 40 GB disk. The handheld used a
Cisco 350 Series Aironet 11Mbps wireless PCMCIA network interface card for
communication. We use a National Instruments PCI DAQ board to sample voltage drop across the iPAQ at 200K samples/sec. The streaming video application
is modelled after the freely available VLC media player for Linux.

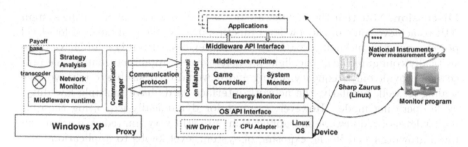

Fig. 17. Prototype Implementation in Dynamo

Fig. 17 shows the integration of the game analysis into the Dynamo middleware architecture. The middleware on the device includes four primary components – the *game controller*, the *system and energy monitors* and the *communication manager*. The middleware provides an API interface for applications to specify the QoS requirements and to change QoS requirements for dynamic adaptation. The *game controller* is used to specify the details of the game analysis and to set/modify the dynamic game parameters. The *system monitor* monitors the resource usage of the system and notifies the runtime of changes (e.g. change in the number of applications). The *energy monitor* communicates with the PCI DAQ board as well as interfaces with the low-level OS APIs to monitor the energy usage of the CPU and the network interface. The power-aware API (PAAPI) library for Linux is used to adjust the operating frequency of the CPU. The *communication manager* defines the middleware communication protocol and communicates with the proxy middleware. It uses UDP over IP for communication and a well defined structure interface for exchange of control information. On the proxy the Dynamo middleware uses a module to perform the strategy analysis using a profiled payoff base. A network monitor module maintains an updated state information on the overall congestion level. This information is used by the middleware to adapt the network traffic to the device. Fig. 18 lists a limited set of middleware API used at the low power device and briefly describes each function. It also presents the energy overheads of using the middleware framework and the communication overheads.

Middleware API	API Description	Energy Overhead (Avg.)	
• GetApplicationQoS( ) • SetApplicationQoS( )	-These functions are used to assign QoS (e.g. video quality) and application specific parameters (WCET, utilization etc.)	Middleware Framework	0.6 Watts
• SendDeviceInfo( ) • ReceiveControlInfo( )	-Send device specific information to the proxy -Receive control information from the proxy	Communication (over 10 min. period, 30Bytes • Send & Receive	0.34 – 0.4 W
• GetSystemInfo( ) • GetBatteryInfo( ) • SetCPUFreq( ) • SetNetworkIdleTime( )	-Get the current system state information (#apps, utilization) -residual Battery energy -Set the CPU frequency level -Set the idle time for the network	Video Playback	6.05 Watts
• SetGameParameters( ) • SetThresholdEnergy( )	-Set the game specific parameters -Set a threshold energy level to account for other components		

Fig. 18. Prototype Middleware API and Initial results

Discussion: Note that the middleware needs to utilize a set of operating system API to achieve some of the low-level functionality. While a number of low-level power management knobs exist for handheld devices, currently many have to be statically configured (e.g. backlight intensity levels). Again, current Xscale processors provide only frequency scaling and it would be desirable to have voltage scaling as well. Similarly, the network interface cards have multiple low duty-cycle operating modes. However, support for dynamically exploiting these at higher levels (middleware and application) are still very limited. We are noticing a growing trend in the exposing of system level knobs to applications and middleware through well defined API interfaces, and have designed our framework to incorporate and exploit future enhancements to APIs at the OS and architectural levels. We also concur that some of our approaches can be better incorporated at the OS level, as it currently has a higher degree of control over hardware power management. The discussion of the low-level API is outside the scope of this work.

6   Related Work

The mathematical theory of games was first introduced by Neumann and Morgenstern [13] in 1944. Since then, game theory [21] has evolved into an important tool for analysis of conflict situations and has found invaluable application in the analysis of numerous social and economic conflict models. Traditionally, game theory has been used in computer science for development of computer games (e.g. chess) and in the areas of artificial intelligence. More recently, several interesting research efforts have applied game theoretic analysis to wireless communication systems [17], flow control [3] and routing [23]. In cellular systems users desire to have a high signal to interference (SIR) ratio at the base station (for low error rate, and reliability) coupled with the lowest possible transmit power (for longer battery life). A high transmit power used by a user can increase interference for other users thereby lowering their SIR. This might lead to other users to increase their transmit powers. Game Theory has been extensively used for analysis of such communication systems [17, 16, 8]. The use of game theoretic analysis for dynamic power management of disks has been suggested in [12]. In our work, we have used game theory to analyze the power management of various components in a low-power system, where we propose that the individual power management strategies for the various components should be chosen such that a socially optimal equilibrium condition is achieved. This is in accordance with the classical game theory problem called the "tragedy of the commons" [2, 15, 21].

On the other hand, power management for the individual components for low-power devices have been aggressively researched. Dynamic Voltage Scaling [9, 7] for saving energy consumption of CPUs have been extensively studied. At the application and middleware levels, the primary focus has been to optimize network interface power consumption [10, 4, 5]. A thorough analysis of power consumption of wireless network interfaces has been presented in [10]. Chandra et al. [4]

have explored the wireless network energy consumption of streaming video formats like Windows Media, Real media and Apple Quick Time. In [22], Shenoy suggests performing power friendly proxy based video transformations to reduce video quality in real-time for energy savings. They also suggest an intelligent network streaming strategy for saving power on the network interface. Caching streams of multiple qualities for efficient performance has been suggested in [11]. The GRACE project [25] claims the use of cross-layer adaptations for maximizing system utility. They suggest both coarse grained and fine grained tuning of parameters for optimal gains. In [24], the authors enhance the OS to support process groups which consist of a set of closely related/dependent processes. Coordination between the architecture(cache) optimizations, network and application adaptations through an adaptive middleware framework has been used in [18] to optimize power and utility for multimedia applications. In [19], a middleware framework that partitions reconfigurable middleware components between a low-power device and proxy for improving the costs of computation and communication is presented. Energy efficient battery management strategies have been extensively studied by Rao et al. [6].

7   Conclusions and Future Work

In this paper, we presented a dynamic game theoretic approach for choosing power optimization strategies for multiple components that draw energy from a common resource, the battery. We modelled the components as players in a non-cooperative game and determined how each component should draw battery power. We evaluated two techniques – one in which the components employ strategies that aim to maximize the overall utility of the system (social optimum) and another in which each component uses a best-response strategy for maximizing its own utility. Our performance results indicate that strategies that achieved a socially optimal energy usage provided the maximum energy savings and with similar utility values. We therefore conclude, that in a multi-component system, strategies for each component should be chosen such that they attain a socially optimal energy usage pattern. As an extension of our current efforts, we plan to employ game theoretic analysis for optimizing power consumption and performance of low-power devices by exploiting the knowledge of the distributed environment. It would be interesting to study a more distributed adaptation scheme involving multiple proxies and devices. We also plan on investigating the impact of optimizations on non realtime applications such as browsers and text editors etc..

References

1. A.J.Jones. *"Game Theory: Mathematical Models of Conflict"*. Ellis Horwood, 1980.
2. R. Amir and N. Nanncrup. Information Structure and the Tragedy of the Commons. June 2000.
3. C.Douligeris and R.Mazumdar. "A game theoretic approach to flow control in an integrated environment with two classes of users". In *Computer Network Symposium*, April 1988.

4. S. Chandra. Wireless Network Interface Energy Consumption Implications of Popular Streaming Formats. In *MMCN*, January 2002.
5. S. Chandra and A. Vahdat. Application-specific Network Management for Energy-aware Streaming of Popular Multimedia Formats. In *Usenix Annual Technical Conference*, June 2002.
6. C. F. Chiasserini and R. Rao. Energy Efficient Battery Management. In *IEEE Infocom*, March 2000.
7. K. Choi, K. Dantu, W.-C. Chen, and M. Pedram. Frame-Based Dynamic Voltage and Frequency Scaling for a MPEG Decoder. In *ICCAD 2000*, 2002.
8. D.J.Goodman and N.B.Mandayam. "Power control for wireless data ". In *IEEE Personal Communications*, April 2000.
9. E.Chan, K. Govil, and H. Wasserman. "Comparing algorithms for dynamic speed-setting of a low-power cpu". In *Proc. of MOBICOM*, November 1995.
10. L. Feeney and M. Nilsson. Investigating the Energy Consumption of a Wireless Network Interface in an ad hoc Networking Environment. In *IEEE Infocom*, April 2001.
11. J. Flinn and M. Satyanarayanan. Energy-Aware Adaptations for Mobile Applications. In *SOSP*.
12. S. Irani, S. Shukla, and R. Gupta. "Competitive analysis of dynamic power management strategies for systems with multiple power saving states". In *DATE*, 2002.
13. J.V.Neumann and O.Morgenstern. "Theory of Games and Economic Behavior". In *Princeton University Press*, 1944.
14. P. Kumar and M. Srivastava. Predictive Strategies for Low-Power RTOS Scheduling. In *ICCD*, 2000.
15. D. Levhari and L.Mirman. The Great Fish War: An example using a Dynamic Cournot-Nash Solution. In *Bell Journal of Economics*, 1980.
16. A. B. MacKenzie and S.Wicker. "Game Theoretic approaches to distributed power control in cdma wireless data networks". In *IEEE Globecom*, November 2001.
17. A. B. MacKenzie and S.Wicker. "Game Theory in Communications: Motivation, explanation and application to power control". In *IEEE Globecom*, November 2001.
18. S. Mohapatra, R. Cornea, and ct.al. "Integrated power management for video streaming to mobile handheld devices". In *ACM Multimedia*, 2003.
19. S. Mohapatra and N. Venkatasubramanian. PARM: Power-Aware Reconfigurable Middleware. In *ICDCS-23*, 2003.
20. B. D. Noble, M. Satyanarayanan, D.Narayanan, J.E.Tilton, and J. Flinn. Agile Application-Aware Adaptation for Mobility. In *SOSP*, October 1997.
21. P.K.Dutta. *"Strategies and Games, Theory and Practice"*. MIT Press, Cambridge, MA, 2001.
22. P. Shenoy and P. Radkov. Proxy-Assisted Power-Friendly Streaming to Mobile Devices. In *MMCN*, 2003.
23. T.Roughgarden and E.Tardos. "How bad is selfish routing?". In *IEEE Symposium on Foundations of Computer Science*, 2000.
24. W. Yuan and K. Nahrstedt. Process Group Management in Cross-Layer Adaptation. In *MMCN*, January 2004.
25. W. Yuan, K. Nahrstedt, S. Adve, D. Jones, and R. Kravets. Design and Evaluation of a Cross-Layer Adaptation Framework for Mobile Multimedia Systems. In *MMCN*, January 2003.

Extending a J2EE™ Server
with Dynamic and Flexible Resource Management

Mick Jordan[1], Grzegorz Czajkowski[1], Kirill Kouklinski[2], and Glenn Skinner[1]

[1] Sun Microsystems, Inc., 4150 Network Circle, Santa Clara, CA 95054, USA
{firstname.lastname}@sun.com
[2]School of Computer Science, University of Waterloo, Waterloo, ON N2L 3G1, Canada
kkouklin@math.uwaterloo.ca

Abstract. The Java™ 2 Platform, Enterprise Edition (J2EE™) is the standard
platform for hosting enterprise applications written in the Java programming
language. A single J2EE server can support multiple applications much like a
traditional operating system, but performance levels can be difficult to control,
due to the absence of resource management facilities in the Java platform. The
Resource Management (RM) interface addresses this problem by providing a
flexible and extensible framework for managing resources that is applicable
across a broad spectrum, from low-level resources like CPU time to higherlevel
resources such as database connections. RM has been implemented in the
Multi-tasking Virtual Machine (MVM), a scalable operating environment for
multiple applications based on the concept of isolated computations. This paper
describes the application of MVM and RM to the management of resources in a
J2EE Server and shows that application performance can be controlled flexibly
and easily with low overhead and minimal intrusion.

1 Introduction

The Java™ 2 Platform, Enterprise Edition (J2EE™) [1] is the standard server-side
environment for developing enterprise applications in the Java programming language. J2EE is itself layered on the Java™ 2 Platform, Standard Edition (J2SE™) [2].
In many respects the combination of the J2EE and J2SE platforms subsumes the underlying operating system (OS). For example, a single J2EE server can host several
applications, possibly from different organizations, that must compete for the server
resources. Many of the traditional OS constructs are overlaid or replaced with J2SE or
J2EE counterparts. For example, the J2SE thread model subsumes the native OS
thread model. Similarly, a J2EE *container*, which hosts a component of a J2EE application, shares some characteristics with an OS process. Both developers and administrators interact mainly with the APIs provided by J2EE/J2SE and only experience the underlying OS APIs through the filters provided by J2EE/J2SE. The main
benefit is the portability of the J2EE/J2SE platform between different operating systems.

In practice, however, the J2EE/J2SE platforms omit some important features that
are standard in operating systems. In particular, unlike OS processes, J2EE applications cannot be properly isolated from one another and many resources required for
adequate application performance cannot be controlled with platform facilities. These
deficiencies require administrators to bypass the J2EE/J2SE layers and interact directly with the native OS APIs, where available, thus limiting overall portability.

H.-A. Jacobsen (Ed.): Middleware 2004, LNCS 3231, pp. 439–458, 2004.
© IFIP International Federation for Information Processing 2004

Consider, for example, a J2EE server that has two different applications deployed and executing. These applications are similar to processes in an OS environment. Therefore, it should be possible to control the resources available to each application using operations analogous to those available for processes, for example, controlling the amount of memory or CPU. In current J2EE platforms this capability is notably absent, essentially because the underlying J2SE platform does not provide controls on these familiar resources. Furthermore, the J2EE platform defines additional resources, with no obvious analog in the operating system context, for example, the number of JDBC™ connections available to an application. Currently, J2EE servers provide some ad hoc mechanisms for controlling such resources, but it is not easy to partition them between separate applications within a single server.

The approach most J2EE server vendors take to solve this problem is to directly exploit the underlying OS facilities by exposing these to the J2EE administrator. Essentially, this involves mapping each J2EE application to a distinct server instance, so that the process-based resource management mechanisms of the OS can be utilized. One consequence is that the system's overall resource consumption is increased, due to the increased number of processes. Another is that part of the API cannot be expressed in terms of the Java programming language. Although this can be papered over to some extent by management frameworks and tools, e.g., Java™ Management Extensions (JMX™)[3] and CIM [4], the end result is more complexity and lower performance than would be possible if the facilities were provided directly in the J2EE/J2SE platform.

In previous work [5] we described a flexible and extensible framework for resource management that is expressed entirely in the Java programming language and is capable of efficiently handling all the traditional resources, such as CPU time, memory, and network, as well as programmer-defined resources such as JDBC connections. This work was itself built on earlier work that developed a programming model, and an associated API extension to the Java platform, that supports fully isolated computations. The API development, carried out as a Java Specification Request under the Java Community Process, is described by JSR 121 [6], and introduces the *isolate*, which abstracts the notion of a program in the Java platform, without prescribing a particular implementation. Resource management (or RM) is based on isolates in that an isolate is the fundamental unit of accounting. This solves many difficult problems relating to resource sharing and ownership. We have built a prototype implementation of RM as an extension to the Multi-tasking Virtual Machine (or MVM) [7] that implements isolates within a single Java™ Virtual Machine (JVM™).

In [8] we discussed how isolates might be utilized within a J2EE server, specifically in the context of the J2EE 1.3.1 Reference Implementation (J2EERI) [9]. A key concept was an *application domain*, that encapsulates an entire J2EE application, and is represented using one or more isolates. The main rationale was based on being able to exploit RM to provide J2EE-application-centric resource management.

This paper addresses the applicability of RM to a J2EE server, in the context of J2EERI. We describe how we integrated RM into the J2EERI and provide some initial measurements of its ability to effectively manage resources in a multi-application environment.

The rest of the paper is structured as follows. Section 2 provides an overview of the MVM architecture and the isolate programming model. Section 3 describes the RM framework. Section 4 contains a very brief overview of J2EE and explains how we applied MVM and isolates to J2EERI. Using J2SE resources and adding new, J2EE-specific ones, to J2EERI is described in Section 5. A summary of related work, future work, and conclusions complete the paper.

2 Background on Isolates and the Multi-tasking Virtual Machine

An isolate is a Java application component that does not share any objects with other isolates. The Isolate API [6] allows for the dynamic creation and destruction of isolates. A simple example of the API is the creation of an isolate, that will execute My-Class with a single argument "abc":

new Isolate("MyClass", new String[] {"abc"}).start();

The creating isolate may pass contextual information to its offspring that is required by the application started within the new isolate. Isolates do not share objects, but they can communicate using traditional inter-process communication mechanisms such as sockets and files. The Isolate API also defines an inter-isolate communication mechanism known as *links* for synchronous and unidirectional message passing. Isolates may exchange instances of java.io.Serializable as well as isolate and link references over links. The ability to send links on links is crucial, because there is no central registry of isolates and their communication endpoints – applications must explicitly create any topology they need.

The Isolate API is fully compatible with existing applications and middleware. In particular, applications unaware of the API may be managed as isolates without need for modification. Likewise, middleware can be unaware of or ignore the API.

Our implementation extends the rudimentary life-cycle management features of the Isolate API with the ability to suspend and resume isolates. We found this addition particularly useful when enforcing CPU time consumption policies (Sec. 5.1).

The Isolate API lends itself to various implementation strategies. One approach is to exploit the abstraction of an operating system process to implement the isolate boundaries. An alternative implementation strategy, employed in the design of MVM, is for all isolates to reside within a single instance of the Java™ runtime environment (JRE) that implements the protection boundaries within a single address space[7].

MVM is a general-purpose virtual machine for executing multiple applications written in the Java programming language. It is based on the Java HotSpot™ virtual machine (HSVM) [10] and its client compiler, version 1.3.1 for the Solaris™ Operating Environment.

MVM aggressively and transparently shares significant portions of the virtual machine among isolates. For example, run-time representations of all loaded classes and compiled code are shared, subject to modifications that prevent inter-isolate interference. Runtime modifications make the replication of non-shareable components (e.g., mutable state of classes) transparent. In effect, each application "believes" it executes in its own private JVM, as there is no inter-isolate interference due to mutable runtime data structures visible directly or indirectly by the application code. Certain JRE classes, such as System and Runtime had to be modified to make operations such as System.exit() apply only to the calling isolate. The heaps of isolates are logically disjoint, since the required level of isolation implies that isolates cannot share objects.

In MVM, each isolate transparently benefits from the class loading and method compiling work done by other isolates. This provides a significant reduction in the startup time and memory footprint. Execution time also benefits due to co-locating frequently communicating programs in the same OS process [8].

MVM operates as follows. The first isolate is a simple application called *Mserver* that listens on a socket for connections. The *java* command invoked by the users is replaced with the *jlogin* program, written in C, that connects to *Mserver* and passes to it the command line arguments (the main class name and its arguments, -*D* flags, etc.). *Mserver* creates a new isolate according to the obtained request. Standard input/output/error streams are routed to the *jlogin* process that launched the isolate.

3   Overview of the Resource Management API

This section contains a brief overview of the main features of the RM API [5]. It is important to note that existing applications can still run without modification, even if the JRE classes they depend on exploit the RM framework. Applications that need to control how resources are partitioned (e.g., application servers) can use the API for that purpose. Proactive programs can use the API to learn about resource availability and consumption to improve the characteristics most important in the given case (response time, throughput, footprint, etc.) or to ward off denial of service attacks.

Resources can be exposed through the RM API in a uniform way, regardless of whether they are actually managed by the operating system (e.g., CPU time in JVMs that rely on kernel threading), the run-time system (e.g., heap memory), core classes (e.g., file and network resources), middleware (e.g., JDBC connections), or by the application itself. Retrofitting existing resource implementations to make them exploit the RM API is relatively easy, and the trade-off between the cost and precision of usage accounting is programmable [5].

The unit of management for the RM API is an isolate. This choice makes accountability unambiguous, as each resource in use has exactly one owner.

A *resource domain* encapsulates a usage policy for a resource. All isolates *bound* to a given resource domain are uniformly subject to that domain's policy for the underlying resource. An isolate cannot be bound to more than one domain for the same resource, but can be bound to many domains for different resources. Thus, two isolates can share a single resource domain for, say, CPU time, but be bound to distinct domains for outgoing socket traffic.

The RM API does not impose any policy on a domain; policies are explicitly defined by programs. A resource management policy for a resource controls when a computation may gain access to, or *consume*, a unit of that resource. The policy may specify *reservations*[1] and arbitrary *consume actions* that should execute when a request to consume a given quantity of resource is made by an isolate bound to a resource domain. Consume actions defined to execute prior to the consuming act as programmable *constraints* and can influence whether or not the request is granted. Regardless of the outcome, they can arbitrarily modify the behavior of isolates bound Consume actions defined to execute after the consume event can be thought of as *notifications*.

---

[1] Guaranteed resource availability, which does not imply that a client may consume the resource, as that is also dependent on the resource usage policy of the client's resource domain. to the resource domain.

Figure 1 illustrates these concepts. In this simplified example there is only one managed resource: the number of open sockets. A *Manager* isolate executes in its own resource domain. It starts three isolates that are bound to a separate resource domain, to ensure that the manager and any other service started later are insulated from consumption by the service provided by these three isolates. The second domain has a reservation of 20. This quantity is guaranteed, but only if there are no constraints further limiting the resource's availability. In our example there is one constraint, *Deny*, which is also set to 20; it logs an appropriate information error message before rejecting the request to open more sockets than allowed. Finally two notifications, *HighWatermark* and *LowWatermark,* are set by the isolates in the second domain themselves to detect when the resource is scarce or plentiful and to modify consumption accordingly.

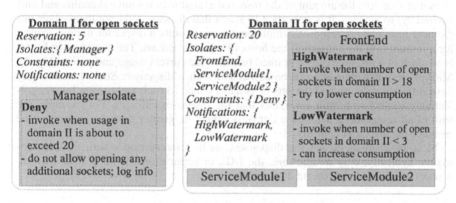

Fig. 1. The Manager isolate controls three isolates with respect to their consumption of sockets. The controlled isolates are bound to the same resource domain (i.e., they share the same policy). Moreover, one of the isolates created two notifications to be informed about resource shortage or abundance.

Resource Attributes. The RM API characterizes a resource as a set of attributes. The attributes provide a programmatic means of learning about the properties of a given resource. Resource characterization relevant to this study includes the *disposable* boolean attribute and the numerical *granularity* of management.

A resource is *disposable* if it is possible to identify a span of program execution over which a given resource instance is considered to be consumed. Outside of this span, the resource instance is available for (re)use. A file descriptor is a disposable resource; CPU time is not. An example of the usefulness of this attribute is in allowing *unconsuming* (i.e., returning to the pool of resources) of disposable resources only. The same operation for a non-disposable resource is erroneous.

The *granularity* of a resource is the minimal indivisible amount of the resource in a given implementation. For example, a heap might be managed as a set of pages; in this case, although the resource's unit is bytes or kilobytes, the deliverable granularity is the underlying page size. RM API method arguments that specify resource quantities are automatically rounded up to the nearest granularity multiple. Requesting to consume a non-multiple of granularity is legal, but the returned value will be a granularity multiple. The rationale behind granularity is to allow managing the tradeoff between accounting precision and its cost. This attribute is important for resource implementers; applications are typically insulated from dealing with it directly.

The resource characterization does not provide any attributes related to bandwidth, and correspondingly the RM API provides no direct means of manipulating consumption rates. However, we observe that the ability to gain control at every resource consumption point implies the ability to delay the consuming thread at each of those points. Thus, to impose a desired consumption rate for a given resource, it suffices to throttle consumption requests until they match that rate. Examples in the following sections expand this point in greater detail.

Resource Dispenser. The bridge between the resource management interface and the code that actually implements (fabricates) a resource is a resource *dispenser*. The dispenser monitors the amount of the resource available to resource domains and thus (indirectly) to isolates. It is important to stress that dispensers do not themselves implement resources. A resource's implementation consults a dispenser upon a request for a resource via the consume() method of ResourceDomain. The dispenser indicates how much of a resource can be granted based on the current usage and policy (Fig. 2). Multiple resource domains can be associated with a dispenser. Such domains may have different policies, and the sets of isolates bound to each are disjoint but are collectively subject to certain invariants that the dispenser enforces. For example, the sum of all reservations across the domains cannot be greater than the amount of the resource the dispenser controls.

Most applications do not see dispensers, as they interact only with resource domains. Typically, only middleware, the JRE, or applications defining their own resources would explicitly create dispensers.

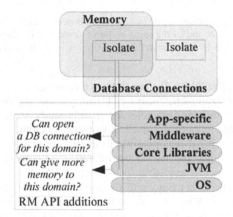

Fig. 2. Resource implementations consult their dispensers when granting a request. The decisions depend on policies defined in resource domains.

Defining Resources. The task of exposing resources through the RM API belongs to virtual machine implementers, to implementers of the JRE, and to developers of libraries defining resources. To make a resource manageable through the RM API, one must subclass ResourceAttributes and Dispenser, and insert consume() and unconsume() calls where appropriate in the resource's implementation.

Figure 2 illustrates this general approach: computations request resources exactly as they would prior to use of the RM API, and small modifications to resource implementations consult programmable consumption policies, deciding whether a given request can be satisfied.

4 J2EERI on MVM

The J2EE specification defines four application types: Java™ Servlets (JavaServer™ Pages), Enterprise JavaBeans ™(EJB™), Applets and (rich) Application Clients; and an array of services, e.g., Java™ Database Connectivity ("JDBC™") and Java™ Message Service (JMS). Instances of these applications are hosted in containers that interpose between the applications and the set of available services. The containers are themselves hosted in servers, e.g., Web, EJB, and JMS, that may occupy one or more Java virtual machines.

The J2EERI implementation is written entirely in the Java programming language. It includes a version of the Tomcat [11] Web server. The JMS service depends on the Cloudscape relational database [12], which is included with the J2EERI and is also written entirely in the Java programming language. At runtime, all servers execute in the same JVM, including the Cloudscape instance that supports JMS.

In earlier work [8], we evaluated several ways in which isolates might be used to restructure a J2EE server, and the J2EERI in particular. While a straightforward approach would place J2EERI implementation modules in isolates, our preferred strategy, which forms the basis of the work described here, uses *application domain* isolates. Each application domain hosts one (or more) complete J2EE applications, and the associated containers and servers. In addition, the application domain isolates are controlled by a separate administrative isolate. This structure has two main advantages. First, it is easy to manage resources on a per application domain basis since RM is based on isolates. Stated differently, this is an application (service) oriented architecture. Second, communication overheads are minimized. Local, pass-by reference interfaces may be used, e.g., EJB local interfaces.

Owing to MVM's efficient runtime meta-data sharing, the cost of replicating the containers and services in each domain is small, on the order of 6MB per domain [8]. Parts of the deployment logic and other sharable components are contained in the administrative isolate. In particular, the administrative isolate is responsible for resource domain management and installs the appropriate callbacks during server startup (Sec. 5.2). Communication between the administrative isolate and application isolates uses the isolate link mechanism.

Optionally an application domain may be further subdivided into isolates that host the major subservers, that is, the Web server, EJB server, and JMS servers. We used the single-isolate variant in this research, but note in passing that the two variants are equivalent from a resource management perspective, due to the fact that several isolates may be bound to the same resource domain. Figure 3 shows the isolate structure of a system we have built with an optional load balancer and three application domains.

Load Balancer. A load balancer directs incoming requests to an appropriate server, based on knowledge of the load on all the servers in a system. Load balancing is standard practice in large J2EE server configurations and is usually realized by a software "plug in" component to a web server. The mechanisms for communication between the load balancer and the servers being balanced are typically ad hoc and server-specific. In principle load balancing can be performed with respect to arbitrary resources, but is typically limited to CPU load and network traffic.

From the perspective of the RM framework, a load balancer is a software component that requries notification of consumption of the appropriate resources on the servers it is attempting to balance. We have implemented a simple CPU load balancer that consists of an HTTP passthrough engine that directs HTTP requests to the least loaded application domain. The load balancing component registers notification consume actions for the CPU resource against all the application domains under its control. It uses the usage information provided in the notification to maintain a load average for each domain. It would be straightforward to add accounting for additional resources into the selection algorithm and we are planning this for future work. A virtue of RM in this context is that the load balancer uses only the standard isolate API and is largely independent of isolate location. In particular, it is possible to load balance to multiple application domains in a single server. This can be used, for example, to direct a specific class of user requests to a lightly loaded (well resourced) application domain, without the need to establish a multi-server infrastructure.

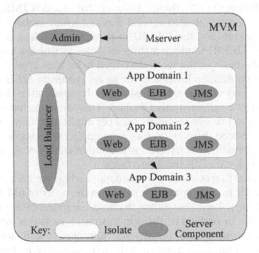

Fig. 3. Isolate structure of modified J2EERI.

5 J2EERI Resources

A J2EE server contains many entities that could be characterized as resources in the RM framework. These range from traditional, low-level, resources such as CPU time, memory, network traffic, and threads, to J2EE-specific resources like JDBC connections, EJB container cache, number of active servlets, and so on. One of the main challenges in using RM effectively is the choice of appropriate resources to manage. This is particularly true of the higher level resources, as there are many entities that could potentially be defined as resources.

Two observations can help with choosing appropriate resources:

- The essential requirement of a J2EE server is to deliver a specified level of service at some minimum "cost". The level of service is typically expressed in terms the client of the service can understand, for example, request throughput and latency. Cost might be specified as some function of resources used, typically traditional resources such as CPU time.
- Higher-level resources depend on lower-level resources for their implementation. For example, a JDBC connection requires memory, CPU cycles, and a socket. A servlet may require a JDBC connection. An application may require several servlets and so on.

The first observation suggests identifying the key resources that contribute to the service level and/or have relevance to the cost function. The second observation implies that defining too many resources, particularly if they have complex dependencies between them, is counterproductive. No human administrator could be expected to understand the inter-dependencies sufficiently well to choose appropriate policies. One particular problem with dependent resources is setting conflicting policies that render higher-level resource policies irrelevant. For example, if network bandwidth to a database is set too low, then a policy that attempts to limit transaction rates may be moot if the maxmum rate can never be achieved because of lack of sufficient network bandwidth. The ultimate solution to this problem is coordinated, automated resource management, but that is beyond the scope of this paper.

5.1 J2SE Resources

MVM supports resource management for CPU time, heap memory, sockets, threads, and network traffic, all of which required changes to either MVM itself or to the appropriate core classes. In this research we have explored the management of CPU time in the J2EERI server. This crucial resource illustrates well how to integrate fine-grain management of standard resouces into an application server.

CPU Time. Efficient and accurate CPU management is challenging to implement. Unlike other resources, there are no explicit points in the program where CPU resources are requested. If code were always interpreted, the main JVM interpreter loop could be modified to issue consume requests periodically. However, achieving the same effect for compiled code would require consume requests to be embedded in many places in the compiled code, a complicated and expensive solution.

Instead, MVM utilizes a polling thread that periodically wakes up, computes the CPU usage for that isolate in the polling period and then invokes the consume() action. This is relatively efficient, depending on the length of the polling period (which, for this resource, is its granularity – see Sec. 3), but does have the property that CPU is actually used before the consume action can impose control.

CPU is an example of a resource that is generally best controlled by limiting the rate of consumption. However, we note in passing that, modulo the polling period, it is straightforward to place an absolute limit on CPU usage to prevent denial of service attacks or to control runaway applications.

The RM API provides a standard rate-adjusting policy that is suitable for many different resources, for example network bandwidth, transaction rate (see Sec. 5.3). The rate is specified as a given threshold value in a given time period, e.g., 100 units in 1 second. The policy is implemented by maintaining a history of resource usage over the interval and, if consumption has been excessive, suspending the isolate on a consume event long enough to bring the rate down to the required level. Given an interval I, a threshold T, history interval H, and usage in history interval U, the formula used to compute the potential length of suspension is $U * (I / T) - H$. If this value is not greater than zero no suspension occurs.

With minor modifications[2], this policy can be applied to controlling CPU usage. For example, 1000ms of CPU time in any 5000ms interval. Or stated in percentage terms, 20% of the CPU in a 5000ms interval.

A variant of this policy simply limits the usage to a specified percentage in every polling period. This is equivalent to the standard policy with the interval set to the polling period and a threshold equal to the given percentage of that period. It has the virtue of requiring no history to be kept, as essentially only the behavior in the most recent polling interval determines the length of suspension, It is also independent of the polling period and arguably more intuitive for an administrator. The virtue of the standard policy is that bursty CPU usage can be tolerated over short periods without suspension, provided that the history interval is large enough. The corollary, however, is that the length of the suspension can be larger in the worst case.

Note that in both variants the potential for overuse is limited to the length of the polling period, which naturally creates pressure to keep it short. However, as we see below, the measurement overhead increases as we reduce the polling period.

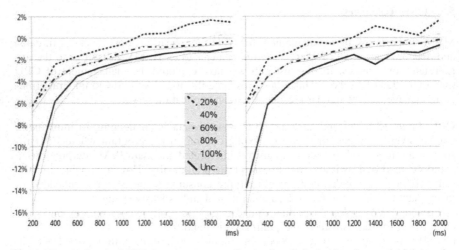

Fig. 4. The overhead of CPU time management for the first (left chart) and second (right) variant, as a function of the polling interval, relative to a server with no RM enabled (lower is worse). Each plot corresponds to the CPU percentage allocated to the test isolate.

---

[2] For CPU usage the polling thread handles the consume event, but we must suspend all user threads in the given isolate, and not the polling thread.

To measure the overhead of CPU time management we executed a CPU-bound servlet while varying the percentage of allocated CPU and the polling period. Figure 4 shows the percentage reduction in throughput for both variants with polling periods from 200ms to 2s and with varying CPU percentage limits[3]. The baseline for comparison was the throughput of the server with RM disabled, multiplied by an appropriate factor to compute the maximum throughput for different target CPU percentages (0.2 for 20%, 0.4 for 40%, etc.). The measurements show that both methods of controlling allocated CPU time have very similar costs, and at a polling period of 2 seconds, there is no discernible overhead. The *Unc* (unconstrained) data is for a server with RM enabled but no CPU resource callbacks installed and, therefore, shows the overhead of the polling thread. Relative to *Unc*, the 100% case shows the additional overhead of executing the callback. We believe imprecision in the Thread.sleep method to be the cause of the overshoots at low percentage limits and are investigating a more precise implementation.

5.2 Integrating Resource Management into J2EERI

Following standard J2EERI conventions, the set of resources to be managed by the server is specified in a properties file. The file may specifiy a subset of the possible resources under RM control if it is not desired to manage certain resources. The set of possible resources includes those provided by the JRE, e.g., CPU time, and additional resources defined specifically for J2EE. Resources are specified using the standard naming convention of Java classes, e.g., server.resource.JDBCConnection.

The associated classes that RM requires for a resource, e.g., the dispenser and resource attributes (Sec. 3), are assumed to have class names formed by standard suffixes to the resource name, e.g., server.resource.JDBCConnectionDispenser.

When MVM starts up, it is passed the file defining the resources to be managed and attempts to instantiate the associated dispenser classes. For reservable resources such as JDBCConnection, the total reservable amount, which is needed by the dispenser, is also specified in the file.

Consume actions applied to a resource are referred to as resource policies and are similarly specified using standardized class names. For example, a consume action that logs the consumption of a resource would be defined and applied in the class server.resource.policy.LogConsumptionPolicy. This class must implement the ResourcePolicy interface and define the method setPolicy.

The application of resource policies is handled by the administrative isolate, again based on information in a properties file. Each application domain enumerates those policies that it wishes to have applied, using the resource class names. The administrative isolate applies a policy by first creating a local resource domain for the resource and binding the application domain isolate to the local resource domain. It then instantiates the policy class and invokes the setPolicy method. For simple policies such as the LogConsumption policy, the setPolicy method simply creates the appropriate consume callback and registers it with the local resource domain. Note that the administrative isolate neither interprets nor depends on the resources or applied poli-

---

[3] All performance data presented in this paper were obtained using the on the Solaris™ 9 Operating System on a Sun 280R server with two 1015Mhz UltraSPARC™ III processors and 4GB of main memory.

cies in any way. Currently the only server code that depends on specific resource types is the load balancer.

Reservations for resources are handled using a generic reservation policy. The amount of the reservation must be specified as an extra argument to the policy in the properties file, and is passed through in a string array to the setPolicy method. Since, initially, the total reservable amount is allocated to the resource domain bound to the administrative isolate, the reservation policy class must first reduce the administrative isolate's allocation and then allocate it to the application domain isolate.

A strength of the RM framework is that generic policies like Reservation and Log-Consumption can be specified once and applied to a wide variety of resources.

The following is a simplified version of the LogConsumption policy[4]:

```
public class LogConsumptionPolicy implements ResourcePolicy, Notification {
        public void setPolicy(ResourceDomain admin, ResourceDomain target) {
                localDomain.setPersistentNotification(this);
        }
        public long notify(ResourceDomain d, long previousUsage, long currentUsage) {
                String resourceName = domain.getResourceAttributes().getName();
                long consumedUnits = currentUsage – previousUsage;
                log("Consumed additional " + consumedUnits + " of " + resourceName);
        }
}
```

5.3 J2EE-Specific Resources

From a variety of potential J2EE-specific resources we chose to focus attention on several resources related to database management, namely connections, statements, and transactions. Defining these three resource types allows for controlling both the absolute and rate availability of these resources to application domains (Sec 3.2).

J2EE application performance is often critically dependent on the performance of the underlying database and on the extent to which data can be cached in the application server. We do not address caching mechanisms in this paper but observe that they depend in part on resources such as the size of the EJB caches and the availability of heap memory, that are manageable with the RM framework.

The performance of the underlying database is generally outside the control of MVM/RM as the database system is typically not implemented in the Java programming language. Those databases, such as Cloudscape [12] and Pointbase [13], that are implemented in the Java programming language are rarely used in enterprise system deployments. Nor are the sources readily available, thus making it difficult to apply RM to their implementations.

A database is accessed from a J2EE application using the JDBC API or, more generally, through the Java Connector Architecture (JCA), that provides a standard way to interact with legacy enterprise information systems. The JDBC driver therefore acts a proxy for the database server and several of the JDBC classes effectively represent resoures that are provided by the database. By controlling access to these proxy resources we can, to some extent, control the use of database resources.

In the following sections we describe the chosen resources, their correspondence to database resources, and their integration into J2EERI.

---

[4] Some of the class and method names in the RM API are different than in the example; the modifications better convey the intuitive meaning behind the code.

Connections

A fundamental JDBC resource is a *connection*, which represents an active session with the database server. A connection is required to perform any interaction with the database. Connections are relatively expensive to set up and a database server can only support a relatively small number of connections, certainly many fewer than the number of concurrent users that might be accessing an application hosted on a J2EE server. A solution to this mismatch is connection pooling, where a fixed number of connections are held open to the database, and shared between the sessions corresponding to the J2EE application clients. An application opens and closes pooled connections in the normal way, but actual database connection open and close operations only take place when necessary, for example, when there are insufficient open connections to handle the load. Connection pool management is one of the more complex areas of a production J2EE server. The administrator typically provides some input to the pool manager in the form of minimum and maximum numbers of open connections. Tuning these values can often have a significant effect on application performance.

Typically, then, from a resource management perspective, a J2EE server can be characterized as having a hard-wired connection management policy, that is tunable by a small set of fixed controls. The hard-wired policy cannot be changed nor is it easy to apply different policies to different databases, beyond altering the fixed controls.

The J2EERI connection pool manager has no externally controllable properties. It attempts to share connections where possible, e.g., when opened with the same transaction, otherwise it grows the pool without limit[5]. It uses a periodic recycling mechanism to detect connections that have not been used recently, closing and removing them from the pool.

To manage connections, we defined a J2EERI server resource called JDBCConnections, which is disposable and has a granularity of one (see Sec. 3). It was straightforward to use the Reservation policy to limit the maximum number of connections that the pool can open. Each application domain can be assigned a subset of the global limit that is set when the dispenser is created. Further, these reservations can be changed dynamically, although since allocated resources cannot be revoked[6], the reduced reservation only takes effect on a subsequent allocation.

Manually setting fixed connection pool parameters is essentially a trial and error process in current servers and therefore does not adapt well to dynamic changes. While throughput is increased, up to a point, by more connections, database request latency also increases. While an area for future work, it would be possible to use RM to create a connection pool policy that adjusted the number of open connections to maintain optimal throughput, given a target range for request latency.

Transactions

An entity that is not usually considered a controllable resource in a J2EE server is a *transaction*. Every interaction with a database must take place under a transaction, which ensures the standard ACID properties associated with a database. A transaction

---

[5] The underlying database effectively imposes the limit.
[6] Except by destroying the isolate, which releases all of its resources.

corresponds to database server resources, such as data that must be kept in case a transaction needs to abort and locks that are needed to keep concurrent transactions from interfering with each other. Committing a transaction requires action on part of the database server to make relevant data durable, which typically requires disk activity. If the transaction rate is too high the database server can get behind on commits, slowing all clients down.

Controlling the rate of transactions that an application domain can issue is therefore useful. Assuming we can modify the code in the JDBC driver that initiates a transaction to issue a consume() action against the transction resource, it is then straightforward to use one of the rate controlling callbacks to limit the transaction rate.

To control transactions we defined a server resource JDBCTransactions, which is nondisposable and has a default granularity of 25.

Statements

Transactions typically consist of more than one JDBC statement execution. A JDBC statement is a representation of a SQL statement that is understood by the database server. JDBC provides two essential variants of statement. A plain statement is sent to the database server as a simple text string, requiring the database to compile the SQL before it can be executed. A JDBC statement therefore corresponds to database server resources relating to SQL compilation, which can be resource intensive. The second variant is a prepared statement that the database server compiles once and further can be parameterized to accept different arguments on each call. Prepared statements are therefore less expensive to execute than plain statements.

In certain cases, it might be useful to control statement execution. For example, it would be relatively simple to limit or deny non-prepared statement execution. One could also control the rate of statement execution, although care must be taken not to conflict with controls on transaction execution rate.

To control statements we defined a server resource JDBCStatements, which has the same attributes as the JDBCTransactions resource.

Experiments

To test the utility and ease of implementation of the above JDBC resources, we modified the MySQL JDBC driver [14] to insert the appropriate RM calls. One issue this immediately raised was that of resource naming. A JDBC driver is required to work with any compliant J2EE server and a J2EE server may utilize several different JDBC drivers. Different servers might wish to define and control different resources and name them differently. Rather than attempt to define a global naming scheme, we instead decided to establish mappings between J2EE server resource names and JDBC driver resource names, that are defined in a server configuration file and propagated to the system properties table. For example, the following mapping is established betwen the server resource name and the driver resource name:

server.resource.JDBCConnections= com.mysql.jdbc.resource.connection

When the driver wishes to acquire the connection resource domain, it looks up its name for the resource in the system properties and retrieves the server resource name. If the mapping does not exist, the driver simply ignores that resource and does not issue consume calls during execution. Therefore the driver can continue to work with a server that is not enabled for resource management[7].

The modifications to the driver were straightforward, amounting to a handful of lines in the com.mysql.jdbc.Connection class.

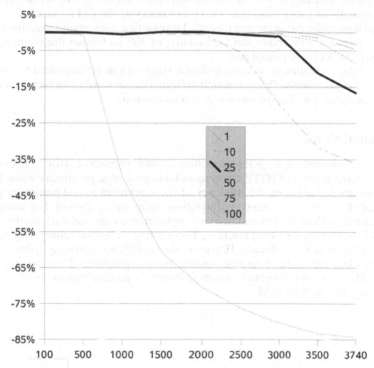

Fig. 5. Percentage difference in actual transaction rate against expected transaction rate for different resource granularities.

The rate-based policy mentioned earlier is very suitable for controlling transaction rate. For example to limit an application to 10 transactions per second, one would specify JDBCTransactions{10, 1000} as the policy.

To test the effectiveness of this policy we used a simple micro-benchmark, similar to that used in the CPU test, that consists of a loop whose body is a transaction that issues an SQL select statement. The benchmark is run for a fixed time interval and reports the transaction rate every 2 seconds. When run with no constraints on transaction rate, the benchmark achieves 3740 transactions per second. To test the ability to control the rate dynamically, we ran the test with a policy that adjusts the maximum allowed number of transactions from 100 through 3740 in increments of 100, in an interval of 1 second, changing the rate every 30 seconds. To measure the effect of resource granularity, we ran tests with the granularity set to 1, 10, 25, 50, 75 and 100. Figure 5 compares the measured transaction rate against the expected transaction rate.

---

[7] By using reflection the driver can also be independent of the RM API at compile time.

A granularity of 1 adds considerable overhead, which is seen by the sharp reduction at high applied rates. This is to be expected: with granularity equal to 1, the time to consult the current resource policy, which includes an inter-isolate communication, is added to each transaction's execution time. However, at granularities of 50 and above, the maximum reduction is 8.5% and is less than 2.5% across 90% of the range, since only at most 2% of transactions incur the cost of querying the RM framework.

Figure 6 plots the measured and requested transaction rates against time for a subset of the transaction rate range and a granularity of 100, and shows that the measured rate closely tracks the requested rate.

Both of these experiments have very similar results when the controlled resource is the number of statements. This correlation indicates that in some cases these resources are interchangeable with respect to resource management.

6 Related Work

J2EE servers currently manage resources they control (pooling of JDBC connections, EJB cache size, number of HTTP server threads) in their own, proprietary ways. Little public information exists on the efficiency of these approaches, and portability problems related to non-standardized configuration management abound. For managing resources not implemented in middleware, application servers fall back on the capabilities of the underlying virtual machine. These rarely go beyond setting heap size or managing the number of threads. However, the underlying operating systems typically provide a richer set of resource management capabilities. Thus, the extent to which a J2EE system can control system resources is dictated largely by its internal partitioning into multiple JVMs.

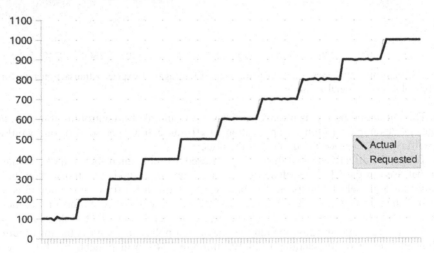

Fig. 6. Responsiveness of controlling the rate of transactions.

Falling back on a process abstraction is often inefficient and can suffer from a dual responsibility: in commodity operating systems a process often serves as both a unit of protection and a unit of resource management. Several researchers have pointed out problems stemming from this conflation. For example resource containers [15] were explicitly designed to decouple these two responsibilities. A resource container is associated with a request; the request can traverse multiple protection domains, but all of its resource activities are "charged" against the same container. Resource containers are a generalization of the well-known *paths* abstraction, introduced in the Scout OS [16]. In some respects resource domains resemble resource containers. The resemblance is not complete, though: isolates are required as basic units of resource management in our model, and flexibility is achieved by dynamic association with resource domains.

A resource adaptation framework described in [17] introduces concepts similar to the abstractions existing in the RM API. Most notably the set of resources is extensible and the binding of computations to resources is flexible. The focus of the work is to simplify resource adaptation for middleware platforms through a uniform API and to define interfaces to partition resources among computations, while our work is equally concerned with implementation and performance issues.

We note the existence of management frameworks, such as JMX [3] and JSR-77 [18] that are used in several production J2EE servers. However, when applied to resource management as defined in this paper, these frameworks lack significant functionality. Nevertheless, their high-level approach to management could provide a convenient coordination and provisioning layer, complementing the low-level functionality of the RM API.

The *defensive programming* approach [19] advocates systematic annotation of programs with code watching for denial-of-service attacks. Whenever such abuse takes place, appropriate programmable action is taken. Similarly to that work, we argue the importance of intra-process protection.

In the *staged event-driven architecture* (SEDA) [20], applications consist of a network of stages connected by explicit queues. Each stage admits another request from its queue when this would not lead to exceeding the stage's capacity. SEDA controls each stage's load through mechanisms such as dynamic thread pool sizing and batch size adjusting. Monitoring CPU-related resources (e.g., the number of threads) guides controlling the sizes queue, in effect managing the load of each stage. The architecture presented here can complement SEDA – fine-grain control over a wide set of resource types produces more usage information that can later be fed into admission policy of each of the request handling stages. Coupling SEDA's explicit architectural approach with isolates to create a modular, easy to manage, scalable, overload-averse application server merits investigation.

In [5] we reviewed the state of the art in resource management geared specifically for the Java platform. In summary, systems such as JRes [21] and J-SEAL2 [22] account for CPU time and memory used by programs by a combination of bytecode editing and native code. Neither of these early systems is adequate for our purpose of efficient, flexible, uniform, and extensible management of resources in an application server. Both JRes and J-SEAL2 incur overheads around 20% of the execution time, even if there are no constraints. The set of resources managed is not extensible, and neither system can fully account for resources consumed by the run-time system and some core classes.

Modifications of the virtual machine, such as KaffeOS [23], alleviate some of these problems. KaffeOS implemented the process abstraction within the JVM, so that mistrusting programs can coexist within the same underlying address space. However,

456 Mick Jordan et al.

KaffeOS's resource management focuses on CPU time and heap memory only and is not designed for application-specific resources.

The Real-Time Java Specification [24], which requires custom virtual machines, is specialized for real-time platforms, with a fixed set of resources, while the RM API's goals include extensibility, flexibility, and cross-scenario applicability that are likely to appeal much more to non-RT programmers.

The .NET platform [25] defines *application domains,* similar to the notion of isolates. Instances of System.AppDomain are virtual processes, isolating applications from one another. AppDomains are being used in some .NET servers, e.g., ASP.NET. We are not aware of APIs for managing resources available to individual domains.

7 Future Work

In this research we have only studied a small subset of the total set of resources that could be managed in a J2EE server. We plan to extend the work to additional low-level resources, especially heap memory and threads, as well as to other J2EE resources such as EJB caches.

Work is also underway to extend the Isolate programming model, RM, and MVM to clusters of separate machines. This will allow us to investigate the utility of these mechanisms in large, horizontally scaled, multi-tier J2EE configurations.

However, manual control of resources really does not scale to a system as large and complex as a J2EE server. In that context, the RM framework should be seen as a tool to assist in the automated management of resources that is driven by a service level definition and a resource cost function. Solving this problem in the general case requires a global optimizer that fully understands the resource dependencies and can automate the application of appropriate resource policies. We plan to evaluate the potential for connecting an appropriate optimization engine to the RM framework.

8 Conclusions

An area where safe language platforms seriously lag behind operating systems is that of resource management facilities. In general, multi-resource load balancing and fine-grained and efficient resource usage monitoring are difficult to accomplish without going beyond the safe language, through mechanisms such as native code or shell scripts that ask the OS to handle RM-related matters. The lack of a standard, programmatic way to partition resources available to virtual machine(s) among Java applications has led to a number of awkward solutions and may discourage some developers from using safe languages. The situation, already problematic in J2SE, is exacerbated in application servers, as the deployed applications rely on more services and resources, implemented by J2EE but without standardized and adequate resource management programming interfaces.

In this paper we demonstrated that an application server can be equipped with flexible, extensible, and efficient mechanisms for fine-grained resource management. The presented architecture builds on a virtual machine that supports multi-tasking and is capable of managing standard resources. The prototype enables uniform management of an extended set of resource types, significantly reduces the complexity of provisioning resources for code deployed in application servers, and allows for precise and inexpensive usage monitoring. Moreover, the presented RM extensions and their dependence on isolates as opposed to OS processes can free application server architects and administrators from requiring multiple virtual machines in their designs, further simplifying the design and management of J2EE execution environments.

From the perspective of resource implementers we found two features of the resulting prototype particularly useful: ease of retrofitting existing resource implementations to make them fit into the RM framework, and the programmable cost/precision tradeoff of the RM API.

Even without extensive tuning, the current prototype is already satisfactory for practical use, with very low – in some cases not measurable – overheads. It demonstrates the potential for a complete and controlled environment for enterprise applications and forms a good basis for further research.

Trademarks: Sun, Sun Microsystems, Java 2 Platform, Standard Edition, J2SE, Java 2 Platform Enterprise Edition, J2EE, Java Management Extensions, JMX, Java Database Connectivity ("JDBC"), JDBC, Java Virtual Machine, JVM, Java runtime environment, Java HotSpot, Java Servlet, JavaServer Pages, Enterprise JavaBeans, EJB, Java Message Service, Java Community Process, JCP, Solaris 9 Operating System are trademarks or registered trademarks of Sun Microsystems Inc. In the U.S. and other countries. All SPARC trademarks are used under license and are trademarks of registered trademarks of SPARC International Inc. In the U.S. and other countries.

References

1. Sun Microsystems, Inc.: Java 2 Platform, Enterprise Edition (J2EE).
   http://java.sun.com/j2ee/index.jsp
2. Gosling, J., Joy, B., Steele, G. and Bracha, G.: The Java Language Specification. 2nd Edition. Addison-Wesley (2000)
3. Sun Microsystems, Inc.: Java Management Extensions.
   http://java.sun.com/products/Java- Management/
4. Distributed Management Task Force: Common Information Model (CIM) Standards.
   http://www.dmtf.org/standards.cim
5. Czajkowski, G., Hahn, S., Skinner, G., and Soper, P., Bryce C.: A Resource Management Interface for the Java Platform. Sun Microsystems TR 2003-124 (2003)
6. Java Community Process: JSR-121: Application Isolation API Specification.
   http://jcp.org/jsr/detail/121.jsp
7. Czajkowski, G., and Daynes, L.: Multitasking without Compromise: A Virtual Machine Evolution. ACM OOPSLA'01, Tampa, FL
8. Jordan, M., Daynes, L., Czajkowski, G., Jarzab, M., Bryce. C.: Scaling J2EE™ Application Servers with the Multi-Tasking Virtual Machine. Sun Microsystems TR 2004-135 (2004)
9. Sun Microsystems, Inc.: Java 2 Platform, Enterprise Edition (J2EE) - Version 1.3.1 Release. http://java.sun.com/j2ee/sdk_1.3/
10. Sun Microsystems, Inc. Java HotSpot™ Technology. http://java.sun.com/products/hotspot
11. The Apache Software Foundation: Apache Tomcat. http://jakarta.apache.org/tomcat
12. IBM Corporation: The Cloudscape database.
    http://www.ibm.com/software/data/cloudscape/

13. Pointbase: The Pointbase Database, http://www.pointbase.com
14. MySQL AB: MySQL Connector/J. http://www.mysql.com/products/connector-j/
15. Bang, G., Druschel, P., and Mogul, J.: Better Operating System Features for Faster Network Servers. Wokshop on Internet Server Performance, Madison, WI (1998)
16. Mosberger, D., and Peterson, L.: Making Paths Explicit in the Scout Operating System, Proceedings of OSDI '96, Seattle, WA (1996)
17. Parlavantas, N., Blair, G.S., and Coulson, G.: A Resource Adaption Framework for Reflective Middleware. Proceedings of the 2nd Intl. Workshop on Reflective and Adaptive Middleware, Ri Janeiro, Brazil (2003)
18. Java Community Process: JSR-77: Java 2 Enterprise Edition Management Specification. http://jcp.org/jsr/detail/77.jsp
19. Qie, X., Pang, R., and Peterson, L.: Defensive Programming: Using an Annotation Toolkit to Build DoS-Resistant Software. 5th OSDI, Boston, MA (2002)
20. Welsh, M., Culler, D., and Brewer D.: SEDA An Architecture for Well-Conditioned, Scalable, Internet. 18th SOSP, Banff, Canada (2001)
21. Czajkowski, G., and von Eicken, T.: JRes: A Resource Accounting Interface for Java.
22. Binder, W., Hulaas, J., and Villazon, A.: Portable Resource Control in Java: The J-SEAL2 Approach. 16th ACM OOPSLA, Tampa Bay, FL (2001)
23. Back, G., Hsieh, W., and Leprau, J.: Processes in KaffeOS: Isolation, Resource Management, and Sharing in Java. 4th OSDI, San Diego, CA (2000)
24. Bollella, G., Gosling, J., Brosgol, B., Dibble, P., Furr, S., Hardin, D., and Turnbull, M.: The Real-Time Specification for Java. Addison-Wesley (2000)
25. Microsoft Corp. .NET Web Page. http://www.microsoft.com/net (2002)

Developing and Managing Software Components in an Ontology-Based Application Server

Daniel Oberle, Andreas Eberhart, Steffen Staab, and Raphael Volz

Institute for Applied Informatics and Formal Description Methods (AIFB)
University of Karlsruhe
Germany
lastname@aifb.uni-karlsruhe.de

Abstract. Application servers provide many functionalities commonly needed in the development of a complex distributed application. So far, the functionalities have mostly been developed and managed with the help of administration tools and corresponding configuration files, recently in XML. Though this constitutes a very flexible way of developing and administrating a distributed application, e.g. an application server with its components, the disadvantage is that the conceptual model underlying the different configurations is *only implicit*. Hence, its bits and pieces are difficult to retrieve, survey, check for validity and maintain. To remedy such problems, we here present an ontology-based approach to support the development and administration of software components in an application server. The ontology captures properties of, relationships between and behaviors of the components that are required for development and administration purposes. The ontology is an *explicit* conceptual model with formal logic-based semantics. Therefore its descriptions of components may be queried, may foresight required actions, e.g. preloading of indirectly required components, or may be checked to avoid inconsistent system configurations – during development as well as during run time. Thus, the ontology-based approach retains the original flexibility in configuring and running the application server, but it adds new capabilities for the developer and user of the system. The proposed scheme has been prototypically implemented in KAON SERVER, an application server running components that support a range of various semantic technologies – thus applying semantic technologies to itself[1].

1   Introduction

Application Servers are component-based middleware platforms that offer an environment in which users can deploy components developed by themselves or by third-party providers [1]. As a sophisticated middleware, application servers provide functionality such as dynamic loading, naming services, load balancing, security, connection pooling, transactions, or persistence.

Despite the bundled functionality, realizing a complex distributed application remains all but an easy task. For instance, managing component dependencies,

---

[1] The software is available for download at http://kaon.semanticweb.org/

H.-A. Jacobsen (Ed.): Middleware 2004, LNCS 3231, pp. 459–477, 2004.

versions, and licenses is a typical problem in an ever-growing repository of programming libraries. In Microsoft environments, this is often referred to as "DLL Hell". Configuration files, even if they are more or less human-readable XML, do not provide an abstraction mechanism to tame the complexity issues arising in such systems.

Our approach is supplementary to the Object Modelling Group's *Model-Driven Architecture (MDA)* [16], in which models abstract from low-level and often platform-specific implementation details. While MDA allows to separate *conceptual concerns* from *implementation-specific concerns*, currently MDA has not been applied for run time relevant characteristics of component management, such as which version of an application interface requires which versions of libraries.

The ability to compile platform-specific configuration files from our conceptual model is a first and immediately obvious advantage of our approach. We do not apply MDA in this paper to tailor a modeling language for component management, since its lack of (logical) formality disallows run time interpretability. We consider this interpretability to be central for component management, for example to query the application server whether configurations are valid or whether further components are needed.

Therefore, the logical next step in developing and managing complex applications is the use of an *explicit conceptual model that is executable, too*, meaning it may be queried and reasoned with, i.e. an ontology. The goal of this paper is to show how ontologies may be defined that support the developer in creating new software or in running new components in the complex environment of an application server. Given software components described by semantic metadata, which conforms to the ontology, inferencing allows for finding APIs that come with certain capabilities (development time support) or for pre-loading components that are required by other components (run time support).

The reader may note that though an application server is not the only software that may be supported in that way, it is a very worthy challenge. The reasons are that the needs are huge in this area and at the same time ontologies may fruitfully contribute to this complex, but nevertheless reasonably restricted domain of application.

We shortly present some motivating use cases for our approach of an explicit conceptual model (section 2). We embed our approach into a generic architecture for an ontology-based application server and briefly refer to its prototypical implementation that supports semantic technology components [20] (section 3). We introduce the well-known J2EE Pet Store demo (section 4) which will be referred to in subsequent sections as a source of examples. As a major contribution of this paper, we describe the ontologies that have been developed since the inception of the architecture implementation (section 5) and highlight some of the new management capabilities provided to developers of the application server (section 6). Finally, related work and conclusions are discussed in sections 7 and 8.

2   Motivation

The first subsection considers use cases for semantic metadata of components and APIs that target development time support. Subsection 2.2 focusses on the run time use cases.

2.1   Use Cases of Semantic Metadata for Development Time Support

Today, the introspection feature of object-oriented languages provide syntactic metadata of classes, fields, and methods along with their parameters, return types, and possible exceptions. Similar information is available from WSDL Web Service metadata [5], whereas component libraries such as dynamic linked libraries or Java archives only carry very little information. We believe that rich, semantic metadata can provide added value to the user. Consider the following use cases:

Component Dependencies and Versioning. Libraries often depend on other libraries and a certain archive can contain several libraries at once. Given this information, a system can assist the developer in locating all the required libraries[2]. Furthermore, the user might be notified when two libraries require different versions of a certain third component. For instance, the multitude of versions of XML parsers causes a lot of trouble. We envision a system, which reasons with this kind of information in order to make an educated suggestion or to display inconsistencies.

Licensing. Similar to the component dependencies, we can describe licensing, trustworthiness and quality. Including an external module in one's software has effects on the licensing options. For instance, using external GPL licensed code prohibits distributing the bundle under a LGPL license. Along the same lines, ISO software certification or a security guideline of a government agency might prohibit certain external components to be used in mission critical software. In all of these cases, it would be useful to model development constraints and reason with these and semantic metadata to avoid problems.

Capability Descriptions. Database interfaces typically offer some method to execute an SQL command. However, the behavior of specific database implementations can vary dramatically. Earlier versions of MySQL do not support transactions or subqueries. In this case, component capabilities adhering to standard interfaces can be made explicit to the developer.

Service Classification and Discovery. Given APIs with similar functionality, one will find different methods and services with essentially the same functionality. We suggest associating these implementations with a common service taxonomy. This will allow the user to discover implementations for a certain taxonomy entry and to classify a given service.

---

[2] This idea is the basis of the RPM package manager: http://www.rpm.org/. Our goal is to generalize this approach and integrate it with other tools and services for the end user.

Semantics of Parameters. Parameters and return types of methods and services are often implicitly encoded in the respective names. Providing meaningful names is considered to be an important practice when developing software systems. However, in addition, it is desirable to associate the names with concepts and relations of a common, agreed-upon domain ontology. Like the point mentioned before, this will allow more powerful searches over a large unfamiliar API. These descriptions can even be used to generate a sequence of method invocations in order to achieve a goal specified [8].

Automatic Generation of Component and Service Metadata. Development toolkits usually provide functionality for creating stubs and skeletons or for automatically generating interface metadata à la java2wsdl. With an entire set of new markup languages like BPEL4WS [2] or OWL-S [13] emerging, tool support for these new languages is needed. Whereas WSDL [5] tools can obtain almost all of the required input directly from the source code, richer descriptions in these languages require additional metadata. If the respective metadata are already available within the system, automatically generated BPEL4WS or OWL-S descriptions can be a side product of a unified framework.

2.2   Use Cases of Semantic Metadata for Run Time Support

Application servers handle issues like load balancing, distributed transactions, session management, user rights or access controls. All of these tasks are orthogonal to specific application issues in that they reappear in just about any scenario. Consequently, it makes sense for an application server to manage these issues in an application independent way. This means that the responsibility is shifted from the coding to the deployment process.

While it is always a good idea to reduce the amount of source code that has to be written, the deployment process can be quite tricky in itself. Consider the J2EE platform as an example. The specification describes the structure of XML deployment metadata[3]. J2EE implementations like JBoss (cf. [9]) provide a set of tools, which help the user to generate such metadata. However, the tools merely act as an input mask, which generates the specific XML syntax for the user. This is definitely a nice feature, however, she or he must fully understand the quite complicated concepts that lie behind the options for the transactional behavior for instance. The current deployment tools do not help to avoid or even actively repair configurations that may cause harmful system behavior. Consider the following situations:

Access Rights. The access control mechanisms of application servers are based on users and roles to whom access can be granted for certain resources and services. In addition, services can be run using the credentials of the caller or those of another user that runs the service on behalf of the caller. This is often referred to as the authentication problem [10]. It is quite evident, that access rights within a large business process can be very complex. A system should be able to assist the user in suggesting suitable settings and in determining

---

[3] Also called deployment descriptor, cf. http://java.sun.com/j2ee/j2ee-1_4-fr-spec.pdf

potential flaws in the security design. We believe that formal reasoning over group memberships or resources being accessed by processes running on behalf of other users will prove to be valuable here.

Error Handling. Modern programming languages make heavy use of exceptions. Exceptions are raised and propagated along the calling stack in order to be handled at the appropriate level. In order to avoid the embarrassing situation that an exception is not handled at all and simply passed to the user interface or business partner, a consistency check can be put in place. Similar to the argument made in the previous example, rules describing how exceptions are thrown, passed across the calling stack, and being caught or not can be applied in this scenario.

Transactional Settings. Resources such as databases and message queues offer transactional recovery. This notion is extended to regular software components, which access transactional resources. Methods can be declared to not support transactions, to initiate a new transaction, or to participate in the caller's transaction. Again, a chain of calls across many components can contain inconsistent settings such as a component which requires a transaction calling one that does not support transactions. A formalization of invocations and the possible transactional settings can be applied here.

Secure Communication. Confidential data might be made accessible to business partners only. Settings on the application server typically determine that a digital signature has to be checked before the request is passed along and that a service can only be bound to a secure communication line or protocol. Similar to the arguments made above, a system should be able to detect, that a confidential resource is accidentally made accessible via a non-encrypted communication channel.

The contribution of this paper is to show how some of these use cases of semantic metadata work. The claim that we make is that all of them – and many more – can be handled in a generic way using an ontology and corresponding semantic metadata.

3   An Ontology-Based Application Server

The various examples make it evident that there is a need for a conceptual model. The advantage of such a model is twofold. The model abstracts from the specifics of implementations such as J2EE with their proprietary configuration and deployment formats. Instead it focuses on and reflects the underlying, well defined and agreed-upon concepts such as users, access rights or transaction settings. Furthermore, general domain knowledge about these concepts can be formalized and reasoned with. This is a valuable basis for a variety of value-added services.

We use ontologies as a representation of the conceptual model. Like conceptual database schemata, ontologies define concepts and concept relationships (associations). Ontologies differ from schemata mainly in two ways. First, ontologies aim at capturing the *shared* understanding, which often includes linguistic

464   Daniel Oberle et al.

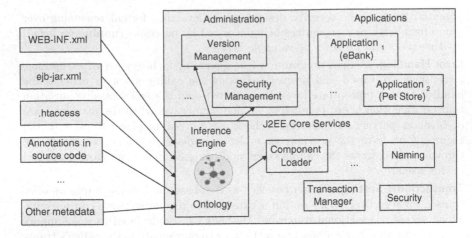

Fig. 1. System architecture of the application server. Semantic metadata and the ontology are loaded into the inference engine. Value-added services and tools leverage the reasoning capability embedded in the application server.

issues as well. Issues such as performance, compact storage, and other application specific features do not play a role. Second, ontologies contain axioms, which further define domain concepts and allow to reason with them. Components are described in terms of the ontology what results in semantic metadata.

Ontologies play a key role in area of the Semantic Web [3] and based on this work, several representation languages have been standardized within the World Wide Web Consortium (W3C)[4]. Consequently, we have chosen these languages as the basis for our work.

The following subsections survey both the overall system architecture of an ontology-based application server and our implementation called KAON SERVER.

3.1   Architecture

Figure 1 shows the overall system architecture. The left side outlines potential sources, which provide input for the framework. This includes web and application server configuration files, annotated source code, or metadata files. This information is parsed and converted into semantic metadata, i.e. metadata in terms of the ontology. Thus, this data is now available conforming to a harmonizing conceptual model. The semantic metadata and the ontology are fed into the inference engine which is embedded in the application server itself. The reasoning capability is used by an array of tools at development and at run time. The tools either expose a graphical user interface (e.g. security management) or provide core functionality (e.g. the dynamic component loader).

---
[4] The W3C also standardized HTML, XML etc.

3.2 Implementation

This section gives a concrete example of how the overall system architecture can be realized. For a detailed discussion the reader is referred to [20].

The aforementioned architecture is implemented in a system called KAON SERVER which is part of the KArlsruhe ONtology and Semantic Web Toolsuite (KAON) [12]. We made use of the Java Management Extensions (JMX [11]) – an open technology for component management. With JMX it becomes possible to configure, manage and monitor Java applications at run time, as well as break applications into components that can be exchanged. Basically, JMX defines interfaces of managed beans (*MBeans*) which are JavaBeans that represent JMX manageable resources. MBeans are hosted by an *MBeanServer* which allows their run time deployment and manipulation. All management operations performed on the MBeans are done through interfaces on the MBeanServer.

JMX only provides an API specification with several available implementations. We have chosen *JBossMX* which is the core of the open-source JBoss application server [9] that augments J2EE by dynamic component deployment. This choice allows us to inherit all the functionality provided by JBoss in the form of its MBeans (Servlet Containers, EJB Containers etc.). We deploy our inference engine as an additional MBean and augment the existing component loader and dependency management to exploit the inferencing. A version and security management tool allows to browse and query the ontology at run time. Thus, it is possible to use the KAON SERVER as a "semantically enhanced JBoss"[5].

4   The J2EE Pet Store Demo

The J2EE Pet Store Demo is a sample application by Sun Microsystems to demonstrate how to use the capabilities of the J2EE platform. We use the Pet Store example to illustrate the different use cases of ontologies and semantic metadata in the remainder of the paper. To be self-contained, we introduce the Pet Store briefly in this section.

The Pet Store illustrates the typical design decisions and tradeoffs a developer makes when building a distributed application and shows how to use JavaServer Pages (JSP), Servlets, Enterprise JavaBeans (EJB) and the Java Message Service (JMS)[6] Pet Store is a decoupled enterprise architecture that can interoperate with existing data sources and business partners' systems, all built on top of the J2EE platform. The sample application comprises four separate sub-applications that cooperate to fulfill the enterprise's business needs, each of which is a J2EE application:

Pet Store e-Commerce Web Site. Web application for end-users for purchasing merchandise through a Web browser. Servlets and Servlet filters are used to receive and process HTTP requests. JSPs define an application view template and the contents of the areas of the template. EJBs are used to implement business processes and to represent and manipulate business data.

---

[5] The KAON SERVER can be obtained at http://kaon.semanticweb.org
[6] http://java.sun.com/developer/releases/petstore/

Pet Store Administration Application. A Web application that enterprise administrators use to view sales statistics and manually accept or reject orders. While being a Web application, its user interface is a rich client that uses XML messaging, rather than an HTML Web browser

Order Processing Center. A process-oriented application that manages order fulfillment by providing several services to other enterprise participants. It receives and processes XML documents containing orders from the Web site via the Java Messaging Service (JMS), a message-oriented middleware. In addition, it provides the admin application with order data using XML messaging over HTTP, sends emails to customers acknowledging orders using JavaMail, sends XML order documents to suppliers via JMS and it maintains the purchase order database.

Supplier. A process-oriented application that manages shipping products to customers by providing the following services: It receives XML order documents from the Order Processing Center via JMS, it triggers shipment of products to customers, it provides manual inventory management through a Web-based interface and it maintains the inventory database.

Throughout the subsequent sections we will refer to the Pet Store application as a source of examples as it uses a multitude of XML configuration files: the standard J2EE deployment descriptor for the Pet Store Web site (*application.xml*), the standard J2EE deployment descriptor for the Pet Store Web-tier components (*web.xml*), several J2EE deployment descriptors for the Pet Store EJB-tier components (*ejb-jar.xml*) as well as vendor-specific deployment descriptors and XML files specific to the application (for defining screens, control screen flow, user sign-on, binding request URLs to HTML actions, etc.).

5   The KAON SERVER Ontology

This section details the ontology used in the KAON SERVER. It is subdivided in an ontology dealing with development use cases and run time use cases. Both are interrelated and split into several modules. They are further discussed in subsections 5.1 and 5.2[7].

5.1   Ontology Modules for Development Use Cases

In this section we present our ontology, which allows to conceptualize the development use cases introduced in section 2.1 by semantic metadata of components and their APIs. Note that we only give a short overview due to the lack of space. The interested reader is referred to [19]. The ontology is divided into several modules (cf. Figure 2) which are explained in the following[8]:

---

[7] Note that the ontologies are expressed in the KAON language [18] that is equivalent to Datalog. For the sake of readability, however, we will express axioms in FOL (First Order Logic) syntax throughout the paper.

[8] Names of the uses cases introduced in section 2.1 are written in sans serif.

API Description. The *API Description* module offers a framework for taxonomically describing the functionality offered by methods of APIs (e.g. the SupplierOrderEJB's setter methods are instances of a method "AddData") and accordingly several types of APIs (e.g. StoreAPI). It also allows to express the semantics of parameters. This kind of information is used to perform service classification and discovery as well as for automatic generation of component and service metadata. E.g. by inspecting the API it becomes evident that SupplierOrderEJB's setOrderID takes a String as argument. However, semantically enriched information, in this case specifying that the argument is information typically attached to an Order, facilitates discovery and can also be used to enrich automatically generated Web Service metadata.

Component. Simply consists of one concept that groups together *Profile* and *Grounding* information (explained below) about every kind of component.

Profile. We use the *Profile* module to express capability descriptions of a component. For example, a database adapter component would have an attribute specifying the SQL dialect used. Information of this type might be used for service classification and discovery.

Grounding. Basically, the *Grounding* module allows to express the mapping between the existing syntactic metadata (e.g. the Pet Store's application.xml, web.xml or ejb-jar.xml) and the semantic metadata. In order to express the mapping between the *API Description* and the source code we came up with a conceptualization of IDL terms which is grouped together in the *Implementation* module (see below).

Implementation. This module contains implementation level details of a component responding to the use case of component dependencies and versioning. Code details are described, like the class name or required archives. Besides, each component has a certain version and potentially depends on others. Along the same lines, some components will not work properly, if a conflicting component is loaded at the same time. These relationships are modelled by *dependsOn* and *conflictsWith* which are transitive and symmetric associations, respectively[9]. Components can be in different states (active, available, serialized, etc.) that are captured by an attribute of the same name. We also model the signature whose methods and parameters are expressed according to the *IDL* module (see below).

IDL. We have conceptualized a small subset of the IDL (Interface Description Language [21]) specification into an ontology-module that allows describing signatures of interfaces. The ontology module features concepts like *Interface*, *Operation* or *Parameter*.

Domain Ontology Modules. While the ontology modules presented so far formalize generic knowledge only, domain ontology modules grasp knowledge specific to a certain application. First, **Domain Profiles** may distinguish component types in a particular application server. While most J2EE servers support Servlets and EJBs, newer ones also introduce MBeans. In addition, Microsoft's

---

[9] That means $\forall c1, c2, c3 \ : \ dependsOn(c1, c3) \ \leftarrow \ dependsOn(c1, c2) \ \wedge$ $dependsOn(c2, c3)$ and $\forall c1, c2 : conflictsWith(c1, c2) \leftrightarrow conflictsWith(c2, c1)$.

468   Daniel Oberle et al.

.NET architecture introduces further idiosyncracies. Second, **Domain API Descriptions** contain sets of APIs and functionality types (methods) that are typically offered by components in a certain domain. An analysis of the Pet Store world results in a domain ontology conceptualizing Orders, Suppliers and Animals, for instance. It is then possible to semantically enrich information about the API, such as setContactInfo's parameter being a mailing address. Both submodules can be easily replaced in a new domain.

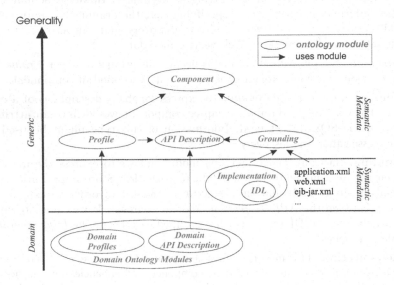

Fig. 2. Ontology Modules for use cases supporting development.

Like discussed in [17, 19] we used OWL-S as a starting point for building the ontology. OWL-S [13] is an ontology expressed in the Ontology Web Language (OWL [15]). Its aims are to enable automatic Web Service discovery, invocation, composition and execution monitoring [22]. Several interesting design principles are realized by OWL-S that inspired our work: separation of semantic and syntactic metadata, separation of generic and domain knowledge and modularization. Our current state of work comprises a full analysis, yet our formalization still lacks the individual groundings. The *Component, Profile, Implementation* and *Domain* modules are already used within the KAON SERVER[10].

5.2   Ontology Modules for Run Time Use Cases

In this section we describe part of our ontology for run time use cases. It conceptualizes interceptors, libraries, archives, security aspects and their interrelation-

---
[10] The ontologies ship with the KAON SERVER distribution and are also separately available at http://kaon.semanticweb.org. The site features a screenshot of browsing the ontologies with a graphical user interface.

ships. We have modelled most of the modules. However, they are not yet used within the KAON SERVER.

Due to space limitations, we focus on the security use case. The J2EE specification distinguishes the key concepts of realm, user, group, and role. We extend these basic notions by introducing additional concepts and some important associations and axioms in the following subsections.

Concepts

Resource. The J2EE specification distinguishes security issues on the web, application, and persistence tiers. Even though the physical ways of accessing these resources differ a lot, the notions of access control and security are the same at all three levels. In our ontology, resources can be web resources, components or databases (tables or SQL views). These are identified by URLs, class names and database URIs (usually server URI augmented by table or view name), respectively.

Method. Resources have methods, which constitute the most fine grained level for access control. Methods are identified in combination with the resource. Web methods are identified by the resource URL and the protocol's method such as HTTP GET. Methods of components are identified by their class name and the method identifier consisting of name and signature[11]. In the case of database resources, methods correspond to operations such as delete, insert, update, or select, which can be granted individually by the database management system. Message queues can be treated similarly to databases with a logical queue behaving like a table and the methods being send and receive instead of select, update etc.

ResourceGroup. Systems usually allow declaring security settings for an entire set of resources. A web container allows URL patterns such as `<url-pattern>/secure/*</url-pattern>`. A similar wildcard notation can encompass all methods of a class.

ACL. The right to access a ResourceGroup, Resource or Method is formalized as a concept *AccessRight*. This was necessary to circumvent ternary associations that cannot be modelled in KAON and other Semantic Web languages like RDF and OWL. Subsumption reasoning capabilities allow us to specialize AccessRight in Read, Write, Modify and Execute. An Access Control List (ACL) is comprised of one or more AccessRights.

Invocation and RequestContext. The definitions so far captured the static aspects of security. At run time, any kind of resource is accessed by an incoming request. The request is associated with context information, e.g. on whose behalf the request is carried out. The context is propagated from tier to tier, unless an explicit context change takes place. We model this situation by *Invocation* and *RequestContext* concepts which are interrelated (cf. Figure 3 and *associatedWith* below).

---

[11] Methods can be overloaded such that the same method name is used with different parameter lists. Consequently, the signature needs to be included in the method identification.

Associations

definedOnx and grantedFor$y$. Like mentioned before, AccessRights might be defined on ResourceGroups, Resources or even Methods, and they might be granted for Roles, UserGroups or even Users.

executes and Accesses. During processing, resources can use other resources. This might be "cart.jsp" invoking the shopping cart EJB, the product entity bean accessing the respective database table, or also an SQL view reading other tables and views. In our ontology, Resources execute Invocations and Invocations in turn access Resources (cf. also Figure 3).

associatedWith. We associated an Invocation with a RequestContext, where each RequestContext carries information about authentication or transactions. This kind of modeling was necessary to capture context propagation. An example would be an administrator who authenticates himself using HTTP basic authentication and accesses the administration webpage. The script on this page, run using the admin credentials, connects to an EJB with the respective security setting. The call succeeds, because the user information will be propagated and the service will also run using the administrator's credentials. An explicit context switch will happen when the "run as" paradigm is used or if a component connects to a database by explicitly stating a username and password. In the Pet Store, this happens when an entity bean reads tuples from the database. The container carries out the actual JDBC call using the user id specified during deployment, instead of the context associated with the end user request that triggered the initial call.

Axioms

invokes. For convenience we defined a transitive association *invokes* by axioms. It abbreviates *executes* and *accesses* in the following way:

$$\forall r1, r2, i : invokes(r1, r2) \leftarrow executes(r1, i) \wedge accesses(i, r2)$$

$$\forall r1, r2, r3 : invokes(r1, r3) \leftarrow invokes(r1, r2) \wedge invokes(r2, r3)$$

Roles, Users, and Groups. Further axioms are necessary to fully model the domain described so far. As we mentioned before, users can be associated to groups and access is granted via the role indirection. The effect of the resulting relationships can be captured by the following rules:

$$\forall ar, r, ug : grantedForUserGroup(ar, ug) \leftarrow AccessRight(ar) \wedge Role(r) \wedge UserGroup(ug) \wedge inRole(ug, r) \wedge grantedForRole(ar, r)$$

$$\forall ar, r, u : grantedForUser(ar, u) \leftarrow AccessRight(ar) \wedge Role(r) \wedge User(u) \wedge inRole(u, r) \wedge grantedForRole(ar, r)$$

$$\forall ar, u, ug : grantedForUser(ar, u) \leftarrow AccessRight(ar) \wedge User(u) \wedge UserGroup(ug) \wedge member(u, ug) \wedge grantedForUserGroup(ar, ug)$$

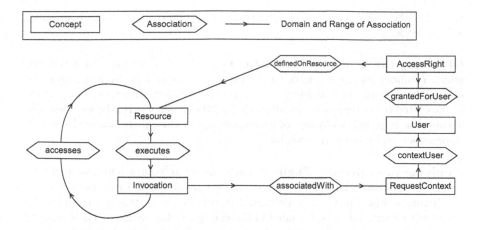

Fig. 3. Snippet of the security module.

A similar rule can be defined for permissions on groups of resources:

$\forall ar, r, rg : definedOnResource(ar, r) \leftarrow AccessRight(ar) \wedge Resource(r) \wedge ResourceGroup(rg) \wedge partOf(r, rg) \wedge definedOnResourceGroup(ar, rg)$

As we may recognize with this small example, it is preferable to specify complex interactions with a few logical rules rather than with extensive coding.

6 Examples

This section provides examples for both development and run time use cases. The first subsection discusses where semantic metadata of components support the developer in versioning problems, the latter recaps the security use case.

6.1 Development Time Example

One of the most relevant use cases for our ontology and semantic metadata is the versioning problem. In the ontology, we distinguish components such as an MBean and libraries such as a certain XML parser. Each of them has a certain version and potentially depends on others. Along the same lines, some components will not work properly, if a conflicting component is loaded at the same time.

The formalization (cf. Implementation ontology module in 5.1) is quite generic and can be applied in several application contexts, e.g. from within an IDE during development as well as during run time or in a JMX enabled dynamic component loader. All scenarios share the notion of a component being *available* to the system[12]. In the following, we discuss the example of the classpath environment

---

[12] Note that the technical details of this availability depends on the scenario.

variable, where only the first occurrence of a class, starting from the beginning, will be loaded.

Obtaining the Semantic Metadata. In a first step, we need to determine which components are available to the system. This is done by inspecting the classpath environment variable as well as the Java lib/ext directory. The archive is associated to its semantic metadata via its MD5 hash. Currently, we manually specify the semantic metadata of a component. In the future, we envision this information to be publicly available[13].

Applying the Inference Engine. Given the set of components, we can now determine whether all required components are available and whether there are conflicting component versions present. The rule below evaluates if components are missing and need to be included in the classpath, for instance. These queries can be evaluated using the version management tool shown in Figure 4.

$$\forall c1, c2 : missing(c2) \leftarrow Component(c1) \land$$
$$state(c1, "available") \land dependsOn(c1, c2) \land state(c2, "unavailable")$$

Conflicts can be discovered using this rule:

$$\forall c1, c2 : conflict(c1, c2) \leftarrow Component(c1) \land state(c1, "available") \land$$
$$conflictsWith(c1, c2) \land state(c2, "available")$$

6.2   Run Time Example

This section introduces two examples for a run time use case. Since section 5.2 focused on security, we also take an example from this use case. The following text illustrates how the necessary information is loaded into the KAON SERVER, provides two examples of how inferencing can be applied and shortly presents the security management tool.

Obtaining the Semantic Metadata. There are several ways of extracting the required information from configuration files, source code, or registries. Our goal is not to provide a complete set of parsers and extraction tools at this point. Instead, we aim at demonstrating the feasibility of our approach in providing a proof of concept in extracting a reasonable amount of information.

Information about the available resources is obtained by reading the file system of the web container and the application server. Database management systems often make metadata on tables, users, and rights available via SQL. In J2EE, the access control lists are specified in the ejb-jar.xml and WEB-INF.xml deployment descriptors for the web and the application server tiers. Various realms can manage the user, group, and role information. We worked with the JDBC realm, where the data is read from tables in a database, making it also easily available to our tool. Arguably the most complicated step is determining

---

[13] The feasibility of such an approach is demonstrated by the RPM package managing system (http://www.rpm.org).

the invocations from one resource to others. We propose a shallow analysis of the source code and SQL statements to pick up the commonly used patterns such as resolving a JNDI home interface reference. Furthermore, the ejb-ref tag in the beans' deployment descriptors provides hints as to which other beans are used. Obviously, we are restricted to static code analysis, which is also used by development environments. Note that this is not really a problem if the complete invocation graph is not extracted automatically, since the system does not actively intervene in the deployment process. It merely helps the user to assess the situation before making an educated decision.

Applying the Inference Engine – Indirect Permissions. An interesting example for reasoning over security settings is to see which resources a user gets indirect access to. For instance, the customer table, accessible only by the database admin, is indirectly readable to other users via the customer entity bean, since this bean performs a context switch. Thus, the call is carried out using admin rights on behalf of the user. This case is definitely not a bug; however, it might be useful to assess the combined effect of various security settings by analyzing the result of such a query. First, the axiom below introduces a convenience predicate *permission* that is true when an AccessRight is granted for a User u on a Resource r. Note that it captures permissions also when access is granted for a UserGroup only but the User is a member (because of the axioms introduced in 5.2).

$$\forall ar, u, r : permission(u, r) \leftarrow User(u) \wedge Resource(r) \wedge AccessRight(ar) \wedge$$
$$grantedForUser(ar, u) \wedge definedOnResource(ar, r)$$

Second, the following axiom recursively extends the definition above that any User having permissions to a Resource, implicitly has indirect access to all resources, which are indirectly invoked by it. The same can be expressed for ResourceGroups, Methods and Roles, UserGroups or combinations.

$$\forall u1, u2, r1, r2, i, ct : permission(u1, r2) \leftarrow permission(u1, r1) \wedge$$
$$Resource(r2) \wedge invokes(r1, r2) \wedge accesses(i, r2) \wedge Invocation(i) \wedge$$
$$associatedWith(i, ct) \wedge RequestContext(ct) \wedge$$
$$contextUser(ct, u2) \wedge permission(u2, r2)$$

Applying the Inference Engine – Non-accessible Resources. Given the access control and collaboration information, we can determine security misconfigurations. Assume the order-processing bean accidentally grants access only to customers. Furthermore, this bean invokes the order message queue without switching user contexts. The message queue, however, is only accessible to the order-processing role. Also assume that no user or group is in both the roles customer and order-processing. From this situation, we can infer that any call from the bean to the message queue must fail due to a security violation. We can formulate a rule, which helps to find such cases. A violation is present, if a component invokes another one by propagating the security context, and no overlap exists in the permission sets.

$$\forall r : inaccessible(r) \leftarrow \nexists u.permission(u, r)$$

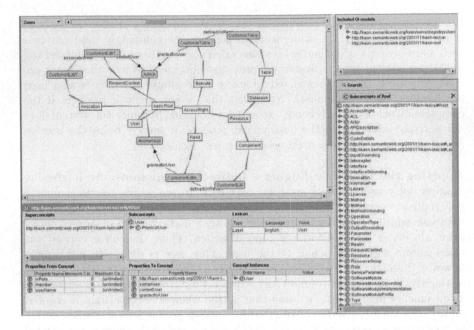

Fig. 4. Screenshot of the version and security management tool. Concepts are represented by rectangles, instances by rounded boxes, associations (also called properties in the figure) by labelled edges. Subconcept associations are represented by non-labelled edges. Clicking on "Search" allows the user to enter an arbitrary query.

Security Management Tool. Our tool allows the user to query the inference engine about any concept in the ontology. For instance, one can retrieve the users who are able to indirectly read a database table. As schematically introduced in Figure 1, Figure 4 shows our version and security management tool that allows to browse the ontology and execute queries at run time. The users who are able to indirectly access the customer table are retrieved by a query.

We plan to realize a more convenient user interface in order to hide the base query language from the user. Furthermore, we would like to develop a watchdog that actively checks for inconsistencies such as a role with no assigned users or groups, empty groups, or, as shown in section 5.2, clashes in the security settings for inter-resource invocations.

7   Related Work

The current generation of application servers uses XML-based configuration files, some of which follow fixed XML schemata. The individual schemata represent static conceptualizations of fragments of the complete configuration. Our ontology-based approach aggregates individual aspects in a platform-independent and extensible way.

Classical Software Reuse Systems also describe software modules for efficient and precise retrieval. However, techniques like the faceted classification [7] are limited to the representation of the provider's features. In analogy, software reuse shares a representation of modules that is based on functionalities achieved by the software, roles and conditions [14]. [6] introduce a software repository system that uses an ontological representation language for describing information about requirements, designs and implementations of software. However, none of these approaches take into account the run time use cases that occur in application server settings. These efforts either describe different kinds of components or concentrate solely on syntactic or semantic metadata without blending them together like in our approach.

[4] shows how description logics can be used to augment CORBA IDL specifications such that *Compatibility testing of IDL specifications, Local consistency checking, More thorough treatment of exceptions* is possible. However, this approach just augments the syntactic part of an API's description. It does not deal with semantic information about method functionality and does not describe component configurations.

Microsoft's System Definition Model (SDM)[14] takes a similar approach to ours in including information about software, hardware, and network in a unified system model. SDM targets design, deployment, and operation. The first actual software tool implementing this strategy will be the next version of the Visual Studio development environment. Unfortunately, not much detailed information is available at this point. Nevertheless, SDM illustrates the trend of representing different system aspects in a common framework.

As a way to abstract from low-level and platform-specific problems, the paradigm of *Model-Driven Architectures (MDA)* [16] has gained wide-spread influence. The principal idea of MDA is to separate *conceptual concerns*, such as which component is using which other component, from *implementation-specific concerns*, such as which version of an application interface requires which versions of windows libraries. MDA achieves this separation by factorizing the two concerns, specifying them separately and compiling them into an executable. Like mentioned in the introduction, MDA has not been applied for run time relevant characteristics of component management. Also, it lacks logical formality what disallows to query the application server at run time.

8   Conclusions and Future Work

In this paper we have presented our approach, an ontology as an explicit, executable conceptual model for administrating an application server. Though we are still dealing with a preliminary version of the ontologies, we could demonstrate small, sophisticated and yet very practical examples of how to improve the development and maintenance of software components for and in an application server.

---

[14] http://www.microsoft.com/windowsserversystem/dsi/sdm.mspx

476   Daniel Oberle et al.

Doing so, our intention was to substantiate a twofold message: First, ontologies and corresponding semantic technology provide huge, practical benefits for handling middleware environments – which we think are *underestimated*. Second, the bread and butter issues of developing and administrating services and components will outlive the utmost fancy issues like automatic composition of services – which we think are *overestimated in feasibility as well as with regard to practical benefits.*

Acknowledgements

We are indebted to Marta Sabou, Vrije Universiteit Amsterdam, The Netherlands, as well as Debbie Richards, MacQuarie University Sydney, Australia, for their fruitful work on the ontology presented in section 5.1.

This work is financed by WonderWeb, an EU Information Society Technologies (IST) funded project (http://wonderweb.semanticweb.org) IST-2001-33052, and by SmartWeb, a German BMBF funded project (http://smartweb.semanticweb.org).

References

1. G. Alonso, F. Casati, H. Kuno, and V. Machiraju. *Web Services*. Springer, Sep 2003.
2. T. Andrews, F. Curbera, H. Dholakia, Y. Goland, J. K. F. Leymann, K. Liu, D. Roller, D. Smith, S. Thatte, I. Trickovic, and S. Weerawarana. Business Process Execution Language for Web Services Version 1. Specification, May 2003. http://www.ibm.com/developerworks/library/ws-bpel/.
3. T. Berners-Lee, J. Hendler, and O. Lassila. The Semantic Web. *Scientific American*, pages 28–37, May 2001.
4. A. Borgida and P. Devanbu. Adding more "DL" to IDL: Towards more knowledgeable component inter-operability. In *Proceedings of the 21st international conference on Software engineering*. IEEE Computer Society Press, 1999.
5. E. Christensen, F. Curbera, G. Meredith, and S. Weerawarana. Web Services Description Language (WSDL). http://www.w3.org/TR/wsdl, Mar 2003. W3C Note.
6. P. Constantopoulos, M. Jarke, J. Mylopoulos, and Y. Vassiliou. The software information base: A server for reuse. *VLDB Journal*, 4(1):1–43, 1995.
7. R. P. Diaz. Implementing faceted classification for software reuse. *Communications of the ACM*, 34(5):88–97, May 1991.
8. A. Eberhart. Ad-hoc Invocation of Semantic Web Services. In *IEEE International Conference on Web Services, July 6-9, 2004, San Diego, California, USA*, 2004.
9. M. Fleury and F. Reverbel. The JBoss Extensible Server. In M. Endler and D. C. Schmidt, editors, *Middleware 2003, ACM/IFIP/USENIX International Middleware Conference, Rio de Janeiro, Brazil, June 16-20, 2003, Proceedings*, volume 2672 of *Lecture Notes in Computer Science*, pages 344–373. Springer, 2003.
10. J. Gray and A. Reuter. *Transaction Processing: Concepts and Techniques*. Morgan Kaufmann, 1993.

11. J. Lindfors and M. Fleury. *JMX - Managing J2EE with Java Management Extensions*. Sams, 2002. The JBoss Group.
12. A. Maedche, B. Motik, and L. Stojanovic. Managing multiple and distributed ontologies in the Semantic Web. *VLDB Journal*, 12(4):286–302, 2003.
13. D. Martin, M. Burstein, G. Denker, J. Hobbs, L. Kagal, O. Lassila, D. McDermott, S. McIlraith, M. Paolucci, B. Parsia, T. Payne, M. Sabou, E. Sirin, M. Solanki, N. Srinivasan, and K. Sycara. OWL-S 1.0 draft release. http://www.daml.org/services/owl-s/1.0/, Dec 2003.
14. P. Massonet and A. van Lamsweerde. Analogical reuse of requirements frameworks. In *3rd IEEE International Symposium on Requirements Engineering (RE'97), January 5-8, 1997, Annapolis, MD, USA*, pages 26–39. IEEE Computer Society, 1997.
15. D. L. McGuinness and F. van Harmelen. Web Ontology Language (OWL) Overview.
   http://www.w3.org/TR/owl-features/, Feb 2004. W3C Recommendation.
16. S. J. Mellor, K. Scott, A. Uhl, and D. Weise. Model-Driven Architecture. In *Advances in Object-Oriented Information Systems, OOIS 2002 Workshops, Montpellier, France, September 2, 2002, Proceedings*, volume 2426 of *Lecture Notes in Computer Science*, pages 290–297. Springer, 2002.
17. P. Mika, D. Oberle, A. Gangemi, and M. Sabou. Foundations for Service Ontologies: Aligning OWL-S to DOLCE. In *The Thirteenth International World Wide Web Conference Proceedings*, pages 563–572. ACM, May 2004.
18. B. Motik, A. Maedche, and R. Volz. A conceptual modeling approach for building semantics-driven enterprise applications. In R. Meersman and Z. Tari, editors, *On the Move to Meaningful Internet Systems, 2002 - DOA/CoopIS/ODBASE 2002 Confederated International Conferences DOA, CoopIS and ODBASE 2002 Irvine, California, USA, October 30 - November 1, 2002, Proceedings*, volume 2519 of *Lecture Notes in Computer Science*. Springer, 2002.
19. D. Oberle, M. Sabou, and D. Richards. An ontology for semantic middleware: extending DAML-S beyond web-services. Technical Report 426, University of Karlsruhe, Institute AIFB, 76128 Karlsruhe, Germany, 2003.
20. D. Oberle, S. Staab, R. Studer, and R. Volz. Supporting Application Development in the Semantic Web. *ACM Transactions on Internet Technology (TOIT)*, 4(4), Nov 2004.
21. Object Modelling Group. IDL / Language Mapping Specification - Java to IDL, Aug 2002. 1.2.
22. OWL Services Coalition. OWL-S: Semantic Markup for Web Services. OWL-S v1.0 White Paper, Nov 2003.

Portable and Efficient Distributed Threads for Java

Eli Tilevich and Yannis Smaragdakis

College of Computing
Georgia Institute of Technology, Atlanta, GA 30332
{tilevich,yannis}@cc.gatech.edu
http://j-orchestra.org

Abstract. Java middleware mechanisms, such as Java RMI or CORBA implementations, do not support thread coordination over the network: synchronizing
on remote objects does not work correctly and thread identity is not preserved
for executions spanning multiple machines. The current approaches dealing
with the problem suffer from one of two weaknesses: either they require a new
middleware mechanism, making them less portable, or they add overhead to the
execution to propagate a thread identifier through all method calls. In this paper
we present an approach that works with an unmodified middleware implementation, yet does not impose execution overhead. The key to our technique is the
bytecode transformation of only stub routines, instead of the entire client application. We argue that this approach is portable and can be applied to mostly any
middleware mechanism. At the same time, we show that, compared to past
techniques, our approach eliminates an overhead of 5.5-12% (of the total execution time) for applications from the SPEC JVM suite.

1 Introduction

The Java programming language offers high-level support for both distributed programming and concurrency, but the two mechanisms are unaware of each other. Java
has an integrated middleware mechanism (Java RMI [15]). Any object can make its
methods remotely accessible by implementing a `Remote` interface. This enables distributed programming without separate interface definitions and IDL tools. At the
same time, Java supports the easy creation and monitor-style synchronization of
threads. Any Java object is mapped to a unique monitor, with a single mutex and condition queue. Java code can synchronize and wait on any object. Nevertheless, synchronization does not carry over to remote objects. The problem is dual. First, synchronization operations (like `synchronized`, `wait`, `interrupt`, etc.) do not get
propagated by Java RMI. For instance, attempting to explicitly lock the mutex of a
remote object will lock the mutex of its RMI stub object instead. Second, thread identity is not maintained over the network. For instance, a thread that calls a remote
method may self-deadlock if the remote operation happens to call back the original
site.

In this paper, we present a mechanism that enables Java thread synchronization in a
distributed setting. Our mechanism addresses monitor-style synchronization (mutexes
and condition variables) which is well-suited for a distributed threads model. (This is
in contrast to low-level Java synchronization, such as volatile variables and atomic
operations, which are better suited for symmetric multiprocessor machines.)

Our work is not the first in this design space. Past solutions fall in two different
camps. A representative of the first camp is the approach of Haumacher et al. [5]

H.-A. Jacobsen (Ed.): Middleware 2004, LNCS 3231, pp. 478–492, 2004.

where a replacement of Java RMI is proposed that maintains correct multithreaded execution over the network. If employing special-purpose middleware is acceptable, this approach is sufficient. Nevertheless, it is often not desirable to move away from standard middleware, for reasons of portability and ease of deployment. Therefore, the second camp, represented by the work of Weyns, Truyen, and Verbaeten [18], advocates transforming the client application instead of replacing the middleware. Unfortunately, clients (i.e., callers) of a method do not know whether its implementation is local or remote. Thus, to support thread identity over the network, *all* method calls in an application need to be automatically re-written to pass one extra parameter – the thread identifier. This imposes both space and time overhead: extra code is needed to propagate thread identifiers and adding an extra argument to every call incurs a run-time cost. Weyns, Truyen, and Verbaeten [18] quantify this cost to about 3% of the total execution time of an application. Using more representative macro-benchmarks (from the SPEC JVM suite) we found the cost to be between 5.5 and 12% of the total execution time. A secondary disadvantage of the approach is that the transformation becomes complex when application functionality can be called by native system code, as in the case of application classes implementing a Java system interface.

The technique we describe in this paper addresses both the problem of portability and the problem of performance. We follow the main lines of the approach of Weyns, Truyen, and Verbaeten: we replace all monitor operations in the bytecode (such as `monitorenter`, `monitorexit`, `Object.wait`) with calls to operations of our own distribution-aware synchronization library. Nevertheless, we avoid instrumenting every method call with an extra argument. Instead, we perform a bytecode transformation on the generated RMI stubs. The transformation is general and portable: almost every RPC-style middleware mechanism needs to generate stubs for the remotely invokable methods. By transforming those when needed, we can propagate thread identity information for all remote invocations, without unnecessarily burdening local invocations. Our approach also has the advantage of simplicity with respect to native system code. Finally, our implementation is fine-tuned, making the total overhead of synchronization be negligible (below 4% overhead even for empty methods and no network cost).

Our technique is implemented in the context of the J-Orchestra system [17]. J-Orchestra is an *automatic partitioning* system for Java programs: given a Java application and under user guidance, J-Orchestra can split the application into parts that execute on different machines. For a large subset of Java, the resulting distributed application will behave exactly like the original centralized one. Beyond J-Orchestra, the distributed synchronization technique described in this paper is applicable to other partitioning systems (e.g., Addistant [16], AdJava [3], FarGo [6]), language tools for distribution (e.g., Java Party [4][11], Doorastha [2]), or stand-alone mechanisms for distributed Java threads (e.g., Brakes [18]).

2 Background: Problem and Application Context

2.1 Distributed Synchronization Complications

Modern mainstream languages such as Java or C# have built-in support for concurrency. Java, for example, provides the class `java.lang.Thread` for creating and managing concurrency, monitor methods `Object.wait`, `Object.notify`, and `Object.notifyAll` for managing state dependence, and `synchronized` methods and code blocks for maintaining exclusion among multiple concurrent activities. (An excellent reference for multithreading in Java is Lea's textbook [7].)

Concurrency constructs usually do not interact correctly with middleware implementations, however. For instance, Java RMI does not propagate synchronization operations to remote objects and does not maintain thread identity across different machines.

To see the first problem, consider a Java object `obj` that implements a `Remote` interface `RI` (i.e., a Java interface `RI` that extends `java.rmi.Remote`). Such an object is remotely accessible through the `RI` interface. That is, if a client holds an interface reference `r_ri` that points to `obj`, then the client can call methods on `obj`, even though it is located on a different machine. The implementation of such remote access is the standard RPC middleware technique: the client is really holding an indirect reference to `obj`. Reference `r_ri` points to a local RMI "stub" object on the client machine. The stub serves as an intermediary and is responsible for propagating method calls to the `obj` object. What happens when a monitor operation is called on the remote object, however? There are two distinct cases: Java calls monitor operations (locking and unlocking a mutex) implicitly when a method labeled `synchronized` is invoked and when it returns. This case is handled correctly through RMI, since the stub will propagate the call of a synchronized remote method to the correct site. Nevertheless, all other monitor operations are not handled correctly by RMI. For instance, a `synchronized` block of code in Java corresponds to an explicit mutex lock operation. The mutex can be the one associated with any Java object. Thus, when clients try to explicitly synchronize on a remote object, they end up synchronizing on its stub object instead. This does not allow threads on different machines to synchronize using remote objects: one thread could be blocked or waiting on the real object `obj`, while the other thread may be trying to synchronize on the stub instead of on the `obj` object. Similar problems exist for all other monitor operations. For instance, RMI cannot be used to propagate monitor operations such as `Object.wait`, `Object.notify`, over the network. The reason is that these operations cannot be indirected: they are declared in class `Object` to be `final`, which means that the methods can not be overridden in subclasses including the `Remote` interfaces required by RMI.

The second problem concerns preserving thread identities in remote calls. The Java RMI runtime, for example, starts a new thread for each incoming remote call. Thus, a thread performing a remote call has no memory of its identity in the system. Fig. 1

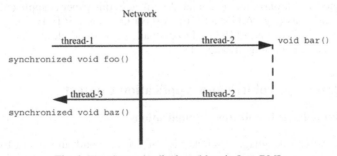

Fig. 1. The zigzag deadlock problem in Java RMI.

demonstrates the so-called "zigzag deadlock problem", common in distributed synchronization. Conceptually, methods `foo`, `bar`, and `baz` are all executed in the same thread – but the location of method `bar` happens to be on a remote machine. In actual RMI execution, thread-1 will block until `bar`'s remote invocation completes, and the RMI runtime will start a new thread for the remote invocations of `bar` and `baz`. Nevertheless, when `baz` is called, the monitor associated with thread-1 denies entry to thread-3: the system does not recognize that thread-3 is just handling the control flow of thread-1 after it has gone through a remote machine. If no special care is taken, a deadlock condition occurs.

2.2 J-Orchestra

Our technique for correct and efficient monitor-style distributed synchronization has been applied in the context of J-Orchestra. J-Orchestra is a system that rewrites existing Java programs at the bytecode level into distributed programs that can be executed on multiple machines. The transformation is done automatically, once the user specifies (through a GUI) which parts of the code should be available on which machine. The emphasis is on the correctness of the partitioning process: for a large subset of Java, J-Orchestra-partitioned applications behave just like the original centralized ones [17]. That is, J-Orchestra emulates many of the language mechanisms of a Java VM over a collection of distinct VMs.

The reason we bring up the context of our work is that the need for correct distributed synchronization is even more pronounced in the case of J-Orchestra than in the case of regular distributed programming. Since J-Orchestra creates distributed applications automatically (i.e., without programmer intervention, beyond choosing locations for code parts) it is important to maintain the same synchronization mechanisms over a network as for a single machine. Furthermore, J-Orchestra is mainly applicable when an application needs to be distributed to take advantage of unique resources of different machines, instead of parallelism. For example, J-Orchestra can be used to partition a traditional Java application so that its GUI runs on one machine, its computation on another, sensor input is produced and filtered on a third machine and file storage occurs on a fourth. Nevertheless, the entire application may only have a single thread, even though it uses libraries that employ synchronization. J-Orchestra will partition this application so that its logic is still single-threaded, yet the implementation consists of multiple Java threads (at least one per machine), only one of which can be active at a time. Thus, with J-Orchestra, the deadlock problems resulting from the lack of remote thread identity can exhibit themselves even for a single-threaded application!

Other than the context and motivation, however, the discussion in the rest of this paper is not specific to J-Orchestra. Indeed, our technique can be applied to any system in the literature that supports distributed communication and threading.

3 Solution: Distribution-Aware Synchronization

As we saw, any solution for preserving the centralized concurrency and synchronization semantics in a distributed environment must deal with two issues: each remote method call can be executed on a new thread, and standard monitor methods such as `Object.wait`, `Object.notify`, and `synchronized` blocks can become invalid when distribution takes place. Taking these issues into account, we maintain per-site "thread id equivalence classes," which are updated as execution crosses the network boundary; and at the bytecode level, we replace all the standard synchronization constructs with the corresponding method calls to a per-site synchronization library. This synchronization library emulates the behavior of the monitor methods, such as `monitorenter`, `monitorexit`, `Object.wait`, `Object.notify`, and `Object.notifyAll`, by using the thread id equivalence classes. Furthermore, these synchronization library methods, unlike the `final` methods in class `Object` that they replace, get correctly propagated over the network using RMI when necessary so that they execute on the network site of the object associated with the monitor.

In more detail, our approach consists of the following steps:

- Every instance of a monitor operation in the bytecode of the application is replaced, using bytecode rewriting, by a call to our own synchronization library, which emulates the monitor-style synchronization primitives of Java
- Our library operations check whether the target of the monitor operation is a local object or an RMI stub. In the former case, the library calls its local monitor operation. In the latter case, an RMI call to a remote site is used to invoke the appropriate library operation on that site. This solves the problem of propagating monitor operations over the network. We also apply a compile-time optimization to this step: using a simple static analysis, we determine whether the target of the monitor operation is an object that is known statically to be on the current site. This is the case for monitor operations on the `this` reference, as well as other objects of "anchored" types [17] that J-Orchestra guarantees will be on the same site throughout the execution. If we know statically that the object is local, we avoid the runtime test and instead call a local synchronization operation.
- Every remote RMI call, whether on a synchronized method or not, is extended to include an extra parameter. The instrumentation of remote calls is done by bytecode transformation of the RMI stub classes. The extra parameter holds the thread equivalence class for the current calling thread. Our library operations emulate the Java synchronization primitives but do not use the current, machine-specific thread id to identify a thread. Instead, a mapping is kept between threads and their equivalence classes and two threads are considered the same if they map to the same equivalence class. Since an equivalence class can be represented by any of its members, our current representation of equivalence classes is compact: we keep a combination of the first thread id to join the equivalence class and an id for the machine where this thread runs. This approach solves the problem of maintaining thread identity over the network.

We illustrate the above steps with examples that show how they solve each of the two problems identified earlier. We first examine the problem of propagating monitor operations over the network. Consider a method as follows:

```
//original code
void foo (Object some_remote_object) {
  this.wait();
  ...
  some_remote_object.notify();
  ...
}
```

At the bytecode level, method `foo` will have a body that looks like:

```
//bytecode
aload_0
invokevirtual       java.lang.Object.wait
...
aload_1
invokevirtual       java.lang.Object.notify
...
```

Our rewrite will statically detect that the first monitor operation (`wait`) is local, as it is called on the current object itself (`this`). The second monitor operation, however, is (potentially) remote and needs to be redirected to target machine using an RMI call. The result is shown below:

```
//rewritten bytecode
aload_0
//dispatched locally
invokestatic jorchestra.runtime.distthreads.wait_
...
aload_1
//get thread equivalence info from runtime
invokestatic jorchestra.runtime.ThreadInfo.getThreadEqClass
//dispatched through RMI;
//all remote interfaces extend DistSyncSupporter
invokeinterface jorchestra.lang.DistSynchSupporter.notify_
...
```

(The last instruction is an interface call, which implies that each remote object needs to support monitor methods, such as `notify_`. This may seem to result in code bloat at first, but our transformation adds these methods to the topmost class of each inheritance hierarchy in an application, thus minimizing the space overhead.)

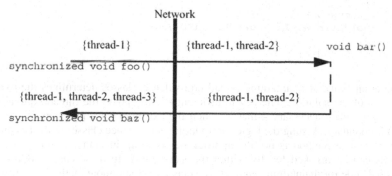

Fig. 2. Using thread id equivalence classes to solve the "zigzag deadlock problem" in Java RMI.

Let's now consider the second problem: maintaining thread identity over the network. Fig. 2 demonstrates how using the thread id equivalence classes can solve the "zigzag deadlock problem" presented above. These thread id equivalence classes enable our custom monitor operations to treat all threads within the same equivalence class as the same thread. (We illustrate the equivalence class by listing all its members in the figure, but, as mentioned earlier, in the actual implementation only a single token that identifies the equivalence class is passed across the network.) More specifically, our synchronization library is currently implemented using regular Java mutexes and condition variables. For instance, the following code segment (slightly simplified) shows how the library emulates the behavior of the bytecode instruction monitorenter. (For readers familiar with monitor-style concurrent programming, our implementation should look straightforward.) The functionality is split into two methods: the static method monitorenter finds or creates the corresponding Monitor object associated with a given object: our library keeps its own mapping between objects and their monitors. The member method enter of class Monitor causes threads that are not in the equivalence class of the holder thread to wait until the monitor is unlocked.

```
public static void monitorenter (Object o) {
  Monitor this_m = null;
  synchronized (Monitor.class) {
      this_m = (Monitor)_objectToMonitor.get(o);
      if (this_m == null) {
          this_m = new Monitor();
          _objectToMonitor.put(o, this_m);
      }
  } //synchronized
  this_m.enter();
}

private synchronized void enter () {
  while (_timesLocked != 0 &&
         curThreadEqClass != _holderThreadId)
    try { wait(); } catch(InterruptedException e) {...}

  if (_timesLocked == 0) {
      _holderThreadId = getThreadID();
  }
  _timesLocked++;
}
```

The complexity of maintaining thread equivalence classes determines the overall efficiency of the solution. The key to efficiency is to update the thread equivalence classes only when necessary – that is, when the execution of a program crosses the network boundary. Adding the logic for updating equivalence classes at the beginning of every remote method is not the appropriate solution: in many instances, remote methods can be invoked locally within the same JVM. In these cases, adding any additional code for maintaining equivalence classes to the remote methods themselves would be unnecessary and detrimental to performance. In contrast, our solution is based on the following observation: the program execution will cross the network boundary only after it enters a method in an RMI stub. Thus, RMI stubs are the best location for updating the thread id equivalence classes on the client site of a remote call.

Adding custom logic to RMI stubs can be done by modifying the RMI compiler, but this would negate our goal of portability. Therefore, we use bytecode engineering on standard RMI stubs to retrofit their bytecode so that they include the logic for updating the thread id equivalence classes. This is done completely transparently relative to the RMI runtime by adding special delegate methods that look like regular remote methods, as shown in the following code example. To ensure maximum efficiency, we pack the thread equivalence class representation into a long integer, in which the less significant and the most significant 4 bytes store the first thread id to join the equivalence class and the machine where this thread runs, respectively. This compact representation significantly reduces the overhead imposed on the remote method calls, as we demonstrate later on. Although all the changes are applied to the bytecode directly, we use source code for ease of exposition.

```
//Original RMI stub: two remote methods foo and bar
class A_Stub ... {
 ...
 public void foo (int i) throws RemoteException {...}
 public int bar () throws RemoteException {...}
}

//Retrofitted RMI stub
class A_Stub ... {
 ...
 public void foo (int i) throws RemoteException {
    foo__tec (Runtime.getThreadEqClass(), i);
 }
 public void foo__tec (long tec, int i) throws
                                        RemoteException
 {...}

 public int bar () throws RemoteException {
    return bar__tec (Runtime.getThreadEqClass());
 }
 public int bar__tec (long tec) throws RemoteException {...}
}
```

Remote classes on the callee site provide symmetrical delegate methods that update the thread id equivalence classes information according to the received long parameter, prior to calling the actual methods. Therefore, having two different versions for each remote method (with the delegate method calling the actual one) makes the change transparent to the rest of the application: neither the caller of a remote method nor its implementor need to be aware of the extra parameter. Remote methods can still be invoked directly (i.e., not through RMI but from code on the same network site) and in this case they do not incur any overhead associated with maintaining the thread equivalence information.

4   Benefits of the Approach

The two main existing approaches to the problem of maintaining the centralized Java concurrency and synchronization semantics in a distributed environment have involved either using custom middleware [5] or making universal changes to the distributed program [18]. We argue next that our technique is more portable than using custom middleware and more efficient than a universal rewrite of the distributed program. Finally, we quantify the overhead of our approach and show that our implementation is indeed very efficient.

4.1 Portability

A solution for preserving the centralized concurrency and synchronization semantics in a distributed environment is only as useful as it is portable. A solution is portable if it applies to different versions of the same middleware (e.g., past and future versions of Java RMI) and to different middleware mechanisms such as CORBA and .NET Remoting. Our approach is both simple and portable to other middleware mechanisms, because it is completely orthogonal to other middleware functionality: We rely on bytecode engineering, which allows transformations without source code access, and on adding a small set of runtime classes to each network node of a distributed application. The key to our transformation is the existence of a client stub that redirects local calls to a remote site. Using client stubs is an almost universal technique in modern middleware mechanisms. Even in the case when these stubs are generated dynamically, our technique is applicable, as long as it is employed at class load time.

For example, our bytecode instrumentation can operate on CORBA stubs as well as it does on RMI ones. Our stub transformations simply consist of adding delegate methods (one for each client-accessible remote method) taking an extra thread equivalence parameter. Thus, no matter how complex the logic of the stub methods is, we would apply to them the same simple set of transformations.

Some middleware mechanisms such as the first version of Java RMI also use server-side stubs (a.k.a. *skeletons*) that dispatch the actual methods. Instead of presenting complications, skeletons would even make our approach easier. The skeleton methods are perfect for performing our server-side transformations, as we can take advantage of the fact that the program execution has certainly crossed the network boundary if it entered a method in a skeleton. Furthermore, having skeletons to operate on would eliminate the need to change the bytecodes of the remote classes. Finally, the same argument of the simplicity of our stub transformations being independent of the complexity of the stub code itself equally applies to the skeleton transformations.

In a sense, our approach can be seen as adding an orthogonal piece of functionality (concurrency control) to existing distribution middleware. In this sense, one can argue that the technique has an aspect-oriented flavor.

4.2   The Cost of Universal Extra Arguments

Our approach eliminates both the runtime and the complexity overheads of the closest past techniques in the literature. Weyns, Truyen, and Verbaeten [18][19] have advocated the use of a bytecode transformation approach to correctly maintain thread identity over the network. Their technique is occasionally criticized as "incur[ring] great runtime overhead" [5]. The reason is that, since clients do not know whether a method they call is local or remote, every method in the application is extended with an extra argument – the current thread id – that it needs to propagate to its callees. Weyns et al. argue that the overhead is acceptable and present limited measurements where the overhead of maintaining distributed thread identity is around 3% of the total execution time. Below we present more representative measurements that put this cost at between 5.5 and 12%. A second cost that has not been evaluated, however, is that of complexity: adding an extra parameter to all method calls is hard when some clients cannot be modified because, e.g., they are in native code form or access the method through reflection. In these cases a correct application of the Weyns et al. transformation would incur a lot of complexity. This complexity is eliminated with our approach.

It is clear that some run-time overhead will be incurred if an extra argument is added and propagated to every method in an application. To see the range of overhead, we wrote a simple micro-benchmark, where each method call performs one integer arithmetic operation, two comparisons and two (recursive) calls. Then we measured the overhead of adding one extra parameter to each method call. Table 1 shows the results of this benchmark. For methods with 1-5 integer arguments we measure their execution time with one extra reference argument propagated in all calls. As seen, the overhead varies unpredictably but ranges from 5.9 to 12.7%.

Table 1. Micro-benchmark overhead of method calls with one more argument.

#params	1 (base)	1+1	2+1	3+1	4+1	5+1
Execution time (sec) for 10^8 calls	1.945	2.059	2.238	2.523	2.691	2.916
Slowdown relative to previous	-	5.9%	8.7%	12.7%	6.7%	8.4%

Nevertheless, it is hard to get a representative view of this overhead from micro-benchmarks, especially when running under a just-in-time compilation model. Therefore, we concentrated on measuring the cost on realistic applications. As our macro-benchmarks, we used applications from the SPEC JVM benchmark suite. Of course, some of the applications we measured may not be multithreaded, but their method calling patterns should be representative of multithreaded applications, as well.

We used bytecode instrumentation to add an extra reference argument to all methods and measured the overhead of passing this extra parameter. In the process of instrumenting realistic applications, we discovered the complexity problems outlined earlier. The task of adding an extra parameter is only possible when all clients can be modified by the transformation. Nevertheless, all realistic Java applications present examples where clients will not be modifiable. An application class can be implementing a system interface, making native Java system code a potential client of the class's methods. For instance, using class frameworks, such as AWT, Swing, or Applets, entails extending the classes provided by such frameworks and overriding some methods with the goal of customizing the application's behavior. Consider, for example, a system interface `java.awt.TextListener`, which has a single method `void textValueChanged (TextEvent e)`. A non-abstract application class extending this interface has to provide an implementation of this method. It is impossible to add an extra parameter to the method `textValueChanged` since it would prevent the class from being used with AWT. Similarly a Java applet overrides methods `init`, `start`, and `stop` that are called by Web browsers hosting the applet. Adding an extra argument to these methods in an applet would invalidate it. These issues can be addressed by careful analysis of the application and potentially maintaining two interfaces (one original, one extended with an extra parameter). Nevertheless, this would result in code bloat, which could further hinder performance.

Since we were only interested in quantifying the potential overhead of adding and maintaining an extra method parameter, we sidestepped the complexity problems by avoiding the extra parameter for methods that could be potentially called by native code clients. Instead of changing the signatures of such methods so that they would take an extra parameter, we created the extra argument as a local variable that was passed to all the callees of the method. The local variable is never initialized to a useful value, so no artificial overhead is added by this approach. This means that our measurements are slightly conservative: we do not really measure the cost of correctly maintaining an extra thread identity argument but instead conservatively estimate the cost of passing one extra reference parameter around. Maintaining the correct value of this reference parameter, however, may require some extra code or interface duplication, which may make performance slightly worse than what we measured.

Another complication concerns the use of Java reflection for invoking methods, which makes adding an extra argument to such methods impossible. In fact, we could not correctly instrument all the applications in the SPEC JVM suite, exactly because some of them use reflection heavily and we would need to modify such uses by hand.

The results of our measurements appear in Table 2. The table shows total execution time for four benchmarks (compress – a compression utility, javac – the Java compiler, mtrt – a multithreaded ray-tracer, and jess – an expert system) in both the original and instrumented versions, as well as the slowdown expressed as the percentage of the differences between the two versions, ranging between 5.5 and 12%. The measurements were on a 600MHz Pentium III laptop, running JDK 1.4.

Table 2. Macro-Benchmarks.

Benchmark	compress	javac	mtrt	jess
Original version (sec)	22.403	19.74	6.82	8.55
Instrumented version (sec)	23.644	21.18	7.49	9.58
Slowdown	5.54%	7.31%	9.85%	12.05%

The best way to interpret these results is as the overhead of pure computation (without communication) that these programs would incur under the Weyns et al. technique if they were to be partitioned with J-Orchestra so that their parts would run correctly on distinct machines. We see, for instance, that running jess over a network would incur an overhead of 12% in extra computation, just to ensure the correctness of the execution under multiple threads. Our approach eliminates this overhead completely: overhead is only incurred when actual communication over distinct address spaces takes place. As we show next, this overhead is minuscule, even when no network communication takes place.

4.3 Maintaining Thread Equivalence Classes Is Cheap

Maintaining thread equivalence classes, which consists of obtaining, propagating, and updating them, constitutes the overhead of our approach. In other words, to maintain the thread equivalence classes correctly, each retrofitted remote method invocation includes one extra local method call on the client side to obtain the current class, an extra argument to propagate it over the network, and another local method call on the server side to update it. The two extra local calls, which obtain and update thread equivalence classes, incur virtually no overhead, having a hash table lookup as their most expensive operation and causing no network communication. Thus, the cost of propagating the thread equivalence class as an extra argument in each remote method call constitutes the bulk of our overhead.

In order to minimize this overhead, we experimented with different thread equivalence classes' representations. We performed preliminary experiments which showed that the representation does matter: the cost of passing an extra reference argument (any subclass of java.lang.Object in Java) over RMI can be high, resulting in as much as 50% slowdown in the worst case. This happens because RMI accomplishes the marshalling/unmarshalling of reference parameters via Java serialization, which involves dynamic memory allocation and the use of reflection. Such measurements led us to implement the packed representation of thread equivalence class information into a long integer, as described earlier. A long is a primitive type in Java, hence the additional cost of passing one over the network became negligible.

To quantify the overall worst-case overhead of our approach, we ran several microbenchmarks, measuring total execution time taken by invoking empty remote methods with zero, one java.lang.String, and two java.lang.String parameters. Each remote method call was performed 10^6 times. The base line shows the numbers for regular uninstrumented RMI calls. To measure the pure overhead of our approach, we used an unrealistic setting of collocating the client and the server on the same machine, thus eliminating all the costs of network communication. The measurements were on a 2386MHz Pentium IV, running JDK 1.4. The results of our measurements appear in Table 3.

Table 3. Overhead of Maintaining Thread Equivalence Classes.

No. of Params	Base Line (ms)	Maintaining Thread Equivalence Classes (ms)	Overhead (%)
0	145,328	150,937	3.86%
1	164,141	166,219	1.27%
2	167,984	168,844	0.51%

Since the remote methods in this benchmark did not perform any operations, the numbers show the time spent exclusively on invoking the methods. While the overhead is approaching 4% for the remote method without any parameters, it diminishes gradually to half a percent for the method taking two parameters. Of course, our settings for this benchmark are strictly worst-case – had the client and the server been separated by a network or had the remote methods performed any operations, the overhead would strictly decrease.

5 Discussion

As we mentioned briefly earlier, our distributed synchronization technique only supports monitor-style concurrency control. This is a standard application-level concurrency control facility in Java, but it is not the only one and the language is actively evolving to better support other models. For example, high-performance applications may use `volatile` variables instead of explicit locking. In fact, use of non-monitor-style synchronization in Java will probably become more popular in the future. The upcoming JSR-166 specification will standardize many concurrent data structures and atomic operations. Although our technique does not support all the tools for managing concurrency in the Java language, this is not so much a shortcoming as it is a reasonable design choice. Low-level concurrency mechanisms (volatile variables and their derivatives) are useful for synchronization in a single memory space. Their purpose is to achieve optimized performance for symmetric multiprocessor machines. In contrast, our approach deals with correct synchronization over middleware – i.e., it explicitly addresses distributed memory. The technique we presented in this paper is likely to be employed in a cluster or even a more loosely coupled network of machines. In this setting, monitor-style synchronization makes perfect sense.

On the other hand, in the future we can use the lower-level Java concurrency control mechanisms to optimize our own library for emulating Java monitors. As we saw in Section 3, our current library is itself implemented using monitor-style programming (`synchronized` blocks, `Object.wait`, etc.). With the use of optimized low-level implementation techniques, we can gain in efficiency. We believe it is unlikely, however, that such a low-level optimization in our library primitives will make a difference for most client applications of our distributed synchronization approach.

Finally, we should mention that our current implementation does not handle all the nuances of Java monitor-style synchronization, but the issue is one of straightforward engineering. Notably, we do not currently propagate `Thread.interrupt` calls to all the nodes that might have threads blocked in an invocation of the `wait` method. Even though it is not clear that the `interrupt` functionality is useful for distributed threads, our design can easily support it. We can replace all the calls to `Thread.interrupt` with calls to our synchronization library, which will obtain the equivalence class of the interrupted thread and then broadcast it to all the nodes of the application. The node (there can be only one) that has a thread in the equivalence class executing the `wait` operation of our library will then stop waiting and the operation will throw the `InterruptedException`.

6   Related Work

The technique described in this paper was applied in the context of J-Orchestra, but can be re-used in multiple different contexts. For instance, our implementation of correct synchronization can be combined with a mechanism for capturing and migrating threads, as in the Brakes system [18]. So far, we have not explored thread migration at all in the context of J-Orchestra. In fact, J-Orchestra prohibits the migration of all objects that can be potentially passed to native code (based on a heuristic analysis) in an effort to ensure the correctness of the resulting partitioned application. Thus, thread objects explicitly cannot be mobile in a J-Orchestra-partitioned application: a thread always executes on the site where it was created. This fits well the requirements of the system, i.e., to ensure correct distributed execution even for completely unsuspecting centralized Java applications.

Several projects have concentrated on offering distributed capabilities for Java applications. Examples include CJVM [1] and Java/DSM [21]. Nevertheless, most of these approaches are in the Distributed Shared Memory (DSM) space, instead of in explicit middleware support for synchronization. As a result, communication is not explicit and the programming model is one of shared memory with relaxed consistency semantics, instead of one of communicating distributed objects. Furthermore, DSMs do not support the portability and ease of deployment goal of our technique. An application deployed on a DSM will require a specialized run-time system and system library. Our distributed synchronization approach adds correct synchronization handling on top of traditional Java middleware.

Our technique has wide applicability in the space of automatic partitioning systems. Several such systems have been proposed recently, including Addistant [16], AdJava [3], FarGo [6], and Pangaea [13][14]. To our knowledge, J-Orchestra is the first automatic partitioning system to concentrate on the correctness of partitioning multithreaded programs. It is worth noting that a partitioning system cannot just transparently inherit distributed synchronization capabilities from its underlying middleware. Even with specialized middleware that tries to handle distributed synchronization issues (e.g., KaRMI [10][12]), a partitioning system will need to transform an application so that Java monitor commands, like `monitorenter`, are propagated to a remote site.

Language tools for distribution, such as JavaParty [4][11], can also benefit from our technique. JavaParty already supports distributed synchronization [5] through a combination of language-level transformation (to intercept monitor actions) and specialized middleware [12]. As discussed earlier, our approach enables the same functionality over standard Java middleware, such as RMI.

Our technique also complements work on offering versions of RMI optimized for parallel computing on cluster machines [8][9]. In a parallel computing setting, it is advantageous to have distributed synchronization as a technique that can be transparently added to a middleware implementation.

Finally, there are approaches to richer middleware that would simplify the implementation of our technique. For instance, DADO [20] enables passing custom information between client and server of a remote call. This would be an easy alternative to our custom bytecode transformations of stubs and skeletons. Nevertheless, using DADO would not eliminate the need for bytecode transformations that replace monitor control methods and synchronization blocks.

7 Conclusions

In this paper we presented a technique for correct monitor-style synchronization of distributed programs in Java. Our technique addresses the lack of coordination between Java concurrency mechanisms and Java middleware. We argue that the technique is important because it comprehensively solves the problem and combines the best features of past approaches by offering both portability and efficiency. Furthermore, we believe that the value of our technique will strictly increase in the future. With the increased network connectivity of all computing resources, we expect a need for distributed programming models that look more like centralized programming models. In such a setting, the need for correct and efficient distributed synchronization will become even greater.

Acknowledgments. This research was supported by the NSF through grants CCR-0238289 and CCR-0220248, and by the Georgia Electronic Design Center.

References

1. Yariv Aridor, Michael Factor, and Avi Teperman, "CJVM: a Single System Image of a JVM on a Cluster", in Proc. *ICPP'99*.
2. Markus Dahm, "Doorastha – a step towards distribution transparency", *JIT,* 2000. See http://www.inf.fu-berlin.de/~dahm/doorastha/.
3. Mohammad M. Fuad and Michael J. Oudshoorn, "AdJava – Automatic Distribution of Java Applications", 25th *Australasian Computer Science Conference (ACSC)*, 2002.
4. Bernhard Haumacher, Jürgen Reuter, Michael Philippsen, "JavaParty: A distributed companion to Java", http://wwwipd.ira.uka.de/JavaParty/
5. Bernhard Haumacher, Thomas Moschny, Jürgen Reuter, and Walter F. Tichy, "Transparent Distributed Threads for Java", *5th International Workshop on Java for Parallel and Distributed Computing*, in conjunction with the *International Parallel and Distributed Processing Symposium (IPDPS 2003)*, Nice, France, April 2003.
6. Ophir Holder, Israel Ben-Shaul, and Hovav Gazit, "Dynamic Layout of Distributed Applications in FarGo", *Int. Conf. on Softw. Engineering (ICSE)* 1999.
7. Doug Lea, "Concurrent Programming in Java -- Design Principles and Patterns", Addison-Wesley, Reading, Mass., 1996.
8. Jason Maassen, Rob van Nieuwpoort, Ronald Veldema, Henri E. Bal, Aske Plaat, "An Efficient Implementation of Java's Remote Method Invocation", *Proc. of ACM Symposium on Principles and Practice of Parallel Programming, Atlanta, GA May 1999*.
9. Jason Maassen, Rob van Nieuwpoort, Ronald Veldema, Henri E. Bal, Thilo Kielmann, Ceriel Jacobs, and Rutger Hofman, "Efficient Java RMI for Parallel Programming", *ACM Transactions on Programming Languages and Systems (TOPLAS)*, 23(6):747-775, November 2001.
10. Christian Nester, Michael Phillipsen, and Bernhard Haumacher, "A More Efficient RMI for Java", in Proc. *ACM Java Grande Conference*, 1999.
11. Michael Philippsen and Matthias Zenger, "JavaParty - Transparent Remote Objects in Java", *Concurrency: Practice and Experience*, 9(11):1125-1242, 1997.
12. Michael Philippsen, Bernhard Haumacher, and Christian Nester, "More Efficient Serialization and RMI for Java", *Concurrency: Practice & Experience*, 12(7):495-518, May 2000.
13. Andre Spiegel, "Pangaea: An Automatic Distribution Front-End for Java", 4th *IEEE Workshop on High-Level Parallel Programming Models and Supportive Environments (HIPS '99)*, San Juan, Puerto Rico, April 1999.
14. Andre Spiegel, "Automatic Distribution in Pangaea", *CBS 2000*, Berlin, April 2000. See also http://www.inf.fu-berlin.de/~spiegel/pangaea/
15. Sun Microsystems, Remote Method Invocation Specification, http://java.sun.com/products/jdk/rmi/, 1997.
16. Michiaki Tatsubori, Toshiyuki Sasaki, Shigeru Chiba, and Kozo Itano, "A Bytecode Translator for Distributed Execution of 'Legacy' Java Software", *European Conference on Object-Oriented Programming (ECOOP)*, Budapest, June 2001.
17. Eli Tilevich and Yannis Smaragdakis, "J-Orchestra: Automatic Java Application Partitioning", *European Conference on Object-Oriented Programming (ECOOP)*, Malaga, June 2002.
18. Danny Weyns, Eddy Truyen, and Pierre Verbaeten, "Distributed Threads in Java", *International Symposium on Distributed and Parallel Computing (ISDPC)*, July 2002.
19. Danny Weyns, Eddy Truyen and Pierre Verbaeten, "Serialization of Distributed Threads in Java", *Special Issue of the International Journal on Parallel and Distributed Computing Practice, PDCP* (to appear).
20. Eric Wohlstadter, Stoney Jackson and Premkumar Devanbu, "DADO: Enhancing Middleware to Support Crosscutting Features in Distributed, Heterogeneous Systems", *International Conference on Software Engineering (ICSE)*, 2003.
21. Weimin Yu, and Alan Cox, "Java/DSM: A Platform for Heterogeneous Computing", *Concurrency: Practice and Experience*, 9(11):1213-1224, 1997.

Platform Independent Model Transformation Based on TRIPLE

Andreas Billig[1], Susanne Busse[2], Andreas Leicher[2], and Jörn Guy Süß[2]

[1] Fraunhofer ISST, Berlin, Germany
`Andreas.Billig@isst.fhg.de`
[2] Technische Universität Berlin, Germany
`{sbusse,aleicher,jgsuess}@cs.tu-berlin.de`

Abstract. Reuse is an important topic in software engineering as it promises advantages like faster time-to-market and cost reduction. Reuse of models on an abstract level is more beneficial than on the code level, because these models can be mapped into several technologies and can be adapted according to different requirements. Unfortunately, development tools only provide fixed mappings between abstract models described in a language such as UML and source code for a particular technology. These mappings are based on one-to-one relationships between elements of both levels. As a consequence, it is rarely possible to customize mappings according to specific user requirements.
We aim to improve model reuse by providing a framework that generates customized mappings according to specified requirements. The framework is able to handle mappings aimed for several component technologies as it is based on an ADL. It is realized in TRIPLE to represent components on different levels of abstraction and to perform the actual transformation. It uses feature models to describe mapping alternatives.

1 Introduction

In general, software development consists of several steps from which one is the design. The design is often expressed by a modeling language such as UML and sketches the specification of a system. It is common practice to translate the result of the design into source code. This is done either manually or automatically. Unfortunately, the link between design and source code often ends after the transformation step and the design is not kept up-to-date any longer. This has several disadvantages, particularly for reuse.

At present, reuse mainly manifests itself in artifacts: Either source code or commercials off-the-shelf (COTS) are reused. However, this kind of reuse is restricted to a small number of situations, where we can directly reuse an artifact. If we, for example, develop a system based on the .Net technology and we have an existing component that exactly fulfills a particular service but is written in CORBA, we can't directly reuse that component. Instead, we have to construct appropriate wrapper code to adapt the component to the actual environment. This often brings some disadvantages such as performance penalties etc. Unfortunately, we cannot simple extract the design from existing code and build an

H.-A. Jacobsen (Ed.): Middleware 2004, LNCS 3231, pp. 493–511, 2004.

adapted component from it, because code is the result of the amalgamation of both design and technology. It is difficult to recognize design in large projects, because it tends to get lost in the brittle structure of libraries and code. As a consequence, design reuse is hard to achieve, as it is not supported in current software development.

For that reason, Model-Driven Development [12] proposes to model systems on a higher level of abstraction – independent of a particular technology – and to automatically transform a design into code. This kind of development promises faster time-to-marked and cost reduction because specifications on a more abstract level simplify development. If we for example have the design specification of the CORBA component mentioned above, we can automatically generate a .Net version of this component based on the abstract design. More precisely, the exact extent of the generation depends on the degree of modeled information in the design model. If it only comprises interface definitions, we only can generate platform specific interfaces. However, we assume that a platform independent component specification additionally includes pre- and post conditions, behavior descriptions, and a state model of the component. Therefore, only a small amount of source code has to be generated manually.

The OMG however proposes Model-Driven Development by their Model Driven Architecture (MDA). The MDA [13] targets fully automated component generation. Therefore, it distinguishes two kinds of models: platform independent models (PIM) and platform specific models (PSM). We refer to a PSM if it is based on a particular form of technology such as Enterprise JavaBeans, JavaBeans, and Jini etc. A PSM is normally described in a modeling language such as UML and corresponds in a one-to-one fashion to an implementation of the system. For example, the OMG provides several UML profiles (PSM) that describe a platform such as Enterprise JavaBeans or CORBA in UML [15]. These profiles also define mappings in order to automatically generate source code. Contrary to these models, platform independent models (PIM) can be defined without reference to a platform, and therefore without describing a particular form of technology. Such kinds of models are usually specified using a modeling language without using platform specific elements, e.g. platform specific types. Figure 1 shows the core concept of Model-Driven Development. It distinguishes the different kinds of models as well as model transformations between them. In particular, it presents two mappings between a platform independent model and the Enterprise JavaBeans technology respectively the .Net Platform.

Unfortunately, the proposed advantages of Model-Driven Development can't yet realized with MDA, because automatic model transformations are required to gain an advantage towards traditional source code development. Currently, the MDA lacks a transformation language to perform necessary mappings [7]. Therefore, the OMG issued the Request for Proposal for Query/Views/Transformations (QVT) [14].

Another problem of today's software development concerns the lack of customization of particular model transformations. A transformation should be applied according to specific user requirements. For example, a platform indepen-

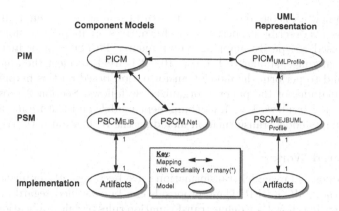

Fig. 1. Model-Based Transformation in MDA

dent component should be transformed into an EntityBean or a SessionBean according to particular requirements. Unfortunately, existing software development tools (such as Rose, ArgoUML etc.) do not support platform independent models. They often provide source code mappings only for one or a small number of technologies: These mappings are defined as one-to-one relationships between UML classes and source code classes. As a consequence, it is rarely possible to customize these mappings according to user requirements.

1.1 Objectives

We propose an ontology-based framework that provides customizable PIM-to-PSM mappings. The framework is based on a platform independent component specification that is constructed according to the component definition used in an Architecture Description Language (ADL). It is capable of handling mappings aimed for several platforms such as Enterprise JavaBeans, CORBA, .Net, COM etc. A user can add mappings for each platform of interest. Each mapping defines a relationship between the platform independent component model and a platform specific component model.

Furthermore, the framework allows defining several PIM-to-PSM mappings for each specific platform. Each mapping can be associated with a particular concept or feature that describes a situation when the mapping should be applied. Thus, a particular mapping is selected based on the requirements of a specific situation. For example, in this paper we start with one platform independent component specification and generate two different EJB models according to user requirements: One is optimized for data throughput between distributed components and one is optimized for local communication. A developer can specify certain properties such as quality of service attributes that should be taken into account in a particular situation. The framework chooses the appropriate mapping based on the specified properties and generates optimized platform specific EJB components.

The framework is based on FEATURE MODELS [5] as well as on TRIPLE [16]. Feature models describe properties and alternatives for model transformations. They are used to specify mapping requirements. TRIPLE is a deductive programming language, similar to F-Logic [10]. It is used to select the appropriate mapping and to perform the model transformation based on this mapping.

The remainder of the paper is organized as follows: Section 2 provides an overview of the framework with its component models and feature models. Section 3 explains model transformation including the realization with Triple.

1.2   Related Work

Several proposals for model transformation have been recently published in response to the OMG's RFP. These proposals can be classified regarding several categories such as how they define transformation rules or rule application strategies. Czarnecki and Helsen [6] provide a classification of model transformation approaches. According to this classification our approach, which is based on TRIPLE is a declarative relational model-to-model approach. Other model transformation languages are based directly on UML. [18] for example defines an extension of the Object Constraint Language OCL using database manipulation operations of SQL. We use an existing language – TRIPLE – to define mappings. Thus, the model transformation is "automatically" done by the inference engine. It allows declaring transformations in a very flexible and compact syntax, similar to F-Logic[1]. Additionally, the TRIPLE concept of parameterized contexts allows a modularization of rule sets and enables the re-use of mappings by parameterized mapping specifications.

Additionally, our approach uses feature model instances, which describe mapping variants to parameterize mappings. Feature models are important in the context of product line engineering and domain analysis ([5,4]). They are used to describe variants within a system family and to generate applications as instances of this system family from the application's specification.

Mostly, the generative approach is used on the implementation level. [2] defines the KobrA methodology for a component-based engineering with UML very similar to our approach. KobrA also contains the specification of variable parts of a system and feature models called decision models. But these concepts are only discussed in the context of product line engineering. We use them to support the general development process wherein alternative realizations must be chosen according to the requirements. Additionally, [2] discusses no explicitly specification of relationships between decisions and realizing system variants so that the transformation has to be done manually.

2   Overview of the Ontology-Based Framework

Our framework provides the frame for model transformation. It therefore has to model both platform independent components and platform specific com-

---

[1] As described in [7] a great advantage is the ability to express the model and instance level in an uniform way and to define multiple targets in a single rule.

ponents for each technology of interest. Furthermore, it includes properties as well as feature models to describe the customization of a model transformation. This section provides an overview of the architecture of our framework and the platform independent conceptual models. As an example for platform specific models we present the Enterprise JavaBeans model which is used in the given example.

2.1 General Architecture of the Framework

Figure 2 shows an overview of the framework's architecture. It is based on a knowledge base that provides reasoning and transformation capabilities. It mainly consists of models describing platform independent and platform specific components as well as of transformation rules. These rules transform a PIM model into a PSM model based on a feature model instance that describes user requirements. A property model allows marking model elements with feature values. The mappings are parameterized both on those marks and on the feature models. The figure does not show the behavioral model, as we do not map its specification at present.

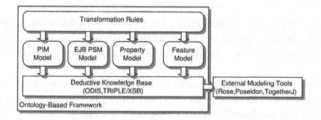

Fig. 2. The Architecture of our Framework

2.2 Platform Independent Models

The conceptual model handles component descriptions on an architectural level. It consists of three sub models representing each of the relevant areas of component descriptions as well as of a feature model to describe customized mappings. These models are shown in figure 3.

The structural model consists of elements that are found in most ADL: components, connectors, interfaces, as well as their relationships and subordinate elements such as operations. Moreover, it distinguishes instance and type elements, in order to describe both architectural styles and system configurations[2]. This model constitutes a type system, which can be specialized into technology specific types.

The behavioral model restricts components and connectors by means of pre- and post-conditions, as well as by protocols (order of method invocations). This

---

[2] Figure 3 shows only component types as we only use component types in our example.

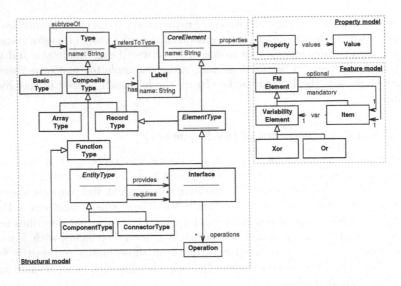

Fig. 3. Platform Independent Models of the Framework

allows verifying behavioral equivalence of components by using appropriate tools such as model checkers and theorem provers. However, this model is not shown in Figure 3, because we do not regard this information for transformation of EJB components.

The property model defines an ontology that describes architectural and technical properties of components. In particular, it provides a classification, which can be used to describe differences between components. Therefore, we integrated two well-known taxonomies from Allen/Shaw and Medvidovic/Mehta, which respectively describe architectural styles and communicational properties. In the context of model transformation, it is used to annotate components with their specific roles and to state user requirements on these elements. This is the basis for customized mappings, described in the next section.

Feature models describe alternatives to customize a mapping. They are graphically expressed in feature diagrams. Feature models play an important role in the area of domain analysis. Introduced in FODA [9] they serve as a description of the features of domain entities using and-or-trees enhanced with some useful elements to express variability. According to Deursen [19] they contain elements representing

- optional and mandatory features pointed to by a simple edge ending with an empty circle or a filled circle, respectively,
- alternative features pointed to by edges connected by an arc,
- non-exclusive features, also called *or-features*, pointed to by edges connected by a filled arc,
- and constraints over feature dependencies specified beside the feature diagram.

2.3   A Platform Specific Component Model for EJB

EJB components are described according to the EJB Profile for UML [8]. They mainly consist of a home interface, a remote interface and an implementation class. We use a slightly adapted form of the profile, because it doesn't support EJB2.x local interfaces. Figure 4 shows a simplified specification of the EJB model.

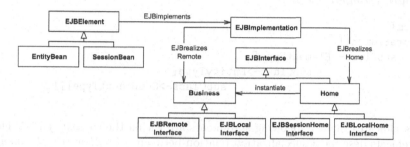

Fig. 4. The EJB Component Model

It is important to notice that the EJB specification and the Profile do not model connectors. Thus, we have to translate connectors from the platform independent level into EJB Components, if they include business logic. Otherwise, we do not need to model a connector at all, because, it is solely a relationship that we can configure in the EJB deployment descriptor.

2.4   Triple Realization

The framework is realized with Triple. Triple is based on F-Logic, which provides a logical foundation for object-oriented features. The design of Triple is influenced by the Resource Description Framework (RDF) [20], which is commonly known in the knowledge representation community. RDF is a general representation language for information structures. It provides basic constructors for the definition of concepts and their relations. Furthermore, it describes knowledge by Tuples (S, P, O): S is a subject, the entity to be described. P is a predicate that states the relation of interest, O stands for an Object, which is either a literal or another resource.

Despite the similarity to RDF, Triple describes tuples of the form (S, P, O, C). It introduces a 'context' as a new construct that allows specifying views of an object in different contexts. In our framework each core model is described within a separate context. This feature is extremely helpful because is divides up facts into chunks that can be used as separate units. Furthermore, it allows creating contexts on the fly by defining mapping rules.

Information specified in RDF can be validated against a schema definition, described by RDFS. The metamodels described above are schema definitions that correspond to RDFS. Instances (Facts) can be checked against these definitions.

An RDF statement can be formalized in Triple as follows

```
Subject[predicate -> object]@context.
```

Subject, predicate and object are normal parts of RDF whereas context refers to a particular tupel space as explained above. If the context is omitted the statement is valid in every possible context. The following example statement declares a *'context'* block:

```
@picm{
  CoreElement[
     subClass->ElementType[
                   subClass->EntityType[
                                subClass->ComponentType]]].
}
```

This indicates that all following statements are within the context *'picm'*. The statements describe a specialization relation between *'CoreElement'*, *'Element-Type'*, *'EntityType'*, and *'ComponentType'*. Thus, Triple statements can be nested, which is extremely useful if we get to more complicated statements. Alternatively, we can state the example as

```
CoreElement[subClass->ElementType].
ElementType[subClass->EntityType].
EntityType[subClass->ComponentType].
```

We also can define instances for these schema definitions:

```
ComponentType[typeOf->Planner].
```

defines *'Planner'* as an instance of *'ComponentType'*.

As a final example, we define the platform specific component model for EJB expressed in Triple. Figure 5 shows the corresponding Triple statements.

The main focus of this paper concerns model transformation. Triple supports these transformations by mapping constructs. We show two examples: The first example describes a parameterized mapping by defining a parameterized context. It describes a kind of 'copy' operation that replicates all facts within the context A into the context B.

```
FORALL A,B @ picm(A,B) {
    FORALL S,P,O
        S[P->O]@A --> S[P->O]@B
}
```

The second example is a mapping rule within the actual context. It is not parameterized and generates for each *'Interface'* an equal named *'ComponentType'*.

```
FORALL Z Interface[typeOf->Z] --> ComponentType[typeOf->Z]
```

```
Class [
    typeOf -> { EJBElement, EJBImplementation, EJBEntityBean, SessionBean,
                Home, Business, EJBSessionHomeInterface, EJBLocalHomeInterface,
                EJBRemoteInterface, EJBLocalInterface } ].

EJBElement [
    subClass -> EntityBean;
    subClass -> SessionBean ].
EJBInterface [
    subClass -> Home [
        subClass -> EJBSessionHomeInterface;
        subClass -> EJBLocalHomeInterface ];
    subClass -> Business [
        subClass -> EJBRemoteInterface;
        subClass -> EJBLocalInterface ]
    ].

Property [ typeOf -> { EJBRealizesHome, EJBRealizesRemote, EJBImplements,
                       instantiate } ].

EJBRealizesHome    [ domain -> EJBImplementation; range -> Home ].
EJBRealizesRemote  [ domain -> EJBImplementation; range -> Business ].
EJBimplements      [ domain -> EJBElement; range -> EJBImplementation ].
instantiate [ domain -> Home; range -> Business ].
```

Fig. 5. Platform Specific Component Model for EJB expressed in Triple

3   PIM-PSM Model Transformation Explained

In this section we present our approach on PIM-to-PSM transformations. Thereby we also regard variants of transformations using feature modelling to determine an appropriate mapping. After describing our approach to model transformation in general, we explain it using an example.

3.1   Customized Model Transformation

In difference to common practice we do not map a PIM directly into source code. Instead, it is mapped into a PSM expressed in UML. The appropriate mapping is chosen according to selected requirements. A PIM-PSM transformation is based on three elements:

- the platform independent model that should be mapped. In our context this will be a PIM represented as an instance of the metamodel described in the last section. Especially, the elements like components are annotated with further properties that can be used to customize a model transformation to the specific situation.
- a feature model instance describing requirements that should be considered in the transformation. It is used to choose an appropriate mapping. So, the feature modelling allows the customization of a model transformation.
- mappings that define rules for possible transformations. Mappings formally specify design knowledge that is used when realizing a system with a specific middleware technology. They enable the automatization of the transformation process.

A PIM-PSM transformation is done as following: At first, the developer designs a system modelling it independent from platform technologies. In a second step, he specifies his requirements on the PIM-PSM transformation by choosing features from the feature model describing possible variants of available transformation rules. The chosen features are called *feature model instances* (FI). In contrast to a feature model it is an instance model that does not contain any variants. In the last step, a development tool transforms the PIM according to the specified requirements.

Formally, the basis for the customized model transformation is a set of transformation rules. Each rule takes the PIM and the feature model instance (FI) as input arguments and specifies the PSM appropriate for the given situation. In our framework all participating models – PIM, feature model, and PSM – are represented as instances of corresponding metamodels that can be translated into the TRIPLE-based format. On this basis a mapping can be defined as a TRIPLE-mapping with parameterized contexts:

```
FORALL PIM, FI @ pim2psmMapping(PIM, FI) {

    // Transformation rule 1
    FORALL <...necessary variables...>
      <...constraint...> @ PIM,  <...constraint...> @ FI
      -->
        <...PSM elements...>

    // Transformation rule 2
    ...
}
```

3.2   Example

Our running example comes from federated information systems. We describe two possible PIM-to-PSM transformations from the platform independent model to EJB specific models regarding specific requirements on distribution and optimization.

3.2.1 Platform Independent Model (PIM).
The PIM of our example consists of two components that are part of a mediator (see figure 6). A mediator is a kind of middleware that performs queries against heterogeneous distributed data sources ([21]). If a client queries a mediator calling the `execute` operation, the mediator first calculates which data sources are capable to answer the query or part of it (Planner component). Then, it queries these sources, integrates the answers and delivers the result back to the client.

The Planner calculates its plans based on specified interfaces of the data sources. These interface descriptions are called query capabilities (QC). A query capability, shown on the right side of the figure, consists of parameters that a data source can process as well as of result attributes returned by the data source. In figure 6, the QCManager component stores the query capabilities (QC) of managed data sources. The Planner uses QC, obtained by the QCManager, to decide which data sources have to be queried. These query plans are provided to the execution component of a mediator.

The figure also shows some annotations that are used for the transformation later on. These annotations are properties describing a component's role regarding its interoperation with another component. For example, the Planner is a client using the interface of the QCManager.

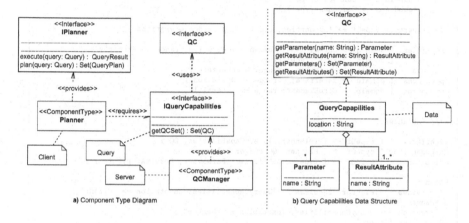

a) Component Type Diagram

b) Query Capabilities Data Structure

Fig. 6. Example – PIM Component Type View

Specification with TRIPLE. The formal specification of the PIM within our framework uses the TRIPLE representation of the UML metamodel and the PIM metamodel defined in the last chapter. It defines the elements of figure 6 as instances of the metamodels.

3.2.2 Variants of the PIM-PSM Transformation.
The PIM of the QC-Manager is used as a starting point to exemplify two PSM transformations for the Enterprise JavaBeans platform. We present two customized transformations according to specific requirements (criteria) for our example: We regard physical distribution of mediator components and performance of communication measured in the number of procedure calls between components and the amount of transmitted data. In general, several factors influence performance. In distributed systems, performance can be improved by minimizing distributed transactions, remote procedure calls, the amount of transmitted data etc. Figure 8 shows the feature diagram related to our example.

The developer chooses the features from the feature model that should be considered in a specific transformation. We will examine a local PSM transformation optimized for the amount of transmitted data, as well as a distributed PSM transformation optimized for the amount of remote procedure calls. Both are realized with the EJB platform.

```
...
picm := "http://cis.cs.tu-berlin.de/modeltrafo#picm".
uml := ... .

//// Schema:

Class [ typeOf -> { Property, CoreElement, EntityType,
                    ElementType, ConnectorType, ComponentType } ].

CoreElement [
    subClass -> ElementType [
      subClass -> EntityType [
        subClass -> ConnectorType;
        subClass -> ComponentType ] ] ].

rdf:Property [ typeOf -> {properties, requires, provides,operations} ].

properties  [ domain -> CoreElement; domain -> Operation; range -> Property ].
requires    [ domain -> EntityType; range -> Interface ].
provides    [ domain -> EntityType; range -> Interface ].
operations  [ domain -> Interface;  range -> Operation ].
annotation  [ domain -> CoreElement; range -> Literal ].
...

//// Instances:

Interface      [ typeOf -> { IPlanner, IQueryCapabilities, QC } ].
ComponentType  [ typeOf -> { Planner, QCManager } ].
uml:Class      [ typeOf -> { IQueryCapabilities, Parameter, ResultAttribute } ].

Planner [
    provides -> IPlanner; requires -> IQueryCapabilities; annotation -> "Client" ].
QCManager [
    provides -> IQueryCapabilities; annotation -> "Server" ].
IQueryCapabilities [
    operations -> op1 [
       name -> "getQCSet"; result -> Set(QC); annotation -> "Query" ] ].
QueryCapabilities [
    realizes -> QC; aggregates -> { Parameter, ResultAttribute };
    annotation -> "Data" ].
```

Fig. 7. Example – Triple Specification of the Platform Independent Model

Specification with TRIPLE. The features chosen by the developer determine which transformation is appropriate for the specific application. To manage transformation variants in our framework we use a TRIPLE representation again. Figure 9 shows an instance of the feature metamodel namely the feature model (FM) shown in figure 8, which is used for the mapping selection. A feature model instance (FI) is a feature model without any variants. It represents the features chosen by the developer and is the input for the PIM-PSM transformation. For example the FI at the end of figure 9 requests a transformation based on remote distribution and optimized procedure calls (distributed configuration).

3.2.3 PIM-PSM Transformation. Starting from the PIM of a mediator and the feature model for EJB architectures we show two possible transformations to a EJB-based PSM. In our example the transformation is based on patterns [11, 1] that were developed to optimize EJB communication and performance. We will discuss a local and a distributed configuration of the mediator components.

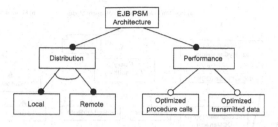

Fig. 8. Feature diagram for EJB-based architectures

```
...
fm := "http://cis.cs.tu-berlin.de/modeltrafo#featureModel".

//// Instance of the feature metamodel as input for mapping selection:

Item [ typeOf -> { EJB_PSM_Architecture, Distribution, Performance,
                   Local, Remote, Optimized_procedure_calls, Optimized_transmitted_data} ].
Xor  [ typeOf -> xor1 ].

EJB_PSM_Architecture [
    mandatory -> Distribution [
        var -> xor1 [
            mandatory -> {Local, Remote} ] ];
    mandatory -> Performance [
        optional -> {Optimized_procedure_call, Optimized_transmitted_data} ] ].

//// Instance of the feature model as a result of a mapping selection:

EJB_PSM_Architecture [
    mandatory -> Distribution [
        mandatory -> Remote ];
    mandatory -> Performance [
        mandatory -> Optimized_procedure_call ] ].
```

Fig. 9. Example – Feature Models in TRIPLE

Example: Local Configuration. This transformation is done according to the features that were chosen by the developer: both components are co-located and optimized for the amount of transmitted data. Using the patterns in [11,1] the transformation results in the PSCM shown in figure 10. The Planner component as a client in this example is mapped into a Session Bean, because it is used as a business logic component, e.g. it provides computations. The QCManager, which includes the QC data structure (determined by the relationship to an element with a Data annotation), is mapped into three Entity Beans, as it presents persistent data. We don't need an extra QCManager Bean as this component would introduce another layer of indirection. Instead, we directly access the persistence layer. This leads to optimized data transfer, as we don't have to collect all data of the persistence layer and send it to the Planner component. Instead, data is returned in form of a set of references to locally available QC Entity Beans. The operation to get all QC is renamed to findQCSet as described in the profile. If the Planner needs parameters or return attributes, additional calls are performed to obtain the queried entities.

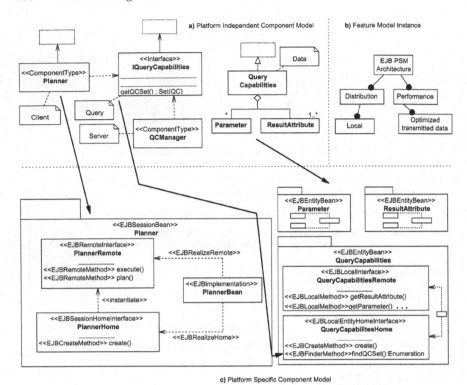

Fig. 10. Example – PIM-PSM Transformation for a Local Configuration

In order to save space, only the Planner component in figure 10 shows all parts of an EJB according to the profile. Otherwise, we only show interesting parts of a bean and represent other elements as small boxes.

Example: Distributed Configuration. The distributed transformation optimizes remote procedure calls between distributed Planner components and a single QCManager component. Again, the transformation is based on the chosen features from the feature model. Regarding the EJB platform, several patterns for performance optimization were developed. We will use the Data Transfer Object pattern (DTO)[11, 1] and the Data Transfer Object Factory pattern (DTOF)[11] for the PIM-to-PSM transformation in this example.

Figure 11 shows the mapping result. The QCManager component is mapped into a stateless session bean following the DTOF pattern that provides a facade to the persistence layer consisting of three Entity Beans. The QCManager locally assembles Data Transfer Objects for each query by calling the Entity Beans. In difference to the local mapping these objects are copies of persistent data. Thus, a query of the Planner component results in a single remote procedure call.

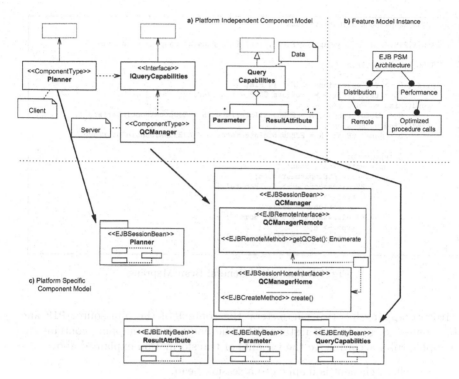

Fig. 11. Example – PIM-PSM Transformation for a Distributed Configuration

Specification with TRIPLE. The specification of the mappings for our transformation described before consists of two parts: the first one defines the general mapping from PIM elements to EJB, the second one defines the mapping depending on the possible features.

Figure 12 shows the general mapping definition from PIM models to session or entity beans. The arguments of the bean mapping are the resource variables X, PIM, and Kind. PIM is the context of the mapping source, X is the element from that source which shall be mapped, and Kind states whether a session or an entity bean shall be the result. The mapping definition consists of one rule which expresses the following: If a element with an appropriate provides/realizes-structure can be derived within the source context (left hand side of the rule) then a bean and the remote/home interfaces corresponding to the Enterprise EJB standard will be generated (right hand side of the rule). The instantiation of the type-variables in the target structure depends on Kind. The target operation TF is the result of a special predicate convertst called with the source operation F. This predicate adds the stereotypes defined by the EJB profile.

Figure 13 shows the specific PIM-to-PSM-mapping depending on possible feature model instances. Within the utility mapping util two specific FIs are considered: the distributed and the local configuration variant. The mapping

```
... // namespaces and abbreviations

FORALL X,PIM,Kind  @ beanMapping(X,PIM,Kind) { // general mapping to a bean

 FORALL B,R,H,Y,F,TF,P

   ( X [ P -> Y [ operations -> F ] ]@ PIM,
          convertst(F,TF),(P = provides OR P = realizes)),
   cond( Kind = "Entity",
          B = EJBEntityBean, R = EJBLocalInterface, H = EJBLocalHomeInterface ),
   cond( Kind = "Session",
          B = SessionBean, R = EJBRemoteInterface, H = EJBSessionHomeInterface ),
   -->
      X [ type -> B;
           implements -> X||'Bean' [
               type -> EJBImplementation;
               EJBRealizesRemote -> X||'Remote' [
                   type -> R;
                   operations -> TF ];
               EJBRealizesHome ->   X||'Home' [
                   type -> H;
                   instantiate -> X||'Remote' ] ]
}
```

Fig. 12. Example – General Bean Mapping

pim2psmMapping has two parameters: the context of the pim source PIM and
the context of the feature instance FI. The body of the mapping contains the
mapping rules according to the variants of transformation explained above:

- Any client element is mapped to a session bean.
- A server will become a session bean if the variant of remote distribution is
  chosen.
- All aggregated elements of a data element are mapped to entity beans.
- A data element x also become an entity bean. If the variant of local data is
  chosen then an EJB conform conversion of any Query-annotated operation
  which uses the interface of x is placed within the home interface of the
  generated bean.

4   Conclusions

In this paper, we presented a model transformation framework that is able to
express and process customized PIM-to-PSM mappings. Contrary to existing
tools, the framework handles several component technologies as it is based on
the platform independent component model (PICM). PICM allows describing
components on different levels of abstraction. Thus, it provides the foundation
for PIM-to-PSM mappings, which is a feature that is not provided by existing modeling tools. As PICM is based on an architecture description language
(ADL), it facilitates easy integration of new component-based technologies. However, instead of using an existing ADL, PICM is based on TRIPLE/RDF. Its main
purpose is to perform explicit reasoning on the selection of component mappings
and to allow declarative rule specifications between model representations.

```
... // namespaces and abbreviations

FORALL FI  @ fm:util(FI) { // utility predicates for feature model instances

   fm:Distribution [ fm:mandatory -> fm:Remote ] @ FI,
   fm:Performance [ fm:mandatory -> fm:Optimized_procedure_call ] @ FI  -->  remoteCall.

   fm:Distribution [ fm:mandatory -> fm:Local ] @ FI,
   fm:Performance [ fm:mandatory -> fm:Optimized_transmitted_data ] @ FI  -->  localData.
}

FORALL PIM, FI  @ pim2psmMapping(PIM, FI) { // pim-to-psm mapping

   FORALL X,T
      X [ annotation -> "Client" ] @ PIM,   T @ beanMapping(X,PIM,"Session")
      --> T.

   FORALL X,T
      X [ annotation -> "Server" ] @ PIM,   T @ beanMapping(X,PIM,"Session"),
      remoteCall @ fm:util(FI)
      --> T.

   FORALL T,X,Y

      X [ annotation -> "Data"; aggregates -> Y ] @ PIM,  T @ beanMapping(Y,PIM,"Entity")
      --> T.

   FORALL X,Ifc,T,F,TF,U,H

      X [ annotation -> "Data"; realizes -> Ifc ] @ PIM,  T @ beanMapping(X,PIM,"Entity")
      -->
         T,
         ( localData @ fm:util(FI),
           F [ annotation -> "Query" ] @ PIM, use(F,Ifc), convert(F,TF),
           U [ EJBRealizesHome -> H ] @ beanMapping(X,PIM,"Entity")
           -->
              H [ operations -> TF ] ).
}
```

Fig. 13. Example – Specific PIM-PSM Transformation Rules

TRIPLE/RDF is a model representation and transformation language. It is suitable to represent and interrelate terminological structures such as feature models as well as conceptual models like UML class diagrams. It allows describing both the model and the instances in a uniform and simple syntax.

The second contribution of the paper is the combination of mappings with feature models. A feature model facilitates the selection of particular mappings depending on certain user requirements. This gives our framework the flexibility to choose appropriate model transformations in a particular situation. To the best of our knowledge there is no existing modeling tool for component-based systems that provide this flexibility.

Currently, the model transformation tasks are realized by services of the Ontology-Based Domain Repository ODIS [3]. Future developments will integrate the presented model transformation framework as a service in the Evolution and Validation Environment (EVE) [17]. EVE allows executing arbitrary services on UML models that were extracted from UML modeling tools. EVE is based on a MOF repository and uses XMI to get models from these tools. At present it supports ArgoUML and Rational Rose. As a consequence, we will be able to directly transform UML models, which were created with a modeling tool, into representations in several component technologies either as UML PSM or as source code. This will be a further step in the direction of a model-driven software engineering.

References

1. ALUR, D., CRUPI, J., AND MALKS, D. *Core J2EE Patterns: Best Practices and Design Strategies*. Prentice Hall / Sun Microsystems Press, 2001.
2. ATKINSON, C., BAYER, J., BUNSE, C., KAMSTIES, E., LAITENBERGER, O., LAQUA, R., MUTHIG, D., PAECH, B., WÜST, J., AND ZETTEL, J. *Component-based Product Line Engineering with UML*. Component Software Series. Addison-Weseley, 2002.
3. BILLIG, A. ODIS - Ein Domänenrepository auf der Basis von Semantic Web Technologien. In *Tagungsband der Berliner XML Tage* (2003), XML-Clearinghouse. english version: http://www.isst.fhg.de/~abillig/Odis/xsw2003.
4. CLEMENTS, P., AND NORTHROP, L. *Software Product Lines: Practices and Patterns*. Kluwer, 2001.
5. CZARNECKI, K., AND EISENECKER, U. *Generative Programming - Methods, Tools, and Applications*. Addison-Wesley, 2000.
6. CZARNECKI, K., AND HELSEN, S. Classification of model transformation approaches. In *Proceedings of the 2nd OOPSLA Workshop on Generative Techniques in the Context of the Model Driven Architecture* (Anaheim, October 2003).
7. GERBER, A., LAWLEY, M., RAYMOND, K., STEEL, J., AND WOOD, A. Transformation: The missing link of MDA. *Lecture Notes in Computer Science 2505* (2002).
8. GREENFIELD, J. UML Profile For EJB. Tech. rep., Rational Software Corporation, May 2001. http://www.jcp.org/jsr/detail/26.jsp, Java Community Process (JCP).
9. KANG, K., COHEN, S., HESS, J., NOVAK, W., AND PETERSON, A. Feature-Oriented Domain Analysis (FODA) Feasibility Study. Tech. Rep. CMU/SEI-90-TR-21, Software Engineering Institute, Carnegie Mellon University, nov 1990.
10. KIFER, M., LAUSEN, G., AND WU, J. Logical foundations of object-oriented and frame-based languages. *Journal of the ACM 42* (Juli 1995), 741–843.
11. MARINESCU, F. *EJB Design Patterns: Advanced Patterns, Processes, and Idioms*. John Wiley & Sons, Inc., 2002.
12. MELLOR, S. J., CLARK, A. N., AND FUTAGAMI, T. Model-driven development. *IEEE Software 20*, 5 (2003), 14–18.
13. MILLER, J., AND MUKERJI, J. Model Driven Architecture(MDA). Tech. Rep. ormsc/2001-07-01, Object Management Group(OMG), Architecture Board ORMSC, July 2001.
14. OBJECT MANAGEMENT GROUP (OMG). *Request for Proposal: MOF 2.0 Query / Views / Transformations RFP*, April 2002. http://www.omg.org/cgi-bin/apps/do_doc?ad/2002-04-10.pdf.
15. OMG. *UML Profile for CORBA Specification V1.0*, 2000.
16. SINTEK, M., AND DECKER, S. TRIPLE - A Query, Inference, and Transformation Language for the Semantic Web. In *Proceedings of International Semantic Web Conference ISWC 2002* (2002), Lecture Notes in Computer Science, Bd. 2342, Springer.

17. SÜSS, J. G., LEICHER, A., WEBER, H., AND KUTSCHE, R.-D. Model-centric engineering with the evolution and validation en vironment. In *UML 2003 - The Unified Modeling Language: Modeling Lan guages and Applications, 6th International Conference, San Francisco, CA, USA* (2003), P. Stevens, J. Whittle, and G. Booch, Eds., vol. 2863 of *LNCS*, Springer, pp. 31 – 43.

18. SÜSS, J., LEICHER, A., AND BUSSE, S. OCLPrime - Environment and Language for Model Query, Views, and Transformations. In *OCL 2.0 - Industry standard or scientific playground?, Workshop on the 6th Int. Conf. UML 2003* (2003).

19. VAN DEURSEN, A., AND KLINT, P. Domain-specific language design requires feature descriptions. *Journal of Computing and Information Technology* (2001).

20. W3C. Resource Description Framework (RDF) Model and Syntax Specification. URL: http://www.w3.org/TR/1999/REC-rdf-syntax-19990222/.

21. WIEDERHOLD, G. Mediators in the Architecture of Future Information Systems. In *Readings in Agents*, M. N. Huhns and M. P. Singh, Eds. Morgan Kaufmann, San Francisco, CA, USA, 1997, pp. 185 – 196.

Author Index

Lecture Notes in Computer Science

For information about Vols. 1–3172

please contact your bookseller or Springer

Vol. 3219: M. Heisel, P. Liggesmeyer, S. Wittmann (Eds.), Computer Safety, Reliability, and Security. XI, 339 pages. 2004.

Vol. 3217: C. Barillot, D.R. Haynor, P. Hellier (Eds.), Medical Image Computing and Computer-Assisted Intervention – MICCAI 2004. XXXVIII, 1114 pages. 2004.

Vol. 3216: C. Barillot, D.R. Haynor, P. Hellier (Eds.), Medical Image Computing and Computer-Assisted Intervention – MICCAI 2004. XXXVIII, 930 pages. 2004.

Vol. 3215: M.G.. Negoita, R.J. Howlett, L.C. Jain (Eds.), Knowledge-Based Intelligent Information and Engineering Systems. LVII, 906 pages. 2004. (Subseries LNAI).

Vol. 3214: M.G.. Negoita, R.J. Howlett, L.C. Jain (Eds.), Knowledge-Based Intelligent Information and Engineering Systems. LVIII, 1302 pages. 2004. (Subseries LNAI).

Vol. 3213: M.G.. Negoita, R.J. Howlett, L.C. Jain (Eds.), Knowledge-Based Intelligent Information and Engineering Systems. LVIII, 1280 pages. 2004. (Subseries LNAI).

Vol. 3212: A. Campilho, M. Kamel (Eds.), Image Analysis and Recognition. XXIX, 862 pages. 2004.

Vol. 3211: A. Campilho, M. Kamel (Eds.), Image Analysis and Recognition. XXIX, 880 pages. 2004.

Vol. 3210: J. Marcinkowski, A. Tarlecki (Eds.), Computer Science Logic. XI, 520 pages. 2004.

Vol. 3209: B. Berendt, A. Hotho, D. Mladenic, M. van Someren, M. Spiliopoulou, G. Stumme (Eds.), Web Mining: From Web to Semantic Web. IX, 201 pages. 2004. (Subseries LNAI).

Vol. 3208: H.J. Ohlbach, S. Schaffert (Eds.), Principles and Practice of Semantic Web Reasoning. VII, 165 pages. 2004.

Vol. 3207: L.T. Yang, M. Guo, G.R. Gao, N.K. Jha (Eds.), Embedded and Ubiquitous Computing. XX, 1116 pages. 2004.

Vol. 3206: P. Sojka, I. Kopecek, K. Pala (Eds.), Text, Speech and Dialogue. XIII, 667 pages. 2004. (Subseries LNAI).

Vol. 3205: N. Davies, E. Mynatt, I. Siio (Eds.), UbiComp 2004: Ubiquitous Computing. XVI, 452 pages. 2004.

Vol. 3203: J. Becker, M. Platzner, S. Vernalde (Eds.), Field Programmable Logic and Application. XXX, 1198 pages. 2004.

Vol. 3202: J.-F. Boulicaut, F. Esposito, F. Giannotti, D. Pedreschi (Eds.), Knowledge Discovery in Databases: PKDD 2004. XIX, 560 pages. 2004. (Subseries LNAI).

Vol. 3201: J.-F. Boulicaut, F. Esposito, F. Giannotti, D. Pedreschi (Eds.), Machine Learning: ECML 2004. XVIII, 580 pages. 2004. (Subseries LNAI).

Vol. 3199: H. Schepers (Ed.), Software and Compilers for Embedded Systems. X, 259 pages. 2004.

Vol. 3198: G.-J. de Vreede, L.A. Guerrero, G. Marín Raventós (Eds.), Groupware: Design, Implementation and Use. XI, 378 pages. 2004.

Vol. 3196: C. Stary, C. Stephanidis (Eds.), User-Centered Interaction Paradigms for Universal Access in the Information Society. XII, 488 pages. 2004.

Vol. 3195: C.G. Puntonet, A. Prieto (Eds.), Independent Component Analysis and Blind Signal Separation. XXIII, 1266 pages. 2004.

Vol. 3194: R. Camacho, R. King, A. Srinivasan (Eds.), Inductive Logic Programming. XI, 361 pages. 2004. (Subseries LNAI).

Vol. 3193: P. Samarati, P. Ryan, D. Gollmann, R. Molva (Eds.), Computer Security – ESORICS 2004. X, 457 pages. 2004.

Vol. 3192: C. Bussler, D. Fensel (Eds.), Artificial Intelligence: Methodology, Systems, and Applications. XIII, 522 pages. 2004. (Subseries LNAI).

Vol. 3191: M. Klusch, S. Ossowski, V. Kashyap, R. Unland (Eds.), Cooperative Information Agents VIII. XI, 303 pages. 2004. (Subseries LNAI).

Vol. 3190: Y. Luo (Ed.), Cooperative Design, Visualization, and Engineering. IX, 248 pages. 2004.

Vol. 3189: P.-C. Yew, J. Xue (Eds.), Advances in Computer Systems Architecture. XVII, 598 pages. 2004.

Vol. 3188: F.S. de Boer, M.M. Bonsangue, S. Graf, W.-P. de Roever (Eds.), Formal Methods for Components and Objects. VIII, 373 pages. 2004.

Vol. 3187: G. Lindemann, J. Denzinger, I.J. Timm, R. Unland (Eds.), Multiagent System Technologies. XIII, 341 pages. 2004. (Subseries LNAI).

Vol. 3186: Z. Bellahsène, T. Milo, M. Rys, D. Suciu, R. Unland (Eds.), Database and XML Technologies. X, 235 pages. 2004.

Vol. 3185: M. Bernardo, F. Corradini (Eds.), Formal Methods for the Design of Real-Time Systems. VII, 295 pages. 2004.

Vol. 3184: S. Katsikas, J. Lopez, G. Pernul (Eds.), Trust and Privacy in Digital Business. XI, 299 pages. 2004.

Vol. 3183: R. Traunmüller (Ed.), Electronic Government. XIX, 583 pages. 2004.

Vol. 3182: K. Bauknecht, M. Bichler, B. Pröll (Eds.), E-Commerce and Web Technologies. XI, 370 pages. 2004.

Vol. 3181: Y. Kambayashi, M. Mohania, W. Wöß (Eds.), Data Warehousing and Knowledge Discovery. XIV, 412 pages. 2004.

Vol. 3180: F. Galindo, M. Takizawa, R. Traunmüller (Eds.), Database and Expert Systems Applications. XXI, 972 pages. 2004.

Vol. 3179: F.J. Perales, B.A. Draper (Eds.), Articulated Motion and Deformable Objects. XI, 270 pages. 2004.

Vol. 3178: W. Jonker, M. Petkovic (Eds.), Secure Data Management. VIII, 219 pages. 2004.

Vol. 3177: Z.R. Yang, H. Yin, R. Everson (Eds.), Intelligent Data Engineering and Automated Learning – IDEAL 2004. XVIII, 852 pages. 2004.

Vol. 3176: O. Bousquet, U. von Luxburg, G. Rätsch (Eds.), Advanced Lectures on Machine Learning. IX, 241 pages. 2004. (Subseries LNAI).

Vol. 3175: C.E. Rasmussen, H.H. Bülthoff, B. Schölkopf, M.A. Giese (Eds.), Pattern Recognition. XVIII, 581 pages. 2004.

Vol. 3174: F. Yin, J. Wang, C. Guo (Eds.), Advances in Neural Networks - ISNN 2004. XXXV, 1021 pages. 2004.

Vol. 3173: F. Yin, J. Wang, C. Guo (Eds.), Advances in Neural Networks – ISNN 2004. XXXV, 1041 pages. 2004.